김앤북의 체계적인
합격 알고리즘

기초 학습 → 문제 풀이 → 실전 적용 → 합격

김영편입 영어

MVP Vocabulary 시리즈

MVP Vol.1   MVP Vol.1 워크북   MVP Vol.2   MVP Vol.2 워크북   MVP Starter

기초 이론 단계

문법 이론   구문독해

기초 실력 완성 단계

어휘 기출 1단계   문법 기출 1단계   독해 기출 1단계   논리 기출 1단계   문법 워크북 1단계   독해 워크북 1단계   논리 워크북 1단계

심화 학습 단계

어휘 기출 2단계   문법 기출 2단계   독해 기출 2단계   논리 기출 2단계   문법 워크북 2단계   독해 워크북 2단계   논리 워크북 2단계

2021 대한민국 우수브랜드 대상
2024, 2023, 2022 대한민국 브랜드 어워즈 대학편입교육 대상 (한경비즈니스)

실전 단계

연도별 기출문제 해설집   TOP6 대학 기출문제 해설집

김영편입 수학

편입 수학 이론 & 문제 적용 단계

미분법   적분법   선형대수   다변수미적분   공학수학

편입 수학 필수 공식 한 권 정리

공식집

편입 수학 핵심 유형 정리 & 실전 연습 단계

미분법 워크북   적분법 워크북   선형대수 워크북   다변수미적분 워크북   공학수학 워크북

실전 단계

연도별 기출문제 해설집

김앤북의 완벽한
단기 합격 로드맵

핵심이론 → 최신기출 → 실전적용 → 단기합격

자격증 수험서

| 전기기능사 필기 | 지게차운전기능사 필기 | 위험물산업기사 필기 | 산업안전기사 필기 | 전기기사 필기 필수기출 / 전기기사 실기 봉투모의고사 | 소방설비기사 필기 필수기출 시리즈 |

컴퓨터 IT 실용서

SQL · 코딩테스트 · 파이썬 · C언어 · 플러터 · 자바 · 코틀린 · 유니티

컴퓨터 IT 수험서

컴퓨터활용능력 1급실기 · 컴퓨터활용능력 2급실기 · 데이터분석준전문가 (ADsP) · GTQ 포토샵 · GTQi 일러스트 · 리눅스마스터 2급 · SQL 개발자 (SQLD)

영어독해

기출/2단계

김영편입 컨텐츠평가연구소 지음

중고급 난이도의 분야별 기출문제로 실전 독해력 완성

김앤북
KIM&BOOK

PREFACE

어떤 공부를 하든 간에 단계별 학습은 중요합니다. 기초가 튼튼해야 그 위에 자신의 실력을 계속해서 쌓을 수 있기 때문입니다. 따라서 기초를 쌓은 후 그 이론을 바탕으로 쉬운 문제부터 어려운 문제로 실력을 확장해 나가는 것이 단계별 편입영어 학습법입니다.

이 책은 수험생이 자신의 실력을 확장하기 위해 보는 "기출 2단계" 책입니다. 최신 출제 경향이 반영된 중·고급 난이도 기출문제를 수록해, 실전에 보다 가까이 다가갈 수 있도록 했습니다.

"기출 2단계" 책은 문법, 논리, 독해의 3종으로 구성되어 있습니다. 문법과 논리의 경우, 1단계에서 핵심 문법 이론과 유형별 학습법을 각각 기출문제에 적용하는 훈련을 했다면, 2단계에서는 다양한 유형을 한데 섞어 수록해 실전 응용력을 기를 수 있도록 했습니다. 그리고 독해의 경우, 1단계에서 기출문제를 유형별로 학습하는 데 초점을 맞추었다면, 2단계에서는 기출문제를 분야별로 학습하는 데 중점을 두어 다양한 주제를 학습할 수 있도록 구성했습니다.

이 책을 학습하기 전에 한 가지 주의할 점이 있는데, 그것은 자신의 위치가 어디에 있는지부터 파악하고 공부를 시작하라는 것입니다. "기출 2단계"를 공부하면서 문제에 어려움을 느끼거나 해설을 이해하지 못한 수험생의 경우, 2단계를 잠시 덮고 1단계부터 다시 보시길 권합니다.

자신의 실력은 다른 사람이 만들어 주는 것이 아닙니다. 비록 실력이 향상되는 데 시간이 많이 걸리고 그 속도가 더디더라도, 결국에는 우공이산(愚公移山)이라는 고사성어처럼, 어떤 일이든 끊임없이 노력하면 반드시 이루어지게 될 것입니다.

"기출 2단계"를 통해 실전 문제에 대비하고 실력을 확장하는 계기가 될 수 있기를 기원합니다.

김영편입 컨텐츠평가연구소

HOW TO STUDY

출제자의 관점으로 문제를 바라보자!

한번쯤은 출제자의 입장이 되어 볼 필요가 있습니다. '이 문제에서는 무엇을 물어볼까?', '여기쯤에 함정을 파놓으면 어떨까?' 이렇게 출제자의 관점에서 문제를 바라보면, 모든 문제가 완전히 새롭게 보일 수 있습니다.

문제의 난이도를 몸으로 익혀보자!

강물의 깊이를 알면 더 빠르고 안전하게 건널 수 있듯이, 문제의 난이도가 어느 정도인지 파악하게 되면, 문제를 더 노련하게 접근해 풀 수 있습니다. 그리고 난이도를 몸으로 익힐 수 있는 지름길은 없습니다. 다양한 난이도의 기출문제를 가능한 많이 풀어보는 것이 유일한 방법입니다.

제한시간을 설정하자!

실전에 대비할 수 있는 가장 좋은 방법은 실전과 똑같은 환경에서 훈련하는 것입니다. 문제를 풀 때는 반드시 제한시간을 설정하여 학습하시길 바랍니다. 실전에서와 같은 압박감과 긴장감을 조성하기에 가장 좋은 방법입니다.

오답에서 배우자!

편입시험은 정답만 기억하면 되는 OX 퀴즈가 아닙니다. 문제를 풀고 난 후엔 맞힌 문제보다 틀린 문제에 주목해야 합니다. 어째서 정답을 맞히지 못했는지 일련의 사고 과정을 면밀히 되짚어봐야만 틀린 문제를 다시 틀리지 않을 수 있습니다.

문법, 논리, 독해는 원래 한 몸이다!

본 시리즈는 문법, 논리, 독해라는 세 가지 영역을 나눠서 각각을 한 권의 책으로 구성했지만, 영역 구분에 지나치게 신경 쓰며 학습하는 것은 좋지 않습니다. 오히려 독해문제에서 중요 어휘와 문법구문을 정리하는 방식처럼 서로 영역을 통합해 학습하게 되면 더 큰 시너지를 일으킬 수 있습니다.

실전 문제 TEST

o 시험에 자주 출제되는 13가지 분야로 구성했으며, 총 200개의 중·장문 독해 지문을 배치했습니다.

o 출제 빈도에 따라 각 분야별 지문수를 다르게 구성하여, 출제 가능성이 높은 지식을 학습하고 배경지식을 쌓을 수 있게 했습니다.

정답과 해설 ANSWERS & TRANSLATION

o 각 문제에 대한 유형을 표시하여 『김영편입 영어 독해 기출 1단계』에서 익힌 내용을 중·장문 지문에서 다시 한 번 확인하고 심화 학습을 할 수 있도록 했습니다.

o 각 지문을 통해 익힐 수 있는 편입 필수 어휘를 꼼꼼히 정리하였으며, 상세한 분석과 오답에 대한 TIP을 수록하여 문제의 이해도를 높였습니다.

CONTENTS

문제편

01 역사·인물 ·· 10
02 심리·교육 ·· 26
03 문화·예술 ·· 54
04 언어·문학 ·· 84
05 철학·종교 ·· 108
06 사회·정치 ·· 132
07 경제·경영 ·· 158
08 과학·기술 ·· 186
09 우주·지구 ·· 208
10 환경·기상 ·· 226
11 의학·건강 ·· 242
12 생물학·생명과학 ································ 270
13 동물·식물 ·· 292

해설편

- 01 역사·인물 ········· 308
- 02 심리·교육 ········· 316
- 03 문화·예술 ········· 332
- 04 언어·문학 ········· 347
- 05 철학·종교 ········· 359
- 06 사회·정치 ········· 371
- 07 경제·경영 ········· 386
- 08 과학·기술 ········· 400
- 09 우주·지구 ········· 411
- 10 환경·기상 ········· 419
- 11 의학·건강 ········· 427
- 12 생물학·생명과학 ········· 442
- 13 동물·식물 ········· 454

일러두기
본 교재에 수록된 문제들은 100% 편입 기출문제입니다.
문제의 출처(출제연도, 대학)는 각 문제의 해설 부분에 모두 정확히 표기했습니다.

교재의 내용에 오류가 있나요?
www.kimyoung.co.kr ➡ 온라인 서점 ➡ 정오표 게시판
정오표에 반영되지 않은 새로운 오류가 있을 때에는 교재 오류신고 게시판에 글을 남겨주세요. 정성껏 답변해 드리겠습니다.

01

역사·인물

01 역사·인물

01

Although Americans have long celebrated Independence Day on July 4, technically that is not when the colonies voted to become a new nation. That honor belongs to July 2, 1776, which was not only the day the Continental Congress approved a resolution declaring independence from Britain but also the day that John Adams wrote would be celebrated by succeeding generations as the great anniversary festival with "pomp and parade." So, what happened? In a word, paperwork. According to Philip Mead, chief historian at the Museum of the American Revolution, it took two days for the Continental Congress to approve a press release explaining why the delegates had voted the way they did. That document, better known as the Declaration of Independence, arrived at the printer on July 4, 1776, which is why that date appears at the top. But though Adams might have been surprised to see Americans celebrate the Fourth of July, he did play a part in the shift. When he and Thomas Jefferson both died on July 4, 1826, that date became even more Ⓐ_____ in American memory.

1 Which of the following best fits into Ⓐ?

① entertained
② estimated
③ eluded
④ enshrined

2 According to the passage, which of the following is true?

① Philip Mead belonged to the Continental Congress.
② The Declaration of Independence was printed on July 2.
③ Adams hoped independence would be celebrated on July 2.
④ Congress voted for the declaration on July 4.

02

The Celts were the first Indo-European occupants of Britain. The southern British Celts had been first subdued and thereafter ruled and sheltered by the Romans. Julius Caesar's attempt at an early invasion in 55-54 BC did not result in occupation, unlike the results elsewhere in the Roman Empire, in particular Gaul (where the Latin spoken by Caesar's legions became, ultimately, Modern French). It was during the rule of the emperor Claudius (from AD 43) that the Roman invasion was followed by a more permanent occupation and military control. For about 400 years thereafter, Britain was a province of the Roman Empire. By the beginning of the fifth century, however, maintaining occupation forces in that outlying territory became too costly for the Romans, who were constantly subjected to the attacks of the Germanic tribes on the Continent. A highly simplified version of the events that followed is that when the Romans pulled out, with all of them gone by AD 410, the Celts in the south of the island were relatively defenseless. It was then that they invited Germanic mercenary soldiers to come over from northern Europe and protect them from invading Vikings, as well as from the Celts from the north and from Ireland (the Scots and the Picts).

1 Which of the following is true according to the passage?

① The Celts arrived in Britain after the Romans.
② Julius Caesar succeeded in a permanent rule of Britain.
③ The emperor Claudius made Britain part of the Roman Empire.
④ Germanic armies totally expelled the Romans from Britain.
⑤ Germanic mercenary soldiers protected the Scots as well as the Picts.

2 What does the underlined that outlying territory refer to?

① Britain
② Gaul
③ Germany
④ Europe
⑤ Ireland

03

The pictures he created over the following 12 months — depicting blossoming fruit trees, views of the town and surroundings, self-portraits, portraits of Roulin the postman and other friends, interiors and exteriors of the house, sunflowers, and landscapes — marked his first great period. In these works he strove to respect the external, visual aspect of a figure or landscape but found himself unable to suppress his own feelings about the subject, which found expression in emphatic contours and heightened effects of color. Once hesitant to Ⓐ_____ the traditional techniques of painting he worked so hard to master, he now Ⓑgave free rein to his individuality and began squeezing his tubes of oil paint directly on the canvas. Van Gogh's style was spontaneous and instinctive, for he worked with great speed and intensity, determined to capture an effect or a mood while it possessed him.

1 Which of the following best fits in the blank Ⓐ?

① diverge from
② adhere to
③ follow on
④ revisit

2 Which of the words below best describes the feeling of the artist created by the underlined phrase Ⓑ?

① carelessness
② reluctance
③ liberation
④ constraint

3 According to this passage, which of the following statements is NOT true?

① Van Gogh's choice of subject was greatly affected by his moods and emotions.
② Van Gogh generally worked quickly while painting.
③ In his pictures, Van Gogh worked hard to represent the subject objectively, but in vain.
④ During this period, Van Gogh painted some pictures of himself.

04

Nigeria and Cameroon are located in West Africa. Their shared 2,400 km border, which runs from Lake Chad in the north to the Bakassi Peninsula in the south, has been a constant source of conflict between the two nations. This border dispute, which was born of colonial creation, is the outcome of the numerous treaties between the British and German colonial powers, treaties which derived their legality from the Berlin Conference of 1884-1885, at which no Africans were present. Nigerians think that the Bakassi Peninsula is critical to the security, economic (fishing and oil), and geo-strategic interests of Nigeria and also that before the 1913 Anglo-German Agreement, it had been an essential part of Nigerian territory. The 1913 Agreement shifted the Nigeria-Cameroon border towards Nigeria and thus, gave the Bakassi Peninsula to Cameroon. However, clue to post-1913 developments, the Bakassi Peninsula reverted back to Nigeria who continued its governance until the Nigerian Civil War (1967-1970) when Cameroon laid claim to it. Eventually, in 2002, Cameroon took the case to the International Court of Justice who set the border solely based on the 1913 Anglo-German Agreement and not on prior history or subsequent acts, and thereby assigned control of the peninsula to Cameroon.

1   Which of the following is the major topic of the passage?

① The role of oil, fishing, and security in disputes
② The worldwide effects of European colonialism
③ The history of an African border dispute
④ Historical border conflicts between Britain and Germany

2   According to the passage, which of the following is true?

① Nigeria is unconcerned about the border in the north.
② The economy is the sole issue regarding the Bakassi Peninsula.
③ Europeans set the legal Nigeria-Cameroon border.
④ The 1913 agreement moved the border in favor of Nigeria

05

Andrés Segovia Torres was a virtuoso Spanish classical guitarist from Linares, Spain. Many professional classical guitarists today were students of Segovia, or students of his students. Segovia's contribution to the modern-romantic repertoire included not only commissions but also his own transcriptions of classical or baroque works. He is renowned for his expressive performances: his wide palette of tone, and his distinctive musical personality, phrasing and style.

Segovia's first public performance was in Granada at the age of 16 in 1909. A few years later he played his first professional concert in Madrid, which included works by Francisco Tárrega and his own guitar transcriptions of J.S. Bach. Despite the discouragement of his family, who wanted him to become a lawyer, and criticism by some of Tárrega's pupils for his idiosyncratic technique, he continued to pursue his studies of the guitar diligently.

He played again in Madrid in 1912, at the Paris Conservatory in 1915, in Barcelona in 1916, and made a successful tour of South America in 1919. Segovia's arrival on the international stage coincided with a time when the guitar's fortunes as a concert instrument were being revived, largely through the efforts of Miguel Llobet. It was in this changing milieu that Segovia, thanks to his strength of personality and artistry, coupled with developments in recording and broadcasting, succeeded in making the guitar more popular again.

Segovia can be considered a catalytic figure in granting respectability to the guitar as a serious concert instrument capable of evocativeness and depth of interpretation. He can be credited to have dignified the classical guitar as a legitimate concert instrument before the discerning music public, which had hitherto viewed the guitar merely as a limited, if sonorous, parlor instrument.

1 Which of the following is NOT true about Segovia?

① His public debut was made at the age of 16.
② His first professional concert was after a few years of his debut.
③ His family strongly opposed to his being a professional guitarist.
④ His public career began with the tour of South America.

2 Which of the following is true?

① Segoivia stuck to the conventional playing technique.
② All of Tárrega's pupils praised Segovia's idiosyncratic playing technique.
③ Miguel Llobet contributed little to the revival of the guitar as a concert instrument.
④ Segovia played a crucial role in making the guitar a dignified concert instrument.

06

On July 25, 1665, a five-year-old boy named John Morley, of the parish of the Holy Trinity in Cambridge, England, was found dead in his home. When town officials examined his corpse, they noted black spots on his chest, the unmistakable mark of the bubonic plague. Almost at once, the townspeople raced to isolate themselves in the countryside. Among those on the run there was a young scholar of Trinity College named Isaac Newton. Newton's home, a farm called Woolsthorpe, lay about sixty miles north of the university. Suitably distant from the nearest town, it was where, in near total solitude, he would invent calculus, create the science of motion, unravel gravity, and more. The plague established the conditions in which modern science could be created. Or so the story goes.

During his nearly two years down on the farm, Newton produced an unbelievable number of exceptional results. He created major new insights across vital areas of mathematics. He created new physics. He performed experiments to measure gravity's pull, and then began shaping his most famous idea, universal gravitation.

But what's untrue is the idea that Newton unleashed his mind on these problems once the plague had given him the gift of solitude. As his definitive biographer, Richard Westfall, meticulously documented, Newton had begun to think about the most pressing questions in science while still studying for his exams in his rooms at Trinity College during the year before the plague struck. The year before the plague, 1664, was also when Newton first began to think deeply about mathematics. Whatever may have enabled Newton to produce epic works of genius during, before, and after his enforced isolation, the retreat to the country itself couldn't have been the decisive difference. Newton himself said as much. When asked how he worked out gravity, he replied, "_____."

1 Which is most appropriate for the blank?

① By fear of plague
② By working on a farm
③ By grieving for John Morley
④ By thinking on it continually
⑤ By living as lonely as possible

2 Which is not stated or implied according to the passage?

① Plague began to spread in the year of 1665.
② John Morley died from a contagious disease.
③ Newton lived at Cambridge before the plague.
④ Newton kept working during his stay at the farm.
⑤ Richard Westfall omitted some information about Newton's achievements.

07

The war for independence from Britain was a long and economically costly conflict. The New England fishing industry was temporarily destroyed, and the tobacco colonies in the South were also hard hit. The trade in imports was severely affected, since the war was fought against the country that had previously monopolized the colonies' supply of manufactured goods. The most serious consequences were felt in the cities, whose existence depended on commercial activity. Boston, New York, Philadelphia, and Charleston were all occupied for a time by British troops. Even when the troops had left, British ships lurked in the harbors and continued to disrupt trade.

American income from shipbuilding and commerce declined abruptly, undermining the entire economy of the urban areas. The decline in trade brought a fall in the American standard of living. Unemployed shipwrights, dock laborers, and coopers drifted off to find work on farms and in small villages. Some of them joined the Continental army, or if they were loyal to Britain, they departed with the British forces. The population of New York City declined from 21,000 in 1774 to less than half that number only nine years later in 1783.

The disruptions produced by the fighting of the war, by the loss of established markets for manufactured goods, by the loss of sources of credit, and by the lack of new investment all created a period of economic stagnation that lasted for the next twenty years.

1 Why does the author mention the fishing industry and the tobacco colonies?

① To identify the two largest commercial enterprises in America
② To compare the economic power of two different regions
③ To show how the war for independence affected the economy
④ To give examples of industries controlled by British forces

2 Why were the effects of the war felt most in the cities?

① The cities depended on manufacturing and trade.
② The British army destroyed most of the cities.
③ Most of the fighting occurred in the cities.
④ The urban population did not support the war.

3 Why does the author mention the population of New York City in paragraph 2?

① To show that half of New York remained loyal to Britain
② To compare New York with other cities occupied during the war
③ To emphasize the great short-term cost of the war for New York
④ To illustrate the percentage of homeless people in New York

4 What probably occurred during the years right after the war for independence?

① Development of new shipbuilding technology
② A return to traditional methods of manufacturing
③ A shift to an agricultural economy in New York
④ Shortages of money and manufactured goods

08

Andrew Carnegie, a Scottish-American industrialist and philanthropist, was born in 1835 in Scotland, and immigrated to the United States with his parents at age 12. Carnegie started work as a telegrapher, and by the 1860s had investments in railroads, bridges, and oil derricks. He accumulated further wealth as a bond salesman. He built Pittsburgh's Carnegie Steel Company, which he sold to J. P. Morgan in 1901 for $303,450,000. After selling Carnegie Steel, he surpassed John D. Rockefeller as the richest American for the next several years.

As early as 1868, at age 33, Carnegie drafted a memo to himself. He wrote: "... The amassing of wealth is one of the worse species of idolatry. No idol more debasing than the worship of money." In order to avoid degrading himself, he wrote in the same memo he would retire at age 35 to pursue the practice of philanthropic giving for "... the man who dies thus rich dies disgraced." However, he did not begin his philanthropic work in all earnest until 1881, with the gift of a library to his hometown in Scotland.

    Ⓐ_____ Carnegie did not comment on British imperialism, he strongly opposed the idea of American colonies. He opposed the annexation of the Philippines and tried to arrange for independence for the Philippines. As the end of the Spanish-American War neared, the United States bought the Philippines from Spain for $20 million. To counter what he perceived as imperialism on the part of the United States, Carnegie personally offered $20 million to the Philippines so that the Filipino people could buy their independence from the United States. However, nothing came of the offer.

1 Which of the following can be inferred from the passage?

① Carnegie started to invest in railroads, bridges, and oil derricks in 1860.
② Carnegie was not the richest man in America in the 1890s.
③ Carnegie idolized money so that he could accumulate his wealth.
④ Carnegie was given a library as a gift in his hometown in Scotland.

2 Which of the following is most suitable for the blank Ⓐ?

① But
② As
③ When
④ While

3 The third paragraph illustrates Carnegie's philosophy of _____.

① wealth
② anti-imperialism
③ the Philippines
④ idolatry

4 According to the passage, which of the following is true?

① Carnegie started to do things as a philanthropist at age 35.
② Carnegie regarded it a disgrace for a rich man to die.
③ The Philippines gained independence from America thanks to Carnegie's offering of money.
④ Carnegie opposed America's purchase of the Philippines from Spain.

09

Major wars often provide the punctuation marks of history, primarily because they force drastic realignments in the relationships among states. To this rule, the First World War was no exception. Long before the fighting ceased in November 1918, it was evident that the map of Europe must be redrawn and that reallocation of colonies, creation of a new international organization, and change in the economic balance must considerably affect the rest of the world as well. World War I (WWI) heralded the end of European dominance, as the true victors in this predominantly European war were America and Japan: two non-European powers. ⓐEuropean countries were not concerned about their domestic affairs, overlooking the importance of their colonies across the globe. The European victors were bled white and suffered a pyrrhic victory from which none of them ever really recovered. While this fact was not evident at the war's end, it was clear that the forthcoming settlement must far exceed in geographic scope and complexity.

As often happens, the sudden collapse of the enemy took the victors by surprise. Germany had been expected to hold out until mid-1919, and in the autumn of 1918, Allied energy was more concentrated upon winning the war than upon planning the peace. True, some planning was in progress, but not always in the most effectual quarters. ⓑIn the final year of the war, the smaller Allied states pursued their limited, specific aims with energy, but achieved only cautious and qualified commitments. Exile organizations representing ethnic groups within the Central powers did the same with similar results. They recognized that the ultimate court of appeal would consist of Britain, France, and America, but these three, who had the task of planning for much of the world, were also responsible for winning the war. Not surprisingly, that came first.

Of the major Allies, the French were perhaps the best organized in planning ahead, mainly because they knew precisely what mattered to them and because their interests were not really global. ⓒIn London, the Foreign Office was industriously preparing position papers on every conceivable topic, but since its views often did not coincide with those of the Cabinet, and even less with those of Prime Minister David Lloyd George, much of the work proved futile. In the United States, the situation was more obscure. A special organization called the Inquiry had been established late in 1917 under the supervision of the President's confidant, Edward M. House, to research the problems of the peace and to prepare a program designed to preempt those of European leaders. ⓓThe Inquiry, composed largely of academicians and functioning independently of the State Department, was hard at work, but its influence was still uncertain and House himself was in Paris during the closing weeks of WWI. Secretary of State Robert Lansing was preparing his views, which did not coincide with those of the Inquiry and which could be expected to clash with those of the President.

1 위 글의 흐름상 가장 적합하지 <u>않은</u> 문장을 고르시오.

① Ⓐ ② Ⓑ
③ Ⓒ ④ Ⓓ

2 위 글의 내용과 일치하는 것을 고르시오.

① Europe's dominance of world politics ended with the First World War.
② Britain, France, and the United States were prepared for the rapid collapse of Germany.
③ European states gradually recovered from the realignment of power mainly due to the rise of America and Japan.
④ Creation of a new international organization preoccupied the victors before WWI was won.

10

A Historians have often seen 1898 as a clear departure from the past, the point of American emergence into world politics. Yet the extent of change can be exaggerated. There was not a sudden increase of American might; since industrialization, the U.S. had been a potential great power. Nor did 1898 mark a sudden, permanent shift in popular interest. After a flurry of arguments over imperialism, most Americans resumed, in the early twentieth century, their habitual concentration on home affairs. However, 1898 did mark a change in American commitments. From this point on, both the U.S. and the European powers assumed that America had some interest in world crises.

B Many reasons have been given for this change. Ⓐ_____: the American economy had reached maturity and therefore America, like other advanced industrial countries, needed new raw materials and foreign markets. Many historians would deny any connection between American expansion abroad and internal American economic development. This connection, however, was frequently made by turn-of-the-century farmers and businessmen, who saw a relationship between domestic prosperity and foreign markets.

C A second explanation for the new departures in foreign policy was the revival and restatement of the traditional idea of America's "manifest destiny" of expansion. However, the change from continental to overseas expansionism needed new justification. One of the most common arguments of late nineteenth-century expansionists was the idea of Anglo-Saxon "racial" superiority. In the 1890's, some claimed superiority over southern African-Americans and new immigrants.

D Another less obvious cause of the change in American policy was the actual situation in great power politics. The imperial activities of the major European nations already engaged in a scramble for territory and influence in the world's underdeveloped regions Ⓑ_____ the American appetite for expansion. Having divided up Africa, the European powers were now eyeing the last two remaining areas for expansion: the Near East and the Far East. Each of these were too important to fall to any single power so the leading nations uneasily supported the independence of both, staking out spheres of economic influence. Everywhere the situation was fluid and dangerous. When a country with a potential might of the U.S. showed an interest in world politics, the country was inevitably seen as a menace by some powers and as a potential ally by others. What happened in 1898 reflected all these forces. Against its will and without quite realizing it, the U.S. became involved in great power politics.

1 Which of the following would be the best title for the above passage?

① America's Overseas Expansion
② Forerunner of American Adventures
③ Peace and Empire in the U.S.
④ The Perils of American Imperialism
⑤ The Mature Economy of America

2 Which of the following would best fit in the blank Ⓐ in paragraph B?

① The public felt that the U.S. had a special interest in the western hemisphere.
② Most believed that American freedom from foreign dangers was permanent and natural.
③ Some of the doctrines were advocated with great force by a group of able young men.
④ The most obvious suggestion embodies the traditional economic interpretation of imperialism.
⑤ Once colonial expansion was completed, public interest in foreign affairs concentrated on traditional concerns.

3 Which of the following can be inserted into the blank Ⓑ in paragraph D?

① whetted
② grieved
③ vindicated
④ dangled
⑤ usurped

4 According to the above passage, which of the following is true?

① Historians have claimed that the year 1898 marks a division in American foreign policy.
② The year 1898 witnessed a sudden change in American people's interest.
③ European nations ceased to support the independence of the countries in the Near East and the Far East.
④ The idea of Anglo-Saxon racial superiority was denied in the 1890's.
⑤ Many historians believed that American overseas expansion was related to its economic crises.

02

심리·교육

02 심리·교육

01

The self-serving bias is the tendency for us to attribute positive events to ourselves and negative ones to external factors. For example, a star athlete interviewed after winning a big game attributes his success to his hard work. The same athlete interviewed a few weeks later after losing a game explains, "Today just wasn't my day." Psychologists say it is human nature to think this way in order to protect our self-esteem and reputation. The advantages of the self-serving bias are: it prevents us from getting depressed in the face of failure, and it allows us to remain Ⓐ_____ about the future. However, blaming negative outcomes on external sources robs us of opportunities to learn from our mistakes and become better people. If we continue to avoid looking honestly at how we contributed to a negative outcome, we will remain Ⓑ_____.

1 Which one of the following ordered pairs best fits into Ⓐ and Ⓑ?

① reticent — positive
② expectant — aloof
③ confident — stagnant
④ foreboding — stable

2 According to the passage, what do we usually do after experiencing a negative event?

① Think of ourselves as responsible
② Listen to critique from other people
③ Try to learn from our mistakes
④ Blame things other than ourselves

02

The modern concept of psychology as a medical science that studies and cures mental, emotional, and behavioral illnesses was just forming when Sigmund Freud began his work in the field. Freud's treatments and theories from the turn of the twentieth century have become cultural norms. While today's popular culture makes fun of his focus on sexual drives, his idea that behavior has unconscious or subconscious motivations is now accepted as fact. Freud was also a main figure in the first explorations of therapy based on simple talking, which is still the core of many modern therapies. Carl Jung was the second influential figure in the formation of the field of psychology. Although he worked with Freud on his theory of complexes, his view was much broader. He took an almost anthropological look at the person in the contexts of culture and religion. Through higher-level analysis, he saw beyond individual illness to a person's personality type. ⒶHis modern influence can be seen in such widely disparate places as Joseph Campbell's popularization of universal myth and the therapeutic tool, the Myers-Briggs Personality Type Indicator.

1. 다음 진술 중 Freud가 믿었던 것을 고르시오.

   ① Psychology should not become a medical science.
   ② People sometimes act based on unconscious motivations.
   ③ Simply talking was not an effective therapy.
   ④ Men have sexual fantasies about their mothers.
   ⑤ There are certain types of human traits.

2. 다음 진술 중 밑줄 친 Ⓐ문장의 의미에 가장 가까운 것을 고르시오.

   ① Joseph Campbell's theory of universal myths and the Myers-Briggs tool are both influenced by him.
   ② His influence can be seen in the way Joseph Campbell's popularization of the universal myth is reflected in the Myers-Briggs Personality Type Indicator.
   ③ His influences included Joseph Campbell's concept of universal myth and the Myers-Briggs tool.
   ④ Even though Joseph Campbell and Myers-Briggs were very different, their ideas are connected by his theories.
   ⑤ According to his theories, Joseph Campbell's concepts and Myers-Briggs Indicator are totally different ideas.

03

Intelligence is often defined as our intellectual potential; something we are born with, something that can be measured, and a capacity that is difficult to change. However, other views of intelligence have emerged. One such conception is the theory of 'multiple intelligences' proposed by Howard Gardner. This theory suggests that traditional psychometric views of intelligence are too limited. In order to capture the full range of abilities that people possess, Gardner theorizes that people do not have just an intellectual capacity, but have many kinds of intelligence, including musical, interpersonal, spatial-visual, and linguistic intelligences. While a person might be particularly strong in a specific area, such as musical intelligence, he or she most likely possesses a range of other abilities. Gardner's theory has come under criticism from some psychologists and educators. These critics argue that Gardner's definition of intelligence is too broad and that his eight different 'intelligences' simply represent talents and personality traits. Despite this, the theory of multiple intelligences enjoys considerable popularity with educators. Many teachers utilize multiple intelligences in their teaching philosophies and work to Ⓐ_____ Gardner's theory into the classroom.

1 Which of the following is the major topic of the passage?

① Traditional psychometric views of intelligence
② Different types of personal talents
③ Criticism against multiple intelligences
④ Gardner's theory of multiple intelligences

2 Which of the following best fits into Ⓐ?

① investigate
② invalidate
③ integrate
④ infiltrate

04

    A behavioral theory asserts that consequences from the environment shape and maintain behaviors. Behaviors that are followed by positive reinforcement are most likely to continue or increase. Ⓐ Conversely, any behavior that is followed by negative consequences such as punishment, should theoretically decrease. Ⓑ However, research has not shown punishment to be an effective means of behavioral intervention. Ⓒ The main reason is that it simply works to stop misbehavior. Ⓓ In fact, it usually stops misbehavior only while the punisher is actually present.

    A behavioral phenomenon called contingency-governed behavior may begin to develop at this time. Contingency-governed behavior means that an individual's behavior depends on the next consequence he perceives. This means that a person will try to get away with an inappropriate behavior if he thinks he will not get caught. Consequently, if the student believes the punisher will not see him or catch him in the misbehavior, he will try to get away with it. The problem behavior cycle escalates. If the student does not get caught, he feels successful, which is a form of positive reinforcement, so he Ⓐ_____ the pattern of problem behavior.

1   Which is the proper order of the sentences Ⓐ-Ⓓ?
① Ⓐ — Ⓑ — Ⓒ — Ⓓ
② Ⓑ — Ⓐ — Ⓓ — Ⓒ
③ Ⓒ — Ⓑ — Ⓓ — Ⓐ
④ Ⓓ — Ⓒ — Ⓑ — Ⓐ

2   Which best fits into the blank Ⓐ?
① continues
② represses
③ desists
④ hampers

3   Which is the best title for the passage?
① Behaviors Change over Time
② Effective Means of Punishment
③ Consequences Shape Behaviors
④ Controversy over Reinforcement

05

   Over the past decade behavioral scientists have come up with some intriguing insights. In one landmark experiment, conducted in an upmarket grocery store in California, researchers set up a sampling table with a display of jams. In the first test they offered a tempting array of 24 different jams to taste; on a different day they displayed just six. Shoppers who took part in the sampling were rewarded with a discount voucher to buy any jam of the same brand in the store. It turned out that more shoppers stopped at the display when there were 24 jams. But when it came to buying afterwards, fully 30% of those who stopped at the six-jam table went on to purchase a pot, against merely 3% of those who were faced with the selection of 24.

   As options multiply, there may be a point at which the effort required to obtain enough information to be able to distinguish sensibly between alternatives outweighs the benefit to the consumer of the extra choice. At this point, choice no longer liberates, but tyrannizes. In other words, the fact that some choice is good doesn't necessarily mean that more choice is better. Consumers find too many options debilitating because of the risk of misperception and miscalculation, of misunderstanding the available alternatives, of misreading one's own tastes, of yielding to a moment's whim and regretting it afterwards, combined with the stress of information acquisition.

1 The best title of the passage would be '_____.'

① Choice and Liberal Democracy
② The Paradox of Choice
③ Free Choice and Economic Growth
④ Information and Human Behavior
⑤ Being Human in a Consumer Society

2 The experiment with the shoppers in the Californian grocery store reveals that _____.

① people believe the perfect choice exists
② shoppers are not put off by more choice
③ too much choice is demotivating
④ if you can have everything in 24 varieties, making decisions becomes easy work
⑤ the more expensive an item is, the more daunting the decision becomes

06

    The major philosophical issue affecting treatment of the gifted is whether education should be aimed at elevating the masses or at nurturing those who evidence the greatest potential. The issue has often been posed as a dichotomy between Ⓐ_____ and democratic equality. Another perspective is that the democratic practice of educating equally individuals of unequal intelligence — that is, having the same expectations and standards for the bright and the dull — is a false conception of equality that leads to Ⓑ_____ and wasted talent. True equality consists rather in providing each individual Ⓒ"_____" (Tsuin-chen, 1961). Throughout history the prevailing philosophy with regard to equality of opportunity has been manifested in the treatment of gifted individuals.

    What society values has also helped determine the definition and identification of gifted individuals over time. When visual arts have been prized — for example, in Renaissance Europe — society has sought out and supported the artistically gifted. Acute needs based on emergencies such as war or famine, and chronic needs existing over time, have also influenced society's identification of gifted individuals. The warrior society of ancient Sparta, for instance, required and hence nurtured individuals gifted with military prowess.

1   Choose a statement that may be inferred from the passage above.

① Parents of gifted children are often overly assertive individuals.
② Gifted individuals should be given an education according to their ability.
③ The definition of gifted individuals has stayed the same over time.
④ Parents of gifted children should provide stimulating materials in the home.
⑤ Economic differences may affect child-rearing practices.

2   Which pair best fits Ⓐ and Ⓑ?

① superiority — competence
② clique — achievement
③ dregs — ordinariness
④ elitism — mediocrity
⑤ extract — skillfulness

3   Which best suits the quote in Ⓒ?

① an equal opportunity to profit by education according to his intelligence
② specialized resources and intensive instructional efforts
③ a supportive home environment as well as personal commitment and excellent teaching
④ stimulating materials in the home
⑤ more elaborate speech, explanation, reasoning, praise, and specific feedback

07

Sentimentality, notoriously, is entirely compatible with a taste for brutality and worse. (Recall the canonical example of the Auschwitz commandant returning home in the evening, embracing his wife and children, and sitting at the piano to play some Schubert before dinner.) People don't become inured to what they are shown — if that's the right way to describe what happens — because of the quantity of images dumped on them. It is passivity that dulls feeling. The states described as Ⓐ_____, moral or emotional anesthesia, are full of feelings; the feelings are rage and frustration. But if we consider what emotions would be desirable, it seems too simple to elect sympathy. The imaginary proximity to the suffering inflicted on others that is granted by images suggests a link between the far-away sufferers — seen close-up on the television screen — and privileged viewer that is simply untrue, that is yet one more mystification of our real relations to power. So far as we feel sympathy, we feel we are not accomplices to what caused the suffering. Our sympathy proclaims our innocence as well as our impotence. To that extent, it can be (for all our good intentions) an impertinent — if not an inappropriate — response. To set aside the sympathy we extend to others beset by war and murderous politics for a reflection on how our privileges are located on the same map as their suffering, and may — in ways we might prefer not to imagine — be linked to their suffering, as the wealth of some may imply the destitution of others, is a task for which the painful, stirring images supply only an initial spark.

1 Choose the best word for blank Ⓐ.

① pathos   ② sympathy
③ apathy   ④ inertia

2 Choose the statement most consistent with the passage.

① The author calls for sympathy for the suffering caused by war and murderous politics.
② An innate tropism toward the gruesome is as natural to human beings as is sympathy.
③ The increase of information in media about calamities taking place in another country makes the spectator a better citizen of the world.
④ Journalism driven by mercantile values and its hunt for more dramatic images is a quintessential feature of modern experience.

08

Researchers have long been intrigued as to whether an ability to avoid, or defer, gratification is related to outcomes in life. The best-known test is the "marshmallow" experiment, in which children who could refrain from eating the confection for 15 minutes were given a second one. Children who could not wait tended to have lower incomes and poorer health as adults. Dr David Lindahl of Stockholm University used data from a Swedish survey in which more than 13,000 children aged 13 were asked whether they would prefer to receive $140 now or $1,400 in five years' time. About four-fifths of them said they were prepared to wait. Unlike previous researchers, Dr Lindahl was able to track all the children and account for their parental background and cognitive ability. He found that the 13-year-olds who wanted the smaller sum of money at once were 32% more likely to be convicted of a crime during the next 18 years than those children who said they would rather wait for the bigger reward. Individuals who are impatient, he believes, prefer instant benefits and are therefore less likely to be deterred by potential punishments. But those who fret that a person's criminal path is set already as a teenager should not despair. Dr Lindahl offers a remedy. When the respondents' education was included in the analysis, he found that higher educational attainment was linked to a preference for delayed gratification. "I therefore suspect that schooling can deter people from crime by making them value the future more," explains Dr Lindahl.

1 The best title of the above passage would be _____.

① Temptation and Punishment
② Human Behavior and Legal Loopholes
③ How to Educate Impatient Children
④ Time Preferences and Criminal Behavior
⑤ Limitations of Higher Education

2 According to the passage, Dr Lindahl's research argues _____.

① educational background and patience are not related
② the "marshmallow" test does not serve any longer as an effective measure of children's self-control
③ kids who delay rewards are more likely to become criminals later
④ patience is not always a virtue
⑤ schooling could make people more likely to postpone rewards

09

Last year my sixth-grade daughter was subjected to science. Her education, week after week, consisted of mindless memorization of big words like "batholith" and "saprophyte" — words that an average Ph. D. scientist wouldn't know. She recited the accomplishments of famous scientists who did things like "improved nuclear fusion" — never mind that she hasn't the vaguest notion of what nuclear fusion means. She did very well (she's good at memorizing things). And now she hates science. My eighth-grade son was also abused by science education. Week after week he had to perform canned laboratory experiments — projects with preordained right and wrong answers. He figured out how to guess the right answers, so he got good grades. Now _____, too.

Science can provide an exhilarating outlet for every child's curiosity. Science education should teach ways to ask questions, and create a framework for seeking answers. In elementary school, because of jargon and mathematical abstraction, my children got the mistaken impression that science is difficult, boring and irrelevant to their everyday interests. Year by year, class by class across America, the number of students who persevere with science education shrinks.

As a professional geologist who has tried to convey some of the wonder and excitement of science to nonscientists, I am saddened and angered to see "the great science turnoff." I know that science is profoundly important in our lives. Informed decision can't be made about where we live, what we eat and how we treat our environment without basic knowledge about our physical world, the knowledge that constitutes scientific literacy.

1 Which is the most appropriate for the blank?

① he has much interest in science
② he hopes to be a scientist
③ he is good at science
④ he hates science

2 According to the passage, which is true?

① Science education should not give children ready-made answers.
② American science education is too advanced for children.
③ Geology can only be understood with the high level of memorizing capability.
④ Students can endure science education with curiosity.

3 Which is the main idea of the passage?

① To persevere with science education is the duty of scientists.
② Science is very important for understanding human world.
③ The professional terms of science should be memorized.
④ Science education should teach how to make questions and find answers.

10

B. F. Skinner, who transformed the landscape of modern psychology, Ⓐ<u>coined</u> the term operant conditioning to explain the acquisition of learning. Operant conditioning is the process by which organisms learn to behave in ways that produce desirable outcomes. The behavior itself is called an "operant" because it is designed to operate on the environment. In other words, in contrast to classical conditioning — which involves the learning of associations between stimuli resulting in a passive response — operant conditioning involves the learning of an association between a spontaneously emitted action and its consequences.

Skinner also used the term reinforcement instead of *reward* or *satisfaction*. Objectively defined, a reinforcer is any stimulus that Ⓑ_____ the likelihood of a prior response. There are two types of reinforcers: positive and negative. A *positive reinforcer* strengthens a prior response through the presentation of a positive stimulus. In contrast, a *negative reinforcer* strengthens a response through the removal of an aversive stimulus.

Skinner was quick to point out that punishment is not a form of negative reinforcement. Although the two are often confused, punishment has the opposite effect: It Ⓒ_____ the likelihood of a prior response. There are two types of punishment. A *positive punisher* weakens a response through the presentation of an aversive stimulus to weaken specific behaviors. In contrast, a *negative punisher* weakens behaviors through the removal of a stimulus typically characterized as positive.

1 Which is closest in meaning to the underlined Ⓐ<u>coined</u>?
① induced ② invented
③ referred ④ repeated

2 Which pair best fits in the blanks Ⓑ and Ⓒ?
① remits — repels
② denies — approves
③ rejects — receives
④ increases — decreases

3 According to the passage, which is true?
① A positive punisher is a stimulus encouraging a behavior.
② A negative reinforcer is a stimulus reducing a behavior.
③ Positive reinforcement improves the probability of a behavior.
④ Negative punishment is the same as negative reinforcement.

11

In one recent experiment, Aimee E. Stahl and Lisa Feigenson of Johns Hopkins showed 11-month-old babies a sort of magic trick. Either a ball appeared to pass through a solid wall, or a toy car appeared to roll off the end of a shelf and remain suspended in thin air. The babies apparently knew enough about everyday physics to be surprised by these strange events and paid a lot of attention to them. Then the researchers gave the babies toys to play with. The babies who had seen the ball vanish through the wall banged it; those who'd seen the car hovering in thin air kept dropping it. It was as if they were testing to see if the ball really was solid, or if the toy car really did defy gravity.

It is not just that young children don't need to be taught in order to learn. Recent studies show that explicit instruction, the sort of teaching that goes with school and "parenting," can be _____. When children think they are being taught, they are much more likely to simply reproduce what the adult does, instead of creating something new.

My lab tried a different version of the experiment with the complicated toy. This time, though, the experimenter acted like a teacher. She said, "I'm going to show you how my toy works." instead of "I wonder how this toy works." The children imitated exactly what she did, and didn't come up with their own solutions. The children seem to work out, quite rationally, that if a teacher shows them one particular way to do something, that must be the right technique, and there's no point in trying something new. But as a result, the kind of teaching that comes with schools and "parenting" pushes children toward imitation and away from innovation.

1 The most appropriate expression for the blank is _____.
① plenteous
② dispensable
③ limiting
④ compensatory
⑤ eluded

2 According to the experiment conducted by Stahl and Feigenson, babies _____.
① didn't believe in the magic
② fell asleep as soon as the experiment began
③ did nothing but observed what the researchers did
④ showed indifference to toys
⑤ wanted to test something unbelievable

3 The best title of the passage would be '_____'.
① Just let them learn by themselves
② Baby's favorite magic show
③ The best toys of babies
④ How to conduct an experiment with children
⑤ Parenting vs. Instruction

12

Imposter syndrome is a psychological pattern in which an individual doubts their accomplishments both in the classroom and in the workplace and has a persistent internalized fear of being exposed as a fraud. Despite Ⓐ_____ evidence of their competence, those experiencing this phenomenon remain convinced that they are frauds and do not deserve all they have achieved. Individuals with impostorism incorrectly attribute their success to luck or regard it as a result of deceiving others into thinking they are more intelligent than they perceive themselves to be. [A] While early research focused on the prevalence among high-achieving women, impostor syndrome has been recognized to affect both men and women equally. [B]

The term imposter phenomenon was introduced in 1978 by Dr. Pauline R. Clance and Dr. Suzanne A. Imes. They defined impostor phenomenon as an individual experience of self-perceived intellectual phoniness or fraud. The researchers investigated the prevalence of this internal experience by interviewing a sample of 150 high-achieving women. [C] Despite the consistent evidence of external validation, these women lacked the internal acknowledgement of their accomplishments. The participants explained how their success was a result of luck while others overestimated their intelligence and abilities. Clance and Imes believed that this mental framework for impostor phenomenon developed from factors such as gender stereotypes, early family dynamics, culture, and attribution style. The researchers determined that the women who experienced impostor phenomenon displayed symptoms related to depression, generalized anxiety, and low self-confidence. [D]

1 Which of the following is most suitable for blank Ⓐ?

① external
② fictitious
③ constitutional
④ intestine

2 Which is the most appropriate place for the sentence below?

All of the participants had been formally recognized for their professional excellence by colleagues, and had displayed academic achievement through degrees earned and standardized testing scores.

① [A]
② [B]
③ [C]
④ [D]

3 According to the passage, which of the following is true?

① Impostor syndrome is caused by co-workers' doubts about high-achieving women.
② Men as well as women can experience impostor phenomenon.
③ All of the 150 high-achieving female participants overcame the syndrome.
④ Those with high-self confidence tend to develop impostorism.

13

We use the terms "college" and "university" interchangeably. "She went to Michigan," we say, or "he goes to Oberlin" — not bothering with the noun that follows the name as if a college and a university were the same thing. They are not. They are, to be sure, interconnected and a college may exist as a division of "school" within a university. But a college and a university have a different purposes. [A] The former is about transmitting knowledge of and from the past to undergraduate students so they may draw upon it as a living resource in the future. The latter is mainly an array of research activities conducted by faculty and graduate students with the aim of creating new knowledge in order to supersede the past. [B] Both of these are worthy aims, and sometimes they converge, as when a college student works with a scholar or scientist doing cutting-edge or groundbreaking research. More often, however, these purposes come into competition if not conflict, especially as one moves up the ladder of prestige. [C] As the man who created one of the world's great universities, the University of California, acknowledged with unusual honesty, "a superior faculty results in an inferior concern for undergraduate teaching." [D] It has been nearly fifty years since Clark Kerr identified this "cruel paradox" as one of our more pressing problems. Today it is more pressing than ever. [E] But what, exactly, is at stake in college, and why should it matter how much or little goes on there? [F] At its core, a college should be a place where young people find help for navigating the territory between adolescence and adulthood. It should provide guidance, but not coercion, for students trying to cross that treacherous terrain on their way toward self-knowledge. It should help them develop certain qualities of mind and heart requisite for reflective citizenship.

1 The underlined "Both of these" refer to _____.

① college and university
② graduate and undergraduate
③ education and research
④ past and future
⑤ tradition and cutting-edge science

2 The underlined "cruel paradox" means that _____.

① a college might be better than a university
② great scholars are not necessarily great teachers
③ college diploma does not guarantee a decent job
④ a university professor may teach better than a college one
⑤ students don't learn much from their college life

3 If the above passage is divided into three paragraphs, the best boundary would be _____.

① A — C
② A — D
③ B — D
④ B — E
⑤ C — F

14

To study social conformity, Philip Zimbardo and Craig Haney (1977) advertised in newspapers for volunteers to take part in a mock prison experiment. The volunteers were randomly assigned roles as "prisoners" and "guards." Both groups were placed in the basement of the Stanford University psychology building and given minimal instructions; they were told to assume their assigned roles and that the guards' job was to "maintain law and order." In only a few hours, the behavior of one group became sharply differentiated from the behavior of the other group. The guards adopted the behavior patterns and attitudes that are typical of guards in maximum security prisons, with most of them becoming abusive and aggressive. Most of the prisoners became passive, dependent, and depressed, although some became enraged at the guards. Suffering among the prisoners was so great that one had to be released in less than thirty-six hours; several other prisoners also had to be released before the intended two-week experiment was ended after six days.

Stereotypical social norms controlled the behavior of both groups. The guards adopted a manner they believed was necessary to simulate their role and maintain order. The prisoners, who were the targets of the guards' abuse, assumed attitudes that accorded with their image of prison life. As the groups became antagonistic, each reinforced the other's behavior. The prisoners expected the guards to be mean and vicious and treated them accordingly. The guards expected the prisoners to be rebellious and acted so as to prevent unruly behavior. A situation of pretense, by virtue of the participants' perceptions, had real effects on the feelings and behavior of everyone involved. As this experiment shows, conformity to social norms is not simply the result of social pressures from one's own group; the influence of other groups in society magnifies the pressure to conform.

1 위 글의 제목으로 가장 적합한 것을 고르시오.

① Psychological Insecurity of Inmates
② Efficacy of Stereotypical Social Norms
③ Behavior Change in a New Environment
④ Influence of Conformity on Social Behavior

2 위 글의 내용과 일치하는 것을 고르시오.

① Conformity prevented the situation from getting worse.
② The participants behaved according to stereotypical social norms.
③ The prisoner group pretended to be passive because of the instructions.
④ Social pressure to conform within a group is mitigated by contact with other groups.

15

Many parents grew up with punishments, and it's understandable that they rely on them. But punishments tend to escalate conflict and shut down learning. They elicit a fight or flight response, which means that sophisticated thinking in the frontal cortex goes dark and basic defense mechanisms kick in. Punishments make us either rebel, feel shamed or angry, repress our feelings, or figure out how not to get caught. In this case, full-fledged 4-year-old resistance would be at its peak.

So rewards are the positive choice then, right? Not so fast. Over decades, psychologists have suggested that rewards can decrease our natural motivation and enjoyment. For example, kids who like to draw and are, under experimental conditions, paid to do so, draw less than those who aren't paid. This is what psychologists call the "overjustification effect" — the external reward overshadows the child's internal motivation.

_____. In one classic series of studies, people were given a set of materials (a box of pins, a candle, and a book of matches) and asked to figure out how to attach the candle to the wall. The solution requires innovative thinking — seeing the materials in a way unrelated to their purpose (the box as a candle holder). People who were told they'd be rewarded to solve this dilemma took longer, on average, to figure it out. Rewards narrow our field of view. Our brains stop puzzling freely. We stop thinking deeply and seeing the possibilities.

The whole concept of punishments and rewards is based on negative assumptions about children — that they need to be controlled and shaped by us, and that they don't have good intentions. But we can flip this around to see kids as capable, wired for empathy, cooperation, team spirit and hard work. That perspective changes how we talk to children in powerful ways. Rewards and punishments are conditional, but our love and positive regard for our kids should be unconditional. In fact, when we lead with empathy and truly listen to our kids, they're more likely to listen to us.

1 Which of the following is most appropriate for the blank?

① Rewards have also been associated with lowering creativity
② However, rewards make kids more attentive to the parents
③ Rewards have also been associated with enhancing creativity
④ Rewards and punishments are vital to enhancing creativity
⑤ Rewards were more effective than punishments in enhancing creativity

2 Which of the following is true according to the passage?

① Neither rewards nor punishments are good solutions.
② First punishments and then rewards are better solutions.
③ First rewards and then punishments are better solutions.
④ More rewards and less punishments are good solutions.
⑤ More punishments and less rewards are better solutions.

16

The school system is viewed by Bourdieu as an institution for the reproduction of legitimate culture through the hidden linkages between scholastic aptitude and cultural heritage. He believes that, despite ideologies of equal opportunity and meritocracy, few educational systems are called upon by the dominant classes to do anything other than reproduce the legitimate culture as it stands and produce agents capable of manipulating it legitimately.

Bourdieu has argued that it is the culture of the dominant group, which is embodied in schools. Educational differences are thus frequently misrecognized as resulting from individual giftedness, rather than from class-based differences, ignoring the fact that the abilities measured by scholastic criteria often stem not from natural "gifts" but from "the greater or lesser affinity between class cultural habits and the demands of the educational system or the criteria which define success within it."

The notion of cultural capital was proposed by Bourdieu in the early 1960s to describe familiarity with bourgeois culture, the unequal distribution of which helps to conserve social hierarchy under the cloak of individual talent and academic meritocracy. This notion includes such things as acquired knowledge (educational or otherwise), cultural codes, manner of speaking and so forth, which are embodied as a kind of "habitus" in the individual and are also objectified in cultural goods.

1 According to the passage, which of the following is NOT true?

① Working-class students may feel like outsiders in the middle-class habitus of higher education.
② Individuals tend to possess innate intelligence based on their social class.
③ Educational institutions ensure the profitability of the cultural capital of the dominant.
④ The dominant culture, by making itself recognized as universal, legitimizes the interests of the dominant group.

2 Which of the following statements can be inferred from the passage?

① According to Bourdieu, every culture is equally valued and equally legitimate.
② According to Bourdieu, schooling produces certain entrenched ways of recognizing that foster existing class stratification.
③ According to Bourdieu, individuals' efficacy is most strongly influenced by mastery experiences throughout all phases of their lives.
④ According to Bourdieu, cultural reproduction is a trivial mechanism through which socioeconomic polarization takes place.

3 What would be the best title of the passage above?

① The importance of individual giftedness in schooling
② The significance of students' achievement in schooling
③ The social responsibility of dominant culture in schooling
④ The reproduction of inequalities in schooling

17

Pedagogy has been defined as the art and science of teaching children. In the pedagogical model, the teacher has full responsibility for making decisions about what will be learned, how it will be learned, when it will be learned, and if the material has been learned. [A] Pedagogy, or teacher-directed instruction as it is commonly known, places the student in a submissive role requiring obedience to the teacher's instructions. It is based on the assumption that learners need to know only what the teacher teaches them. The result is a teaching and learning situation that actively promotes dependency on the instructor.

Up until very recently, the pedagogical model has been applied equally to the teaching of children and adults, and in a sense, is a contradiction in terms. [B] They are often motivated to learn by a sincere desire to solve immediate problems in their lives. Additionally, they have an increasing need to be self-directing. In many ways the pedagogical model does not account for such developmental changes on the part of adults, and thus produces tension, resentment, and resistance in individuals.

The growth and development of andragogy as an alternative model of instruction has helped to remedy this situation and improve the teaching of adults. But this change did not occur overnight. [C] In fact, an important event took place that affected the direction of adult education in North America. Andragogy as a system of ideas, concepts, and approaches to adult learning was introduced to adult educators in the United States by Malcolm Knowles. [D] His contributions to this system have been many and have influenced the thinking of countless educators of adults.

The term andragogy is often interpreted as the process of engaging adult learners with the structure of learning experience. Knowles defined the term as the art and science of helping adults learn. In the first use of the term andragogy, he suggested that it should be distinguished from the more commonly used pedagogy. Later, he modified his early view, stating "andragogy is simply another model of assumptions about adult learners to be used alongside the pedagogical model of assumptions, thereby providing two alternative models for testing out the assumptions as to their 'fit' with particular situations."

1 아래의 문장이 들어갈 위치로 가장 적합한 곳을 고르시오.

The reason is that as adults mature, they become increasingly independent and responsible for their own actions.

① [A]   ② [B]
③ [C]   ④ [D]

2 위 글을 통해 추론할 수 있는 것으로 가장 적합한 것을 고르시오.

① The andragogical model assigns the primary role to teachers in instruction.
② In the pedagogical approach, students remain passive agents to observe teachers' instruction.
③ Recently, the pedagogical model is more welcomed by adults than children.
④ According to Knowles' later view, pedagogy and andragogy are contradictory with each other.

18

Passive-aggressive behaviors are those that involve acting indirectly aggressive rather than directly aggressive. Passive-aggressive people regularly exhibit resistance to requests or demands from family and other individuals often by procrastinating, Ⓐexpressing sullenness, or acting stubborn.

Passive-aggressive behavior may manifest itself in a number of different ways. For example, a person might repeatedly make excuses to avoid certain people as a way of expressing their dislike or anger towards those individuals. In cases where the passive-aggressive person is angry, they might repeatedly claim that they are not mad or that they are fine, even when they are apparently furious and not okay. Denying what they are feeling and refusing to be emotionally open, they are shutting down further communication and Ⓑrefusing to discuss the issue. Deliberately procrastinating is another characteristic of passive-aggressive behavior. When Ⓒconfronting with tasks that they do not want to do or appointments they do not wish to keep, the passive-aggressive individual will drag their feet. If they have been asked to complete a task at work, they will put it off until the very last second. They may even turn it in late in order to punish the person who assigned the task.

So what can you do when confronted by a friend, co-worker, or even a romantic partner who regularly engages in passive-aggression? The first step is to recognize the signs of such behavior. Sulking, backhanded compliments, procrastination, withdrawal, and refusal to communicate are all signs of passive-aggression. When the other person begins acting in such a way, try to keep your anger in check. Instead, point out the other person's feelings in a way that is non-judgmental yet factual. If you are dealing with a child who is clearly upset about Ⓓhaving to do chores: "You seem to be angry at me for asking you to clean your room." The reality is that people usually deny their anger anyway. At this point, it's a good idea to step back and give them time to work through these feelings.

1   Which of the following is NOT a sign of passive-aggression?

① expressing sullenness
② resisting requests from others
③ hesitating in response
④ completing a task at once

2 What is suggested when you meet a friend showing passive-aggression?

① Stay calm and do not let out the anger.
② Point out his/her feelings in a judgmental way.
③ Report to the health institutes immediately.
④ Punish him/her for such a behavior.

3 Which of the following is NOT grammatical?

① Ⓐ 　　　　　② Ⓑ
③ Ⓒ 　　　　　④ Ⓓ

19

Whatever their initial motivations, fundamentalist groups were occasionally successful in pursuing anti-evolution goals in the South and Southwest during the first few decades of the last century. By the end of the 1920s, fundamentalists had introduced anti-evolution bills into a majority of U.S. state legislatures, and had passed some in various southern states. Probably the most famous confrontation between evolution and biblical creationism during that period was the 1925 trial of a schoolteacher, John Scopes, who was convicted of ignoring the ban against teaching evolution in Tennessee schools.

Although many biologists felt that the Scopes trial essentially defeated the intellectual validity of the creationist position, creationists apparently lost little ground in these regions and managed to have an impact on public education far beyond the South and Southwest. As Nelkin pointed out, by influencing textbook adoption procedures in various local and state school boards in the United States, creationists successfully minimized evolutionary explanations in secondary school textbooks for a long time.

The impetus for an increase of evolutionary teaching in U.S. secondary schools was the result of a movement to reform the science curriculum in the late 1950s and early 1960s, when it was realized that science education lagged behind that of other countries, specifically the Soviet Union, which in 1957 had launched the first space satellite, Sputnik. Among these innovations were new high school textbooks in both biological and social sciences that discussed evolution and analyzed changes in human social relationships. By the end of the 1960s anti-evolution laws were either repealed or declared unconstitutional.

Within the last decade, a number of societies and institutes established by fundamentalists for the propagation of creation science/intelligent design have entered the fray with the aim of including creationism in the science curriculum. Despite the name, there is little (if any) recognizable science in creation science. Although considerable literature deals with creationist attacks on evolution, the refusal of fundamentalist creationists to accept the scientific evidence shows no promise of ever being resolved.

1 위 글을 통해 추론할 수 있는 것으로 가장 적합한 것을 고르시오.

① The increase of the evolutionary teaching resulted in the public belief that creationists deteriorated the quality of science education.
② The author is skeptical about the arguments in intelligent design proposed by fundamentalists.
③ Fundamentalists were successful in introducing anti-evolution bills to the entire states of the U.S. in the 1920s.
④ Fundamentalists' essential claims are based on the premises of evolutionary biology.

2 위 글의 제목으로 가장 적합한 것을 고르시오.

① Contribution of Science Education to the Development of Space Science
② Science Curriculum Reform in U.S. Secondary Schools
③ Eulogy to the Propagation of Creationism
④ Creationist-Evolutionist Conflict in the U.S. Science Education

20

A Although many people use the two words "guilt" and "shame" interchangeably, from a psychological perspective, they actually refer to different experiences. Guilt and shame sometimes go hand in hand; the same action may give rise to feelings of both shame and guilt, where the former reflects how we feel about ourselves and the latter involves an awareness that our actions have injured someone else. In other words, shame relates to self; guilt to others.

B According to Dictionary.com, guilt involves the awareness of having done something wrong; it arises from our actions (even if it might be one that occurs in fantasy). Shame may result from the awareness of guilt but apparently is not the same thing as guilt. It's a painful feeling about how we appear to others (and to ourselves) and doesn't necessarily depend on our having done anything. I once said something hurtful at a dinner party, and on some level, I intended it to be hurtful. Afterward, I felt guilty because I could see that I had hurt my friend. More painfully, I also felt ashamed that I was the sort of person who would behave that way. Guilt arose as a result of inflicting pain on somebody else; I felt shame in relation to myself.

C In order to feel guilt about the harm you may have done to somebody else, you must recognize him or her as a distinct individual, to begin with. Thus, a person who struggles with separation and merger issues might not feel true guilt even if he or she were to use that word to describe a feeling. Many people who display narcissistic behavior often suffer from profound feelings of shame but have little authentic concern for other people; they don't tend to feel genuinely guilty. The lack of empathy to be found in narcissistic personality disorder makes real guilt unlikely since guilt depends upon the ability to intuit how someone else might feel.

D When shame is especially pervasive, it can preclude feelings of genuine concern and guilt from developing; the sense of being damaged is so powerful and painful that it crowds out feelings for anyone else. In such cases, idealization often comes into play: other people are then viewed as perfect, the lucky ones who have the ideal shame-free life we crave; powerful envy may be the (unconscious) result. In those cases, we might take pleasure in hurting the person we envy rather than feeling guilty about it.

1 According to the above passage, which of the following is NOT true about guilt?

① Guilt interferes with an other-oriented connection.
② Guilt involves a condemnation of a specific behavior.
③ Guilt-proneness is positively associated with empathy.
④ Guilt requires more sophisticated cognitive abilities than shame.
⑤ The capacity to feel guilt depends on the psychological growth to view other people as separate.

2 Which of the following would be the best title for paragraph Ⓒ?

① The Self in Shame and Guilt
② Shame, Guilt, and Psychoanalysis
③ Authentic Shame and Genuine Guilt
④ Shame and Guilt as Moral Emotions
⑤ The Link between Shame and Interpersonal Sensitivity

3 Which of the following is the best summary of paragraph Ⓓ?

① Shame-free state is the cause of envy.
② Shame can lead to idealization of others.
③ Shame-proneness is often caused by envy.
④ The self-focus of shame can impede sensitivity to others.
⑤ The feelings of shame are induced by the sense of being damaged.

4 Which of the following is the best summary of the author's argument in the above passage?

① Shame and guilt induce different emotions.
② Shame and guilt relate to interpersonal empathy.
③ The self-focus of shame can impede the development of guilt.
④ The difference between shame and guilt can be examined in the role of the self.
⑤ Shame involves negative evaluations of the self while guilt involves positive evaluations of the self.

03

문화·예술

03 문화·예술

01

Ethnocentrism can be seen in many aspects of culture — myths, folktales, proverbs, and even _____. For example, in many languages, especially those of non-Western societies, the word used to refer to one's own tribe or ethnic group literally means "mankind" or "human." This implies that members of other groups are less than human. For example, the term *eskimo*, used to refer to groups that inhabit the arctic and subarctic regions, is an Indian word used by neighbors of the Eskimos who observed their strange way of life but did not share it. The term means "eaters of raw flesh," and as such is an ethnocentric observation about cultural practices that were normal to one group and repulsive to another. On the other hand, if we look at one subgroup among the Alaskan natives, we find them calling themselves *inuit*, which means "real people" (they obviously did not think eating raw flesh was anything out of the ordinary). Here, then, is a contrast between one's own group, which is real, and the rest of the world, which is not so "real." Both terms, *eskimo* and *inuit*, are equally ethnocentric — one as an observation about differences, the other as a self-evaluation. However, *inuit* is now seen as a more appropriate term because of its origin.

1 According to the passage, which of the following best fits the blank?

① food
② language
③ clothing
④ belief

2 According to the passage, which of the following is true?

① Both *eskimo* and *inuit* have the meaning of "mankind" or "human."
② Both the Eskimos and the Inuits eat raw flesh.
③ Those who call themselves *inuit* think they are the only real people in the world.
④ Ethnocentric terms are found in non-Western societies only.

02

Reggae is a music genre that originated in Jamaica in the late 1960s. A 1968 single "Do the Reggay" was the first popular song to use the word, effectively naming the genre and introducing it to a global audience. While sometimes used in a broad sense to refer to most types of popular Jamaican dance music, the term 'reggae' more properly denotes a particular music style that was strongly influenced by traditional *mento* as well as American jazz and R&B. Reggae is instantly recognizable from the counterpoint between the bass guitar and drum downbeat, and the offbeat rhythm section. It is common for reggae to be sung in Jamaican dialect and Jamaican English. Reggae has spread around the world, often incorporating local instruments and fusing with other genres. For instance, Caribbean music in the United Kingdom, including reggae, has been popular since the late 1960s, and has evolved into several subgenres and fusions. In Jamaica, authentic reggae is one of the biggest sources of income.

1 Which of the following is the best title for the passage?

① Origin and Traits of Reggae
② Reggae's International Theme
③ Use of Language in Reggae
④ Popular Reggae Artists

2 According to the passage, which of the following is NOT true?

① Authentic reggae earns Jamaicans a lot of money.
② Reggae music has emerged without international influence.
③ Reggae lyrics are rarely written in American English.
④ There are many different types of reggae across the world.

03

Cultural relativism is the principle that an individual human's beliefs and activities should be understood by others in terms of that individual's own culture. This principle was established as Ⓐ_____ in anthropological research by Franz Boas in the first few decades of the 20th century and later popularized by his students. Boas first articulated the idea in 1887: "… civilization is not something absolute, but … is relative, and … our ideas and conceptions are true only so far as our civilization goes."

However, Boas did not coin the term. The first use of the term recorded in the Oxford English Dictionary was by philosopher and social theorist Alain Locke in 1924 to describe Robert Lowie's "extreme cultural relativism," found in the latter's 1917 book "Culture and Ethnology." The term became common among anthropologists after Boas' death in 1942, to express their Ⓑ_____ of a number of ideas Boas had developed. Boas believed that the sweep of cultures, to be found in connection with any sub species, is so vast and pervasive that there cannot be a relationship between culture and race. Cultural relativism involves specific epistemological and methodological claims. Whether or not these claims necessitate a specific ethical stance is a matter of debate. This principle should not be confused with moral relativism.

1 위 글의 제목으로 가장 적당한 것은?

① Current Debates over Cultural Relativism
② What is Cultural Relativism?
③ Cultural Relativism vs. Moral Relativism
④ Branches of Cultural Relativism

2 위 글의 빈칸 Ⓐ과 Ⓑ에 들어갈 단어로 적당한 것은?

① axiomatic — sympathy
② axiomatic — synthesis
③ unconventional — sympathy
④ unconventional — synthesis

3 위 글의 다음에 올 내용으로 가장 적당한 것은?

① Evaluation of appropriateness of a behavior in other cultures
② Decline of culture relativism research
③ Difference between cultural relativism and moral relativism
④ Thorny issues in cultural relativism

04

On October 21, 1962, an exhibition opened at New York's Sidney Janis Gallery that altered American art history. The exhibition featured new artists who dominated the 1960s. New York's art critics went crazy. A renowned critic said this exhibition "hit the New York art world with the force of an earthquake." Surely, there were contrasting views. The new artists were referred to as 'vulgarists' and even 'sign painters.' Despite polarized views, these artists, priding themselves as descendants of Marcel Duchamp, continued to defy traditional fine art. Andy Warhol was the heart of this movement. He had admired fine art all his life, but Warhol was faithful to this commercial approach until the end. He used 'ready-made' subjects for his paintings, replicated, and copied them in silk-screens, and projected the public's desire through them. His famous *Campbell's Soup Cans* expresses best Andy Warhol's aesthetics. The two words, Ⓐ_____ and Ⓑ_____, split Warho's ego all his life. He wrote, "Business art is the step that comes after art. I wanted to be a business artist. Being good in business is the most fascinating kind of art." He called himself a business artist, but Warhol never quenched his thirst for fine art. The term 'Warholism' signifies the world's love for the artist, but Ⓒcritics refused to rid his work of the commercialism tag. A quarter century has passed since he faced death alone in a New York hospital, but Warhol remains one of our most controversial artists.

1 According to the passage, which of the following is true of Andy Warhol?

① He was a pioneering artist highly influential to his descendants including Duchamp.
② He created materials for his works by himself.
③ His commitment to the commercial approach led him to his abhorrence of fine art.
④ His artworks still receive mixed reviews from critics.

2 From the context, which of the following ordered pairs best fits into Ⓐ and Ⓑ?

① traditional — modern
② art — business
③ old — new
④ replicated — original

3 Which of the following can be inferred from the underlined Ⓒ?

① Warhol's business art was still underestimated by art critics.
② Warhol's name was removed from the history of art.
③ Warhol's business art was finally acknowledged as mainstream art.
④ Warhol cleared himself of the accusation of being a business artist.

05

　　The general answer to <u>all these questions</u> is the same: culture. As Bailey points out, "cultures vary in their ways of thinking and ways of behaving." A As you may have noticed, all of the questions we posed dealt with thinking and behaving. Although culture is not the only stimulus behind your behavior, its omnipresent quality makes it one of the most powerful. B Furthermore, what makes culture so unique is that you share your culture with other people who have been exposed to similar experiences. While your personal experiences and genetic heritage form the unique "you," culture unites people with a collective frame of reference that is the domain of a community, not a characteristic of a single person. C Nolan reaffirms that culture is a group worldview, the way of organizing the world that a particular society has created over time. D This framework or web of meaning allows the members of that society to make sense of themselves, their world, and their experiences in that world. It is this sharing of a common reality that gives people within a particular culture a common fund of knowledge.

1　밑줄 친 "all these questions"의 예로 유추하기에 적절하지 않은 것은?

① Why do some people believe in God?
② Why do some people have genetic disease?
③ Why do some people paint and decorate their entire bodies?
④ Why do some people shake hands when introduced to a stranger?

2　아래의 문장이 들어갈 곳으로 가장 알맞은 곳은?

As Hofstede points out, "Culture is to a human collective what personality is to an individual."

① A　　　　　　　　　② B
③ C　　　　　　　　　④ D

06

Piano Sonata No. 2 is one of the most recognizable works by 19th-century Polish pianist and composer Frédéric Chopin. While the public was almost immediately enchanted by the work, many of the leading critics of the day were less than impressed. One of its most outspoken detractors was celebrated composer Robert Schumann. He, along with other critics of the time, argued that the work's movements did not fit together thematically. Because of this supposed shortcoming, the work was regarded as being Ⓐ_____ in form. In fact, some critics argued that it should not be classified as a sonata at all.

Notwithstanding these harsh appraisals, the work's third movement, titled "Funeral March," received high praise. Celebrated composer Franz Liszt, a friend of Chopin, found this movement nothing short of brilliant. His sentiment was echoed by other musicians, and the Funeral March has become one of the most enduring movements written for the piano. It has also influenced compositions in many genres of modern music, from jazz to electronic.

1 Which of the following is most appropriate for blank Ⓐ?

① opulent
② unorthodox
③ unrelenting
④ excellent

2 What is the main purpose of the passage?

① To review the critical reception of Piano Sonata No. 2
② To analyze the musical structure of Piano Sonata No. 2
③ To examine the influence of various composers on Piano Sonata No. 2
④ To counter the negative assessments of Piano Sonata No. 2

3 Which of the following is correct about Piano Sonata No. 2?

① It was largely disliked by the public upon its release.
② Schumann had mixed feelings about its musical value.
③ Many critics regarded it as having clashing themes.
④ Its third movement was less well received than its other movements.

07

Postmodernism is a broad movement that developed in the mid- to late 20th century across philosophy, the arts, architecture, and criticism, marking a departure from modernism. The term has been more generally applied to describe a historical era said to follow after modernity and the tendencies of this era.

Postmodernism is generally defined by an attitude of skepticism, irony, or rejection toward what it describes as the grand narratives and ideologies associated with modernism, often criticizing Enlightenment rationality and focusing on the role of ideology in maintaining political or economic power. Postmodern thinkers frequently describe knowledge claims and value systems as contingent or socially-conditioned, framing them as products of political, historical, or cultural discourses and hierarchies. Common targets of postmodern criticism include universalist ideas of Ⓐsubjective reality, Ⓑtruth, Ⓒreason, and Ⓓscience. Accordingly, postmodern thought is broadly characterized by tendencies to self-consciousness, self-referentiality, epistemological and moral relativism, pluralism, and irreverence.

Postmodern critical approaches gained popularity in the 1980s and 1990s, and have been adopted in a variety of academic and theoretical disciplines, including cultural studies, philosophy of science, economics, linguistics, architecture, feminist theory, and literary criticism, as well as art movements in fields such as literature, contemporary art, and music. Postmodernism is often associated with schools of thought such as deconstruction, post-structuralism, and institutional critique, as well as philosophers such as Jean-François Lyotard, Jacques Derrida, and Fredric Jameson.

Criticisms of postmodernism are intellectually diverse and include arguments that postmodernism promotes obscurantism, is meaningless, and that it adds nothing to analytical or empirical knowledge.

1 Which of the following is NOT true about postmodernism?

① It aggressively criticizes the fundamental values of modernity.
② It places focal attention on the role of ideology for maintaining political power.
③ It inherits modernism's concept of grand narratives.
④ It is related to deconstruction and post-structuralism.

2 Which of the following is NOT appropriate from the context?

① Ⓐ
② Ⓑ
③ Ⓒ
④ Ⓓ

08

In his book, *The Psychology of Prejudice*, Nelson (2006) asks a sarcastic question: "Where have all the bigots gone?" He observes that it was once common for Whites to openly express racist attitudes and beliefs, advocate for segregation, and denigrate people of color — especially Black Americans — as morally and intellectually inferior. Over many decades, Ⓐ_____, the old-fashioned forms of racism that characterized the segregated Southern States diminished greatly in importance and seemed to have disappeared. Much of this change has been attributed to the landmark rulings of the Supreme Court, the Civil Rights Movement, and the Third World Movements. If one traces the stereotypes of Black Americans over time, for example, early characterizations of them as superstitious, lazy, and ignorant have declined dramatically.

Many race scholars, however, believe that racism has not disappeared, but (1) morphed into a highly disguised, invisible, and subtle form that lies outside the level of conscious awareness, (2) hides in the invisible assumptions and beliefs of individuals, and (3) is embedded in the policies and structures of our institutions. These researchers and scholars do not deny that major advances in positive race-relations have occurred because of legal, political, and social forces against racism, but they cite an increasing body of evidence suggesting that prejudice is alive and well under the labels "modern racism," "symbolic racism," and "aversive racism."

1 Which expression best fits Ⓐ?

① for example
② therefore
③ especially
④ however
⑤ in general

2 Which statement CANNOT be inferred from the passage above?

① The modern forms of racism operate in such a manner as to preserve the nonprejudiced self-image of Whites by offering them convenient rationalizations for their actions.
② Aversive racists truly believe that they are nonprejudiced, espouse egalitarian values, and would never consciously discriminate, but they, nevertheless, harbor unconscious biased attitudes that may result in discriminatory actions.
③ The term "old-fashioned racism" has been used to define its blatant forms.
④ The contemporary manifestation of racism includes hate crimes, physical assaults, and use of racial epithets.
⑤ Symbolic racists are prevented from recognizing their own racial biases or the implicit prejudicial attitudes they harbor toward others.

09

In Christian art, a Pietà is an artwork depicting the Virgin Mary holding the crucified body of Jesus. While these artworks take many forms, they are typically sculptures, with the earliest examples being wooden figures crafted in Germany in the Middle Ages. By the 15th century, the image, which was never explicitly mentioned in the Bible, had made its way to Italy. In 1497, Michelangelo, perhaps the country's most famous sculptor, was commissioned by a French cardinal to create a marble Pietà. This work, which was to adorn the cardinal's tomb after his death in 1499, became one of Michelangelo's masterpieces. He started the sculpture in 1498, and after months of labor, he unveiled it to widespread acclaim. Unlike virtually all his other works, it bears the sculptor's name, which was added after Michelangelo learned that another artist had been falsely credited with its creation. The sculpture exemplifies the Italian Renaissance principles of naturalism, an artistic style that emphasized idealized yet highly lifelike detail. Ⓐ_____, Michelangelo's figures exhibit grossly distorted proportions, with Mary dwarfing the lifeless figure of Jesus. Some view this artistic choice as an attempt to evoke the idea of a child in his mother's arms. However, others argue that the sculpture's proportions were merely intended to provide the viewer with a sense of stability.

1 Which of the following is correct according to the passage?

① Pietàs have been created in a variety of different media.
② Pietàs were developed in Italy before spreading to Germany.
③ Michelangelo started his Pietà after the French cardinal's death.
④ Michelangelo depicted Mary as being small compared with Jesus.

2 Which of the following is closest in meaning to the underlined word credited?

① aggrandized
② acknowledged
③ reimbursed
④ complimented

3 Which of the following is most appropriate for blank Ⓐ?

① Nevertheless
② Consequently
③ For instance
④ To summarize

4 What can be inferred from the passage?

① Michelangelo feared being denied recognition for sculpting his Pietà.
② Michelangelo clarified the reason for his sculpture's odd proportions.
③ Michelangelo's Pietà was regarded as flawed upon its public unveiling.
④ Michelangelo's Pietà surprised Renaissance viewers with its unusual style.

10

No one civilization can possibly utilize in its mores the whole potential range of human behavior. Every society, beginning with some inclination in one direction or another, carries its preference farther and farther, integrating itself more and more completely upon its chosen basis, and discarding those types of behaviors that are uncongenial. Most of those organizations of personality that seem to us more incontrovertibly abnormal have been used by different civilizations in the very foundations of their institutional life. Conversely, the most valued traits of our normal individuals have been looked on in differently organized cultures as aberrant. Normality, in short, within a very wide range, is culturally defined. The very eyes with which we see the problem are conditioned by the long traditional habits of our own society.

It is a point that has been made more often in relation to ethics than in relation to psychiatry. We do not any longer make the mistake of deriving the morality of our own locality and decade directly from the inevitable constitution of human nature. We do not elevate it to the dignity of a first principle. We recognize that morality differs in every society, and is a convenient term for _____. Mankind has always preferred to say, "It is morally good" rather than "It is habitual." But historically the two phrases are synonymous.

1 What would be the best title of the passage above?

① Morality and Cultural Norms
② Aberrant Norms of Human Behavior
③ How to Categorize Civilizations Critically
④ Our Preferences for Normal Individuals

2 Choose the one that best fills in the blank.

① the inevitability of different civilizations
② universally recognizable human traits
③ various types of behaviors
④ socially approved habits

3 Which of the following CANNOT be inferred according to the passage above?

① We tend to believe habitual actions to be morally good.
② Unlike normality, morality is not subject to change in different cultures.
③ Every society discredits behaviors that do not conform to its chosen norms.
④ What is considered aberrant in one society can be considered normal in another.

11

Italy's seminal position as a cultural cornucopia was magnified in 1748 by the discovery of the buried city of Pompeii. Suddenly genuine Roman works were being dug up daily, and the world could admire an entire ancient city.

A Because of renewed interest in studying the ancients, art academies began to spring up around Europe and in the United States. Artists were trained in what the Academy viewed as the proper classical tradition — part of that training sent many artists to Rome to study works firsthand.

B The discovery of Pompeii inspired art theorist Johann Winckelmann to publish *The History of Ancient Art* in 1764, which many consider the first art history book. Winckelmann heavily criticised the waning Rococo as decadent, and celebrated the ancients for their purity of form and crispness of execution.

C The Salons had very traditional standards, insisting on artists employing a flawless technique with emphasis on established subjects executed with conventional perspective and drawing. History paintings, that is, those paintings dealing with historical, religious, or mythological subjects, were most prized. Portraits were next in importance, followed by landscapes, genre paintings, and then still lifes.

D The French Academy, for example, showcased selected works by its members in an annual or biannual event called the Salon, so called because it was held in a large room, the Salon Carré, in the Louvre. Art critics and judges would scout out the best of the current art scene, and accept a limited number of paintings for public view at the Salon. If an artist received this critical endorsement, it meant his or her prestige greatly increased, as well as the value of his or her paintings.

No education was complete without a Grand Tour of Italy. Usually under the guidance of a connoisseur, the tour visited cities like Naples, Florence, Venice, and Rome. It was here that people could immerse themselves in the lessons of the ancient world and perhaps collect an antiquity or two, or buy a work from a contemporary artist under the guidance of the connoisseur. The blessings of the Neoclassical period were firmly entrenched in the mind of art professionals and educated amateurs.

1 위 글의 단락을 논리적 흐름에 맞게 순서대로 배열한 것으로 가장 적합한 것을 고르시오.

① A — C — B — D
② A — D — B — C
③ B — A — D — C
④ B — D — A — C

2 위 글의 내용과 일치하는 것을 고르시오.

① The Grand Tour accompanied by a connoisseur expedited the discovery of Pompeii.
② Johann Winckelmann was an avid supporter of the French Academy.
③ The Salons challenged the traditional artistic conventions and invited aesthetic criticism.
④ The Grand Tour of Italy was an important part in education of the Neoclassical period.

12

For modern listeners, Debussy practically defines French music, by which I mean that the essential qualities of his music (not only his sensuous delicacy but also his aversion to the harmonic behavior characteristic of late-nineteenth-century German music, a dense chromatic motion that tends to constantly, restlessly build to orgiastic climaxes, as in Wagner and Strauss) have come to be seen as essentially "French" qualities. Walsh makes clear, however, that Debussy, far from simply amplifying or exemplifying the dominant tendencies of his musical milieu, consciously and stubbornly swam against the current, especially when it came to the heavy influence of German music on French composers. Wagner was the unavoidable presence in late-nineteenth-century Paris, but Debussy traced the blame for that influence further back, to Gluck. Debussy was quietly radical in his preference for Rameau's "delicate and charming tenderness" over what he perceived as the Germanic "affectation of profundity or the need to double underline everything."

1 윗글의 제목으로 가장 적절한 것은?

① Further Back to Gluck: Root of Debussy's Music
② A Wizardly Gift: To Be Both French and German
③ What Makes Debussy's Music Fundamentally French
④ Rediscovering an Unsung Hero in the History of Music
⑤ Debussy's Alchemy: Textualizing Global Conflicts into Music

2 밑줄 친 "swam against the current"의 의미로 가장 적절한 것은?

① not to cater to the taste of his German audiences
② to control his own personal preferences for French music
③ to withdraw from the world and sink into the inner world of his art
④ not to imitate the formal logic and dense textures of German music
⑤ to curb the contemporary musical tendencies defined by delicacy and charm

13

It makes little sense to imagine the scene of culture as one that one might enter to find bits and pieces of evidence that show an Ⓐ<u>abiding</u> faith in an already established notion of universality. If one were to enter various domains of culture in order to find examples of world citizens, one would Ⓑ_____ from those various examples the selfsame lesson, the selfsame universal bearing. But is the relation between culture and the universal appropriately construed as that between an example and the moral dictum it is said to support? In such cases, the examples are subordinate to the universal, and they all indicate the universal in the same way. The future articulation of the universal, however, can happen only if we find ways to effect cultural translations between those various cultural examples in order to see which versions of the universal are proposed, on what exclusions they are based, and how the entry of the excluded into the domain of the universal requires a radical transformation in our thinking of universality. When competing claims to the universal are made, it seems imperative not to presume that the cultural moments at issue exemplify a(n) Ⓒ_____ universal. The claim is part of the ongoing cultural articulation of universality, and the complex process of learning how to read that claim is not something any of us can do outside of the difficult process of cultural translation. This translation will not be an easy one in which we reduce every cultural instance to a presupposed universality, nor will it be the enumeration of radical particularisms between which no communication is possible.

1 Choose the answer that has the closest meaning to the underlined word Ⓐ above.

① staunch
② coruscating
③ subsiding
④ appending

2 How does the author define the "universal"?

① a religious belief that opposes modern androcentric culture
② a perennial truth that can only be discovered through numerous cultural translations
③ an ideology to be debunked
④ an ongoing approximation of perspectives in a single articulation

3 According to the author, why are cultural translations important for the future expression of the universal?

① It is central to the articulation of a multicultural society based on mutual respect for one another.
② It is needed to recognize and incorporate excluded aspects into better approximations of the universal.
③ It is essential for actualizing timeless truths that can only be articulated through cultural comparisons.
④ An abiding faith should be reinforced by adopting a universal truth that reflects all cultures.

4 Choose the best words for blanks ⓑ and ⓒ above.

① cull — ready-made
② rile up — protean
③ foment — excremental
④ prod — nascent

14

Eugène Delacroix (1798-1863) was an important artist in the French Romantic movement, and some of his greatest works, like *Massacre at Chios*, depicted the horrors of war while also supporting revolutions against oppressive governments. Many of his later paintings depicted Arabic and Jewish culture, often based on sketches that he made while traveling in Spain and North Africa. Delacroix also illustrated books by William Shakespeare, Sir Walter Scott, and Johann Wolfgang von Goethe, and he earned a reputation as a writer on art and other subjects for his *Journals*. His painting *Liberty Leading the People* commemorates France's three-day July Revolution in 1830 when the Trois Glorieuses, a coalition of workers and the middle classes, deposed King Charles X and established a constitutional monarchy under King Louis-Philippe. The July Revolution was prompted by four proclamations signed by Charles that dissolved the National Assembly, ended freedom of the press, and created an electoral system that gave the aristocracy more power. *Liberty Leading the People* combines realism and allegory, with Liberty personified as both a mythical figure or goddess and a woman of the people leading the rebels on the bloodiest day of the revolution. Delacroix created this painting for a May 1831 exhibit celebrating the revolution at the Salon in Paris. But because government officials feared that Delacroix's painting would encourage more insurrections, *Liberty Leading the People* was exhibited only rarely after the Salon until it entered the Louvre in 1874. Now Delacroix's painting is associated with patriotism for the French Republic, so much so that the portrait appeared on the back of the hundred-franc note for fifteen years.

1 Which does NOT describe Delacroix's career?

① artist
② writer
③ illustrator
④ journalist

2 According to the passage, which is true?

① France's July Revolution in 1830 ended up in abolishing monarchy permanently.
② Some of Delacroix's great works reflect the ideals of the French Romanticism.
③ In France's July Revolution in 1830 workers, the middle classes and the aristocracy joined their force to overthrow the oppressive king's regime.
④ Delacroix made his paintings on Arabic and Jewish culture directly from his memory of traveling experiences in Arabic and Jewish communities.

3 According to the passage, which is NOT true about *Liberty Leading the People*?

① It is particularly famous for its championing the cause of freedom.
② It describes the revolution scene on the street predominantly in the realistic mode.
③ It is so endeared by the French people that it has been displayed on money for 15 years.
④ It was seldom exhibited in France for decades even after the success of the July Revolution in 1830.

15

The format of the Sun Dance, a traditional Native American ceremonial dance, has always varied from community to community. Ⓐ_____, there are certain features of the dance that many tribes share. Often, the dance must be initiated by a sponsor, someone who takes a vow in the hope of being relieved of a worry, or being blessed in the coming year. [A] It is almost always performed near the time of summer solstice. Most Sun Dances begin with the erection of a circular lodge around a solemnly chosen and cut central pole. During the next three or four days, periods of dancing, accompanied by singing and drumming, are interspersed with periods of rest and meditation. Dancers do not eat or drink during the entire period of the dance, although some do chew on bear root to keep their mouths moist. Toward the end of the dance, participants experience visions and receive blessings. [B]

Early Europeans were repulsed by some tribes' practice of self-mortification in the ceremony. [C] Dancing and straining against the ropes, they eventually tore loose from the skewers. Through this ritual, participants literally suffer on behalf of their community and call upon the Creator to pity and assist them in the fulfillment of their vows. [D] This aspect of the ritual was the main reason federal officials prohibited it between the late 1870s and 1935. Despite the ban, however, many tribes continued to hold the Sun Dance surreptitiously in remote areas of their reservations or to enact it without its objectionable features.

1 Which of the following is most suitable for the blank Ⓐ?
　① Therefore　　　　② Hence
　③ Nevertheless　　　④ Meanwhile

2 Which is the most appropriate place for the sentence below?

Male dancers had their breasts or backs skewered and tied to a central lodge pole.

　① [A]　　　　② [B]
　③ [C]　　　　④ [D]

3 According to the passage, which of the following is NOT true?
　① Dancers are allowed to bite a certain plant root to moisten their mouths.
　② An individual can initiate the Sun Dance as a sponsor.
　③ Some aspects of the Sun Dance are common to many tribes.
　④ The Sun Dance was not performed during the prohibition period.

4 According to the passage, the main objective of the self-mortification is to _____.

① test the participants' limits to endure physical sufferings
② show the participants' courage and determination to help the community
③ induce the Creator to help the participants fulfill their vows
④ experience visions of the tribal future and participants' pity toward the Creator

16

Most critics, especially the highbrow kind, deplored the mass culture of the 1950s. And there was plenty to deplore. The preponderance of popular fare — Hollywood spectaculars, "horror" comics, hammering rock-and-roll music — had only one redeeming virtue: transience. Television was everyone's whipping boy; and in contemplating its fare, even middlebrow columnist Harriet Van Horne was crying cultural doom: "Our people are becoming less Ⓐ_____ by the minute. As old habits decline, such as reading books and thinking thoughts, TV will absorb their time. By the 21st Century our people doubtless will be squint-eyed, hunchbacked and fond of the dark."

There were real cultural dangers, no doubt of it. In this age of economic boom and mass media, culture, like toothpaste, was produced and consumed at a fearful rate; and this Ⓑ_____ pressure did tend to lower the quality of the product. Yet the situation was not so dismal as the pessimists claimed. For one thing, the much abused media seemed quite responsible at times. In 1956, the National Broadcasting Company paid out $500,000 to present the premier of Laurence Olivier's film version of Shakespeare's *Richard III*. Fifty million people tuned in, and about half of them stayed on through its entire three hours. *Life* magazine in 1952 regaled — or challenged — its several million readers by devoting a whole issue to the publication of Ernest Hemingway's new novel, *The Old Man and the Sea*.

There were other oases in the cultural wasteland. In painting, a group of innovators led by Jackson Pollock moved the capital of the art world from Paris to New York. Egghead humor, as purveyed by sharp-tongued satirists such as Mort Sahl, graduated from small clubs to big audiences on network variety shows. Paperback publishers propagated millions of copies of standard classics at prices low enough($0.25 to $1.35) to attract cultural window-shoppers. Classical music was riding a spectacular wave of national interest. In mid-decade the country boasted some 200 symphony orchestras, up 80 per cent since 1940, and 2,500 towns offered concert series, an increase of 150 per cent in the same period. Music, in fact, went a long way toward proving that America's cultural oases might yet become bigger than the wasteland itself: in 1955 some 35 million people went to classical music performances — more than twice the year's attendance at major league baseball games.

1 빈칸 Ⓐ와 Ⓑ에 들어가기에 가장 적합한 것을 고르시오.

① obdurate — opportune
② thoughtful — facilitative
③ literate — relentless
④ impulsive — unremitting

2 위 글을 통해 추론할 수 있는 것으로 가장 적합한 것을 고르시오.

① The prevailing mood of the 1950s was pessimism, as there was much more talk of avant-garde in literary and intellectual circles.
② Despite the decadence of the mass culture, the culture of the 1950s was not so bleak.
③ During the 1950s, a number of people found their oases in new and controversial styles of music like rock-and-roll.
④ As the popularity of television and three penny magazines grew, movie lost viewers.

17

Dada artists showed their disapproval of and contempt for traditional culture and artistic conventions and continually tried to undermine them. A striking example of this is Marcel Duchamp's infamous act of drawing a mustache on a reproduction of Leonardo da Vinci's *Mona Lisa*, an act which the art establishment considered irreverent and ill-conceived. Dada sought to represent the opposite of whatever art stood for. If conventional art had at least an implied message, Dada was to have no meaning. Thus, the interpretation of Dada works depended wholly on the viewer.

Dada opened up and explored whole new approaches to creativity. No longer constrained by artistic traditions, Dada artists found themselves free to experiment with the creative process. For example, the painter Jean Arp took sheets of paper and tore them roughly into squares, which he then dropped unto a sheet of paper on the floor, gluing them wherever they landed. Arp was so pleased with the randomness and improvisation of this method that he used it to create one of his best known works, *Collage Arranged According to the Laws of Chance*.

Marcel Duchamp, perhaps the most influential of the Dada artists, was famous for his readymades, which were intended to be an overt criticism of the strictly conventional use of mediums within art. [A] These were common mass-produced objects, such as soup cans and bottle racks, that the artists modified in some way or combined with other objects. [B] The artist conferred the status of art upon them simply by exhibiting them in a gallery. [C] Duchamp's most outrageous ready-made sculpture, *Fountain*, was simply a porcelain urinal. [D]

1 According to paragraph 1, which of the following is true of Dada artists?

① They used classical art styles in their works.
② They were at odds with the established art world.
③ They attempted to destroy famous works of art.
④ The artists' messages are implied in their art.

2 Which of the following can be inferred from the passage about Jean Arp?

① He was the first to invent the technique of collage.
② He did not think it necessary to have control over his art.
③ He preferred to create art with a minimum effort.
④ He thought it important to apply scientific knowledge to his art.

3 Which is the most appropriate place for the sentence below?

It was signed and dated as any work of art would be.

① A
② B
③ C
④ D

18

Fauvism was the first avant-garde art movement of the 20th century. Spearheaded by a trio of young, Paris-based painters — Henri Matisse, André Derain and Maurice de Vlaminck — it was characterized by intense, expressive, non-naturalistic color, along with loose brushwork and simplified forms. Active from around 1905 to 1910, the Fauvists drew on — and advanced — several, recent currents of art: chiefly that of the Impressionists, Pointillists, Gauguin and Van Gogh, who refused to use colors in a way that literally corresponded to the subjects they were describing. As Matisse put it, "when I put down a green, it doesn't mean grass; and when I put down a blue, it doesn't mean the sky." Color, in short, was completely set free.

The movement's name derives from the French word for wild beast — fauve — and was coined by the stunned art critic, Louis Vauxcelles, when writing a review of the Autumn Salon exhibition in Paris in 1905. Seeing a Quattrocento-style sculpture displayed in the same room as eye-popping paintings by Matisse, Derain, and so on, he said, was like witnessing "Donatello chez les fauves" (Donatello among wild beasts). The label stuck, and Fauvism was born.

Fauvism was only made possible by advances in industrial manufacturing in the 19th century, which created new and brighter-colored paint pigments. The group often used these straight from the tube, without mixing — which is to say, in the strongest possible form — in defiance of Academy practice and, indeed, of Western artistic convention generally.

Even though the Fauvists made revolutionary art, it's fair to say they didn't have the personalities of "Ⓐ_____." Before becoming a painter, Matisse was a lawyer, for example, while Derain was an engineer.

Given the brilliant colors and spontaneous brushwork, the movement on which Fauvism had the greatest impact was probably German Expressionism. However, by subordinating everything — including the realistic depiction of subjects — to the interplay of colors, the Fauves also opened the way to abstraction.

1 Which of the following best fits in Ⓐ?

① good humor
② obedience
③ rationality
④ wild beast

2 Which of the following is NOT a characteristic of Fauvism?

① revolutionary artistic style
② use of intense and expressive color
③ carefully designed brushwork
④ rejection of artistic convention

3 **Which of the following is true?**

① Gauguin refused to accept Fauvist techniques.
② Matisse coined the term "Fauvism."
③ Fauvism was not related to the advances of paint pigment.
④ For Fauvism, color was more important than the realistic drawing of subjects.

19

One of the central claims of feminist thought is that biological 'sex' is a separate thing from 'gender', which is a matter of cultural convention. Notions as to which traits 'masculinity' and 'femininity' involve vary from one society to another. What is thought of as 'feminine' behaviour in one context might be seen as more 'masculine' behaviour in another. [A] People conform to the cultural norms as to 'male behaviour' and 'female behaviour' set by the social context in which they live. From being born onwards, they are socialized into accepting unconsciously, and acting upon the basis of, such norms. A central element of growing up involves learning how to be 'male' or how to be 'female.' [B] And the person comes to think that the culturally derived gender norms that have shaped them are actually natural and unchangeable. In this way, ways of thinking and acting that we tend to think are naturally either 'feminine' or 'masculine' are in fact the products of the inculcation of specific cultural expectations. [C]

As a result, we might think that cultural norms of gender would influence a person as they grow up not just in terms of their ways of thinking, but also in terms of their corporeality, that is, the ways in which they move and experience their bodies. In most societies, men tend to occupy more positions of power than women. In patriarchal form of social organization, men as a group both have more power than women and also have power over women. [D] In a society like that, cultural forces tend simultaneously to reflect and to justify this situation. Men are seen as being somehow naturally superior to women. This superiority is taken as if it were an unchanging fact of life. Gender norms characteristic of a patriarchal society create an essence of 'femininity' that is not a natural essence, but a _____. 'Femininity' generally is defined in negative ways, stressing the inferiority of the female psychologically and physically.

1 Choose the best expression for the blank.

① linguistic expression
② historical accident
③ social change
④ cultural fabrication

2 Choose the best place where the following sentence should be put.

Generally these learning processes happen at an unconscious and semi-conscious psychological level.

① [A]   ② [B]
③ [C]   ④ [D]

3 Which of the following is NOT true, according to the passage?

① In most societies, cultural norms reflect the way things actually are, and are accepted as natural.

② Culture exerts influence not only on the way we think but also on the way we use our bodies.

③ In a patriarchal society, men's superiority to women is regarded as an unchanging fact of life.

④ The ideas of what constitutes femininity or masculinity are not identical in all social organizations.

20

No artist has reinvented the visible world in a more radical way than Picasso. In his stringent early Cubist paintings, composed with fragmentary geometric planes, the differences between figure and ground are hardly distinguishable, testing the limits of representation. After the First World War, he developed a very different kind of painting, Ⓐ_____ both flat and suggestive of intangible depth, hard-edged and often brightly coloured. Recently, T. J. Clark focuses on those paintings of the 1920s and 30s in his book, *Picasso and Truth*. A Picasso's works from this period have now become so familiar that their complexity and radical strangeness are often taken for granted, even overlooked. Clark's book sets out to explore just how radical and how strange these paintings are.

Ugliness and monstrosity cannot always be co-opted into another form of beauty; they are sometimes meant to shake the very foundations of the viewer's beliefs and reveal new kinds of truth. Clark sees Picasso as a kind of wizard, who had the uncanny gift of being able to see the world around him in a clearer, more truthful way than his contemporaries. Clark's book attempts to show how Picasso extends and even redefines conventional notions of truth through complex relationships between spaces and objects and subject matter, most especially through a courageous engagement with monstrosity. B

Because Picasso's works of these years departed so radically from accepted norms, they were often greeted with hostility or puzzlement. In 1932, the psychologist Carl G. Jung famously compared Picasso's paintings to the pictures made by schizophrenics, and called him an "underworld" personality who followed "the demonic attraction of ugliness and evil." C Although Clark does not mention Jung in this context, he casts his own similar position in a positive light, celebrating rather than damning the eerie power of Picasso's paintings. Clark acknowledges that Picasso's art contains pathological elements, but he sees them as reflections of the pathology of an age rather than of an individual. D

1 According to the passage, which of the following does NOT properly describe Picasso's art?

① monstrous
② representational
③ pathological
④ anti-foundational

2 Choose the best one for blank Ⓐ.

① imaginatively
② unexpectedly
③ memorably
④ paradoxically

3 Choose the best place for the following sentence.

For him, Picasso's art is a judgement on a century that was rife with disaster.

① A ② B
③ C ④ D

4 Which of the following is NOT true, according to the passage?

① Picasso's art radically departed from the conventional interpretations of the visible world.
② Clark did not recognize Picasso's demonic attraction of evil as Carl G. Jung once did.
③ Clark's book aims to shed new light on the ways in which Picasso's art appears strange and radical.
④ In terms of Picasso's monstrocity, Clark held a more historical interpretation than any other.

04

언어 · 문학

01

　　Languages spoken at high altitudes are more likely to contain a certain kind of sound using short bursts of air, according to a new study. "I had this hypothesis that certain sounds might be more common at high altitudes," said study author Everett. "When I actually looked at the data, the distribution was pretty overwhelming," he said. Using an online database that categorizes languages based on their features, Everett analyzed the locations of about 600 of the world's 7,000 languages. He found that 92 of the languages contained ejective consonants. Ejectives are sounds produced with an intensive burst of air and are not found in the English. Moreover, most of the languages containing ejectives were spoken in, or near, five out of six high-altitude regions around the world. Ejectives are easier to produce at high altitudes because air pressure decreases with altitude, and it takes less effort to compress less-dense air. But there is one high-altitude region where the spoken languages did not contain ejectives: the Tibetan plateau. People there have a unique adaptation to high altitude that may account for this fact.

1　Which of the following is the main idea of the passage?

①　Geography can influence the emergence of language sound.
②　Some sounds are louder than others at high altitudes.
③　People tend to use consonants more than vowels.
④　At high altitudes, the climate affects language use.

2　Which of the following is true of the passage?

①　Ejectives are easy to pronounce for native speakers of English.
②　The decrease of air pressure can facilitate the pronunciation of ejectives.
③　There are no high elevation regions where ejectives are absent.
④　Ejectives are very common in languages around the world.

02

Many critics of Emily Brontë's novel *Wuthering Heights* see its second part as a counterpoint that comments on, if it does not reverse, the first part, where a romantic reading receives more confirmation. Seeing the two parts as a whole is encouraged by the novel's sophisticated structure, revealed in its complex use of narrators and time shifts. Granted that the presence of these elements need not argue for an authorial awareness of novelistic construction, their presence does encourage attempts to unify the novel's heterogeneous parts. However, any interpretation that seeks to unify all of the novel's diverse elements is bound to be somewhat unconvincing. This is not because such an interpretation necessarily stiffens into a thesis (although rigidity in any interpretation of this or of any novel is always a danger), but because *Wuthering Heights* has recalcitrant elements of undeniable power that, ultimately, resist inclusion in an all-encompassing interpretation. In this respect, *Wuthering Heights* shares a feature of *Hamlet*.

1 According to the passage, which of the following is true about the second part of *Wuthering Heights*?

① It annuls the sophisticated structure of the novel.
② It strengthens the force of the first part.
③ It provides less substantiation for a romantic reading.
④ It unifies the complex elements in the novel.

2 According to the passage, the author would be most likely to agree that critics should _____.

① try to claim for an authorial awareness of novelistic construction
② not be inflexible when they analyze the novel's diverse elements
③ blindly accept the interpretations of other critics
④ not argue that the complex use of narrators or of time shifts indicates a sophisticated structure

03

One of the most important characteristics of the new murder mystery was the new demands it placed on readers, requiring that they play an active role in shaping the narrative and assigning guilt for the crime. Whereas execution sermons had required only that readers accept on clerical authority their official version of an uncontestable truth, the new legal narratives effectively treated readers as Ⓐ<u>recipients</u> who must cast a vote for conviction or acquittal.

The anonymous reader who wrote in the margin of a convicted murderer's printed self-exculpation, "This statement is universally regarded as a lie from beginning to end," was responding to this expectation of his role as reader. But murder mysteries required that readers do more than just vote. They made readers actively shape the narrative, sifting through evidence, piecing the fragments together, tracking, detecting, probing, "unveiling" — effectively taking on themselves the responsibility for crafting the master narrative of the event after Ⓑ<u>the withdrawal</u> of the Providential Narrator.

To this end, the murder mystery narrative pulled readers into the Ⓒ<u>investigation</u> of the crime, offering visual illustrations of key evidence, and graphic illustrations of scenes of the crime — both architectural facades and interior scenes, maps aimed at assisting the readers in Ⓓ<u>reconstructing</u> the crime in three-dimensional space, and architectural floor plans that paid special attention to the murderer's mode of access(the rear window, the unlocked door), sometimes tracking his path with a dotted line, increasingly noting the precise location of the victim's body.

1 위 글의 요지로서 가장 적합한 것을 고르시오.

① The readers of modern society want to know the conclusion of the mystery in advance.
② The new murder mystery has not been attractive to most readers.
③ The readers of the new murder mystery should be agile to catch the narrative.
④ The new modern mystery tends to distract the reader's interest with its narrative.

2 위 글에서 논지의 흐름상 가장 적합하지 <u>않는</u> 것을 고르시오.

① Ⓐ   ② Ⓑ
③ Ⓒ   ④ Ⓓ

04

A lingua franca is a language or mixture of languages used as a medium of communication by people whose native languages are different. It is also known as a trade language, contact language, and global language. The term "English as a lingua franca" refers to the teaching, learning, and use of English as a common means of communication for speakers of different native languages. The status of English is such that it has been adopted as the world's lingua franca for communication in Olympic sport, international trade, and air-traffic control. Unlike any other language, English has spread to all five continents and has become a truly global language. According to Nicholar Ostler, however, we need to draw a distinction between a language which is spread through nurture, a mother tongue, and a language that is spread through recruitment, a lingua franca. The latter is a language you consciously learn because you need to. A mother tongue is a language you learn because you can't help it. The reason English is spreading around the world at the moment is because of its utility as a lingua franca. Globish, a simplified version of English used around the world, will be there as long as it is needed, but since it's not being picked up as a mother tongue, it's not typically being spoken by people Ⓐ_____. It is not getting effectively to first base, the most crucial base for long-term survival of a language.

1 Which of the following is the major topic of the passage?

① Superiority of mother tongues
② English as a lingua franca
③ How to develop Globish
④ Survival of a language

2 Which of the following best fits into Ⓐ?

① outside their own country
② for business purposes
③ in American colleges
④ to their children

3 According to the passage, a lingua franca CANNOT be defined as _____.

① a language used by people with different native languages
② a trade language, contact language, and global language
③ a language unconsciously learned from one's parents
④ a language that is spread through recruitment

05

Dr. Thomas Bowdler, an English physician, thought parents should read Shakespeare's plays to their children. Although Shakespeare may be an immortal bard, his plays do contain profanity and <u>suggestive</u> scenes that may not be appropriate for family reading. So in 1818, Bowdler decided to publish a family edition of Shakespeare. In his preface, Bowdler noted that he carefully edited "those words and expressions which cannot, with propriety, be read aloud to a family." Outraged critics attacked Bowdler and coined the new word "bowdlerize" to describe the deletion of parts of a book or play that are deemed offensive. Interestingly, the bowdlerized edition of Shakespeare proved to be a commercial success, thus, perhaps, vindicating Bowdler's judgment. The controversy over bowdlerized books did not end with Thomas Bowdler. In her book *The Language Police*, Diane Ravitch argues that American students are compelled to read bland texts that have been bowdlerized by publishers and textbook committees who cut or change _____ material from books, even classics.

1 Which has the closest meaning to the underlined word?

① rigorous
② obscene
③ beneficial
④ relevant

2 What would be the most likely reason that critics were outraged?

① Bowdler edited Shakespeare's plays and eventually impaired literary masterpieces.
② Bowdler damaged Shakespeare's books to invent a new set of printing type of letters.
③ Bowdler deleted parts of Shakespeare's plays to make them cheap and bring commercial success.
④ Bowdler suggested parents to read aloud Shakespeare's inappropriate plays to their children.

3 Which is the most appropriate for the blank?

① controversial
② contrasting
③ converted
④ concordant

06

Pidgins and creoles are the outcome of the need of people not sharing a language to communicate. They differ from national and international languages in that a pidgin does not begin as an already existing language or dialect selected to serve this purpose; it is rather a particular combination of two languages. Loreto Todd has the following to say about pidgins and creoles:

A pidgin is a marginal language which arises to fulfil certain restricted communication needs among people who have no common language. In the initial stages of contact the communication is often limited to transactions where a detailed exchange of ideas is not required and where a small vocabulary, drawn almost exclusively from one language, suffices. The syntactic structure of the pidgin is less complex and less flexible than the structures of the language that were in contact, and though many pidgin features clearly reflect usages in the contact languages, others are unique to the pidgin.

A creole arises when a pidgin becomes the mother tongue of a speech community. The simple structure that characterized the pidgin is carried over into the creole but since a creole, as a mother tongue, must be capable of expressing the whole range of human experience, the lexicon is expanded, and frequently a more elaborate syntactic system evolves.

Since creoles are often not regarded as "real" languages and consequently considered as inferior, it is worth noting that, for example, both French and English may be the outcome of pidgins — in the first case through contact between native Gauls and occupying Romans, and in the second through contact between the native Anglo-Saxons and the Danes who settled on the east coast of England.

1 윗글의 내용과 일치하지 <u>않는</u> 것은?

① A pidgin usually develops from two different languages.
② The vocabulary of the pidgin is typically drawn from the two languages that were in contact.
③ A creole can usually express a wider range of human experiences than a pidgin.
④ The structures of the languages that were in contact are generally more flexible than the structure of the pidgin.

2 윗글의 내용으로 추론할 수 있는 것은?

① French is possibly a creole.
② English is possibly a pidgin.
③ Pidgins develop to promote the exchange of philosophical ideas.
④ A creole becomes a pidgin when a speech community accepts it as its mother tongue.

07

    Don Quixote is a novel published in two parts by Spanish writer Miguel de Cervantes, and is one of the most widely read classics of Western literature. Originally conceived as a parody of the chivalric romances that had long been in literary vogue, Ⓐ<u>it</u> describes realistically what befalls an aging knight who, his head bemused by reading such romances, sets out on his old horse Rocinante, with his pragmatic squire, Sancho Panza, to seek adventure. Widely and immediately translated (first English translation in 1612), the novel was a great and continuing success and is considered a prototype of the modern novel.

    When first published, *Don Quixote* was usually interpreted as a comic novel. After the French Revolution, Ⓑ<u>it</u> was better known for its central ethic that individuals can be right while society is quite wrong and seen as disenchanting. In the 19th century, it was seen as a social commentary, but no one found it easy to tell "whose side Cervantes was on." Many critics came to view the work as a tragedy in which Don Quixote's idealism and nobility are viewed by the post-chivalric world as insane, and are defeated and rendered useless by common reality. By the 20th century, Ⓒ<u>the novel</u> had come to occupy a canonical space as one of the foundations of modern literature.

    In addition to spawning countless works of critical discussion, *Don Quixote* inspired artists in every medium. Notable adaptations included a classic 1869 ballet; the 1965 musical play *Man of La Mancha*, which first opened on Broadway in 1968; and a 1972 film version directed by Arthur Hiller. Another notable film adaptation was *The Man Who Killed Don Quixote* (2018), a loose retelling of Cervantes's novel by the director Terry Gilliam, whose attempts to make the film over the course of nearly three decades were beset by various complications, delays, and cancellations, turning Gilliam into a quixotic figure himself, as detailed in the 2002 documentary Ⓓ<u>*Lost in La Mancha*</u>.

1 Which of the following does NOT refer to the same thing?

① Ⓐ   ② Ⓑ
③ Ⓒ   ④ Ⓓ

2 Which of the following is NOT true about the work *Don Quixote*?

① It is highly praised as a model of modern novel.
② It has been interpreted differently in different times.
③ Post-chivalric world embraced the novel's idealism.
④ It has been adapted in many fields of arts.

3 Which of the following is NOT true?

① *Don Quixote* is still highly regarded by the critics.
② Don Quixote sought adventure as if he were a knight.
③ Cervantes was considered to have shown no clear political stance.
④ Terry Gilliam reproduced *Don Quixote* in the form of ballet.

08

Language is such a dominant feature of our mental world that it is tempting to equate language with thought. Some theorists have even argued that language is simply a means of expressing thought. The linguistic relativity hypothesis maintains that language shapes the nature of thought. This idea was championed by Benjamin Whorf. The most frequently cited example of linguistic relativity comes from the Inuit in Canada. Their language has many different terms for frozen white flakes of precipitation, for which we use the word *snow*. Whorf believed that because they have so many terms for snow, the Inuit perceive and think about snow differently than do English speakers. Whorf has been criticized for the anecdotal nature of his observations, and some controlled research has cast doubt on Whorf's hypothesis. Eleanor Rosch studied the Dani, an isolated agricultural tribe living in New Guinea. They have only two terms for colors that roughly refer to "dark" and "light". If Whorf's hypothesis were correct, you would expect the Dani _____. But in Rosch's experiments, they learned shades of color just as well as people who have many more color terms in their first language. More recent evidence shows that language may influence color processing. Researchers compared English children with African children from a cattle-herding tribe in Namibia known as the Himba. The English have 11 basic color terms, but the Himba, who are largely isolated from the outside world, have only five. Researchers showed a series of colored tiles to each child and then asked the child to choose that color from an array of 22 different colors. The youngest children, both English and Himba, who knew few or no color names, tended to confuse similar colors. But as the children grew and acquired more names for colors, their choices increasingly reflected the color terms they have learned.

1 What is the passage mainly about?

① the leading features of language and thought
② the significance of Whorf's theory
③ the invalidity of equation between language and thought
④ the influence of linguistic theory on thought

2 Which of the following is NOT true?

① Language affects how we think about color.
② The Inuit use many different terms for snow, leading Whorf to propose that they think about snow differently than do English speakers.
③ Recent studies on color processing point to an influence of language on thought.
④ Language forms the nature of thoughts.

3 Which of the following best fills in the blank?

① to have problems perceiving and learning different shadows of color
② to have no problem perceiving and learning different shadows of color
③ to have problems perceiving and learning color words
④ to have no problem perceiving and learning color words

09

I will start with some basic assumptions, points that are widely accepted. First, language is/was primarily spoken. It is of course well-known that human communication is multi-modal, and that gesture may support spoken speech. Sign language is these days recognized as "full" language, but it is unlikely that such gestures were ever developed into a fully-fledged system in the early decades of language. [A]

Second, with regard to location, Africa is widely believed to be the area of origin for human language, though the exact location, once thought to be the Rift Valley, is still debated, and some southern African sites are under investigation. The notion of polygenesis is now thought to be unlikely, and claims about other possible areas of origin, such as China, have mostly faded. [B]

Third, in relation to date, language is of relatively recent origin, certainly compared with the evolution of the human species. [C] At one time, full language was dated fairly late, around 50,000 years ago. But the likely date has been creeping back. Somewhere between 100,000 and 50,000 is now a plausible guess as to the time of fully developed language, though increasingly, researchers are trying to reconstruct a possible proto-language. The proto-language possibly emerged in stages, the earliest of which might have been in existence for millennia. [D]

Fourth, the relationship of human language to animal communication is becoming clearer. The extent to which it is continuous or discontinuous with animal communication has been widely discussed. The various constituents of language need to be assessed separately, since they contain different degrees of overlap, with auditory mechanisms showing strong overlap, the brain medium and articulatory mechanisms displaying little overlap. [E]

1 Which is the best place for the following sentence?

The vocal-auditory channel is therefore considered by most researchers to be primary.

① [A]
② [B]
③ [C]
④ [D]
⑤ [E]

2 According to the passage, which of the following is not stated or implied?

① Human language originated in China as well as in Africa.
② Not only speaking but also gesture is a mode of human communication.
③ There was possibly a proto-language before language was fully developed.
④ Human language was developed much later than the evolution of the human species.
⑤ Human language and animal communication have something in common in hearing mechanisms.

10

The New Negro: An Interpretation (1925) is an anthology of fiction, poetry, and essays on African and African-American art and literature edited by Alain Locke, who lived in Washington, DC and taught at Howard University during the Harlem Renaissance. As a collection of the creative efforts coming out of the burgeoning New Negro Movement or Harlem Renaissance, the book is considered by literary scholars and critics to be the definitive text of the movement. This book included Locke's title essay "The New Negro," as well as nonfiction essays, poetry, and fiction by many of the African American writers.

The New Negro dives into how the African Americans sought social, political, and artistic change. Ⓐ_____ accepting their position in society, Locke saw the New Negro as championing and demanding civil rights. In addition, his anthology sought to change old stereotypes and replaced them with new visions of black identity that resisted simplification. The essays and poems in the anthology mirror real life events and experiences. The anthology reflects the voice of middle class African American citizens that wanted to have equal civil rights like the white, middle class counterparts.

A theme used by Locke commonly is this idea of the Old vs the New Negro. The Old Negro according to Locke was a product of stereotypes and judgments that were put on them, not ones that they created. They were forced to live in a shadow of themselves and others' actions. The New Negro is a Negro that now has an understanding of oneself. They at one point lacked self-respect and self-dependence which has created a new dynamic and allowed the birth of the New Negro. They have become the Negro of today which is also the changed Negro. Locke speaks about the migration having an effect on the Negro leveling the playing field and increasing the realm of how the Negro is viewed because they were moved out of the southern parts of U.S. and into other areas where they could start over. The migration in a sense transformed the Negro and fused them together as they all came from all over the world, all walks of life, and all different backgrounds.

1 Which of the following best fits in Ⓐ?

① In behalf of
② In case of
③ In light of
④ Instead of

2 Which of the following is NOT true about the book *The New Negro*?

① It was written by Alain Locke alone.
② It includes works from a variety of literary genre.
③ It deals with African Americans' effort for a new identity.
④ It reflects the real life experiences well.

3 Which of the following is NOT a feature of the New Negro?

① crave for a new identity
② quest for black supremacy
③ knowledge of oneself
④ demand for civil rights

11

The withdrawal of the problem of discourse in the contemporary study of language is the price we must pay for the tremendous achievements brought about by Ferdinand de Saussure's famous *Course in General Linguistics*. His work relies on a fundamental distinction between language as *langue* and *parole*. *Langue* is the code — or the set of codes — on the basis of which a particular speaker produces *parole* as a particular message.

To this main dichotomy are connected several subsidiary distinctions. A message is individual, its code is collective. The message and the code do not belong to time in the same way. A message is a temporal event in the succession of events which constitute the diachronic dimension of time, while the code is in time as a set of contemporaneous elements, i.e., as a synchronic system. The code is anonymous and not intended. In this sense it is unconscious, not in the sense that drives and impulses are unconscious according to Freudian metapsychology, but in the sense of a nonlibidinal structural and cultural unconscious.

More than anything else, a message is arbitrary and contingent, while a code is systematic and compulsory for a given speaking community. This last opposition is reflected in the affinity of a code for scientific investigation; particularly in a sense of the word 'science' which emphasizes the quasi-algebraic level of the combinatory capacities implied by such finite sets of discrete entities as phonological, lexical, and syntactical systems. Even if *parole* can be scientifically described, it falls under many sciences including acoustics, physiology, sociology, and the history of semantic changes, whereas *langue* is the object of a single science, the description of the synchronic systems of language.

1 Which of the following would make the best title for the passage?

① Freud's influence on the study of language
② *Parole* as the object of a single science
③ *Langue* as a code vs. *parole* as a message
④ The collective nature of a message as *langue*

2 Which of the following can be inferred from the passage?

① Freud's notion of instinctive unconsciousness affects greatly on the study of *langue*.
② Saussure discarded the notion of discourse to study language scientifically.
③ A study of *parole* needs to focus on the quasi-algebraic nature of language.
④ *Langue* is a collection of succeeding events over time.

3 According to the passage, which of the following is NOT the characteristics of *parole*?

① It is a personal and atemporal instantiation of a code.
② It is individual, although it is based on a collective code.
③ It can be investigated from different points of view in many sciences.
④ It is an event which occurs in a continuous dimension of time.

12

Have you ever had the experience of knowing part of a word that you wanted to say (e.g., the first letter), but were unable to retrieve the whole word? This is known as the "tip-of-the-tongue" phenomenon. The guesses subjects make when they are unable to access the desired word often provide information about the possible structure of our mental dictionary.

The guesses made by people suffering from the tip-of-the-tongue phenomenon tend to be substitutions that Ⓐrespect word type boundaries; nouns are substituted for nouns, verbs for verbs, and so forth. This suggests that words of the same grammatical class are stored together, which is consistent with the results of the word association data analysis. The research revealed that the tip-of-the-tongue states are subject to the "bathtub effect." The first and last parts of words are best remembered in the same way that the head and feet of a person in a bathtub may be visible, but not his or her middle. For example, a study found that subjects were most likely to experience a tip-of-the-tongue phenomenon when the first and last parts were Ⓑsimilar to the correct or intended term. For example, if the target word in a tip-of-the-tongue state was "sextant" (a navigational instrument used to measure angular distances, such as the altitude of the moon and stars), "sextet" was more likely to be mistakenly "recognized" by subjects than "compass," which is semantically similar. _____, while 70 percent of the tip-of-the-tongue errors were similar in sound to the target, only 30% were similar in meaning. This suggests that once subjects have in mind a certain word based on its meaning, they can be tricked into accepting Ⓒa semantic relative of the intended word. Thus, both meaning and phonology play a part in accessing and producing lexical items. Knowing the meaning may lead subjects to the right lexical entry, but if the phonology is not completely specified, phonological neighbors of the target word may be Ⓓinaccurately produced or recognized.

1 Which of the following is NOT the correct expression in the flow of the passage?

① Ⓐ
② Ⓑ
③ Ⓒ
④ Ⓓ

2 What is the best expression for the blank?

① However
② In fact
③ Instead
④ As a result

3 Which of the following is NOT true according to the passage?

① The tip-of-the-tongue phenomenon is sensitive to grammatical category distinction.
② The "bathtub effect" is a solution to the tip-of-the-tongue phenomenon.
③ Both sound and meaning contribute to explaining why the tip-of-the-tongue phenomenon occurs.
④ The beginnings and endings of words are prominent in the lexical store.

13

Let us recall that the Grimms first heard the tale of "Hansel and Gretel" told by Dortchen Wild some time between 1808 and 1810 and wrote it down in the Ölenberg manuscript of 1810 under the title "Das Brüderchen und das Schwesterchen" ("The Little Brother and the Little Sister"). It was very short and much different from the text that they published in the first edition of the *Children and Household Tales* in 1812. In a recent study Gerhard Neumann examines "Hansel and Gretel" as exemplary for the genre of the fairy tale and argues that Hansel and Gretel leave their home to undergo a psychological socialization in which they must realize that their mother and home are both loving and cruel and they must learn to come to terms with this ambivalence in order to survive. Neumann's study, however, disregarded the textual and intertexual development of the tale and overlooked important issues of poverty, abandonment, and patriarchy. A critical reading should focus on textual changes that the Grimms made to minimize the role of the father as victimizer and to depict a *stepmother* as aligned with a witch who wants to devour the children. Over the course of forty-seven years the Grimms kept changing the tale, adding some important motifs and incidents. Today the 1857 version, *Kinder- und Hausmärchen* (*Children's and Household Tales*) is considered to be the most definitive and "authentic." But how can any text that was first told by Dortchen Wild and that was written down, translated from the Grimms' perspective, and then edited and revised numerous times, be considered "authentic" or "original"? This question reveals a major problem — our non-recognition of translation. Translation is vital in the history of the oral folk tale. In some ways, translation is the overcoming of what Freud calls "das Unheimliche," the uncanny in life, so that which is strange becomes familiar and we feel comfortable with it. The translator takes that which is "*un-heimlich*," not homey, and transforms it into something "*heimlich*," homey, so that we are not threatened by what we otherwise cannot understand.

1 The author addresses Freud's concept of the uncanny in life to demonstrate that _____.

① "Hansel and Gretel" is an exemplary fairy tale that shows the process of children's psychological socialization

② the Grimms minimize the role of the mother as victimizer in their translation of "Hansel and Gretel"

③ to translate is to interpret someone else's words as faithfully as possible according to the original intention

④ translation involves the interrogation and reiteration of a text into one's own language so that a foreign narrative becomes familiar

2 Choose the statement that can be BEST inferred from the passage.

① The Ölenberg manuscript includes the first version of "Hansel and Gretel," which is considered the most authentic text.
② Dorchen Wild told Wilhelm Grimm a story in which a mother attempts to devour her stepchildren.
③ Gerhard Neumann's study examines the middle-class attitudes regarding poverty and famine in nineteenth-century Germany.
④ The tale of "Hansel and Gretel" went through many editions in the first half of the nineteenth century.

14

Ⓐ Words often have two types of meaning: denotation and connotation. Denotation refers to the actual dictionary definition of the word, without the attachment of an emotional response. For example, if you look up the word *aggressive*, you will find that it means "Ⓐunprovokedly offensive, Ⓑquite amicable, Ⓒvigorously energetic, and Ⓓboldly assertive." If used to describe a type of treatment for a deadly disease, *aggressive* carries a positive emotional response. On the other hand, if your friend complains that a salesperson is aggressive, the picture you get of that salesperson is not necessarily positive. Thus, the word *aggressive* evokes both positive and negative emotions depending on the context in which the word is used. Your connotations for words become part of your assumptions and thus influence your inferences.

Ⓑ Writers and speakers consciously use connotative language to shape your inferences. They do this by choosing words with universal connotations. Thus, they expect you to respond emotionally in a certain way to the word choice. For example, imagine yourself in an art history class where the instructor is discussing some of the later paintings by the impressionist Claude Monet. The instructor carefully avoids including opinions about Monet because he wants his students to learn to evaluate paintings for form and style. (1)_____, in commenting on a later Monet painting, he says that "the apparently random choice of reds and oranges is a departure from the more serene blues and greens that Monet used in earlier paintings of the same scene." *Random*, when used to refer to an artist's color choice, has a more negative connotation. On the other hand, *serene* holds a more positive connotation. The instructor's use of the words *random* and *serene* helps you infer that (2)_____.

1 According to the paragraph Ⓐ, which has a positive connotation of *aggressive*?

① Aggressive behavior is a sign of emotional distress.
② People complain that salespersons are usually aggressive in today's competitive market.
③ My friend has been diagnosed with an aggressive form of cancer.
④ The doctor took an aggressive approach to treating the infection.

2 Identify the one underlined part that should be rewritten in the paragraph Ⓐ.

① unprovokedly offensive
② quite amicable
③ vigorously energetic
④ boldly assertive

3 Which is the most appropriate for the blank (1) in the paragraph B?

① Thus
② However
③ Otherwise
④ Moreover

4 Which is the most appropriate for the blank (2) in the paragraph B?

① he preferred Monet's later paintings to his earlier ones
② he is impressed with both Monet's later and earlier paintings
③ he is not as impressed with Monet's later paintings as he is with his earlier ones
④ he is not impressed with either Monet's earlier paintings or his later ones

15

There have been various attempts to determine what literature is. You can regard it, for example, as 'imaginative' writing in the sense of fiction — writing which is not literally true. But even the briefest reflection on what people commonly include under the heading of literature suggests that this will not do. Seventeenth-century English literature includes Shakespeare, Webster, Marvell and Milton; but it also stretches to the essays of Francis Bacon, the sermons of John Donne, Bunyan's spiritual autobiography and whatever it was that Sir Thomas Browne wrote. It might even at a pinch be taken to encompass Hobbes's *Leviathan* or Clarendon's *History of the Rebellion*. French seventeenth-century literature contains, along with Corneille and Racine, La Rochefoucauld's maxims, Bossuet's funeral speeches, Boileau's treatise on poetry, Madame de Séignés letters to her daughter and the philosophy of Descartes and Pascal. Nineteenth-century English literature usually includes Lamb (though not Bentham), Macaulay (but not Marx), Mill (but not Darwin or Herbert Spencer).

A distinction between 'fact' and 'fiction', then, seems unlikely to get us very far, not least because the distinction itself is often a questionable one. It has been argued, for instance, that our own opposition between 'historical' and 'artistic' truth does not apply at all to the early Icelandic sagas. In the English late sixteenth and early seventeenth centuries, the word 'novel' seems to have been used about both true and fictional events, and even news reports were hardly to be considered factual. Novels and news reports were neither clearly factual nor clearly fictional: our own sharp discriminations between these categories simply did not apply. Gibbon no doubt thought that he was writing the historical truth, and so perhaps did the authors of *Genesis*, but they are now read as 'fact' by some and 'fiction' by others; Newman certainly thought his theological meditations were true but they are now for many readers 'literature.' Moreover, if 'literature' includes much 'factual' writing, it also excludes quite a lot of fiction. *Superman* comic and Mills and Boon novels are fictional but not generally regarded as literature, and certainly not as Literature. If literature is 'creative' or 'imaginative' writing, does this imply that history, philosophy and natural science are uncreative and unimaginative? Certainly not.

1 The above passage is most likely to be part of an essay whose topic is _____.

① The various usage of the word 'novel'
② The opposition between 'historical' and 'artistic'
③ The distinction between fact and fiction
④ The meaning and definition of literature

2 Which of the following is most likely to be inferred from the above passage?
① Literature can be thought of as fictional writing, that is, writing which is not literally true.
② History, philosophy and natural science cannot be imaginative because they are based on fact.
③ There were periods when the factual writing and the fictional writing were not clearly distinguished.
④ The distinction between 'fact' and 'fiction' is very helpful when one tries to identify what literature is.

3 According to the above passage, literature cannot be limited to 'fictional' writing because _____.
① people, who are not specialists on literature, commonly think that only fictional writings are included in literature
② factual writings, such as those in history, philosophy, and natural science are neither creative nor imaginative
③ seventeenth-century English literature includes Shakespeare, Webster, Marvell and Milton
④ factual writings are often regarded as literature, and fictional writings are not always included in literature

05

철학·종교

05 철학·종교

01

In the fifth century B.C., the Greek philosophers tried to overcome the sharp contrast between the views of Parmenides and Heraclitus. In order to reconcile the idea of unchangeable Being of Parmenides with that of eternal Becoming of Heraclitus, they assumed that the Being is manifest in certain invariable substances, the mixture and separation of which gives rise to the changes in the world. This led to the concept of the atom, the smallest invisible unit of matter, which found its clearest expression in the philosophy of Democritus. The Greek atomists drew a clear line between spirit and matter, picturing matter as being made of several basic building blocks. These were purely passive and intrinsically dead particles moving in the void. The cause of their motion was not explained, but was often associated with external forces which were assumed to be of spiritual origin and fundamentally different from matter. In subsequent centuries, this image became an essential element of Western thought, of dualism between mind and matter, between body and soul.

1 What is the passage mainly about?

① The origin of Western dualism
② The main problem of Western thought
③ The relationship between spirit and matter
④ The uncanny world of the Greek philosophers

2 Which of the following is NOT true, according to the passage?

① Parmenides and Heraclitus were two opposing poles of the Greek thought.
② Parmenides and Heraclitus once worked together to reconcile their ideas.
③ The Greek atomists believed in the two different worlds of spirit and matter.
④ The tradition of Western thought has been largely embedded in the dualistic world view.

02

When faced with a decision to make, utilitarians prefer to create a list of pros and cons. One of the main ethical theories, utilitarianism Ⓐ_____ that the key to determining what makes an act morally right or wrong is its consequences.

Whether people's intentions are good or bad is irrelevant; what matters is whether the result of their actions is good or bad. Happiness is the ultimate goal of human beings and the highest moral good. Thus, if there is great unhappiness because of an act, then that action can be said to be morally wrong. Utilitarians believe that people should carefully weigh the potential consequences of an action before they take it.

Another problematic aspect of utilitarianism is that it deems it acceptable to use another person as a means to an end and sacrifice the happiness of one or a few for the happiness of many.

1 Choose the best word for Ⓐ.
① denies
② posits
③ questions
④ discredits

2 Which one is true?
① Using utilitarianism to make a moral decision is not always easy.
② Utilitarians believe that consequences are irrelevant.
③ A pro/con list is the only way to make the right decision for utilitarians.
④ Utilitarians believe sacrifices are not necessary in life.

3 Which one is NOT true?
① Utilitarians might use people as a means to an end.
② Utilitarians believe that actions that create a lot of unhappiness are morally wrong.
③ Utilitarians assert that having good or bad intentions is not important.
④ Utilitarians think that potential consequences should be weighed after the actions are taken.

03

In the 17th century, religion provided a logical and comfortable accounting for a person's place within the world and the universe beyond it, both in life and in the hereafter. The Great Chain of Being, a cornerstone of Elizabethan cosmology, was a structure that, in its beautiful simplicity and perfection, made every part of the natural world accountable in a Ⓐ_____. With God at the top, the chain descended through the angels to humans, lower animals, and finally to inanimate objects. All was ordered in a way that accounted for a person's position in respect to the environment. Predestination, like the Great Chain of Being, was a tenet of all Protestant religions of the 17th century. One's place in the afterlife was foreordained at birth, and there was nothing that one could do to alter it. In other words, no amount of misbehavior or exemplary behavior would change the predestined course of events.

1 Which of the following best fits into Ⓐ?

① gigantic cycle
② religious event
③ predestined disorder
④ hierarchical arrangement

2 According to the passage, which of the following is NOT true?

① Seventeenth century religion offered its own logical accounts for people's positions in the universe.
② Admirable Protestant behavior improves your chances for a better afterlife.
③ Humans are not at the top of the Great Chain of Being.
④ Protestant religions of the time held that a person's fate was predetermined.

04

　　The ancient Greek philosopher Plato did a lot to change the way we think about the world, in everything from mathematics to ethics to logic. But perhaps one of his most influential contributions to philosophy was the Theory of Forms. In basic terms, Plato's Theory of Forms asserts that the physical world is not really the "real" world. ⒶInstead, ultimate reality exists beyond our physical world. Plato discusses this theory in a few different dialogues, including the most famous one, called "The Republic." It is also likely that Plato inherited some of this theory from his mentor, Socrates.

　　Plato's philosophy asserts that there are two realms: the physical realm and the spiritual realm. The physical realm is the material stuff we see and interact with on a daily basis. This physical realm is changing and imperfect, as we know all too well. The spiritual realm, Ⓑhowever, exists beyond the physical realm. Plato calls this spiritual realm the Realm of Forms (also called the Realm of Ideas or Realm of Ideals). Plato's Theory of Forms asserts that the physical realm is only a shadow, or image, of the true reality of the Realm of Forms.

　　So what are these Forms, according to Plato? The Forms are abstract, perfect, unchanging concepts or ideals that (1)_____. They exist in the Realm of Forms. ⒸEven though the Forms are abstract, that doesn't mean they are not real. In fact, the Forms are more "real" than any individual physical objects. ⒹBut concepts like Redness, Roundness, Beauty, Justice, or Goodness are Forms (and thus they are commonly capitalized). Individual objects like a red book, a round ball, a beautiful girl, a just action, or a good person reside in the physical realm and are simply different examples of the Forms.

1　Which of the following best fits in the underlined (1)?

① change in the course of time
② transcend time and space
③ vary their forms in different times
④ exist only within the realm of space

2　Which of the following is NOT appropriate?

① Ⓐ
② Ⓑ
③ Ⓒ
④ Ⓓ

3　Which of the following is true?

① Plato offered a new way of seeing the world.
② Plato's philosophy was succeeded by Socrates.
③ According to Plato, the physical realm casts a shadow over the spiritual realm.
④ According to Plato, the abstract nature of the Forms makes themselves unreal in the real world.

05

Mr. Makari's highly engaging story begins with René Descartes. Ever since Greek philosophy had merged with Christianity, the soul had been regarded as the "unifying link between nature, man and God," Mr. Makari writes. By the 17th century, however, Christendom was in crisis, and many found it hard to reconcile the notion of an incorporeal soul with a mechanical world that was increasingly understood as made up of matter. Descartes tried to satisfy the demand of skeptical naturalists by narrowing the concept of the soul to a "thing that thinks," yet that was separate from the body. The French philosopher thus breathed new life into the Christian belief in an immortal soul. At the other end of the Ⓐ_____ stood Thomas Hobbes, who thought there was no such thing as "immaterial substance." In his view the soul, rather than being rational and Godlike, was "material, prone to illness and errors." Ⓑ_____. And they were to demonstrate the importance of Mr. Makari's narrative as more than just an intellectual exercise. After Hobbes concluded that men were controlled by animal feelings that inevitably produced conflict, his proposed solution was to hand over power to an absolute monarch.

1 Select the statement most consistent with the passage.
① European philosophy became increasingly religious in the seventeenth century.
② Mr. Makari charts the rise of modern secular philosophy.
③ Hobbes advocated modern forms of demagoguery based on humans' tendency to "illness and errors."
④ Descartes emphasized the insignificance of the mechanical world.

2 Choose the best sentence that fits blank Ⓑ above.
① Hobbes's views were consistent with those of Descartes but extrapolated them one step further
② Hobbes corroborated Descartes's ideas by translating his notion of the immaculate soul into material terms
③ The disparate views on the nature of the "thing that thinks" were to have monumental implications
④ Rather than "I think, therefore I am," Hobbes famously posited, "I think, therefore I am," but "I am, therefore I think, too"

3 Choose the best word for blank Ⓐ above.
① diaspora   ② bulwark
③ obscurity   ④ gamut

06

Religion can inspire people to altruism or ruthless cruelty, and can have both effects at different times. Dissecting this paradox should come naturally to Karen Armstrong. British-born and a former Roman Catholic nun, she has written more than a dozen books on religious history at its broadest, expounding her view that faith is a legitimate part of human experience, whether or not its claims are true. In her latest work, "Fields of Blood," Ms Armstrong does not add to the many existing theories on offer. Instead she presents a vast overview of religious and world history, sketching the early evolution of all global faiths. Then, with giant strokes and plenty of (not totally accurate) detail, she studies the influence of the Christian West on the world over the past 500 years. It is not obvious how all this coheres, until you realize which demons she is fighting. Ms Armstrong is not trying to prove anything; more to disprove several things. First, the idea that religion is a gratuitous cause of violence, whose elimination would promote peace. And second, the view that Islam is an egregious case of a religion that inspires violence. Her third bogeyman combines the first two: the idea that because the "Christian" West has shed more religious baggage than the Muslim world has, it must restrain an incorrigibly violent Islam.

1 Ms Armstrong argues in her books that _____.

① religion is fundamentally authoritarian
② religion has acted as a powerful tool for eliminating human violence
③ the dark side of religion has been exaggerated
④ a religious belief is meaningful only if its claims are proven right
⑤ faith is necessary to human life regardless of its basis in truth

2 The underlined part implies that _____.

① Islam is a religion of peace
② Christianity brings out the worst in people
③ the Christian West is more religious than the Muslim world
④ the Christian West is a more benign global force
⑤ the Christian West can learn from the Muslim world

07

One of the most central doctrines of Hume's philosophy, stated in the very first lines of the *Treatise*, is his notion that the mind consists of its mental perceptions, or the mental objects which are present to it, and which divide into two categories: impressions and ideas. Hume's *Treatise* thus opens with the words: "All the perceptions of the human mind resolve themselves into two distinct kinds, which I shall call IMPRESSIONS and IDEAS." Hume states that "I believe it will not be very necessary to employ many words in explaining this distinction" and commentators have generally taken Hume to mean the distinction between feeling and thinking. Controversially, Hume may regard the difference as in some sense a matter of degree, as he takes "impressions" to be distinguished from ideas, on the basis of their force, liveliness, and vivacity. Ideas are therefore _____. For example, experiencing the painful sensation of touching the handle of a hot pan is more forceful than simply thinking about touching a hot pan. According to Hume, impressions are meant to be the original form of all our ideas, and Don Garret has thus coined the term "the copy principle" to refer to Hume's doctrine that all ideas are ultimately all copied from some original impression, whether it be a passion or sensation, from which they derive. Hume's writings on ethics began in the *Treatise*. His views on ethics are that "moral decisions are grounded in moral sentiment." It is not knowing that governs ethical actions, but feelings. Arguing that reason cannot be behind morality, he wrote: "Morals excite passions, and produce or prevent actions. Reason itself is utterly impotent in this particular. The rules of morality, therefore, are not conclusions of our reason." Hume's sentimentalism about morality was shared by his close friend Adam Smith. And Hume and Smith were mutually influenced by the moral reflections of their older contemporary Francis Hutcheson. Peter Singer claims that Hume's argument that morals cannot have a rational basis alone "would have been enough to earn him a place in the history of ethics".

1 Choose the most appropriate one for the blank.

① the grounds of ethics
② faint impressions
③ the imitations of morality
④ forceful reasons

2 Which of the following statement is true?

① Ethical actions arise from knowledge.
② Hume attempted to set a moral ground on the basis of reason.
③ In *Treatise*, Hume explored some epistemological problems.
④ To Hume the distinction between feeling and thinking is virtually meaningless.

08

Wittgenstein asked simply, what is language? Why and how do the squawks a person makes, and the squiggles they draw, conjure up all that is in the world? Anthony Quinton, a British philosopher, compared his instincts to those of Sir Isaac Newton, who had troubled to ask why stones fall to the ground when others had been content enough to say, "They just do."

Wittgenstein's answer was the picture theory of language, a neat demonstration of the relation between words and the real world. He argued that all meaningful thoughts that people have are arrangements of pictures, which, when expressed in language as "propositions," can be communicated to others. [A] This is what "the cat sat on the mat" has in common with complex sentences. At least in the cases of tangible things like felines, that might seem obvious. [B] But Wittgenstein was breaking new ground. The idea came to him as he read a report about a court case involving a car crash. Learning that a lawyer had used toy cars and dolls to explain the smash, he grasped the pictorial basis of language. [C] He applied this view to the central philosophical problems, and concluded that, since philosophy largely discusses things that are not demonstrable in the world and cannot therefore be pictured, many of its propositions are not meaningful. [D] He preferred to focus on the few areas that could be meaningfully discussed with language. That led him to a final, definitive proposition: "Whereof one cannot speak, thereof one must be silent."

1 Which of the following is the most appropriate place for the following sentence to be inserted in?

In other words, most philosophy is "nonsense."

① [A]   ② [B]
③ [C]   ④ [D]

2 In this passage, Wittgenstein is compared to Newton because _____.

① both of them kept asking questions about what seems like a matter of course
② both of them thought that only questions in natural science are meaningful
③ both of them were interested in the relation between nature and language
④ both of them showed instincts which are studied by later philosophers and scientists

3 According to the passage, which of the following is most likely to be true about Wittgenstein's thought?

① Lawyers' demonstration of car accidents with toys and dolls are useful because accidents cannot be pictured.
② We can think about things in the world and speak about them with language because it just does.
③ Newton's question about why things fall to the ground are not significant because it is about an abstract notion, that is gravity.
④ If a thing cannot be described like a picture, it cannot be expressed with language and therefore is meaningless.

09

But that's putting it too negatively. If I were interested in preserving religious faith, I would be very afraid of the positive power of evolutionary science precisely because it is _____. The difficult problem for any theory of biological design is to explain the massive statistical improbability of living things. Statistical improbability in the direction of good design — "complexity" is another word for this. The standard creationist argument — there is only one; they're all reduced to this one — takes off from a statistical improbability. Living creatures are too complex to have come about by chance; therefore, they must have had a designer. This argument, of course, shoots itself in the foot. Any designer capable of designing something really complex has to be even more complex himself, and that's before we even start on the other things he's expected to do, like forgive sins, bless marriages, and listen to prayers. Complexity is the problem that any theory of biology has to solve, and you can't solve it by postulating an agent that is even more complex, thereby simply compounding the problem. Darwinian natural selection is so stunningly elegant because it solves the problem of explaining complexity in terms of nothing but simplicity. Essentially, it works by providing a smooth ramp of gradual, step-by-step increment. But here, I only want to make the point that the elegance of Darwinism is corrosive to religion, precisely because it is so elegant, so parsimonious, so powerful, so economically powerful. It has the sinewy economy of a beautiful suspension bridge. The God theory is not just a bad theory. It turns out to be — in principle — incapable of doing the job required of it. So, returning to tactics and the evolution lobby, I want to argue that rocking the boat may be just the right thing to do. My approach to attacking creationism is — unlike the evolution lobby — to attack religion as a whole.

1 Choose the best answer to fill in the blank.

① omnipotent
② tacit
③ fertile
④ atheistic

2 What would be the best title of the passage above?

① Religion in the age of evolution
② Complexity of natural selection
③ Elegance in creationism
④ Statistical improbability in science

10

Philosophy, like all other studies, aims primarily at knowledge. The knowledge it aims at is the kind of knowledge which gives unity and system to the body of the sciences, and the kind which results from a critical examination of the grounds of our convictions, prejudices, and beliefs. But it cannot be maintained that philosophy has had any very great measure of success in its attempts to provide definite answers to its questions. If you ask a mathematician, a mineralogist, a historian, or any other man of learning, what definite body of truths has been ascertained by his science, his answer will last as long as you are willing to listen. But if you put the same question to a philosopher, he will, if he is Ⓐcandid, have to confess that his study has not achieved positive results such as those achieved by other sciences. It is true that Ⓑthis is partly accounted for by the fact that, as soon as definite knowledge concerning any subject becomes possible, this subject ceases to be called philosophy and becomes a separate science. The whole study of the heavens, which now belongs to astronomy, was once included in philosophy; Newton's great work was called 'the mathematical principles of natural philosophy'. Ⓒ_____, the study of the human mind, which was a part of philosophy, has now been separated from philosophy and has become the science of psychology. Thus, to a great extent, the uncertainty of philosophy is more apparent than real: those questions which are already capable of definite answers are placed in the sciences, while those only to which, at present, no definite answer can be given, remain to form the residue which is called philosophy.

1 The main topic of this passage is _____.

① the difficulty in defining the goal and the object of philosophy
② the relation between astronomy, psychology and philosophy
③ the joy and happiness of investigating knowledge in philosophy
④ the measure of successful investigation in philosophy

2 Which can be used instead of Ⓐ?

① terrific
② insincere
③ discontented
④ forthright

3 What is ⓑthis referring to?

① The critical investigation of the grounds of our prejudices, convictions, and beliefs made by philosophy
② The definite body of truths ascertained by various types of sciences including philosophy
③ The lack of definite answers to the knowledge philosophy aims at
④ The fact that subjects with concrete answers become a separate science such as astronomy and psychology

4 Which is most suitable for ⓒ?

① In contrast
② Similarly
③ Therefore
④ Nevertheless

11

The explanation of religion as a phenomenon rooted in social structure and the material world, does not always satisfy those who seek a more spiritual and individual basis for religion. Through the years, philosophers and social scientists have suggested a number of other factors such as: awe over the power of nature, fear of death, the need to interpret dreams, guilt over the wish to kill one's parents, and original sin. Some sociologists speak of a human need for transcendence, to escape the limits of one's own senses and to feel that one's life has significance beyond daily experience.

These possible sources, however, cannot explain the endless variety of belief systems or how they change over time. For this type of analysis we must pay attention to the group's particular culture and social structure. Do gathering bands, for example, tend to develop belief systems different from those of agricultural tribes? If the origins of belief lie in the uncertainties of human existence, then we would expect differences simply on the basis of varying modes of subsistence. In line with that thinking, anthropologist Marvin Harris suggests that the kinds of gods people worship reflect the nature of social relationships within the society. In simple gathering or hunting bands, the gods, like the people they guide, are basically an egalitarian bunch, with little distinction between male and female. These gods were important in creating the group but they leave daily life largely to the skills of the native population and to lesser divinities. In contrast, in agricultural societies, especially those with centralized states and well-defined social classes, the gods themselves are highly stratified and insist on strict obedience to standards of conduct and morality.

There is also evidence that important ritual functions were performed by women, such as the vestal virgins in ancient Europe, druid priestesses in Britain, and members of women's cults in early Roman history. Statues of a mother goddess from ancient Crete and wall paintings from Stone Age Turkey suggest an even more central role for women, not only in religious ritual but in the society as a whole. Indeed, there is evidence of widespread mother worship throughout the world, from prehistoric to contemporary societies.

1 위 글의 제목으로 가장 적합한 것을 고르시오.

① Cross-Cultural Perspectives in Belief Systems
② Gender Difference Reflected in Belief Systems
③ Social Structure and Individual Basis in Religion
④ The Universal Role of Women in Religious Rituals

2 위 글을 통해 추론할 수 있는 것으로 가장 적합한 것을 고르시오.

① A human's pursuit of the transcendence may explain the various forms of belief systems.
② Inter-societal relationships affected the formation of gods people believed in.
③ Gods were not distinctive in gender in the society of hunting bands.
④ According to the ancient Greek relics, women were believed to support religious rituals.

12

What is phenomenology? And why should anthropologists, as well as students of history, psychology, education, or political economy be interested in it? Within philosophy, phenomenology is as diverse as its practitioners. Indeed, an introduction to philosophical traditions of phenomenology finds it important to warn readers Ⓐ to overstate the degree to which phenomenology "coheres into an agreed method, or accepts one theoretical outlook, or one set of philosophical theses about consciousness, knowledge, and the world." Some of this diversity continues Ⓑ to be a feature of anthropological uses of phenomenology. Yet we also argue for a heuristic narrowing of the range of its meanings. We do so in order to widen its potential applicability, making it more instructive to anthropology as well as to aligned disciplines. What might appear to be a paradox — restricting meaning in order to expand its use — is in fact in keeping with phenomenology's own teachings. For preliminary purposes, we offer a serviceable definition of phenomenology: phenomenology is Ⓒ an investigation of how humans perceive, experience, and comprehend the sociable, materially assembled world that they inherit at infancy and in which they dwell.

Framed in this way, phenomenology in anthropology is a theory of perception and experience that pertains to every man, woman, and child in every society. As such, it is relevant not just to locals in the fieldwork sites that anthropologists step into and out of, but also to anthropologists and philosophers in their own regional lives, surrounded like everyone everywhere by significant others, human and non-human. Phenomenology therefore has a decidedly universalistic dimension. But it is also determinedly particularistic. The phenomenology we privilege sets out Ⓓ to show how experience and perception are constituted through social and practical engagements. There is a temporal, cumulative dimension to phenomenological descriptions of people's activities and concerns, which comes through most profoundly in phenomenology's subtle vocabulary of the orientations that inhabit our bodies and guide people's actions and perspectives.

1 Which of the following is most likely to be the topic of this passage?

① How one can distinguish between phenomenology and anthropology
② How we can identify anthropological approach in phenomenology
③ How phenomenological methods can be applied to anthropology
④ How social sciences can ignore non-empirical methodologies such as phenomenology

2 According to the passage, which of the following is true?

① Phenomenology can be defined as a philosophical discipline based on a unified methodology.
② Phenomenology mainly focuses on people's perception, experience, and understanding of the world.
③ By adopting phenomenological methodologies in anthropology, researchers narrowly focus on locals in fieldworks.
④ Phenomenological anthropology emphasizes universal aspects of human lives, without considering particular aspects.

3 Which of the following is the most appropriate place for the word "not" to be inserted in?

① Ⓐ ② Ⓑ
③ Ⓒ ④ Ⓓ

13

Critical thinkers learn to recognize fallacies. Most fallacies are flashy shortcuts that look good at first but turn out to be based on dubious assumptions and careless generalizations. Some common logical fallacies are ad hominem, circular reasoning, red herring, either/or argument, and bandwagon. A

First, ad hominem makes a personal attack on an opponent rather than focusing on the issue under discussion. Ad hominem arguments become smear tactics when a speaker or a writer attacks an opponent's personality or motives. The speaker who resorts to the abusive rhetoric may well be avoiding the real issues, such as whether a proposal is practical. B

Second, circular reasoning — also called begging the question — happens when instead of supporting a claim, the writer simply restates the claim in different words. Take this faulty argument: "The death penalty is wrong because the state should not have the power to end a criminal's life." But that's exactly what the death penalty is — state-<u>sanctioned</u> execution. C

Third, red herring involves diverting the audience's attention from the main issue by bringing up an irrelevant point. People who fear they have a weak case may employ a red herring by bringing in some emotionally charged but irrelevant point in the hope they can distract their audience.

Fourth, either/or argument implies that one must choose between only two options — right/wrong, good/bad, moral/immoral, and so forth. This is another simplistic reasoning that glosses over complex issues and instead attacks the opposition. D

Lastly, bandwagon tactic argues that an activity or a product must be worthwhile because it is popular. As millions of people have pointed out, popularity doesn't necessarily guarantee merit. E

1 According to the passage, which of the following would be the best definition of logical fallacy?
① Apparently wrong argument
② Emotionally charged argument
③ Shoddy imitations of well-reasoned argument
④ Logically reasoned argument
⑤ Abusive and insulting argument

2 The underlined word "<u>sanctioned</u>" can be best replaced by _____.
① punished   ② benefitted
③ violated   ④ endorsed
⑤ named

3 According to the Passage One, what kind of logical fallacy does the following sentence use?

A legislator arguing for a bill that would raise taxes on alcohol to provide low-cost housing claims that those who oppose the bill are heartless people more concerned with keeping down the price of their evening cocktails than with helping others.

① Ad hominem
② Circular reasoning
③ Red herring
④ Bandwagon
⑤ Either/or argument

4 According to the Passage One, what kind of logical fallacy does the following sentence use?

We should not raise taxes to build the new airport because doing so would cost taxpayers more money.

① Ad hominem
② Circular reasoning
③ Red herring
④ Bandwagon
⑤ Either/or argument

5 The following sentence could be added to the passage.

But don't confuse this type of fallacy with relevant questions about a person's credibility. It's perfectly legitimate to question an opponent whose qualifications or motives are dubious, as long as those considerations are relevant to the issues being discussed.

Where would the sentence best fit?

① A
② B
③ C
④ D
⑤ E

14

The word "Shaman" comes from the Evenki, a Siberian people, but shamans can be found in practically every corner of the planet — including in shamanic centers now in London, Boston, and many other Western cities. Shamans believe that unseen spirits permeate the world around us, act upon us, and govern our fates. By turns doctors, priests, mystics, psychologists, village elders, oracles, and poets, they are the designated negotiators with this hidden reality, and they occupy an exalted position within their societies.

There is no precise definition of shamanism. "It would be better to speak of 'shamanisms,' in the plural," says Marjorie Mandelstam Balzer, an anthropologist at Georgetown University. Beliefs, practices, and rituals vary from person to person, she told me, because the path to becoming a shaman is above all a highly individual one. Similarities do exist, though: The ecstatic trance, or soul journey, as it is sometimes called, is a signature phenomenon. But how shamans employ their instruments and spiritual insights varies greatly, as can the ritual's ultimate purpose. Many shamans work alone, while others join large urban organizations that act as trade unions.

Most shamans in Central Asian countries, where Islam predominates, regard themselves as devout Muslims, and their rites are infused with the mystic traditions of Sufism. Swathed in virginal white smocks, they conduct their rituals at Muslim holy sites, and every ceremony includes extensive prayers from the Koran. In Siberia and Mongolia, shamanism has merged with local Buddhist traditions — so much so that it's often impossible to tell where one ends and the other begins.

As shamanism's popularity has grown, its rituals have become major events — and even big business. On an August day in a sun-drenched meadow in Russia's Republic of Buryatiya, in Siberia, some two dozen people in indigo robes from a local shamanic group called Tengeri (Sky Spirits) performed an energetic ritual called a tailgan, in honor of a sacred spot on a nearby mountain. Shamanism represents more than spiritual rebirth and good business. It is also a catalyst for the post-Soviet cultural revival among the native peoples of Buryatiya. On the shore of Lake Baikal, the world's deepest body of fresh water and one of the most sacred sites in Siberia, observers may witness shamanism as self-determination — a ceremony by Buryats for Buryats.

1 Which of the following would be best for the title?

① The Popularity of Shamanism
② The Origins of Shamanism
③ The Uniformity of Shaman Rituals
④ The Rigidity of Shaman Tradition

2 What makes it hard to define shamanism in precise terms?

① ethnicity
② individuality
③ religiosity
④ ubiquity

3 Which of the following is NOT true?

① Shamanism attracts the westerners due to its Asian origin.
② Today's shamanism often leads to business opportunities.
③ Local shamanism contributes to cultural pride.
④ Shamanism varies in its styles and practices.

15

Kant rejects maximizing welfare and promoting virtue. Neither, he thinks, respects human freedom. So Kant is a powerful advocate for freedom. But the idea of freedom he puts forth is demanding — more demanding than the freedom of choice we exercise when buying and selling goods on the market. What we commonly think of as market freedom or consumer choice is not true freedom, Kant argues, because it simply involves satisfying desires we haven't chosen in the first place. So, if we're capable of freedom, we must be capable of acting not according to a law that is given or imposed on us, but according to a law we give ourselves. But where could such a law come from? Kant's answer: from reason. We're not only sentient beings, governed by the pleasure and pain delivered by our senses; we are also rational beings, capable of reason. If reason determines my will, then the will becomes the power to choose independent of the dictates of nature or inclination. (Notice that Kant isn't asserting that reason always does govern my will; he's only saying that, insofar as I'm capable of acting freely, according to a law I give myself, then it must be the case that reason can govern my will.) Of course, Kant isn't the first philosopher to suggest that human beings are capable of reason. But his idea of reason, like his conceptions of freedom and morality, is especially demanding. Thomas Hobbes called reason the "scout for the desires." David Hume called reason the "slave of the passions." Reason's work, for the utilitarians, is not to determine what ends are worth pursuing. Its job is to figure out how to maximize utility by satisfying the desires we happen to have. Kant rejects this subordinate role for reason. For him, reason is not just the slave of the passions. If that were all reason amounted to, Kant says, we'd be better off with instinct. Kant's idea of reason — of practical reason, the kind involved in morality — is not instrumental reason but "pure practical reason, which legislates a priori, regardless of all empirical ends." But how can reason do this? Kant distinguishes two ways that reason can command the will, two different kinds of imperative. One kind of imperative, perhaps the most familiar kind, is a hypothetical imperative. Hypothetical imperatives use instrumental reason: If you want X, then do Y. If you want a good business reputation, then treat your customers honestly. Kant contrasts hypothetical imperatives, which are always conditional, with a kind of imperative that is unconditional: a categorical imperative. "If the action would be good solely as a means to something else," Kant writes, "the imperative is hypothetical. If the action is represented as good in itself, and therefore as necessary for a will which of itself accords with reason, then the imperative is categorical." The term categorical may seem like jargon, but it's not that distant from our ordinary use of the term. By "categorical," Kant means unconditional. So, for example, when a politician issues a categorical denial of an alleged scandal, the denial is not merely emphatic; it's unconditional — without any loophole or exception. Similarly, a categorical duty or categorical right is one that applies regardless of the circumstances.

1 You can infer from the passage that for empiricist philosophers including the utilitarians, reason is _____.

① instrumental   ② categorical
③ unconditional   ④ practical

2 Which of the following statement is true?
① Kant's exalted idea of freedom incorporates the principles of the greatest happiness.
② Kant's notion of practical reason is based upon a practical aspect of empirical truth.
③ Maximizing utility is the ultimate goal of both Kant and utilitarians, though they pursued it in different ways.
④ A categorical imperative is founded upon the good itself rather than its consequences.

06

사회·정치

06 사회·정치

01

There hasn't always been quite such optimism about love's longevity as there is today. For the Greeks, inventors of democracy and a people not amenable to being pushed around by despots, love was a disordering and thus preferably brief experience. Later, during the reign of courtly love, love was illicit and usually fatal. Passion meant suffering; the happy ending didn't yet exist in the cultural imagination. The innovation of happy love didn't even enter the vocabulary of romance until the 17th century. Before the 18th century — when the family was primarily an economic unit of production rather than a hothouse of Oedipal tensions — marriages were business arrangements between families; participants had little to say on the matter. Some historians consider romantic love a learned behavior that really only took off in the late 18th century along with the new fashion for reading novels, though even then affection between a husband and wife was considered to be in questionable taste. Historians disagree, of course. Some tell the story of love as an eternal and unchanging essence; others, as a progress narrative over stifling social conventions. But has modern love really set us free? No. We feel like failures when love dies.

1 In which course is this passage most likely to be assigned reading?

① Medicine
② American History
③ Sociology
④ Human biology

2 Which of the following is NOT true of the passage?

① Marriage was a business bridegrooms controlled.
② The Greeks considered love to be a mental problem.
③ The popularity of reading novels altered perceptions of romance.
④ Love's portrayal in the past was generally inconsistent with current views.

3 Which of the following is the best title for the passage?

① Love's Longevity: A Fantasy
② Love's Business Arrangement: Practicality
③ Love as Eternal Truth
④ Love as a Never-Changing Social Form

02

A The next wave of new immigrants came between 1870 and 1900. Among the newcomers were many Chinese, who were mostly men and lived in California. Many worked in the minefields and railroad construction sites. Others worked at menial jobs as cooks, laundrymen, or servants. However, the Chinese faced harsh racial prejudice. In 1882, the U.S. Congress passed the Chinese Exclusion Act, banning nearly all Chinese from coming into the country.

B The United States is a nation of immigrants. Before the 1840s, about 60,000 immigrants arrived each year. During the 1840s and 1850s, the number of people coming to the United States increased dramatically. Over three million Irish and Germans crossed the Atlantic for America at this time.

C Most Irish immigrants lived in extreme poverty. Most settled in the slums of Boston and New York and worked in low-paying jobs. Irish women worked as kitchen maids while men took dangerous jobs at low wages. Ⓐ_____, most German immigrants came with more money and training than the Irish. They were able to buy land in the Midwest. Many became farmers in states such as Ohio and Wisconsin.

1 Which one is the right order?

① C — A — B
② B — A — C
③ B — C — A
④ C — B — A

2 Which one is NOT TRUE?

① The number of immigrants increased significantly around the mid-19th century in the U.S.
② Most Irish immigrants lived in the poor sections of cities.
③ All Chinese immigrants have been banned since 1882.
④ Most German immigrants came with greater wealth than Irish immigrants.

3 Choose the best expression for Ⓐ.

① Similarly
② In contrast
③ As a result
④ As such

03

Over the past 15 years, my country has gone through a colossal political revolution. The traditional secular elite that identifies with the nation's modernist founder, Mustafa Ataturk, has been replaced by religious conservatives who, until recently, were largely powerless and marginalized. The religious conservatives have by now come to dominate virtually all institutions of the state, as well as the media and even much of the business sector.

This political revolution has had an inadvertent outcome. It has tested the ostensible virtues of these religious conservatives — and they have failed. They have failed the test so terribly that it raises the question of whether religiosity and morality really go hand in hand, as so many religious people like to claim. The religious conservatives morally failed because they ended up doing everything that they once condemned as unjust and cruel. For decades, they criticized the secular elite for nepotism and corruption, for weaponizing the judiciary and for using the news media to demonize and intimidate their opponents.

1 What does the underlined their opponents refer to?

① The secular elite
② The religious conservatives
③ The judiciary and the media
④ The followers of Mustafa Ataturk

2 Which of the following is true of the new political leaders?

① They are moral as well as conservative.
② They do not believe religious people are moral.
③ They are being accused of using their power unfairly.
④ They used to stand in the same political position as Mustafa Ataturk.

04

The real objection to capital punishment doesn't lie against the actual extermination of the condemned, but against our brutal American habit of putting it off so long. _____, every one of us must die soon or late, and a murderer, it must be assumed, is one who makes that sad fact the cornerstone of his metaphysic. But it is one thing to die, and quite another thing to lie for long months and even years under the shadow of death. No sane man would choose such a finish. All of us, despite the Prayer Book, long for a swift and unexpected end. Unhappily, a murderer, under the irrational American system, is tortured for what, to him, must seem a whole series of eternities. For months on end he sits in prison while his lawyers carry on their idiotic buffoonery with writs, injunctions, mandamuses, and appeals. In order to get his money (or that of his friends) they have to feed him with hope. Now and then, by the imbecility of a judge or some trick of juristic science, they actually justify it. But let us say that, his money all gone, they finally throw up their hands. Their client is now ready for the rope or the chair. But he must still wait for months before it fetches him.

1 What would be the best expression for the blank?
① Therefore
② Nevertheless
③ Unfortunately
④ However
⑤ After all

2 Which of the following CANNOT be inferred from the given passage?
① American capital punishment system is not reasonable.
② Leaving anyone to wait for his/her death for such a long time is cruel.
③ No one wants a sudden, unanticipated death.
④ Lawyers are part of irrational American juristic system.
⑤ The Prayer Book is against the swift and unexpected death.

3 Which can best replace the underlined imbecility?
① irrelevance
② stupidity
③ intelligence
④ miscalculation
⑤ corruption

4 What would be the writer's attitude towards American juristic system?
① sarcastic
② furious
③ supportive
④ sympathetic
⑤ pedantic

05

At the beginning of the twentieth century, scholars from a wide array of disciplines began to think that narratives are central to human thinking and motivation. In their attempts to understand social movements, sociologists have begun to think of the contagion of narratives as Ⓐcentral to social change. For example, sociologist Francesca Polletta, who studied the sit-in social movement of the 1960s in which white Americans participated in protests of discrimination against blacks, reported that students described the demonstrations as Ⓑunplanned like a fever and over and over again, spontaneous. These demonstrations were often driven by a particular popular narrative about blacks demanding service at lunch counters that were labeled as "white only," accompanied by young white Ⓒsupporters who showed moral outrage at the exclusion of blacks.

The sit-in story emerged from a single story about a protest in 1960 involving four students from Greensboro College. The story revolved around polite young black people who Ⓓobeyed orders to leave the lunch counter where blacks were not served. The young people sat patiently, waiting to be served until the restaurant closed, and they returned the next day with more young people. The story went viral, through word of mouth and through news media attention, and the sit-ins spread throughout much of the United States. The story's spread was not entirely unplanned. Activists tried to promulgate the story, but they were not in tight control of the social movement, which was largely Ⓔviral. The word sit-in, coined in 1960, was a true epidemic.

1 윗글의 제목으로 가장 적절한 것은?
① Who's Making Sense of Narrative Change
② Why Some Narratives Have Become Obsolete
③ The Centrality of Narratives in Social Movements
④ Unsung Heroes in the History of Social Activism
⑤ Diverse Evidence on the Inflammatory Nature of Narratives

2 밑줄 친 Ⓐ~Ⓔ 중에서 문맥상 낱말의 쓰임이 적절하지 않은 것은?
① Ⓐ   ② Ⓑ
③ Ⓒ   ④ Ⓓ
⑤ Ⓔ

06

While Fascism is engaged in the struggle to acquire power, it has to make an appeal to a considerable section of the population. Both in Germany and in Italy, it arose out of Socialism, by rejecting whatever was anti-nationalistic in the orthodox programme. It took over from Socialism the idea of economic planning and of an increase in the power of the State, but the planning, instead of being for the benefit of the whole world, was to be in the interests of the upper and middles class in one country. And these interests it seeks to secure, Ⓐ_____ by increased efficiency, Ⓑ_____ by increased oppression, both of wage-earners and of unpopular sections of the middle class itself. In relation to Ⓒ<u>the classes which lie outside the scope of its benevolence</u>, it may, at best, achieve the kind of success to be found in a well-run prison; more than this it does not even wish to do.

1 Choose the best words or phrases for blanks Ⓐ and Ⓑ.
   ① more — than
   ② no less — than
   ③ as much — as
   ④ not so much — as

2 Which of the following serves best as an example of Ⓒ?
   ① an entrepreneur   ② a clerk
   ③ an aristocrat   ④ a beggar

3 Choose the statement LEAST consistent with the passage.
   ① Both the orthodox doctrines of Fascism and Socialism include nationalism.
   ② Both the orthodox doctrines of Fascism and Socialism emphasize the power of the State.
   ③ The idea of economic planning is crucial to the orthodox doctrines of Fascism.
   ④ The orthodox doctrines of Fascism make a great appeal only to a portion of the population.

07

In this first decade of the twenty-first century, the world community is confronted with staggering problems. There are 6 billion people on our globe and forecasters project that the world population will reach 10 billion by 2050. Those people will need food, shelter, and an education that will allow them to lead fulfilled lives. The twentieth century saw great advances in many fields, but these advances did not come without costs. Acid rain, for example, polluted our vegetation, wild life, and the very bodies of millions of people. Together, the people of the world need to stop the systemic despoiling of our planet. Weaponry, such as nuclear devices and improvised explosive devices, daily threaten the world's peace and progress. Religious fanaticism, hunger, and poverty have bred a desperate terrorism in many corners of the world. It is no overstatement to say that we are in a race for global survival.

1 What would be the best title for the above passage?

① Great Advances Made in the Twentieth Century
② Global Warming, Vegetation, and Wildlife
③ Great Advances Made with Significant Costs Paid
④ How to Lead Fulfilled Religious Lives
⑤ Desperate Terrorism and Global Survival

2 Which can best replace the underlined staggering?

① stimulating
② suspicious
③ abundant
④ astounding
⑤ stagnant

3 Which statement is NOT TRUE according to the given passage?

① The rapid growth of world population foreshadows serious problems to be dealt with.
② At a significant cost, we have made great technical advances in different areas.
③ Problems including nuclear devices and religious fanaticism are considered relatively easier to stop.
④ It is not an exaggeration to say that we need to resolve issues threatening the global community.
⑤ It is not likely that we can afford to provide enough resources to the growing population.

08

However, most Jews in the North remained too insecure in their status to act altruistically toward blacks in a consistent way. Instead, they usually fell into a much more ambivalent pattern, continuously asserting their social superiority as whites but expressing concern and sympathy for blacks when it did not bring their own status into question. The issue of residential segregation provides an instructive example. Jews supported neighborhood "protective" associations in New York and Chicago, but the Jewish press often found it appropriate to criticize such movements. The editors of the *American Hebrew*, however, ultimately understood the dilemma faced by status-conscious Jews, who they thought would surely encourage black social advancement, education, and self-sufficiency as long as "the negro advanced anywhere Ⓐbut in their own neighborhood." Many Jews who lived in transitional neighborhoods avoided the uncomfortable question of residential restriction altogether, preferring to sell their homes to African Americans and move. In this manner, they were able to fulfill their contradictory desires to put distance between themselves and the changing neighborhood and to avoid participating directly in the segregation efforts. These dual impulses were at work in 1919, when members of Chicago's Temple Isaiah voted to relocate away from the encroaching "Black Belt" but ignored the pleas of the Hyde Park-Kenwood Association not to sell to an African American congregation.

1 According to the above passage, which of the following is NOT true?

① The social status of Jews in the North was not secure enough.
② The issue of residential restriction indicated that Jewish Americans were altruistic.
③ Jews were supportive of the education and social uplift of African Americans.
④ The Jewish American attitude towards race-relations was ambivalent.

2 Which of the following is closest in meaning to Ⓐbut?

① yet
② only
③ still
④ except

3 Which of the following can be inferred from the above passage?

① Jews emphasized their whiteness by keeping their neighborhoods white.
② Jews were consistent in their actions for African Americans.
③ The residential issue often brought Jews' status into question.
④ Jews often felt torn between their impulses for inclusion and distinctiveness.

09

The writers of the Constitution wanted to make sure that the people's rights would always be safe and _____ the central or federal government would never become too powerful. A government ought to have three major powers: to make laws, to carry out those laws, and to provide justice under law. ⒶShould these three functions be in the hands of one person, there would be a great danger Ⓑthat that person could use the power for personal profit rather than for the people. ⒸTo guard against this possibility, the Constitution established three branches of government: the legislature to make laws; the executive to carry out the laws; and the judiciary to watch over the rights of people as described in the Constitution. The powers of these three branches of the government are described carefully in the Constitution. The reason Ⓓfor describing the powers of the three branches was to prevent any one branch _____ becoming stronger than the others. Each part of the government can only function in relation to the others. This system not only balances power between the three branches, but also Ⓔprovide a check on each branch by the others. This system means that at all times the people's rights and interests are being carefully guarded.

1 Which is the best title for the passage?

① System of Checks and Balances
② Ways of Making a Powerful Government
③ Collaboration between Governments
④ People's Rights and Interests
⑤ Benefits of the Constitution for People

2 Which are the most suitable words for the blanks?

① which — to
② whether — to
③ that — for
④ which — from
⑤ that — from

3 Select the part grammatically wrong.

① Ⓐ
② Ⓑ
③ Ⓒ
④ Ⓓ
⑤ Ⓔ

10

Under a government which imprisons any unjustly, the true place for a just man is a prison. The proper place today, the only place which Massachusetts has provided for her freer and less Ⓐ_____ spirits, is in her prisons, to be put out and locked out of the State by her own act, as they have already put themselves out by their principles. It is there that the fugitive slave, and the Mexican prisoner on parole, and the Indian come to plead the wrongs of his race, should find them; on that separate, but more free and honorable, ground, where the State places those who are not with her, but against her — the only house in a slave State in which a free man can abide with honor. If any think that their influence would be lost there, and their voices no longer afflict the ear of the State, that they would not be as an enemy within its walls, they do not know by how much truth is stronger than error, nor how much more eloquently and effectively he can combat injustice who has experienced a little in his own person. Cast your whole vote, not a strip of paper merely, but your whole influence. A minority is powerless while it conforms to the majority; it is not even a minority then; but it is irresistible when it clogs by its whole weight. If the alternative is to keep all just men in prison, or give up war and slavery, the State will not hesitate which to choose. If a thousand men were not to pay their tax-bills this year, that would not be a violent and bloody measure, as it would be to pay them, and enable the State to commit violence and shed innocent blood. This is, in fact, the definition of a Ⓑ_____ revolution, if any such is possible. If the tax-gatherer, or any other public officer, asks me, as one has done, "But what shall I do?" my answer is, "If you really wish to do anything, resign your office." When the subject has refused allegiance, and the officer has resigned his office, then the revolution is accomplished.

1   빈칸 Ⓐ와 Ⓑ에 들어가기에 가장 적합한 것을 고르시오.

  ① desponding — peaceable
  ② courageous — radical
  ③ obdurate — belligerent
  ④ discursive — restive

2   위 글에서 저자가 주장하는 바와 가장 일치하는 것을 고르시오.

  ① Massachusetts should prepare enough prisons in which the dissidents are put out and locked out of the State.
  ② A minority becomes a majority if it fights fiercely against injustice.
  ③ The public officer should resign if the subject pledges allegiance to the State.
  ④ Refusal to pay tax-bills could be one of the most disobedient actions that the subjects could take.

11

It is not often realized that women held a high place in southern European societies in the 10th and 11th centuries. As a wife, the woman was protected by the setting up of a dowry or *decimum*. Admittedly, the purpose of this was to protect her against the risk of desertion, but in reality its function in the social and family life of the time was much more important. The *decimum* was the wife's right to receive a tenth of all her husband's property. The wife had the right to withhold consent, in all Ⓐ_____ the husband would make. And more than just a right: the documents show that she enjoyed a real power of decision, equal to that of her husband.

Women seemed perfectly prepared to defend their own inheritance against husbands who tried to exceed their rights, and on occasion they showed a fine fighting spirit. A case in point is that of Maria Vivas, a Catalan woman of Barcelona. Having agreed with her husband Miro to sell a field she had inherited, for the needs of the household, she insisted on Ⓑ_____. None being offered, she succeeded in dragging her husband to the Ⓒ_____ to have a contract duly drawn up assigning her a piece of land from Miro's personal inheritance.

1 Which pair best fits Ⓐ and Ⓑ?

① transactions — compensation
② treaties — negotiation
③ exchanges — enactment
④ dealings — settlement
⑤ auctions — indemnity

2 Choose a statement that may be inferred from the passage above.

① The legal standing of the wife in marriage was higher than that of a single woman.
② The legal standing of the wife in marriage was lower than that of her husband.
③ The wife received one-tenth of her husband's land.
④ The husband could sell his wife's inheritance if his father-in-law agreed.
⑤ The wife had a powerful economic position.

3 Which profession best fits Ⓒ?

① scribe
② tinker
③ mason
④ smith
⑤ forger

12

A slew of factors have combined in recent years to create the impression that the world is run by plutocrats, oligarchs and semi-detached politicians in the interests of the few not the many.

A quarter of a billion people are on the move around the world, providing more ammunition than ever before for right-wing populists who argue that political elites have failed to get a handle on the kind of immigration that they say threatens jobs, wages and social cohesion.

Meanwhile, the number of billionaires has jumped fivefold in the last 20 years, to more than 2,200, according to *Forbes*, as globalization opened up new markets for entrepreneurs to tap while at the same time making it possible to shield capital, assets and income from the taxman. The world's eight richest people own as much as the poorest 3.5 billion. The amount of money gained by the financial elite is put at as much as £10 trillion.

But there are also many non-economic factors that may offer partial explanations for populism's rise: a cultural backlash against elites, a technological revolution that has rewired our politics, a convergence of now indistinguishable left and right political parties on a technocratic centre.

1 The best title of the passage would be _____.
① How can you spot a populist?
② What is populism?
③ Who are the populists?
④ Why have the populists emerged now?
⑤ What's the opposite of a populist?

2 As a factor which has created a backdrop for populism, _____ is NOT mentioned in the passage.
① cultural elitism
② tax evasion
③ mass migration
④ soaring inequality
⑤ ideological confrontation

3 According to the passage, populism is against _____.
① political elites of the right
② political elites of the left
③ corrupt elites
④ the wicked businessmen
⑤ the ordinary masses

13

The objective profile of the United States, then, may be traced throughout Disneyland, even down to the morphology of individuals and the crowd. All its values are exalted here, in miniature and comic-strip form. Embalmed and pacified. Whence the possibility of an ideological analysis of Disneyland: digest of the American way of life, panegyric to American values, idealized transposition of a contradictory reality. To be sure. But this conceals something else, and that "ideological" blanket exactly serves to cover over a third-order simulation: Disneyland is there to conceal the fact that it is the "real" country, all of "real" America, which is Disneyland (just as prisons are there to conceal the fact that it is the social in its entirety, in its banal omnipresence, which is Ⓐ_____). Disneyland is presented as imaginary in order to make us believe that the rest is real, when in fact all of Los Angeles and the America surrounding it are no longer real, but of the order of the hyperreal and of simulation. It is no longer a question of a false representation of reality (ideology), but of concealing the fact that the real is no longer real, and thus of saving the reality principle. The Disneyland imaginary is neither true nor false: it is a deterrence machine set up in order to rejuvenate in reverse the fiction of the real. Whence the debility, the Ⓑ_____ degeneration of this imaginary. It is meant to be a(n) Ⓑ_____ world, in order to make us believe that the adults are elsewhere, in the "real" world, and to conceal the fact that real childishness is everywhere, particularly among those adults who go there to act the child in order to foster illusions of their real childishness.

1 Choose the best word for the blank Ⓐ above.

① abject
② carceral
③ epicene
④ blithe

2 According to the logic of the passage, what is NOT hyperreal?

① Universal Studios
② reality television shows
③ Grand Canyon
④ McDonald's

3 Which statement CANNOT be inferred from the passage?

① Adulthood is no longer possible in America.
② Ideology permeates quotidian life.
③ Disneyland is a metonym for American culture.
④ The Disneyland imaginary hides the fact that the real is no longer real.

4 Choose the best word for the blank Ⓑ above.

① dystopian
② prosaic
③ meretricious
④ infantile

14

John C. Calhoun, the great statesman of the pre-Civil War South, thought you could have responsible constitutional government without Ⓐforcing minorities to submit to the will of the majority. He advocated giving minorities the veto power over majority decisions which Ⓑaffects their vital interests. The trouble with this remedy, of course, is that it makes government ineffective on all crucial issues, and gives a minority the supreme power of _____ of the majority will. The English political philosopher John Stuart Mill proposed another remedy, which has become part of electoral procedure in many countries: proportional representation. Mill Ⓒpointed out that it was possible for a minority to attain a sizable vote and yet be without any representation in the national lawmaking body. Mill felt that "minority representation" should accompany majority rule, that the minority should have a voice, though not the supreme power. He also suggested a system of "plural voting" which would grant more votes to the more highly educated or intelligent persons. There is no doubt that proportional representation gives a more just representation to various political convictions. But it Ⓓhas tended to make governments unstable, with no single party able to attain a majority. I think we all agree that the majority should be prevented from taking away certain human rights. Nor should the majority Ⓔbe allowed to impose its religious beliefs, political convictions, or mode of life on minorities.

1 According to the passage, which of the following is NOT true about Mill?

① granting minority to have a voice
② giving more votes to the more highly educated persons
③ sympathizing with "minority representation"
④ rectifying proportional representation
⑤ suggesting a system of "plural voting"

2 According to the passage, governments can be made unstable by _____.

① proportional representation ② supreme power
③ the majority will ④ any political unit
⑤ a political philosopher

3 Which of the following is most appropriate to fill in the blank?

① verification ② nullification
③ vindication ④ clarification
⑤ externalization

4 Which of the following underlined words is grammatically INCORRECT?

① Ⓐ ② Ⓑ
③ Ⓒ ④ Ⓓ
⑤ Ⓔ

15

All societies are based on imagined hierarchies, but not necessarily on the same hierarchies. In most cases the hierarchy originated as the result of a set of _____ and was then perpetuated and refined over many generations as different groups developed vested interests in it. A For instance, many scholars surmise that the Hindu caste system took shape when Indo-Aryan people invaded the Indian subcontinent about 3,000 years ago, subjugating the local population. The invaders established a stratified society, in which they occupied the leading positions (priests and warriors), leaving the natives to live as servants and slaves. The invaders, who were few in number, feared losing their privileged status and unique identity. B To forestall this danger, they divided the population into castes, each of which was required to pursue a specific occupation or perform a specific role in society. Each had different legal status, privileges and duties. Mixing of castes — social interaction, marriage, even the sharing of meals — was prohibited. And the distinctions were not just legal — they became an inherent part of religious mythology and practice. The rulers argued that the caste system reflected an eternal cosmic reality rather than a chance historical development. Concepts of purity and impurity were essential elements in Hindu religion, and they were harnessed to buttress the social pyramid. C Pious Hindus were taught that contact with members of a different caste could pollute not only them personally, but society as a whole, and should therefore be abhorred. Such ideas are hardly unique to Hindus. Throughout history, and in almost all societies, concepts of pollution and purity have played a leading role in enforcing social and political divisions and have been exploited by numerous ruling classes to maintain their privileges. D It probably has its roots in biological survival mechanisms that make humans feel an instinctive revulsion towards potential disease carriers, such as sick persons and dead bodies. If you want to keep any human group isolated — women, Jews, Roma, gays, blacks — the best way to do it is convince everyone that these people are a source of pollution.

1 Choose the most appropriate one for the blank.

① ultimate economic advantages
② accidental historical circumstances
③ extant theological myths
④ inherent cosmic realities

2 Choose the most appropriate place for the sentence below.

The fear of pollution is not a complete fabrication of priests and princes, however.

① A   ② B
③ C   ④ D

16

The places that now consider themselves to be democracies are with a handful of exceptions run by the process generally known as representative democracy. That qualifying adjective should make you sit up and think. The starting point of modern democracy is the belief that every sane adult is entitled to an equal say in the conduct of public affairs. Some people are richer than others, some are more intelligent, and nobody's interests are quite the same as anybody else's: but all are entitled to an equal voice in deciding how they should be governed. There is therefore something odd in the fact that in most democracies this voice is heard only once every few years, in elections in which voters choose a president or send their representatives to an elected parliament: and that between those elections, for periods of anything up to seven years, it is the presidents and parliamentarians who do all the deciding, while the rest of the democracy is expected to stand more or less quietly on one side, either nodding its head in irrelevant approval or growling in frustrated disagreement. This is part-time democracy.

There exists in a few places a different way of doing it, called direct democracy. In this straightforward version, the elected representatives are not left to their own devices in the periods between elections. The rest of the people can at any time call them to order, by cancelling some decision of the representatives with which most of the people do not agree or, sometimes, by insisting that the representatives do something they had no wish to do, or perhaps had never even thought about. The machinery by which this is done is the referendum, a vote of the whole people.

1 The best title of the passage would be '_____'.
① Why democracy does not work
② How modern democracy failed
③ Democracies in the 21st century
④ How to turn autocracy into democracy
⑤ Two different processes of running democracy

2 In this passage, the author argues that representative democracy is part-time democracy because _____.
① most representatives work part-time
② some people are not allowed to vote
③ people's voice is heard only in elections
④ all people are entitled to an equal say in public affairs
⑤ people can cancel some decisions of the representatives at any time

3 The underlined part "left to their own devices" means '_____'.

① allowed to remain unchanged
② allowed to resist changes
③ allowed to do as they wish
④ allowed to hold their status
⑤ allowed to stay in power

17

People seem to feel that there is some essential difference between beggars and ordinary "working" men. They are a race apart — outcasts, like criminals. Working men "work," beggars do not "work"; they are parasites, worthless in their very nature. It is taken for granted that a beggar does not "earn" his living, as a bricklayer or a literary critic "earns" his. He is a mere <u>social excrescence</u>, tolerated because we live in a humane age, but essentially despicable. Yet if one looks closely one sees that there is no essential difference between a beggar's livelihood and that of numberless respectable people. Beggars do not work, it is said; but, then, what is work? A navvy works by swinging a pick. An accountant works by adding up figures. A beggar works by standing out of doors in all weathers and getting varicose veins, chronic bronchitis, etc. It is a trade like any other; quite useless, of course — but, then, many reputable trades are quite useless. And as a social type a beggar compares well with scores of others. He is honest compared with the sellers of most patent medicines, high-minded compared with a Sunday newspaper proprietor, amiable compared with a hire-purchase tout — in short, a parasite, but a fairly harmless parasite. He seldom extracts more than a bare living from the community, and, what should justify him according to our ethical ideas, he pays for it over and over in suffering. I do not think there is anything about a beggar that sets him in a different class from other people, or gives most modern men _____.

1 Choose the closest in meaning to the underlined "<u>social excrescence</u>."
① bulwark of society
② watching of society
③ nuisance to society
④ arbiter in society

2 Choose the one the best fills in the blank.
① the rationale for immortalizing him
② a reason to venerate him
③ an excuse for proselytizing him
④ the right to despise him

3 What is the best title for the passage?
① The Ignominy of Beggary
② The Ups and Downs of Being a Beggar
③ Begging For Respect
④ Beggars: On the Same Grounds

4 What is the tone of the passage?
① ironic
② euphoric
③ confessional
④ nostalgic

18

A For, whether intended or not, the effect of obedience to the law is to uphold the authority of those who make decisions about what the law should be, and how it is to be enforced. To uphold this authority is to aid in maintaining aspects of the distribution of power to make decisions for society. Similarly, all violations of the law constitute political behavior; every violation of law is ipso facto a defiance of constituted authority. It threatens the maintenance of the existing pattern of distribution of the power to make decisions for society. If the incidence of violations of law continues to increase, political authority eventually atrophies; that is axiomatic.

B An attempt to define political stability must begin by clarifying the concepts of politics and political structure. Political behavior is any act by any member of a society that affects the distribution of the power to make decisions for that society. Political behavior is ubiquitous. Members of society behave politically insofar as, in obeying or disobeying the laws of the society, they support or undermine the power stratification system. Obedience to the law constitutes political behavior just as much as contesting elections does.

C We have clearly not defined the political in the usual sense of demarcating particular acts that are political from those that are not. Nor do we intend to offer such a definition, because it is misleading to delineate the political in that fashion. Strictly speaking, there is no human act, even so simple as wearing hair long, that is intrinsically nonpolitical. This is true because the "politicalness" of an act is not a quality inherent in that act but rather a characterization of it according to the context in which we study it, and the context in which it occurs.

D To illustrate, we would not ordinarily consider long hair a form of political behavior. Yet a puritanical despot might decide that this act corrupts and consequently command everyone to cut his hair short. Suppose that shortly after such a decree has been widely and intensively publicized, all the men invited by the despot to a state ceremony arrive with long hair. In the circumstances, we would legitimately conclude that these men were committing a very bold act of political disobedience.

1 위 글의 단락을 논리적 흐름에 맞게 순서대로 배열한 것으로 가장 적합한 것을 고르시오.

① D — B — C — A
② B — A — C — D
③ A — C — B — D
④ B — A — D — C

2 위 글의 주제로 가장 적합한 것을 고르시오.

① Psychological effects of individual and group behaviors in organized society
② Knowing the concepts of political election and obedience
③ The contribution of cultural power to stabilize society
④ Defining the political stability in the relations between politics and political structure

19

When in 1997 the United States Congress passed a law requiring that juveniles aged 14 or older charged with federal crimes be tried as adults and incarcerated in adult prisons, they were following the lead of every state in the country.

But despite the tremendous popularity in lowering the age of adulthood by the criminal justice system, there's no evidence that it works to lower crime. In fact, ironically, the evidence shows the opposite.

Certainly, there are juvenile psychopathic murderers from whom, if released, the public could never be assured of protection. But as nightmarish as are those headline cases of brutal murders by juveniles, they make up an infinitesimal fraction of serious youth crimes. Most juveniles who are tried in adult courts and sent to adult prisons are sent there for lesser crimes than homicide and will be released someday.

Every study available so far shows that those juveniles who are sent to adult prison have higher recidivism rates than those who remain in juvenile facilities. That means that juveniles sent to adult prison tend to endanger the public and get rearrested at much higher rates once they've been released.

The reason youths who have served time in adult prison are so much more dangerous when released than their counterparts who have served time in juvenile facilities is that, for those who are capable of having their lives turned around, they stand the best chance of picking up the life skills they need in juvenile facilities. For most — but not all — education and treatment in youth facilities that are set up to try to save kids really does work.

Certainly, rehabilitation doesn't have a 100 percent success rate, particularly in those rare instances when the youngster either is incapable of or not open to it. One teenager I spoke with, whom I'll call ⒶJesse, had abandoned a fine family with seemingly caring working-class immigrant parents and successful siblings for an essentially homeless life of no school, fighting and crime. He couldn't articulate to me why he preferred his rootless life.

1 Which of the following can be inferred from the passage?

① Every juvenile crime can be prevented by appropriate parental guidance regardless of each juvenile's personality.

② The portion of brutal murders by juveniles is not small enough to be ignored but has gradually decreased.

③ The juveniles in juvenile facilities are likely to endanger the public less than those in adult prison, once both of them were released.

④ There is no evidence that lowering the age of adulthood by the criminal justice system actually increases crime.

2 What is the main purpose of the passage?

① To explain criminal justice system relating to juveniles in America before 1997
② To inform the reader of the negative effect of sending juveniles to adult prison
③ To describe the relation between ages and crime rates
④ To provide examples for juvenile crimes which raise serious issues

3 Why does the author mention a teenager, ⒶJesse in the passage?

① To provide an example of a juvenile who got unsuccessful rehabilitation
② To analyze the difference between adult prisons and juvenile facilities
③ To criticize the complicated situation of American criminal justice system
④ To portray the life of an average adolescent in a juvenile facility

20

In the 16th century, Sir Thomas More described an imaginary ideal society in his book *Utopia*. His Utopians would allow only slaves to kill animals because they did not want free citizens to experience the cruelty associated with killing living things. In modern slaughterhouses, cattle have often been killed with a lot of unnecessary suffering: animals stressed by abject fear and pain.

Temple Grandin, a renowned animal behavioral scientist, is leading authority on improving conditions at processing plants, advising the U.S. government on the federal Human Slaughter Act (calling for painless killing), and writing guidelines for the American Meat Institute. A An example of her practical designs: slaughterhouse ramps where cattle walk single file, able to see only three animals ahead, with the walkway turning in 180 degree curves so the cattle cannot see anything unexpected that will make them balk. When there are high walls, no shadows, no loud noises, no hitting, no slippages underfoot, the animals proceed without fear, and industry efficiency improves. Although many animal welfare advocates say we should avoid eating meat entirely, livestock animals serve a human purpose. B

Animal activists have also alerted people to the cruel conditions of the veal industry. Deprived of their mothers at birth, male veal calves are put in tiny pens alone, chained at the neck, unable to walk — all in order to keep their meat very tender. Raised on a liquid diet, Ⓐ<u>deficient</u> in iron and fiber, full of chemicals, antibiotics, and hormones, the calves are literally dragged to the slaughter at about 4 months old. Such conditions are now banned in Britain, and many consumers and chefs in the U.S. resist buying or preparing veal raised in this way. C

There is also a growing switch from red meat to poultry. But chickens tightly confined in battery cages in huge factory-like warehouses are also fed antibiotics and hormones. D Transportation and slaughter conditions are often appalling. Consequently, consumers have become interested in stores which use only "care-free" eggs and "organic" chickens. Despite the added cost, this trend is growing, fed by consumer disgust with the treatment of animals and worries over the industrialization of the food supply.

1 According to the passage, which of the following is NOT true?

① Temple Grandin believes that human beings owe animals a peaceful death.
② Slaughtering veal in cruel conditions is illegal in Britain today.
③ Grandin's inventions are purely profit-oriented.
④ Many American chefs resist preparing veal raised in inhumane conditions.

2 Which of the following can be inferred from the passage?

① Consumers are gradually eating more chicken than veal because of the high-quality meat.
② Utopians believed that slaves could kill animals with greater efficiency than free men.
③ People use their buying power to show their disapproval of the veal industry.
④ Grandin's inventions make the cattle unable to see anything at all in front of them.

3 Which of the following is the closest in meaning to the underlined Ⓐdeficient?

① unendurable ② insufficient
③ unseemly ④ incompetent

4 The author's main purpose in writing this passage is to _____.

① emphasize the great legacy of Temple Grandin's achievements
② discuss the inhumane conditions of animals in slaughterhouses these days
③ explain how livestock animals react to Grandin's designs
④ show how the veal industry raises the young cows to make their meat tender

5 Which is the most appropriate place for the sentence below?

And Grandin believes humans should recognize their caretaking role toward these animals.

① Ⓐ ② Ⓑ
③ Ⓒ ④ Ⓓ

07

경제·경영

07 경제·경영

▶▶▶ ANSWERS P.386

01

Trade protectionism is used by countries when they think their industries are being damaged by unfair competition by other countries. It is a defensive measure, and it is usually politically motivated. It can often work, in the short run. However, in the long run it usually does the opposite of its intentions. It can make the country, and the industries it is trying to protect, less competitive on the global marketplace. Countries use a variety of ways to protect their trade. One way is to enact tariffs, which tax imports. This immediately raises the price of the imported goods, and therefore less competitive when compared to locally produced goods. This works especially well for a country like the U.S., which imports a lot of its goods. The most famous example is the Smoot-Hawley Tariff of 1930. It was originally designed to protect farmers from agricultural imports from Europe, which was stepping up farming after the destruction of World War I. However, by the time the bill made it through Congress, it had slapped tariffs on many more imports. As so often happens with tariffs, other countries Ⓐ_____. This tariff war restricted global trade, and was one reason for the extended severity of the Great Depression.

1 Which of the following is NOT mentioned in the passage?

① Trade protectionism is not conductive to booming global trade.
② Trade protectionism often works well in the long run.
③ One way of trade protectionism is to impose heavy tariffs upon imports.
④ The Great Depression was extended by the US trade protectionism.

2 Which of the following is a most suitable word for the blank Ⓐ?

① accepted
② dwindled
③ retaliated
④ confused

02

Assessing how well employees are performing is a key part of any organization's human resource management. Most companies conduct a performance appraisal once or twice a year. Popular methods include "Management by Objectives," which compares set goals with the employee's actual performance, "Ⓐ_____" appraisals, in which coworkers review one another, "Ⓑ_____" appraisals, whereby the employee is assessed by everybody from senior managers to coworkers, customers, and suppliers, and even "Self-Appraisal," with workers evaluating themselves.

If done well, a detailed performance evaluation can bring benefits. It can help to identify and reward success, motivating employees to excel further. It can be used to determine raises or promotions based on merit. It can also help to highlight areas for improvement or further training. At the very least, it gives the employee a better understanding of the company's needs and expectations.

1 빈칸 Ⓐ, Ⓑ에 들어갈 가장 알맞은 것을 고르시오.

① Peer-to-Peer — 360 Degree
② Unilateral — All-around
③ Communicative — Top-down
④ Reciprocal — Bottom-up

2 위 글의 내용과 맞는 것을 고르시오.

① Performance appraisal is insignificant to upgrading a company's product quality.
② Performance appraisal is most effective when it is done by a company's management.
③ Performance appraisal can bring numerous personal benefits to employees.
④ Performance appraisal forces employees to conform to the company's policies.

03

One phase of the business cycle is the expansion phase. This phase is a twofold one, including recovery and prosperity. ⓐIt is not prosperity itself but expectation of prosperity that triggers the expansion phase. During the recovery period there is ever-growing expansion of existing facilities, and new facilities for production are created. More businesses are created and older ones expanded. Improvements of various kinds are made. There is an ever-increasing optimism about the future of economic growth. Much capital is invested in machinery or heavy industry. More labor is employed. More materials are required. As one part of the economy develops, other parts are affected. ⓑFor example, a great expansion in automobiles results in an expansion of the steel, glass, and rubber industries. Roads are required; thus the cement and machinery industries are stimulated. ⓒDemand for labor and materials results in greater prosperity for workers and suppliers of raw materials, including farmers. This increases purchasing power and the volume of goods bought and sold. Thus, prosperity is diffused among the various segments of the population. ⓓThis prosperity period may continue to rise and rise without an apparent end. However, a time comes when this phase reaches a peak and stops spiraling upwards. This is the end of the expansion phase.

1 윗글의 흐름상 가장 적합하지 않은 것을 고르시오.
① ⓐ　　　　　　　　　　② ⓑ
③ ⓒ　　　　　　　　　　④ ⓓ

2 윗글을 통해 추론할 수 있는 것으로 가장 적합한 것을 고르시오.
① When consumers lose their confidence in the market, a recession follows.
② In the expansion phase, many parts of the economy are mutually benefited.
③ Luxury goods such as jewelry are unaffected by industrial expansion.
④ The creation of new products is crucial in the prosperity period.

04

'Product placement', also called 'embedded marketing,' is a merchandising strategy for brands to reach their target audiences by embedding their products into another form of media. This placement of branded goods or services is often found in entertainment, namely in movies or television. For examples of branded product placement in the media, think of movies you've seen. If the lead actor is drinking a clearly labeled 'Coke' or using a clearly labeled 'Samsung' cell phone, then this is product placement. In most cases, large brands will have paid huge sums of money for their brand to be placed in movies. While the product placement cost can be high, the payout can be even higher for the brand. For example, Hershey embedded its chocolate into the movie *E.T.* and their profits jumped by 65%. Aside from an increase in profits, product placement can also boost brand recognition. *The Journal of Management and Marketing Research* estimates that 57.5% of television viewers recognized a brand embedded in a show when the brand was also advertised during the show. Even if that doesn't translate to immediate sales, higher brand recognition will benefit your business in Ⓐ_____.

1 According to the passage, what are the two benefits of product placement?

① Increases in profits and brand awareness
② Increases in profits and decreases in costs
③ Economical advertising and creative branding
④ Trendy advertising and efficient branding

2 Which of the following best fits into Ⓐ?

① a creative way
② a short time
③ the mean time
④ the long run

05

　　A company has a great product and naturally wants consumers to think of it as the best they can buy. So the marketing team rolls out an advertising campaign showing why the product is superior to the competition in terms of features and price, and is rewarded with robust sales. Instead of being able to bask in that success, however, the company starts to hear a lot of complaints and get a lot of returns. Clearly, the strategy Ⓐ_____. But why? It turns out that comparative ads and "Ours is the best!" product positioning activate something known as the maximizing mind-set, which leads people to regard anything that's less than perfect as a waste of money. Our research has found that although some people are "maximizers" by nature, and others tend to be content with "good enough," those attitudes aren't fixed. The maximizing mind-set can be induced by situations that encourage people to make comparisons and to look for the very best. When marketing messages inadvertently induce it, the results may be post-purchase regret and brand switching at the slightest hint of Ⓑ_____.

1 빈칸에 들어갈 표현으로 가장 적절한 것은?

① failed — adversity
② recoiled — improvement
③ backfired — disappointment
④ floundered — gratification

2 위 글의 내용과 가장 거리가 먼 것은?

① Comparative ads do not always pay off.
② Maximizers tend to entice other people to make comparisons.
③ The maximizing mind-set is contingent upon situations.
④ Consumers with a maximizing mind-set are inclined to seek after the very best.

06

The rise of a handful of vast corporate powerhouses whose business models have no instructive precedent from the analogue-era forces a reappraisal of the way capitalist economies work. The top seven highest valued companies in the world are all in the technology sector. Titans such as Alphabet (which owns Google) and Facebook specialize in products that do not exist in three-dimensional space. Apple and Amazon sell real-world objects as well as concepts, but their fortunes and market dominance have been built on nebulous concepts — models, brands and algorithms.

Wealth is no longer in factories, pipelines or retail outlets. Their capital is not anchored to specific fields. That makes them hard to regulate and hard to tax. These are patterns of economic globalization that pre-date the digital revolution. While some intangibles like software and data strongly rely on computers, others do not: brands, for example.

What makes the new era different is the extent to which value has become detached from the tangible, and the corresponding social and economic consequences. This is the dynamic described by Jonathan Haskell and Stian Westlake as "capitalism without capital". In their book of that title, the authors illuminate ways in which the scale of intangibility deforms the familiar mechanisms of a market economy.

1 The underlined "capitalism without capital" means _____.

① the collapse of capitalist economy
② capitalism with the intangible capital
③ the importance of global network in business
④ the inequality of wealth in capitalism
⑤ the global expansion of tangible assets in capitalism

2 The best headline of the above editorial is "_____."

① The Necessity of Globalism in Capitalism
② The Globalization of Capitalism
③ The Rise of the Intangible Wealth
④ The Changing Nature of Capitalism
⑤ The Guide to the Success in the New Era

07

Corporations can be either public or private. The stock of a public corporation can be bought by the general public. A In contrast, that of a private corporation, such as Gallo Wine, Levi Strauss, or United Parcel Service, is owned by only a small group of people and is usually not sold to the general public. The controlling stockholders may be family members, a management group, or even employees of the company. B

Corporations have several advantages. The biggest advantage is limited liability: The liability of investors is limited to the amount of money they personally invested in the company. C In case of failure, the courts may seize and sell a corporation's assets but cannot dispose of the investors' personal possessions at will. For example, if you invest $1,000 in a company and it goes bankrupt, you may lose no more than that amount. In other words, $1,000 is the limit of your liability. D Another advantage is continuity. Because it has a legal life, which is independent of the biological lives of its owners, a corporation can, Ⓐ_____, last forever. Shares of stock, for example, may be inherited by future generations. Finally, corporations have the upper hand in raising money. By selling more stock, for instance, they can easily increase the number of investors and the amount of funds.

1 Choose the best place for the following.

Because unknown stocks don't tend to attract buyers, most new corporations start out as private corporations.

① A
② B
③ C
④ D

2 Choose the best expression for Ⓐ.

① just like everything else in life
② at least in theory
③ never
④ by no means

3 Which is TRUE?

① It is impossible for a private corporation to issue stock to the public.
② The liability of an investor in a corporation is virtually unlimited.
③ A corporation can continue even after the death of the initial investors.
④ An employee of a private corporation is not allowed to own its stock.

08

Although nations may choose different economic systems, all must be concerned with producing. Any discussion of economic systems requires an understanding of what have been described as the ingredients of production. All production involves four separate factors: natural resources, labor, capital, and entrepreneurship.

Natural resources — the materials nature provides — are necessary for the production of the things we want. Some economists prefer to call this factor land. The minerals in the ground, forests, waterfalls, and fertile soil are all examples of a nation's resources; they are important in determining its production, particularly because they are becoming more scarce.

To adapt natural resources for human use, we must apply work. This is done by labor, the second factor of production. The skill and the amount of labor will also be important in determining production. India has more than twice the labor force of the United States, but the greater skill of the U.S. worker leads to far more productivity. Superior education has allowed the United States to capitalize on the use of machines.

The third factor of production is capital. Most people think of capital as money. To the _____, capital is any man-made instrument of production — that is, a good used to further production. Frequently, it will mean a tool or a machine. It can also mean the rolled steel that is used in automobile production. If great amounts of capital are placed in skilled hands, productivity can be increased tremendously.

1 According to the passage, which is NOT true?
① The quality of labor is related to education and skill levels.
② Forests can be an element of natural resources.
③ Capital, one of the ingredients of production, is identical to money.
④ Natural resources are generally dwindling.

2 Which is the most appropriate for the blank?
① cardiologist
② economist
③ environmentalist
④ anthropologist

3 Which is most likely to follow the passage?
① An explanation of entrepreneurship
② A principle of productivity
③ A summary of the ingredients of production
④ An introduction of economic systems

09

It is possible for a product to become _____. When a product is so new, so innovative, or so well marketed that it dominates the marketplace and the mindset of the consumer, it can be easy to associate the product's brand name with the product itself. When a type of product is nearly universally known or referred to by the brand name of one version of the product, the brand name becomes a victim of "genericism." Aspirin (acetylsalicylic acid), the escalator (moving stairs), and the pogo stick (hopping toy) are all former brand names whose success and popularity led to such general and widespread use of the names that the inventors or parent companies were unable to maintain their trademark protections and even lost their competitive advantage against similar products described with the term that had once been a definitive brand name. All it takes is one court ruling for a term that has shifted away from its identity as a trusted brand name to become forever identified as a generic product. When this happens, a company is likely to lose a profitable beachhead within the consumer consciousness. The loss of revenue due to a shift to genericism is compounded by the large amounts of money companies spend in an attempt to keep it from happening. Despite spending millions of dollars in legal and public relations campaigns, the company Kimberly-Clark has been fighting an uphill battle to keep people from referring to all forms of tissues as Kleenex.

1 윗글의 내용과 가장 거리가 먼 것은?
① Genericism is a by-product of a company's successful marketing of a product.
② Kimberly-Clark doesn't want people to refer to all forms of tissues as Kleenex.
③ Aspirin and the escalator are often considered brand names rather than the names of products nowadays.
④ Companies are usually unable to protect their trademarks when they become a generic term for a product.
⑤ Companies often spend a lot of money to prevent their trademarks from becoming a generic term for a product.

2 빈칸에 들어갈 가장 적절한 것은?
① a victim of its own success
② popular regardless of its quality
③ unpopular because of its brand name
④ a big success regardless of marketing strategies
⑤ nothing but a failure due to marketing strategies

10

For many business owners, getting the most out of staff is a perennial problem. In the case of fruit farmers, perhaps "perennial" is the wrong word: Workers show up for the summer harvest only.

Tough work for the fruit-pickers, the business is also a headache for the owner, who must offer a pay scheme that both satisfies minimum-wage laws and motivates workers in an industry in which slacking is an understandable temptation. So an unlikely alliance was formed between the owner of a large British fruit-farm business and a team of economists. The economists designed and administered pay schemes in order to research the nexus between _____.

The economists turned their attention to incentives for low-level managers, who would also be temporary immigrant workers but who would be responsible for on-the-spot decisions such as which workers were assigned to which row in the field. The economists found that managers tended to do their friends favors by assigning them the easiest rows. This made life comfortable for insiders but was unproductive since the most efficient assignment for fruit picking is for the best workers to get the best rows. The economists responded by linking managers' pay to the daily harvest. The result was that managers started favoring the best workers rather than their own friends, and productivity rose by 20 percent.

1 Which of the following is most appropriate for the blank?

Ⓐ pay
Ⓑ workers' backgrounds
Ⓒ workplace friendships
Ⓓ workers' productivity

① Ⓐ and Ⓑ
② Ⓑ and Ⓓ
③ Ⓐ, Ⓒ and Ⓓ
④ Ⓐ, Ⓑ and Ⓓ
⑤ Ⓑ, Ⓒ and Ⓓ

2 What did the experimented pay scheme show?

① Financial incentives trump social ties.
② Low-level managers favor their friends.
③ Workers prioritize social networks over money.
④ All the pay schemes have their own merits.
⑤ Only the businesses that practice new pay schemes can survive.

11

The neoliberal state should favor strong individual private property rights, the rule of law, and the institutions of freely functioning markets and free trade. These are the institutional arrangements considered essential to guarantee individual freedoms. The state must therefore use its monopoly of the means of violence to preserve these freedoms at all costs. By extension, the freedom of businesses and corporations (legally regarded as individuals) to operate within this institutional framework of free markets and free trade is regarded as a fundamental good. Private enterprise and entrepreneurial initiative are seen as the keys to innovation and wealth creation. Intellectual property rights are protected (for example through patents) so as to encourage technological changes.

Neoliberals are particularly assiduous in seeking the privatization of assets. Enclosure and the assignment of private property rights are considered the best way to protect against the so-called "tragedy of the commons". Sectors formerly run or regulated by the state must be turned over to the private sphere and be deregulated (freed from any state interference). Privatization and deregulation combined with competition, it is claimed, eliminate bureaucratic red tape, increase efficiency and productivity, improve quality, and reduce costs, both directly to the consumer through cheaper commodities and services and indirectly through reduction of the tax burden.

1 According to the passage, which of the following is NOT true?

① In situations where property rights are hard to define, it is not recommended that the state uses its power to impose or invent market systems.
② The assumption that individual freedoms are guaranteed by freedom of the market and of trade is a cardinal feature of neoliberal thinking.
③ The sanctity of contracts and the individual right to freedom of action, expression, and choice must be protected.
④ Competition — between individuals, between firms — is held to be a primary virtue.

2 Which of the following is NOT the characteristics of the neoliberal state?

① It seeks to transfer control of economic factors to the private sector from the public sector.
② It is a less regulatory state with regards to private life.
③ It emphasizes the efficiency of market competition and the role of individuals in determining economic outcomes.
④ It tries to protect social justice and redistribution at all costs.

3 What is the meaning of the "tragedy of the commons"?

① The tendency for markets to grow more imperfect, causing social inequality
② The tendency for individuals to irresponsibly exploit public property resources
③ The tendency for companies to ignore investing in quality-enhancing factors
④ The tendency for societies to self-protect against unregulated market exchange

12

Many people enjoy benefits from sports without ever paying the team or event organizer. They bask in civic pride because they live in a major league city, or they bask in national pride when their nation's athletes win Olympic medals. They line the streets of Manhattan for tickertape parades when the Yankees win the World Series, or pack Trafalgar Square in London and the beaches of Rio de Janeiro to celebrate their cities' being awarded the Olympic Games.

This complicates benefit-cost analysis of government policies supporting sports. In principle, measuring the benefits from ticket purchases and cable subscriptions is easy. Market data on ticket prices and sales, for instance, allow estimation of demand functions, and consumer and producer surplus. Such methods use revealed preference data, so called because people's purchases reveal their preferences for sports over alternative goods and services.

But no markets exist for tickertape parades and office conversations about last night's game. No league or team collects statistics measuring national pride or the value fans place on checking the highlights at ESPN.com or the league standings in their local newspapers. Crompton calls such benefits 'psychic income' and says they are perhaps the greatest _____ benefits produced by sports.

In this respect, sport resembles the environment. Both produce important benefits in the nature of non-rival and non-excludable public goods. No one disputes that many people value public goods such as scenic vistas, survival of endangered species, and clean air. But no one has to go to the corner shop or to an online seller to buy them. In other words, as in sports, many of the benefits are difficult to value because there are no revealed preference data with which to estimate demand and consumer surplus. Fortunately for sports economists, environmental economists have developed a method to measure the benefits of non-traded public goods.

1 Choose the one that would best fill in the blank.
① intangible
② pervasive
③ flamboyant
④ succulent

2 Which of the following is NOT mentioned?
① where Londoners gather for celebrations
② a definition of 'revealed preference data'
③ reasons for fans checking their team's league standings
④ an analogy between sport and the environment

3 What is the most likely purpose of this passage?
① to introduce a method to measure 'psychic income'
② to criticize government subsidization of sport teams
③ to emphasize the importance of government sports policies
④ to illustrate hidden benefits of sporting events

13

Detractors describe the valuation of Bitcoin as nothing more than a speculative bubble. Legendary investor Warren Buffett said, "it's a gambling device." Critics find its story similar to Ⓐthat of the famous tulip mania in the Netherlands in the 1630s, when speculators drove up the price of tulip bulbs to such heights that one bulb was worth Ⓑabout as much as a house. That is, Bitcoins have value today because of public excitement. ⒸWith Bitcoin to achieve its spectacular success, people had to become excited enough by the Bitcoin phenomenon to take action to seek out unusual exchanges to buy them.

For Bitcoin's advocates, labeling Bitcoin as a speculative bubble is the ultimate insult. Bitcoin's supporters often point out that public support for Bitcoin is not fundamentally different from public support for many other things. For example, gold has held tremendous value in the public mind for thousands of years, but the public could just as well have accorded it little value if Ⓓpeople had started using something else for money. People value gold primarily because they perceive that other people value gold. In addition, it is pointed out that bubbles can last a long time. Long after the seventeenth-century tulip mania, rare and beautiful tulips continued to be highly valued, Ⓔthough not to such extremes. To some extent, tulip mania continues even today in a diminished form. The same might happen to Bitcoin.

1 밑줄 친 Ⓐ~Ⓔ 중에서 어법상 적절하지 않은 것은?

① Ⓐ ② Ⓑ
③ Ⓒ ④ Ⓓ
⑤ Ⓔ

2 윗글의 내용과 일치하는 것은?

① Tulip mania disappeared a long time ago.
② The value of gold is based on people's belief that other people also value gold.
③ The famous tulip bubble is one reason many people become Bitcoin enthusiasts.
④ Warren Buffet supports Bitcoin because he can identify why people believe in its value.
⑤ Critics do not value Bitcoin primarily because its volatile prices can lead to price fluctuations of many commodities.

14

The central thesis of *Capital in the Twenty-first Century* by Thomas Piketty is that inequality is not an accident, but rather a feature of capitalism, and can only be reversed through state interventionism. The book thus argues that, unless capitalism is reformed, the very democratic order will be threatened.

Piketty bases his argument on a formula that relates the rate of return on capital (*r*) to economic growth (*g*), where *r* includes profits, dividends, interest, rents and other income from capital and *g* is measured in income or output. He argues that when the rate of growth is low, then wealth tends to accumulate more quickly from *r* than from labor and tends to accumulate more among the top 10% and 1%, increasing inequality. Thus the fundamental force for divergence and greater wealth inequality can be summed up in the inequality *r* > *g*. He analyzes inheritance from the perspective of the same formula.

The book argues that there was a trend towards higher inequality which was reversed between 1930 and 1975 due to unique circumstances: the two world wars, the Great Depression and a debt-fueled recession destroyed much wealth, particularly that owned by the elite. These events prompted governments to undertake steps towards redistributing income, especially in the post-World War II period. The fast, worldwide economic growth of that time began to reduce the importance of inherited wealth in the global economy.

The book argues that the world today is returning towards "patrimonial capitalism," in which much of the economy is dominated by inherited wealth: the power of this economic class is increasing, threatening to create an oligarchy. Piketty cites novels by Honoré de Balzac, Jane Austen and Henry James to describe the rigid class structure based on accumulated capital that existed in England and France in the early 1800s.

Piketty proposes that a progressive annual global wealth tax of up to 2%, combined with a progressive income tax reaching as high as 80%, would reduce inequality, although he concedes that such a tax "would be politically impossible."

1 Which of the following is NOT true?

① Inequality is an inevitable part of capitalism.
② The lower the rate of growth, the more the income of the rich.
③ Oligarchy presupposes the absence of inherited money.
④ Annual global wealth tax could help to reduce inequality.

2 Which of the following is NOT Piketty's suggestion?

① state's intervention   ② reformation of capitalism
③ progressive income tax   ④ patrimonial capitalism

15

What sets a product apart from the others with which it competes? Appearance and quality aside, branding is probably the most direct way to distinguish an item from its peers on the market shelf. Consequently, most products sold in the United States and the Western world carry an identification indicating a particular name, place, or organization of manufacture.

According to the American Marketing Association, a brand is a name, term, sign, symbol, or design — or a combination of these — intended to identify the goods or services of one seller or group of sellers and to differentiate them from those of competitors. A brand name is that part of a brand that can be vocalized. A trademark is a brand, or part of a brand, given legal protection because it is capable of exclusive appropriation.

[A] Most importantly, branding offers the consumer confidence in product consistency. Assuming that the manufacturer makes a consistent product, branding helps convey the message that the item being purchased is similar in quality and performance to those products of the same brand that have previously been used.

[B] Branding identifies a particular manufacturer's product. By branding its products, an organization makes it possible for the customer to note easily a particular product and repeat the purchase if satisfaction resulted from the initial purchase.

[C] At the same time, branding represents a dual-edged sword. If the previous purchase of that particular brand resulted in dissatisfaction, then by being able to easily identify the product or service, the customer is able to avoid repeat purchase on subsequent occasions.

For example, Maytag washing machines have, for years, been considered by many consumers to be the finest products in their field. Hence, the company's fabled "lonely repairman." This image of a smooth-running, long-lasting product was no accident. The organization attempted to build a sound product and, at the same time, ensure that servicing of the product was equally good. Consequently, consumers who owned Maytag washing machines and needed to purchase new ones more often than not would "think" Maytag when making their purchases. In essence, the consumer in such a case bets on the consistency of product and performance indicated by a brand name. In the case of more frequently purchased products, such as toothpaste or detergent, brand identification facilitates continued and frequent repurchases, an indicator of consumer brand loyalty.

1 위 글의 밑줄 친 문장들을 바른 순서대로 나열한 것으로 가장 적합한 것을 고르시오.

① [B] — [A] — [C]
② [B] — [C] — [A]
③ [C] — [A] — [B]
④ [C] — [B] — [A]

2 위 글의 내용과 일치하는 것을 고르시오.

① Branding sometimes discourages consumers' repurchase of products.
② The influence of branding is stronger in the Western world than in the U.S.
③ Consumers are more affected by branding than appearance of products.
④ The purchase of washing machines is more subject to branding than that of detergent.

16

A Stagflation is a combination of the words stagnation and inflation. It describes an economic condition characterized by slow growth and high unemployment (economic stagnation) mixed with rising prices (inflation).

The term appeared as early as 1965, when British Conservative Party politician Ian Macleod in a speech to the House of Commons said: "We now have the worst of both worlds, not just inflation on the one side or stagnation on the other, but both of them together. We have a sort of 'stagflation' situation and history in modern terms is indeed being made."

B After all, unemployment and inflation rates generally move in opposite directions. However, as the "Great Inflation" period of the 1970s ultimately proved, stagflation is real, and it can have a devastating effect on the economy.

C Stagflation and inflation are related, but they shouldn't be confused. The term inflation refers to a sustained increase in the average price level of all goods and services, not just a few of them, in an economy over time. Inflation happens when the money supply grows at a faster rate than the economy can produce goods and services.

Stagflation happens when inflation exists in tandem with slow economic growth and high unemployment. Typically, these economic conditions don't occur together. Unemployment and inflation tend to be inversely correlated. So, as unemployment rates increase, inflation usually decreases and vice versa. Of course, as the stagflation of the 1970s illustrated, this relationship isn't always stable or predictable.

D Stagflation is a perfect storm of economic ills: slow economic growth, high unemployment, and high prices. The two root causes of stagflation economists generally agree upon are supply shocks and fiscal and monetary policies. For households, stagflation means people are earning less money while spending more on everything from food and medicine to housing and consumer products. As consumer spending slows, corporate revenue declines, exacerbating the overall effect on the economy.

1 Which of the following is best for the following sentence?

Initially, many economists believed stagflation wasn't possible.

① A
② B
③ C
④ D

2 Which of the following is NOT true?

① Slow growth and high unemployment with rising prices characterize stagflation.
② Stagflation is a made-up word describing a British economic situation in the 1960s.
③ During the stagflation, people tend to earn less money and spend even less.
④ The primary causes of stagflation are supply shocks and fiscal and monetary policies.

17

On the future course of the economy, economists' predictions differ greatly. Optimists suggest that the economy has already hit the Ⓐ_____, but pessimists warn of the Ⓑ_____ of a double-dip recession. They must be eager to predict when the crisis will be over, but it is not an easy job. One American economist once said, Ⓒ"The only function of economic forecasting is to make astrology look respectable."

As it must have been frustrating to make wrong predictions, some economists try to go beyond the traditional indexes and seek their answers from completely unrelated fields. Lawrence Summers, a famous economist, recently said the free fall of the American economy has stopped. As proof, he pointed to the number of people searching for the phrase "economic recession" on Google, which in the beginning of the year had Ⓓ_____ to four times more than usual but has now Ⓔ_____ conspicuously.

Alan Greenspan, another famous economist, is said to have examined the amount of garbage, number of customers at dry cleaners and the sales of men's underwear. He did so because households produce more garbage and send more clothes to the dry cleaners when the economy is strong. On the contrary, if sales of men's underwear dwindle, it means the economy has abruptly turned bad.

1 Choose the best expression for Ⓐ and Ⓑ.

① apex — advent
② bottom — advent
③ bottom — end
④ apex — end

2 What does the underlined Ⓒ mean?

① Economic forecasting is a function of astrology.
② Economic forecasting is as unreliable as astrology.
③ Astrology is as trustworthy as the economy.
④ Astrology can be a more respectable science with the help of economics.

3 Choose the best expression for Ⓓ and Ⓔ.

① soared — dropped
② extended — dropped
③ soared — rebounded
④ extended — rebounded

4 Which one is NOT true?

① Summers believed the statistical data of Googling could be an appropriate indicator for the economy.

② Greenspan believed that people tend to use the dry cleaners more often in an economic crisis.

③ Greenspan believed that men tend to spend less money buying underwear during a recession.

④ Greenspan believed that more garbage from households could be a positive sign for the economy.

18

The fashion industry is a product of the modern age. Prior to the mid-19th century, virtually all clothing was handmade for individuals, either as home production or on order from dressmakers and tailors. ⒶBy the beginning of the 20th century — with the rise of new technologies such as the sewing machine, the rise of global capitalism and the development of the factory system of production, and the proliferation of retail outlets such as department stores — clothing had increasingly come to be mass-produced in standard sizes and sold at fixed prices. ⒷAlthough the fashion industry developed first in Europe and America, today it is an international and highly globalized industry, with clothing often designed in one country, manufactured in another, and sold in a third. ⒸThe fashion industry has long been one of the largest employers in the United States, and it remains so in the 21st century. However, employment declined considerably as production increasingly moved overseas, especially to China. Because data on the fashion industry typically are reported for national economies and expressed in terms of the industry's many separate sectors, aggregate figures for world production of textiles and clothing are difficult to obtain. However, by any measure, the industry inarguably accounts for a significant share of world economic output. ⒹThe fashion industry consists of four levels: the production of raw materials, principally fibres and textiles but also leather and fur; the production of fashion goods by designers, manufacturers, contractors, and others; retail sales; and various forms of advertising and promotion. These levels consist of many separate but interdependent sectors, all of which are devoted to the goal of satisfying consumer demand for apparel under conditions that enable participants in the industry to operate at a profit.

1 Which of the following is NOT one of the factors that has contributed to the development of mass production in fashion industry?

① introduction of sewing machines
② expansion of outsourcing practices
③ expansion of retail outlets
④ rise of global capitalism

2 Which of the following is NOT identified as one of the levels of fashion industry?

① advertising and promotion
② employment and education
③ production of raw materials
④ production of fashion goods

3 Where should the following sentence be added?

For example, an American fashion company might source fabric in China and have the clothes manufactured in Vietnam, finished in Italy, and shipped to a warehouse in the United States for distribution to retail outlets internationally.

① A   ② B
③ C   ④ D

19

The leisure class lives by the industrial community rather than in it. Its relations to industry are of a pecuniary rather than an industrial kind. Admission to the class is gained by exercise of the pecuniary aptitudes — aptitudes for acquisition rather than for serviceability. There is, therefore, a continued selective sifting of the human material that makes up the leisure class, and this selection proceeds on the ground of fitness for pursuits of wealth. But the scheme of life of the class is in large part a heritage from the past, and embodies much of the habits and ideals of the earlier barbarian period. This archaic, barbarian scheme of life imposes itself also on the lower orders, with more or less mitigation. In its turn the scheme of life, of conventions, acts selectively and by education to shape the human material, and its action runs chiefly in the direction of conserving traits, habits, and ideals that belong to the early barbarian age — the age of prowess and predatory life.

The most immediate and unequivocal expression of that archaic human nature which characterizes man in the predatory stage is the fighting propensity proper. In cases where the predatory activity is a collective one, this propensity is frequently called the martial spirit, or, latterly, patriotism. It needs no insistence to find assent to the proposition that in the countries of civilized Europe the hereditary leisure class is endowed with this martial spirit in a higher degree than the middle classes. Indeed, the leisure class claims the distinction as a matter of pride, and no doubt with some grounds. War is honorable, and warlike prowess is eminently honorific in the eyes of the generality of men; and this admiration of warlike prowess is itself the best voucher of a predatory temperament in the admirer of war. The enthusiasm for war, and the predatory temper of which it is the index, prevail in the largest measure among the upper classes, especially among the hereditary leisure class. Moreover, the ostensible serious occupation of the upper class is that of government, which, in point of origin and developmental content, is also a predatory occupation.

1 Which of the following is the best topic for the passage?

① The characteristics of the leisure class
② The barbaric heritage in predatory age
③ The fighting trait of European society
④ The rise and fall of the barbaric warriors

2 Which of the following is the most important requirement for the membership of the leisure class?

① serviceability
② courage
③ money-making ability
④ predatory temper

3 Which of the following is NOT true about the leisure class?

① Their mode of life has become the standard for that of the lower classes.
② Their status enables them to create war-like attitudes totally different from previous ages.
③ The fighting propensity is still continued in the name of patriotism in modern times.
④ The warlike attitudes are easily found in most members of the leisure class.

20

Email is the most common form of written communication in the business world. Although emails are often seen as less formal than business letters, they still need to be professional in tone and structure, and are quite different from the casual messages you send to friends and family. However, business emails are not just letters sent via a computer — they have a style of their own which is important to understand. One of the most important things to remember when emailing to business colleagues is to be concise. Many professionals receive a multitude of emails throughout the day and often don't have the time to read thoroughly each piece of correspondence. Because the recipient may have to evaluate which incoming messages have the greatest priority, choose the contents of the subject line carefully and use it to give a clear summary of the email's purpose. Email messages being sent outside of the company should end with a closing signature that includes the sender's full name and business affiliation. Most email programs provide an option whereby a closing signature may be created and automatically appended to all outgoing messages. It is good business practice to use the 'reply' option to an existing message rather than opening a 'new message' page. The 'reply' gives the recipient a link, commonly called a thread, to the original message, and a path to follow if several replies to one message pile up. Or, if the incoming message is lengthy and only certain items require a response, the sender can copy only those relevant parts and paste them into a 'new message', then key in the appropriate responses.

1 글의 내용에 의하면, 업무상 이메일이 간결해야 하는 이유는?

① Because email is the most common form of written communication in the business world.
② Because email is still considered a professional way of communication in the business world.
③ Because computers can process more efficiently when email follows a certain style of its own.
④ Because many professionals are usually too busy to read all the emails that they receive each day.
⑤ Because it is not polite and also ineffective to write lengthy emails to business colleagues.

2 밑줄 친 the 'reply' option과 가장 잘 부합하는 것은?

① It is recommended to make a reply with a new message page instead of an existing message page.
② It is recommended to make a reply to every message showing a link or a thread to the original message.
③ It is recommended to include the original message and to show a path to guide previous messages in the reply.
④ It is recommended to make just one reply to the recipient although he has sent several messages.
⑤ It is recommended to include all the original messages with appropriate responses although they may be lengthy.

3 윗글의 내용과 부합하지 않는 것은?

① Business emails should be written more professionally compared with casual emails to friends and family.
② Brief business emails are preferred to lengthy business emails among many professionals.
③ The contents of the subject line should indicate the priority level of the message.
④ When enclosing a closing signature, the sender's full name and company name should be stated.
⑤ When incoming email is lengthy, only the relevant parts of the message can be replied in a new page.

08

과학·기술

08 과학·기술

01

Perkin, Nobel, and Fleming benefited from happy accidents, but their discoveries were not purely accidental. Their discoveries are examples of serendipity, which means the wise use of fortuitous accidents. Serendipity has played a role in many important scientific achievements including the discovery of the x-ray, insulin, and DNA. For serendipity to play a role in scientific discovery, researchers must be keenly observant, open to multiple possibilities, and curious about the unexpected. If Perkin had not noted the color of the substances as he cleaned up after his experiment, he would not have discovered an artificial dye. It was the first artificial dye that could be manufactured inexpensively for people of average means to wear the color purple. If Nobel had not permitted himself to ask the question *Can *collodion be used in explosives?* he would not have invented **gelignite. If Fleming had not been curious about the mold in one of his dishes, he would not have discovered the antibiotic *penicillin* which has relieved so much human suffering.

*Collodion, a common treatment for the wound at the time
**Gelignite, the first and less dangerous explosive than dynamite

1 Which is the best title for the passage?

① History of Explosives
② Happy Accidents in Science
③ Role of Responsible Scientists
④ Significance of Well-designed Researches

2 According to the passage, which is NOT true?

① Nobel's invention of a new explosive was a sheer accident.
② Perkin discovered the first artificial dye for the color purple.
③ Perkin's discovery allowed people of average means to afford to wear the purple.
④ Fleming's curiosity about the mold in his dish resulted in his discovery of *penicillin*.

02

Blockchain is an enormous digital record open for anyone with internet access to see. This record is not maintained by any individual or organization, but by approximately 9,000 computers in a distributed network. The computers' owners volunteer to add their machines to the network because, in exchange for their computer's services, they sometimes receive payment. All the information in the record is permanent. It cannot be changed because each of the computers keeps a copy of the record. If you wanted to hack the system, you would have to hack every computer on the network which has so far proved impossible, despite many trying. The collective power of all these computers is greater than the world's top 500 supercomputers combined. New information is added to the record every few minutes, but it can be added only when all the computers signal their approval, which they do when they receive satisfactory proof that the new information is correct. Everybody knows how the system works, but nobody can change how it works because it is Ⓐ_____.

1 According to the passage, which of the following is true of blockchain?

① Its information is secure.
② It consists of 500 supercomputers.
③ Owners can delete its information.
④ People pay to become part of it.

2 From the context, which of the following best fits into Ⓐ?

① uncontrolled
② fully automated
③ regularly updated
④ freely available

03

It was in the 1920s that the idea of freezing fresh vegetables into preserved, edible rectangles first caught hold, when inventor Clarence Birdseye developed a high-pressure, flash-freezing technique that operated at especially low temperatures. The key to his innovation was the flash part: comparatively slow freezing at slightly higher temperatures causes large ice crystals to form in food, damaging its fibrous and cellular structure and robbing it of taste and texture. Birdseye's supercold, superfast method allowed only small crystals to form and preserved much more of the vitamins and freshness. In the 90 years since, food manufacturers have added a few additional tricks to improve quality. Some fruits and vegetables are peeled or blanched before freezing, for example, which can cause a bit of oxidation — the phenomenon that makes a peeled apple or banana turn brown. But blanching also deactivates enzymes in fruit that would more dramatically degrade color as well as flavor and nutrient content. What's more, the blanching process can actually increase the fibrous content of food by concentrating it, which is very good for human digestion.

1 The best title of the above passage would be _____.

① Technological Leap in Food Storage
② Side Effects of Food Additives on Health
③ Marketing History of Healthy Foods
④ How to Buy Bargain Foods in Supermarket
⑤ Marketing Strategies of Food Manufactures

2 According to the passage, which of the following is true?

① There is no relation between the speed of freezing and the nutrients in foods.
② Fiber and nutrient contents can stay high in frozen foods.
③ Birdseye's freezing method was innovative but it costed a lot.
④ Peeling is preferable to blanching, which destroys the flavor of foods.
⑤ Unlike other nutrients, vitamins are considerably affected by freezing.

04

Further justification for the photon nature of light came from an experiment conducted by Arthur H. Compton in 1923. In his experiment, Compton directed an x-ray beam toward a block of graphite. He found that the scattered x-rays had a slightly longer wavelength than the incident x-rays, and hence the energies of the scattered rays were lower. The amount of energy reduction depended on the angle at which the x-rays were scattered. The change in the wavelength between a scattered x-ray and an incident x-ray is called the Compton shift. In order to explain this effect, Compton assumed that if a photon behaves like a particle, its collision with other particles is similar to a collision between two billiard balls. Hence, the x-ray photon carries both measurable energy and momentum, and these two qualities must be conserved in a collision. If the incident photon collides with an electron initially at rest, the photon transfers some of its energy and momentum to the electron.

1 What would be the best title of the passage above?
① The paradox of photon studies
② The nature of Compton effect
③ The sequence of x-ray
④ The discovery of x-rays

2 According to the passage above, which one is true concerning Compton effect?
① The scattered photon has less energy than the incident photon.
② The scattered photon has more energy than the incident photon.
③ The scattered photon has shorter wavelength than the incident photon.
④ The scattered photon has the same wavelength as the incident photon.

3 What can be inferred from the given passage when the incident photon collides with an electron initially at rest?
① The incident photon loses energy.
② The incident photon gains energy.
③ The incident photon produces a chain of multiple collision.
④ The incident photon prevents the loss of energy.

05

Ethics may be profoundly affected by an adoption of the scientific point of view; that is to say, the attitude that men of science, in their professional capacity, adopt towards the world. This attitude includes a high (perhaps an unduly high) regard for the truth, and a Ⓐrefusal to come to unjustifiable conclusions which expresses itself on the plane of religion as agnosticism. And along with this is found a deliberate Ⓑemancipation of emotion until the last possible moment, on the ground that emotion is stumbling-block on the road to truth. So a rose and a tape-worm must be studied by the same methods and viewed from the same angle, even if the work is ultimately to lead to the killing of the tape-worms and the propagations of roses. Again, the scientific point of view involves the Ⓒcultivation of a scientific esthetic which rejoices in the peculiar forms of beauty which characterize scientific esthetic theory. Those who find an intimate relation between the good and the beautiful will Ⓓrealize the importance of the fact that a group of men so influential as scientific workers are pursuing a particular kind of beauty. _____, since the scientist, as such, is contributing to an intellectual structure that belongs to humanity as a whole, his influence will inevitably fall in favour of ethical principles and practices which transcend the limits of nation, colour, and class.

1 Which is the most appropriate for the blank?
① Instead
② Finally
③ Nevertheless
④ Intriguingly

2 Which of the underlined words is NOT appropriate?
① Ⓐ
② Ⓑ
③ Ⓒ
④ Ⓓ

3 According to the passage, which is true?
① Science doesn't impinges upon ethics.
② Science has its own concept of the beautiful.
③ A deliberate oppression of emotion is an impetus to finding the beautiful.
④ Aesthetics has no relation with ethics.

06

Dalton's concept of an atom was far more detailed and specific than Democritus'. The first hypothesis states that atoms of one element are different from atoms of all other elements. Dalton made no attempt to describe the structure or composition of atoms. But he realized that the different properties shown by elements such as hydrogen and oxygen can be explained by assuming that hydrogen atoms are not the same as oxygen atoms. The second hypothesis suggests that, to form a certain compound, we need not only atoms of the right kinds of elements, but the specific numbers of these atoms as well. Dalton's second hypothesis supports another important law, the law of multiple proportions. According to this law, if two elements can combine to form more than one compound, the masses of one element that combine with a fixed mass of the other element are in ratios of small whole numbers. Dalton's theory explains the law of multiple proportions quite simply: Compounds differ in the number of atoms of each kind that combine. For example, carbon forms two stable compounds with oxygen, namely, carbon monoxide and carbon dioxide. On the basis of Dalton's atomic theory, we can define an atom as the basic unit of an element that can enter into chemical combination. Dalton imagined an atom that was both extremely small and indivisible. However, a series of investigations that began in the 1850s and extended into the 20th century clearly demonstrated that atoms actually possess internal structure.

1 The passage above is mainly about _____.
① Dalton's contribution to the atomic theory
② the negative effect of Dalton's theory
③ Dalton's unintended discovery of an atom
④ the immoral aspect of Dalton's theory

2 Which of the following is true?
① Democritus' atomic theory was not widely accepted by many of his contemporaries.
② Dalton failed to formulate a definition of the indivisible building blocks of matter.
③ According to Dalton's hypothesis, compounds composed of atoms need to have specific numbers of the atoms.
④ Dalton made a serious effort to depict the atomic structure.

07

The word 'metaverse' is often traced to Neal Stephenson's 1992 dystopic, cyberpunk novel *Snow Crash*, and many see a more recent inspiration in the dazzling warren of experiences at the heart of Ernest Cline's 2011 novel *Ready Player One*. However, the metaverse is far from the stuff of sci-fi. It's not even new. Online communities have existed since the mid-1980s, and grew in the 1990s with chatrooms, AOL instant messenger, and the first social media sites. The game *World of Warcraft* became a persistent social scene for millions in the early 2000s, and communities have continued to sprout up within and around games. Today, logging onto *Fortnite*, joining a chat with friends over a console platform and launching into a game with them is, especially to younger generations, just as social an experience as most physical interactions. Whether in virtual reality (VR), augmented reality (AR), or simply on a screen, the promise of the metaverse is to allow a greater overlap of our digital and physical lives in wealth, socialization, productivity, shopping, and entertainment. These two worlds are already interwoven, no headset required: Think about the Uber app telling you via location data how far away the car is; think about how Netflix gauges what you've watched before to make suggestions. At its core, the metaverse is a(n) Ⓐ_____ of our current Internet.

1 Which of the following is the best title for the passage?

① The Retreat of the Metaverse
② Metaverse: It's around the Corner
③ The Metaverse Has Already Arrived
④ How the Metaverse Will Change our Lives

2 According to the passage, which of the following is true?

① The metaverse is only a figment of sci-fi authors' imaginations.
② Playing *Fortnite* is a physical interaction but not a social one.
③ The metaverse allows for our digital and physical lives to overlap.
④ The word 'metaverse' first appeared in *Ready Player One*.

3 Which of the following best fits into Ⓐ?

① decay
② evolution
③ abbreviation
④ manipulation

08

Heat is everywhere. It's raw energy, and it boils down to matter in motion. Atoms and molecules, the building blocks of everything around us including ourselves, move constantly and randomly; the faster they move, the warmer the substance they make up. Every object in this world — no matter how frigid it may seem — contains some heat. Even a jug of ice water harbors so much molecular motion that if you gently place a drop of ink on the surface, it will diffuse evenly throughout the liquid within hours. In fact, if you could extract and store all the thermal energy contained in a single snowy ski slope in January, you could heat your house with it for days. Scientists have determined that, at least in theory, there's a point called absolute zero where all motion — and hence all heat — ceases to exist. But it remains unattainably cold: -460°F.

Heat always travels in whatever direction tends to equalize temperatures; that is, from region of high thermal energy and relative warmth to colder areas. Bring enough heat together in one place, and you may be able to overcome the forces of attraction between atoms and molecules, causing a change of state from solid to liquid or liquid to gas. Such changes require additional energy, called latent heat, which doesn't raise the substance's temperature but is needed just to change state. Consequently, _____ to raise the temperature of a quart of water from 210°F (liquid) to 220°F (steam) than it does to raise its temperature from 85°F (liquid) to 95°F (liquid).

1 Which of the following is NOT true according to the passage?

① Heat moves to colder places.
② Even cold water has thermal energy.
③ People have not experienced absolute zero.
④ A ski slope does not contain thermal energy in winter.
⑤ A drop of ink on the surface of ice water will diffuse throughout the water.

2 Which of the following is most appropriate for the blank?

① it takes more energy
② it gets more dangerous
③ it requires less heat
④ it becomes less expensive
⑤ it gets more perceivable

09

What is the insight in which the scientist tries to see into nature? Can it indeed be called either imaginative or creative? To the literary man the question may seem merely silly. He has been taught that science is a large collection of facts; and if this is true, then the only seeing which scientists need to do is, he supposes, seeing the facts. He pictures them, the colorless professionals of science, going off to work in the morning into the universe in a neutral, unexposed state. They then expose themselves like a photographic plate. And then in the darkroom or laboratory they develop the image, so that suddenly and startlingly it appears, printed in capital letters, as a new formula for atomic energy.

Men who have read Balzac and Zola are not deceived by the claims of these writers that they do no more than record the facts. The readers of Christopher Isherwood do not take him literally when he writes "I am a camera." Yet the same readers solemnly carry with them from their schooldays this foolish picture of the scientist fixing by some mechanical process the facts of nature. I have had of all people a historian tell me that science is a collection of facts, and his voice had not even the ironic rasp of one filing cabinet reproving another.

It seems impossible that this historian had ever studied the beginnings of a scientific discovery. The Scientific Revolution can be held to begin in the year 1543 when there was brought to Copernicus, perhaps on his deathbed, the first printed copy of the book he had finished about a dozen years earlier. The thesis of this book is that the earth moves around the sun. When did Copernicus go out and record this fact with his camera? What appearance in nature prompted his outrageous guess? And in what odd sense is this guess to be called a _____ record of fact?

1 Which does the underlined part refer to?

① scientists ② Balzac and Zola
③ colorless professionals of science ④ literary people

2 According to the passage, which is NOT true?

① Scientist as well as writers need to see nature with imagination.
② Isherwood wrote in one of his works that he was a camera.
③ One book that Copernicus wrote was brought to him in 1543.
④ The Scientific Revolution started with recording the facts about nature.

3 Which is the most appropriate for the blank?

① slanted ② biased
③ neutral ④ complete

10

　　The posthuman subject is an amalgam, a collection of heterogeneous components, a material-informational entity whose boundaries undergo continuous construction and reconstruction. Consider the six-million-dollar man, a paradigmatic citizen of the posthuman regime. As his name implies, the parts of the self are indeed owned, but they are owned precisely because they were purchased, not because ownership is a natural condition preexisting market relations. Similarly, the presumption that there is an agency, desire, or will belonging to the self and clearly distinguished from the wills of others is undercut in the posthuman, for the posthuman's collective heterogenous quality implies a distributed cognition located in disparate parts. We have only to recall Robocop's memory flashes that interfere with his programmed directives to understand how the distributed cognition of the posthuman complicates individual agency. If human essence is freedom from the wills of others, the posthuman is "post" not because it is necessarily unfree but because there is no a priori way to identify a self-will that can be clearly distinguished from an other-will. Although these examples foreground the cybernetic aspect of the posthuman, it is important to recognize that the construction of the posthuman does not require the subject to be a literal cyborg. Whether or not interventions have been made on the body, new models of subjectivity emerging from such fields as cognitive science and artificial life imply that even a biologically unaltered Homo sapiens count as posthuman. The defining characteristics involve the construction of subjectivity, not the presence of nonbiological components.

1　Which of the following is NOT the characteristic of the posthuman?
　　① an entity of hybrid components
　　② an agency of the distributed cognition
　　③ a model of a new subjectivity
　　④ a species of biologically altered parts

2　Which of the following can be inferred from the passage?
　　① There is a humanist presumption that is never weakened in the posthuman.
　　② The posthuman is represented only through bodily interventions.
　　③ The construction of the posthuman subjectivity is not altogether artificial.
　　④ The posthuman gives way to the biological aspect of Homo sapiens.

3　Why does the author mention Robocop in the passage?
　　① To put an emphasis on the mechanism of artificial intelligence
　　② To put the case that cognition is distributed and complicated
　　③ To give a further example of the current market relations
　　④ To offer an in-depth analysis of the posthuman anxiety

11

Our present ideas about the motion of bodies date back to Galileo and Newton. Before Ⓐ<u>them</u> people believed Aristotle, who said that the natural state of a body was to be at rest and that it moved only if driven by a force or impulse. It followed that Ⓑ_____, because it would have a greater pull toward the earth.

The Aristotelian tradition also held that one could work out all the laws that govern the universe by pure thought: it was not necessary to check by observation. So no one until Galileo bothered to see whether bodies of different weights did in fact fall at different speeds. It is said that Galileo demonstrated that Aristotle's belief was false by dropping weights from the leaning tower of Pisa. The story is almost certainly untrue, but Galileo did do something equivalent; he rolled balls of different weights down a smooth slope. The situation is similar to that of heavy bodies falling vertically, but it is easier to observe because the speeds are smaller. Galileo's measurements indicated that each body increased its speed at the same rate, no matter what its weight.

1 Which one does Ⓐ refer to?
① our present ideas
② bodies
③ weights
④ Galileo and Newton

2 Choose the best expression for Ⓑ.
① a light body should fall much faster than a heavy one
② a light body should fall more faster than a heavy one
③ a heavy body should fall faster than a light one
④ a heavy body should fall less faster than a light one

3 Which one can be inferred?
① If bodies of different weights fall without much air resistance, they hit the ground at the same time.
② The speed between two bodies would be twice as strong if one of the bodies had its mass doubled.
③ As a similar example provided by a car, the more powerful the engine, the greater the acceleration.
④ It shows that the real effect of weight is always to change the speed of a body.

4 Which one is true?

① Aristotle's belief was falsified by Newton's observation of dropping two bodies.
② Galileo is the first one who attempted to check the old belief by experiment.
③ It is still believed that a body moves only if driven by a force or impulse.
④ Galileo's first measurements showed that two bodies fall at different speeds.

12

Moore's Law originated in a four-page 1965 magazine article written by Gordon Moore, then at Fairchild Semiconductor and later one of the founders of Intel. In it, he predicted that the number of components on a single integrated circuit would rise from the then-current number of roughly 26 to roughly 216 in the following ten years — that is, the number of components would double every year. He based this prediction on four empirical data points and one null data point, fitting a straight line on a graph plotting the log of the number of components on a single chip against a linear scale of calendar years. Intel later amended Moore's Law to say that "the number of transistors on a chip roughly doubles every two years."

Moore's Law is rightly seen as the fundamental driver of the information technology revolution in our world over the last fifty years. Doubling the number of transistors every so often has made our computers twice as powerful for the same price and in general improved them in every possible way by a factor of 2 on a clockwise schedule.

But why does it happen? Automobiles have not obeyed Moore's Law; neither have batteries, nor clothing, nor food production, nor the level of political discourse. All but the last have demonstrably improved due to the influence of Moore's Law, but none has had the same relentless exponential improvements. The most elegant explanation for what makes Moore's Law possible is that digital logic is all about an abstraction — and, in fact, a one-bit abstraction, a yes/no answer to a question — and that abstraction is independent of physical bulk.

In a world that consists entirely of piles of red sand and piles of green sand, the size of the piles is irrelevant. A pile is either red or green, and you can take away half the pile, and it's still either a pile of red sand or a pile of green sand. And repeated halving at a constant rate makes an exponential. That's why Moore's Law works for digital technology and doesn't work for technologies that require physical strength. Digital technology uses physics to maintain an abstraction and nothing more.

1 위 글의 제목으로 가장 적합한 것을 고르시오.

① The Effects of Semiconductors on the Development of Modern Computing Powers
② The Role of Powerful Computers in the Revolution of the Information Technology
③ An Account of Exponential Improvements of Digital Technology
④ Abstract Digitization and Its Implications for the Future Computer Industry

2 위 글의 내용과 일치하지 <u>않는</u> 것을 고르시오.

① The amended Moore's Law predicts that the number of transistors on integrated circuits doubles approximately every two years.
② Moore's prediction can be diagramed on a graph using the log of the transistor counts and the year of their introduction.
③ Moore's prediction has it that the capabilities of digital devices improve at roughly exponential rates.
④ Moore's Law does not apply for automobiles since manufacturing these products requires more digital technologies.

13

⒜ Developments in computing technologies have allowed scientists to make major advancements in AI even though the simulated reconstruction of a human brain is still unattainable. ⒝ People expect machines that act human should look human as well. ⒞ For instance, Honda revealed in 2000, ASIMO, a 130-centimeter humanoid robot. ASIMO, which stands for Advanced Step in Innovative Mobility, was created to assist individuals who have difficulty with mobility complete common everyday tasks. ASIMO can walk, and it can navigate unbalanced terrain like stairs, attaining a top speed of six kilometers per hour. With its two camera "eyes," the robot is programmed to determine direction and distance, respond to human gestures, and recognize and name up to ten individuals. ⒟

However, the prospect of designing machines capable of possessing human qualities has also created many fears and anxieties. In the 1968 dystopian novel by Philip K. Dick entitled, *Do Androids Dream of Electric Sheep?*, androids appear human and have implanted human memories, Ⓐ<u>but are unable to understand others' feelings</u>. They are forced to do difficult or dangerous work Ⓑ_____ humans. When six of these androids start a rebellion, a bounty hunter is called upon to track them down and destroy them. The novel begs the questions, "What distinguishes machines from humans?" and "Is it moral to destroy a machine that believes that it is human?"

1 Choose the best place for the following.

To promote interest in the sciences, ASIMO often makes appearances in public in which he performs choreographed dances and displays his understanding of voice commands.

① Ⓐ ② Ⓑ
③ Ⓒ ④ Ⓓ

2 Why does the author mention Ⓐ<u>but are unable to understand others' feelings</u>?

① To persuade readers that androids possess morals
② To claim that emotions are the most important characteristic in androids
③ To criticize Philip K. Dick's depiction of non-human intelligence
④ To point out what differentiates humans and androids

3 Which one is TRUE?

① People generally imagine that machines with human-like abilities also have a human-like appearance.
② ASIMO's design is based on the design of the androids from Philip K. Dick's novel.
③ Implanted human memories are the critical factors dividing robots like ASIMO from humans.
④ Philip K. Dick's anxieties about the creation of ASIMO are due to sympathetic androids.

4 Which one does NOT appropriately replace Ⓑ?

① instead of   ② in place of
③ in hopes of   ④ in lieu of

14

　　The paradox that had troubled Einstein for a decade was this. In the mid-1800s, after a close study of the experimental work of the English physicist Michael Faraday, the Scottish physicist James Clerk Maxwell succeeded in uniting electricity and magnetism in the framework of the electromagnetic field. If you've ever been on a mountaintop just before a severe thunderstorm or stood close to a Van de Graaf generator, you have a visceral sense of what an electromagnetic field is, because you've felt it. In case you haven't, it is somewhat like a tide of electric and magnetic lines of force that permeate a region of space through which they pass. When you sprinkle iron filings near a magnet, for example, the orderly pattern they form traces out some of the invisible lines of magnetic force. When you take off a wool sweater on an especially dry day and hear a crackling sound and perhaps feel a momentary shock or two, you are witnessing evidence of electric lines of force generated by electric charges swept up by the fibers in your sweater. Beyond uniting these and all other electric and magnetic phenomena in one mathematical framework, Maxwell's theory showed — quite unexpectedly — that electromagnetic disturbances travel at a fixed and never-changing speed, a speed that turns out to equal that of light. From this, Maxwell realized that visible light itself is nothing but a particular kind of electromagnetic wave, one that is now understood to interact with chemicals in the retina, giving rise to the sensation of sight. Moreover (and this is crucial), Maxwell's theory also showed that all electromagnetic waves — visible light among them — are the epitome of the peripatetic traveler. They never stop. They never slow down. Light always travels at light speed.

　　All is well and good until we ask: what happens if we chase after a beam of light, at light speed? Intuitive reasoning, rooted in Newton's laws of motion, tells us that we will catch up with the light waves and so they will appear stationary; light will stand still. But according to Maxwell's theory, and all reliable observations, there is simply no such thing as stationary light: no one has ever held a stationary clump of light in the palm of his or her hand. Hence the problem. Luckily, Einstein was unaware that many of the world's leading physicists were struggling with this question (and were heading down many a spurious path) and pondered the paradox of Maxwell and Newton largely in the pristine privacy of his own thoughts.

1 According to the above passage, which of the following is <u>not</u> an instance of experiencing the electromagnetic field?
① The feeling one can have on a mountaintop just before a severe thunderstorm
② The pattern iron filings show when they are spread near a magnet
③ The cracking sound one can hear when taking off a wool sweater in a dry day
④ The recognition that light travels at a fixed and never-changing speed

2 According to the above passage, which of the following is the problem Einstein faced?

① The pattern of iron filings near a magnet is different from that which can be found on a wool sweater.
② Even though one would chase after a beam of light at light speed, the light can never be stationary.
③ Light is just a kind of electromagnetic wave, but it can interact with chemicals in the retina.
④ Light can permeate a region of space as a tide of electric and magnetic lines of force.

3 Which of the following is least likely to be inferred from the above passage?

① Both Maxwell and Newton recognized the paradox between the laws of motion and the speed of light.
② Maxwell managed to unite electricity and magnetism via a thorough investigation of Faraday's experiment.
③ According to Maxwell's theory, the prediction on light speed based on Newton's laws of motion is not borne out.
④ Both the pattern of iron filings near a magnet and the sound of a wool sweater can be explained by the electromagnetic field.

15

A What did you think of the last commercial you watched? Was it funny? Confusing? Would you buy the product? You might not remember or know for certain how you felt, but increasingly, machines do. New artificial intelligence technologies are learning and recognizing human emotions, and using that knowledge to improve everything from marketing campaigns to healthcare.

B These technologies are referred to as "emotion AI." Emotion AI is a subset of artificial intelligence (the broad term for machines replicating the way humans think) that measures, understands, simulates, and reacts to human emotions. It's also known as affective computing or artificial emotional intelligence. The field dates back to at least 1995, when MIT Media lab professor Rosalind Picard published "Affective Computing." ❶ Javier Hernandez, a research scientist with the Affective Computing Group at the MIT Media Lab, explains emotion AI as a tool that allows for a much more natural interaction between humans and machines. ❷

C While humans might currently have the upper hand on reading emotions, machines are gaining ground using their own strengths. Machines are very good at analyzing large amounts of data, explained MIT Sloan professor Erik Brynjolfsson. They can listen to voice inflections and start to recognize when those inflections correlate with stress or anger. Machines can analyze images and pick up subtleties in micro-expressions on humans' faces that might happen even too fast for a person to recognize. ❸

D "We have a lot of neurons in our brain for social interactions. We're born with some of those skills, and then we learn more. It makes sense to use technology to connect to our social brains, not just our analytical brains," Brynjolfsson said. "Just like we can understand speech and machines can communicate in speech, we also understand and communicate with humor and other kinds of emotions. ❹ And machines that can speak that language — the language of emotions — are going to have better, more effective interactions with us. It's great that we've made some progress; it's just something that wasn't an option 20 or 30 years ago, and now it's on the table." ❺

1 Which of the following would be the best title for the above passage?

① Language of Emotions
② New Artificial Intelligence Technology
③ More Natural Interaction Between Humans and Machines
④ Effective Communication in Computing
⑤ Artificial Emotional Intelligence

2 According to the above passage, which of the following is NOT true about emotion AI?

① It was developed for more emotional interactions between humans and machines.
② The study of emotion AI began 25 years ago or earlier.
③ It can be used to improve marketing campaigns.
④ It uses voice inflections in recognizing emotions.
⑤ It analyzes facial expressions.

3 The following part was removed from the passage. In which part may the following sentences be inserted to support the argument made by the author?

"Think of the way you interact with other human beings; you look at their faces, you look at their body, and you change your interaction accordingly," Hernandez said. "How can [a machine] effectively communicate information if it doesn't know your emotional state, if it doesn't know how you're feeling, and if it doesn't know how you're going to respond to specific content?"

① ❶
② ❷
③ ❸
④ ❹
⑤ ❺

4 Which of the following is true according to the above passage?

① Machines read emotions better than humans do.
② Machines can read emotions by analyzing large amounts of data.
③ Artificial intelligence is now being replaced by emotion AI that reacts to human emotions.
④ Emotion AI replicates social interaction in human brain functions.
⑤ Affective computing is an earlier version of emotion AI.

09

우주 · 지구

09 우주·지구

01

　Further encouragement for the existence of black holes came in 1967 with the discovery by a research student at Cambridge, Jocelyn Bell-Burnell, of objects in the sky that were emitting regular pulses of radio waves. At first Bell and her supervisor, Antony Hewish, thought they might have contact with an alien civilization in the galaxy. In the end, however, they came to the less romantic conclusion that these objects, which were given the name pulsars, were in fact rotating neutron stars that were emitting pulses of radio waves because of a complicated interaction between their magnetic fields and surrounding matter. This was bad news for writers of space westerns, but very hopeful for the small number of us who believed in black holes at that time: it was the first positive evidence that neutron stars existed. A neutron star has a radius of about ten miles, only a few times the critical radius at which a star becomes a black hole. If a star could collapse to such a small size, it is not reasonable to expect that other stars could collapse to even smaller size and become black holes. How could we hope to detect a black hole, as by its very definition it does not emit any light? It might seem a bit like looking for a black cat _____. Fortunately, there is a way. As John Michell pointed out in his pioneering paper in 1783, a black hole still exerts a gravitational force on nearby objects.

1 The passage above is mainly about _____.

① the legacy of black hole
② the function of black hole
③ the discovery of black hole
④ the latent power of black hole

2 Choose the one that best fills in the blank.

① in a coal cellar
② in an inflated balloon model
③ through a triangular-shaped piece of glass
④ with concave lens telescope

3 **Which of the following is true?**

① Bell and Hewish contacted with an alien civilization in the galaxy.
② A star can be enlarged to a gigantic size and become a black hole.
③ The existence of black holes was fully known in 1967.
④ A black hole can exercise a gravitational force on nearby matters.

02

Scientists long believed that gradual changes in global climate caused the extinction of the dinosaurs. In 1979, however, a team from Berkeley discovered in Italy a layer of clay from about the time of the dinosaurs' disappearance, with an iridium level some thirty times greater than that of the clays in the adjacent strata. Since iridium settles fairly evenly over time and is extraterrestrial in origin, the researchers concluded that the high iridium level of this clay must have resulted from a sudden, catastrophic event. Scientists differ over the exact nature of the event. The possibility that a stellar explosion caused the deposition has been discounted because certain radioactive isotopes are largely absent from the clay. If the material had originated within the solar system, the earth must have collided with an astral body large enough to distribute the iridium-rich material around the globe. There is no geological evidence of the impact of such massive objects, but Grieve argues that the clay layers could have settled as fallout after an atmospheric explosion. Kyte asserts that a comet, disrupted by the earth's gravitational field, would have produced a deluge of falling debris without creating major craters. The Berkeley group suggests that an asteroid may have landed in the sea. Whatever the type of event, the Berkeley team argues that it disrupted the planetary ecology by suspending vast clouds of matter in the stratosphere. The effects of the impact would have increased as the blockage of sunlight impeded photosynthesis, causing a massive disruption at the base of the global food chain.

1 저자의 의도로 가장 적절한 것은?

① rebutting a traditional assumption
② discussing the implications of a discovery
③ suggesting a new course of investigation
④ summarizing and assessing differing theories

2 "The Berkeley Group"의 주장을 뒷받침할 수 있는 근거로 가장 알맞은 것은?

① a drop in the number of plant fossils in the strata above those studied in Italy
② a discovery of dinosaur fossils in the strata older than the iridium-rich clay layer in Italy
③ a discovery of elevated levels of iridium in the rocks above and below the clay strata in Spain
④ a development of a consensus among scientists on the probability of a comet's impact with the earth

03

　　Up until the 1920s, everyone thought the universe was essentially static and unchanging in time. Then it was discovered that the universe was expanding. Distant galaxies were moving away from us. This meant they must have been closer together in the past. If we extrapolate back, we find we must have all been on top of each other about 15 billion years ago. This was the Big Bang, the beginning of the universe. But was there anything before the Big Bang? If not, what created the universe? Why did the universe emerge from the Big Bang the way it did? We used to think that the theory of the universe could be divided into two parts. First, there were the laws like Maxwell's equations and general relativity that determined the evolution of the universe, given its state over all of space at one time. And second, there was no question of the initial state of the universe. We have made good progress on the first part, and now have the knowledge of the laws of evolution in all but the most extreme conditions. But until recently, we have had little idea about the initial conditions for the universe. However, this division into laws of evolution and initial conditions depends on time and space being separate and distinct. Under extreme conditions, general relativity and quantum theory allow time to behave like another dimension of space. This removes the distinction between time and space, and means the laws of evolution can also determine the initial state. The universe can spontaneously create itself out of nothing. Moreover, we can calculate a probability that the universe was created in different states. These predictions are in excellent agreement with observations by the WMAP satellite of the cosmic microwave background, which is an imprint of the very early universe. We think we have solved _____. Maybe we should patent the universe and charge everyone royalties for their existence.

1　Choose the sentence that best fills in the blank.
① the chance of spreading out into space
② the mystery of creation
③ the future of the human race
④ the question of the universe through observation

2　Which of the following is true?
① It is undeniable that galaxies are moving closer to us.
② The evolutionary law cannot be applied to the initial state of the universe.
③ The distinction between time and space can disappear in an extreme condition.
④ The calculation of the age of the universe is not supported by any empirical observation.

04

The tides present a striking paradox, and the essence of it is this: the force that sets them in motion is cosmic, lying wholly outside the earth and presumably acting impartially on all parts of the globe, but the nature of the tide at any particular place is a local matter, with astonishing differences occurring within a very short geographic distance. When we spend a long summer holiday at the seashore we may become aware that the tide in our cove behaves very differently from that at a friend's place twenty miles up the coast, and is strikingly different from what we may have known in some other locality. If we are summering on Nantucket Island our boating and swimming will be little disturbed by the tides, for the range between high water and low is only about a foot or two. But if we choose to vacation near the upper part of the Bay of Fundy, we must _____ ourselves to a rise and fall of 40 to 50 feet, although both places are included within the same body of water — the Gulf of Maine. Or if we spend our holiday on Chesapeake Bay we may find that the time of high water each day varies by as much as 12 hours in different places on the shores of the same bay.

1 Which of the following is the best title for the passage?

① The importance of cosmic influence on the tides of the earth
② How local geography determines the nature of the tides
③ How to make the most of our summer holiday at the seaside
④ The importance of choosing the right place for summer holiday

2 Which of the following best fills in the blank?

① manifest
② divert
③ accommodate
④ evacuate

3 According to the passage, which of the following is true?

① The cosmic influence on the tides varies from place to place.
② In Nantucket Island, the range between high tide and low is relatively large.
③ Both Nantucket Island and the upper part of the Bay of Fundy are located in the Gulf of Maine.
④ On the shores of Chesapeake Bay, the time of high water is the same everywhere.

05

A Typically below unconfined aquifers are confined aquifers and are topped with an impermeable layer of stone and clay. Therefore, while there is some part that remains unconfined to allow for water recharge, most of the groundwater remains under high pressure. If a well should be drilled into the rock, the groundwater will rise to the surface.

B Deep underground are large deposits of water. These reservoirs can be found in every kind of environment including deserts. The total amount of this groundwater is significantly more than the sum of all lakes and rivers. Most of the water existing underground is found in aquifers, layers of porous rock that can store water. Scientists categorize them into two types: unconfined and confined. The unconfined aquifer lies under a layer of permeable material. As a result, it can easily receive water from the surface, and the water table surface fluctuates up and down, depending on the rate of water recharge.

C Confined and unconfined aquifers are refilled by groundwater. However, the rate for them differs. Most groundwater is the result of rain penetrating the soil. The water will then trickle down to the lower layers until it reaches the aquifer. Confined aquifers recharge at a slower rate than unconfined. This is mainly because the water has more difficulty entering them. In tropical regions, recharge occurs during the rainy seasons. In more temperate regions, it happens during the winter.

1 Choose the appropriate order of the paragraphs.
① A — C — B
② B — A — C
③ C — A — B
④ C — B — A

2 According to the passage, confined aquifers _____.
① receive water from the water table
② are always found with unconfined aquifers
③ recharge faster than unconfined aquifers
④ are subjected to high pressure

3 Which is the best title of the passage?
① The Need to Protect Aquifers from Overuse
② The Importance of Regulating Groundwater Aquifers
③ The Process of Water Storage Within the Earth
④ The Problems with the Use of Groundwater

06

After traveling 300 million miles through the solar system, NASA's InSight spacecraft descended through the Martian sky and touched down safely on the smooth surface of Elysium Planitia. ⒶA

Using a robotic arm, the lander will first install a super-sensitive seismometer on the Martian surface, where it will listen for meteorite impacts and Marsquakes. ⒷB The seismic waves from these events will give scientists a clearer picture of the planet's internal structure. InSight will then release its heat probe, a self-hammering 16-inch nail that will burrow down as deep as 16 feet over the course of several weeks. The instrument will measure how much heat escapes from Mars' interior, which will reveal the amount of heat-producing radioactive elements it contains and how Ⓐ_____ active the planet is today. ⒸC The spacecraft also has two X-band antennas on its deck that make up a third instrument, called RISE. ⒹD Radio signals from RISE will be used to track the wobble of Mars' orbit. This will help researchers understand the size and state of the Martian core. Together, these experiments will crack open Mars and spill the planetary secrets scientists have sought for decades.

1 The author's main purpose in writing this passage is to _____.

① discuss Martian internal structure and heat-producing radioactive elements
② emphasize the safe landing of InSight on Mars after a long journey
③ explain the experiments InSight will perform to reveal Mars' secrets
④ show how the wobble in the rotation of Mars is related to its magnetic field

2 Which is the most appropriate place for the sentence below?

Unlike the space agency's rovers, InSight is a lander designed to study an entire planet from just one spot.

① A
② B
③ C
④ D

3 Which of the following is most suitable for the blank Ⓐ?

① astronomically
② geologically
③ geometrically
④ astronautically

4 According to the passage, which of the following is true?

① NASA managed to land spacecraft safely on the surface of Mars three times.
② The deck of InSight spacecraft has a total of five instruments that can reveal Martian secrets.
③ The seismic waves will be used in tracking the wobble in the rotation of Mars.
④ A self-hammering nail will measure the amount of heat coming from the inside of Mars.

07

Of what materials is the earth composed, and in what manner are these materials arranged? These are the first inquiries with which Geology is occupied, a science which derives its name from the Greek *ge*, the earth, and *logos*, a discourse. Previously to experience we might have imagined that investigations of this kind would relate exclusively to the mineral kingdom, and to the various rocks, soils, and metals, which occur upon the surface of the earth, or at various depths beneath it. But, in pursuing such researches, we soon find ourselves led on to consider the successive changes which have taken place in the former state of the earth's surface and interior, and the causes which have given rise to these changes; and what is still more singular and unexpected, we soon become engaged in researches into the history of the animate creation, or of the various tribes of animals and plants which have, at different periods of the past, inhabited the globe.

All are aware that the solid parts of the earth consist of distinct substances, such as clay, chalk, sand, limestone, coal, slate, granite, and the like; but previously to observation it is commonly imagined that all these had remained from the first in the state in which we now see them — that they were created in their present form, and in their present position. The geologist soon comes to a different conclusion, discovering proofs that the external parts of the earth were not all produced in the beginning of things in the state in which we now behold them, nor in an instant of time. On the contrary, he can show that they have acquired their actual configuration and condition gradually, under a great variety of circumstances, and at successive periods, during each of which distinct races of living beings have flourished on the land and in the waters, the remains of these creatures still lying buried in the crust of the earth.

1 Which of the following modes of writing is included in the first paragraph?

① criticism ② narration
③ classification ④ definition

2 Which is the closest in meaning to the underlined part?

① channel ② trajectory
③ mutation ④ shape

3 According to the passage, which is true?

① Although geology was first thought to be a study of earth changes, further study shows that the history of animals and plants are part of the subject as well.
② Although geology was first thought to be a study of minerals, further study shows that animals and plants are part of the subject as well.
③ Although geology was first thought to be a study of the earth's surface, further study shows that the depths beneath the surface are part of the subject as well.
④ Although geology was first thought to be a study of the history of creation, further study shows that animals and plants are part of the subject as well.

08

Most astronomy data today are gathered automatically through robotic systems that collect far more information than the world's roughly 10,000 professional astronomers could ever evaluate in their lifetimes. However, there are at least one million amateur astronomers, who now have a way to get in on the action and make real contributions. [A] In 2007, a group of astronomers wrote a web-based application called Galaxy Zoo, which created a clever, gamelike user interface for a database of astronomical information collected by the Sloan Digital Sky Survey. [B] It turns out that people can do certain kinds of galaxy classifications visually that computers are not yet very good at. So the project made it fun for the public to participate in the classifications, which also helped the astronomers test a theory that spiral galaxies tended to rotate clockwise. [C] Galaxy Zoo was launched with a data set made up of a million galaxies imaged with a robotic telescope. Participants looked at the images and classified the galaxies as "right-handed" (meaning they rotated clockwise) or "left-handed" (rotating counterclockwise). With so many galaxies, the team thought it might take at least two years for the site's visitors to work through them all. Within 24 hours of its launch, however, the site was receiving 70,000 classifications an hour, and more than 50 million classifications were received by the project during its first year, from almost 150,000 people. The effort refuted the idea that most spiral galaxies were right-handed. It turns out that only half of them were. [D] Even more amazing, a Dutch schoolteacher participating in the project found a strange galaxy that so baffled astronomers it ended up getting the attention of the Hubble telescope. [E] In 2008, Microsoft introduced the WorldWide Telescope (WWT) and gave astronomers and the general public access to interactive 3-D images of the sky, planets, and galaxies. Visitors can view the images through a standard browser and visualize the same data that professional astronomers use. WWT incorporates the Galaxy Zoo classifications and more. Visualization tools such as the WWT can actually transform scientists' ability to gain insights from data, sometimes with the help of ordinary citizens.

1 Where would the best points be to divide this essay into paragraphs?

① at points [A], [B], and [D]
② at points [A], [C], and [D]
③ at points [B], [C], and [D]
④ at points [A], [C], and [E]
⑤ at points [B], [D], and [E]

2 Which of these sentences incorrectly paraphrases an idea from the passage?

① As a result of the Galaxy Zoo project, astronomers discovered that there was no special tendency of galaxies to rotate either clockwise or counterclockwise.
② There is so much information available for astronomers to analyze that there are not enough professional astronomers to analyze all the information.
③ Computers are not as good as people at some kinds of astronomy tasks, such as deciding whether a galaxy is "right handed" or "left handed."
④ When astronomers created the Galaxy Zoo program they did not expect to get results as quickly as they actually got them.
⑤ Visualization tools on the internet mean that amateur astronomers in modern times can do better work than professional astronomers could do in the past.

09

The earth's motion has two components. It *rotates* on its axis, the imaginary line about which the earth is spinning, and it *revolves* around the sun in its orbit. As for the earth's rotation, there are lots of evidence and arguments. The sun, planets, and stars rise in the east and set in the west because the earth rotates. Also observers in the Northern Hemisphere can see that the northern stars move counterclockwise in circles centered on the North Star. These observations, however, could be explained not only by a rotating earth but also by a stationary earth with a moving sky. Hence, we need stronger arguments such as the following.

First, the earth is not exactly spherical; the distance through the earth at its equator is 12,756 km while the distance from one pole to the other is only 12,713 km. So the earth has a bulging shape, and scientists explain it by using the idea of *inertia*, the tendency of moving matter to continue moving in the same direction. If the matter making up the planet were not held in place by the planet's gravity, it would fly out from the rotating planet, like mud from a spinning wheel. The earth's surface is moving fastest at its equator where its matter bulges out against the inward pull of gravity. Hence the bulge at the equator results.

Another piece of evidence comes from the earth's wind patterns. If the earth were not spinning but it retained the same atmospheric heat distribution, the wind patterns would be much simpler; the heated air at the equator would move toward the poles, and the cold air from the higher latitudes would move back toward the equator. The motion would be straight north and south. However, we actually observe a curved wind pattern because the earth's rotation deflects the wind.

Finally, we know by direct observation that the earth is rotating: Astronauts on the moon saw the earth's entire surface in each twenty-four-hour day. The moon does not revolve around the earth once each day. Therefore, _____.

1 Fill in the blank with the best expression.

① the earth must be rotating
② other planets must not be revolving, either
③ the earth not only rotates but also revolves
④ the reports from the astronauts should be revised

2 What is the best title for the passage?

① The Distinction between Rotation and Revolution
② Evidence for the Earth's Rotation
③ Methods of Astronomical Observations
④ The Interaction between Inertia and Gravity on Earth

3 Which of the following is the undeniable argument for the earth's rotation?

① The sun and stars rise in the east and set in the west.
② The earth's wind patterns are not straight but curved.
③ The northern stars move counterclockwise in circles centered on Polaris.
④ The distance from one pole to the other is equivalent to the distance through the earth at the equator.

10

In April 1920, Harlow Shapley and Heber Curtis argued over the scale of the universe in the great auditorium of the Smithsonian's Natural History Museum in Washington. In this discussion, Curtis argued that the cosmos consists of many separate "island universes" — that the so-called spiral nebulae were distant systems of stars outside our milky way. Shapley argued that spiral nebulae were merely gas clouds in the milky way. He further placed the Sun much of the way out near the edge of the galaxy — the entire universe, in his view — whereas Curtis believed the Sun to be near the galaxy's center. Curtis was right about the large size of the universe but wrong about the Sun's place in the galaxy, whereas Shapley was wrong about the smaller universe and right about the Sun's location in it.

With the advent of many extragalactic distance measurements, new arguments erupted concerning the "Hubble Constant," the expansion rate of the universe. A group of astronomers staged a second great debate in 1996. The age and the size of the universe are, of course, interrelated, and both depend critically on the Hubble Constant. In the same auditorium used by Shapley and Curtis, galaxy researchers Sidney van den Bergh and Gustav Tammann argued over the question. Van den Bergh offered evidence supporting a high value of the constant, suggesting a young age and correspondingly small size of the universe. Tammann argued for a low value of the constant, which would indicate an older, larger universe. Neither van den Bergh nor Tammann succeeded in convincing astronomers from the other camp.

Despite this, astronomers can set some limits on what must be true. Using powerful telescopes, astronomers see galaxies 10 or 12 billion light-years away. A light year equals about 10 trillion kilometers, so the "horizon" of visibility is some 24 billion light-years in diameter. But that's from our viewpoint. What about the horizons as seen from distant galaxies? It's possible the universe is much larger than the portions we can see. This will be the case in the likely event that the inflation hypothesis, put forth by MIT's Alan Guth, proves correct. This idea suggests the extremely young universe experienced a moment of hypergrowth so severe it ballooned from the size of a subatomic particle to a softball's size in an instant. If inflation occurred, then _____.

Here's where it gets weird: If inflation happened, then it may have happened in many places beyond the visible horizon. If this is so, then other universes might exist beyond our ability to detect them. Science begs off this question, as by definition science is about creating and experimenting with testable ideas. For now, it's wondrous to know we live in a universe that's at least 150 billion trillion miles across.

1 Choose the one that best fills in the blank.

① it may be much bigger than we might expect
② all bets are off as to determining the size of the universe
③ theories regarding our milky way must be reassessed
④ there may be more than one universe to contend with

2 What is the main idea of the passage?

① Scientists generally agree about the shape of our universe.
② The validation of the Big Bang Theory depends on how large the universe is.
③ Despite scientific advancements the size of our universe still remains a mystery.
④ True science is not about idle speculation but about provable facts.

3 Choose the one that does not accord with the passage.

① There are no real victors in the Shapley-Curtis debate on cosmology.
② The universe's rate of expansion depends on the Hubble Constant.
③ The farthest galaxy we can see is more than 20 billion light-years away.
④ Scientists accept the existence of multiple universes, based on experimentation.

10

환경·기상

10 환경·기상

01

Birds are everywhere. We see them every day flying over our heads or hopping around our backyards. But scientists say that bird populations are declining rapidly, especially in North America. Approximately 29% of the continent's total bird population has been lost since 1970. Ⓐ_____, it has been found that common bird species, such as sparrows and blackbirds, are disappearing at an alarming rate, even faster than rare bird species. According to a new study, almost every group of birds is facing difficulty. Grassland bird populations have suffered the greatest loss, having declined by 53%. Forest-dwelling birds, which outnumber grassland birds, are also disappearing fast. One billion have been lost. Shorebirds, which migrate over entire hemispheres, are also showing sharp, consistent population losses. Their total population has dropped by 37% within the past 50 years. Even invasive species, which are often able to adapt to different environments, have not been able to escape this fate. As birds are indicator animals, whose well-being can reflect an ecosystem's overall health, scientists say that this massive population loss should be taken as a warning about the state of North American ecosystems in general.

1 Which of the following is most appropriate for blank Ⓐ?

① Finally
② Therefore
③ However
④ Moreover

2 Which bird group has experienced the largest decline in percentage terms in North America?

① shorebirds
② invasive birds
③ grassland birds
④ forest-dwelling birds

3 What can be inferred from the passage?

① The fate of birds points to potential threats posed to other animals.
② Bird species are declining mainly because of invasive species.
③ The most common bird species are proving the best able to adapt.
④ Bird numbers are falling most along common bird migration routes.

02

Modern forecasting methods are fairly accurate when it comes to short-range predications, but the longer the forecast, the more chances there are that the forecasts are going to be incorrect. ⒶThe current method of mathematically calculating weather conditions confines accurate predictions to about five days in advance due to the chaotic nature of the weather. ⒷMeteorologists combine the results of the computational data collection methods with the actual atmospheric conditions occurring in the present. ⒸCurrent information concerning the temperature, dew point, and winds at various levels is gathered throughout the day all around the world to provide clues that are compared to computer models based on past conditions to come up with probable weather patterns. ⒹAs a result, an experienced meteorologist who has seen a great variety of weather conditions and is knowledgeable about the changes and shifts that they are likely to make stands nearly as good of a chance at accurately predicting future weather conditions as a computer-generated model does.

1 Which has the closest meaning to the underlined word?

① changes
② degrees
③ speeds
④ elevations

2 Choose the most suitable position of the following sentence in the above passage.

However, though the science and methodology of meteorological methods have improved, there are still large gaps in the understanding of atmospheric and weather-related activity.

① Ⓐ
② Ⓑ
③ Ⓒ
④ Ⓓ

3 According to the passage, which is NOT true?

① Computer-generated models are quite reliable to predict longer-term weather patterns.
② Experienced meteorologists can make predictions as accurately as computer-generated models do.
③ Accurate weather predictions can only be made for the near future since weather changes rapidly.
④ The modern forecasting takes data into account, particularly temperature, humidity and wind patterns to determine future weather patterns.

03

Nature challenges humans in many ways, through disease, weather, and famine. For those living along the coast, one unusual phenomenon capable of catastrophic destruction is the tsunami. A tsunami is a series of waves generated in a body of water by an impulsive disturbance. Earthquakes, landslides, volcanic eruptions, explosions, and even the impact of meteorites can generate tsunamis. Starting at sea, a tsunami slowly approaches land, growing in height and losing energy through bottom friction and turbulence. Still, just like any other water waves, tsunamis <u>unleash</u> tremendous energy as they plunge onto the shore. They have great erosion potential, stripping beaches of sand, undermining trees, and flooding hundreds of meters inland. They can easily crush cars, homes, vegetation, and anything they collide with. To minimize the devastation of a tsunami, scientists are constantly trying to anticipate them more accurately and more quickly. Because many factors come together to produce a life-threatening tsunami, foreseeing them is not easy. Ⓐ_____ this, researchers in meteorology persevere in studying and predicting tsunami behavior.

1 In the first sentence, why does the author mention weather?
① because tsunamis are caused by bad weather
② because tsunamis are more destructive than weather phenomena
③ as an example of a destructive natural force
④ as an introduction to the topic of coastal storms

2 Which of the following is closest in meaning to the underlined word <u>unleash</u>?
① release ② consume
③ contain ④ sustain

3 Which of the following is most appropriate for blank Ⓐ?
① In line with ② Despite
③ Contrary to ④ Compared with

4 Which sentence best expresses the essential information of this passage?
① Tsunamis could become a new source of usable energy in the near future.
② Tsunamis do more damage to the land than flooding.
③ Tsunamis can have an especially catastrophic impact on coastal communities.
④ Scientists can predict and track tsunamis with a fair degree of accuracy, reducing their potential impact.

04

All of us have come to expect that reliable sources of energy will be available forever. We drive our cars wherever and whenever we want. When the gas tank gets low, we simply pull into the nearest gas station. ⓐ At home, whenever we need to change the temperature, prepare food, we simply turn on the nearest appliance. ⓑ What is the source of all this energy that we use so carelessly? In most of the world, energy is created by burning fossil fuels — coal, natural gas, and oil. The problem is that these resources are Ⓐ_____. At our current rate of use, by the year 2080, the world's supply of oil will be almost gone. ⓒ The best solution to this worldwide problem is to find alternative sources of energy to meet our future needs. The current leading alternatives to fossil fuels are fusion and solar energy. ⓓ Fusion is a nuclear reaction that results in an enormous release of energy. It is practically pollution-free and is probably our best long-range option. Unfortunately, it will not be available for at least twenty years. ⓔ The other possible energy source, solar power, is the source of all energy, except nuclear, on Earth. When people think of solar energy, they generally think of the many ways that individual homeowners can utilize the power of the sun for heating water and buildings. But solar energy can also be utilized to generate electricity and to purify fuels for automobiles. ⓕ It is clear that for us to have sufficient energy sources for the 21th century, it will be necessary to pursue the development and encourage the use of alternative energy sources worldwide. If we ignore this problem, what will become of our children? What will life be like for them in the year 2050?

1 When the above passage can be divided into three paragraphs, which would be the best boundary?
① B and C
② B and D
③ B and E
④ C and E
⑤ C and F

2 What is most appropriate for the blank Ⓐ?
① artificial
② finite
③ polluted
④ dangerous
⑤ ineffective

3 What is the main idea of the passage?
① necessity of finding pollution-free energy
② importance of the energy-saving plan
③ necessity of increasing the efficiency of appliances and vehicles
④ importance of finding new energy sources
⑤ potentiality of solar energy

05

Around 18,000 years ago, the majority of modern-day Britain was covered by an ice age, according to Wessex Archaeology. This period of glaciation persisted for thousands of years until around 12,000 years ago after a warming climate brought the icy expanse to an end. In its wake, the areas that today are the North Sea and the English Channel were filled with grassy marshland, wooded valleys and swamps, according to *National Geographic*. This area of land, known as Doggerland, connected Britain with mainland Europe and spanned over 18,000 square miles.

The beginning of the end for Britain's connection to Continental Europe began around 8,200 years ago when a massive tsunami struck Doggerland. Off of the coast of Norway, an enormous underwater landslide, known as the Storegga Slide, shifted more than 720 cubic miles of material through the water, according to research published in the journal *Nature Climate Change*. This is 300 times the annual sediment output from all the world's rivers.

The Storegga Slide was likely triggered by seismic activity following a period of deglaciation across Norway, according to the journal *Marine and Petroleum Geology*. The rapid movement and displacement of water caused by the slide generated enough energy to create the tsunami. The enormous wave would have reached heights of up to 66 feet, according to *Nature Climate Change*. The tsunami swallowed up Doggerland. It crashed into the north-east of Britain and travelled 25 miles inland, making it a newly formed island, according to the BBC.

1 What is the passage mainly about?

① The beginning of global warming
② Britain's separation from mainland Europe
③ Effects of the Storegga Slide on Continental Europe
④ The role of Doggerland in the formation of modern-day Britain

2 According to the passage, which of the following is true?

① The period of glaciation continued for about 18,000 years.
② The underwater landslide caused the rapid displacement of water.
③ The majority of contemporary Britain disappeared around 8,200 years ago.
④ Doggerland was formed when mainland Europe was struck by a tsunami.

06

Sustainable living deals with the practice of decreasing your demand on natural resources by ensuring you recycle what you use to the best of your ability. Sometimes that can mean not choosing to Ⓐ_____ a product that is made using practices that don't promote sustainability, and sometimes it means altering how you do things so that you can start playing more of an active part in the cycle of life.

People know that global warming, climate change, damaging the ozone layer, and losing resources are real and their Ⓑ_____ on human and animal lives can be catastrophic. It is time for individuals to adopt actions for sustainable living by changing their lifestyle. For example, basic measures such as using public transportation more frequently, reducing energy consumption, and becoming more eco-friendly can go a long way in minimizing your environmental impact and making this planet a safe and clean place.

1 Which one is NOT TRUE?

① Sustainable living involves changing your lifestyle to minimize your environmental impact.
② Sustainable living involves using more natural resources by buying more products.
③ Sustainable living involves trying your best to recycle what you use.
④ Sustainable living involves using less energy.

2 Which one CANNOT be inferred from the passage?

① You can help promote sustainability by walking or biking to work more often.
② You can reduce your energy consumption by using more natural light than light bulbs.
③ You can become eco-friendly by reusing items.
④ You can help reduce your environmental impact by increasing your imprint on the world.

3 Choose the best word for Ⓐ and Ⓑ.

① consume — compact   ② consult — compact
③ consume — impact   ④ consult — impact

4 Choose the best title.

① Ways to Recycle
② Benefits of Public Transportation
③ Harming the Ozone Layer
④ How to Live a Sustainable Life

07

Environmentalists say that Ⓐ_____. Of course it is. Just look at West Virginia, where whole Appalachian peaks have been knocked into valleys to get at the coal underneath and streams run orange with acidic water. Or look at downtown Beijing, where the air these days is often thicker than in an airport smoking lounge. Air pollution in China, much of it from burning coal, is blamed for more than a million premature deaths a year. That's on top of the thousands who die in mining accidents, in China and elsewhere.

These problems aren't new. In the late 17th century, when coal from Wales and Northumberland was lighting the first fires of the industrial revolution in Britain, the English writer John Evelyn was already complaining about the "stink and darkness" of the smoke that wreathed London. Three centuries later, in December 1952, a thick layer of coal-laden smog descended on London and lingered for a long weekend, provoking an epidemic of respiratory ailments that killed as many as 12,000 people in the ensuing months.

Coal, to use the economists' euphemism, is fraught with Ⓑ"externalities" — the heavy costs it imposes on society. It's the dirtiest, most lethal energy source we have. But by most measures it's also the cheapest, and we depend on it. So the big question today isn't whether coal can ever be "clean." It can't. It's whether coal can ever be clean enough — to prevent not only local disasters but also a radical change in global climate.

In 2012 the world emitted a record 34.5 billion metric tons of carbon dioxide from fossil fuels. Coal was the largest contributor. Cheap natural gas has lately reduced the demand for coal in the U.S., but everywhere else, especially in China, demand is surging. During the next two decades several hundred million people worldwide will get electricity for the first time, and if current trends continue, most will use power produced by coal. Even the most aggressive push for alternative energy sources and conservation could not replace coal — at least not right away.

1 Which of the following best fits in Ⓐ?

① clean coal is a myth
② coal is blessing to civilization
③ coal is not changing the scenery
④ coal burning is less fatal than mining

2 Which of the following is closest in meaning to Ⓑ"externalities"?

① the direct costs in producing coal
② the costs that coal miners pay to society
③ the indirect costs that society has to pay
④ the costs that consumers do not have to pay

3 Which of the following is NOT true?

① Burning coal has claimed many human lives for long.
② Coal causes environmental concerns around the world.
③ The biggest reason we depend on coal is that it's cheap.
④ Natural gas reduces the demand for coal in China.

08

A The atmosphere is divided into five layers. It is thickest near the surface and thins out with height until it eventually merges with space. Ozone is found in the two different parts of the Earth's atmosphere: the troposphere and the stratosphere. The former is ground level ozone, a human health irritant and component of smog, while the latter accounts for the vast majority of atmospheric ozone that protects human health as it absorbs ultraviolet radiation from the sun, thereby preventing the radiation from hitting Earth's surface and harming living organisms from this biologically dangerous radiation. ❶

B The term 'ozone hole' refers to recent depletion of this protective layer of stratospheric ozone over the polar regions. People, plants, and animals living under the ozone hole are harmed by the solar radiation now reaching the Earth's surface — where it causes health problems from eye damage to skin cancer. ❷

C Scientists discovered that the ozone layer was thinning in the lower stratosphere, with particularly dramatic ozone loss — known as the ozone hole — in the Antarctic springtime. This is caused by increasing concentrations of ozone-depleting chemicals in the stratosphere, called chlorofluorocarbons or CFCs, which remain in the atmosphere for decades to over a century. When the sun comes out again in the polar spring, the ice particles melt, releasing the ozone-depleting molecules which in turn do their dirty work, breaking apart the molecular bonds in ultraviolet radiation-absorbing ozone. ❸

D The ozone hole, however, is not the mechanism of global warming. Ultraviolet radiation represents less than one percent of the energy from the sun — not enough to be the cause of the excess heat from human activities. Global warming is caused primarily from putting too much carbon into the atmosphere when coal and oil are burned to generate electricity or to run our cars. These gases spread around the planet like a blanket, capturing the solar heat that would otherwise be radiated out into space. ❹

E Both of these environmental problems do, however, have a common cause — human activities that release gases into and alter the atmosphere. Ozone depletion occurs when CFCs — formerly found in aerosol spray cans and refrigerants — are released into the atmosphere. These gases, through several chemical reactions, cause the ozone molecules to break down, reducing ozone's ultraviolet radiation-absorbing capacity. ❺

1 Which of the following questions is NOT answered in the passage?

① What is the ozone hole?
② What causes the ozone hole?
③ How does the ozone hole influence people?
④ How does the ozone hole contribute to global warming?
⑤ Does climate change have an impact on the stratospheric ozone layer?

2 The following is removed from the passage. In which parts ❶~❺ may it be inserted to support the argument made by the author?

Because our atmosphere is one connected system, it is not surprising that ozone depletion and global warming are related in some other ways. For example, evidence suggests that climate change may contribute to thinning of the protective ozone layer.

① ❶
② ❷
③ ❸
④ ❹
⑤ ❺

3 According to the passage, which of the following is NOT true?

① The "ozone hole" in the troposphere do harm to people and animals.
② Ozone depleting molecules are released from the ice particle due to global warming.
③ CFCs, a human-developed compound, are quite destructive and long-lived in the atmosphere.
④ The thickness of the polar stratospheric ozone layer represents the intact function of its protection by the atmosphere.
⑤ As carbon chemicals and other heat-trapping gases rise into the atmosphere, spread around the globe, and act like a blanket holding in heat around Earth.

09

Mercury pollution is a global problem. Emissions from gold mining, coal burning, and other industrial processes travel through the atmosphere, eventually falling to Earth as rain or snow. The poison can make its way to fish and the humans who eat them, where it can damage the developing nervous system, causing problems with memory and language in children exposed in the womb.

When mercury lands in wetlands and lake sediment, microbes change the metallic element into a dangerous compound called methylmercury that builds up in food webs. Concentrations are highest in larger, predatory fish. Public health agencies regularly test such fish in many lakes, sometimes leading to warnings to limit consumption.

[A] To get a clear understanding, a large research project began an experiment in 2001 using a kind of chemical tracer: enriched stable isotopes of mercury. These forms of the element behave the same way chemically, but they can be distinguished from typical mercury in the environment. For 7 years, the researchers added one isotope of mercury to the water of Lake 658, part of a remote Canadian research station called the Experimental Lakes Area where 58 lakes and their watershed have been reserved for science. They also sprayed different isotopes from an airplane onto the surrounding wetland and upland to study how it moves into the lake.

[B] Since the 1980s, regulations to control air pollution have gradually lowered emissions of mercury in North America and Europe, but sources elsewhere are still increasing, particularly small-scale gold mining in Latin America and coal burning power plants in Asia. In 2013, nations agreed to an international treaty, called the Minamata Convention on Mercury, that requires signers to ban mercury in products such as light bulbs and batteries, as well as reducing industrial emissions.

[C] But how quickly do these measures have an effect? One hurdle to answering that question has been the complicated behavior of mercury in ecosystems, which makes it hard to figure out how much of a given decline in mercury concentrations in fish is due to reductions in air pollution rather than to factors such as excessive nutrients, invasive species, and other ecological changes.

Soon after the experiment began, isotopically labeled methylmercury began to accumulate in invertebrates living in the lake, such as zooplankton. It also rose in yellow perch and other small fish that eat the zooplankton, and increased by about 40% in larger fish such as pike, which eat smaller fish. After the first 7 years of the experiment, the researchers stopped adding the isotopic mercury and continued to check the concentrations in the animals living in the lake. During the next 8 years of the study, concentrations of isotopic mercury dropped by up to 91% in the small fish. Concentrations also fell in populations of the larger fish. Only a small amount of the mercury that was added to the surrounding land ended up in fish, and these levels also fell quickly.

The exact benefits to particular lakes will be difficult to predict, researchers say, because local conditions, such as the size of the surrounding watershed and rates of methylation, influence how much mercury ends up in fish. And even if all atmospheric emissions cease, some mercury — the legacy of past air pollution — will continue to enter lakes from the surrounding watershed.

1 위 글의 단락을 논리적 흐름에 맞게 순서대로 배열한 것으로 가장 적합한 것을 고르시오.

① B — A — C
② B — C — A
③ C — A — B
④ C — B — A

2 위 글의 요지로 가장 적합한 것을 고르시오.

① The long-term experiment was supported by the international authorities to prevent mercury contamination.
② Researchers analyzed the factors of raising the concentrations of mercury.
③ Lengthy experiment demonstrated environmental recovery by cutting mercury contamination.
④ Local conditions yielded the different results in terms of the concentrations of mercury.

10

Ⓐ At the Institute of Geosciences at Johannes Gutenberg University Mainz (JGU), Dr. Michael Deininger investigated Ⓐhow regional climate systems have changed since the beginning of the current interglacial period some 10,000 years ago and what conclusions can be drawn from this. ❶ "We were able to accurately reconstruct summer precipitation in the monsoon regions in Africa and South America, compare this data with changes in precipitation in the northern mid-latitudes, and relate this to changes in temperature," Deininger explained. The study also involved scientists from Australia, Brazil, Mexico, Ireland, Austria, and South Africa. ❷

Ⓑ As Ⓑthe Earth is heated stronger at the equator than at the poles due to the differing distribution of solar radiation, a temperature gradient develops which, to put it in simple terms, causes atmospheric circulation to transport energy toward the poles. ❸ Changes to this solar radiation-related temperature difference will in turn influence the atmospheric circulation, and thus, also regional precipitation patterns.

Ⓒ The new study shows that over the past 10,000 years, changes to regional precipitation in the northern latitudes, Africa, and South America have more or less been synchronous. ❹ "We argue that these regional climate variations are connected and that they are mainly caused by alterations to solar radiation and the associated temperature differences between the tropics and polar regions," stated Deininger.

Ⓓ The researchers involved in the study Ⓒwere particularly interested in the question of whether it is possible to learn from the past to benefit the future. With the current level of global warming, the temperature gradient between the equator and the poles is being reduced — especially due to the fact that warming in the Arctic has a particularly marked effect. ❺ This can weaken the westerly winds in mid-latitudes in the Northern Hemisphere, cause a weaker South American monsoon and a stronger African monsoon, while at the same time lead to lower precipitation levels in the summer rainfall zone of Southeast Africa. The consequences of this could be shifts in regional rainfall patterns, Ⓓpotentially caused droughts in some areas, and flooding in others. "In the future, we need to recognize Ⓔthe fundamental role the variation in temperature difference plays in controlling our climate system," concluded Dr. Deininger.

1 Which of the following is the best title for the above passage?

① Arctic Warming Contributing to Drought
② The Arctic Heated Up Three Times More Than Planet Average
③ A Reconstruction of Global Average Surface Temperature Change
④ The Differences in Temperature Between the Tropics and the Poles
⑤ Change in Global Precipitation Patterns as a Result of Climate Change

2 Choose the underlined phrase that must be changed for the sentence to be grammatically correct.
① Ⓐ how regional climate systems have changed
② Ⓑ the Earth is heated stronger
③ Ⓒ were particularly interested in the question
④ Ⓓ potentially caused droughts
⑤ Ⓔ the fundamental role the variation in temperature difference plays

3 The following sentence is removed from the above passage. In which part may it be inserted to support the argument made by the author?

To do this, the paleoclimatologist looked at data for rainfall time series recorded in various climate archives.

① ❶
② ❷
③ ❸
④ ❹
⑤ ❺

4 According to the passage, which of the following is NOT true?
① The researchers are interested in what we can learn from the past to benefit the future.
② Dr. Michael Deininger teamed up with scholars from other countries to conduct the research.
③ The research team succeeded in reconstructing summer precipitation in African and South American monsoon areas.
④ The study revealed that changes to regional precipitation in the researched regions took place sequentially.
⑤ Temperature rise in the Arctic has an extremely noticeable influence.

11 의학·건강

11 의학·건강

01

People who repeatedly gain and lose weight acquire a permanent, long-term change in their metabolism. Their metabolism slows down, so that they consume less food energy than others. The result is that the excess energy in their food becomes stored as fat. This means that crash dieting is self-defeating. Experiments on rats have shown that alternating underfeeding with overfeeding results in a lower metabolic rate. The lower rate enabled the rats to gain weight more easily, with less food than they would ordinarily need. Further, a study of high school wrestlers found that some of them lost and regained weight as often as 10 times during the wrestling season. In the off-season, they were no fatter than those whose weight did not vary, but their metabolic rate was substantially lower. The implication is that people who crash-diet and then regain weight are likely to _____.

1 빈칸에 들어갈 가장 알맞은 것을 고르시오.

① crash-diet again and again
② control their weight fairly easily
③ be eager to keep their metabolic rate low
④ experience more and more difficulty in losing it

2 위 글의 내용과 맞는 것을 고르시오.

① Human beings and rats repeatedly gain and lose weight.
② High school wrestlers are recommended to crash-diet in the off-season.
③ The metabolic rate has a lot to do with the ability to lose weight.
④ Alternating underfeeding with overfeeding does not affect rats' metabolism.

02

   The most common treatment for post-traumatic stress disorder is known as exposure-based therapy. This asks those afflicted to imagine the sights and sounds that traumatized them, and helps them confront those memories. It often works. But not always. And it would undoubtedly be better if troops did not develop the condition in the first place. With this in mind, a team of engineers, computer scientists and psychologists led by Dr Skip Rizzo propose a form of psychological vaccination. By _____, Dr Rizzo hopes to inure squaddies to anything they might witness on the field of battle. The idea of doing this developed from Dr Rizzo's work using virtual reality to help with exposure-based therapy. Such VR enables the sights, sounds, vibrations and even smells of the battlefield to be recreated in the safety of a clinic, and trials suggest it can help those who do not respond to standard exposure-based therapy. The success of such simulation led Dr Rizzo to wonder if a similar regime, experienced before actual battle, might prepare troops mentally in the way that traditional training prepares them physically. His preliminary results suggest it might.

1 Which of the following is most appropriate for the blank?
   ① making soldiers relive the horrors of war as they come back
   ② presenting soldiers with the horrors of war before they go to fight
   ③ preparing soldiers more physically for battle
   ④ using a variety of stress-reduction tactics
   ⑤ speeding up the healing process with virtual training courses

2 According to the passage, Dr Rizzo's method of treatment _____.
   ① is not a complete break from the exposure-based therapy
   ② is likely to create problems because it is based on video games
   ③ does not work for those with severe physical limitations
   ④ suggests that an actual battlefield cannot be replaced by a virtual one
   ⑤ tends to be less harmful than conventional shock therapy

03

A key strategy for eating well is to select foods that offer significant amounts of nutrients but a small number of calories. A If a particular food has a high ratio of nutrients to calories, it is a nutritionally dense food. B The procedure for determining the nutrient density of food consists of adding the percentage of the recommended dietary allowance for the eight essential nutrients listed on the package label for one serving and dividing by the number of calories per serving. C The higher the score, the higher the nutritional quality (nutrient density) of the food. If two foods have the same number of calories per serving but one has more nutrients, it is more nutritionally dense. D The concept of nutrient density can help the health-conscious and weight-conscious person make informed choices. E With the number of foods available and the promises and claims that come with them, people need a way to evaluate foods. Nutrient density is one technique that consumers can use to select food.

1 Which is the best place in the passage for the following sentence?

This ratio, called nutrient density, provides a quantitative basis for judging the nutritional quality of food.

① A
② B
③ C
④ D
⑤ E

2 What is the main topic of the passage?

① Nutrient density to evaluate foods
② Nutritional information for older people
③ Ways of calculating nutrient density of foods
④ Relations between nutrients and calories in foods
⑤ Importance of taking nutritionally balanced foods for weight loss

04

Subtle changes in the way a person walks can be an early warning sign of cognitive decline and a signal of the need for advanced testing. The findings are the first to link a physical symptom to Alzheimer's, which up until now required doctors to begin a diagnosis by focusing on cognition and administering lengthy neurological exams. Monitoring deterioration and other changes in a person's gait is Ⓐ_____ because it doesn't require any expensive technology or take a lot of time to assess. The disease affects 5.4 million mostly older people in the United States, numbers expected to spike to 16 million in 2050 as baby boomers age. Walking requires a perfect and Ⓑ_____ integration of multiple areas of the brain. Walking changes occur because the disease interferes with the circuitry between these areas of brain. In the Mayo Clinic, researchers measured the stride length and velocity of more than 1,340 participants through a computerized gait instrument at two or more visits 15 months apart. They found that study participants with lower velocity and length of stride experienced significantly larger declines in cognition, memory, and executive function.

1 Which of the following is the best title for the passage?

① A Solution to Cognitive and Memory Decline
② How to Prevent Alzheimer's by Changing Gait
③ The Faster You Walk, the Healthier You Become
④ Walking Changes: An Early Warning of Alzheimer's

2 Which of the following ordered pairs best fits into Ⓐ and Ⓑ?

① ideal — simultaneous
② challenging — instant
③ preferred — stationary
④ accurate — intermittent

05

Since bones deteriorate with age, it makes sense to take in more calcium as we get older to lower the risk of fractures. But how much is enough?

A report from Swedish researchers suggests that for women over 50, anywhere from 700 to 900 mg of calcium a day is ideal for preventing bone fractures. Higher levels than that had no additional impact on fracture risk. The researchers studied more than 60,000 women who reported their dietary and supplemental calcium intake as well as their fracture rates over 19 years. Women who got less than 750 mg of calcium per day had a 26% higher risk of fracture than women consuming about 900 mg daily, but those who got more — up to 1,185 mg a day — did not lower their risk of fracture any further than those taking 900 mg.

The findings suggest that the calcium consumption recommended for women over 50 by U.S. dietary guidelines — 1,200 mg daily — may be too high. It's not that calcium doesn't help promote bone health; it's just that exceeding the threshold may not increase its benefit.

1 Which of the following is true about the report in the passage?
① Intake of too much calcium negates its benefits.
② More calcium is not necessarily better for preventing bone fractures.
③ The more you take calcium, the lower the risk of fractures becomes.
④ Women under 50 should take in more calcium than those who are over 50.
⑤ Most women are deficient in calcium and prone to fractures.

2 How much of calcium a day does the underlined threshold refer to?
① 600 mg
② 700 mg
③ 900 mg
④ 1,185 mg
⑤ 1,200 mg

06

Once the domain of childhood curiosity, the question of why we can't tickle ourselves is now exciting neuroscientists. To understand their interest, consider this: every time your body moves, it creates sensations that could potentially confuse you in all kinds of ways. Just imagine the chaos if every time one of your hands brushed your leg, you assumed that someone was fondling or attacking you. Being able to distinguish between your movement and the actions of others is a central part of our sense of self and agency.

To find an answer to the question, Sarah-Jayne Blackemore scanned subjects' brains as her colleagues tickled the palms of their hands and as the participants attempted to do so themselves. From the resulting brain activity, she concluded that whenever we move our limbs, the brain's cerebellum produces precise predictions of the body's movements and then sends a second shadow signal that damps down activity in the somatosensory cortex where tactile feelings are processed. The Ⓐ_____ is that when we tickle ourselves, we don't feel the sensations with the same intensity as we would if they had come from someone else, and so we remain calm.

1 Which is the passage mainly about?

① the importance of childish curiosity
② the unreliability of human sensation
③ a recent advancement in brain scanning technology
④ a brain mechanism for distinguishing self and others

2 Which best fits into the blank Ⓐ?

① result
② reason
③ evidence
④ prediction

3 Which is true according to the passage?

① People who are easy to tickle are intelligent.
② Palms are the most sensitive part of the human body.
③ People believe that they are attacked when tickled by themselves.
④ We cannot tickle ourselves because we predict that we will be tickled.

07

We talk about food in the negative: What we shouldn't eat, what we'll regret later, what's evil, dangerously tempting, unhealthy. ⒶThe effects are more insidious than any overindulgent amount of "bad food" can ever be. By fretting about food, we turn occasions for comfort and joy into sources of fear and anxiety. And when we avoid certain foods, we usually compensate by consuming too much of others. All of this happens under the guise of science. But a closer look at the research behind our food fears shows that many of our most demonized foods are actually fine for us. Consider salt. It's true that, if people with high blood pressure consume a lot of salt, it can lead to cardiovascular events like heart attacks. It's also true that salt is overused in processed foods. But the average American consumes just over three grams of sodium per day, which is actually in the sweet spot for health. Eating too little salt may be just as dangerous as eating too much. This is especially true for the majority of people who don't have high blood pressure. Regardless, Ⓑexperts continue to push for lower recommendations. ⒸMany of the doctors and nutritionists who recommend avoiding certain foods fail to properly explain the magnitude of their risks. In some studies, processed red meat in large amounts is associated with an increased relative risk of developing cancer. The absolute risk, however, is often quite small.

1 What does the underlined Ⓐ mean?

① The effects of food fears
② The effects of "bad food"
③ The effects of eating too much
④ The effects of eating processed food

2 The author agrees _____.

① with both Ⓑ and Ⓒ
② with Ⓑ, but not with Ⓒ
③ with Ⓒ, but not with Ⓑ
④ with neither Ⓑ nor Ⓒ

08

Health problems ranging from a mild headache to severe cognitive impairment can result from exposure to air pollution. A pollutant's capacity to affect health depends on many factors, such as proximity of the person to the pollutant, age of the person exposed, and duration of his or her exposure. Reactions to pollutants vary among individuals, but patterns of ill health — particularly when experienced by an entire family in a home or by multiple workers in an office building — may be an aid in diagnosing the condition and resolving the problem. However, the phenomenon of "sick building syndrome" (in which a large number of workers or residents report symptoms like headache or sore throat but no physical cause can be found) shows that diagnosis is not always easy or even possible.

According to the categories established for diagnostic evaluation by the American Medical Association, indoor air pollutants can be classified into the following groups: combustion products, biological pollutants, volatile organic compounds, and heavy metals. Any of these categories could be further broken down according to several bases. For example, biological pollutants could be classified according to their pathogenicity — their likelihood of causing disease, regardless of whether or not the disease is significantly uncomfortable.

1 The American Medical Association in the passage classifies four groups of indoor air pollutants. Which is NOT included in any of the four?
① tobacco smoke
② organic folic acid
③ molds and bacteria
④ lead and mercury

2 According to the passage, which is NOT a factor of health problems caused by air pollution?
① How close the person is to the pollutant
② How old the person is
③ How long the person contacts the pollutant
④ How knowledgeable the person is about the pollutant

09

Although Europe had experienced many serious outbreaks of disease, the most devastating of all struck in the mid-14th century, killing between one-third and half the continent's population. Known as the Black Death, the plague may have spread to Europe from Central Asia. Theories abound on what caused the disease, although it is widely supposed to have been *Yersinis pestis*, a bacterium carried by fleas on rodents. The infection has three variants: bubonic plague, which is characterized by buboes, or swellings, of the neck, groin, and armpits; pneumonic plague, which infects the lungs; and septicemic plague, or blood poisoning. The plague was transmitted via Constantinople in 1347 and reached most parts of Europe during 1348 and 1349. It caused widespread terror and panic, and most attempts to fight its spread were useless. By 1350, the Black Death had largely run its course, but with somewhere between 25 and 50 million Europeans dead, a sudden _____ of labor may have contributed to profound social changes. The peasantry found their diminished numbers led to a greater demand for their services, which meant that their living conditions and legal rights greatly improved.

1 Which of the following is most appropriate for the blank?

① shortage
② integration
③ division
④ abundance
⑤ diversification

2 Which of the following is <u>not</u> true according to the passage?

① Fleas are believed to have spread the plague.
② By 1350 the Black Death reached its peak.
③ The symptoms of the plague were classified into three categories.
④ The Black Death was the most catastrophic event in the history of Europe.
⑤ The Black Death made it possible for European society to change for the better.

10

A good run can transform you, at least temporarily, into a brand new person. Current research in neurogenesis has been trying to account for why this is the case. Until recently, the prevailing theory was that the number of neurons in your brain was finite, and after you reached adulthood, no more could be created. Ⓐ_____, studies have shown that neurons can be produced throughout your life, but under only one condition: hard exercise. Ⓑ_____, the location of the new brain cells is in the hippocampus, a region of the brain associated with learning and memory. So if you exercise enough to sweat for 30 to 40 minutes, the part of your brain that remembers things will grow. In addition, the same amount of exercise leads to brain development in the frontal lobe, the frontal executive network system. This part of the brain is associated with goal-setting, planning, focus and concentration, and time management. Moreover, the frontal lobe is linked with emotion regulation. So people who have had a long run feel better. Ⓒ_____, running, not pharmaceuticals, may be the best medicine for people with depression or anxiety disorders. Finally, runners almost always let their minds wander as they exercise. This daydreaming has a positive impact on creativity and problem-solving skills.

1 Which one of the following ordered sets best fits into Ⓐ, Ⓑ, and Ⓒ?

① However — Therefore — Furthermore
② Furthermore — Therefore — However
③ However — Furthermore — Therefore
④ Furthermore — However — Therefore

2 Which of the following is NOT listed as a benefit of hard exercise?

① Increased muscular coordination
② Improved ability to concentrate
③ Improved creativity and problem solving
④ Increased number of neurons in the hippocampus

3 According to the passage, which of the following is true?

① Previous theories about neurons have been confirmed.
② Both daydreaming and concentration are promoted by running.
③ A larger hippocampus enhances emotional regulation.
④ People with depression should run for less than half an hour.

11

The Ebola virus causes an acute, serious illness which is often fatal if untreated. Ebola virus disease (EVD) first appeared in 1976 in 2 <u>simultaneous</u> outbreaks, one in Nzara, Sudan, and the other in Yambuku, Democratic Republic of Congo. The latter occurred in a village near the Ebola River, from which the disease takes its name. Ebola is introduced into the human population through close contact with the blood, secretions, organs or other bodily fluids of infected animals such as fruit bats, monkeys and porcupines found ill or dead.

Ebola then spreads through human-to-human transmission via direct contact with the blood, secretions, organs or other bodily fluids of infected people, and with surfaces and materials contaminated with these fluids. Health-care workers have frequently been infected while treating patients with suspected or confirmed EVD. This has occurred through close contact with patients when infection control precautions are not strictly practiced. People remain infectious as long as their blood and body fluids, including semen and breast milk, contain the virus.

1 What does the word "<u>simultaneous</u>" in this passage tell readers?

① that the Ebola virus outbreak in Sudan happened subsequent to the one in the Democratic Republic of Congo
② that the Ebola virus outbreak in Sudan happened at about the same time as the one in the Democratic Republic of Congo
③ that the Ebola virus outbreak in Sudan was a cause of the one in the Democratic Republic of Congo
④ that the Ebola virus outbreak in Sudan was just as significant as the one in the Democratic Republic of Congo

2 Which of the following best expresses the author's opinions about the Ebola virus in this passage?

① Ebola is a disease which just started to appear in the past year.
② People contract the Ebola virus only with direct contact with other victims.
③ Few health-care workers are willing to take care of patients with the Ebola virus since Ebola is very contagious through human contact.
④ Medical researchers have warned that close contact with people who have been infected by the Ebola virus is very dangerous, and therefore such people should take special precautions.

12

We don't typically overbreathe, overdrink, or overmate — so why do we overeat? There are at least three reasons. First, overeating can result from biochemical abnormalities. For example, obese people are often leptin-resistant — that is, their brains do not respond to the chemical message that shuts hunger off — and even leptin injections don't help them. For such people the urge to eat is incredibly compelling, and they can't just to stop eating any more than you could just decide to stop breathing. Second, we often eat even when we are not really hungry. For example, we may eat to reduce negative emotions such as sadness or anxiety, we may eat out of habit ("I always have ice cream at night"), and we may eat out of _____ ("Everyone else is ordering dessert"). Third, nature designed us to overeat. For most of our evolutionary history, the main food-related problem facing our ancestors was starvation, and we evolved two strategies to avoid it. First, we developed a strong attraction to foods that provide large amounts of energy per bite — in other words, foods that are calorically rich — which is why most of us prefers hamburgers and milk-shakes to celery and water. Second, we developed an ability to store excess food energy in the form of fat, which enabled us to eat more than we needed when food was plentiful and then live off our reserves when food was scarce.

1 Which of the following statements is likely to follow the final sentence?
① We are beautifully engineered for a world in which food is generally low-cal and scarce.
② Our bodies respond to dieting by reducing the heart beating rate or increasing our metabolism, which is the rate at which energy is used.
③ Once our bodies have added a fat cell, that cell is pretty much there to stay.
④ Many of Candyland's goods tend to be high in saturated fat, which is not related to the chemical messengers that tell us to stop eating.

2 Which of the following best fills in the blank?
① radical conformity   ② social obligation
③ rational conformity   ④ social disparity

3 According to passage, which of the following is NOT true?
① Evolution is related to overweight or obesity.
② People tend to make a decision out of habit.
③ Eating may reduce negative feelings like worries and grief.
④ Leptin injection contributes to saving the reserved fat.

13

Immunology is the study of the body's defense against infection. We are continually exposed to microorganisms, many of which cause disease, and yet become ill only rarely. How does the body defend itself? When infection does occur, how does the body eliminate the invader and cure itself? And why do we develop long-lasting immunity to many infectious diseases encountered once and overcome? These are the questions addressed by immunology, which we study to understand our body's defenses against infection at the cellular and molecular levels.

[A] Jenner had observed that the relatively mild disease of cowpox, or vaccinia, seemed to confer protection against the often fatal disease of smallpox, and in 1796, he demonstrated that inoculation with cowpox protected the recipient against smallpox. His scientific proof relied on the deliberate exposure of the inoculated individual to infectious smallpox material two months after inoculation. This scientific test was his original contribution.

[B] The beginning of immunology as a science is usually attributed to Edward Jenner for his work in the late 18th century. The notion of immunity — that surviving a disease confers greater protection against it later — was known since ancient Greece. Variolation — the inhalation or transfer into superficial skin wounds of material from smallpox pustules — had been practiced since at least the 1400s in the Middle East and China as a form of protection against that disease and was known to Jenner.

[C] Jenner called the procedure vaccination. This term is still used to describe the inoculation of healthy individuals with weakened or attenuated strains of disease-causing agents in order to provide protection from disease. Although Jenner's bold experiment was successful, it took almost two centuries for smallpox vaccination to become universal. This advance enabled the World Health Organization to announce in 1979 that smallpox had been eradicated, arguably the greatest triumph of modern medicine.

1 위 글의 단락을 논리적 흐름에 맞게 순서대로 배열한 것으로 가장 적합한 것을 고르시오.

① [B] — [A] — [C]
② [B] — [C] — [A]
③ [C] — [A] — [B]
④ [C] — [B] — [A]

2 위 글의 내용과 일치하는 것을 고르시오.

① Edward Jenner was not aware of the existence of smallpox pustules.
② The occurrence of smallpox cannot be prevented by variolation.
③ Cowpox can be prevented by using vaccination.
④ Edward Jenner was informed of variolation practiced in the past.

14

There are several pro tips for long and healthy life. First, diet. Weight loss likely explains many of the positive changes, such as lower blood pressure and better blood-sugar levels. But some experts speculate that fasting also makes the body more resistant to stress, which can have beneficial effects at the cellular level. One expert says, "Diet is by far the most powerful intervention to delay aging and age-related diseases."

In the past couple of years, scientists have shown that Ⓐ_____ behavior, like sitting all day, is a risk factor for earlier death. They found that hours spent sitting are linked to increased risks of Type 2 diabetes and nonalcoholic fatty liver disease. You can't exercise away all the bad effects of sitting too much. But the good news is that doing anything but sitting still — even fidgeting counts — can add up. People who logged the least physical activity had the highest risk of a heart event in the next ten years, which isn't shocking. But to the surprise of the researchers, moving just a little bit more during the day — like doing chores around the house — was enough to lower the risk of a heart event.

By now it's clear to scientists that our emotions affect our biology. Studies have shown for years that anger and stress can release stress hormones like adrenaline into our blood, which trigger the heart to beat faster and harder. Stress may even have an effect on how well our brains hold up against Alzheimer's disease. The researchers found that people who held more negative views of aging earlier in life had greater loss in the volume of their hippocampus, a region of the brain whose loss is linked to Alzheimer's disease. This is not the first time research has suggested that Ⓑ_____.

1 Which best fits in the blank Ⓐ?

① active
② abrupt
③ sedentary
④ vociferous

2 According to the passage, which is NOT one of the pro tips for long and healthy life?

① not sitting still for long
② doing excessive exercise
③ keeping to a regimen of diet
④ having an optimistic attitude

3 Which best fits in the blank Ⓑ?

① how we feel about aging can affect how we age
② stress and exercise are interrelated with each other
③ Alzheimer's disease is linked to positive views of aging
④ anger and stress have no direct bearing on Alzheimer's disease

15

The human ear contains the organ for hearing and the organ for balance. Both organs involve fluid-filled channels containing hair cells that produce electrochemical impulses when the hairs are stimulated by moving fluid.

The ear can be divided into three regions: outer, middle, and inner. The outer ear collects sound waves and directs them to the eardrum separating the outer ear from the middle ear. The middle ear conducts sound vibrations through three small bones to the inner ear. The inner ear is a network of channels containing fluid that moves in response to sound or movement.

To perform the function of hearing, the ear converts the energy of pressure waves moving through the air into nerve impulses that the brain perceives as sound. Vibrating objects, such as the vocal cords of a speaking person, create waves in the surrounding air. These waves cause the eardrum to vibrate with the same frequency. The three bones of the middle ear amplify and transmit the vibrations to the oval window, a membrane on the surface of the cochlea, the organ of hearing. Vibrations of the oval window produce pressure waves in the fluid inside the cochlea. Hair cells in the cochlea convert the energy of the vibrating fluid into impulses that travel along the auditory nerve to the brain.

The organ for balance is also located in the inner ear. Sensations related to body position are generated much like sensations of sound. Hair cells in the inner ear respond to changes in head position with respect to gravity and movement. Gravity is always pulling down on the hairs, sending a constant series of impulses to the brain. When the position of the head changes — as when the head bends forward — the force on the hair cells changes its output of nerve impulses. The brain then interprets these changes to determine the head's new position.

1 What can be inferred about the organs for hearing and balance?

① Both organs evolved in humans at the same time.
② Both organs send nerve impulses to the brain.
③ Both organs contain the same amount of fluid.
④ Both organs are located in the ear's middle region.

2 Hearing involves all of the following EXCEPT _____.

① motion of the vocal cords so that they vibrate
② stimulation of hair cells in fluid-filled channels
③ amplification of sound vibrations
④ conversion of wave energy into nerve impulses

3 It can be inferred from paragraphs 2 and 3 that the cochlea is a part of _____.

① the outer ear
② the eardrum
③ the middle ear
④ the inner ear

4 What can be inferred from paragraph 4 about gravity?

① Gravity has an essential role in the sense of balance.
② The ear converts gravity into sound waves in the air.
③ Gravity is a force that originates in the human ear.
④ The organ for hearing is not subject to gravity.

16

As you get older, little growths called skin tags might start popping up on your body. You'll recognize them because they're thinner at the base and get wider at the top. They aren't painful or dangerous like cancerous moles, but there's a very good reason you'll want them removed. People have used all kinds of crazy methods to try removing skin tags on their own, says Dr. Rossi, MD, dermatologic surgeon. He's heard of people tying strings around them, burning them, trying to pick them off with their fingers, and even slamming books against them. A dermatologist, on the other hand, can snip away skin tags quickly and cleanly.

For one thing, dermatologists have sterile instruments, but using your own could lead to an infection. A Plus, while dermatologists can use local anesthesia and have supplies to stop the blood, you could bleed uncontrollably with at-home methods. B Even hospital medications claiming to dissolve the skin tags could be bad news, says Dr. Rossi. "You could burn the skin or make marks," he says. "There could be unintended consequences."

But there's an even bigger reason you should visit an expert. C After dermatologists remove a growth, they'll look at it under a microscope. "There are things that look like skin tags but are cancerous," says Dr. Rossi. That doesn't mean you should freak out if you do find a skin tag. D Plus, checking a skin tag is a "Ⓐ_____" to get your doctor to check the rest of your body for skin cancer and atypical or malignant growths, says Dr. Rossi.

1 Choose the best title.
① How to Handle Skin Tags
② The Consequences of Skin Tags
③ The Benefits of Home-Treatment of Skin Tags
④ The Cause of Skin Tags

2 Which one is NOT TRUE?
① Skin tags have a circular cone shape.
② People try a variety of ways to remove skin tags.
③ Most skin tags are cancerous.
④ It is good to get your body checked when a skin tag is found.

3 Choose the best place for the following.

Most will just be benign, but you won't know for sure until you've asked.

① A   ② B
③ C   ④ D

4 Choose the best expression for Ⓐ.

① good excuse
② dangerous process
③ useless method
④ necessary evil

17

When we digest a slice of bread, we break the carbohydrates into simple sugars and its proteins into amino acids. At the same time, we also break down and rebuild the proteins of our own skin, muscles, and bones. All organisms continually break down macromolecules and reuse the building blocks.

Organisms have to assemble and disassemble macromolecules easily. The bonds that hold macromolecules together must be strong enough so that the macromolecules will not fall apart. But the bonds must not be so strong that organisms can't easily take them apart when they need to. Like children's pop beads and Legos bricks, the building blocks of life easily snap together and easily snap apart.

Amazingly, biological building blocks all snap together in the same way. The building blocks of all the major macromolecules join by the same simple chemical reaction. In every case, enzymes (molecules that help make and break chemical bonds) remove two hydrogen atoms and one oxygen atom from between pairs of building blocks, forming a bond. Removing two hydrogens and an oxygen — the equivalent of one molecule of water — is called a dehydration condensation reaction, because one water molecule is removed.

To snap apart macromolecules, organisms reverse the dehydration condensation reaction, adding one water molecule to each pair of building blocks. Enzymes detach each small molecule from a macromolecule by adding one molecule of water, a process called hydrolysis [Greek, *hydro* = water + *lysis* = breaking].

Although all the building blocks are joined by similar dehydration condensation reactions, the exact bonds that form are different in each case. For example, sugars form *glycosidic bonds*, while amino acids form *peptide bonds*.

1 What is the topic of the passage?

① the way organisms store and consume energy
② the types of chemical bonds formed by enzymes
③ the intricate structure of bonds holding macromolecules together
④ the role of enzymes in the mechanism of the building blocks of life

2 Based on the passage, choose the best words for the blanks in the following statement.

Enzymes link two building blocks by _____ the equivalent of one water molecule.
Enzymes add a water molecule to _____ a long chain into two single building blocks.

① taking away — break
② taking away — form
③ adding — break
④ adding — form

3 Which of the following is NOT true according to the passage?

① All living things including humans constantly break down macromolecules.
② Macromolecular bonding is so strong that building blocks do not snap apart.
③ How biological building blocks are linked is identical for all the major molecules.
④ The bonds that form from dehydration are different in each case.

18

People have been interested in how the brain works for centuries, and the study of language provides a unique opportunity to deepen our understanding of this complex organ. We've come a long way since the practices of the early Egyptians, who considered the heart, not the brain, the center of intelligence. We've also moved forward since the early nineteenth century, when Franz Joseph Gall proposed that certain areas of the brain control certain behaviors. Though this idea of localization is still of use today, Gall's work led to the (quite unscientific) theory of phrenology, the study of the connection between personality traits and the bumps of the skull. Now, with electroencephalography (EEG), positron emission tomography (PET) scans, and functional magnetic resonance imaging (fMRI), we've come a long way! Language disorders that result from trauma to the brain provide a rich resource for information leading to our understanding of the brain and at the same time expand our knowledge of the innateness of human language.

People who experience damage to the brain, particularly to the frontal lobe of the left hemisphere, typically experience certain kinds of language disorders and deficits. Such language-related disorders and deficits, called aphasia, provide us with insights into the areas of the brain that seem to be primarily responsible for language. The two major types of disorder are Broca's aphasia, named after Paul Broca, a French physician, who first described it in the 1860s; and Wernicke's aphasia, named after German physician Karl Wernicke, who first described this type of language deficit in the 1870s. Their research led to a new field of neuroscience. There are many different aphasias, including agraphia, alexia, and anomia.

Both Broca's and Wernicke's aphasias provide evidence for the separation of language from other cognitive abilities, for patients with these language disorders can be in command of other faculties that aren't closely tied to language. They test well on nonverbal IQ tests, and they can set clocks, read maps, make things, and carry out commands, suggesting that at least in some ways, Ⓐ_____.

1 Which of the following best fits in Ⓐ?

① cognitive disorder leads to different types of aphasia
② language and cognition are dependent upon each other
③ cognitive abilities are derived from other language abilities
④ language abilities are separated from other cognitive abilities

2 Which of the following is true about Broca and Wernicke?

① They were born in the 20th century.
② They were French nationals.
③ They were physicians.
④ They established phrenology.

3 Which of the following is NOT true?

① The early Egyptians thought the heart was the center of intelligence.
② Phrenology has been accepted as a scientific theory.
③ Agraphia, alexia, and anomia are types of aphasia.
④ Gall's idea of localization is currently useful.

19

[A] The Spanish flu, also known as the 1918 flu pandemic, was a deadly pandemic in recent history. It spread worldwide during the year 1918-1919. The virus infected 500 million people — about a third of the world's population at the time. The death toll was estimated to be at least 50 million worldwide, possibly as high as 100 million. This makes it the severest pandemic in human history.

[B] The outbreak of the Spanish flu was caused by an H1N1 virus with genes of avian origin. Historians now believe that World War I could have been partly responsible for spreading the virus. Lack of hygiene and malnourishment may have also been responsible for weakening the immune system. For example, a 2007 analysis of medical journals from the period of the pandemic found that the viral infection was no more aggressive than previous influenza strains. Instead, malnourishment, overcrowded medical camps and hospitals, and poor hygiene, all exacerbated by the recent war, promoted bacterial superinfection.

[C] There is no agreement about the origin of the virus. The 1918 flu was first observed in Europe, the United States, and parts of Asia before swiftly spreading around the world. It is believed that censorship was the main reason why this pandemic was referred to as the Spanish flu. To maintain morale, World War I censors minimized early reports of illness and mortality in Germany, the United Kingdom, France, and the United States. However, newspapers were free to report the epidemic's effects in neutral Spain, such as the grave illness of King Alfonso XIII, and these stories created a false impression of Spain as especially hard hit. This gave rise to the name 'Spanish flu'. Historical and epidemiological data are inadequate to identify with certainty the pandemic's geographic origin, with varying views as to its location.

[D] Nearly a century after the Spanish flu struck, the World Health Organization (WHO) called on scientists, national authorities and the media to follow best practices in naming new human infectious diseases to minimize unnecessary negative effects on nations, economies, and people. More modern terms for this virus include the "1918 influenza pandemic," the "1918 flu pandemic," or variations of these.

1 According to the passage, which of the following is true about the 1918 flu pandemic?

① It was far more serious than previous types of influenza.
② It was later coined to lessen the negative effects of its initial name.
③ It was named as the Spanish flu because of its first outbreak in Spain.
④ It was assessed not to have killed more than 50 million people worldwide.

2 Which of the following is the topic of the paragraph ⓑ in the passage?

① When did the flu's superinfection vanish once and for all in Europe?
② Who minimized reports on the outbreak of the Spanish flu?
③ Which journals found that the Spanish flu was not aggressive?
④ What caused the Spanish flu?

3 Which of the following is the topic of the paragraph ⓒ in the passage?

① Why was the censorship imposed?
② When did Spain make a report on the pandemic?
③ Where did the 1918 flu pandemic start?
④ Which country was hard hit by the Spanish flu?

20

Vogelstein, a cancer geneticist, and Cristian Tomasetti, an applied mathematician, put forth a mathematical formula to explain the genesis of cancer in a research paper. Here's how it works: Take the number of cells in an organ, identify what percentage of them are long-lived stem cells, and determine how many times the stem cells divide. ⓐWith every division, there's a risk of a cancer-causing mutation in a daughter cell. Thus, Tomasetti and Vogelstein reasoned, the tissues that host the greatest number of stem cell divisions are those most vulnerable to cancer. ⓑAlthough the randomness of cancer might be frightening, those in the field see a positive side, too. When Tomasetti crunched the numbers and compared them with actual cancer statistics, he concluded that this theory explained two-thirds of all cancers.

"Using the mathematics of evolution, you can really develop an engineerlike understanding of the disease," says Nowak, who has worked with Tomasetti and Vogelstein. "It's a baseline risk of being an animal that has cells that need to divide." The idea emerged during one of the pair's weekly brainstorming sessions in Vogelstein's office. They returned to an age-old question: How much of cancer is driven by environmental factors, and how much by genetics? ⓒTo solve that, Tomasetti reasoned, "I first need to understand how much is by chance and take that out of the picture."

By "chance" Tomasetti meant the roll of the dice that each cell division represents, leaving aside the influence of deleterious genes or environmental factors such as smoking or exposure to radiation. He was most interested in stem cells because they endure — meaning that a mutation in a stem cell is more likely to cause problems than a mutation in a cell that dies more quickly. Tomasetti searched the literature to find the numbers he needed, such as the size of the stem cell "compartment" in each tissue. Plotting the total number of stem cell divisions over a lifetime against the lifetime risk of cancer in 31 different organs revealed a correlation. ⓓAs the number of divisions rose, so did risk.

Colon cancer, for example, is far more common than cancer of the duodenum, the first stretch of the small intestine. This is true even in those who carry a mutated gene that puts their entire intestine at risk. Tomasetti found that there are about 10^{12} stem cell divisions in the colon over a lifetime, compared with 10^{10} in the duodenum. Mice, by contrast, have more stem cell divisions in their small intestine — and more cancers — than in their colon. The line between mutations and cancer isn't necessarily direct. "It may not just be whether a mutation occurs," says Bruce Ponder, a longtime cancer researcher.

1 위 글의 흐름상 가장 적합하지 않은 것을 고르시오.

① ⓐ ② ⓑ
③ ⓒ ④ ⓓ

2 위 글을 통해 추론할 수 있는 것으로 가장 적합한 것을 고르시오.

① The number of stem cell divisions has to do with the productivity of their daughter cells.
② For mice, more stem cell divisions lead to less risk of cancers.
③ Cells with short life span do not incur cancer-causing mutation as often as stem cells.
④ In rodents, colon cancer is more frequently observed than duodenum cancer.

3 위 글의 제목으로 가장 적합한 것을 고르시오.

① The Simple Math that Explains Why You May Get Cancer
② The Proactive Research Agenda that Intrigue Extensive Arguments
③ The Best Solution to Prevent You from Having Cancer
④ The Effective Method to Explore the Stem Cell that Causes Cancer

12

생물학·생명과학

12 생물학·생명과학

01

Not all relationships between animals are predatory. Some are mutualistic, meaning that both organisms in a relationship benefit from each other. ⒜ For example, insects that eat nectar from a flower also help the flower. The flower's pollen sticks to the insects as they eat, and then the pollen drops off as they fly to another flower.

Some are parasitic, meaning that one organism benefits while another organism suffers. ⒝ Think about fleas on a dog. The fleas bite the dog to get energy from its blood, and in return the poor dog gets itchy welts and other possible diseases. In this kind of relationship, the flea is called a parasite and the dog is called a host. ⒞

Some exhibit commensalism, meaning that one organism is helped while the other organism is neither helped nor harmed. A great example of commensalism is the relationship between a remora and a whale. ⒟ The remora has a sucker on the top of its head that attaches to the whale's top, mouth, or underside. Through this attachment, the remora can travel around more easily and eat any debris that falls from the whale. The whale is left Ⓐ_____.

1 Which of the following would be most appropriate for the blank Ⓐ?

① unharmed
② perilous
③ mediocre
④ salutary

2 Which is the most appropriate place for the sentence below?

Tapeworms, ticks, and lice are other examples of parasites.

① A
② B
③ C
④ D

3 According to the passage, which of the following is true?

① The relationship between a remora and a whale is predatory.
② Flowers serve as pollinators.
③ All organisms depend on other organisms for survival.
④ Fleas cause the host harm.

02

To avoid being eaten, ladybugs and other insects have evolved bright colors and markings — signals to predators that they taste foul or are toxic. But if every bird must first sample one of these bugs to discover that they're inedible, the insects would likely vanish before their warning colors could evolve. Now, scientists report that Ⓐ<u>a bit of bird social learning helps the insects out</u>. The scientists filmed a great tit opening a white paper packet stamped with a black square. Inside were bits of almond soaked with a bitter fluid. The bird pecked at the almond and almost instantly dropped the nut, shook its head, and wiped its beak repeatedly on its perch — a tit's way of saying it's inedible. The researchers then showed the video to 15 other great tits. When these birds later foraged in an aviary containing packets stamped either with the black square or a black cross, those that had watched the film were 32% less likely than birds that hadn't seen the video to choose packets marked with squares. Wild birds, of course, don't watch videos to learn what's inedible. But other research has shown they do watch each other. From this we can safely claim that they are clearly paying attention when Ⓑ_____.

1 Which of the following is the best title for the passage?

① Survival Strategies of Birds and Insects
② Great Tits Unlock Secrets of Symbol Decoding
③ Insects Develop Warning Colors for Self-Protection
④ Birds Learn from Other Birds about Food Suitability

2 Which of the following is implied by Ⓐ?

① Even a little bit of learning can make a great impact on insect-eating birds.
② Birds that learn from others have survival advantages over others that don't.
③ Birds don't have to taste all the insects and thus insects are spared.
④ Even birds benefit from learning while insects cannot take advantage of it.

3 Which of the following best fits into Ⓑ?

① another bird says "yuck!"
② its friend exclaims "bravo!"
③ a packet is marked "come on!"
④ its companion says "yummy!"

03

Decades of research suggest that the neurotransmitter dopamine plays a critical role in how we perceive time. Some studies have found that increasing dopamine speeds up an animal's internal clock, leading it Ⓐ_____ the passage of time; others have found that dopamine compresses events and makes them seem more fleeting; still others have uncovered both effects, depending on context. Dopamine's association with time perception is intriguing, in part because the neurotransmitter is better known for its function in reward and reinforcement learning processes. When we receive an unexpected reward, for instance — in what's known as a prediction error — we experience a rush of the chemical, which teaches us to continue pursuing that behavior in the future. It's likely more than a coincidence that dopamine is so fundamental to both time perception and learning processes. Drugs like methamphetamine and neurological disorders like Parkinson's alter both processes and also involve changes in dopamine. And learning itself — the association of a behavior with its outcome — requires the linking of one event with another in time. "Really, at the very core of reinforcement learning algorithms is Ⓑ_____," said a neuroscientist.

1 빈칸 Ⓐ에 들어가기에 가장 적절한 것은?

① to predict
② to terminate
③ to undersize
④ to remember
⑤ to overestimate

2 빈칸 Ⓑ에 들어가기에 가장 적절한 것은?

① prediction error
② Parkinson's disease
③ learning process
④ information about time
⑤ research in neuroscience

3 윗글의 내용과 가장 잘 부합하는 것은?

① Time means just one thing to the brain.
② Dopamine does not accelerate our internal clock.
③ Dopamine has nothing to do with how we perceive time.
④ An unexpected reward for a behavior can make us repeat it.
⑤ It is a coincidence that dopamine plays a role in time perception.

04

In the dozen years since *The Selfish Gene* was published its central message has become textbook orthodoxy. This is paradoxical, but not in the obvious way. It is not one of those books that was reviled as revolutionary when published, then steadily won converts until it ended up so orthodox that we now wonder what the fuss was about. Quite the contrary. From the outset the reviews were gratifyingly favourable and it was not seen, initially, as a controversial book. Its reputation for contentiousness took years to grow until, by now, it is widely regarded as a work of radical extremism. But over the very same years as the book's reputation for extremism has escalated, its actual content has seemed less and less extreme, more and more the common currency. The selfish gene theory is Darwin's theory, expressed in a way that Darwin did not choose but whose aptness, I should like to think, he would instantly have recognized and delighted in. It is in fact a logical outgrowth of orthodox neo-Darwinism, but expressed as a novel image. Rather than focus on the individual organism, it takes a gene's-eye view of nature. In the opening pages of *The Extended Phenotype* I explained this using the metaphor of the Necker cube. This is a two-dimensional pattern of ink on paper, but it is perceived as a transparent, three-dimensional cube. Stare at it for a few seconds and it will change to face in a different direction. Carry on staring and it will flip back to the original cube. Both cubes are equally compatible with the two-dimensional data on the retina, so the brain happily alternates between them. Neither is more correct than the other. My point was that there are two ways of looking at natural selection, the gene's angle and that of the individual. If properly understood they are equivalent; two views of the same truth. You can flip from one to the other and it will still be the same neo-Darwinism.

1 **The selfish gene theory is _____.**

① a different way of seeing, not a different theory
② not only a different way of seeing but also a different theory
③ neither a different way of seeing nor a different theory
④ a different theory, not a different way of seeing

2 **Which of the following statement can be inferred?**

① Radical extremism can be facilitated by the presentation of different ways of looking at the same things.
② The metaphor of the Necker cube undermines the reputation for extremism.
③ The most important contribution of a scientist can make is to provide a new theory.
④ The Necker cube example gives insight into having multiple perspectives.

05

　　In the late 1890s two German psychologists, Georg Müller and Alfons Pilzecker, found out that it takes an hour or so for memories to become fixed, or "consolidated", in the brain. Subsequent studies confirmed the existence of short-term and long-term forms of memory and provided further evidence of the importance of the consolidation phase during which the former are turned into the latter. In the 1960s, University of Pennsylvania neurologist Louis Flexner made a particularly intriguing discovery. After injecting mice with an antibiotic drug that prevented their cells from producing proteins, he found that the animals were unable to form long-term memories but could continue to store short-term ones. The implication was clear: long-term memories are not just stronger forms of short-term memories. A Storing long-term memories requires the synthesis of new proteins. Storing short-term memories does not. More recent research turned to the issue of the physical workings of both short-term and long-term memory. B The results demonstrated that the more times an experience is repeated, the longer the memory of the experience lasts. Repetition encourages consolidation. Particularly, when researchers examined the physiological effects of repetition on neuronal signals, they discovered something amazing. C Not only did the concentration of neurotransmitters in synapses change, altering the strength of the existing connections between neurons, but the neurons grew entirely new synaptic terminals. The formation of long-term memories, in other words, involves not only biochemical changes but anatomical ones. D That explains why memory consolidation requires new proteins. Proteins play an essential role in producing structural changes in cells.

1 아래의 문장이 들어갈 위치로 가장 적합한 곳을 고르시오.

The two types of memory entail different biological processes.

① A　　　　　　　　　　　② B
③ C　　　　　　　　　　　④ D

2 윗글을 통해 추론할 수 있는 것으로 가장 적합한 것을 고르시오.

① Use of antibiotic drugs prevents humans from recalling even quite recent experiences.
② Short-term memory is a key predictor for how long we can hold consolidated information in mind in an active manner.
③ Relatively fewer neurotransmitters are expected to be released in the brain synapses when long-term memory is formed.
④ Retaining information in the brain for a longer period is most likely to be accompanied by anatomical changes of synapses.

06

If we didn't already know that Rudolph the Red-Nosed Reindeer was special, that shiny nose of his could have resulted from the one-in-a-million transfer of genetic material from a brilliant colored coral found in the Red Sea. Perhaps it entered his mother's bloodstream when she scraped against the coral during a crash water landing while pregnant with Rudolph and then the DNA was passed to her unborn calf. At least that's what a smart scientist from Johns Hopkins University speculated might explain the nose that guided Santa and his sleigh on that famous foggy Christmas eve. "Mobile genetic elements," said Steve Farber, a Hopkins biology professor, "are derived from viruses and have the amazing ability to cut and insert chunks of DNA into the genome of its host."

While most children and probably most of their parents accept the beloved holiday creatures as they are, scientists want us to understand the world around us, even if it's in a cherished Christmas storybook. Rather than suspending disbelief, scientists tend to look to peer-reviewed studies first to see if there is some solid explanation for what they've witnessed, or they craft their own trials, Farber said. Rudolph might be as easy as a Ⓐ_____ test to identify the coral DNA. And his offspring would carry the same Ⓐ_____ rearrangements containing it as well.

"I've proposed a number of ways this could happen, if you're willing to forgo the impossibilities in the system. I'm just having fun," added Bah, a researcher.

1 Which of the following best fits in Ⓐ?

① experimental
② synthetic
③ genetic
④ environmental

2 Which of the following would be best for the title?

① Why Is Rudolph's Nose So Bright?
② Scientific Examination of Rudolph Is Popular
③ Christmas Stories Are Very Scientific
④ The DNA of Rudolph Is Completely Analyzed

3 Which of the following is true about Rudolph?

① He is not a deer.
② He is historically true.
③ His nose is not really bright.
④ He may have glowing genes.

07

In its modern form, suggestions for improving the human gene pool came under the name eugenics, a term coined by Francis Galton in 1883 from the Greek words *eu* (good) and *gen* (birth). ⒶAfter reading the works of Darwin, Galton became concerned with the heredity of quantitative characteristics, especially intelligence. From 1865 on, he promoted the idea that the evolution of human traits through natural selection could be substituted by their evolution through selective breeding. ⒷComing from a brilliant family himself, Galton was impressed by the way in which intellectual and personality traits tend to run in families. Convinced that such traits were inherited, and drawing on his knowledge of animal breeding, he concluded that, "judicious marriages over several generations" could "produce a highly gifted race of men," and thus thwart the "reversion to mediocrity" he believed to be threatening society as a result of excessive breeding by those who were not superior.

Galton's ideas were taken up and developed by many prominent thinkers. ⒸStudies have shown that as socio-economic conditions improve, average intelligence scores also improve, although genetic differences between individuals remain. Like the Social Darwinists, however, early eugenicists reflected their own personal and cultural biases as to which traits they deemed undesirable, and strong racist and class-based biases played a part from the beginning. ⒹDavenport, an influential leader of the early twentieth century eugenics movement, exemplified this racist approach by using New Englanders as the standard of comparison for all American social groups irrespective of their country of origin. According to Davenport and other members of his Eugenics Record Office (which from 1910 to 1944 collected an enormous database of information about American families), particular groups could be characterized by social characteristics with identifiable hereditary components: Italian violence, Jewish mercantilism, Irish pauperism, and so on.

1 위 글에서 논지의 흐름상 가장 적합하지 않은 것을 고르시오.

① Ⓐ　　　　　　　　② Ⓑ
③ Ⓒ　　　　　　　　④ Ⓓ

2 위 글의 내용과 일치하지 않은 것을 고르시오.

① The term, *eugenics*, was first invented by Francis Galton.
② Irish pauperism is a typical hereditary component in eugenics.
③ Galton argued that selective breeding can enhance human traits.
④ Racial discrimination prejudice was gradually infiltrated in eugenics.

08

Scientists nowadays point out that morality in fact has deep evolutionary roots pre-dating the appearance of humankind by millions of years. All social mammals, such as wolves, dolphins, and monkeys, have ethical codes, adapted by evolution to promote group cooperation. For example, when wolf cubs play with one another, they have 'fair game' rules. If a cub bites too hard or continues to bite an opponent that has rolled on his back and surrendered, the other cubs will stop playing with him. In chimpanzee bands, dominant members are expected to respect the property rights of weaker members. If a junior female chimpanzee finds a banana, even the alpha male will usually avoid stealing it for himself. If he breaks this rule, he is likely to lose status. Apes not only avoid taking advantage of weak group members, but sometimes actively help them. A male pygmy chimpanzee called Kidogo, who lived in the Milwaukee County Zoo, suffered from a serious heart condition that made him feeble and confused. When he was first moved to the zoo, he could neither orient himself nor understand the instructions of the human care-takers. When the other chimpanzees understood his Ⓐ_____, they intervened. They often took Kidogo by the hand and led him wherever he needed to go. If Kidogo became lost, he would utter loud distress signals and some ape would rush to help.

1 Which of the following is the best title for the passage?
  ① Violations of 'Fair Game' Rules by Primates
  ② The Evolutionary History of Social Mammals
  ③ Cooperative Animal Behavior as the Origin of Morality
  ④ Similarity of Human and Chimpanzee Morality

2 Which of the following best fits into Ⓐ?
  ① prerogative   ② predicament
  ③ personality   ④ preference

3 According to the passage, which of the following is NOT true?
  ① All social beings prefer group cooperation to ethical codes.
  ② Low status apes expect dominant ones to respect their possessions.
  ③ If a wolf cub keeps biting too hard, the other cubs will stop playing with him.
  ④ Other chimpanzees helped Kidogo because they knew he was ill.

09

Only a decade ago, the biological concept of race seemed finally to have met its end. The Human Genome Project, which mapped the entire human genetic code, proved that race could not be identified in our genes. On June 26, 2000, when President Bill Clinton unveiled the draft genomic sequence, he famously declared that "human beings, regardless of race, are 99.9 percent the same." Contrary to popular misconception, we are not naturally divided into genetically identifiable racial groups. Biologically, there is one human race. Race applied to human beings is a political division: it is a system of governing people that classifies them into social hierarchy based on invented biological demarcations.

But reports of the demise of race as a biological category were premature. Instead of hammering the last nail in the coffin of an obsolete system, the science that emerged from sequencing the human genome was shaped by a resurgence of interest in race-based genetic variation. Some scientists are claiming that clusters of genetic similarity detected with novel genomic theories and computer technologies correspond to antiquated racial classifications and prove that human racial differences are real and significant. Others are searching for genetic differences among races that can explain staggering inequalities in health and disease as well as variations in drug responses. There has been a corresponding explosion of race-based biotechnologies. In 2005, the U.S. Food and Drug Administration (FDA) approved the first race-specific drug, BiDil, _____.

1 What is the main topic of the passage?

① The demise of race as a political system
② The development of biotechnologies
③ The dispute over genetic categorization of race
④ A common struggle for the equal dignity of all of humankind

2 Which of the following CANNOT be inferred from the passage?

① We are witnessing the emergence of a new form of racial politics.
② Genomic science and biotechnologies play a role in today's reinvention of racial order.
③ The state power which controled the life and death of populations no longer relied on classifying them by race.
④ Some scientists are resuscitating biological theories of race by using genomic research.

3 Which of the following is most suitable for the blank?

① to treat heart failure in black patients
② to identify the race of criminal suspects
③ to increase racial fairness
④ to divide human beings into different racial groups

10

A "biological annihilation" of wildlife in recent decades means a sixth mass extinction in Earth's history is under way and is more severe than previously feared, according to research. Scientists analyzed both common and rare species and found billions of regional or local populations have been lost. They blame human overpopulation and overconsumption for the crisis and warn that it threatens the survival of human civilization, with just a short window of time in which to act.

Previous studies have shown species are becoming extinct at a significantly faster rate than for millions of years before, but even so extinctions remain relatively rare giving the impression of _____. The new work instead takes a broader view, assessing many common species which are losing populations all over the world as their ranges shrink, but remain present elsewhere.

1 According to the passage, which of the following is NOT correct about "a sixth mass extinction"?

① It is partly caused by human overpopulation.
② It is in progress, but its speed becomes slower.
③ It is seriously happening all over the world.
④ It endangers the continuation of human civilization.
⑤ It means a disappearance of regional bio-species from the earth.

2 Which of the following is most appropriate for the blank?

① a gradual loss of biodiversity
② a sudden disappearance of species
③ a whole extinction of human race
④ a partial end of biological types
⑤ an enduring continuity of biological variety

11

   Many of us are somewhat familiar with the second law of thermodynamics, the unwavering propensity of energy to disperse and, in doing so, transition from high-quality to low-quality forms. There is growing evidence that life, the biosphere, is no different. It has often been said that life's complexity contravenes the second law, indicating the work either of a deity or some unknown natural process, depending on one's bias. Yet the evolution of life and the dynamics of ecosystems obey the second law's mandate, functioning in large part to dissipate energy. They do so not by burning brightly and disappearing but through stable metabolic cycles that store chemical energy and continuously reduce the solar gradient. Photosynthetic plants, bacteria, and algae capture energy from the sun and form the core of all food webs. Other kinds of life-forms consume these "producers," making the most of the available energy pool. Then, virtually all organisms, including humans, are sunlight transmogrified, being _____ in the flow of energy. Viewed from a thermodynamic perspective, ecological succession — that is, changes in the species structure of an ecological community over time — is a process that maximizes the capture and degradation of energy. Similarly, the tendency for life to become more complex over the past 3.5 billion years — as indicated by increasing complexity in anatomical forms, metabolic pathways, and trophic interactions, as well as increasing biomass and biodiversity — is not due simply to natural selection, as most evolutionists still argue, but also to nature's efforts to grab more and more of the sun's flow. The slow burn that characterizes life enables ecological systems to persist over deep time, changing in response to external and internal perturbations.

1 Choose the closest in meaning to the underlined "contravenes."

① clarifies
② corroborates
③ disproves
④ asseverates

2 Which of the following can be inferred from the passage?

① Energy keeps flowing and in the process interrupts the substance of life.
② Nearly all living organisms are agents that capture and disperse energy.
③ Evolution of organisms made it possible to stop energy from dispersing.
④ Changes in metabolism and anatomy in life-forms reflect life's process of continuous simplification.

3 Choose the one that best fills in the blank.

① timeless microcosms
② insulated cocoons
③ temporary waypoints
④ permanent reservoirs

4 What is the main purpose of the passage?

① to offer a counterargument to a thermodynamic perspective on life
② to refute the evolutionary theory using data repudiating natural selection
③ to water down the importance of solar energy as the source of life itself
④ to explain the history of life through the second law of thermodynamics

12

From the outside, humans are pleasingly symmetrical, with arms, legs, and eyes that have matching right and left sides. But inside, it's a different story: our heart is on the left; our liver is on the right. Lungs and kidneys are also asymmetric. Now researchers have pinned down a gene that helps developing organs find their proper place.

Scientists have identified other genes that break the initial symmetry of a developing round embryo, and help organs pick sides. But the way researchers tracked this one down was unique, says Daniel Grimes, a developmental biologist. The research, he says, could lead to a better understanding of why organ formation goes awry, as it does in some people.

Developmental biologists have long known that the off-center placement of the heart and other organs is linked to a group of cells called the left-right organizer, which transiently forms in an early embryo. In 1998, based on studies in mice, Japanese researchers proposed that twirling cilia — hairlike appendages on a subset of organizer cells — send embryonic fluid to the left but not to the right, helping organs form in the correct place. The flow activates certain genes just on that left side, altering what grows next, they and others have speculated. The same thing happens in fish and frogs, researchers later found.

But surprisingly, there are no such cells with twirling cilia in developing chicks and pigs, even though their hearts still form to one side. There have been "many confusing results in the literature that are hard to reconcile," Grimes says. He and others think these so-called motile cilia evolved early in animal evolution but were lost in the branches of the animal family tree leading to birds and to the "even-toed" mammals such as pigs, but not humans.

Developmental biologists, Bruno Reversade and Christopher Gordon, wondered whether this disparity could hint at a way to track down new genes responsible for breaking body symmetry. They and their colleagues simply looked for genes active in developing mice, fish, and frogs, but inactive at the stage of development in pigs and birds where there was no longer any fluid flow and thus no need for those genes.

The researchers discovered five such genes, they report this month in *Nature Genetics*. Reversade knew his team was on the right track because three of these genes were already known to be important in flow-induced loss of symmetry.

1 위 글의 제목으로 가장 적합한 것을 고르시오.

① Searching for Genes Breaking Body Symmetry
② The Preemptive Steps to Find Embryonic Fluids
③ Exploring Secrets of Twirling Cilia in Gene Therapy
④ Diverse Perspectives on the Role of the Early Embryo

2 위 글을 통해 추론할 수 있는 것으로 가장 적합한 것을 고르시오.

① The left-right organizer does not function in the embryonic period.
② According to the study in mice, twirling cilia enable organs to be built in the proper position.
③ In the case of even-toed mammals, twirling cilia help hearts grow in one side.
④ In the end, Reversade and Gordon found it difficult to identify the genes which break body symmetry.

13

Ⓐ The first brains appeared on earth about 500 million years ago, spent a leisurely 430 million years evolving into the brains of the earliest primates and another 70 million years evolving into the brains of the first protohumans. Then, something happened and the soon-to-be-human brain experienced an unprecedented growth spurt that more than doubled its mass in a little over two million years, transforming it from the one-and-a-quarter-pound brain of Homo habilis to the nearly three-pound brain of Homo sapiens. ❶

Ⓑ Now if you were put on a hot-fudge diet and managed to double your mass in a very short time, we would not expect all of your various body parts to share equally in the gain. ❷ Similarly, the dramatic increase in the size of the human brain did not democratically double the mass of every part so that modern people ended up with new brains that were structurally identical to the old ones, only bigger. Rather a disproportionate share of the growth centered on a particular part of the brain known as the frontal lobe. ❸

Ⓒ Scientists noticed that although patients with frontal lobe damage often performed well on standard intelligence tests, they showed severe impairment on any test that involved planning. They even found it practically impossible to say what they would do later that afternoon. ❹ This finding helps us assume that the frontal lobe is a time machine that allows each of us to vacate the present and experience the future before it happens. No other animals have a frontal lobe quite like ours, which is why we are the only animal that thinks about the future as we do. ❺ If the story of the frontal lobe tells us how people conjure their imaginary tomorrows, it doesn't tell us why.

1 Which of the following is the best title for the above passage?

① The Steady Evolution of the Human Brain
② The Importance of Brain Size
③ Amazing Human Brain Power Demystified
④ Future-Planning Brain Areas
⑤ Impact of Brain Damage on Time-Concept

2 Which of the following CANNOT be inferred from the passage?

① The size of the protohuman's brain is less than half the size of the human brain.
② It is still unknown what caused the rapid growth of the human brain.
③ The human brain has disproportionately evolved.
④ Patients with frontal lobe damage cannot understand how time proceeds.
⑤ The human brain is different from other brains not only in size but in structure.

3 The following sentence is removed from the passage. In which part may it be inserted to support the argument made by the author?

Your belly and buttocks would probably be the major recipients of newly acquired flab, while your tongue and toe would remain relatively svelte and unaffected.

① ❶
② ❷
③ ❸
④ ❹
⑤ ❺

4 Which of the following would most likely to be discussed after the above passage?
① Why we should study the human brain
② Why people should prepare for the unexpected future
③ Why animal brains work differently from human brains
④ Why the severly impaired frontal lobe cannot be easily treated
⑤ Why people think about the consequences of their actions in advance

14

　　For Darwin, and for several generations of biologists after him, evolution was conceived of as "descent with modification." Consider first "descent." According to this conception of evolution, evolution occurs only in lineages, which are populations of organisms that are related by descent. A population, in the biological sense, is a group of reproductively interacting organisms. As organisms in a population reproduce, they create a new generation, which itself reproductively interacts to spawn yet another generation of reproductively interacting organisms. This process creates a temporally extended sequence of populations, the later of which are descended from the earlier by reproduction, and such a temporal sequence of populations is a lineage. In a lineage, offspring tend to inherit their characteristics from their parents, so that offspring resemble their parents more than they resemble unrelated organisms in their lineage. "Descent," then, indicates a lineage of organisms that are characterized by hereditary similarity between parents and their offspring.

　　"Modification" refers to change across generations in the distribution of characteristics, or traits, in a lineage. A trait can be any one of an organism's observable properties, from an organ or bit of morphology to a form of behavior. As the organisms in a population reproduce to create a new generation, there may or may not be changes in the frequencies of traits from one generation to the next. If one generation of a human population is 65 percent brown-eyed, 25 percent green-eyed, and 10 percent blue-eyed, for example, and if the percentages of these eye colors are different in the next generation, then there has been "modification" of that lineage. Thus, for Darwin and several generations of biologists after him, evolution was change in the frequencies of hereditary characteristics across generations in a lineage. It is important to note that, according to this definition, evolution should not concern changes that individual organisms undergo during their lifetimes. Ⓐ_____, evolution should consist only in the changes across generations within a lineage in the frequencies of characteristics of organisms.

1 According to the passage above, a population in the biological sense is most appropriately defined as a group of organisms which _____.
① can interact with each other to produce offspring
② can undergo changes during their lifetime
③ can modify themselves to survive temporal sequences
④ can be related with any of other organisms

2 Which of the following is most appropriate for the blank Ⓐ?
① Rather　　　　　　　　② By the way
③ Nevertheless　　　　　④ However

3 Which of the following is least likely to be inferred from the passage above?

① Any observable property an organ has can be a target of evolutionary modification.
② Only changes which are found across generations in a lineage can be regarded as evolution.
③ Modification in a lineage is always helpful for organisms to adapt to the environment.
④ Hereditary similarity in a lineage of organisms is a result of recursive reproduction in a population.

4 Which of the following is most likely to follow the passage above?

① The difference between the conception of "descent" and "modification"
② Problems in the definition of evolution made by Darwin and his followers
③ The change of eye-colors across generations of various human populations
④ The reason why offspring sometimes do not resemble their parents

15

A Many interpreters argue that (1)<u>the most likely scenario</u> has wolf wannabe dogs Ⓐ<u>first taking advantage of the calorie bonanzas</u> provided by humans' waste dumps. By their opportunistic moves, those emergent dogs would be behaviorally and ultimately genetically adapted for reduced tolerance distances, less hair-trigger flight, puppy developmental timing with longer windows for cross-species socialization, and more confident parallel occupation of areas also occupied by dangerous humans.

B Studies of Russian fur foxes selected over many generations for differential tameness show many of the morphological and behavioral traits associated with domestication. These foxes might model the emergence of a kind of proto- "village dog," genetically close to wolves but Ⓑ<u>behaviorally quite different from and receptive to human attempts</u> to further the domestication process. Both by deliberate control of dogs' reproduction and by unintended but nonetheless potent consequences, humans could have contributed to shaping the many kinds of dogs that appeared early in the story. Human life ways changed significantly in association with dogs. Flexibility and opportunism are the name of the game for both species, who shape each other throughout the still ongoing story of co-evolution.

C Scholars use versions of this story to question sharp divisions of nature and culture in order to shape a more generative discourse for technoculture. Darcy Morey believes that the distinction between artificial and natural selection is empty because all the way down the story is about differential reproduction. Ed Russell, an environmental historian, argues that the evolution of dog breeds is a chapter in the history of biotechnology. He emphasizes human agencies and regards organisms as engineered technologies, but Ⓒ<u>in a way that has the dogs active</u>, as well as in a way to foreground the ongoing co-evolution of human cultures and dogs.

D Co-evolution has to be defined more broadly than Ⓓ<u>biologists habitually do</u>. Certainly, the mutual adaptation of visible morphologies like flower sexual structures and the organs of their pollinating insects is co-evolution. But it is a mistake to see the alterations of dogs' bodies and minds as biological and the changes in human bodies and lives as cultural, and so not about co-evolution. At the least, I suspect that human genomes contain a considerable molecular record of the pathogens of their companion species, including dogs. Immune systems are not a minor part of nature cultures; they determine Ⓔ<u>where organisms, including people, can live and with whom</u>. The history of the flu is unimaginable without the concept of the co-evolution of humans, pigs, fowl, and viruses.

1 Which of the following is the best title for the above passage?

① The Conflicted Evolutionary Theory of Dogs
② The Domestication of Animals and Its Influence on Culture
③ The Interaction Between Nature and Culture in Co-evolution
④ Immunity of Human Culture in Evolutionary Theory
⑤ Co-evolutionary Factors Alter Dogs' Biology

2 Choose the underlined phrase that must be changed for the sentence to be grammatically correct.

① Ⓐ first taking advantage of the calorie bonanzas
② Ⓑ behaviorally quite different from and receptive to human attempts
③ Ⓒ in a way that has the dogs active
④ Ⓓ biologists habitually do
⑤ Ⓔ where organisms, including people, can live and with whom

3 According to the passage, which of the following is NOT true?

① Disease is a matter not only of biology but of sociology.
② The weaning period of a wolf is shorter than that of a dog.
③ Domestication is an emergent process of co-habiting, involving agencies of many sorts.
④ Human genes have been altered by organisms causing disease in the companion species.
⑤ There is a dispute whether dogs are genetically closer to Russian fur foxes than to wolves.

4 Which of the following best explains the scenario in the underlined (1)<u>the most likely scenario</u> in paragraph Ⓐ?

① the best way to settle the dispute about dogs' origin
② the most interesting movie script about dogs
③ the most convincing story about the influence of biology on culture
④ the most useful ways to train the wolf into the dog
⑤ the most plausible story about how the dog first emerged

13

동물·식물

13 동물·식물

01

A 9-year study has uncovered some unusual behavior by common bottlenose dolphins living off the coast of Slovenia. Within one population of this species, the animals have divided into two groups that avoid contact by hunting at different times of day — a social strategy not known in marine mammals. Researchers used photographs of the dolphins' dorsal fins to individually identify them. They made many observations of 38 of the animals, carefully recording the time, date, and location of each sighting. The marine mammals divided into two major groups of 19 and 13 animals each, with six animals loosely making up a third group. The 19 members of the larger group tended to hang out — and likely hunt — while following fishing trawlers in the Bay of Trieste, which is located at the eastern top of Italy's "boot." The second group's cadre of 13 never associated with boats when in the Bay of Trieste. Although the dolphins hunted in the same area, they rarely saw each other, the researchers discovered, because the larger group was in that area only between 7 a.m. and 1 p.m. local time, whereas the smaller group showed up between 6 p.m. and 9 p.m. Other studies have documented groups of dolphins that divide up the waters where they hunt, but this is the first time these marine mammals have been shown to timeshare the sea. Although they don't know why — or how — the dolphins set these schedules, the fact that the animals are never in the same place likely diminishes unfriendly encounters and reduces direct competition for food.

1 위 글의 제목으로 가장 적합한 것을 고르시오.

① Predator's Intelligence: Threat to the Prey
② Dolphins' Timesharing with Peers in the Sea
③ Demystifying the Mistery of Dolphins' Training
④ The Repertoire of Dolphins' Problem-Shooting Skills

2 위 글을 통해 추론할 수 있는 것으로 가장 적합한 것을 고르시오.

① Bottlenose dolphins have found the communication strategies of recalling their habitats.
② There is intense and antagonistic tension between two dolphin groups.
③ Photos of the dolphins' dorsal fins help researchers recognize each dolphin.
④ Some bottlenose dolphins educated as a leader are able to tell the time.

02

Australia has seven species of stinging trees, the most painful of which is probably *Dendrocnide moroides*. This small shrub grows in light-filled clearings in rainforests and has leaves up to 50 cm wide. These leaves are covered in fine hairs, which make them look soft to the touch. When they come into contact with skin, however, they inject a painful toxin. This toxin takes effect immediately, reaching maximum intensity within half an hour, and persists for days or weeks. Rubbing or washing the affected area does little to relieve the stinging, as the hairs tend to be lodged in the skin. Just being in the Ⓐ_____ of these plants is hazardous, as they fill the air nearby with particles that can cause serious respiratory damage. Despite the potency of its toxin, the plant is consumed by several insect species and a marsupial called the red-legged pademelon.

1 Which of the following is most appropriate for blank Ⓐ?

① existence
② similarity
③ vicinity
④ appearance

2 How long does it take for the stinging to reach its peak?

① Less than half an hour
② Half an hour to an hour
③ A few hours to a full day
④ A few days to a few weeks

3 What should people probably do if they are stung by *Dendrocnide moroides*?

① Rub the affected area
② Apply pressure to the skin
③ Remove any remaining hairs
④ Wash the area around the sting

03

Professor Constantine Slobodchikoff and his colleagues have been decoding the communication system of prairie dogs, rodents not known for their smarts. And yet, Slobodchikoff's team has evidence that prairie dogs have a complex language, which they are starting to understand. When prairie dogs see a predator, they warn one another using high-pitched chirps. To the untrained ear, these chirps may all sound the same, but they are not. Slobodchikoff thinks the alarm calls are Ⓐ"Rosetta Stone" in decoding prairie-dog language, because they occur in a context people can understand, enabling interpretation. In his research, Slobodchikoff records the alarm calls and subsequent escape behaviors of prairie dogs in response to approaching predators. Then, when no predator is present, he plays back these recorded alarm calls and films the prairie dogs' escape responses. If the escape responses to the playback match those when the predator was present, this suggests that Ⓑ_____. And indeed, there seems to be. Slobodchikoff has discovered they have distinct calls pertaining to different predators. The calls even specify the color, size, and shape of the predator.

1 Which of the following is the main theme of the passage?

① Scientists began to understand the language of prairie dogs.
② Scientists observed prairie dogs' peculiar escape behavior.
③ Prairie dog language is structurally comparable to human language.
④ Prairie dogs have an elaborate system of conveying diverse emotions.

2 What motivates Slobodchikoff to liken the calls to Ⓐ?

① Presence of interpretive clues
② Absence of concrete data in the past
③ Restrictive nature of the call vocalization
④ Historical significance in language science

3 Which of the following best fits into Ⓑ?

① their escape responses exhibit great variation
② encoded information is beyond comprehension
③ meaningful information is encoded in the calls
④ their responses are biologically programmed reflexes

04

The sharks considered dangerous to man have to be divided into two classes, the known man-eaters and the reputed man-eaters. The known man-eating species of shark are few. Of these, the white shark is the most ferocious and dangerous known to man. Often called by Australians the white pointer, this shark is also known throughout the rest of the world under a variety of names which include the white death, the great white shark, the grey shark, the grey death, and the grey pointer. Without a doubt this is the most terrible monster the seas have produced in recent times. It has been recorded to be a length of almost 40 feet, with a specimen of 39 feet being captured off the Hawaiian Islands in the late 1930s, and another estimated at 36 feet in length at Port Fairy in Victoria. Such an animal must have weighed several tons or more. The white shark is found in every ocean and sea of the world. It is most prolific in cooler waters, although still common and often encountered in tropical and semitropical regions.

Since men first took to the sea in ships, the white shark has been known and feared, instilling terror into the _____ of sailors. Perhaps the "ghostly" white appearance of this huge shark has earned it its evil reputation, for there is something unreal and sinister about the great beast. The white shark has been known to follow sailing vessels for days, even weeks, gliding silently near the keel or close to the stern, watching and waiting. It has been recorded in the old sailing days that the hungry monster has reached out of the ocean to snatch some helpless seaman from the side of his becalmed ship.

1 According to the passage, which is true?

① Sharks can be classified into three groups based on the degree of danger.
② Australians often call the white shark the great grey shark.
③ White sharks are usually observed in Australia, the Hawaiian Islands, and Canada.
④ The white shark is more commonly found in temperate zones than in hot areas.

2 Which is the most appropriate for the blank?

① silliest
② tallest
③ warmest
④ hardiest

05

Plants can detect competing plants through various cues, such as the reduction in light quantity or in the ratio of red to far-red wavelengths (R:FR), which occurs when light is filtered through leaves. Such competition cues induce three types of avoidance responses: plants try to outgrow and shade their neighbors; plants become shade-tolerant, adapting to perform better under limited light conditions; or they grow sideways, away from their neighbors. But can plants choose among these responses and match them to the relative size and density of their competitors? To answer this question, researchers used an experimental setup that simulated different light-competition settings. They used vertical stripes of transparent green filters that mimic competing plants in that they reduce both light quantity and R:FR. By changing both the height and density of this simulated vegetation, the researchers could present different light-competition scenarios to the plants. The results demonstrated that plants can indeed choose to respond to competition in an optimal way. When the simulated competitors were short and densely packed, plants showed the highest vertical growth. However, under tall, well-spaced-out neighbors, plants grew the farthest sideways. Lastly, under simulated tall and densely-packed neighbors, which could not be outgrown vertically or laterally, plants displayed the highest shade tolerance behavior. The findings of this study reveal that Ⓐplants can evaluate the density and competitive ability of their neighbors and tailor their responses accordingly.

1 According to the passage, which of the following is true?

① Shade tolerance allows plants to grow sideways, away from their competitors.
② Red to far-red wavelength ratio appears when plants are intolerant of their neighbors.
③ Green filters can be successfully used to simulate neighboring vegetation.
④ Plants can choose to grow vertically but not horizontally.

2 According to the passage, which of the following is NOT an example of a plant's avoidance response?

① Trying to grow higher than tall, densely-packed competitors
② Growing sideways when its competitors are tall and spread out
③ Improving shade tolerance when it cannot outgrow its competitors
④ Increasing height when the competitors are short and growing close together

3 Which of the following can be inferred from Ⓐ?

① Plants can miscalculate their competitors' ability but still survive.
② We need to examine the density and height of neighboring vegetation when we plant.
③ Plants can analyze their situation and select the best course of action.
④ A plant's ability to compete has a limited effect on how it responds to competition.

06

Conflict is seen in all socially living animals, occurring over scarce resources such as food, space, or mates. But in the late 20th century, our view of animal conflict changed. In the older view, threats and other aggressive displays were held to reduce actual violence by spacing individuals and arranging them in a stable hierarchy, and field research seemed to support this view. Only humans, it was said, kill our own kind, because weapons distance us from our victims, making submissive displays and other natural restraints on violence ineffective.

We now know this is false. It persisted in part because of lack of opportunity to observe animal killings. If a baboon* troop had the same violent death rate as humans do, it could take centuries to observe even a single killing. But as field observations accumulated, deadly violence was seen in many species.

An example is competitive infanticide, first studied in Hanuman langurs.* At the core of langur groups are female relatives and their young; males may stay for a year or more but are ultimately transient. At some point new males appear, drive off the previous ones, and take their places. They soon kill all infants below six months of age; females resist for a time, but without success, and they soon become fertile again and mate with the new males. Various forms of competitive infanticide were described in chimpanzees, lions, wild dogs, and many other species.

* baboon, langur: 원숭이의 일종

1 Which of the following does the passage mainly discuss?
① human cruelty
② natural selection
③ animal violence
④ interracial struggle

2 What was the finding in the late 20th century?
① That it is only humans that kill their own kind.
② That threats reduce actual violence among animals.
③ That weapons make submissive displays ineffective.
④ That conflict among animals may involve killing.

3 According to the passage, which of the following is true?
① Unlike many other animals, baboons never kill each other.
② Male chimpanzees were seen to kill infants of other males.
③ Male langur relatives constitute the core of langur groups.
④ Female langurs will probably kill the males that commit infanticide.

07

It's a sound you will probably never hear, a sickened tree sending out a distress signal. But a group of scientists has heard the cries, and they think some insects also hear the trees and are drawn to them like vultures to a dying animal. Researchers with the U.S. Department of Agriculture's Forest Service fastened sensors to the bark of parched trees and clearly heard distress calls. According to one of the scientists, most drought-stricken trees transmit their torment in the 50- to 500-kilohertz range. The unaided human ear can detect no more than 20 kilohertz. Red oak, maple, white pine, and birch all make sightly different sounds in the form of vibrations at the surface of the wood.

The scientists think that the vibrations are created when the water columns inside tubes that run the length of the tree break, a result of too little water flowing through them. These fractured columns send out distinctive vibration patterns. Because some insects communicate at ultrasonic frequencies, they may pick up the trees' vibrations and attack the weakened trees. Researchers are now running tests with potted trees that have been deprived of water to see if the sound is what attracts the insects. "Water-stressed trees also smell differently from other trees, and they experience thermal changes, so insects could be responding to something other than sound," one scientist said.

1 Which of the following could be considered a cause of the trees' distress signal?

① torn roots
② attacks by insects
③ lack of water
④ formation of water columns

2 It can be inferred from the passage that the sounds produced by the trees _____.

① serve as a form of communication with other trees
② cannot be heard by the unaided human ear
③ are the same no matter what type of tree produces them
④ fall into the 1-20 kilohertz range

3 Which of the following is closest in meaning to the underlined word?

① agony   ② circumstance
③ requisite   ④ beckon

4 Which of the following is NOT mentioned as a possible factor in drawing insects to weakened trees?

① thermal change
② change in color
③ sound
④ smell

08

The cosmos is one of a genus of tropical herbs, numbering about twenty species. It is a tall, graceful, late-flowering annual or perennial, of many different varieties and feathery foliage. The word "cosmos" is derived from the Greek term, *kosmos*, and signifies "an ornament or beautiful thing." And after seeing the lovely graceful cosmos in bloom, one feels that this flower has indeed been rightly named. It is native to tropical and semitropical America. Its American ancestors are said to have come from the warmer uplands of Mexico. The early kinds grown in the U.S. could not stand cold, for the cosmos glories in the sun. Often frost killed the plants before their seeds had ripened. However, new ones have been developed that now make the cosmos a fall as well as a summer flower.

The fact that cosmos flowers late, when many other plants have completed their work, makes it of more value to gardeners and flower lovers. For it truly comes into its own at the first frosts. This late, aster-like blossom, with its filmy leaves, not only is most attractive in garden beds or against walls but the cut flowers make beautiful bouquets for indoor decorations.

The most commonly cultivated type in the U.S. may grow to heights of from 7 to 10 feet, though some are not so tall. It has smooth stems, and its brightly rayed, showy flowers have yellow disks. The rays are in a variety of colors including white, pink, red, purple, shell, yellow, orange — in fact, almost any hue except blue. The early primitive kinds had flowers only about an inch across. But various breeders have worked with this desirable plant, and have in some cases shortened the stems and increased the size of the blooms, some of which grow singly, others in clusters.

1 Choose the one closest in meaning to the underlined part.

① the cosmos grows better at the time of the first frost
② the first frosts are not conducive in making the cosmos grow
③ when the first frosts come, the cosmos blooms to its fullest
④ the cosmos has developed skills to cope with frosts on its own

2 Which of the following CANNOT be inferred about the "cosmos"?

① It was originally a fall flower but now has developed into a summer one.
② Some types live for a few growing seasons.
③ The meanings of its name seems to suit the flowers well.
④ The origins of the ones found in the U.S. can be traced to Mexico.

3 According to the passage, which aspect is associated with why the cosmos is valued?

① It lasts a longer time than other kinds of cut flowers.
② It is a rare flower that cannot be found in warmer climates.
③ It is easy to cultivate since it does not need much water to grow.
④ It is pleasing to look at when planted in garden beds.

4 According to the passage, which of the following is NOT true about the appearance of the cosmos?

① Not all blooms are found in clusters.
② The color of the rays varies widely but does not include blue.
③ The average height is 7–10 feet with some types growing taller.
④ The stems are smooth and all flowers have yellow disks.

09

Komodo dragons have lived on some of Indonesia's islands for thousands of years. One story tells that the Komodo dragon was first discovered during World War I, when an airplane crash landed in the waters around Komodo Island. The story tells how the pilot swam to the island, where he was surrounded by terrifying, huge lizards. It sounds like something out of an action movie; however, the story is actually a myth. We don't know exactly when Komodo dragons were first discovered, but the existence of the Komodo dragon was confirmed in 1926. This was the year that the explorer Douglas Burden led an expedition to Komodo. He was working for the American Museum of Natural History. He returned from his trip with twelve dead specimens and two living Komodo dragons.

The Komodo dragon is the largest living lizard in the world. Some Komodo dragons can be 3m long and can weigh more than 130kg. This means that Komodo dragons are the heaviest lizards on Earth. They have long heads with short snouts, scaly skin, short legs, and big, strong tails. The largest dragon ever found was 3.13m long and weighed 166kg! Komodo dragons are the top predators on the islands where they live. They will eat nearly anything, including carrion, smaller dragons, wild horses and pigs, large water buffalo and sometimes unlucky humans! Although the Komodo dragon can run briefly at 20km per hour, the reptiles usually hunt using camouflage and patience. They can spend hours in one place, waiting for their prey. When their unfortunate victim passes, the dragons attack and rip it to pieces. Their saliva has more than fifty types of bacteria. If the prey animal is bitten and escapes, it usually dies of blood poisoning quite quickly. If this happens, the dragons follow and locate the dead or dying animal by using their excellent sense of smell. Many large carnivores, such as tigers, do not eat 25 to 30 per cent of their prey. They leave the stomach, hide, bones, and feet. However, Komodo dragons are less wasteful and leave only about 12 per cent of their prey. They eat bones, feet, fur and skin — they even eat the stomach! A Komodo dragon can eat 80 per cent of its own body weight. However, when they feel scared or nervous, Komodo dragons can throw up the contents of their stomachs. This makes them lighter so they can escape more easily.

1 The existence of Komodo dragons was known to the world by _____.

① a pilot who swam to Komodo Island after his plane crashed in the waters
② an expedition team leader from the American Museum of Natural History
③ a rescue team who went to search for a missing pilot in Komodo Island
④ a fisherman who captured a huge lizard in Komodo Island

2 Which of the following is a characteristic of Komodo dragons?

① Komodo dragons can run fast for long.
② Komodo dragons are wasteful of their food.
③ Komodo dragons can vomit when they need to.
④ Komodo dragons do not eat dead animals.

3 How does a Komodo dragon find its prey that is bitten and escapes?

① By tracing the prey's blood drops
② By following the dying prey's smell
③ By waiting in camouflage for the prey to die
④ By dropping its own saliva on the prey's way

10

A Though red squirrels are a solitary and territorial species, a 22-year study of these squirrels in the Yukon suggests that they have a higher chance of survival and a greater number of offspring Ⓐwhen living near the same neighbors year after year. ❶ These benefits were even more pronounced in older squirrels, who the data suggested could sharply offset the effects of aging by maintaining all of their neighbors from one year to the next. ❷

B "Red squirrels live on their individual territory, and they rarely come into physical contact with one another, but Ⓑgiven the value of familiar neighbors, our study raises this really interesting possibility that they might cooperate with their competitors," says first author Erin Siracusa, a postdoctoral researcher at the University of Exeter. ❸ "What this cooperation looks like, whether it's sharing of food resources, or actively alarm-calling to warn their neighbors of predators, or potentially even forming coalitions to protect the neighboring territories from usurpers, we don't know. But I would argue Ⓒbased on our findings that despite their solitary nature, red squirrels do engage in social interactions and can have important social relationships." ❹

C While it's known that social relationships play a key role for animals that live in groups, Siracusa was interested in learning how social relationships affect solitary, territorial species — who rarely physically interact with their own kind. ❺

D Siracusa had previously observed that red squirrels with stable social relationships — established in part through defensive calls known as "rattles" that the squirrels make to identify themselves — were less likely to intrude on each other's territories and pilfer each other's cache. "Once they live next to each other long enough to agree on these territory boundaries, they sort of enter into this gentleman's agreement, saying, 'Okay, we've established these territory boundaries. We know where they are. We're not going to waste our time and energy Ⓓto fight over these boundaries anymore,'" she says. This reduced aggression in familiar neighbors, known as the "dear enemy" phenomenon, has been established in many species previously, but researchers Ⓔhaven't been able to easily tie the phenomenon to a fitness advantage.

1 Which of the following would be the best summary of the research findings in the above passage?

① The benefits of the familiarity among older squirrels were more pronounced.
② Territorial red squirrels live longer when they are friendly with their usurpers.
③ The red squirrels establish boundaries to reduce aggression in familiar neighbors.
④ The red squirrels developed a mechanism that works to minimize the costs of territoriality.
⑤ The longer the red squirrels lived near each other, the more likely they were to survive into the next year and produce more offspring.

2 According to the above passage, which of the following is NOT true about the red squirrels?

① They are a solitary and territorial species.
② They rarely come into physical contact with their kind.
③ They form coalitions with new comers to protect their territories.
④ They are in social relationships with their neighbors.
⑤ They use rattle calls to protect their boundaries.

3 The following sentence is removed from the passage. In which part may it be inserted to support the argument made by the author?

Surprisingly, the findings show that it didn't matter whether the squirrels' neighbors were related to them; these fitness benefits instead depended on familiarity, or the length of time the same squirrels lived next to each other.

① ❶
② ❷
③ ❸
④ ❹
⑤ ❺

4 Choose the underlined word or phrase that must be changed for the sentence to be correct.

① Ⓐ when living
② Ⓑ given the value of familiar neighbors
③ Ⓒ based on our findings
④ Ⓓ to fight over these boundaries
⑤ Ⓔ haven't been able to

해설편

01 역사·인물

01 2018 한국외대

미국인들은 오랫동안 7월 4일에 독립기념일을 기념해왔지만, 엄밀히 말하면 그 날은 식민지 주들이 표결하여 새로운 국가가 된 날이 아니다. 그 기념일은 원래는 1776년 7월 2일인데, 이날은 대륙회의(미국 독립 혁명 당시 미국 13개 식민지의 대표자 회의)가 영국으로부터 독립을 선언하는 결의안을 승인한 날일 뿐 아니라, 존 애덤스(John Adams)가 '화려한 퍼레이드'가 열리는 위대한 기념일로서 다음 세대에 의해 기념될 것이라고 쓴 날이기도 했다. 아니, 무슨 일이 있었는가? 한마디로 말해서, 서류 처리 문제가 있었다. 미국 독립 혁명 박물관의 수석 역사학자인 필립 미드(Philip Mead)에 따르면, 대륙회의에 참석한 대의원들이 왜 실제로 했던 그 방식으로 투표했는지를 설명하는 보도 자료를 대륙회의가 승인하는 데 이틀이 걸렸다고 한다. 미국 독립 선언서로 더 잘 알려진 그 문서는 1776년 7월 4일에 인쇄소에 도착했고 이러한 이유로 독립 선언서의 상단에는 그 날짜(7월 4일)가 표시돼 있다. 그러나 애덤스는 미국인들이 7월 4일을 기념하는 것을 보고 놀랄지 모르겠지만, 그는 그 날짜 변경에 한 몫을 했다. 그와 토머스 제퍼슨(Thomas Jefferson) 둘 모두 1826년 7월 4일에 사망했을 때, 그 날은 미국인의 기억 속에 더욱 고이 간직되었다.

technically ad. 엄밀히 따지면[말하면]
honor n. 명예, 영예, 영광; 서훈(敍勳); 의례, 의식
resolution n. 결의안
declare v. 선언하다, 공표하다
succeeding a. 계속되는, 잇따른, 다음의
pomp n. (공식 행사·의식의) 장관, 화려함
approve v. 승인하다
press release 보도 자료, 대언론 공식 발표
delegate n. 대리인, 대의원
shift n. 변화

1 ④ ▶ 빈칸완성
미국의 독립기념일은 원래는 7월 2일이었지만, 7월 4일에 기념을 하게 된 이유에 대해 설명하는 글인데, 마지막 문장에서 존 애덤스와 토머스 제퍼슨도 7월 4일에 사망했다고 했으므로 미국 역사에서 7월 4일은 뜻깊은 날이라고 볼 수 있다. 따라서 빈칸에는 '소중히 하다', '(마음속에) 간직하다'라는 의미의 ④ enshrined가 적절하다. ① 즐겁게 하다 ② 추정하다 ③ 교묘히 피하다

2 ③ ▶ 내용일치
두 번째 문장에서 독립기념일은 원래는 1776년 7월 2일이었으며, 존 애덤스는 "이날이 '화려한 퍼레이드'가 열리는 위대한 기념일로서 다음 세대에 의해 기념될 날이다."라고 했으므로, 존 애덤스는 독립기념일을 7월 2일에 기리기를 희망했다고 볼 수 있다. 따라서 ③이 정답이다.

02 2019 인하대

켈트족은 최초의 인도-유럽 어족의 영국 점령자들이었다. 영국 남부의 켈트족들은 로마인들에 의해 처음으로 정복되었고, 그 후로는 그들의 지배와 보호를 받았다. 기원전 55-54년에 있었던 줄리어스 시저(Julius Caesar)의 초기 침략 시도는 로마 제국의 다른 곳, 특히 갈리아(이곳에서는 시저의 군대가 사용하던 라틴어가 결국 현대의 프랑스어가 되었다.)에서의 결과와는 달리 점령으로 이어지진 않았다. 로마인들의 침략이 보다 항구적인 점령과 군사적 통제로 이어진 것은 (서기 43년부터 시작된) 클라우디우스(Claudius) 황제의 통치 기간 동안이었다. 그 후 약 400년 동안 영국은 로마 제국의 속주(屬州)가 되었다. 그러나 5세기 초 무렵, 저 동떨어진 곳에 위치한 영토에 점령군을 유지하는 것이 로마인들에게 비용 면에서 매우 부담스럽게 되었는데, 이는 로마인들이 유럽대륙에서 게르만족의 공격에 끊임없이 시달리고 있었기 때문이다. 그 후에 일어난 사건들을 아주 간략하게 설명하자면, 로마인들이 철수하여 서기 410년에 모두 사라졌을 때, 영국 남부의 켈트족들은 상대적으로 무방비 상태에 있었다. 그때 그들은 북유럽으로부터 게르만 용병들을 끌어들여 북유럽과 아일랜드의 켈트족(스코틀랜드족과 픽트족)의 침략으로부터 뿐만 아니라 바이킹들의 침략으로부터 그들을 보호하도록 했다.

occupant n. 점유자, 점거자
subdue v. 정복하다; 위압하다, 압도하다
thereafter ad. 그 후, 그 이래로
rule v. 다스리다, 통치하다
shelter v. 숨기다, 감추다; 비호하다, 보호하다
invasion n. 침입, 침략
occupation n. 점유, 점령; 직업
legion n. (고대 로마의) 군단; 군대
emperor n. 황제
permanent a. 영속적인; 불변의
province n. 지방, 지역; 속주(屬州, 고대 로마의 지배를 받던 국외의 토지)
outlying a. 중심을 떠난; 동떨어진; 외진

1 ③ ▶ 내용일치
"로마인들의 침략이 보다 항구적인 점령과 군사적 통제로 이어진 것은 클라우디우스(Claudius) 황제의 통치 기간 동안이었으며, 그 후 약 400년 동안 영국은 로마 제국의 속주(屬州)가 되었다."라고 돼 있으므로, ③이 본문의 내용과 일치하는 진술이다. ① 켈트족이 먼저 왔고, 이후에 그곳에 온 로마인들의 지배를 받았다. ② 줄리어스 시저의 침략이 점령으로 이어지지는 않았다. ④ 본토와 멀리 떨어져 있는 영국에 군대를 주둔시키는 비용이 부담되어 스스로 철수한 것이다. ⑤ 게르만 용병의 보호 대상은 영국 남부에 있던 켈트족이었다.

2 ① ▶ 지시대상
로마인들이 점령하고 있으나 섬인 까닭에 유럽 대륙에 위치한 로마제국과 멀리 떨어져 있는 '영국'을 가리키고 있다.

territory n. 영토, 영지; 속령
costly a. 값이 비싼, 비용이 많이 드는
constantly ad. 항상; 변함없이
be subjected to ~을 당하다
tribe n. 부족, 종족
the Continent <영국 제도와 구별하여> 유럽 대륙
simplify v. 단순화하다, 간단하게 하다
pull out 철수하다, 빠져나가다
defenseless a. 무방비의; 방어할 수 없는
mercenary n. 용병

03 2022 덕성여대

그가 그 후 12개월 동안 그린 그림들 — 꽃이 피어오르는 과일 나무, 마을과 주변의 경치, 자화상, 우체부 룰랭(Roulin)과 다른 친구들의 초상화, 집의 내부와 외부, 해바라기, 그리고 풍경들을 묘사한 그림들 — 은 그의 첫 번째 위대한 시기의 특징이었다. 이 작품들에서 그는 인물이나 풍경의 외부적, 시각적 측면을 중시하려고 노력했지만, 그림의 소재에 대한 자신의 감정을 억누를 수 없었고, 그 감정은 뚜렷한 윤곽과 강화된 색채의 효과로 나타났다. 그가 숙달하려고 열심히 노력했던 전통적 회화 기법에서 벗어나기를 한때 주저하기도 했지만, 이제 그는 자신의 개성을 자유롭게 발휘했고 캔버스에 직접 유화 물감을 짜기 시작했다. 반 고흐(Van Gogh)의 스타일은 무의식적이고 본능적이었다. 왜냐하면 그는 어떤 효과나 분위기가 자신을 사로잡고 있는 동안 그것을 포착하기로 결심하고서 엄청난 속도와 강도로 그려냈기 때문이다.

1 ① ▶ 빈칸완성
과거 한때의 상황과 지금의 상황이 대조를 이루어야 한다. 지금 개성 있는 그림을 그리고 있다는 것은 과거에는 그렇지 못했다는 것이고, 이는 전통에서 벗어나지 않으려 했다는 말로 바꿔 표현할 수 있으므로, 빈칸에는 ①이 들어가는 것이 가장 적절하다. ② ~을 고수하다 ③ ~을 뒤따라가다 ④ 다시 찾아가다

2 ③ ▶ 부분이해
give free rein은 '완전한 자유를 주다'라는 의미이므로, 예술가에게 해방감을 느끼게 해주었을 것으로 볼 수 있다. ① 부주의 ② 거리낌 ④ 속박

3 ① ▶ 내용일치
그가 그림의 소재로 삼았던 대상, 즉 나무, 마을, 친구, 집의 안팎, 해바라기, 풍경 등은 그의 감정과는 무관하고 그가 단순히 자신 주변에 있는 것들을 그려냈음을 의미한다. 따라서 ①이 정답으로 적절하다. ③ "그는 인물이나 풍경의 외부적, 시각적 측면을 중시하려고 노력했지만, 그림의 소재에 대한 자신의 감정을 억누를 수 없었고, 그 감정은 뚜렷한 윤곽과 강화된 색채의 효과로 나타났다."를 통해 옳은 진술임을 알 수 있다.

depict v. 그리다; 묘사하다
blossom n. 꽃이 피다
self-portrait n. 자화상
portrait n. 초상화
interior n. 내부
exterior n. 외부
landscape n. 풍경, 경치
strive v. 노력하다
suppress v. 억압하다, 억누르다
subject n. 주제; (그림·사진 등의) 대상[소재]
emphatic a. 강조하는; 뚜렷한, 눈에 띄는
contour n. 윤곽, 윤곽의 미
heighten v. (효과·속도·인기 따위를) 더하다, 강화시키다, 증대[증가]시키다
hesitant a. 머뭇거리는, 주저하는
give free rein 완전한 자유를 주다
individuality n. 개성
squeeze v. 압착하다, 짜다
spontaneous a. 자발적인; 무의식적인
instinctive a. 본능적인, 직감적인
intensity n. 강함, 격렬함; (빛 등의) 강도[세기]
determine v. 결심시키다; 결정하다
possess v. 소유하다; ~의 마음을 사로잡다

04 2021 한국외대

나이지리아(Nigeria)와 카메룬(Cameroon)은 서아프리카에 위치해 있다. 북쪽의 차드(Chad) 호수에서 남쪽의 바카시(Bakassi) 반도에 이르는, 양국이 공유하고 있는 2,400km의 국경은 두 국가 사이에 끊임없는 분쟁의 원인이었다. 식민지 건설에서 발생한 이 국경 분쟁은 식민지 열강이었던 영국과 독일 사이의 수많은 조약들의 결과인데, 그 조약들은 그 어떤 아프리카인도 참석하지 않았

shared a. 공유하는
dispute n. 논쟁, 분규, 분쟁
treaty n. 조약

던 1884-1885년의 베를린 회담에서 그 적법성을 얻어낸 조약이었다. 나이지리아인들은 바카시 반도가 나이지리아의 안보와 경제적 이익(어업과 석유), 그리고 지전략적(地戰略的) 이익에 매우 중요하다고 생각하고 있으며, 또한 1913년 영국과 독일의 협정 체결 이전에는 그 반도가 순전히 나이지리아 영토의 일부였다고 생각한다. 1913년 협정에 따라 나이지리아-카메룬 국경이 나이지리아 쪽으로 옮겨졌고 그래서 바카시 반도가 카메룬에게로 넘어갔다는 것이다. 그러나 1913년 이후의 사태 진전으로 인해 바카시 반도는 나이지리아로 다시 되돌아갔고, 나이지리아가 계속 통치한 상태에서 나이지리아 내전(1967-1970)에 이르렀고, 이 내전이 발발할 때 카메룬이 바카시 반도에 대한 소유권을 주장했다. 결국, 2002년에 카메룬은 이 사건을 국제사법재판소에 회부했고, 국제사법재판소는 오로지 1913년 영국과 독일 협정에만 근거하고 그 이전의 역사나 그 후의 여러 조치들은 무시한 채 국경을 결정시켰으며, 바카시 반도에 대한 통치를 카메룬에게 배정했다.

colonial powers 식민지 열강들
legality n. 적법성, 합법성
critical a. 중요한
development n. 발전; 새로 전개된 사건
revert v. (본래 상태·습관·신앙으로) 되돌아가다
governance n. 통치, 관리
lay claim 권리를 주장하다
take a case to court 사건을 재판에 부치다
eventually ad. 결국
solely ad. 오로지
prior a. 이전의
subsequent a. 그다음의
assign v. 맡기다, 배정하다

1 ③   ▶ 글의 주제
   나이지리아와 카메룬의 국경 분쟁과 그 배경에 대한 내용이므로, 주제로 적절한 것은 ③이다.

2 ③   ▶ 내용일치
   나이지리아와 카메룬의 국경분쟁이 영국과 독일이 맺은 여러 조약들의 결과라고 했고, 이 조약들은 아프리카인이 하나도 참석하지 않은 회담에서 그 적법성을 얻었다고 했으며, 국경을 옮긴 1913년 협정도 영국과 독일이 체결한 것이었다고 했으므로, 결국 두 나라 사이의 국경은 유럽인들에 의해 정해졌다고 할 수 있다. 따라서 ③이 옳은 진술이다. ④ 국경이 나이지리아 쪽으로 옮겼다는 것은 나이지리아의 영토가 줄어들어 나이지리아에게는 불리하게 됐다는 것을 의미한다.

---

05   2019 숭실대

안드레스 세고비아 토레스(Andrés Segovia Torres)는 스페인 리나레스 출신의 클래식 기타의 거장이었다. 오늘날 전문 클래식 기타리스트로 활동하는 많은 사람들은 세고비아의 문하생이었거나 그의 문하생들의 문하생이었다. 세고비아가 현대 낭만주의 연주 목록에 기여한 것은 그의 작품들 뿐만 아니라 고전이나 바로크 작품을 자신의 방식대로 편곡한 것도 포함되었다. 그는 표현력이 풍부한 연주로 명성이 높은데, 그의 넓은 음색과 독특한 음악성, 표현, 스타일이 그것이다.
세고비아의 첫 번째 대중공연은 1909년에 16세의 나이에 그라나다에서 있었다. 몇 년 후에 그는 마드리드에서 프로페셔널 연주가로서의 첫 콘서트를 열었는데, 이 콘서트에는 프란시스코 타레가(Francisco Tárrega)의 작품과 J.S. 바흐(J.S. Bach)의 작품을 기타로 편곡한 작품이 포함되어 있었다. 그가 변호사가 되길 원했던 가족의 제지와 그의 특이한 연주 기법에 대한 타레가의 일부 문하생들의 비판에도 불구하고, 그는 기타 공부를 부지런히 계속했다.
그는 1912년에 마드리드에서, 1915년은 파리음악원에서, 1916년은 바르셀로나에서 다시 연주를 했고, 그리고 1919년에는 남아메리카에서 성공적인 순회 연주를 했다. 국제적인 무대에서의 세고비아의 등장은 콘서트 악기로서 기타의 운명이 주로 미구엘 료벳(Miguel Llobet)의 노력으로 되살아나던 시기와 동시에 일어났다. 이러한 변화하는 환경에서, 세고비아는 녹음과 방송의 발전과 더불어 그의 성격적인 장점과 예술가적 기교 덕분에 기타를 다시 더 대중적으로 만드는 데 성공했다.
세고비아는 생각을 불러일으키고 해석을 깊이 있게 할 수 있는 본격적인 연주회용 악기로서의 품위를 기타에 부여하는 데 촉매적인 역할을 한 인물로 여겨진다. 그때까지 기타를 듣기에는 좋지만 단지 제한된 실내 악기로만 생각했던 통찰력 있는 음악 애호가들 앞에서, 그는 클래식 기타를 정당한 연주회용 악기로 품격을 높였다는 평을 받고 있다.

virtuoso n. (음악 분야에서) 거장, 명인 a. 고도의 기교를 보여 주는
repertoire n. 레퍼토리, 상연 목록, 연주 곡목
commission n. (주문 제작된) 작품, 제작물
transcription n. 편곡, 녹음
be renowned for ~로 명성이 높다
palette n. 색채의 범위[종류]
distinctive a. 독특한, 특색 있는
phrasing n. 프레이징(선율을 작은악절(phrase)로 구분하기); 구절법
discouragement n. 낙심, 좌절
pupil n. 학생, 문하생, 제자
idiosyncratic a. 특유의, 특이한
pursue v. 추구하다; 밀고 나가다
diligently ad. 부지런히, 열심히, 애써
coincide v. 동시에 일어나다
fortune n. 운, 운명, 미래
milieu n. 주위, 환경
strength n. 장점, 이점
artistry n. 예술적 수완[재능, 효과]
succeed in ~에 성공하다
catalytic a. 촉매(觸媒) 작용의, 접촉 반응의
grant v. 주다, 수여하다

1 ④   ▶ 내용파악
   세고비아는 16살에 첫 번째 대중공연을 그라나다에서 했고, 1912년 마드리드, 1915년 파리음악원, 1916년 바르셀로나 공연에 이어, 1919년 남미투어를 성공적으로 마쳤다고 했다. 따라서 그의 경력은 그라나다 공연과 함께 시작되었다고 볼 수 있다. ④가 정답이다.

2 ④　▶ 내용일치
마지막 단락에서 세고비아는 클래식 기타를 본격적인 연주회용 악기로 품격을 높였다고 했으므로 ④가 이 글의 내용과 일치한다.

respectability n. 존경할 만함, 훌륭함
evocativeness n. 불러일으킴; 생각나게 함
dignify v. 위엄[품위] 있어 보이게 하다
discerning a. 통찰[식별]력이 있는, 명민한
hitherto ad. 지금까지; 그때까지
sonorous a. 듣기 좋은, 낭랑한
parlor a. 실내의; 말뿐인, 겉으로만의

06　2021 인하대

1665년 7월 25일, 영국 케임브리지(Cambridge) 성 삼위일체 교구의 존 몰리(John Morley)라는 5살짜리 소년이 자택에서 죽은 채 발견되었다. 마을 관리들이 그의 시체를 검시했을 때, 그의 가슴에 있는 검은 반점에 주목했는데, 이 반점은 흑사병의 명백한 특징이었다. 거의 곧바로, 마을주민들은 서둘러 스스로를 시골지역에 격리시켰다. 이렇게 흑사병을 피해 달아난 사람들 중에는 아이작 뉴턴(Isaac Newton)이라는 케임브리지 대학교 트리니티 칼리지의 젊은 학생도 있었다. 뉴턴의 집은 울즈소프(Woolsthorpe)라 불리는 농장이었는데, 이 농장은 케임브리지 대학교로부터 북쪽으로 60마일 가량 떨어진 곳에 있었다. 그 농장은 가장 가까운 도시에서 적당히 떨어져 있었는데, 그 곳에서 거의 완전히 고독한 상태로, 그는 미적분학을 발명했고, 운동학을 만들어냈으며, 중력을 밝혀내는 등의 업적을 이루었다. 흑사병이 현대 과학이 만들어지는 환경을 조성해주었다. 아니 사람들의 말로는 그렇다.

그 농장에서 머물렀던 거의 2년 동안, 뉴턴은 놀라운 결과물을 믿기 힘들 정도로 많이 만들어냈다. 그는 수학이라는 매우 중요한 영역 전체에 걸쳐 주요한 새로운 통찰을 형성했고, 새로운 물리학을 만들어냈다. 그는 중력을 측정하는 실험을 실시한 다음, 그의 가장 유명한 개념인 만유인력을 구체화하기 시작했다.

그러나 사실과 다른 것은 흑사병이 뉴턴에게 고독이라는 선물을 안겨주자, 뉴턴이 이들 문제에 몰두하게 되었다는 것이다. 뉴턴에 대한 최고의 전기 작가인 리처드 웨스트폴(Richard Westfall)이 꼼꼼하게 기록한 것처럼, 흑사병이 발병하기 전 1년 동안 뉴턴은 트리니티 칼리지에 있는 그의 방에서 여전히 시험공부를 하면서, 과학에서 가장 시급한 문제들에 대해 생각하기 시작했다. 흑사병이 발병하기 전 해인 1664년에 뉴턴은 처음으로 수학에 대해 깊이 생각하기 시작했다. 강제 격리 기간 동안, 그리고 이 기간 전후로, 무엇이 뉴턴으로 하여금 천재적인 연구들을 방대하게 해낼 수 있게 했든 간에, 시골에서의 칩거가 그 자체로 결정적인 차이일 수는 없었을 것이다. 뉴턴 자신도 그 정도의 말은 했다. 어떻게 중력을 이해하게 되었는지를 물었을 때, 그는 "그것에 대해 끊임없이 생각해서"라고 대답했다.

parish n. (교회·성당의) 교구
corpse n. 시체
chest n. 가슴
bubonic plague 흑사병
scholar n. 장학생
in solitude 혼자서
calculus n. 미적분학
unravel v. 해결하다
gravity n. 중력
Or so the story goes 소문으로는 그렇다
exceptional a. 아주 뛰어난, 비범한, 빼어난
universal gravitation 만유인력
unleash v. (반응을) 불러일으키다
definitive a. 결정적인; 최고의
biographer n. 전기(傳記) 작가
meticulously ad. 꼼꼼하게
pressing a. 다급한
strike v. (질병 등이) 발생하다
epic a. 서사시적인; 방대한
retreat n. 칩거
work out 이해하다

1 ④　▶ 빈칸완성
빈칸 앞 문장에서 뉴턴 자신도 그 정도의 말은 했다고 했는데 '그 정도의(as much) 말'에 해당하는 것이 빈칸에 들어가야 한다. 그것은 흑사병 전에 수학에 대해 깊이 생각하기 시작했으며 시골로의 칩거 자체가 큰 차이를 가져다주는 것은 아니었다는 내용의 말이다. 따라서 빈칸에는 ④의 '그것에 대해 끊임없이 생각해서'가 들어가는 것이 적절할 것이다.

2 ⑤　▶ 내용일치
리처드 웨스트폴은 뉴턴에 대한 최고의 전기 작가이며, 뉴턴에 대해 꼼꼼히 기록했다고 했다. 따라서 뉴턴의 업적에 대해 누락했다고 보기는 어려우므로, ⑤가 정답이다.

07   2013 동덕여대

영국을 상대로 벌인 독립전쟁은 길고 경제적으로 많은 비용이 들어간 전쟁이었다. 뉴잉글랜드의 어업은 일시적으로 파괴되었고 남부의 담배 재배지역 역시 큰 타격을 입었다. 이미 미국의 공산품 공급을 독점하고 있던 국가(영국)를 상대로 전쟁을 시작한 이래로 수입 무역은 혹독한 영향을 받았다. 가장 심각한 폐해는 상업 활동에 의존하여 살아가고 있는 도시들에서 나타났다. 보스턴, 뉴욕, 필라델피아, 그리고 찰스턴은 모두 한동안 영국 군대에게 점령당했다. 심지어 군대가 떠난 다음에도, 영국 선박들은 항구에 숨어있으면서 무역을 계속 방해했다.

미국이 조선업과 무역에서 얻던 수입은 급격하게 감소하였고, 이는 도시 지역의 경제 전체를 약화시켰다. 교역의 감소는 미국인의 생활수준의 하락을 가져왔다. 직장을 잃은 조선공들, 항만 노동자들, 그리고 통 제조업자들은 일을 찾기 위해서 농장으로 그리고 작은 마을로 빠져나갔다. 일부는 미국군에 입대했고, 영국에 충성심을 가지고 있던 일부는 영국군과 함께 떠났다. 뉴욕시의 인구는 1774년 21,000명에서 겨우 9년 뒤인 1783년에는 절반에도 못 미치는 수로 줄어들었다.

교전, 기존의 제조업 시장의 상실, 신용 원천의 상실, 그리고 새로운 투자의 부족, 이 모두로 인해 생겨난 혼란은 향후 20년 동안이나 지속되었던 경기 침체기를 만들어 냈다.

1 ③   ▶ 내용파악
본문에서는 독립전쟁으로 인해 어업이 파괴되었고 담배 재배지역도 타격을 입었다고 했다. 이 두 사업은 저자가 독립전쟁의 경제적 피해를 보여주기 위해 언급한 여러 가지 예들 중 일부이다. 그러므로 ③이 정답으로 가장 적절하다.

2 ①   ▶ 내용파악
본문 첫 번째 단락의 네 번째 문장에서 언급한 바와 같이 도시가 상업에 기반을 두고 있었기 때문에 가장 큰 피해를 입었다고 했으므로 ①이 정답으로 적절하다.

3 ③   ▶ 내용파악
본문은 전쟁으로 인해 뉴욕시 인구가 농장이나 작은 마을로 일거리를 찾아 빠져나갔다고 언급했다. 전쟁으로 야기된 경제 인구 손실을 극명하게 보여주고자 인구 변화 수치를 언급했다고 할 수 있다. 그러므로 ③이 정답으로 적절하다. ① 일부의 인구가 영국에 대한 충성심을 잃지 않은 채 영국군과 함께 떠났다고는 했지만 그 인구가 뉴욕시 인구의 절반이라는 언급은 없으므로 옳지 않다. ② 보스턴, 뉴욕, 필라델피아, 그리고 찰스턴의 무역업이 방해를 받았다는 언급만 있을 뿐 뉴욕과 다른 도시를 비교하는 말은 본문에 없으므로 옳지 않다. ④ 뉴욕 노숙자 인구에 관한 언급은 본문 어느 곳에도 없으므로 옳지 않다.

4 ④   ▶ 내용파악
기존의 제조업 시장을 잃어버렸고 전쟁으로 인해 신용도 또한 떨어졌다고 본문의 마지막 단락에서 말하고 있다. 그러므로 전쟁 이후 몇 년간은 제조업 시장의 부재로 인한 공산품 부족과, 신용도 하락으로 인한 자본 유치의 어려움이 생겨났을 것으로 예측할 수 있으므로 ④가 정답으로 가장 적절하다. ① 조선기술의 낙후로 조선업이 어려움을 겪었다는 언급은 없다. 전쟁으로 인해 조선업과 무역에서 얻던 수입이 감소하자 일자리가 줄었을 것이고, 이로 인해 기술자들이 공장이나 작은 마을로 빠져나갔다고 했으므로 옳지 않다. ② 제조 방법의 문제에 대한 언급은 없으므로 옳지 않다. ③ 뉴욕시의 경제문제는 상업 경제로 야기된 것이 아니라, 상업 경제가 타격을 입자 노동자들이 도시를 떠나기 시작하면서 생긴 것이라 할 수 있다. 또한 전쟁으로 인해 전반적인 신용도 하락과 투자 부족 또한 경기 침체의 원인이라고 언급하고 있다. 그러므로 뉴욕시가 다시 농업경제로 돌아갈 것이란 추측은 적절하지 않다.

---

temporarily ad. 일시적으로, 임시로
colony n. 식민지; 집단; 군집
hard-hit a. 심각한 영향을 받은, 큰 타격을 입은
monopolize v. 독점하다; 독차지하다
manufactured a. 제작된
consequence n. 결과; 중요성
troop n. 병력, 군대
lurk v. 숨다; 숨어있다
harbor n. 항구
shipbuilding n. 조선[업, 술]
commerce n. 상업; 무역
abruptly ad. 갑자기
undermine v. 몰래 손상시키다; 약화시키다
shipwright n. 배 대목, 조선공
dock laborer 항만 노동자
cooper n. 통 제조업자
drift v. 떠가다, 표류하다; 이동하다
Continental Army (독립전쟁 당시의) 미국군
disruption n. 붕괴; 분열; 중단
credit n. 신용, 신용거래
stagnation n. 침체, 정체; 불경기

08 2020 세종대

스코틀랜드계 미국인 기업가이자 자선사업가인 앤드류 카네기(Andrew Carnegie)는 1835년 스코틀랜드에서 태어나 12세 때 부모님과 함께 미국으로 이주했다. 카네기는 전신 기사로 일을 시작했고, 1860년대에는 이미 철도, 교량, 석유 시추탑에 투자하고 있었다. 그는 채권 판매원으로 더 많은 부(富)를 축적했다. 그는 피츠버그의 카네기 철강회사를 세웠고, 그것을 1901년에 J. P. 모건(Morgan)에게 3억 345만 달러에 팔았다. 카네기 철강회사를 매각한 후에, 그는 존 D. 록펠러(John D. Rockefeller)를 뛰어넘어 이후 몇 년 동안 가장 부유한 미국인이었다.

일찍이 1868년에, 33세였던 카네기는 자신에게 보내는 메모의 초안을 작성했다. 그는 "... 부를 축적하는 것은 가장 나쁜 종류의 우상숭배에 속한다. 돈을 숭배하는 것보다 인간을 더 타락시키는 우상은 없다."라고 썼다. 스스로 품위를 떨어뜨리는 일이 없도록 하기 위해, 그는 똑같은 메모 속에 자신이 35세에 은퇴할 것이며 "... 부자인 채로 죽는 것은 수치이기" 때문에 박애주의적인 기부를 할 것이라고 썼다. 그러나 그는 스코틀랜드의 고향에 도서관을 선물한 1881년까지 자선사업을 본격적으로 시작하지 않았다.

카네기는 영국의 제국주의에 대해서는 아무런 언급을 하지 않았지만, 미국의 식민지 사상에 대해서는 강하게 반대했다. 그는 필리핀의 합병을 반대했고 필리핀의 독립을 주선하려 했다. 스페인-미국 전쟁이 끝나갈 무렵, 미국은 스페인으로부터 필리핀을 2천만 달러에 사들였다. 카네기는 자신이 미국의 제국주의라고 인식한 것에 반대하기 위해, 필리핀인들이 미국으로부터 독립을 쟁취할 수 있도록 개인적으로 필리핀인들에게 2천만 달러를 주겠다고 제안했다. 하지만, 그 제안은 아무 성과도 없었다.

1 ② ▶ 내용추론
1901년에 카네기 철강회사를 J. P. 모건(Morgan)에게 매각한 후에 미국에서 가장 부유한 사람이 되었으므로, 1890년대에는 그가 미국에서 가장 부유한 사람이 아니었음을 알 수 있다. 따라서 ②가 정답으로 적절하다. ① 1860년에 시작한 것이 아니라 그 이전에 시작되어 1860년대에는 이미 하고 있었다. ③ 카네기는 부를 축적하는 것이 가장 나쁜 종류의 우상숭배에 속한다고 생각했다. ④ 카네기 자신이 스코틀랜드의 고향에 도서관을 지어준 것이다.

2 ④ ▶ 빈칸완성
여러 나라를 식민지로 두는 것이 제국주의이므로, 'imperialism = idea of colonies'의 관계가 성립한다. 같은 사안에 있어서 영국과 미국에 대해 다른 태도를 보이고 있으므로, 빈칸에는 역접의 접속사 While이 적절하다.

3 ② ▶ 내용파악
세 번째 문단에서는 카네기가 '미국의 제국주의적 정책과 사상에 반대'했으며, 필리핀 독립에 힘을 보태려 했다는 사실을 예로 들면서 이야기하고 있다.

4 ④ ▶ 내용일치
마지막 문단에 "카네기는 미국이 스페인으로부터 필리핀을 사들여 합병하는 것에 반대하고 필리핀의 독립을 주선하려 했다."는 것과 관련된 내용이 있으므로, ④가 본문의 내용과 일치하는 진술이다. ① 46세였던 1881년에 도서관을 고향에 기증하는 것으로 자선활동을 시작했다. ② 재산을 사회에 환원하지 않고 부자인 상태로 죽는 것이 수치스럽다고 했다. ③ 미국으로부터의 독립을 위해 필리핀인들에게 2천만 달러를 주겠다고 제안했지만 아무 성과도 없었다고 했다.

---

industrialist n. 실업가, 기업가
philanthropist n. 박애주의자, 자선가
immigrate v. (영주할 목적으로) 타국에서 이주해오다; (새로운 거주지로) 이주하다
telegrapher n. 전신 기사
investment n. 투자, 출자
oil derrick 채유탑(採油塔), 석유 시추탑
accumulate v. (조금씩) 모으다, 축적하다
surpass v. ~보다 낫다, ~을 능가하다
draft v. 초안[원고]을 작성하다
amass v. (재산을) 축적하다
idolatry n. 우상숭배; 맹목적 숭배
debase v. (가치·품위 등을) 떨어뜨리다, 저하시키다
worship n. 숭배, 예배
degrade v. 지위를 낮추다; 타락시키다
pursue v. 추구하다, 추적하다
philanthropic a. 박애주의의
disgrace v. 망신시키다, 면목을 잃게 하다
in earnest 진지하게, 본격적으로
imperialism n. 제국주의
oppose v. 반대하다, 대항하다
colony n. 식민지
annexation n. 합병
arrange v. 마련하다, 준비하다
near v. 접근하다, 다가오다
counter v. 반대하다, 거스르다
perceive v. 지각하다, 인식하다

09 2022 중앙대

주요한 전쟁들은 종종 역사를 구분하는 일종의 구두점을 제공하는데, 주된 이유는 그 전쟁들이 국가 사이의 관계의 철저한 재편성을 강제하기 때문이다. 이러한 원칙에 제1차 세계대전도 예외가 아니었다. 1918년 11월에 전쟁이 끝나기 오래 전부터 유럽의 지도가 다시 그려져야 하고, 식민지의 재할당, 새로운 국제 조직의 창립, 그리고 경제 균형의 변화가 세계의 다른 지역에도 필경 상당한 영향을 미칠 것이라는 것이 분명했다. 제1차 세계대전은 유럽 지배의 종말을 예고했는데, 주로 유럽에서 진행된 이 전쟁의 진정한 승전국이 비유럽 열강인 미국과 일본이었기 때문이다. <유럽 각국은 국내 문제에 대해 우려하지 않았고, 전 세계에 있는 자신들의 식민지의 중요성도 간과했다.> 유럽의 승전국들은 가진 모든 것을 잃었고, 그들 중 어느 국가도 실질적으로 회복하지 못할 정도로 막대한 희생을 치른 승리를 거둔 셈이었다. 이 사실은 전쟁이 끝날 당시에는 분명하지 않았지만, 다가올 전후의 체제는 지리적 범위와 복잡성 면에서 훨씬 더 클 것이 분명했다.

종종 그러하듯, 적의 갑작스러운 몰락은 승자들을 깜짝 놀라게 했다. 독일은 1919년 중반까지 버티리라 예상되었지만, 1918년 가을, 동맹국의 에너지는 평화를 계획하는 일보다 전쟁을 승리로 이끄는 일에 더욱이 집중되었다. 물론 일부 평화 계획이 진행 중이긴 했으나 항상 가장 효과적인 쪽으로 진행되는 것은 아니었다. 전쟁 마지막 해, 동맹국 중에 작은 나라들은 제한된 구체적 목표를 침착하게 추구했지만 신중하고 한정된 약속만을 얻어냈을 뿐이었다. 독일 쪽 동맹국 내의 민족 집단들을 대변하는 추방 단체들도 같은 일을 했고 비슷한 결과를 얻었다. 그들은 최고 항소 법원이 영국과 프랑스와 미국으로 이루어지리라는 것을 알고 있었지만, 이 세 나라는 세계 많은 지역을 위한 계획을 과제로 갖고 있으면서 전쟁을 승리로 이끌 책무도 있었다. 당연히 전쟁의 승리가 먼저였다.

주요 동맹국들 중 프랑스가 주로 자기들에게 무엇이 중요한지 정확히 알고 있었고, 그들의 관심이 실제로 그다지 전 세계적인 것이 아니었기 때문에 아마도 계획을 가장 조직적으로 세운 열강이었을 것이다. 런던에서는 외무부가 생각할 수 있는 모든 주제에 관해 입장 표명서를 열심히 준비하고 있었지만 외무부의 입장은 종종 내각의 입장과 일치하지 않았고 심지어 수상이었던 데이비드 로이드 조지(David Lloyd George)의 입장과는 더욱이 일치하지 않았기 때문에 많은 노력이 헛일로 판명되었다. 미국의 경우 상황은 더 애매모호했다. 1917년 말 '인콰이어리(탐구)'라는 특수 기구가 대통령의 친구 에드워드 M. 하우스(Edward M. House)의 감독 하에 평화의 문제를 연구하고 유럽 지도자들의 프로그램을 선취하기 위한 프로그램을 준비하기 위해 설립되었다. 인콰이어리는 대개 국무부와 독립적으로 일하는 학자들로 이루어져 있어 연구를 열심히 했지만, 그 영향력은 여전히 불확실했고 하우스 자신도 대전이 끝나는 몇 주 동안 파리에 있었다. 국무부 장관 로버트 랜싱(Robert Lansing)은 자신의 견해를 준비하고 있었는데, 그의 견해는 인콰이어리의 견해와 맞지 않았고 대통령의 견해와도 충돌할 것으로 예상될 수 있었다.

1 ① ▶ 문맥상 적절하지 않은 문장 고르기
Ⓐ의 문장 내용은 "유럽 각국은 국내 문제에 대해 우려하지 않았고, 전 세계에 있는 자신들의 식민지의 중요성도 간과했다."인데, 이는 제1차 세계대전의 여파와 결과를 다루는 글의 흐름에 맞지 않는다. 따라서 Ⓐ가 글의 흐름상 적합하지 않은 문장이다.

2 ① ▶ 내용일치
"제1차 세계대전은 유럽 지배의 종말을 예고했다고 했고, 유럽의 승전국들은 가진 모든 것을 잃었고, 그들 중 어느 국가도 실질적으로 회복하지 못할 정도로 막대한 희생을 치르고 승리를 거둔 셈이었다."고 했으므로 ①이 글의 내용과 일치한다.

---

punctuation n. 구두점
realignment n. 재편성, 조정
state n. 국가
reallocation n. 재할당, 재배치
overlook v. 간과하다
bleed ~ white ~를 짜낼 수 있는 데까지 짜낸다
pyrrhic victory 피로스(고대 그리스의 왕)의 승리 (막대한 희생을 치른 승리)
take someone by surprise ~을 깜짝 놀라게 하다
Central Powers 동맹국(제1차 세계대전 중에 연합국에 대항해서 공동으로 싸웠던 독일, 오스트리아, 헝가리; 때로 터키, 불가리아를 포함)
futile a. 무익한, 헛된

10 2020 아주대

A 역사학자들은 종종 1898년을 미국이 과거로부터 분명히 벗어나 세계정치에 등장했던 시점으로 꼽는다. 그러나 그 변화의 정도는 과장될 수 있다. 산업화 이후에 미국은 잠재적인 강대국이 되었으므로 미국의 힘이 갑자기 커진 것은 아니었다. 1898년에 대중들의 관심사가 갑자기 영구적으로 변한 것도 또한 아니었다. 제국주의에 대한 거센 논쟁이 있은 후, 20세기 초 대부분의 미국인들은 습관적으로 다시 국내 문제에 집중하기 시작했다. 그러나 1898년에는 미국의 참여에 분명히 변화가 있었다. 이때부터 미국과 유럽 열강들 모두 미국이 세계 위기에 어느 정도 관심을 갖고 있다고 가정했다.

B 이러한 변화에 대해 많은 이유가 제시되었다. 가장 분명한 제안은 제국주의에 대한 전통적인 경제적 해석을 구체화하고 있다. 즉, 미국 경제가 성숙기에 이르렀고, 따라서 미국도 다른 선진국들과 마찬가지로 새로운 원자재와 외국 시장을 필요로 했다는 것이다. 많은 역사가들은 미국의 해외 팽창과 미국의 국내 경제 발전 사이의 연관성을 부인할 것이다. 그러나 세기의 전환기의 농민들과 기업인들은 자주 이 둘을 연관 지었는데, 이들은 국내 번영과 해외 시장의 관계를 간파하고 있었던 것이다.

C 대외정책에서의 새로운 출발에 대한 또 하나의 설명은 미국이 팽창해야 할 "명백한 사명"을 갖고 있다는 전통적 사상이 부활하고 수정 제시되었다는 것이다. 그러나 미(美) 대륙 내에서의 팽창이 해외 팽창으로 변모하는 데에는 새로운 정당한 명분이 필요했다. 19세기 말 팽창주의자들의 가장 일반적인 주장 중 하나는 앵글로 색슨족이 "인종적으로" 우월하다는 사상이었다. 1890년대에, 일부 사람들은 남부의 아프리카계 미국인들과 새로운 이민자들에 대한 우월성을 주장했다.

D 미국 정책 변화의 좀 덜 분명한 또 다른 원인은 열강 정치의 실제 상황이었다. 이미 세계 저개발 지역에서 영토와 영향력 쟁탈전을 벌이고 있던 주요 유럽 국가들의 제국주의 활동은 미국의 팽창 욕구를 자극했다. 아프리카를 분할한 유럽 열강들은 이제 마지막으로 남은 두 팽창대상 지역인 근동과 극동을 주시하고 있었다. 이들 각 지역은 너무나 중요해서 그 어느 강대국이든 독차지하게 되어서는 안 되었기에 주요 국가들은 불안해하면서도 두 지역의 독립을 지지했고 저마다 경제적 영향력의 영역을 분명하게 표시했다. 모든 곳의 상황이 유동적이고 위태로웠다. 미국과 같이 잠재력을 가진 나라가 세계 정치에 관심을 보였을 때 그 나라는 불가피하게도 일부 강대국들에게는 위협으로, 또 다른 강대국들에게는 잠재적 동맹국으로 간주되었다. 1898년에 일어난 일은 이 모든 요소들을 반영했다. 미국은 자신의 의지와는 반대로, 그리고 전혀 깨닫지 못한 채, 열강 정치에 관여하게 되었다.

departure n. 출발, 이탈
flurry n. 일진광풍
imperialism n. 제국주의
resume v. 다시 시작하다
commitment n. 헌신; 참여
embody v. 구체화하다
maturity n. 성숙
turn-of-the-century a. 세기가 바뀌는 시점의
restatement n. 수정재표시, (재무제표의) 수정
manifest destiny 명백한 사명(설)(미국이 북미 전체를 지배할 운명을 갖고 있다는 주장); (일반적으로) 영토 확장론
justification n. 정당한 이유, 명분
scramble n. 쟁탈전
whet v. (식욕·흥미 등을) 돋우다
uneasily ad. 불안하게
stake out (울타리를 치거나 하여) ~이 자기 것임을 분명히 표시하다
fluid a. 유동적인
menace n. 위협
ally n. 동맹

1 ① ▶ 글의 제목
이 글은 미국이 1898년 이후 세계정치에 뛰어들면서 세계에 대한 팽창주의적 정책을 펴게 된 이유를 분석하고 있다.

2 ④ ▶ 빈칸완성
"경제는 성숙기에 이르렀고, 다른 선진국들과 마찬가지로 새로운 원자재와 외국 시장을 필요로 했다."는 진술에 비추어 볼 때, B 단락은 미국의 제국주의적 팽창의 원인을 경제적 원인에서 찾는 분석임을 알 수 있다. 따라서 경제와 관련된 내용인 ④가 빈칸에 적절하다.

3 ① ▶ 빈칸완성
whet appetite for ~는 '~에 대한 식욕을 돋우다' 또는 '~에 대한 욕망을 자극하다'는 의미이다. ② 비통해 하다 ③ 옹호하다 ④ 매달리다 ⑤ 빼앗다

4 ① ▶ 내용일치
"역사학자들은 종종 1898년을 미국이 과거로부터 분명히 벗어나 세계정치에 등장했던 시점으로 꼽는다."고 하였으므로 ①이 본문의 내용과 일치한다.

02 심리·교육

01 2018 한국외대

자기 본위 편향은 우리가 긍정적인 사건은 우리 자신 때문으로, 부정적인 사건은 외부적인 요인 때문으로 보는 경향이다. 예를 들면, 큰 경기에서 승리한 후에 인터뷰를 한 유명 운동선수는 그의 성공을 자신이 열심히 훈련한 결과라고 생각한다. 몇 주 후에 경기에서 지고 나서 한 인터뷰에서 그 같은 운동선수는 "오늘은 그저 운이 없네요."라고 이유를 댄다. 심리학자들은 자존심과 평판을 지키기 위해서 이런 방식으로 생각하는 것이 인간의 본성이라고 말한다. 자기 본위 편향의 이점은 우리가 실패에 직면했을 때 우울해지지 않도록 해주며 우리가 미래에 대해 자신감을 유지하게 해준다. 그러나 부정적인 결과를 외부적인 요인 탓으로 돌리는 것은 실수로부터 배워 더 나은 사람이 될 수 있는 기회를 우리에게서 앗아간다. 만약 우리가 어떻게 해서 부정적인 결과를 초래했는지 솔직히 살펴보는 것을 계속해서 회피한다면, 우리는 정체된 채로 있을 것이다.

self-serving bias 자기 본위[이기적] 편향
tendency n. 경향, 성향
attribute A to B A를 B의 결과라고 생각하다
external a. 외부의, 외적인
athlete n. 경기자, 운동선수
self-esteem n. 자존심, 자부심
reputation n. 평판, 명성
blame A on B A의 책임을 B에게 지우다
rob A of B A에게서 B를 빼앗다

1 ③   ▶ 빈칸완성
빈칸 ⓐ에는 자기 본위 편향의 이점이 들어가야 하는데, 실패에 직면했을 때 우울하지 않게 해준다고 한 다음 순접의 접속사 and가 왔으므로, 미래를 긍정적으로 바라볼 수 있게 해준다는 의미가 될 수 있도록 하는 expectant와 confident가 들어갈 수 있다. 한편, 부정적인 결과를 외부적인 요인 탓으로 돌리게 되면 실수를 통해 배울 수 없고 더 나은 사람이 될 수 없다고 했으므로, 정체되어 발전이 없다는 의미가 될 수 있도록 빈칸 ⓑ에는 stagnant가 적절하다. 따라서 ③이 정답이다. ① 삼가는 ─ 긍정적인 ② 기대하는 ─ 무관심한 ④ 불길한 ─ 안정적인

2 ④   ▶ 내용파악
자기 본위 편향은 '우리 자신에게 일어난 부정적인 사건을 외부적인 요인 탓으로 돌리는 경향'인데, 자존심과 평판을 지키기 위해서 이런 방식으로 생각하는 것이 인간의 본성이라고 했으므로, 부정적인 사건을 경험하면 내가 아닌 외부적인 요인을 탓한다고 볼 수 있다. 따라서 ④가 정답이다.

02 2015 상명대

정신적, 감정적, 행동성 질환을 연구하고 치료하는 의학으로서의 심리학의 현대적인 개념은 지그문트 프로이트(Sigmund Freud)가 이 분야에서 연구를 시작했을 때 막 형성되고 있었다. 20세기의 전환기에 나온 프로이트의 치료법과 이론은 이제 문화적인 규범이 되었다. 오늘날의 대중문화는 성욕에 대한 그의 관심을 장난스럽게 다루지만, 행동이 무의식적이거나 잠재의식적인 동기를 갖고 있다는 그의 생각은 현재 사실로서 인정받고 있다. 프로이트는 또한 단순한 이야기하기에 기반을 둔 치료법을 처음 시도한 주요 인물인데, 이것은 여전히 많은 현대 치료법의 핵심이다. 칼 융(Carl Jung)은 심리학 분야가 형성되는 데 있어서 두 번째로 영향력 있는 인물이었다. 그는 무의식에 있는 관념과 감정의 복합체에 관한 이론을 프로이트와 함께 연구했지만, 그의 견해는 훨씬 더 폭이 넓었다. 그는 문화와 종교의 맥락에서 인간에 대한 거의 인류학적인 견해를 취했다. 더 높은 수준의 분석을 통해, 그는 개인적인 질병을 넘어 인간의 성격 유형에게로 눈길을 던졌다. 그가 끼친 현대적인 영향은 조셉 캠벨(Joseph Campbell)의 보편적인 신화의 대중화와 MBTI(마이어 브릭스 유형지표, the Myers-Briggs Type Indicator)라는 치료 수단처럼 서로 전혀 다른 여러 분야에서 찾아볼 수 있다.

concept n. 개념, 생각; 구상
psychology n. 심리학
treatment n. 대우, 처리; 치료; 치료법
cultural norm 문화 규범
make fun of ~을 놀리다, 비웃다
drive n. 충동, 본능적 욕구
unconscious a. 무의식의, 부지중에; 모르는
subconscious a. 잠재의식의
motivation n. 자극, 유도; 동기, 동기 부여
exploration n. 탐사, 탐험; 탐구, 조사; 검사, 검진
complex n. 복합체; 강박 관념; 이상심리
anthropological a. 인류학의
context n. 문맥, 맥락
disparate a. 다른, 공통점이 없는

1 ②   ▶ 내용파악
세 번째 문장에서 프로이트의 일부 이론은 웃음의 대상이 되기도 하지만, "행동이 무의식

적이거나 잠재의식적인 동기를 갖고 있다는 그의 생각은 현재 사실로서 인정받고 있다." 라고 했으므로, 프로이트는 "사람들이 무의식적인 동기에 기초하여 행동을 한다."고 믿었음을 알 수 있다.

2 ④　▶ 부분이해
조셉 캠벨의 보편적인 신화와 마이어 브릭스 유형지표(MBTI)는 전혀 공통점이 없지만 둘 모두 칼 융의 이론에서 영향을 받았음을 확인할 수 있다고 했으므로, ④가 밑줄 친 Ⓐ를 설명한 것으로 적절하다. 참고로 ①과 ③에는 두 이론이 전혀 다르다는 의미가 포함되어 있지 않아서 정답이 될 수 없다.

myth n. 신화, (많은 사람들의) 근거 없는 믿음
therapeutic a. 치료법의

03　2022 한국외대

지능은 종종 우리의 지적 잠재력으로 정의된다. 바로 우리가 가지고 태어난 것으로, 측정할 수 있으면서도, 바꾸기 어려운 능력을 일컫는다. 그러나 지능에 대한 다른 견해들이 나타났다. 그런 개념 가운데 하나는 하워드 가드너(Howard Gardner)가 제안한 '다중 지능' 이론이다. 이 이론은 지능에 대한 전통적인 심리측정학적 견해가 너무 제한적이라는 의견을 제시한다. 사람들이 가지고 있는 모든 범위의 능력을 포착하기 위해, 가드너는 사람들이 지적 능력만을 가지고 있는 것이 아니라 음악적, 대인 관계적, 공간-시각적, 언어적 지능을 포함하는 많은 종류의 지능을 가지고 있다는 이론을 내세웠다. 어떤 사람이 음악적 지능과 같은 특정 영역에서 특히 강할 수 있지만, 그 사람은 틀림없이 다른 능력도 다채롭게 가지고 있을 것이라는 것이다. 가드너의 이론은 일부 심리학자와 교육자들로부터 비판을 받게 되었다. 가드너를 비판하는 이 사람들은 지능에 대한 가드너의 정의가 지나치게 광범위하고 그가 말하는 8가지 서로 다른 '지능'은 단순히 재능과 성격적 특성을 나타낸다고 주장한다. 그럼에도 불구하고, 다중 지능 이론은 교육자들 사이에서 상당한 인기를 누리고 있다. 많은 교사들이 그들의 교육 철학에 다중 지능을 활용하고 가드너의 이론을 교실에 융합시키기 위해 노력하고 있다.

1 ④　▶ 글의 주제
가드너의 다중 지능 이론을 소개하면서, 이에 대해 비판하는 사람들이 있기는 하지만 학습 현장에서 이 이론이 상당한 인기를 누리고 있음을 이야기하고 있다. 따라서 ④가 정답으로 적절하다.

2 ③　▶ 빈칸완성
많은 교사들이 가드너의 다중 지능을 활용하고 있다면 그것을 학습 공간에 녹아들 수 있도록 했을 것이므로, 빈칸에는 '융합시키다'라는 의미의 ③이 가장 적절하다. ① 조사하다 ② 무효로 하다 ④ 침투시키다

intelligence n. 지능
define v. (말의) 정의를 내리다, 뜻을 밝히다
intellectual a. 지적인, 지력의
potential n. 잠재력
capacity n. 능력, 재능
conception n. 개념, 생각
psychometric a. 정신측정의, 심리측정의
limited a. 제한된
possess v. 소유하다, 가지고 있다
theorize v. 이론을 세우다
interpersonal a. 사람과 사람 사이의, 개인 간의
spatial-visual a. 공간-시각적인
linguistic a. 언어의, 언어학의
criticism n. 비판, 비평
critic n. 비평가, 평론가
trait n. 특색, 특성
considerable a. 중요한; 상당한, 적지 않은
utilize v. 활용하다

04　2018 국민대

행동이론은 환경에서 비롯된 결과가 행동을 정하고 유지시킨다는 주장을 한다. 긍정적인 강화가 뒤따르는 행동은 지속되거나 늘어날 가능성이 매우 높다. Ⓐ 이와는 반대로, 처벌과 같은 부정적인 결과가 뒤따르는 모든 행동은 이론적으로는 줄어들어야 한다. Ⓑ 그러나 이제껏 처벌이 행동개입(behavioral intervention)의 효과적인 수단이라는 것을 보여준 연구는 없었다. Ⓒ 그러한 주된 이유는 처벌이 단지 나쁜 행실을 멈추게 하는 데만 효과가 있기 때문이다. Ⓓ 사실, 처벌은 대개 처벌을 하는 사람이 실제로 있는 동안에만 나쁜 행실을 막을 수 있다.
이 시점에서 '유관 지배 행동(contingency-governed behavior)'이라 불리는 행동 현상이 생겨나기 시작할지도 모른다. 유관 지배 행동이란 개인의 행동은 개인이 느끼는 다음번에 있을 결과에 좌우된다는 것을 의미한다. 이는 만약 어떤 사람이 자신의 부적절한 행동이 발각되지 않을 거라 생각한다면, 그는 그 일을 저지르고 처벌을 받지 않고 무사히 빠져나가려 하는 경향이 있다는 것을 뜻한

behavioral a. 행동의[에 관한]
assert v. 단언[역설]하다, 주장하다
consequence n. 결과, 결말
environment n. (생태학적·사회적·문화적인) 환경
shape v. 모양 짓다, 형체를 이루다
maintain v. 지속하다, 유지하다
positive a. 단정적인, 명확한; 긍정적인
reinforcement n. 보강, 강화, 증원; 상을 주는 학습
conversely ad. 거꾸로, 반대로

다. 결과적으로, 만약 나쁜 행실을 하는 자기를 처벌하는 사람이 보지 못하거나 발각하지 못할 거라 믿는다면, 그 학생은 그 행실을 저지르고 처벌을 받지 않고 무사히 빠져나가려 할 것이다. 문제가 되는 행동은 반복되면서 더 심해진다. 그 학생이 발각되지 않는다면, 그는 성공했다고 느끼는데, 이것은 일종의 긍정적인 강화여서 그는 문제 있는 행동 양식을 계속하게 된다.

1 ① ▶ 문장배열
환경에서 비롯된 결과가 행동을 정하고 유지시킨다는 행동이론의 내용 중 '긍정적인' 강화가 뒤따르는 행동의 특성에 대해 언급한 상황이므로, 이 내용에 이어서는 '부정적인' 결과가 뒤따르는 행동에 대한 내용이 와야 한다. 그러므로 A가 맨 처음에 와야 한다. A의 내용과 관련하여 실제로는 그렇지 않음을 언급한 B가 그 다음에 와야 하고, B의 내용에 대한 이유를 언급한 C와 C의 내용을 부연설명하고 있는 D가 뒤이어 와야 한다.

2 ① ▶ 빈칸완성
두 번째 문장에서 "긍정적인 강화가 뒤따르는 행동은 지속되거나 늘어날 가능성이 매우 높다."고 했으므로, 자신의 부적절한 행동이 발각되지 않음으로 인해 긍정적인 강화의 일종인 성공을 느끼게 된다면, 그는 이러한 행동을 '계속할 것임'을 알 수 있다. 따라서 빈칸에는 ①이 들어가야 한다. ② 억누르다 ③ 중지하다 ④ 방해하다

3 ③ ▶ 글의 제목
본문에서는 개인의 행동이 환경에서 비롯되는 결과에 의해 좌우된다는 '행동이론'과 개인의 행동은 그 자신이 느끼는 다음번에 있을 결과에 좌우된다는 것을 의미한다는 '유관 지배 행동'에 관하여 주로 이야기하고 있다. 그러므로 글의 제목으로는 ③이 적절하다.

punishment n. 벌, 처벌
theoretically ad. 이론적으로
effective a. 효과적인, 유효한, 효력이 있는
intervention n. 조정, 중재; 개입, 간섭
misbehavior n. 버릇없음, 무례; 나쁜 행실, 부정행위
phenomenon n. 현상; 사건
contingency n. 우연, 우발사건
contingency-governed behavior 유관 지배 행동(행동에 수반뇌어 일어나는 결과에 지배되는 행동)
perceive v. 지각하다, 감지하다; 인식하다
inappropriate a. 부적절한, 부적당한
get away with (비교적 가벼운 처벌을) 받다, (나쁜 짓을 하고도) 처벌을 모면하다[그냥 넘어가다]
escalate v. 확대되다, 증가되다

05 2020 성균관대

지난 10년에 걸쳐 행동과학자들은 몇 가지 흥미로운 통찰을 생각해냈다. 캘리포니아의 고급 식료품점에서 행해진 한 획기적인 실험에서, 연구원들은 여러 잼들을 진열해놓은 시식대를 설치했다. 첫 번째 실험에서 그들은 24가지의 다양한 잼들을 맛볼 수 있도록 멋지게 배치했다. 다른 날에, 그들은 단지 6개의 잼만 진열했다. 시식회에 참여한 손님들은 상점에서 같은 브랜드의 잼을 구입할 수 있는 할인 상품권을 받았다. 24개의 잼이 진열되었을 때 더 많은 쇼핑객들이 진열대에 들른 것으로 판명되었다. 그러나 후속 구매에 관한 한, 6개의 잼 진열대에 들린 손님들 중 적어도 30%가 잼을 구매했는데, 이것은 24개를 선택해야 했던 사람들 중 단지 3%만이 구입한 것과 비교된다.
선택 대상의 수가 증가함에 따라, 선택할 여러 대체물들을 현명하게 서로 구별할 수 있을 만큼 충분한 정보를 취득하는 데 필요한 노력이 선택 대상이 더 늘어난 소비자들에게 주는 이익보다 더 커지는 시점이 있을지도 모른다. 이 시점에서 선택은 더 이상 자유를 주는 것이 아니라 압박을 주는 것이다. 다시 말해, 얼마간의 선택이 좋다는 사실이 반드시 더 많은 선택이 더 좋다는 것을 의미하는 것은 아니다. 소비자들은 선택 대상이 너무 많은 것이 사람을 무력하게 만든다는 것을 알게 되는데, 이는 정보 취득의 스트레스와 아울러, 잘못 인식하고 잘못 계산할 위험과, 이용 가능한 대체물들을 오해할 위험과, 자신의 취향을 잘못 파악할 위험과, 순간적인 변덕에 굴복하고는 나중에 후회할 위험을 초래하기 때문이다.

1 ② ▶ 글의 제목
이 글에서 시식대 실험을 통해 행동과학자들이 밝혀낸 사실은 선택 대상이 어느 정도 있는 것은 좋지만 너무 많이 있으면 스트레스가 되고 잘못 선택할 위험이 있어 오히려 좋지 않다는 사실이다. 따라서 글의 제목으로 적절한 것은 ② '선택의 역설'이다.

2 ③ ▶ 내용파악
24개의 잼이 진열되었을 때 더 많은 쇼핑객들이 진열대에 들른 것으로 판명되었지만, 후속 구매 면에서는 6개의 잼만 진열되어 있을 때 더 많이 구매했다. 이것은 선택 대상이 너무 많을 때는 구매 의욕이 꺾인다는 것을 말한다. 따라서 ③이 정답이다.

come up with ~을 내놓다, 제안하다
intriguing a. 흥미를 자아내는; 음모를 꾸미는
upmarket a. (상품 등이) 고급품 시장[고소득층]용의, 고급이며 고가인
tempting a. 유혹하는, 매력적인
array n. 배치, 배열, 열거
discount voucher 할인 쿠폰
selection n. 선발, 선택
option n. 선택, 취사
multiply v. 증가시키다; 곱하다
alternative n. (2개의 것 중) 한 쪽; 대안
outweigh v. ~보다 뛰어나다, 중대하다
at this point 이 시점에서
liberate v. 해방하다, 자유롭게 하다
tyrannize v. 압제하다
debilitate v. 약하게 하다
miscalculation n. 오산, 판단 착오
yield v. 항복하다, ~에 굴하다
whim n. 변덕, 일시적 기분

06 2013 이화여대

타고난 재능이 있는 사람들을 다루는 데 영향을 미치는 주요한 철학적인 문제점은 교육의 목표를 대중의 수준을 끌어올리는 데 둘 것인가 혹은 가장 큰 잠재력을 드러내는 사람들을 교육하는 데 둘 것인가 하는 것이다. 그러한 문제점은 종종 엘리트주의와 민주주의적 평등 사이의 이분법으로 제기돼왔다. 또 다른 관점은 지능이 동등하지 않은 개인들을 동등하게 교육하는 것의 민주주의적 실천 — 다시 말해, 똑똑한 사람들과 우둔한 사람들에 대해 동일한 기대와 기준을 갖는 것 — 은 평등의 잘못된 개념으로, 이것은 (뛰어난 사람을) 평범하게 만들고 재능을 허비하게 만든다는 것이다. 진정한 평등이란 오히려 '각자의 지능에 따른 교육을 통해 이익을 얻을 수 있는 공평한 기회'를 각 개인에게 제공하는 데 있다(1961, 쓴첸). 역사를 통틀어, 기회의 평등과 관련한 지배적 철학이 타고난 재능이 있는 개인을 다루는 데에서 분명히 나타났다.

시간이 지나면서, 사회가 가치 있게 여기는 것도 또한 타고난 재능이 있는 개인에 대한 정의와 식별을 결정하는 데 도움을 주었다. 시각 예술이 높은 평가를 받았을 때에는 — 가령, 르네상스 시기의 유럽에서는 — 사회에서 예술적 재능을 타고난 사람들을 찾아서 지원했다. 전쟁이나 기아와 같은 비상사태에 기초한 급성(긴급한) 필요와, 오랜 시간에 걸쳐 늘 존재하는 만성(장기적) 필요가 또한 사회가 타고난 재능이 있는 개인을 식별하는 데 영향을 미쳤다. 예를 들어, 고대 스파르타의 무인 사회에서는 군인다운 용맹스러움을 갖춘 개인들이 필요했으며 따라서 그런 사람들을 길러냈다.

1 ② ▶ 내용추론
본문에서는 일률적인 교육이 아니라 '능력에 맞는 교육과 교육 기회의 평등'을 강조하고 있으므로, ②가 본문을 통해 추론할 수 있는 진술이다. ① 본문의 내용과 무관한 편견에 가까운 진술이다. ③ 두 번째 문단 첫 번째 문장의 "사회가 가치 있게 여기는 것도 또한 타고난 재능이 있는 개인에 대한 정의와 식별을 결정하는 데 도움을 주었다."라는 내용과 배치된다. ④, ⑤ 상식적인 관점에서는 그럴 수 있겠으나, 본문의 내용을 통해 유추할 수 있는 내용이 아니다.

2 ④ ▶ 빈칸완성
빈칸 Ⓐ 앞에 a dichotomy between이라는 표현이 있는데, dichotomy는 '대상을 둘로 나눠서 생각하는 이분법'이라는 뜻이므로, Ⓐ에는 and 뒤의 democratic equality와 대조를 이루는 표현이 들어가야 한다. 민주주의적 평등이란 모든 사람을 똑같이 대하는 것이므로, 이것과 반대되는 개념은 '소수의 뛰어난 사람들이 사회나 국가를 지배하고 이끌어야 한다고 믿는 태도나 입장'이다. 따라서 elitism이 적절하다. 한편, 지능이 같지 않은 사람들에게 똑같은 교육을 받게 하면, 뛰어난 사람의 경우 자신에게 맞는 수준의 교육을 받지 못하게 되어, 보통 사람이 되고 말 가능성이 크므로 빈칸 Ⓑ에는 mediocrity가 적절하다. ① 우월 — 능력 ② 파벌 — 성취 ③ 찌꺼기 — 보통 ⑤ 발췌 — 능숙

3 ① ▶ 빈칸완성
빈칸 ⓒ를 포함하고 있는 문장의 바로 앞에서 '지능이 동등하지 않은 개인들을 동등하게 교육하는 것을 비판'하고 있고, 이어지는 문장에서는 '기회의 평등'에 대해 언급하고 있으므로, 빈칸에는 앞서 언급한 두 가지 사항을 모두 이야기하고 있는 표현이 들어가는 것이 적절하다. 따라서 ①이 여기에 부합하는 진술이다.

treatment n. 취급, 대우; 처리
gifted a. 타고난 재능이 있는; 유능한
elevate v. 올리다, 높이다; 향상시키다
nurture v. 양육하다; 교육하다
evidence v. 입증하다; (감정 등을) 겉으로 드러내다
potential n. 잠재력; 가능성
dichotomy n. 이분법; 분열
perspective n. 전망; 시각; 견지
standard n. 표준, 기준; 규범
dull a. 둔감한, 우둔한; 지루한
conception n. 개념, 생각
prevailing a. 우세한; 유력한; 널리 보급돼 있는
manifest v. 명백히 하다; 명시하다; (감정을) 나타내다
definition n. 한정; 정의
identification n. 신원의 확인; 동일시
famine n. 기근, 굶주림
chronic a. 만성의; 상습적인
prowess n. 용감, 용감한 행위

07 2017 서강대

감상적인 태도가 잔혹한 취향과 양립 가능하며 그보다 더할 수 있다는 것은 주지의 사실이다. (아우슈비츠의 사령관이 저녁에 귀가하여 자신의 부인 및 아이들과 포옹하고 저녁 식사 전에 피아노 앞에 앉아 슈베르트의 곡을 연주했다고 하는 전형적인 예를 떠올려 보라.) 사람들이 그들 앞에 보이는 것에 단련되는 것은 — 만약 단련이라는 표현이 이 상황을 기술하는 적절한 방식이라고 한다면 — 단지 그들에게 쏟아지는 이미지들의 양 때문이 아니다. 감정을 무디게 하는 것은 수동성이다. 흔히 냉담함, 도덕적 또는 감정적 무감각으로 기술되는 상태들은 감정들로 가득 차 있다. 그 감정들은 분노와 좌절이다. 그러나 만약 우리가 어떤 감정들이 바람직할까 생각해보면, 너무나 쉽게 동정심을 꼽는 것 같다. 타인들에게 가해지는 고통을 이미지를 통해 보게 될 때 느끼는 그들과의 가상의 근접

sentimentality n. 감상적임, 감상적 태도
notoriously ad. 악명 높게도; 주지의 사실로서
compatible a. 양립 가능한
brutality n. 잔인성, 야만성
canonical a. 정전으로 인정받는, 규범적인
commandant n. 사령관
inure v. 익숙케 하다, 단련하다

성은 TV의 근접 촬영으로 비춰지는 먼 곳의 고통 받는 이들과 그것을 지켜보는 특권적 시청자들 사이에 하나의 연결을 암시하지만 그것은 분명히 허구적인 것이며, 우리가 권력과 맺고 있는 실질적 관계들에 대한 또 하나의 신비화이다. 우리가 동정심을 느끼는 한, 우리는 그 고통을 야기한 것들과 공범이 아님을 느낀다. 우리의 동정심은 우리의 무력함과 더불어 우리의 결백을 분명히 보여준다. 그런 만큼, 동정심은 (우리의 선한 의도에도 불구하고) 비록 부적절한 반응은 아닐지라도, 무례한 (뻔뻔스런) 반응이다. 전쟁과 폭정으로 괴로워하고 있는 타인들에 대한 우리의 동정심을 한쪽으로 제쳐두고, 어떤 이들의 부가 다른 이들의 궁핍을 의미할 수도 있기에, 우리의 특권이 그들의 고통과 같은 지도 위에 어떻게 위치해 있는지, 그리고 우리의 특권이 그들의 고통과, 어쩌면 상상하고 싶지 않은 방식으로, 어떻게 연결되어 있는지를 성찰해보는 것이 우리의 과제이며, 고통스럽게 우리를 동요시키는 저 이미지들은 이 과제를 시작하도록 첫 점화를 시켜줄 뿐이다.

1 ③ ▶ 빈칸완성
빈칸의 바로 다음에 언급되어 있는 '도덕적 또는 감정적 무감각'이 앞의 내용과 동격관계에 있음을 고려할 때, 가장 가까운 의미를 띤 것은 '냉담함, 무관심'을 뜻하는 ③ apathy이다. ① 연민 ② 동정 ④ 타성; 무력

2 ② ▶ 내용일치
필자는 첫 번째 문장에서 "감상적인 태도가 잔혹한 취향과 양립 가능한 것은 주지의 사실이다."라고 하였고, 그러한 감상적 태도의 대표적인 예로 동정심을 들었다. 그러므로 ②의 진술은 본문에 비추어 타당하다. ① "고통 받는 이들에 대한 동정심은 무례한 반응이므로 한쪽으로 제쳐두자."고 하였으므로 틀린 진술이다. ③ '디 니은 세계시민회 현상'에 대한 언급은 없으므로 무관한 진술이다. ④ 상업적 가치와 자극적 이미지의 추구가 언론을 지배한다는 것은 본문과 무관하다.

anesthesia n. 마취, 무감각증
sympathy n. 공감, 동정심
proximity n. 근접, 가까움
mystification n. 신비화
accomplice n. 공범, 공범관계
proclaim v. 선포하다, 공표하다; 분명히 보여주다
impotence n. 무력, 무기력
impertinent a. (연장자나 더 중요한 사람에게) 무례한, 버릇없는; 관계없는, 적절하지 못한
set aside ~을 한쪽으로 제쳐두다
beset v. 괴롭히다
murderous a. 살기등등한, 잔인한
reflection n. 심사, 숙고
destitution n. 빈곤, 궁핍
initial a. 처음의, 최초의
tropism n. (생물의) 향성(向性); (주의·사물에 대한) 지지(支持)
gruesome a. 섬뜩한, 소름끼치는, 잔혹한
mercantile a. 상업적인
quintessential a. 본질적인, 정수(精髓)의

08 2015 성균관대

연구원들은 욕구충족을 피하거나 미루는 능력이 인생에 있어서의 결과와 관련되어 있는지에 대해 오랫동안 흥미를 가지고 있어 왔다. 가장 잘 알려진 실험은 '마시멜로' 실험이다. 이 실험에서 15분 동안 과자를 먹는 것을 참은 아이들은 과자를 하나 더 받았다. 기다리지 못한 아이들은 성인이 되었을 때 수입이 낮고 건강이 안 좋은 경향이 있었다. 스톡홀름 대학의 데이비드 린달(David Lindahl) 박사는 스웨덴에서 조사된 한 연구 자료를 사용했는데, 그 연구에서는 13세의 아이들 13,000명 이상에게 지금 140달러를 받고 싶은지 아니면 5년 후에 1,400달러를 받고 싶은지를 물어보았다. 이 아이들 중 약 5분의 4는 기다릴 준비가 되어 있다고 말했다. 이전의 연구원들과는 달리, 린달 박사는 모든 아이들을 추적할 수 있었으며 아이들의 부모의 배경과 인지능력을 확인할 수 있었다. 그는 더 적은 돈을 즉시 받길 원했던 13세 아이들은 나중에 더 큰 보상을 받기 위해 기다리겠다고 말했던 아이들보다 향후 18년 동안 범죄로 유죄판결을 받을 가능성이 32%나 더 높았음을 확인했다. 그는 조급한 사람들은 즉각적인 혜택을 선호하고, 따라서 잠재적인 처벌에 의해 억제되는 경향이 낮다고 생각한다. 그러나 한 사람의 범죄 행로가 이미 10대에 정해져 있다는 사실이 괴로운 사람들이 절망할 필요는 없다. 린달 박사는 해결책을 제공한다. 응답자들의 교육을 분석에 포함시켰을 때, 그는 교육정도가 더 높은 것이 지연된 욕구충족을 선호하는 것과 관련돼 있음을 확인했다. "따라서 저는 학교 교육이 사람들로 하여금 미래를 더 가치 있게 여기게 만듦으로써 사람들이 범죄를 저지르는 것을 막을 수 있다고 생각합니다."라고 린달 박사는 설명한다.

1 ④ ▶ 글의 제목
삶 전반에서 욕구충족을 지연시키는 아이들이 조급한 아이들보다 범죄를 저지를 가능성이 낮다고 설명하고 있는 글이다. '마시멜로' 실험에 이어, 린달 박사의 실험에서 나중에 더 큰 보상을 받길 원한 아이들의 경우 성인이 되었을 때 유죄판결을 받을 확률이 낮다고 했으므로, 이 글의 제목으로는 ④ '시차 선호(미래의 이익과 비교된 현재의 이익을 더 선호하는 것)와 범죄 행동'이 적절하다.

intrigue v. 강한 흥미[호기심]를 불러일으키다
avoid v. 피하다, 회피하다
defer v. 연기하다, 늦추다
gratification n. 만족시킴, 희열, 욕구충족
refrain from ~을 삼가다
confection n. 과자, 캔디
track v. 추적하다, 뒤쫓다
account for ~을 해명하다, ~의 이유가 되다
at once 즉시, 당장
be convicted of ~로 유죄판결을 받다
fret v. 초조하다, 안달이 나다, 괴로워하다
educational attainment 교육정도
preference n. 선호, 애호(for)

2 ⑤   ▶ 내용파악
"린달 박사는 높은 교육정도가 지연된 욕구충족을 선호하는 것과 관련되어 있음을 확인했다."라고 했으므로, ⑤가 린달 박사가 주장하는 바이다.

09 2021 단국대

지난해에 6학년인 나의 딸은 과학 과목을 공부해야 했다. 그녀의 교육은 매주 보통 박사 학위를 가진 과학자도 모를 단어인 "저반(底盤)"과 "부생(腐生) 식물"과 같은 어려운 단어를 생각 없이 암기하는 것으로 이루어져 있었다. 그녀는 "개선된 핵융합"과 같은 일들을 한 유명한 과학자들의 업적을 읊었지만, 핵융합이 무엇을 의미하는지 전혀 모르고 있다는 것은 아무런 걱정을 할 것이 없다. 그녀는 아주 좋은 성적을 받았다(그녀는 암기를 잘한다). 그런데 지금은 과학을 싫어한다. 8학년인 나의 아들 또한 과학 교육에 시달렸다. 매주 그는 사전에 옳고 그른 답이 이미 정해져 있는 판에 박힌 실험실 실험을 해야 했다. 그는 정답을 알아맞히는 방법을 알아냈고, 좋은 점수를 받았다. 지금 그 또한 과학을 싫어한다.

과학은 모든 아이들의 호기심을 즐겁게 배출하는 수단을 제공할 수 있다. 과학 교육은 질문을 하는 방법을 가르치고, 답을 찾기 위한 틀을 만들어야 한다. 초등학교에서, 전문 용어와 수학적 추상(이론) 때문에 나의 아이들은 과학은 어렵고, 지루하여, 일상의 관심사와 무관하다는 잘못된 인상을 갖게 됐다. 해마다, 미국 전역의 학급마다 과학을 끈기 있게 배우는 학생들의 수가 줄어들고 있다.

과학의 경이로움과 즐거움을 일반인들에게 얼마간 전하려고 했던 전문 지질학자로서 나는 "과학에 대한 흥미상실 현상"을 보고 슬프기도 하고 화가 나기도 한다. 나는 과학이 우리의 삶에서 매우 중요하다는 것을 알고 있다. 우리의 물리적인 세계에 대한 기본 지식, 과학적 이해능력을 이루는 지식이 없으면, 우리는 우리가 사는 곳, 먹는 것, 환경을 다루는 방법에 대해 정보에 입각한 결정을 내릴 수 없다.

1 ④   ▶ 빈칸완성
빈칸 앞에서 필자의 6학년 딸이 의미도 모르고 과학 개념, 과학자의 업적 등을 외워 좋은 성적을 냈지만, 지금은 과학을 싫어한다(now she hates science)고 했다. 그리고 이와 비슷한 경우에 해당하는 8학년 아들 또한 답이 미리 정해져 있는 실험을 했고 좋은 점수를 받았다고 했다. 빈칸에는 아들이 과학에 대해서 어떻게 생각하는지에 대한 내용이 적절한데, 빈칸 뒤의 too를 고려하면, 8학년 아들 또한 6학년 딸처럼 과학을 싫어한다(he hates science)는 흐름을 만드는 ④가 빈칸에 적절하다.

2 ①   ▶ 내용일치
필자는 좋은 점수를 받았음에도 정작 과학을 싫어하게 된 자녀들의 사례를 소개하면서, 과학 교육은 질문을 하는 방법을 가르치고, 답을 찾기 위한 틀을 만들어야 한다는 자신의 의견을 개진했다. 따라서 ①이 글의 내용과 일치한다.

3 ④   ▶ 글의 요지
필자는 과학 교육에 흥미를 잃은 딸과 아들의 사례를 예로 들며, 현재 미국의 암기식 과학 교육 방법이 잘못되었으며, 아이들의 호기심을 자극할 수 있도록 과학 교육은 질문을 하는 방법을 가르치고, 답을 찾기 위한 틀을 만들어야 한다고 주장하고 있다. 따라서 ④가 글의 요지로 적절하다.

---

mindless a. 지성이 없는, 무심한, 생각이 모자라는
memorization n. 기억, 암기
big words 자랑, 허풍, 어려운 말
batholith n. 저반(底盤)(화성암이 불규칙하게 형성된 큰 덩어리)
saprophyte n. 부생(腐生) 식물(균류)
recite v. 읊다, 암송하다
vague a. 막연한, 애매한, 명확치 않은
abuse v. 남용하다, 학대하다
canned a. 미리 준비된, 판에 박힌
preordained a. 이미 정해져 있는
exhilarating a. 아주 신나는[즐거운]
outlet n. 발산[배출] 수단
jargon n. (특정 분야의 전문·특수) 용어
abstraction n. 관념, 추상적 개념
persevere v. (끝까지) 해내다, 끈기 있게 노력하다
shrink v. 줄어들다
geologist n. 지질학자
turnoff n. 흥미를 잃게 하는 것[사람]
profoundly ad. (영향 등을) 깊이
literacy n. 글을 읽고 쓸 줄 아는 능력; 지식, 능력

10 2019 국민대

현대 심리학의 지형을 바꾸어놓은 버러스 프레드릭 스키너(B. F. Skinner)는 학습의 습득을 설명하기 위해 조작적 조건화라는 용어를 새로 만들었다. 조작적 조건화는 유기체가 바람직한 결과를 만들어내는 방식으로 행동하는 법을 배우는 과정이다. 그런 행동을 '조작적'이라고 부르는데, 왜냐하면 그런 행동은 그 환경에서 작동하기로 고안되었기 때문이다. 다시 말해, 수동적인 반응을 일으키는 자극들 간의 연상학습을 포함하는 고전적 조건화와는 대조적으로, 조작적 조건화는 자발적으로 발산된 행동과 그에 따른 결과 간의 연상학습을 포함한다.

스키너는 또한 '보상'이나 '만족' 대신에 강화라는 용어를 사용했다. 객관적으로 정의하면, 강화인자는 이전에 있었던 반응이 일어날 가능성을 증가시키는 자극이다. 강화인자에는 두 가지 종류가 있는데, 하나는 긍정적 강화인자고 다른 하나는 부정적 강화인자다. '긍정적 강화인자'는 긍정적인 자극을 표출함으로써 이전에 있었던 반응을 강화시킨다. 이에 반해, '부정적 강화인자'는 혐오자극을 제거함으로써 반응을 강화시킨다.

스키너는 처벌이 부정적 강화의 형태는 아니라고 재빨리 지적했다. 비록 처벌과 부정적 강화가 종종 헛갈리지만, 처벌에는 역효과가 있다. 즉, 처벌은 이전에 있었던 반응이 일어날 가능성을 줄여준다. 처벌에는 두 가지 종류가 있다. '긍정적 처벌인자'는 특정 행동을 약화시킬 목적으로 혐오자극을 표출함으로써 반응을 약화시킨다. 이에 반해, '부정적 처벌인자'는 긍정적이라고 일반적으로 특징지어지는 자극을 제거함으로써 행동을 약화시킨다.

operant conditioning 조작적 조건화
classical conditioning 고전적 조건화
association n. 연상, 연상되는 것
stimulus n. 자극제, 자극
reinforcement n. (상벌 따위에 의한) 강화
positive reinforcer 긍정적 강화인자, 정적 강화인자(어떤 행동이 일어난 직후에 강화인자를 제공함으로써 그 행동의 빈도 혹은 확률이 높아지도록 하는 것)
presentation n. <심리학> 표출
negative reinforcer 부정적 강화인자(바라지 않는 어떤 것을 제거함으로써 바람직한 행동의 강도와 빈도를 증가시키는 것)
aversive stimulus 혐오자극(미래의 행동 발생 가능성을 감소시킬 수 있는 모든 유형의 자극)

1 ② ▶ 동의어
본문에서 coin은 '(새로운 낱말 어구를) 만들다'라는 뜻으로 쓰였으므로, ②의 invented가 정답이다. ① 유도하다 ③ 가리키다 ④ 반복하다

2 ④ ▶ 빈칸완성
강화는 보상이나 만족 대신에 쓰이는 용어라고 했으므로, 강화인자 역시 보상이나 만족과 같이 긍정적인 결과와 관련된 말이 될 것이다. 따라서 빈칸 ⑧ 역시 긍정적인 내용인 increases가 적절하다. 한편, 처벌에는 역효과가 있다고 했으므로, 빈칸 ⓒ에는 부정적인 내용인 decreases가 적절하다. 따라서 ④가 정답이다. ① 용서하다 — 격퇴하다 ② 부인하다 — 승인하다 ③ 거부하다 — 받다

3 ③ ▶ 내용일치
긍정적 강화인자는 긍정적인 자극을 표출함으로써 이전에 있었던 반응을 '강화시킨다'고 했으므로 ③이 정답이다. ① 긍정적 처벌인자는 특정 행동을 약화시킬 목적으로 혐오자극을 표출함으로써 반응을 '약화시킨다'고 했다. ② 부정적 강화인자는 혐오자극을 제거함으로써 반응을 '강화시킨다'고 했다. ④ 부정적 처벌인자는 긍정적이라고 일반적으로 특징지어지는 자극을 제거함으로써 행동을 '약화시킨다'고 한 반면, 부정적 강화인자는 혐오자극을 제거함으로써 반응을 '강화시킨다'고 했으므로, 서로 다르다.

11 2022 성균관대

최근의 한 실험에서, 존스홉킨스(Johns Hopkins) 대학의 에이미 스탈(Aimee E. Stahl)과 리사 페이겐슨(Lisa Feigenson)은 11개월 된 아기에게 일종의 마술을 보여주었다. 공이 단단한 벽을 통과하는 것처럼 보이거나 장난감 자동차가 선반 끝으로 굴러 떨어져 허공에 매달려 있는 것처럼 보이게 했다. 아기들은 이러한 기이한 사건들에 놀라고 많은 관심을 기울일 만큼 일상 물리학에 대해 충분히 알고 있었다. 그러고 나서 연구원들은 아기들에게 가지고 놀 장난감을 주었다. 공이 벽을 뚫고 사라지는 것을 본 아기들은 공을 두드렸고, 차가 허공에 매달려 있는 것을 본 아기들은 계속 차를 떨어뜨렸다. 그것은 마치 공이 정말로 단단한지 혹은 장난감 자동차가 중력을 거스르는지 알아보기 위해 실험하는 것과 같았다.

이것은 어린아이들이 배우기 위해 가르침을 받을 필요가 없다는 것은 아니다. 최근 연구는 학교수업과 "자녀양육"에 수반되는 그런 종류의 가르침인 명시적 교육이 제한적일 수 있음을 보여준다. 아이들은 자신들이 가르침을 받고 있다고 생각할 때, 그들은 새로운 것을 만들어내는 대신 어른들이

solid a. 단단한, 고체의
roll off 굴러 떨어지다
physics n. 물리학
vanish v. 사라지다
bang v. 탁 치다; 쿵 울리다; 쾅 쏘다
hover v. (허공을) 맴돌다
defy v. (사물을) 무시하다, 문제시하지 않다
gravity n. 중력
explicit a. 분명한, 명백한
instruction n. 설명, 교육

하는 것을 단순히 재현할 가능성이 훨씬 더 높다.
내 연구실은 복잡한 장난감으로 다른 버전의 실험을 했다. 하지만 이번에는 실험자가 선생님처럼 행동했다. 그녀는 "이 장난감이 어떻게 움직이는지 궁금해요." 대신 "내 장난감이 어떻게 작동하는지 보여줄게요."라고 말했다. 아이들은 그녀가 한 것을 정확히 따라했고, 그들만의 해결책을 떠올리지 못했다. 아이들은 아주 합리적으로, 선생님이 아이들에게 무언가를 하는 어떤 특정한 방법을 보여준다면, 그것은 올바른 방법임에 틀림없으며 새로운 것을 시도하는 것은 의미가 없다고 생각하는 것처럼 보인다. 그러나 결과적으로 학교와 "자녀양육"에 수반되는 그런 종류의 교육은 아이들을 모방으로 몰아넣고 혁신에서 멀어지게 한다.

reproduce v. 다시 만들어 내다, 재생[재현]하다
imitate v. 모방하다, 흉내 내다
come up with (해답·돈 등을) 찾아내다[내놓다]
solution n. 해법, 해결책
rationally ad. 합리적으로, 이성적으로
innovation n. 혁신, 쇄신

1 ③   ▶ 빈칸완성
빈칸 다음 문장에서 아이들은 자신들이 가르침을 받고 있다고 생각할 때 어른들이 하는 것을 단순히 재현할 가능성이 높다고 했으므로, 학교수업과 자녀양육에 수반되는 명시적 교육은 새로운 것을 만들어내는 것이 아니라 어른들을 모방하는 것일 수 있다. 따라서 명시적 교육은 '제한적'이라고 볼 수 있으므로 ③이 빈칸에 적절하다. ① 풍부한 ② 불필요한 ④ 보상의 ⑤ 피하는

2 ⑤   ▶ 내용파악
첫 번째 단락에서 스탈과 페이겐슨은 아이들에게 공이 단단한 벽을 통과하는 것처럼 보이거나 장난감 자동차가 선반 끝으로 굴러 떨어져 허공에 매달려 있는 것처럼 보이는 실험을 했다고 했다. 그리고 나서 이들은 아기들에게 가지고 놀 장난감을 주었는데, 공이 벽을 뚫고 사라지는 것을 본 아기들은 공을 두드렸고, 차가 허공에 매달려 있는 것을 본 아기들은 계속 차를 떨어뜨렸다고 했다. 그것은 마치 공이 정말 단단한지 아니면 장난감 자동차가 중력을 거스르는지 알아보기 위해 실험하는 것과 같았다고 했는데, 이는 아기들이 생각하기에 일어나기 어려운 것을 시험해 보기 위한 행동이었으므로 ⑤가 정답이다.

3 ①   ▶ 글의 제목
아이들은 가르침을 받고 있다고 생각할 때, 새로운 것을 만들어내는 대신 어른들이 하는 것을 단순히 재현할 가능성이 훨씬 더 높으며, 학교와 "자녀양육"에 수반되는 명시적 교육은 아이들을 모방으로 몰아넣고 혁신에서 멀어지게 한다고 했다. 이 글은 '아이들이 스스로 배울 수 있는 환경의 중요성'에 대해 설명하고 있으므로 ①이 제목으로 적절하다.

12 2021 세종대

가면(假面) 증후군은 개인이 교실과 직장에서 자신이 이뤄낸 성과를 스스로 의심하고 사기꾼으로 드러날까 봐 끊임없이 마음속으로 두려워하는 심리적 성향이다. 그들의 역량을 보여주는 외적인 증거가 있음에도 불구하고, 이러한 현상을 경험하는 사람들은 자신들이 사기꾼이고 자신들이 성취한 모든 것에 대해 스스로가 자격이 없다고 여전히 확신하고 있다. 가면 증후군을 가진 사람들은 자신들의 성공을 운이 좋았던 탓으로 잘못 돌리거나, 다른 사람들을 속여서 스스로가 인식하는 것보다 더 똑똑하다고 생각하게 만든 결과로 간주한다. 초기 연구는 성공한 여성들 사이에 (가면 증후군이) 널리 퍼져 있는 것에 초점을 맞췄지만, 가면 증후군은 남녀 모두에게 똑같이 영향을 미치는 것으로 인식되어 왔다.

가면 현상이라는 용어는 폴린 클랜스(Pauline R. Clance) 박사와 수잔 임스(Suzanne A. Imes) 박사가 1978년에 도입한 용어다. 그들은 가면 현상을 스스로 인식한 지적 허위나 사기를 개인적으로 경험하는 것이라고 정의했다. 연구원들은 표본으로 선택된 150명의 성공한 여성들을 인터뷰함으로써 이와 같은 내적 경험을 한 사람이 얼마나 널리 퍼져 있는지를 조사했다. <모든 참가자들은 동료들로부터 뛰어난 업무 능력을 공식적으로 인정받았으며, 수여받은 학위와 표준화된 시험 점수를 통해 학업 성취도를 보여주었다.> 외부의 인정을 보여주는 일관된 증거에도 불구하고, 이 여성들은 자신들의 성과에 대한 내면적 인정이 부족했다. 다른 사람들은 자신들의 지능과 능력을 과대평가한 반면, 인터뷰에 참여했던 여성들은 자신들의 성공이 운이 좋아서 그렇게 된 것이라고 설명했다. 클랜스와 임스는 가면 현상에 대한 이와 같은 심리적 틀이 성(性) 고정관념, 어린 시절의 가족 동태, 문화, 그리고 귀인(歸因) 방식과 같은 요인들부터 생겨난다고 믿었다. 연구원들은 가면 현상을 경험한 여성들이 우울증, 전반적인 불안감, 낮은 자신감과 관련된 증상을 보인다고 판단했다.

imposter syndrome 가면 증후군(자신이 이뤄낸 업적을 스스로 받아들이지 못하는 심리 현상)
persistent a. 고집하는, 완고한; 영속하는, 끊임없는
internalize v. 내면화하다, 주관화하다
expose v. 노출시키다; (환경 따위에) 접하게 하다
fraud n. 사기, 협잡; 사기꾼
competence n. 적성, 자격, 능력
convinced a. 확신한
deserve v. ~할 만하다, 받을 가치가 있다
impostorism n. 가면 증후군
attribute v. (~에) 돌리다, (~의) 탓으로 하다
deceive v. 속이다
perceive v. 지각하다, 감지하다; 인식하다
prevalence n. 보급, 유행; 우세
affect v. 영향을 미치다; (병·고통이 사람·인체를) 침범하다, 해치다

1 ①　　▶ 빈칸완성
주절의 '자신들이 사기꾼이고 자신들이 성취한 모든 것들에 대해 스스로가 자격이 없다고 확신하는 것'은 '내적인(internal) 심리상태'를 가리키며, 이것과 양보, 대조 관계에 있는 '증거(evidence)'는 '외적인(external)' 속성을 가진 것이라 할 수 있다. ② 허구의 ③ 구조상의 ④ 내부의

2 ③　　▶ 문장삽입
주어진 문장은 "모든 참가자들은 동료들로부터 뛰어난 업무 능력을 공식적으로 인정받았으며, 수여받은 학위와 표준화된 시험 점수를 통해 학업 성취도를 보여주었다."라는 의미로, 인터뷰에 참가한 여성들이 외부로부터 인정을 받은 사람들이라는 것을 밝히는 내용이므로 ⓒ에 위치하는 것이 적절하다. 이런 외부적 인정은 ⓒ 다음의 Despite구가 잘 가리키고 있다.

3 ②　　▶ 내용일치
"가면 증후군은 남녀 모두에게 똑같이 영향을 미치는 것으로 인식되고 있다."라는 첫 단락 마지막 부분을 통해 ②가 옳은 진술임을 알 수 있다.

term n. 용어
introduce v. 소개하다; 받아들이다
define v. 정의하다; 규정하다
phoniness n. 허위
consistent a. 일치하는; 시종일관된
external a. 외부의, 외적인
validation n. 입증; 인정, 인증
lack v. 부족하다
acknowledgement n. 승인; 자백
overestimate v. 과대평가하다
framework n. 뼈대, 틀
factor n. 요인, 요소
gender stereotype 성(性) 고정관념
dynamics n. 역학; 활력
attribution n. (원인 따위를 ~에) 돌림, 귀속(歸屬)
depression n. 우울증
generalized a. 일반화된
self-confidence n. 자기 확신

13　　2017 성균관대

우리는 'college'와 'university'란 용어를 상호교환해서 사용한다. 우리는 "그녀가 미시건 대학에 다녔다." 또는 "그가 오벌린 대학에 다닌다."라고 말을 할 때 마치 college와 university가 같은 의미를 가지고 있는 것처럼 이름 뒤에 오는 명사에 신경을 쓰지 않고 말한다. 두 용어는 같은 것이 아니지만, 확실하게 두 용어는 서로 관련되어 있으며 college는 university내의 '학부'로서 존재할지도 모른다. 그러나 college와 university에는 서로 다른 목적이 있다. college는 학생들이 미래를 살아가는 자원으로 지식을 이용하도록 과거의 지식을 대학생들에게 전하는 것과 관련되어 있다. university는 과거를 대체하기 위한 새로운 지식 창출을 목적으로 교수와 대학원생들이 하는 다수의 연구 활동이 주를 이룬다.
B 이 둘은 모두 가치 있는 목적이며, 대학생이 최첨단 또는 혁신적인 연구를 하는 학자 또는 과학자와 함께 연구를 할 때 때때로 이 둘의 목적이 수렴된다. 그러나 종종 이런 목적들은, 갈등은 아니라 하더라도, 경쟁에 놓이게 되는데, 연구의 수준이 높아질수록 특히 더 그러하다. 세계에서 가장 우수한 종합대학 중 하나인 캘리포니아 주립대학교를 설립한 사람이 이례적으로 정직하게 인정했듯이, "(연구) 수준이 높은 우수한 교수일수록 결과적으로 학부 학생을 가르치는 데 대한 관심은 낮아지게 된다." 클라크 커(Clark Kerr)가 우리의 보다 절실한 문제 중 하나로 이런 '잔인한 역설'을 확인한 이후 이것은 거의 50년 동안 이어졌다. 오늘날은 그 어느 때보다 더 절실하다.
E 그러나 정확히 대학에서 문제가 되는 것은 무엇이고, 대학에서 얼마만큼의 일이 이루어지고 있느냐 하는 것이 왜 중요한 것일까? 가장 중요한 점으로, 대학은 젊은이들이 청소년기와 성인기 사이에 있는 영역을 통과하는 데 도움이 될 수 있는 장소가 되어야 한다. 대학은 자기 인식을 위해 그런 힘난한 상황을 건너기 위해 노력하는 학생들을 위해 강제가 아니라 안내를 해주어야 한다. 대학은 학생들이 사려 깊은 시민의 자질에 필요한 특정한 자질의 정신과 마음을 기르는 것을 도와야 한다.

1 ③　　▶ 지시대상
are 다음의 보어로 aims(목적)가 있으므로 Both of these가 가리키는 것은 college와 university가 될 수 없으며, 그 앞에 설명된 college의 목적인 transmitting knowledge(지식전달)와 university의 목적인 creating new knowledge(신지식 창출)를 가리킨다고 해야 한다. 지식전달은 곧 교육이나 교수(teaching)이며 신지식 창출은 곧 연구이므로 밑줄 친 Both of these가 가리키는 것은 ③이다.

interchangeably ad. 상호교환해서
bother v. 신경 쓰다, 애를 쓰다
interconnect v. 서로 관련되다
division n. (조직의) 분과[부, 국]
transmit v. (지식·보도 따위를) 전하다, 전파시키다
undergraduate student 대학생
draw upon ~을 이용하다, ~에 의지하다
an array of 다수의
research activity 연구 활동
faculty n. (대학의) 학부; 교수; 교직원
graduate student 대학원생
with the aim of ~을 지향하여, ~을 목표로
supersede v. 대체하다, 대신하다
converge v. (생각·정책·목적 등이) 수렴되다
cutting-edge a. 최첨단의
groundbreaking a. 획기적인, 혁신적인
move up the ladder 승진[출세]하다
prestige n. 명성, 신망
pressing a. 긴급한, 절박한
at stake 성패가 달려 있는, 위태로운
adolescence n. 청소년기, 사춘기
adulthood n. 성인(임), 성년
core n. 핵심; 정수
coercion n. 강제; 위압

2 ②　▶ 부분이해
클라크 커가 확인한 cruel paradox는 앞 문장에 언급된 "수준이 높은 우수한 교수일수록 결과적으로 학부 학생을 가르치는 데 대한 관심은 낮아지게 된다."는 모순적인 상황을 의미한다고 볼 수 있다. 따라서 훌륭한 교수들이 반드시 잘 가르치는 것은 아니라고 볼 수 있으므로 cruel paradox가 의미하는 것은 ②이다.

3 ④　▶ 단락나누기
사람들이 상호교환해서 사용하는 college와 university의 차이점을 설명하고, 그리고 B college와 university의 목적인 교육과 연구 사이의 중대한 역설에 대해 언급하고, 마지막으로 E college가 나아가야 할 방향에 대해 설명하고 있으므로 ④가 정답이다.

treacherous a. 믿을 수 없는, 방심할 수 없는
terrain n. 영역, 분야
requisite a. 필요한, 없어서는 안 될

14 2013 중앙대

사회적 순응을 연구하기 위해 필립 짐바르도(Philip Zimbardo)와 크래그 헤이니(Craig Haney)(1977)는 모의 교도소 실험에 참여할 지원자 모집광고를 신문에 냈다. 지원자들에게 무작위로 '죄수'와 '교도관'의 역할이 주어졌다. 두 집단의 사람들을 스탠포드 대학 심리학 건물 지하실의 가짜 교도소에 집어넣고는 최소한의 지시만 내렸다. 그들에게 주어진 역할을 맡으라고 말해주고 교도관의 임무는 '법과 질서를 유지하는' 것이라고 말해주기만 했다. 단 몇 시간 만에 한 집단의 행동이 다른 집단의 행동과 분명히 구분되었다. 교도관들은 경비가 가장 엄중한 교도소의 전형적인 행동방식과 태도를 취했는데, 대부분이 폭력적이고 공격적이 되었다. 몇몇 죄수들은 교도관들에 대해 격분하기도 했지만 대부분의 죄수들은 수동적이고 의존적이며 우울해지기도 했다. 죄수들의 고통이 너무 커서 한 죄수는 36시간이 채 지나지 않아 석방시켜야 했으며 여러 명의 다른 죄수들도 예정된 2주간의 실험이 끝나기 전인 실험시작 6일이 지난 후에 석방시켜야 했다.
전형적인 사회규범들이 두 집단의 행동을 통제했다. 교도관들은 그들의 역할을 그대로 하고 질서를 유지하기 위해 필요하다고 믿는 태도를 택했다. 교도관들의 학대의 대상인 죄수들은 교도소 생활에 대해 그들이 생각하는 이미지와 일치하는 태도를 취했다. 그 두 집단들이 적대적이 되었을 때 각 집단은 다른 집단의 행동을 강화시켰다. 죄수들은 교도관들이 비열하고 사악할 것으로 예상했고 그에 따라 그들을 대했다. 교도관들은 죄수들이 반항적일 것으로 예상했으며 다루기 힘든 행동을 막기 위한 조치를 취했다. 실험참가자들의 인식 때문에, 이러한 거짓 상황이 실험에 포함된 모든 사람의 감정과 행동에 실제적인 영향을 미쳤다. 이 실험에서 나타나는 것처럼, 사회규범에 따르는 것은 단순히 자신이 속한 집단의 사회적 압력의 결과인 것은 아니며, 사회의 다른 집단의 영향 또한 규범에 따르도록 하는 압력을 가중시키는 것이다.

1 ④　▶ 글의 제목
본문에서 집단이 사회규범에 따르게 되는 것(conformity)은 사회 내의 다른 집단의 영향으로 규범을 따르라는 압력이 커지기 때문이라고 했으므로 ②의 경우에 '전형적인 사회 규범의 효과'라고 한다면 conformity의 개념이 없으므로 틀렸으며 ④에서 다른 집단의 영향으로 규범에 순응하게 되고 이에 따라 그에 상응하는 사회적 행동을 하게 되므로 '순응이 사회적 행위에 미치는 영향'이라고 한 것이 맞다. 더군다나 마지막 문장에 실험 결과를 나타내는 '이 실험이 보여주는 것처럼(as this experiment shows) 사회규범에 순응하는 것(conformity to social norms)'이 무엇인지를 나타내는 부분이 나온다. 실험을 인용한 글에서는 그 실험의 결과, 결론을 나타내는 부분이 핵심이므로 이점에 착안하여 정답을 도출해내도 된다.

2 ②　▶ 내용일치
두 번째 단락 첫 번째 문장에서 전형적인 사회규범이 두 집단의 행동을 통제했다고 했으므로 실험참가자들(두 집단)이 전형적인 사회규범에 따라 행동한 것이다. ① 순응으로 인해 이 실험의 상황이 더 악화되었으므로 틀린 진술이다. ③ 지시사항 때문에 수동적인 척 한 게 아니라 정말로 수동적이 된 것이다. ④ 집단 내에서 규범에 따르도록 하는 사회적인 압력이 다른 집단과의 접촉으로 완화되는 게 아니라 더 강화된다고 마지막 문장에서 언급하고 있으므로 틀린 진술이다.

conformity n. 순응; 일치
volunteer n. 지원자, 자원 봉사자
take part in ~에 참여[참가]하다, 가담하다; 협력하다
mock v. 조롱하다 a. 모의의; 가짜의
randomly ad. 무작위로
assign v. 부여하다, 배정하다, 할당하다
prisoner n. 죄수
guard n. 경호원; 교도관, 간수
basement n. 지하실
instruction n. (pl.) 지시, 명령
differentiate v. 분리[구분]하다
typical a. 전형적인, 대표적인
maximum security 가장 삼엄한 경비
abusive a. 학대하는; 욕설을 퍼붓는; 폭력적인
aggressive a. 공격적인
passive a. 수동적인
dependent a. 의지하고 있는, 의존하는
depressed a. 의기소침한; 우울한; 불경기의
enraged a. 분개하는
stereotypical a. 전형적인, 진부한
simulate v. 흉내 내다; 가상 모의실험을 하다
accord with ~와 일치하다
antagonistic a. 적대적인
mean a. 비열한
vicious a. 사악한
rebellious a. 반항적인
unruly a. 다루기 힘든, 제어하기 힘든
pretense n. 가식, 핑계; 주장
by virtue of ~때문에, 덕분에
magnify v. 확대하다; 과장하다; 심화하다

15 2019 인하대

많은 부모들이 벌(罰)을 받으면서 자랐기 때문에, 그들이 처벌에 의존하는 것은 이해할 만한 일이다. 그러나 처벌은 갈등을 증폭시키고 (경험에 따른) 학습을 차단하는 경향이 있다. 처벌은 '싸움 혹은 도망'이라는 반응을 이끌어내는데, 이는 전두엽에서 일어나는 정교한 사고(思考)가 작동을 멈추고 기본적인 방어 메커니즘이 작동하기 시작한다는 것을 의미한다. 처벌은 우리로 하여금 반항하게 만들고, 수치심이나 분노를 느끼게 하며, 감정을 억누르거나, 혹은 들키지 않는 방법을 알아내려 하게 만든다. 이 경우에, 어엿한 4살배기 아이라면 격하게 반항하게 될 것이다.

그렇다면 보상이 긍정적인 선택이다, 그런가? 속단지 마라. 수십 년에 걸쳐, 심리학자들은 보상이 우리가 본래부터 가지고 있는 동기와 즐거움을 감소시킬 수 있다는 말을 해왔다. 예를 들어, 그림 그리기를 좋아하는 아이들에게, 실험 조건 하에서, 돈을 주면서 그림을 그리도록 하면, 그 아이들은 돈을 받지 않은 아이들보다 그림을 덜 그린다. 이는 심리학자들이 "과잉정당화 효과"라고 부르는 것으로, 외부적인 보상이 아이의 내적인 동기를 가려 버린다는 것이다.

보상은 또한 창의력을 저하시키는 것과도 관련지어져 왔다. 일련의 권위 있는 한 연구에서, 사람들에게 한 세트의 재료들(핀이 들어 있는 상자, 양초, 종이성냥)을 주고는, 양초를 벽에 붙이는 방법을 알아내도록 했다. 그 문제를 해결하는 데는 혁신적인 사고가 필요하다. 즉, 재료들을 목적과 무관한 방식으로(상자를 양초의 받침대로) 보아야 하는 것이다. 이 난제를 해결하면 보상을 받을 거라는 말을 들은 사람들은 해결 방법을 알아내는 데 평균적으로 더 많은 시간이 걸렸다. 보상은 우리의 시야를 좁게 만든다. 우리의 뇌는 자유롭게 이리저리 생각해보는 것을 멈추게 된다. 우리는 깊이 생각하고 여러 가능성들을 살펴보는 것을 중단한다.

처벌과 보상에 대한 전반적인 개념은 아이들에 대한 부정적인 가정을 바탕으로 하고 있다. 아이들은 우리가 통제하고 우리가 원하는 모습으로 만들어야 하며 아이들은 좋은 의도를 가지고 있지 않다는 것이다. 그러나 아이들이 공감, 협동, 팀 정신, 근면에 대한 역량을 갖추고 있음을 우리가 깨닫게 되면, 우리는 이 가정을 뒤집을 수 있다. 그러한 관점은 우리가 아이들에게 말하는 방식을 크게 바꾼다. 보상과 처벌은 조건적이지만, 아이들에 대한 우리의 사랑과 긍정적인 관심은 무조건적이어야 한다. 사실, 우리가 공감하면서 이끌고 아이들의 말에 진심으로 귀를 기울일 때, 아이들도 우리의 말에 더 귀를 기울일 것이다.

1 ① ▶ 빈칸완성

이어지는 사례에서는 "어려운 과제를 사람들에게 주고 그 난제를 해결하면 보상을 받을 거라고 하는 경우, 평균적으로 해결방법을 알아내는 데 더 많은 시간이 걸렸다."는 것을 말하고 있는데, 이는 곧 보상이 문제를 해결하는 능력이나 창의력의 발휘를 방해한다는 것이므로, 빈칸에는 ①이 적절하다. 문단 후반부의 "보상은 우리의 시야를 좁게 만든다. 우리의 뇌는 자유롭게 이리저리 생각해보는 것을 멈추게 된다. 우리는 깊이 생각하고 여러 가능성들을 살펴보는 것을 중단한다."라는 내용을 통해서도 이를 확인할 수 있다.

2 ① ▶ 내용일치

마지막 문단에 글의 요지가 담겨 있는데, "처벌과 보상 모두 아이들에 대한 부정적인 가정에 바탕을 둔 것이며, 아이들이 가진 역량을 깨닫게 되면 이러한 가정을 하지 않게 된다. 아이들에게는 보상과 처벌보다는 사랑과 관심으로 다가가야 한다."로 요약할 수 있다. 그러므로 본문에서는 처벌과 보상 모두 좋은 해결책으로 여기지 않고 있음을 알 수 있다. 따라서 ①이 본문의 내용과 일치하는 진술이다.

---

escalate v. 단계적으로 확대시키다
conflict n. 갈등, 충돌, 대립
elicit v. (진리·사실 따위를 논리적으로) 이끌어 내다
sophisticated a. 정교한, 복잡한; 고도로 세련된
frontal cortex 전두엽
go dark (작동 등을) 정지하다, 멈추다
kick in 효과가 나타나기 시작하다
rebel v. 배반하다; 반항하다, 반대하다
sham v. 창피주다, 모욕시키다
repress v. 억누르다, 제지하다
full-fledged a. 깃털이 다 난; 완전히 성장한; 자격을 제대로 갖춘
resistance n. 저항, 반항
reward n. 보수, 포상, 보상
Not so fast 서두르지 마라, 그렇게 덤비지 마라
motivation n. 자극; 동기부여
overjustification n. 과잉정당화
external a. 외부의, 외적인
overshadow v. 가리다, 어둡게 하다; (비교하여) ~보다 중요하다[낫다]
internal a. 내부의, 내적인
classic a. 일류의; 권위 있는; 전형적인, 대표적인
a book of matches (떼어 쓰는) 종이성냥
unrelated a. 관계없는
dilemma n. 궁지, 딜레마
narrow v. 좁게 하다, 좁히다
puzzle v. 이리저리 생각하다, 머리를 짜내다
concept n. 개념
assumption n. 가정, 억측; 가설
intention n. 의도, 의향
empathy n. 공감, 감정이입
cooperation n. 협력, 협동, 제휴
perspective n. 전망, 견지, 시각
unconditional a. 무조건적인

---

16 2020 홍익대

부르디외(Bourdieu)는 학교 제도를 학문적 적성과 문화적 전통의 숨은 연결을 통해 정통(正統) 문화를 재생산하는 제도로 간주한다. 그는 기회 균등과 능력주의의 이념에도 불구하고, 지배계급은 정통 문화를 있는 그대로 재현하는 것과 그 문화를 정통적 방식으로 조작할 수 있는 행위자를 만들어내는 것만을 위해 거의 모든 교육 제도를 요구한다고 생각한다.

부르디외는 그것이 지배 집단의 문화이며, 이 문화가 학교에서 구현되고 있다고 주장해왔다. 따라서 교육의 차이는 계급적 차이에서가 아니라 개인의 재능에서 비롯되는 것으로 잘못 인식되는 경우

---

institution n. 제도, 관례, 관습
reproduction n. 재생, 재현
legitimate a. 합법적인, 적법의; 기존의 규칙[원칙, 기준]에 맞는
scholastic a. 학교의, 학교교육의

가 많은데, 이는 학문적 기준에 의해 측정되는 능력이 종종 천부적인 "재능"에서 비롯되는 것이 아니고 "계층 문화적 습관들과 교육 제도의 요구나 교육 제도 안에서의 성공을 정의하는 기준 사이의 유사성이 더 크거나 더 적음"에서 비롯된다는 사실을 무시한 결과다.

문화자본이라는 개념은 1960년대 초에 부르주아 문화와의 친밀도(숙지도)를 설명하기 위해 부르디외가 제안한 것인데, 부르주아 문화의 불평등한 분배는 개인의 재능과 학문적 능력주의를 빙자한 사회적 서열 유지에 도움이 된다. 이 개념에는 습득한 지식(교육적인 지식 혹은 그 밖의 지식), 문화적 코드, 말하는 방식 등이 포함되며, 이는 개인에게서 일종의 "아비투스"로 구현되고 문화적 상품에서도 구체화된다.

1 ② ▶ 내용일치
"교육의 차이는 계급적 차이에서가 아니라 개인의 재능에서 비롯되는 것으로 잘못 인식되는 경우가 많다."라고 했는데, 여기서 타고난 지능은 개인의 재능과 관계된 선천적인 것으로 후천적인 사회적 계층에 기초해서 생겨나는 것이 아니므로, ②가 옳지 않은 진술이다.

2 ② ▶ 내용추론
부르디외는 학교 제도를 지배계급의 정통 문화를 있는 그대로 재현하기 위한 제도로 간주하고 있으므로, ②가 정답으로 적절하다.

3 ④ ▶ 글의 제목
'기회 균등과 능력주의의 이념에도 불구하고, 지배계급은 정통 문화를 있는 그대로 재현하는 교육제도만을 원하고 있음'을 말하고 있는 글인데, 이는 곧 기회 균등과 능력주의가 실현되지 못하고 있다는 것이므로, 이것을 아우를 수 있는 제목으로는 ④가 적절하다.

aptitude n. 소질, 재능; 적성
heritage n. 상속재산; 전통; 유산
meritocracy n. 실력주의, 능력주의
dominant a. 지배적인, 유력한
reproduce v. 재생하다; 재현하다
manipulate v. (사람·여론 등을) (부정하게) 조종하다; (시장·시가 등을) 조작하다
embody v. (사상·감정 따위를) 구체화하다, (주의 등을) 구현하다, 실현하다
recognize v. 인지하다; 인정하다
giftedness n. 타고난 재능이 있음, 머리가 매우 좋음
criterion n. (비판·판단의) 기준, 표준
stem v. 유래하다, 일어나다, 생기다
affinity n. 친밀감; (밀접한) 관련성
define v. (말의) 정의를 내리다, 뜻을 밝히다
notion n. 관념, 개념
propose v. 제안하다, 제의하다
describe v. 묘사하다, 기술하다
familiarity n. 친밀, 친숙; 정통함
distribution n. 분배, 배분
conserve v. 보존하다, 보호하다
hierarchy n. 계급제도
under the cloak of ~의 가면을 쓰고
acquired a. 취득한, 획득한
habitus n. 습관, 버릇; 친숙한 사회 집단의 습속[습성]; 아비투스(권력 기반의 사회질서가 생산, 지각, 경험하게 되는 일상생활의 장이라는 뜻으로, 프랑스의 사회학자 피에르 부르디외가 도입한 용어)
objectify v. 객관화하다, 구체화하다

---

17 2014 중앙대

교육학은 아동들을 가르치는 기술이자 과학으로 정의되어 왔다. 교육학적 모델에서, 교사는 무엇이 학습되어야 할지, 어떻게 학습되어야 할지, 언제 학습되어야 할지, 그리고 학습내용이 학습되었는지 여부에 관해 결정할 전적인 책임이 있다. 교육학, 즉 흔히 알려져 있는 교사주도적인 가르침이라는 것은 학생에게 교사의 지시에 복종해야 하는 순종적 역할을 부여한다. 그것은 학습자는 교사가 그들에게 가르치는 것만을 알 필요가 있다는 가정에 입각해 있다. 그 결과 교사에게 의존하는 경향을 적극적으로 조장하는 교수-학습 상황이 생겨난다.

아주 최근까지 이러한 교육학적 모델은 아동을 가르칠 때와 성인을 가르칠 때에 똑같이 적용되어 왔는데, 이는 어떤 의미에서는 용어적으로 모순이다. <그 이유는 성인은 성숙함에 따라 점점 더 독립적이 되고 자신의 행동에 대해 책임을 지기 때문이다.> 그들은 종종 그들의 삶에 놓인 즉각적인 문제들을 해결하려는 진지한 욕구에 의해 배우려는 동기를 갖게 된다. 뿐만 아니라, 그들은 점점 더 스스로 결정을 하려는 욕구를 가진다. 여러 가지 면에서 교육학적 모델은 성인의 측면에서 벌어지는 그런 발달상의 변화들을 해명하지 않는데, 그 결과 개인 내부에 긴장, 분노, 그리고 저항을 양산하게 된다.

교육에 대한 대안적 모델로서의 성인 교육학의 성장과 발전은 이러한 상황을 바로잡고 성인교육을 향상시키는 데 도움이 되었다. 그러나 이런 변화는 하루아침에 일어난 것이 아니었다. 사실, 북미의

pedagogy n. 교육학
pedagogical a. 교육학의
material n. (특정 활동에 필요한) 자료, 소재
teacher-directed a. 교사 주도적
instruction n. 훈련, 교수, 교육; 설명; 지시
submissive a. 순종적인, 고분고분한
obedience n. 복종, 순종
dependency n. 의존, 종속
instructor n. 강사, 교사
account for ~을 해명하다, ~의 이유가 되다
andragogy n. 성인 교육학
remedy v. 바로잡다, 개선[교정]하다
engage A with B A와 B의 관계를 맺다

성인교육의 방향에 영향을 미친 중대한 사건이 있었다. 성인학습에 대한 사상, 개념, 접근법의 체계로서의 성인 교육학은 말콤 놀즈(Malcolm Knowles)에 의해 미국의 성인 교육자들에게 도입되었다. 그 체계에 대한 그의 기여는 상당한 것이었으며, 무수히 많은 성인 교육자들의 사고에 영향을 미쳤다.

성인 교육학이라는 용어는 성인 학습자들을 학습체험 구조와 연결시키는 과정으로 종종 해석된다. 놀즈는 이 용어를 성인들이 학습하는 것을 돕는 기술이자 과학이라고 정의하였다. 최초로 성인 교육학이라는 용어를 사용하면서, 그는 좀 더 보편적으로 사용되는 교육학이라는 용어와 구별되어야 한다고 주장하였다. 이후에, 그는 자신의 초기 견해를 수정하면서 "성인 교육학은 기존 교육학의 가설적 모델과 더불어 사용되어야 할 성인 학습자들에 관한 또 하나의 모델에 불과한 것으로서, 결국 성인들의 특정 상황에서의 '적합성'에 관한 가정들을 검증하기 위한 두 개의 대안적인 모델이 제공되는 셈이다."라고 말하였다.

modify v. 수정하다
thereby ad. 그것에 의해서, 그것으로
test out ~를 시험해 보다

1 ② ▶ **문장삽입**
주어진 문장은 "성인이 성숙함에 따라 독립적이고, 책임성이 높아지기 때문이다."는 것으로서, 앞서 나온 어떤 내용의 이유를 설명하는 것이다. 두 번째 단락의 첫 번째 문장에서 기존의 교육학적 모델을 성인에게 그대로 적용할 경우 용어적 모순이 발생한다고 하였다. 주어진 문장은 그러한 '용어적 모순이 발생하는 이유'를 제시하는 것으로, ⒷⒷ의 위치에 들어가는 것이 적절하다. 전체적으로 볼 때, 첫 번째 단락은 일반 교육학의 대상과 특성, 두 번째 단락은 일반 교육학의 내용을 그대로 성인에게 적용할 때 생길 수 있는 문제점, 세 번째 단락은 성인 교육학에 대한 제안과 그 기원, 네 번째 단락은 두 교육학적 모델의 관계기 다루어지고 있다.

2 ② ▶ **내용추론**
교육학적 모델에서는 "학생에게 교사의 지시에 복종해야 하는 순종적 역할을 부여한다."고 하였으므로, ②가 추론 가능한 내용이다. ① 네 번째 단락에서, 성인 교육학 모델의 주된 방식은 '성인들이 학습하는 것을 돕는 것'이라고 하였으므로, '교사의 역할이 교육에서 주요하다'고 한 추론은 적절하지 않다. ③ 두 번째 단락에서, 성인들에게 기존 교육학적 모델을 그대로 적용하면 '긴장, 분노, 저항'이 야기된다고 하였으므로 '성인들에게서 기존 교육학적 모델이 더 환영받는다'는 것은 적절한 추론이 아니다. ④ 네 번째 단락을 보면, 놀즈는 자신의 초기의 견해를 수정하여 '기존 교육학 모델과 자신의 성인 교육학 모델은 성인들의 특정한 상황에 따라 제공되어야 할 대안들'이라고 함으로써 그 둘의 관계가 모순적이거나 대립적 관계가 아닌 상호 보완적 관계에 있음을 시사했으므로 적절한 추론이 아니다.

18 2021 숭실대

수동적 공격성은 직접적으로 공격성을 보이기보다 간접적으로 공격적인 행동을 하는 것을 포함하는 행동이다. 수동적 공격성을 보이는 사람들은 종종 일을 미루거나, 뚱한 표정을 보이거나, 고집스러운 행동을 함으로써 가족과 다른 사람들의 요청이나 요구에 대해 자주 반감을 드러낸다.

수동적 공격성은 여러 가지 다른 방법들로 나타날지도 모른다. 예를 들면, 어떤 사람은 다른 사람들에 대한 자신의 혐오나 분노를 표현하는 방법으로 특정한 사람들을 피하기 위해 반복적으로 변명을 할지도 모른다. 수동적 공격성을 보이는 사람이 화를 내는 경우, 겉으로 보기에는 몹시 화가 나있고 괜찮지 않은데도 자신들이 화가 나있지 않으며 괜찮다고 거듭해서 주장할지도 모른다. 그들이 느끼고 있는 것과 감정적으로 마음을 여는 것을 거부하면서 그들은 더 이상의 의사소통을 하지 않고 그 문제를 논하는 것을 거부한다. 의도적으로 해야 할 일을 미루는 것은 수동적 공격성의 또 다른 특징이다. 하고 싶지 않은 일이나 지키고 싶지 않은 약속에 직면하면 수동적 공격성을 보이는 사람들은 일부러 늑장을 부릴 것이다. 만약 그들이 직장에서 업무를 완수하도록 요구받는다면 마지막 순간까지 그 업무를 미룰 것이다. 그들은 그 일을 맡긴 사람들을 곤란하게 하기 위해 그 과제를 심지어 늦게 제출할지도 모른다.

그래서 당신이 종종 수동적 공격성을 보이는 친구, 동료, 심지어 연인과 부딪힌다면 무엇을 할 수 있을까? 첫 번째 단계는 그러한 행동의 징후를 인식하는 것이다. 부루퉁함, 빗대어 말하는 칭찬, 꾸물거림, 움츠리는 태도, 그리고 의사소통의 거부 등은 수동적 공격성의 모든 징후들이다. 다른 사람들

passive-aggressive behavior 수동적 공격성
procrastinate v. 미루다
sullenness n. 시무룩함, 뚱함
stubborn a. 완고한, 고집스러운
manifest v. (특히 감정·태도·특질을 분명히) 나타내다
make excuses 변명하다
furious a. 몹시 화가 난
deliberately ad. 고의로, 의도[계획]적으로
drag one's feet 일부러 꾸물거리다, 열심히 하지 않다
put off 미루다, 연기하다
sulk v. 부루퉁하다, 샐쭉하다
backhanded a. 서투른, 빗대어 말하는
compliment n. 칭찬(의 말), 찬사
withdrawal n. 움츠림; 취소

이 이런 행동을 한다면, 당신은 화를 억누르도록 노력하라. 대신, 판단하지 않고 사실에 입각한 방식으로 다른 사람들의 감정을 지적하도록 하라. 만약 하기 싫은 일을 하는 것에 대해 매우 화가 난 아이를 대해야 한다면, "너는 방을 청소해 달라고 한 것에 대해 나에게 화가 난 것처럼 보이는구나."라고 말할 수 있다. 현실에서 사람들은 어쨌든 일반적으로 그들이 화가 나 있는 것을 부정한다. 이 시점에서 한 발짝 물러서서 그들에게 이런 감정을 헤쳐 나갈 시간을 주는 것이 좋은 생각이다.

keep in check ~을 억제하다, 억누르다
nonjudgmental a. (특히 도덕상의 문제에서) 개인적 판단을 피하는
factual a. 사실에 기반을 둔, 사실을 담은
chore n. 자질구레한 일, 허드렛일

1 ④　▶ 내용파악
　수동적 공격성의 징후들로 '부루퉁함, 빗대어 말하는 칭찬, 꾸물거림, 움츠리는 태도, 의사소통 거부' 등을 들고 있다. 하지만 ④는 해야 할 일을 미루는 것과 반대되는 것이므로 수동적 공격성의 징후로 볼 수 없다.

2 ①　▶ 내용파악
　세 번째 단락에서 수동적 공격성을 보이는 사람을 만났을 때 취할 행동에 대해 제안하고 있다. 친구, 동료 등이 수동적 공격성을 보인다면, 화를 억누르고 사실에 입각한 방법으로 그들의 감정에 대해 이야기하라고 했다. 따라서 ①이 수동적 공격성을 보이는 친구를 만날 때 취해야 할 행동으로 적절하다.

3 ③　▶ 어법
　ⓒ 분사구문의 주어는 the passive-aggressive individual인데, 이들이 하기 싫은 일에 직면하게 되는 것이므로 과거분사 confronted가 되어야 한다. Ⓐ 전치사 by 이하에서 동명사들이 병치되어 있다. Ⓑ 등위접속사 and 앞이 shutting down이므로 refusing은 올바른 표현이다. Ⓓ 전치사 about 뒤의 동명사로 적절하다.

19　2015 중앙대

최초의 동기가 무엇이었든지 간에, (기독교) 근본주의 집단은 지난 세기의 첫 수십 년 동안 미국 남부와 남서부 지역에서 진화론에 반대하는 목표를 밀어붙이는 데 있어 때때로 성공을 거두었다. 1920년대 말 무렵, 근본주의자들은 이미 대다수 미국 주 의회에 '진화론 반대' 법안을 상정했고, 남부 여러 주에서는 일부 법안을 통과시켰다. 아마도 이 기간 동안에 진화론과 성경의 창조론 사이의 가장 유명한 대결은 1925년 고등학교 교사 존 스콥스(John Scopes)의 재판이었을 것인데, 그는 테네시 주의 학교에서 진화론 교육을 금지하는 규정을 무시했다는 혐의로 유죄판결을 받았다.
많은 생물학자들은 스콥스 재판이 창조론 견해의 지적(知的) 타당성을 근본적으로 무너뜨렸다고 여겼지만, 창조론자들은 분명 이들 지역에서 기반을 거의 잃지 않았고, 남부와 남서부 이외의 다른 지역의 공교육에까지 영향을 미쳤다. 넬킨(Nelkin)이 지적했듯이, 미국의 여러 지방 및 주 교육의원회의 교과서 선정절차에 영향을 미침으로써, 창조론자들은 오랜 기간 동안 중등학교 교과서에서 진화론에 의거한 설명을 최소화하는 데 성공했다.
미국 중등학교에서 진화론 교육이 늘어나게 된 계기는 1950년대 말과 1960년대 초에 일어난 과학 교과과정 개혁운동의 결과였다. 이때는 과학교육이 다른 국가들, 특히 1957년에 최초의 인공위성 스푸트니크(Sputnik)호를 발사했던 소련에 비해 뒤처졌다는 것을 깨달은 시기였다. 이런 혁신들 가운데 하나는 진화론을 논의하고 인간의 사회적 관계의 변화를 분석한 생물학과 사회과학 분야의 새 고등학교 교과서였다. 1960년대 말에는 진화론에 반대하는 법들이 폐기되거나 위헌으로 공표되었다.
지난 10년 동안, 창조과학/지적설계론을 선전하기 위해 근본주의자들이 설립한 많은 협회와 대학은 과학 교과과정에 창조론을 포함시킬 목적으로 논쟁을 시작했다. 과학이라는 이름이 붙어 있음에도 불구하고, 창조과학에는 딱히 과학이라고 할 만한 것이 (혹 있다 하더라도) 거의 없다. 상당한 양의 (창조과학) 문헌이 진화론에 대한 창조론의 공격을 다루고 있지만, 근본주의적 창조론자들이 과학적 증거를 인정하기를 거부하는 것은 결코 문제 해결의 가망성이 없다는 것을 보여주고 있다.

initial a. 처음의, 최초의, 시작의, 초기의
motivation n. 자극, 유도; (행동의) 동기 부여
fundamentalist n. 근본주의 신자, 원리주의자
pursue v. 추구하다
bill n. 법안, 의안
legislature n. 입법 기관
confrontation n. 대치, 대립
trial n. 재판, 공판
convict v. ~의 유죄를 입증하다, 유죄를 선언하다
validity n. 정당성, 타당성
adoption n. 채택
minimize v. 최소화하다
impetus n. 자극, 유인; 추진력
curriculum n. 교육과정, 교과과정
lag behind ~보다 뒤떨어지다, 뒤처지다
repeal v. (법률을) 폐지하다
declare v. 선언하다, 선포하다, 공표하다
unconstitutional a. 헌법에 위배되는, 위헌의
institute n. 연구기관, 학회, 협회
propagation n. 선전
intelligent design 지적설계론
fray n. 싸움, 전투, 언쟁, 논쟁
resolve v. 분해하다, 분석하다; 해결하다

1 ②　▶ 내용추론
　마지막 문장에서 창조론자들이 창조과학과 지적설계론을 들고 나와 진화론의 논쟁을 촉발시켰지만, 이들이 과학적 증거자료를 전혀 인정하지 않고 있다는 점에서 논쟁의 해결

가능성이 전혀 없다고 지적하고 있다. 이를 통해, 지적설계론의 주장에 대해 작가는 비판적인 입장에 있음을 알 수 있다. 따라서 정답은 ②가 된다. ①은 resulted in이 아니라 resulted from이어야 한다.

2 ④ ▶ **글의 제목**
본문에서는 20세기 초반부터 20세기 말까지 창조론자와 진화론자의 갈등을 통시적인 흐름을 통해 설명하고 있다. 따라서 글의 제목으로는 ④ '미국 과학교육에 있어 창조론자와 진화론자의 갈등'이 가장 적절하다.

---

20 2022 아주대

A 많은 사람들이 "죄책감"과 "수치심"이라는 두 단어를 같은 의미로 사용하지만, 심리학적 관점에서 보면 실제로는 다른 경험을 나타낸다. 죄책감과 수치심은 때때로 밀접히 연관되어 있다. 하나의 행동이 수치심과 죄책감을 모두 유발할 수 있는데, 전자는 우리 자신에 대해 어떻게 느끼는지를 반영하고, 후자는 우리의 행동이 다른 사람에게 해를 끼쳤다는 인식과 관련이 있다. 다시 말해 수치심은 자기 자신과 관련이 있고, 죄책감은 타인과 관련이 있다.
B Dictionary.com에 따르면 죄책감은 잘못된 일을 했다는 자각과 관련이 있다. 그것은 우리의 행동에서 생겨난다(그것이 비록 환상에서 발생하는 것일지라도). 수치심은 죄책감을 자각하는 데에서 비롯될 수 있지만 분명히 죄책감과 같은 것은 아니다. 그것은 우리가 다른 사람들(그리고 우리 자신에게)에게 어떠해 보이는지에 대한 고통스러운 감정으로서, 우리가 어떤 행동을 한 것에 반드시 의존하는 것은 아니다. 언젠가 디너파티에서 나는 누군가에게 상처를 주는 말을 한 적이 있는데, 어느 정도는 상처를 주려는 의도를 갖고 있었다. 얼마 뒤 나는 내가 친구에게 상처를 줬다는 사실을 깨닫고 죄책감을 느꼈다. 더 고통스러웠던 것은, 내가 그런 식으로 행동하는 부류의 사람이라는 사실에 대해 수치심까지 느꼈기 때문이다. 다른 누군가에게 고통을 가한 결과 죄책감이 들었고, 나 자신과 관련해 수치심을 느꼈다.
C 당신이 다른 사람에게 끼쳤을지도 모르는 해악에 대해 죄책감을 느끼기 위해서는 우선 그 사람을 별개의 개인으로 인정해야 한다. 따라서 분리와 합체 문제(자아와 타자 사이의 경계선이 모호하여 일어나는 정신질환 증세)로 힘들어하고 있는 사람이 자신의 감정을 표현하기 위해 죄책감이라는 단어를 쓰더라도, 그 사람은 진정한 죄책감을 느끼지 않을 수 있다. 자기애적 행동을 보이는 많은 사람들은 종종 깊은 수치심을 느끼지만 다른 사람들에 대한 진정한 관심은 거의 없다. 그들은 진심으로 죄책감을 느끼지 않는 경향이 있다. 죄책감은 다른 사람이 느낄 수 있는 감정을 직감하는 데 달려 있으므로, 자기애적 성격 장애에서 발견되는 공감의 결핍은 참된 죄책감이 발생할 가능성을 거의 없게 만든다.
D 수치심이 유난히 팽배하면, 그 수치심이 진정한 염려와 죄책감이라는 감정의 발달을 막을 수 있다. 자신이 손상되는 것에 대한 의식이 너무나 강력하고 고통스러워서 타인에 대한 감정을 밀어내어 버린다. 그러한 경우에 이상화가 작동하는 경우가 많다. 즉, 타인들을 우리가 갈망하는 수치심 없는 이상적인 삶을 살아가는 완벽하고 운 좋은 사람들로 간주하는 것이다. 그 결과 (무의식적인) 강력한 시기심을 품게 된다. 이런 경우 우리가 시기하던 대상에게 상처를 줄 때 우리는 죄책감을 느끼기보다 그것을 즐기게 될 가능성이 높아진다.

1 ① ▶ **내용파악**
본문에 따르면 '죄책감은 타인과 관련이 있는 것으로, 타인에게 고통을 가했을 때 느껴지는 감정'이다. 따라서 죄책감은 본질적으로 타인과의 연결(또는 회복)을 지향하는 감정이지, 타인과의 연결을 방해하는 감정은 아니다. 한편, C 단락 마지막 문장에서 '죄책감은 다른 사람이 느낄 수 있는 감정을 직감하는 데(공감에) 달려 있으며, 공감의 결핍이 참된 죄책감이 발생할 가능성을 거의 없게 만든다'고 했는데, 이는 공감과 죄책감이 비례한다(양의 상관관계이다)는 말이므로 ③은 타당한 진술이다. 그리고 A, B 단락에서 '죄책감은 우리의 행동이 다른 사람에게 해를 끼쳤다는 인식(awareness)과 관련이 있다', '죄책감은 잘못된 일을 했다는 자각(awareness)과 관련이 있다'는 진술에 비추어 볼 때, ④도 타당한 진술이다.

---

guilt n. 유죄; 죄책감
interchangeably ad. 교환할 수 있게
refer to ~을 나타내다
go hand in hand (두 가지 일이) 밀접히 연관되다
inflict v. (고통·상처를) 가하다, 입히다
to begin with 우선
merger n. 합병
narcissistic a. 자애적(自愛的)인, 자기도취증에 빠진
profound a. 깊은
authentic a. 진짜의, 진정한
empathy n. 공감
intuit v. 직감하다
pervasive a. 만연한, 팽배한
preclude v. 방해하다, 불가능하게 하다
come into play 작동하다
idealization n. 이상화
crave v. 갈망하다

2 ③ ▶ **단락의 제목**
C 단락에서 필자는 '타인에 대한 인정과 관심'이 진정한 죄책감의 원천이라고 하였고, 자기애적 성격 장애자들의 사례를 통해 '타인에 대한 관심과 그들의 고통에 대한 공감이 결핍된 수치심'은 병적인 자기사랑일 뿐, 진실한 수치심은 아니라고 말하고 있다.

3 ④ ▶ **내용파악**
D 단락에서는 수치심은 '타인이 아닌 자기에 집중할 때의 감정으로서 과도할 경우 타인에 대한 진정한 염려와 죄책감이 발달하지 못하게 된다'는 것이 강조되고 있으므로 ④가 단락의 내용을 가장 잘 요약하고 있다.

4 ④ ▶ **내용파악**
필자는 A, B 단락에서 수치심과 죄책감을 구별하였다. '수치심과 죄책감은 서로 다른 감정인데, 수치심은 자기 자신과 관련이 있고, 죄책감은 타인과 관련이 있다'고 하였다. 그리고 이하의 단락들에서 '타인에 대한 관심과 공감에서 기인하는 감정이 죄책감인 반면, 수치심은 자아에 대해 느끼는 감정이며 과도해지면 병적인 자기 집중(자기애)에 빠지고, 타인을 해치는 것까지 마다하지 않을 수 있다'고 하였다. 따라서, 필자의 주장은 '수치심과 죄책감은 자아의 역할에서 그 차이가 있다'로 요약될 수 있다.

03 문화·예술

01 2022 서울여대

자기민족중심주의는 신화, 민간 설화, 속담, 심지어 언어와 같이 많은 문화적인 측면에서도 볼 수 있다. 예를 들어, 많은 언어, 특히 비서구 사회의 언어에서 자신의 종족 또는 민족 집단을 가리키는 데 사용되는 단어는 말 그대로 "인류" 또는 "인간"을 의미한다. 이것은 다른 집단의 구성원은 인간 이하라는 것을 의미한다. 예를 들어, 북극과 북극에 가까운 지역에 사는 집단을 가리키는 데 사용되는 "에스키모(eskimo)"라는 용어는 그들의 낯선 생활을 목격했지만 그 생활 방식을 공유하지 않았던 에스키모의 이웃들이 사용한 인디언 단어이다. 그 말은 "날고기를 먹는 사람들"을 의미하며, 그와 같은 단어는 한 집단에게는 일반적이지만 또 다른 집단에게는 혐오감을 일으키는 문화적 관행에 대한 자기민족중심주의적인 발언이다. 반면, 알래스카 원주민에 속하는 한 하위 집단을 보면, 우리는 그들이 자신들을 "진정한 사람들"이란 의미의 "이뉴잇(inuit)"이라고 부르는 것을 발견하게 된다. (그들은 확실히 날고기를 먹는 것을 이상한 것이라고 생각하지 않았다.) 그런데 여기에는 진정한 자신의 집단과 그다지 "진정하지 않은" 다른 나머지 세상(집단) 사이의 대조가 있다. 에스키모와 이뉴잇 두 용어는 모두 똑같이 자기민족중심주의적인 말이다. 에스키모는 차이점에 대한 발언으로서 자기민족중심적이고, 이뉴잇은 자기평가로서 자기민족중심적이다. 그러나 지금은 이뉴잇이 그것의 기원 때문에 (자기민족중심주의를 보여주기에) 더 적절한 용어로 간주된다.

ethnocentrism n. 자기민족중심주의
myth n. 신화, 전설
proverb n. 속담, 격언
tribe n. 부족, 종족
ethnic a. 인종의, 민족의
literally ad. 문자[말] 그대로
arctic a. 북극의
subarctic a. 아(亞)북극의, 북극에 가까운
raw a. 익히지 않은, 날것의
flesh n. 살, 고기
repulsive a. 역겨운, 혐오스러운
out of the ordinary 특이한, 색다른

1 ② ▶ 빈칸완성
빈칸 다음 문장에서 자기민족중심주의의 여러 측면과 관련하여 '예를 들어, 많은 언어에서'라고 시작하면서 '언어'와 관련한 자기민족중심주의를 설명하고 있으므로 빈칸에는 ② language가 적절하다. ① 음식 ③ 의복 ④ 신념

2 ③ ▶ 내용일치
On the other hand 이하의 두 문장은 이뉴잇 족을 설명하는데, 그들은 자신들을 "진정한 사람들"이라는 의미의 이뉴잇이라 부르고, 여기에 진정한 자신들의 집단과 진정하지 않은 다른 나머지 세상(집단) 사이에 대조가 있다고 했으므로, 이뉴잇 족은 자기들만이 진정한 사람들이라고 자기평가를 한 셈이다. 따라서 ③이 옳은 진술이다. ② 이뉴잇 족은 날고기를 먹는 타부족인 에스키모족의 관행을 이상하게 생각하지 않았을 뿐 그들도 날고기를 먹는지는 알 수 없다.

02 2017 한국외대

레게는 1960년대 후반에 자메이카에서 유래한 음악 장르다. 1968년에 발표된 싱글곡인 "Do the Reggay"는 그 단어(레게)를 사용한 최초의 대중가요였으며, (노래제목으로 인해) 그 장르의 이름을 효과적으로 정하고 전 세계 관객에게 그 장르를 효과적으로 소개하게 되었다. '레게'라는 용어는 때때로 넓은 의미로 대부분의 대중적인 자메이카 댄스 음악 양식을 지칭하는 것으로 사용되기도 하지만, 더 정확하게는 미국 재즈와 리듬 앤 블루스(R&B)뿐만 아니라 전통적인 '멘토(칼립소와 유사한 자메이카의 민속음악)'의 영향을 강하게 받은 특정한 음악 양식을 의미한다. 레게는 베이스 기타와 드럼의 다운비트 사이에서 대위법으로 연주되는 선율과 오프비트(강세를 붙이지 않는 박자) 리듬 악기부로 인해 바로 식별할 수 있다. 레게를 자메이카 방언과 자메이카식 영어로 부르는 것은 흔한 일이다. 레게는 전 세계에 널리 퍼졌으며 종종 현지 악기들과 혼합되고 다른 장르들과 융합되었다. 예를 들면, 레게가 포함된 영국의 카리브해 음악은 1960년대 후반 이후로 인기를 끌어왔으며, 여러 하위 장르와 퓨전 음악으로 진화했다. 자메이카에서 정통 레게음악은 국가의 가장 큰 수입원 중 하나이다.

originate v. 비롯되다, 유래하다
effectively ad. 효과적으로
name v. 이름을 붙이다
denote v. 나타내다, 의미하다
instantly ad. 즉각, 즉시
counterpoint n. 대위법으로 연주되는 선율
downbeat n. <음악> 강박(强拍), 하박(下拍)
offbeat n. <음악> 오프비트, 약한 박자
rhythm section 리듬 악기부(보통 드럼과 베이스로 이뤄지고 가끔은 피아노도 쓰임)
fuse with ~와 융합하다

1 ① ▶ 글의 제목
레게가 1960년대 후반 자메이카에서 생겨난 음악 장르라고 소개하면서, 레게에 대한 정의, 음악적 특징을 설명하고, 다양한 장르의 음악들이 융합된 퓨전 음악으로 발전했다고 이야기하고 있으므로, 글의 제목으로는 ① '레게의 기원과 특징'이 적절하다.

2 ② ▶ 내용일치
레게음악은 '미국 재즈와 리듬 앤드 블루스뿐만 아니라 자메이카 전통 음악인 멘토의 영향을 받은 독특한 음악 형식'이라고 했으므로, 레게음악이 국제적인 영향을 받지 않고 생겨났다고 볼 수 없다. 따라서 ②가 정답이다.

03 2012 경희대

문화상대주의는 한 개인의 믿음과 행동은 그 개인 자신의 문화의 관점에서 다른 사람들에 의해 이해되어야 한다는 원칙이다. 이 원칙은 20세기 초 수십 년 동안에 프란츠 보아스(Franz Boas)에 의한 인류학적 연구에서 자명한 것으로 확립되었고 나중에 그의 제자들에 의해 대중화되었다. 보아스는 1887년에 처음으로 그 생각을 다음과 같이 분명히 표현했다. "문명은 절대적인 것이 아니고 상대적이며 우리의 생각들과 개념들은 우리의 문명에 한정해서만 사실이다."
그러나 보아스는 (문화상대주의라는) 용어를 만들지는 않았다. 옥스포드 영어 사전에 기록된 그 용어의 첫 사용은 로버트 로이(Robert Lowie)가 1917년에 쓴 저서 『Culture and Ethnology』에 나오는 "extreme cultural relativism"을 철학자이자 사회이론가 알렌 로크(Alain Locke)가 설명하기 위해 1924년에 사용한 것이었다. 그 용어는 1942년에 보아스가 죽은 후 인류학자들 사이에서 그가 전개시켰던 많은 생각을 통합한 것을 나타내기 위해 보편화되었다. 보아스는 문화들의 영역은 하위의 종들과 관련해서도 발견되는 것으로 너무 광범위하고 널리 퍼져 있어서 문화와 인종 사이의 연관성은 있을 수 없다고 믿었다. 문화상대주의는 특정한 인식론적·방법론적인 주장들을 포함한다. 이러한 주장들이 특정한 윤리적 입장을 필요로 하는지는 논쟁거리이다. 이 원칙은 도덕적 상대주의와 혼동되어서는 안 된다.

anthropological a. 인류학의
articulate v. 분명히 표현하다
coin v. (신어·신표현을) 만들어 내다
sweep n. 범위, 영역; 쓸어 모은 것
pervasive a. 만연하는; 퍼지는
epistemological a. 인식론(상)의
methodological a. 방법론의
stance n. 입장, 태도
necessitate v. 필요로 하다, 요하다

1 ② ▶ 글의 제목
전체적으로 cultural relativism에 대해 언급하고 있다. 따라서 글 전체 내용을 포괄할 수 있는 제목은 ②의 "문화상대주의란 무엇인가?"이다.

2 ② ▶ 빈칸완성
빈칸 Ⓐ는 동사가 '확립되었다(establish)'인 것과 관련하여 '자명한(axiomatic)'이 적절하고, 빈칸 Ⓑ는 후배 학자들이 선배인 보아스의 많은 생각들을 '통합한 것(synthesis)'이라고 하는 것이 적절하다. 따라서 ②가 정답이다. ① 자명한 — 동정; 공감 ③ 관습에 얽매이지 않는 — 동정; 공감 ④ 관습에 얽매이지 않는 — 종합, 통합

3 ③ ▶ 뒷내용 추론
본문의 마지막에 도덕적 상대주의와 혼동하면 안 된다고 했으므로, 뒤에는 문화상대주의와 도덕적 상대주의의 차이를 설명하는 내용이 오는 것이 가장 적절하다.

04 2015 한국외대

1962년 10월 21일, 뉴욕의 시드니 재니스(Sidney Janis) 갤러리에서 미국 미술사를 바꾼 전시회가 열렸다. 그 전시회는 1960년대를 주름잡았던 새로운 화가들을 크게 다루었다. 뉴욕의 미술 비평가들은 열광했다. 한 저명한 비평가는 이 전시회가 "뉴욕 미술계를 지진과 같은 힘으로 강타했다"라고 말했다. 확실히, 대조적인 견해들도 존재했다. 그 새로운 화가들은 '속물주의자', 심지어는 '간판장이'라고 불렸다. 양극화된 견해에도 불구하고, 스스로에 대해 마르셀 뒤샹(Marcel Duchamp)

exhibition n. 전시, 공개; 전람회, 전시회
alter v. 바꾸다, 변경하다
feature v. 특징으로 삼다; ~의 특징을 이루다
dominate v. 지배하다; 특색지우다, 좌우하다
critic n. 비평가, 평론가

03 문화·예술 333

의 문하생이라는 자부심을 갖고 있었던 이 화가들은 전통적인 순수 미술에 계속해서 도전했다. 앤디 워홀(Andy Warhol)은 이러한 움직임의 중심에 있었다. 그는 평생 동안 순수 미술을 동경해 왔었으나, 마지막까지 자신의 상업적인 접근 방법에 충실했다. 그는 '이미 만들어져 있는' 대상을 자신의 그림들에 활용했고, 실크스크린을 통해 사본을 떠서 복제품을 만들어냈으며, 그것들을 통해 대중이 바라는 바를 분명히 전했다. 『캠벨 수프 통조림(Campbell's Soup Cans)』이라는 유명 작품은 앤디 워홀의 미학(美學)을 가장 잘 나타내고 있다. 예술과 상업이라는 두 단어는 워홀의 일생 동안 그의 자아를 나누어 놓았다. 그는 "상업 미술은 미술의 다음 단계다. 나는 상업미술가가 되고 싶었다. 사업에 수완이 있는 것은 가장 매혹적인 종류의 예술이다."라고 썼다. 그는 스스로를 상업미술가로 불렀다. 그러나 워홀은 순수 미술에 대한 그의 열망을 결코 해소하진 못했다. "워홀리즘"이라는 말은 그 예술가에 대한 세상 사람들의 애정을 나타내지만, 비평가들은 그의 작품에서 상업주의라는 꼬리표를 떼어내길 거부했다. 뉴욕의 병원에서 홀로 죽음을 맞은 지 25년이 흘렀지만, 워홀은 여전히 가장 논란이 되고 있는 예술가 중의 한 명으로 남아있다.

crazy a. 미친 듯한; 열중한, 열광하는
renowned a. 유명한, 이름 높은, 명성이 있는
contrasting a. 대조적인, 대비적인
vulgarist n. 속물주의자
polarize v. 양극화를 초래하다; (빛 등을) 편광시키다
pride v. 자부하다, 자랑하다
descendant n. 자손, 후손, 후예; 제자
defy v. ~에 도전하다; (경쟁·공격 등을) 문제 삼지 않다
faithful a. 충실한, 성실한, 신의 있는
subject n. 주제; 학과, 과목; 대상; 피(被)실험자
replicate v. ~의 사본을 뜨다, 모사하다, 복제하다
project v. (개념 등을) 명확히 전하다
aesthetics n. 미학
quench v. (불 따위를) 끄다; (갈증 따위를) 풀다
controversial a. 논쟁의; 논의의 여지가 있는

1 ④　▶ **내용파악**
"워홀리즘"이라는 말이 만들어질 만큼 워홀을 높게 평가하는 사람들도 있지만, 한편으로는 그의 작품에서 상업주의라는 꼬리표를 떼어내길 거부하고 있는 이들도 있는 상황이다. 그러므로 이런 상황과 맥을 같이 하는 진술인 ④가 정답이다. ① 앤디 워홀이 뒤샹의 문하생에 속한다. ② 이미 만들어져 있는 것들을 자신의 그림에 활용했다고 했다. ③ 스스로를 상업미술가로 여겼지만, 순수 미술에 대한 열망을 결코 해소하진 못했다고 했다.

2 ②　▶ **빈칸완성**
그다음의 인용문에서 사업에 수완이 있는 것은 가장 매혹적인 종류의 예술이라고 한 것이 그가 사업과 예술을 모두 추구했음을 이야기하고 있다. 그러므로 빈칸 ⓐ와 ⓑ 각각에 들어갈 표현은 ②의 art와 business이다. ① 전통적인 — 현대적인 ③ 오래된 — 새로운 ④ 복제된 — 독창적인

3 ①　▶ **부분이해**
밑줄 친 ⓒ는 "비평가들은 그의 작품에서 상업주의라는 꼬리표를 떼어내길 거부했다."라는 의미인데, 이것은 "비평가들은 여전히 그의 작품을 돈벌이를 위한 것으로 본다."는 것이고, 이는 곧 그의 예술성을 인정하지 않는다는 것이 된다. 워홀이 60년대에 비평가들을 열광하게 만들었던 미술계의 움직임을 주도했던 인물임을 감안하면, 그의 예술은 여전히 과소평가되고 있다고 할 수 있다.

05　2017 한양대

이 모든 질문들에 대한 일반적인 대답은 똑같이 문화다. 베일리(Bailey)가 지적하듯이, "문화는 사고방식과 행동방식에 있어서 다양하다." 당신도 알고 있었겠지만 우리가 제기한 모든 질문들은 생각과 행동을 다루었다. 문화가 당신의 행동을 유발하는 유일한 자극제는 아니지만, 문화의 편재성은 문화를 가장 강력한 자극제 중 하나로 만들어 준다. 게다가 문화를 그렇게도 독특하게 만들어 주는 것은 당신이 비슷한 경험을 접해온 다른 이들과 당신의 문화를 공유하고 있다는 사실이다. 당신의 개인적 경험과 유전적으로 물려받은 것이 독특한 '당신'을 형성하고 있지만, 문화는 단 한사람의 특징이 아닌 한 지역사회의 영역인 집단적인 준거기준으로 사람들을 통합시킨다. <홉스테드(Hofstede)가 지적하듯이, "문화와 공동체의 관계는 개성과 개인의 관계와 같다."> 문화란 한 집단의 세계관, 즉 특정 사회가 시간이 흐르면서 만들어낸 세상을 구성하는 방식이라고 놀란(Nolan)이 재확인하고 있다. 이러한 의미의 체계는 그 사회 구성원들이 자신들, 그들의 세상, 그리고 그 세상에서의 경험들을 이해하도록 허용해준다. 특정한 문화 속의 사람들에게 하나의 축적된 공동지식을 제공해주는 것은 바로 이러한 공통된 현실의 공유다.

point out ~을 지적하다, 알려주다
pose v. (문제·질문 등을) 제기하다
deal with ~을 처리하다, 다루다
stimulus n. 자극, 격려, 고무
omnipresent a. 편재하는, 어디에나 동시에 있는
unique a. 독특한, 진기한
genetic a. 유전의; 유전학의
unite v. 묶다, 통합하다, 합치다

1 ②　▶ **부분이해**
이 글의 전반적인 내용은 '문화가 그 문화의 구성원들의 사고와 행동에 대해 맡아 하고 있는 역할'에 관한 것이므로, 유전병에 대한 질문인 ②가 유추하기에 적절하지 않다.

2 ③ ▶ 문장삽입

ⓒ의 앞 문장에서 "문화는 단 한사람의 특징이 아닌 한 지역사회의 영역인 집단적인 준거 기준으로 사람들을 통합시킨다."라고 하여 한 개인과 그 특성, 한 지역사회와 그 집단적 기준인 문화의 관계를 모두 언급했으므로, "개개인이 독특한 자신의 개성이 있는 것처럼 하나의 공동체도 자신의 독특한 문화가 있다."는 내용을 담고 있는 제시문은 ⓒ에 들어가는 것이 적절하다.

06 2022 경기대

피아노 소나타 2번(Piano Sonata No. 2)은 19세기 폴란드의 피아니스트이자 작곡가인 프레데리크 쇼팽(Frédéric Chopin)의 가장 유명한 작품 중 하나다. 대중들은 거의 즉각적으로 그 작품에 매료되었지만, 당대의 많은 유력한 비평가들은 감명을 받지 못했다. 그 작품을 가장 노골적으로 비방했던 사람들 중 한 명은 저명한 작곡가 로베르트 슈만(Robert Schumann)이었다. 그는 당시의 다른 비평가들과 마찬가지로 그 작품의 악장들이 주제적인 측면에서 서로 맞지 않는다고 주장했다. 소위 이러한 결점 때문에 이 작품은 형식면에서 정통이 아닌 것으로 간주되었다. 사실, 일부 비평가들은 아예 소나타로 분류해선 안 된다는 주장을 하기도 했다.

이러한 혹독한 평가에도 불구하고, 이 작품의 제3악장인 "장송 행진곡(Funeral March)"은 큰 찬사를 받았다. 저명한 작곡가이자 쇼팽의 친구였던 프란츠 리스트(Franz Liszt)는 이 악장이 대단히 뛰어나다고 생각했다. 그의 생각은 다른 음악가들의 반향을 불러일으켰고, 장송 행진곡은 불후의 피아노 악장 중의 하나가 되었다. 그것은 또한 재즈에서 전자음악에 이르는 현대 음악의 많은 장르의 작품들에 영향을 미쳤다.

1 ② ▶ 빈칸완성

'그 작품의 악장들이 주제적인 측면에서 서로 맞지 않는다'는 주장과 '아예 소나타로 분류해선 안 된다'는 주장이 있었던 것으로 미루어, 그 작품은 기존의 소나타와는 매우 다른 '특이한' 혹은 '정통이 아닌' 작품으로 간주되었을 것임을 알 수 있다. ① 풍부한 ③ 무자비한 ④ 훌륭한

2 ① ▶ 글의 목적

쇼팽의 피아노 소나타 2번에 대해 슈만을 포함한 당대의 비평가들의 비판적인 반응이 있었지만 그런 혹평에도 불구하고 제3악장은 뛰어나고 후대의 음악에 좋은 영향을 미쳤다는 등, 피아노 소나타 2번의 장점을 밝혀준 글이므로, 글의 목적으로 ①이 가장 적절하다. ④ 부정적인 평가가 잘못되었다고 반박하는 것은 아니다.

3 ③ ▶ 내용파악

'슈만과 다른 비평가들은 그 작품의 악장들이 주제적인 측면에서 서로 맞지 않는다고 주장했다'라고 돼 있으므로, ③이 옳은 진술이다.

enchant v. 매혹하다
outspoken a. 거리낌 없는, 솔직한
detractor n. 비방[중상]하는 사람
celebrated a. 유명한; 세상에 알려진
shortcoming n. 결점, 단점
classify v. 분류하다
notwithstanding prep. ~에도 불구하고
harsh a. 호된, 가혹한
appraisal n. 평가, 감정
funeral n. 장례식
nothing short of 매우 ~한
echo v. 메아리치게 하다, 반향시키다
enduring a. 영속적인
composition n. 작곡; 작품

07 2021 숭실대

포스트모더니즘(Postmodernism)은 20세기 중후반 철학, 예술, 건축, 그리고 비평 등과 관련된 영역에서 발달된 광범위한 (문화) 운동으로, 모더니즘에서 탈피한 것을 특징으로 한다. 이 용어는 현대성의 뒤를 잇고 있다고 말해지는 역사적 시대와 이 시대의 경향을 묘사하는 데 더 일반적으로 적용된다.

포스트모더니즘은 일반적으로 그것이 모더니즘과 연관된 거대 서사와 이데올로기라고 설명하는 것에 대한 회의나 아이러니나 부인의 태도에 의해 정의되며, 종종 계몽주의의 합리성을 비난하고 정치적 또는 경제적 권력을 유지하는 데 있어서 이데올로기의 역할에 중점을 둔다. 포스트모더니즘 사상가들은 자주 지식 주장과 가치 체계를 우발적이거나 사회적으로 조건된 것이라고 설명하면서, 그것들을 정치적, 역사적, 혹은 문화적 담론과 위계질서의 산물이라고 말한다. 포스트모던 비판

describe v. 서술하다, 묘사하다
follow after ~을 찾다, 추구하다
tendency n. 성향, 기질
skepticism n. 회의, 회의론
irony n. 아이러니, 역설적인 점
grand narrative 대서사, 웅장한 서술
Enlightenment n. 계몽 운동
rationality n. 순리성, 합리성

의 일반적인 대상에는 <주관적인> 실재, 진실, 이성 및 과학에 대한 보편적인 사상 등이 포함된다. 그에 따라, 포스트 모던적(탈현대적) 사고는 자의식, 자기지시성, 인식론적·도덕적 상대주의, 다원론, 불경(不敬)에 대한 경향에 의해 광범위하게 특징지어진다.

포스트모던의 비판적 접근은 1980년대와 1990년대에 인기를 얻었으며, 문학, 현대미술, 음악과 같은 분야의 예술운동뿐만 아니라 문화 연구, 과학철학, 경제학, 언어학, 건축, 페미니스트 이론, 문학 비평 등 다양한 학문 및 이론적 분야에서 채택되어 왔다. 포스트모더니즘은 장 프랑수아 리오타르(Jean-François Lyotard), 자크 데리다(Jacques Derrida), 그리고 프레드릭 제임슨(Fredric Jameson)과 같은 철학자뿐만 아니라 해체 이론, 후기 구조주의, 제도비판과 같은 사상유파와 종종 연관되어 있다.

포스트모더니즘에 대한 비판은 지적으로 다양하며 포스터모더니즘이 반계몽주의를 조장하고, 무의미하며, 그것이 분석적 또는 경험적 지식에 아무것도 기여하는 것이 없다는 주장을 포함한다.

self-consciousness n. 자의식
referentiality n. 지시성(문학 작품에서 언급이 있는지 여부)
epistemological a. 인식론(상)의
relativism n. 상대주의
pluralism n. 다원론(多元論)
irreverence n. 불경(不敬), 불손
deconstruction n. 해체 이론[비평]
institutional a. 제도상의, 제도적인
obscurantism n. 반계몽주의, 몽매주의(일부러 이해하기 어렵게 하기 위해 어려운 말을 사용하는 표현법)
meaningless a. 무의미한
empirical a. 경험[실험]에 의거한, 실증적인

1 ③ ▶ 내용파악
두 번째 문단 첫 번째 문장에서 "포스트모더니즘은 일반적으로 모더니즘과 연관된 거대 서사와 이데올로기를 설명하는 것에 대한 회의나 아이러니나 부인의 태도에 의해 정의된다."라고 했으므로 포스트모더니즘은 현대의 대서사의 개념을 이어받은 것이 아니라 오히려 부인했다. 따라서 ③이 정답이다.

2 ① ▶ 문맥상 적절하지 않은 표현 고르기
포스트모던 비판의 일반적인 대상이 나열되어 있는데 ⑧ 진실, ⓒ 이성, ⓓ 과학은 객관적인 것을 바탕으로 하는 반면 Ⓐ는 subjective(수관석인)가 들어가 객관적인 것과는 반대가 된다. 따라서 Ⓐ를 objective reality로 고쳐야 문맥상 적절하다. 그래야 그다음 문장에서 탈현대적 사고가 특징지어지는 주관적이고, 상대적인 개념과 어울리게 된다.

08 2017 이화여대

그의 책 『편견의 심리학(The Psychology of Prejudice)』에서 넬슨(2006)은 "편견에 찬 사람들은 모두 어디로 갔는가?"라는 냉소적인 질문을 던진다. 그는 백인들이 인종 차별적 태도와 신념을 공개적으로 표현하고, 인종차별을 옹호하며, 유색인종들이 — 특히 미국 흑인들이 — 도덕적으로나 지적으로 열등하다고 모욕하는 것이 한때는 흔한 일이었다고 말한다. 하지만, 수십 년에 걸쳐, 인종차별적인 남부 주(州)들의 특징이던 구식 인종차별주의는 그 힘이 크게 줄어들었고 사라진 것처럼 보였다. 이와 같은 변화의 상당 부분은 대법원의 기념비적인 판결, 민권운동, 그리고 제3세계 운동에 기인한 것이었다. 예를 들어, 만약 오랜 시간에 걸친 흑인 미국인들에 대한 고정관념들을 추적해보면, 그들을 미신적이고, 게으르고, 무식하다고 특징짓던 초기의 행태는 크게 줄어들었음을 알 수 있을 것이다.

그러나 많은 인종학자들은 인종차별이 사라지지 않았으며, (1) 의식적 인식 수준 바깥에 있는, 고도로 위장되고, 드러나지 않고, 미묘한 형태로 변모했고, (2) 개인들의 보이지 않는 가정과 신념 속에 숨어 있으며, (3) 우리의 제도들의 정책과 구조 속에 깊이 매립되어 있다고 믿는다. 이들 연구자들과 학자들은 인종차별을 금지하는 법적, 정치적, 사회적 영향력으로 인해, 여러 인종들 사이에 긍정적인 관계를 만드는 데 큰 진전이 있었음을 부인하지는 않는다. 그러나 그들은 편견이 살아 있으며 "현대적 인종차별주의", "상징적 인종차별주의", "혐오적 인종차별주의"라는 이름으로 아직도 건재함을 보여주는 많은 증거들을 열거한다.

sarcastic a. 빈정거리는, 비꼬는
bigot n. 편견이 아주 심한 사람, 편협한 사람
observe v. 지키다, 준수하다; 관찰하다; 말하다
racist a. 인종차별적인
advocate n. 옹호자, 지지자
segregation n. 분리, 격리; 인종차별
denigrate v. 모욕하다, (인격·명예 등을) 훼손하다
characterize v. ~의 특색을 이루다
stereotype n. 고정 관념, 판에 박힌 문구
superstitious a. 미신적인, 미신에 사로잡힌
disguise v. 변장하다, 가장하다
assumption n. 가정, 억측
embed v. (물건을) 끼워 넣다, 묻다; (마음·기억 등에) 깊이 새겨 두다
institution n. 제도, 관례, 관습
aversive a. 기피하는, 혐오의

1 ④ ▶ 빈칸완성
빈칸을 기준으로, 앞에는 '한때는 백인들이 인종차별주의적인 태도와 신념을 공공연히 드러냈다'는 내용이 있고, 뒤에서는 '지난 수십 년에 걸쳐 그러한 상황이 크게 개선됐음'을 언급하고 있다. 빈칸 전후의 내용이 대조를 이루므로, 역접의 접속사 ④ however가 들어가는 것이 적절하다. ① 예를 들면 ② 따라서 ③ 특히 ⑤ 일반적으로

2 ④ ▶ 내용추론
④에서 언급한 '증오 범죄, 신체적 폭행, 인종차별적인 욕설' 등은 모두 인종차별주의를

공공연하게 드러내는 것들인데, "백인들이 인종차별주의를 행동을 통해 공공연하게 드러낸 것은 과거에 흔히 있었던 일이고, 오늘날에는 보다 은밀하고 간접적인 형태로 남아 있다."는 것이 본문의 내용이므로, ④가 본문을 통해 추론할 수 없는 진술이다.

09 2021 경기대

기독교 미술에서, 피에타(Pietà)는 십자가에 못 박힌 예수의 시신을 안고 있는 성모 마리아를 묘사하고 있는 예술작품이다. 이 예술작품들은 여러 형태를 취하지만, 조각상이 일반적이며, 가장 먼저 만들어진 예로는 중세 독일에서 만든 나무 조각상이 있다. 성경에는 결코 명시적으로 언급돼 있지 않지만, 그 형상은 15세기에 이르러 이탈리아로 건너갔다. 1497년, 프랑스 추기경이 아마도 그 나라에서 가장 유명한 조각가였을 미켈란젤로(Michelangelo)에게 대리석으로 피에타를 만들어줄 것을 의뢰했다. 1499년 그 추기경의 사후에 그의 무덤을 장식하게 될 것이었던 이 작품은 미켈란젤로의 걸작 중 하나가 되었다. 그는 1498년에 이 조각상을 만들기 시작했고, 몇 달간의 노력 끝에 그것을 공개하여 널리 갈채를 받았다. 사실상 그의 다른 모든 작품들과는 달리, 이 작품에는 조각가의 이름이 새겨져 있는데, 다른 예술가가 이 작품을 만든 것으로 잘못 인정받았다는 것을 미켈란젤로가 알고 나서 추가한 것이다. 그 조각상은 이탈리아 르네상스의 자연주의 원칙의 전형적인 예인데, 자연주의는 이상화된 모습을 그리면서도 실물과 매우 똑같은 디테일을 강조하는 예술 양식이다. 그럼에도 불구하고, 미켈란젤로가 만들어 낸 형상들은 심하게 왜곡된 비율을 보이는데, 생명이 없는 예수의 형상이 마리아와 대조적으로 왜소하게 보인다. 어떤 이들은 이와 같은 예술적 선택을 어머니의 품에 안긴 아이라는 생각을 불러일으키기 위한 것으로 본다. 그러나 다른 사람들은 그 조각상의 비율이 그저 보는 사람에게 안정감을 주기 위해 그렇게 만든 것이라고 주장한다.

1 ① ▶ 내용일치
"피에타는 여러 형태를 취하지만 조각상이 일반적이며, 독일에서 나무로 조각상을 만들기도 했고, 프랑스 추기경은 대리석으로 피에타를 만들어줄 것을 미켈란젤로에게 의뢰하기도 했다."라는 내용을 통해, '피에타는 조각상 이외의 것도 있고, 조각상 또한 여러 다른 재료들로 만들어졌음'을 알 수 있다. 그러므로 ①이 정답으로 적절하다.

2 ② ▶ 동의어
credit이 '~의 행위자[공로자]로 생각하다[인정하다]'라는 의미로 쓰였으므로, '인정하다'라는 뜻의 acknowledge가 동의어로 적절하다. ① 확대하다 ③ 상환하다 ④ 칭찬하다

3 ① ▶ 빈칸완성
'미켈란젤로의 피에타가 실물과 똑같은 디테일을 강조하는 자연주의의 전형적인 예'라는 점과 '그가 만든 피에타 속의 형상들이 비율적으로 왜곡돼 있는 점'은 서로 상반된 내용으로 양보 관계에 있다. 그러므로 빈칸에는 ①이 들어가야 한다. ② 그 결과로서 ③ 예를 들면 ④ 요약하자면

4 ① ▶ 내용추론
"미켈란젤로의 다른 모든 작품들과는 달리, 그가 만든 피에타에는 조각가의 이름이 새겨져 있는데, 이는 다른 예술가가 이 작품을 만든 것으로 잘못 인정받았다는 것을 미켈란젤로가 알고 나서 추가한 것이다."라는 내용을 통해 ①을 추론할 수 있다.

Pietà n. 피에타(예수의 시체를 안고 슬퍼하는 마리아상)
depict v. 묘사하다, 표현하다
crucify v. 십자가에 못 박다
typically ad. 전형적으로, 일반적으로
sculpture n. 조각, 조각 작품
figure n. 형상; 사람의 모습
craft v. ~을 정교하게 만들다
explicitly ad. 명백히
sculptor n. 조각가
commission v. (일 따위를) 의뢰하다, 주문하다
cardinal n. 추기경
marble n. 대리석
adorn v. 꾸미다, 장식하다
masterpiece n. 걸작, 명작
unveil v. 베일을 벗기다; 제막식을 행하다
widespread a. 널리 보급돼 있는; 광범위한
acclaim n. 갈채, 환호
exemplify v. 예증하다, 예시하다; ~의 좋은 예가 되다
principle n. 원리, 원칙
naturalism n. 자연주의, 사실주의
emphasize v. 강조하다, 역설하다
idealize v. 이상화하다, ~의 이상을 그리다
lifelike a. 살아 있는 것 같은; 실물과 똑같은
detail n. 세부, 세부 묘사
exhibit v. 나타내다, 보이다
grossly ad. 지독히, 극도로
distort v. 왜곡하다
proportion n. 비율; 조화, 균형
dwarf v. 작아 보이게 하다
evoke v. (기억·감정을) 불러일으키다, 환기하다
stability n. 안정, 안정성

10　2014 서강대

그 어떤 문명도 그 문명의 사회적 관습을 이루는 데 있어 가능한 모든 범위의 인간 행위를 이용할 수는 없다. 모든 사회는 어느 쪽이든 한 방향으로 얼마간 기울기 시작해서, 그 선호하는 쪽으로 점점 더 나아가면서, 그 사회가 선택한 기반 위에 점점 더 완전하게 통합되며, 적합하지 않은 유형의 행위들은 버린다. 우리에게는 아무런 논란의 여지없이 비정상적으로 보이는 그런 인성 조합들 대부분을 다른 문명들은 그들의 제도적 생활의 바로 그 토대를 이루는 데 사용해왔다. 정반대로, 우리 문명의 정상적인 개개인들의 가장 존중되는 특징들이 우리와 다르게 조직된 문화들에서는 비정상적인 것으로 간주되어 왔다. 간단히 말해, 매우 넓은 범위에서는, 정상이란 문화적으로 규정되는 것이다. 우리가 문제를 인식하는 바로 그 시각은 우리 사회의 오랜 전통적 관습에 의해 정해진다.
그것은 정신의학과 관련해서라기보다 윤리와 관련하여 더 자주 지적되어온 요점이다. 우리는 우리들이 사는 장소와 시대의 도덕성을 인간 본성의 필연적 구성으로부터 직접 도출해내는 실수를 더 이상 저지르지 않는다. 우리는 그것을 제1원리라는 고귀한 지위로 추켜세우지 않는다. 우리는 도덕성이 사회마다 다르며 사회적으로 인정된 관습들을 가리키는 편리한 용어일 뿐이라는 것을 인정한다. 인류는 항상 "그게 관습적이지."라는 말보다 "그게 도덕적으로 옳아."라는 말을 선호해왔다. 그러나 역사적으로 이 두 표현은 같은 뜻을 나타낸다.

1　①　▶ 글의 제목
　　첫 번째 문단의 주제문은 끝에서 두 번째 문장으로, 'normality(정상적인 것, 규범)는 문화적으로 규정된다'라는 것이 요지이다. 두 번째 문단의 주제문은 첫 번째 문장으로, '그것은 윤리와 관련 있는 요점이다'라는 것이 요지이다. 첫 번째 문단과 두 번째 문단의 요지들을 결합하면, ①의 '도덕성과 문화적 규범'이 글의 제목으로 가장 적절하다.

2　④　▶ 빈칸완성
　　빈칸 다음 문장이 앞 문장에 대한 부연설명이므로 같은 내용을 찾으면 되겠는데, 빈칸 뒤의 문장에서 '도덕적으로 옳다'라는 말과 '관습적이다'라는 말은 동의어라 했으므로, '도덕성은 사회적 관습을 가리키는 편리한 용어'라는 뜻의 ④가 들어가는 것이 적절하다.

3　②　▶ 내용추론
　　normality는 morality와 관련 있는 것이라고 두 번째 문단 첫 번째 문장에서 언급했으므로 같은 성질의 것으로 봐야 한다. 따라서 전치사 Unlike가 아니라 Like로 바뀌어야 맞고, 도덕성은 문화마다 다르게 규정되고 인식된다고 했을 뿐, 변화를 겪지 않는다는 말은 없으므로 ②가 옳지 않은 진술이다. ① 맨 마지막 문장에서 도덕성과 관습적 행동이라는 말이 동의어라고 했으므로, 일반적으로 같은 개념으로 우리가 인식한다고 볼 수 있다. ③ 두 번째 문장에서 비정상적인 행동들은 버린다고 했으므로 옳은 진술이다. ④ 네 번째 문장에 진술돼 있다.

---

utilize v.	활용하다, 소용되게 하다
mores n.	풍습, 관습, 사회적 관행
inclination n.	경향; 경사도
uncongenial a.	마음에 들지 않은; 적합하지 않은
integrate v.	통합시키다; 완전하게 하다
incontrovertibly ad.	반박의 여지가 없이, 확실하게
institutional a.	제도상의, 규격화된, 획일적인
conversely ad.	정반대로, 거꾸로
trait n.	특징, 특색, 특성
aberrant a.	비정상적인, 일탈적인
in short	요컨대
define v.	정의내리다, 규정하다
condition v.	조절하다, 결정하다
psychiatry n.	정신의학
derive v.	~로부터 끌어내다; ~의 기원을 찾다
constitution n.	구성; 기질; 헌법, 관습
dignity n.	위엄; 품위; 명예
term n.	용어; 기간; 관계
norm n.	규범
be subject to	~의 지배를 받다, 영향을 받다
discredit v.	신용을 떨어뜨리다; 믿지 않다

11　2022 중앙대

문화의 보고로서의 이탈리아의 중요한 위상은 묻혀 있던 폼페이라는 도시가 1748년에 발견되면서 더욱 높아졌다. 돌연, 진정한 로마의 유물이 매일매일 발굴되었고 세상은 고대 도시 전체를 숭앙할 수 있게 되었다.
B 폼페이의 발견으로 영감을 받은 미술 이론가 요한 빙켈만(Johann Winckelmann)은 1764년에 많은 사람들이 최초의 미술사책으로 간주하는 『고대 미술의 역사(The History of Ancient Art)』라는 책을 출간했다. 빙켈만은 당시 시들해지고 있던 로코코 양식을 퇴폐적이라며 심하게 비판했고, 고전 시대 사람들이 보여준 형식의 순수성과 명쾌한 솜씨를 높이 평가했다.
A 고대인 연구에 대한 새로운 관심 때문에 유럽과 미국에서 아카데미라는 미술 교육기관이 생겨나기 시작했다. 화가들은 아카데미가 올바른 고전 전통으로 간주하는 전통 속에서 교육을 받았고, 그 교육의 일환으로 아카데미는 많은 화가들을 로마로 보내 예술 작품을 직접 공부하게 했다.
D 가령, 프랑스 아카데미는 회원들의 작품을 선별하여 살롱이라는 연중 1~2회의 행사에서 전시했다. 살롱이라고 불린 것은 그 행사가 루브르 박물관의 살롱 카레라는 커다란 방에서 열렸기 때문이

seminal a.	중대한
cornucopia n.	보물창고, 보고
magnify v.	확대하다
buried a.	매장된
spring up	생겨나다
classical a.	고전적인
firsthand ad.	직접
decadent a.	퇴폐적인
crispness n.	바삭함; 상쾌함; 명쾌함
mythological a.	신화의
showcase v.	전시하다

다. 미술 비평가들과 심사위원들은 당대 미술계의 최고의 작품을 살펴본 다음 제한된 수의 그림을 인정하여 살롱에서 대중에게 관람시키곤 했다. 화가가 이러한 평단의 인정을 받았으면 그것은 화가의 그림의 가치뿐 아니라 화가의 명망도 크게 높아졌다는 뜻이었다.

C 살롱은 매우 전통적인 기준을 갖고 있었으므로, 화가들에게 흠 없는 기법을 사용하라고 주장하고 기존의 소재를 전통적인 원근법과 드로잉으로 그리는 것을 강조했다. 역사화, 다시 말해 역사적, 종교적, 신화적 소재를 다룬 그림들이 가장 귀중하게 여겨졌다. 초상화는 중요성 면에서 그다음을 차지했고, 그다음이 풍경화, 풍속화, 정물화의 순이었다.

그 어떤 교육도 이탈리아 대순회 여행 없이는 완벽하지 않았다. 대개 예술 전문가의 지도하에 진행된 순회에서는 나폴리, 피렌체, 베니스, 로마와 같은 도시들을 방문했다. 바로 이런 곳에서 사람들은 고대 세계의 교훈에 흠뻑 빠질 수 있었고, 아마도 전문가의 지도하에 고대 작품 한두 점을 수집하거나 당대 화가의 작품을 사기도 했을 것이다. 신고전주의 시대의 장점들은 미술 전문가들과 교육받은 아마추어들의 정신 속에 굳건히 뿌리박고 있었다.

biannual a.	연2회의	
critic n.	비평가	
judge n.	심사위원	
prestige n.	명망, 명성	
Grand Tour	유럽 대륙 순회 여행(과거 영·미 부유층 젊은이들이 교육의 일환으로 유럽 주요 도시들을 둘러보던 여행)	
connoisseur n.	(미술품 등의) 감정가, 전문가	
entrenched a.	단단히 자리잡은, 뿌리박힌	

1 ③ ▶ 단락배열
첫 단락에서 언급한 폼페이 유적 발견 다음에 그 발견이 고대인에 대한 찬양을 낳았음을 설명한 B가 오고, 그다음에 고대인 연구에 대한 관심 고조로 생긴 아카데미에 대해 설명한 A가 오고, 그다음에 아카데미의 일례로 프랑스 아카데미를 다룬 D가 오고, 마지막으로 D에 나온 살롱에 대해 부연 설명하는 C가 오는 것이 적절한 순서이다.

2 ④ ▶ 내용일치
마지막 문단에서 이탈리아 순회 여행이 전문가들의 지도하에 이루어졌다고 했고 당시 신고전주의 시대의 사람들이 거기서 고대 세계의 교훈에 흠뻑 빠질 수 있었다고 했으므로, ④ 이탈리아 대순회 여행이 신고전주의 교육의 일부였다고 할 수 있다. ① 폼페이의 발견이 결국 대순회 여행이라는 결과를 낳은 것이다. ② 빙켈만은 로마 예술의 지지자이지 프랑스 아카데미의 지지자란 말은 없다. ③ 살롱은 전통을 옹호했지 전통에 도전한 기관이 아니다.

12 2019 한양대

현대의 음악 애호가들에게 드뷔시(Debussy)는 실질적으로 프랑스 음악을 규정하는 작곡가다. 이 말에서 내가 의미하는 바는 (그의 감각적 섬세함뿐 아니라 와그너(Wagner)와 슈트라우스(Strauss)에서처럼 끊임없이 분주하게 흥분을 고조시키며 클라이맥스로 치닫는 고밀도의 반음계적 전개를 특징으로 하는 19세기 후반 독일 음악의 화성적 양식들에 대한 그의 반감도 포함된) 그의 음악의 본질적 특성들이 이제 본질적으로 "프랑스적" 특징으로 간주되기에 이르렀다는 것이다. 그러나, 월시(Walsh)는 드뷔시가 자신의 음악적 환경의 지배적인 경향을 단순히 확장하거나 구현하기는커녕 의식적으로 완고하게 시대의 조류를 거슬렀음을, 특히 독일 음악이 프랑스 작곡가들에게 미친 심대한 영향과 관련하여 그렇게 했음을, 분명히 한다. 바그너(Wagner)는 19세기 후반 파리에서 피해갈 수 없는 존재였지만, 드뷔시는 독일 음악 영향에 대한 비난을 더 먼 과거로 거슬러 올라가 글루크(Gluck)에게로 던졌다. 드뷔시는 그가 독일적인 "심오한 척하는 가식이나 모든 것을 곱절로 강조하려는 욕구"로 인식되는 것보다도 라모(Rameau)의 "섬세하고 매혹적인 유연함"을 더 선호한 점에서 묵묵히 급진적이었다.

sensuous a.	감각적인
delicacy n.	섬세함
aversion n.	반감
harmonic a.	화성의
chromatic a.	반음계의
orgiastic a.	흥분시키는, 진탕 마시고 노는
amplify v.	확장하다
exemplify v.	구현하다
milieu n.	환경
underline v.	강조하다
affectation n.	가식, 꾸밈
profundity n.	심오함

1 ③ ▶ 글의 제목
이 글은 드뷔시 음악의 프랑스적 특징에 대해 논하고 있다. 드뷔시는 프랑스 음악에 미친 독일 작곡가들의 영향을 비판하고 있으므로 ①과 ②는 적절치 않다.

2 ④ ▶ 부분이해
드뷔시는 당시의 시대적 조류였던 독일 음악의 영향을 거부하고 프랑스적인 특성을 찾으려고 하였다. 본문에서 소개된 독일 음악은 '흥분을 고조시키는 고밀도의 특성', '심오한 척하는 가식', '모든 것을 과다하게 강조하려는 경향' 등의 특징을 지니고 있다. 따라서 ④가 가장 적절하다. ③ '세상으로부터의 철수'는 드뷔시가 세상을 등진 것이 아니므로 부적절하며, ⑤ '섬세함과 매력'은 프랑스 음악의 특징으로 소개된 내용이다.

13 2016 서강대

문화의 장(場)을 기존에 이미 확립된 보편성 개념에 대한 확고한 믿음을 보여주는 이런저런 증거를 찾기 위해 들어가 볼 수 있는 장(場)으로 떠올리는 것은 거의 이치에 맞지 않다. 만약 누군가가 세계 시민의 예를 찾기 위해 문화의 다양한 영역 속으로 들어간다면, 그는 그 다양한 사례들로부터 똑같은 교훈, 똑같은 보편적 의미를 골라 모을 것이다. 그러나 문화와 보편적인 것들과의 관계를 어떤 예와 그것이 지지한다고 말해지는 도덕적 언명 간의 관계라고 해석하는 것이 적절한가? 그런 경우에, 그 예들은 보편적인 것들에 종속된 것이고, 따라서 그것들은 모두 똑같은 방식으로 그 보편적인 것들을 나타낼 것이다. 그러나 그 보편적인 것들 가운데 어떤 것들이 제시되고 있고, 그것들은 어떤 것들을 배제한 토대 위에 있는지, 그리고 그렇게 배세된 것들이 보편적인 것들의 영역 속으로 들어올 수 있으려면 보편성에 대한 우리의 사고가 어떻게 근본적으로 변해야 하는지를 이해하기 위해 다양한 문화적 예들 간의 문화적 번역(변환)을 낳게 할 방법들을 찾을 경우에야 비로소 보편적인 것들에 대한 분명한 미래적 표현이 가능하다. 보편적인 것들에 관한 주장들이 상충할 때, 논쟁의 대상이 되는 문화적 순간들이 기성의 보편성을 예시하는 것이라고는 간주하지 말아야 할 것 같다. 그러한 주장은 보편성에 대한 지속적인 문화적 표현의 일부이고, 그러한 주장을 해독하는 방법을 배우는 복잡한 과정은 우리들 중 그 누구도 문화적 번역의 어려운 과정을 벗어나 해낼 수 있는 것이 아니다. 이러한 번역은 모든 문화적 사례들을 전제된 보편성으로 환원시켜버리는 쉬운 번역이 아닐 것이고, 서로 어떤 소통도 불가능한 급진적인 개별주의들을 열거하는 것도 아닐 것이다.

1 ① ▶ 동의어
①의 abiding은 '영속적인, 변치 않는'이라는 의미이므로, ①의 '확고한'의 의미를 가진 staunch가 정답이다. ② 생기 넘치는, 번뜩이는 ③ 하강하는 ④ 첨부된

2 ② ▶ 내용파악
필자는 기존에 이미 확립된 보편성 개념 하에서 문화적 사례들을 제시할 경우 기존의 보편성 개념에 종속될 수밖에 없으며 기존의 보편성 개념이 배제하고 있는 것들이 반영될 수 있으려면 어렵더라도 다양한 문화적 번역(변환)들을 시도하는 수밖에 없다고 주장한다. "다양한 문화적 예들 간의 문화적 번역을 낳게 할 방법들을 찾을 경우에야 비로소 보편적인 것들에 대한 분명한 미래적 표현이 가능하다."라고 한 다섯 번째 문장이 이를 뒷받침한다.

3 ② ▶ 내용파악
필자는 기존의 보편성 개념이 어떤 것들을 배제하고 있는지 확인하고, 그 배제된 것들이 보편성의 영역 속으로 들어올 수 있을 때 비로소 보편적인 것들에 좀 더 가까워질 수 있다고 말한다. 다섯 번째 문장의 in order to 이하가 단서다.

4 ① ▶ 빈칸완성
빈칸 ⑧에는 '고르다, 선택하다'의 의미의 표현이 적절하며, 빈칸 ⓒ에는 an already established, presupposed와 동등한 의미를 지니고 있는 표현이 와야 한다. 그러므로 ①이 정답이다. ② 짜증나게 하다 — 변화무쌍한 ③ (문제·폭력을) 조장하다 — 배설물의 ④ 촉구하다 — 초기의

enter v. (공식적으로) 제기하다, 진술하다
bits and pieces 잡동사니
abiding a. (믿음 등이) 지속적인, 변치 않는
universality n. 보편성
cull A from B B에서 A를 골라 모으다
selfsame a. 그와 똑같은
bearing n. 관계, 관련; 의미, 취지
construe v. 이해하다, 해석하다
dictum n. 격언, 금언; 언명
subordinate to ~에 종속하는, ~에 부수적인
articulation n. 명확한 표현
effect v. (어떤 결과를) 가져오다; 실행하다
exclusion n. 제외, 배제, 차단
entry n. 입장, 등장; 기회
imperative a. 반드시 해야 하는, 긴요한
exemplify v. 예증[예시]하다
reduce v. 축소하다, 환원시키다
presuppose v. 전제하다
enumeration n. 열거
particularism n. 개별주의; 배타주의
androcentric a. 남성 중심의
perennial a. 지속되는, 영원한
debunk v. 틀렸음을 밝히다, 정체를 폭로하다
approximation n. 근사치, 근접
timeless a. 세월이 흘러도 변치 않는

14 2020 국민대

외젠 들라크루아(Eugène Delacroix)(1798-1863)는 프랑스 낭만주의 운동에 있어 중요한 화가였으며 "키오스섬의 대학살(Massacre at Chios)"과 같은 그의 위대한 작품 중 일부는 폭압 정권에 대항한 혁명을 지지하면서 전쟁의 공포를 묘사했다. 그의 후기 그림들 중에는 스페인과 북아프리카를 여행하면서 한 스케치를 바탕으로 아랍과 유대 문화를 묘사한 것이 많았다. 들라크루아는 또한 윌리엄 셰익스피어, 월터 스콧 경, 요한 볼프강 폰 괴테의 책에 삽화를 그려 넣었으며, 예술과 또 다른 주제들에 대한 글을 자신의 『저널(Journals)』에 실어 문필가로서도 명성을 얻었다. 그의 그림 "민중을 이끄는 자유의 여신(Liberty Leading the People)"은 노동자와 중산층의 연합군, 즉 영광의 3

massacre n. 대학살
depose v. (권력의 자리에서) 물러나게 하다; (국왕을) 폐하다
commemorate v. 기념하다, 축하하다
constitutional a. 헌법의
proclamation n. 포고
dissolve v. 해산시키다

일(Trois Glorieuses)이 샤를 10세(Charles X)를 퇴위시키고 루이 필립(Louis-Philippe)이 통치하는 입헌 군주국을 수립한 1830년 3일간의 프랑스 7월 혁명을 기념하는 작품이다. 7월 혁명은 국민 의회를 해산하고 언론의 자유를 종식시키고 귀족에게 더 많은 권력을 부여하는 선거 제도를 만드는 4개의 포고문에 샤를이 서명함으로써 촉발되었다. "민중을 이끄는 자유의 여신"은 사실주의와 알레고리(비유)를 결합하고 있는 것으로, 자유의 여신은 신화 속의 인물이나 여신으로서 그리고 가장 치열했던 유혈혁명의 날에 반란군을 이끄는 민중의 여성으로서 의인화되어 있다. 들라크루아는 혁명 기념 전시회로 개최된 1831년 5월의 파리 미술 전람회(Salon)에 출품하기 위해 이 그림을 그렸다. 그러나 정부 관리들이 들라크루아의 그 그림이 더 많은 반란을 고무시킬 것을 두려워했기 때문에, "민중을 이끄는 자유의 여신"은 전람회가 끝나고 1874년 루브르 박물관에 들어올 때까지 단지 드물게만 전시되었다. 이제 들라크루아의 그림은 프랑스 공화국에 대한 애국심과 연관되며, 너무나 그렇게 연관되다 보니 그의 초상화는 100프랑짜리 지폐 뒷면에 15년 동안 등장했다.

aristocracy n. 귀족
allegory n. 풍유; 상징
personify v. 의인화하다
insurrection n. 반란, 봉기
patriotism n. 애국심

1 ④ ▶ 내용파악
본문에서 들라크루아가 신문기자로서 활동했다는 내용은 나오지 않는다.

2 ② ▶ 내용일치
입헌 군주국을 수립했다고 했으므로 군주제의 영구적 폐지는 아니어서 ①은 사실이 아니다. 본문에서 '노동자들과 중산층의 연합군(귀족은 제외)'이라고 하였으므로 ③은 틀린 진술이다. 여행 경험을 기억해서가 아니라 여행하면서 한 스케치를 바탕으로 그렸으므로 ④는 틀린 진술이다. 본문에서 들라크루아는 '프랑스 낭만주의 운동에 있어 중요한 화가'라고 하였으므로 ②의 진술은 옳다.

3 ② ▶ 내용파악
본문에서 "민중을 이끄는 자유의 여신"은 '사실주의와 알레고리를 결합하고 있다'고 하였으므로 ②는 옳지 않다.

15 2019 세종대

미국 원주민이 전통 의식에서 췄던 춤인 태양 춤의 형식은 항상 지역사회마다 달랐다. 그럼에도 불구하고, 그 춤의 일정한 특징들은 많은 부족들이 공유하고 있다. 종종, 그 춤은 종교적인 대부(代父)가 시작해야 하는데, 그는 걱정거리에서 벗어나거나 다음 해에 복을 받기를 바라면서 맹세를 하는 사람이다. 태양 춤은 거의 항상 하지(夏至) 무렵에 거행된다. 대부분의 태양 춤은 종교의식에 맞게 선택하고 베어낸 중앙의 나무기둥 주위에 원형의 천막집을 세우는 것으로 시작된다. 그 후 사나흘 동안 노래를 부르고 북을 치면서 춤을 추며, 간간이 휴식과 명상의 시간이 주어진다. 춤추는 사람들은 춤을 추는 시간 내내 먹거나 마시지 않지만, 일부는 입이 마르지 않게 하기 위해 곰 뿌리라는 풀뿌리를 씹기도 한다. 춤이 끝날 무렵, 참가자들은 환상을 경험하고 신의 은총을 받게 된다.
초기 유럽인들은 그 의식에서 자진해서 고행(苦行)을 하는 일부 부족들의 관행에 거부감을 느꼈다. <춤을 추는 남자들은 가슴이나 등이 꼬챙이에 꿰어진 채 중앙에 있는 천막집의 기둥에 매어져 있었다.> 춤을 추며 (중앙기둥과 연결된) 밧줄에 팽팽히 잡아당겨지다가 그들은 마침내 꼬챙이에서 벗어나 자유로워졌다. 이 의식을 통해 참가자들은 그들의 공동체를 대신하여 글자 그대로 고통을 겪고, 신(神)에게 그들을 불쌍히 여기고 그들이 맹세한 바를 완수할 수 있도록 도와줄 것을 청한다. 1870년대 후반부터 1935년 사이에 연방 관리들이 그 의식을 금지한 주된 이유도 그 의식의 이런 측면 때문이었다. 그러나 금지령에도 불구하고, 많은 부족들은 인디언 보호구역 내의 외딴 지역에서 몰래 태양 춤 의식을 거행하거나 불쾌한 요소들을 빼고 공연하기를 계속했다.

format n. 형태, 체재
ceremonial a. 의식의, 의례상의
vary v. 가지각색이다, 다르다
feature n. 특징, 특색
tribe n. 부족, 종족
initiate v. 시작하다, 개시하다
sponsor n. 보증인; 후원인; (종교적인) 대부(代父)
vow n. 맹세, 서약
relieve v. (고통·부담 따위를) 경감하다; (고통·공포 따위로부터) 해방하다; 구원하다
summer solstice 하지(夏至)
erection n. 건설, 조립; 세움
circular a. 원형의, 둥근
lodge n. 오두막집; (북아메리카 원주민의) 천막집
solemnly ad. 엄숙하게; (종교적인) 의식에 맞게
accompany v. 동반하다; (현상 따위가) ~에 수반하여 일어나다
intersperse v. 흩뿌리다, 산재시키다
meditation n. 묵상, (종교적) 명상
chew on 우물거리다, 잘근잘근 씹다

1 ③ ▶ 빈칸완성
빈칸 앞에서는 '태양 춤의 형식이 지역사회마다 달랐음'을 이야기하고 있고 빈칸 뒤에서는 '태양 춤의 일정한 특징들을 많은 부족이 서로 공유함'을 언급하고 있다. 빈칸 전후의 내용이 대조를 이루므로, 빈칸에는 '그럼에도 불구하고'라는 의미의 ③이 적절하다. ① 그런 까닭에 ② 그러므로 ④ 그 사이에

2 ③　　▶ 문장삽입

주어진 문장은 "춤을 추는 남자들은 가슴이나 등이 꼬챙이에 꿰어진 채 중앙에 있는 천막집의 기둥에 매어져 있었다."는 의미이므로, ⓒ 앞에서 언급한 '고행(self-mortification)'을 구체적으로 설명한 것이라 할 수 있다. 그러므로 주어진 문장은 ⓒ에 들어가는 것이 적절하다.

3 ④　　▶ 내용일치

마지막 문장에서 "금지령에도 불구하고, 많은 부족들은 인디언 보호구역 내의 외딴 지역에서 몰래 태양 춤 의식을 거행했다."고 했으므로, ④가 옳지 않은 진술이다.

4 ③　　▶ 내용파악

"이 의식을 통해 참가자들은 그들의 공동체를 대신하여 글자 그대로 고통을 겪고, 신(神)에게 그들을 불쌍히 여기고 그들이 맹세한 바를 완수할 수 있도록 도와줄 것을 요청한다."고 했다. 그러므로 ③이 정답으로 적절하다.

bear root 천궁과 유사한 약초, 풀
moist a. 습기 있는, 축축한
participant n. 참여자
vision n. 환상, 환영(幻影)
blessing n. 축복; 신의 은총
repulse v. 구역질나게 하다, 혐오감을 주다
self-mortification n. 자진하여 고행을 함
strain v. 잡아당기다
tear loose from ~로부터 자유롭게 되다, 달아나다
skewer v. 꼬챙이에 꿰다 n. 꼬챙이
ritual a. 의식의, 제식의
on behalf of ~을 대신하여, ~을 대표하여
pity v. 불쌍히 여기다
fulfillment n. 이행, 수행, 완수; 실천
aspect n. 양상, 모습; 측면
prohibit v. 금지하다
ban n. 금지, 금지령
surreptitiously ad. 내밀하게, 은밀히, 몰래
reservation n. 인디언 보호 거주지
enact v. 법제화하다; (연극을) 공연하다
objectionable a. 못마땅한, 불쾌한

16　2020 중앙대

대부분의 비평가들, 특히 식자층을 대변하는 비평가들은 1950년대 대중문화를 개탄하였다. 그리고 개탄할 만한 것들은 넘쳐났다. 할리우드의 대작들, "공포" 만화들, 머리를 울리는 굉음의 로큰롤 음악 등, 통속적인 내용물들이 우위를 차지한 것에 유일한 보상적 미덕이 있었다면, 그것이 일시적이라는 점이었다. 텔레비전이 비난을 온통 뒤집어썼는데, 텔레비전의 내용을 논하면서 심지어 중간급 칼럼니스트였던 해리엇 반 호른(Harriet Van Horne)조차 문화적 파멸을 개탄하였다. "우리 대중들은 읽고 쓸 줄 아는 능력이 시시각각으로 약해지고 있다. 책을 읽고 다른 사람의 생각을 생각해보는 것과 같은 오래된 습관은 스러져가고, TV가 그들의 시간을 빨아들일 것이다. 21세기 대중들은 사팔눈에 휘어진 등으로 어둠 속에 있기를 좋아할 것이 틀림없다."

실제로 문화적 위험이 존재했음은 의심의 여지가 없다. 경제 호황과 대중 매체의 시대에, 문화는 마치 치약처럼 무서운 속도로 생산되고 소비되었다. 이러한 가치 없는 압력은 제품의 질을 낮추는 경향이 있었다. 그러나 상황은 비관론자들이 주장하는 만큼 그리 암울하지만은 않았다. 우선, 많이 남용되던 미디어들이 당시 꽤 책임 있는 태도를 보였다. 1956년, NBC(National Broadcasting Company)는 50만 달러를 들여 셰익스피어의 『리처드 3세(Richard III)』를 원작으로 한 로렌스 올리비에(Laurence Olivier)의 영화를 방영했다. 5천만 명이 시청했고, 그중 절반 정도는 장장 3시간 동안 끝까지 시청했다. 『Life』지는 1952년 어니스트 헤밍웨이(Ernest Hemingway)의 신작 소설 『노인과 바다(The Old Man and the Sea)』를 전재함으로써 수백만의 독자들을 즐겁게 하거나 자극했다.

문화적 황무지에 또 다른 오아시스들도 있었다. 회화 분야에서, 잭슨 폴록(Jackson Pollock)이 이끌던 혁신가 그룹은 전 세계 예술의 수도를 파리에서 뉴욕으로 옮겨왔다. 모트 살(Mort Sahl)처럼 신랄한 풍자가들이 공급하던 지식인 유머는 작은 클럽을 벗어나, 방송의 버라이어티 쇼를 통해 더 큰 대중들에게 도달하기 시작했다. 구경만하고 사지 못하던 문화적 소외계층을 끌어들이기 위해 문고본 출판사들은 저렴한 가격(0.25불에서 1.35불)으로 수백만 부의 표준 고전 작품들을 보급하였다. 클래식 음악은 놀라운 국민적 관심을 받게 되었다. 1950년대 중반에 미국의 교향악단은 1940년 이후 80퍼센트 증가하여 약 200개에 달했고, 콘서트들은 같은 기간에 150퍼센트 증가한

highbrow a. 식자층의, 교양 있는
deplore v. 한탄하다
preponderance n. 우위, 우세
redeeming a. (결점을) 벌충하는
transience n. 덧없음, 일시적임
fare n. 공연물, 프로내용, 콘텐츠
whipping boy (왕자의 학우로) 왕자를 대신하여 매맞는 소년, 희생양
contemplate v. 숙고하다
middlebrow a. 중간급의
squint-eyed a. 사팔눈의
hunchbacked a. 꼽추의
dismal a. 암울한
regale v. 맘껏 즐기게 하다
egghead n. 인텔리, 지식인
purvey v. 공급하다
sharp-tongued a. 입이 험한, 말이 신랄한
satirist n. 풍자가
propagate v. 전파하다, 번식시키다
ride a wave of ~의 지지를 받다, ~의 혜택을 누리다
go a long way toward ~에 크게 도움 되다

2,500개 도시에서 이어졌다. 사실, 음악은 미국의 문화적 오아시스들이 문화적 황무지 자체보다 더 커질지도 모른다는 것을 입증하는 데 큰 역할을 하였다. 1955년에 약 3천5백만 명의 사람들이 클래식 음악 공연을 관람했는데, 이는 그해 메이저리그 야구 경기 관람객들 숫자의 2배 이상이었다.

1 ③ ▶ **빈칸완성**
빈칸 Ⓐ 다음에 있는 '책을 읽고 다른 사람의 생각을 생각해보는 것과 같은 오래된 습관은 스러져 간다'는 진술을 고려할 때 literate가 적절하고, 빈칸 Ⓑ 앞에 있는 '무서운 속도'라는 표현에서 relentless가 적절함을 알 수 있다. 참고로, relentless pressure는 '엄청난 압력', '극심한 압력' 등의 의미로 자주 사용된다. ① 완고한 — 시의 적절한 ② 사려 깊은 — 촉진하는 ④ 충동적인 — 끈질긴

2 ② ▶ **내용추론**
'1950년대 대중문화에서 개탄할 만한 것들은 넘쳐났다', '상황은 비관론자들이 주장하는 만큼 그리 암울하지만은 않았다', '문화적 황무지에 또 다른 오아시스들도 있었다' 등의 진술에 비추어 볼 때, ②는 타당한 추론이다.

17 2012 동덕여대

다다이즘 예술가들은 전통적 문화와 예술적 관습에 대한 그들의 반감과 경멸감을 드러내며 끊임없이 그것들을 훼손시키기 위해 노력했다. 이러한 것의 극명한 예는 레오나르도 다빈치(Leonardo da Vinci)의 『모나리자(Mona Lisa)』 복제품에 콧수염을 그려 넣은 마르셀 뒤샹(Marcel Duchamp)의 악명 높은 행위인데, 기존의 예술계에서는 불손하고 발상이 잘못된 행위로 여겼다. 다다이즘은 (기존의) 예술이 나타내는 것이 무엇이든 그 정반대의 것을 표현하고자 했다. 종래의 예술이 적어도 하나의 함축적 메시지를 갖고 있었다면, 다다이즘은 어떠한 의미도 갖지 않으려 했다. 따라서 다다이즘 작품들에 대한 해석은 전적으로 보는 사람에게 달려 있었다.

다다이즘은 독창성에 대한 전혀 새로운 접근법을 개척하고 탐구했다. 다다이즘 예술가들은 더 이상 예술적 전통에 제약받지 않으며, 자유롭게 창작과정을 실험할 수 있게 되었다. 예를 들어, 화가 쟝 아르프(Jean Arp)는 종잇장들을 가져다 대충 사각형 모양으로 찢고 나서 그다음 이 종이들을 마룻바닥 위의 한 장의 종이에 흩뿌려 그것들이 어디로 떨어지든지 접착제로 붙였다. 아르프는 이 방법의 임의성과 즉흥성에 너무나 만족한 나머지 이 방법을 이용해 그의 가장 잘 알려진 작품 중 하나인 『우연의 법칙에 의한 사각형들의 콜라주(Collage Arranged According to the Laws of Chance)』를 만들었다.

아마도 다다이즘 예술가들 중 가장 영향력 있는 사람인 마르셀 뒤샹은 예술계 내의 엄격한 관례적 표현수단의 사용에 대한 공공연한 비판을 위한 것인 그의 레디메이드로 유명하다. 이러한 레디메이드는 예술가들이 어떻게든 변형시키거나 다른 물체들과 결합시킨 수프 캔과 보틀랙 같은 일상생활의 대량생산된 물건들이었다. 예술가는 단순히 그 물건들을 미술관에 전시함으로써 그것들에게 예술적 지위를 부여했다. 뒤샹의 가장 충격적인 레디메이드 조각인 『샘(Fountain)』은 그저 하나의 자기로 된 소변기였다. <그것은 어느 예술 작품과 마찬가지로 서명과 날짜가 기록됐다.>

dada(ism) n. 다다이즘(20세기 초의 문예·예술 운동)
convention n. 관습, 관례
contempt n. 경멸, 멸시; 개의하지 않음, 무시
undermine v. (자신감·권위 등을) 약화시키다
striking a. 눈에 띄는, 현저한; 빼어난
reproduction n. 생식, 번식; 복사, 복제; (특히 예술 작품의) 복제품
irreverent a. 불손한, 불경한
ill-conceived a. 계획[구상]이 잘못된
implied a. 함축된, 암시적인
constrain v. 강요하다; 제약하다
randomness n. 임의성, 무질서
improvisation n. 즉석에서 하기; (즉흥시·즉흥곡·즉흥연주 등) 즉석에서 한[지은] 것
ready-made a. 이미 만들어져 나오는; 기성품의 n. <미술> 레디메이드(일상의 기제품을 본래의 용도가 아닌 다른 의미를 부여하여 조각 작품으로 발표한 것)
overt a. 명시적인, 공공연한
bottle rack 보틀랙(포도주 따위의 술병을 뉘어서 놓아두는 격자형 또는 평면으로 된 선반)
confer v. (학위·명예·자격 등을) 부여[수여]하다
outrageous a. 너무나 충격적인; 아주 별난
porcelain n. 자기
urinal n. (남성용) 소변기

1 ② ▶ **내용파악**
첫 번째 단락에서 다다이즘 예술가들은 전통적 문화와 예술적 관습에 반감과 경멸감을 표하고 (기존의) 예술이 나타내는 것이 무엇이든 그 정반대의 것을 표현하고자 했다고 했다. 따라서 be at odds with는 '~와 불화하다, 갈등을 겪다, 뜻이 맞지 않다'라는 의미이므로 ②의 설명이 다다이즘 예술가들에 대한 올바른 진술이다. ① 다다이즘 예술가들은 예술적 전통에 제약받지 않고 자유롭게 새로운 예술 양식을 이용했다고 했다. ③ 유명 예술 작품들을 훼손하려 했다는 내용만 있을 뿐 파괴하려 했다는 내용은 없다. ④ 종래의 예술과 달리 다다이즘은 어떠한 메시지도 갖지 않으려 했다.

2 ② ▶ **내용추론**
"쟝 아르프는 종이를 마룻바닥에 흩뿌리는 방법의 임의성과 즉흥성에 너무나 만족한 나머지 이 방법을 이용해 그의 가장 잘 알려진 작품 중 하나인 『우연의 법칙에 의한 사각형들의 콜라주』를 만들었다."라고 했으므로 자신의 작품에 대한 '통제성'을 필수적으로 생

각하지 않았을 거라 유추할 수 있다. 따라서 ②가 정답으로 가장 적절하다. 임의성과 즉흥성은 통제와 반대되는 개념이다. ① 콜라주 기법을 누가 처음에 발명했는지는 본문을 통해 확인할 수 없다. ③ 창작과정의 노력을 최소화하기 위한 내용은 전혀 언급되지 않았다. ④ 과학적 지식이 예술에 적용된 예의 근거를 찾을 수 없다.

3 ④ ▶ 문장삽입
주어진 문장의 주어(It)는 단수 비인칭대명사로 그것이 의미하는 것은 앞 문장의 「샘」이라는 작품이다. 따라서 Ⓓ에 삽입되는 것이 가장 적절하다. 「샘」이라는 작품이 Ⓒ 앞 문장에 언급된 '단순히 미술관에 전시함으로써 예술적 지위를 부여한 물건들'의 한 예에 해당하므로 Ⓒ에 삽입되기는 부적절하다.

18 2020 숭실대

야수파는 20세기 최초의 아방가르드 예술(전위 예술) 운동이었다. 파리에서 활동하던 젊은 세 명의 예술가인 앙리 마티스(Henri Matisse), 앙드레 드랭(André Derain), 모리스 드 블라맹크(Maurice de Vlaminck)가 주도한 이 운동은 느슨한 붓놀림과 단순화된 형태와 함께, 강렬하고, 표현이 풍부하며, 비사실적(非寫實的)인 색채가 특징이었다. 1905년경에서 1910년까지 활동했던 야수파 화가들은 몇 가지 최근의 예술 사조를 이끌어냈고 발전시켰는데, 주로 인상파화가, 점묘화가, 고갱(Gauguin), 반 고흐(Van Gogh)의 예술 사조였다. 그들은 묘사하고 있는 피사체와 정확하게 일치하는 방식으로 색을 사용하기를 거부한 화가들이었다. 마티스는 "내가 초록색을 칠한다고 해서 그것이 풀을 의미하는 것이 아니듯이, 내가 파란색을 칠한다고 해서 그것이 하늘을 의미하는 것이 아니다."라고 설명했다. 요컨대 색이 완전히 자유로이 사용되었다.

그 운동의 이름은 불어로 야수를 의미하는 fauve에서 유래했으며 1905년 파리에서 열린 가을 살롱 전시회에서 논평의 글을 썼던 유명 미술 평론가 루이 보셀(Louis Vauxcelles)에 의해 만들어졌다. 마티스, 드랭 등의 눈길을 끄는 그림과 같은 방에 전시된 15세기 양식의 조각을 보는 것은 '야수들 사이의 도나텔로'를 보는 것과 같았다고 그는 말했다. 그 명칭이 받아들여지게 됐고 야수파가 탄생하게 되었다.

야수파는 새롭고 밝은 색의 그림물감을 만들었던 19세기 산업 제조의 발전에 의해서 가능해졌다. 야수파는 종종 이 물감들을 예술원의 관행에, 그리고 사실, 서구의 예술적 관행에 반하여, 튜브에서 짜내서, 물과 섞지 않고, 즉 가능한 가장 강력한 형태로, 그대로 사용했다.

야수파 화가들은 혁명적인 작품들을 만들었지만, 그들이 '야수'의 성격을 가지고 있지는 않았다고 말하는 것이 온당하다. 예를 들면, 화가가 되기 전에 마티스는 변호사였고 드랭은 기술자였다.

화려한 색체와 즉흥적인 붓놀림을 고려했을 때 야수파가 가장 큰 영향을 끼친 운동은 아마도 독일 표현주의였을 것이다. 그러나 피사체의 사실적(寫實的) 묘사를 포함하여 모든 것을 색의 상호 작용보다 하위에 둠(경시함)으로써 야수파는 또한 추상주의로 가는 길을 열었다.

Fauvism n. 야수파(1905년부터 파리에서 잠시 유행했던 회화의 한 유파, 강렬한 색채와 비현실적인 소재 묘사가 특징)
avant-garde n. 아방가르드(문학·예술에서 전위적인 사상)
spearhead v. 선봉에 서다, 진두지휘하다
impressionist n. 인상파의 화가
pointillist n. 점묘화가
literally ad. 정말로, 완전히
correspond v. 상당하다, 대응하다
derive from ~에서 유래하다, 파생하다
stunned a. (놀람 등으로) 어리벙벙하게 하는
Quattrocento n. 15세기
eye-popping a. 눈이 휘둥그래질 만한, 깜짝 놀라게 하는, 놀라운
pigment n. 색소, 안료, 물감재료
in defiance of ~를 무시하여, 무릅쓰고
revolutionary a. 혁명[획기]적인
subordinate v. (~보다) 하위에 두다, 경시하다
interplay n. 상호 작용

1 ④ ▶ 빈칸완성
양보의 접속사 Even though가 와서 '작품은 혁명적이고 과격했지만, 이들의 성격은 그 다음 문장의 변호사와 기술자처럼 평범하고 온건했다'는 말이 되어야 한다. 그런데 부정문이므로 빈칸에는 혁명적이고 과격한 성격을 나타내는 ④(야수)가 적절하다. ① 좋은 기분 ② 복종 ③ 합리성

2 ③ ▶ 내용파악
야수파의 특징을 설명하는 말로 loose brushwork(느슨한 붓놀림)와 spontaneous brushwork(즉흥적인 붓놀림)가 제시되어 있으므로, 야수파는 신중하게 계획해서 붓을 놀리지 않는다고 볼 수 있다. 따라서 ③이 정답이다.

3 ④ ▶ 내용일치
마지막 문장에서 야수파는 피사체의 사실적 묘사를 포함하여 모든 것을 색의 상호 작용보다 경시했다고 했으므로, ④가 정답이다.

19 2016 가톨릭대

페미니즘 사상의 핵심주장 가운데 하나는 '생물학적 성(sex)'은 '사회학적 성(gender)'과 다른 별개의 개념이고, 사회학적 성은 문화규약의 문제라는 것이다. '남성성(masculinity)'과 '여성성(femininity)'이 어느 특징과 연관된 것인가에 대한 생각들은 사회마다 다르다. 어떤 상황에서 '여성적'인 행동으로 간주되는 것이 다른 상황에서는 더 '남성적'인 행동으로 간주될지도 모른다. 사람들은 그들이 몸담고 사는 사회적 상황에 의해 정해진 '남성적인 행동'과 '여성적인 행동'에 관한 문화규범에 순응하고 있다. 사람은 태어난 이후 계속해서 사회화 과정을 겪어 가면서, 이런 문화규범을 무의식적으로 수용하고, 이것을 기반으로 해서 행동한다. 성장의 중요한 요소는 '남성적'이 되고 '여성적'이 되는 방법을 학습하는 것을 내포하고 있다. <일반적으로 이런 학습과정은 무의식적이고 반(半) 의식적인 심리 수준에서 발생한다.> 그러면 사람은 그들을 결정지은 문화적으로 파생된 사회학적 성의 규범을 실제로 타고난 불변적인 것으로 생각한다. 우리가 자연스럽게 '여성적'이거나 '남성적'이라고 생각하는 사고와 행동 방식은 실제로는 특정한 문화적 기대가 가르친 결과물이다.

그 결과 우리는 사회학적 성에 대한 문화규범이 자라나는 사람에게 그들의 사고방식 면에서 뿐 아니라 그들의 육체적인 면에서도, 즉 그들이 몸을 움직이고 경험하는 방식 면에서도 영향을 줄 것이라고 생각할지 모른다. 대부분의 사회에서 남성은 여성보다 더 많은 권력 지위를 차지하기 쉽다. 그리고 가부장적 사회구조 하에서는 남성 집단이 여성보다 더 많은 권력을 가지며, 여성을 지배하는 권력도 가진다. 그와 같은 사회에서 문화적 세력들은 이런 상황을 반영하는 동시에 이를 정당화하고 있다. 남성은 여성보다 어떻게든 본래적으로 더 우월한 존재로 간주되고 있으며, 이런 우월성이 마치 삶의 불변하는 사실인 것처럼 받아들여지고 있다. 가부장적 사회에 특징적인 사회학적 성의 규범은 본래적인 본질이 아니라 문화적 조작인 '여성성'의 본질을 만든다. 심리적으로 그리고 육체적으로 여성의 열등성을 강조하면서 '여성성'은 일반적으로 부정적인 방식으로 정의된다.

claim n. 주장; 요구
separate a. 관련이 없는, 별개의
sex n. 생물학적 성(性)
gender n. 사회학적 성(性)
convention n. 협정, 합의, 규약
trait n. 특징, 특색
masculinity n. 남성성
femininity n. 여성성
conform v. (규칙·관습 등에) 따르다, 순응하다(to)
onwards ad. (특정 시간부터) 계속; 앞으로
norm n. 규범; 기준
feminine a. 여성의
masculine a. 남성의
inculcation n. 반복교육, 주입교육
corporeality n. 육체성; 유형성, 구체성
patriarchal a. 가부장제의
simultaneously ad. 동시에, 일제히
superiority n. 우월성
inferiority n. 열등성
fabrication n. 제작; 꾸며낸 일

1 ④ ▶ 빈칸완성
페미니즘 사상에 따르면, sex(생물학적 성)와 gender(사회학적 성)는 서로 다른 개념이며, 사회학적 성은 문화규약의 문제다. 사회학적 성은 특정 문화 속에서 구성원들이 그 문화의 기대치를 학습한 산물이지 고유한 실재는 아니라는 것이다. 예를 들어, "육아는 여자가 해야 한다."라는 주장은 여성성의 실체가 아니라 특정 문화가 만든 개념인 것이다. 따라서 문화규범 안에서 특정한 여성성은 '문화적으로 조작'된 것임을 알 수 있다. ① 언어학적인 표현 ② 역사적 사건 ③ 사회적인 변화

2 ② ▶ 문장삽입
사회학적 성은 특정사회의 문화규범이자 이데올로기이다. 인간은 출생 직후부터 특정한 사회 안에서 사회화 과정을 통해 남녀를 구분하는 사회학적 성의 문화규범을 수용하고, 이를 기반으로 행동하도록 학습을 받는다. 'these learning processes' 이하의 문장은 앞의 학습내용을 말하고 있는 것이므로, 주어진 문장은 B에 오는 것이 가장 적절하다.

3 ① ▶ 내용일치
페미니스트의 주장에 따르면, 사회학적 성은 '생득적이고 본질적인 실재'가 아니라 '특정 문화의 합의규범'이며, 사회학적 성의 목적은 사회 구성원을 특정 문화규범에 순응하기 위해 만든 문화적 조작이다. 이런 점에서, "문화규범이란 사물의 실재 상태를 반영한다."는 페미니즘의 주장과는 전혀 다른 내용임을 알 수 있다.

20 2014 가톨릭대

피카소(Picasso)보다 더 급진적인 방식으로 시각적인 세상을 다른 모습으로 보여준 예술가는 없었다. 단편적인 기하학적인 면들로 구성된 그의 엄격한 초기 입체파 그림들에서는 인물과 배경 사이의 차이점이 거의 구분이 되지 않으며 구상적 표현의 한계를 시험하고 있다. 제1차 세계대전이 끝난 뒤, 그는 역설적으로 편평하면서도 감지할 수 없는 깊이를 암시하고, 현실을 예리하게 묘사하면서도 종종 밝게 채색된 매우 다른 종류의 그림을 그렸다. 최근에 T. J. 클락(T. J. Clark)은 그의 저서인 『Picasso and Truth』에서 1920년대와 1930년대의 피카소 그림들에 초점을 맞추고 있다. 이

reinvent v. 재발명하다, 다른 모습[이미지]을 보여주다
radical a. 급진적인, 과격한; 근본적인
stringent a. 엄중한, 엄격한; 긴박한, 절박한
fragmentary a. 단편적인, 부분적인
geometric a. 기하학적인
distinguishable a. 구분할 수 있는

시기의 피카소 작품들은 지금은 아주 익숙해져서 그림들의 복잡함과 극단적인 생소함이 종종 당연한 것으로 여겨지고 있거나 심지어 간과되기도 한다. 클락의 책은 이 그림들이 얼마나 급진적이고 생소한지를 탐구하고 있다.

추악함과 기괴함이 항상 또 다른 형태의 아름다움이라고 내세워질 수는 없다. 왜냐하면 그러한 것들은 때때로 그림을 보는 사람들의 믿음의 토대를 흔들어 새로운 종류의 진실을 드러내도록 의도되어 있기 때문이다. 클락은 피카소를 동시대인들보다 더 분명하고 더 진실된 방식으로 자신의 주변 세상을 볼 수 있는 초자연적인 재능을 가진 일종의 마법사로 여기고 있다. 클락의 책은 피카소가 어떻게 공간과 물체 그리고 주제 사이의 복잡한 관계를 통해, 특히 기괴함을 대담하게 수용함으로써 틀에 박힌 진실의 개념을 확대하고 심지어 재정의하는지를 보여주고 있다.

이 몇 년간 피카소의 작품들이 보편적인 규범들로부터 아주 급진적으로 이딜되어 있었기 때문에 종종 적대감이나 혼란스러움으로 받아들여졌다. 1932년에 심리학자인 칼 융(Carl G. Jung)은 피카소의 그림을 정신 분열증 환자가 그린 그림과 비교하여 그를 "추악함과 사악함의 악마적 매력"을 추구하는 "저승에서 온" 인간이라 불렀다. 비록 클락은 이러한 맥락에서 융을 언급하지는 않지만 긍정적인 관점에서 그와 비슷한 자신의 의견을 드러내고 피카소 그림들의 섬뜩한 힘을 혹평하기 보다는 오히려 높이 평가하고 있다. 클락은 피카소의 작품에 병적인 요소가 포함되어 있음을 인정하고는 있지만 그는 피카소의 작품들이 한 개인의 병적 상태(병상)라기 보다는 한 시대의 병적 상태를 반영하고 있다고 보고 있다. <그에게 피카소의 그림은 재난으로 가득했던 한 세기에 대한 판단이다.>

1 ② ▶ 내용파악
①, ③, ④는 각각 본문의 내용에 등장하고 있으나 ②는 본문에서 '구상적 표현의 한계를 시험하고 있다'고 했으므로 피카소의 작품은 구상의 한계를 뛰어넘는 비구상적인 것이라 해야 한다. 피카소의 추악하고 기괴한 그림이 그림을 보는 사람들의 믿음의 토대를 흔들어 새로운 종류의 진실을 드러내도록 의도되어 있다고 했으므로 ④는 적절하다.

2 ④ ▶ 빈칸완성
입체파 화풍에서 편평하면서도 무형의 깊이를 연상시키는 매우 다른 종류의 그림을 그렸다는 내용으로 볼 때 역설적이라 할 수 있다. 따라서 ④ paradoxically가 적절하다. ① 상상력이 풍부하게 ② 예기치 않게 ③ 기억할 만하게

3 ④ ▶ 문장삽입
본문의 마지막 문장에서 피카소의 작품들이 한 시대에 대한 병적 상태를 반영한다는 내용으로 비추어 볼 때 "그에게 피카소의 그림은 재난으로 가득했던 한 세기에 대한 판단이다."라는 표현이 맥락상 그 뒤에 자연스럽게 연결될 수 있다.

4 ② ▶ 내용일치
마지막 단락의 중간에 칼 융의 의견에 대해 클락은 긍정적인 관점에서 그와 비슷한 입장을 피력했다는 내용으로 볼 때 완전히 부정한 것으로 볼 수는 없다.

---

intangible a. 무형의, 만질 수 없는
hard-edged a. 선명한; 현실을 예리하게 묘사하는
complexity n. 복잡성
overlook v. 간과하다
ugliness n. 추악함
monstrosity n. 기괴; 기형 동물[식물]
co-opt v. 선임하다, 끌어들이다
reveal v. 드러내다, 밝히다, 폭로하다
wizard n. 마법사
uncanny a. 초자연적인; 이상한
contemporary n. 동시대[동시기]의 사람
extend v. 확장하다, 늘이다
redefine v. 재정의하다
conventional a. 관습적인, 전통적인; 틀에 박힌
engagement n. 약속; 참여, 관여; 고용
depart v. 떠나다, 이탈하다
norm n. 규범
hostility n. 적대감
puzzlement n. 당혹감
schizophrenic n. 정신 분열병 환자
cast v. 던지다
damn v. 혹평하다
eerie a. 무시무시한, 섬뜩한, 기분 나쁜
pathological a. 병적인, 걷잡을 수 없는; 병리학의
reflection n. 반사; 반영
pathology n. 병리학, 병상
monstrous a. 기형의; 괴물 같은
representational a. 구상적인; 구상(具象)파의
anti-foundational a. 기본에 반하는

04 언어·문학

01 2014 한국외대

새로운 연구에 의하면, 고도가 높은 곳에서 사용하는 언어는 공기를 짧게 터뜨려서 내는 특정 종류의 소리를 포함하고 있을 가능성이 더 높다. "저는 특정 소리가 고도가 높은 곳에서 더 흔할지도 모른다는 이러한 가설을 가지고 있었습니다."라고 연구 저자 에버렛(Everett)이 말했다. "실제로 자료를 살펴보았을 때, 그 분포는 매우 압도적이었습니다."라고 그는 말했다. 특징을 바탕으로 언어를 분류하는 온라인 데이터베이스를 이용하여, 에버렛은 세계의 7,000개 언어 가운데 약 600개 언어의 위치를 분석했다. 그는 그 언어들 가운데 92개의 언어에 방출음의 자음이 있다는 것을 발견했다. 방출음은 공기를 강하게 터뜨려서 내는 소리로, 영어에서는 찾아볼 수 없다. 더욱이, 방출음을 가지고 있는 언어의 대부분은 세계에서 고도가 높은 지역 6곳 가운데 5곳 혹은 그 부근에서 사용된 것들이다. 방출음은 고도가 높은 곳에서 내기가 더 쉬운데, 왜냐하면 고도가 높아짐에 따라 기압이 낮아지며, 밀도가 더 낮은 공기를 압축하는 것이 힘이 덜 들기 때문이다. 그러나 고도가 높으면서도 언어에 방출음이 없는 지역이 한 곳 있다. 바로 티벳 고원이다. 그곳의 사람들은 고도가 높은 곳에 독특하게 적응했는데, 그것이 아마도 이러한 사실을 설명해 줄지도 모른다.

1 ① ▶ 글의 요지
'고도가 높은 곳에서 사용하는 언어는 공기를 짧게 터뜨려서 내는 특정 종류의 소리를 포함하고 있을 가능성이 더 높음'을 언급하고서, 방출음을 그 예로 들고 있다. 고도가 높다는 것은 지리적인 개념이므로, 요지로 적절한 것은 ①이 된다.

2 ② ▶ 내용일치
"고도가 높아지면 기압이 낮아지며, 밀도가 더 낮은 공기를 압축하는 것이 힘이 덜 들기 때문에 방출음은 고도가 높은 곳에서 내기가 더 쉽다."라고 돼 있으므로, ②가 본문의 내용과 일치하는 진술이다. ① "방출음은 공기를 강하게 터뜨려서 내는 소리로, 영어에서는 찾아볼 수 없다."라고 돼 있다. ③ 고도가 높은 지역이면서도 언어에 방출음이 없는 곳으로 티벳 고원을 언급하고 있다. ④ 에버렛 전 세계의 7,000개 언어 가운데 약 600개의 위치를 분석했으며, 그 600여 개의 언어 가운데 92개의 언어에 방출음이 있는 것을 발견한 상황이다. 즉, 7,000개의 언어 가운데 92개의 언어에 방출음이 있는 것이므로, 방출음이 흔하다고는 전혀 볼 수 없다.

altitude n. 높이, 고도
contain v. 포함하다; 참다, 억제하다
burst n. 파열, 폭발; 돌발
hypothesis n. 가설, 가정, 전제
distribution n. 분배, 배포; 분포
overwhelming a. 압도적인, 저항할 수 없는
categorize v. 분류하다
analyze v. 분석하다, 분해하다
ejective a. 방출하는, 내뿜는 n. 방출음
consonant n. 자음
intensive a. 강한, 격렬한; 집중적인, 철저한
compress v. 압축하다; 압착하다
less-dense a. 밀도가 더 낮은
plateau n. 고원, 대지
unique a. 유일무이한, 독특한, 특별한
adaptation n. 적응, 적합; 개작
account for 설명하다

02 2013 단국대

많은 비평가들은 에밀리 브론테(Emily Brontë)의 소설 『폭풍의 언덕(Wuthering Heights)』의 두 번째 부분이 첫 번째 부분을 뒤집지는 않는다 하더라도 첫 번째 부분에 대해 설명하는 대위적 요소인 것으로 간주하는데, 첫 번째 부분에서는 낭만적으로 읽는 것이 옳다는 것이 더 많은 확증을 얻는다. 화자들과 시간의 변화들의 복합적인 사용에서 드러나는 소설의 복잡한 구조 때문에 두 부분을 하나로 보는 것이 권장되고 있다. 이러한 요소들의 존재가 소설의 구조에 대한 작가적 인식을 지지하는 근거가 꼭 되어야 할 필요는 없다 하더라도, 그것들의 존재는 소설의 이질적인 부분들을 통합하려는 시도를 장려한다. 하지만 소설의 모든 다양한 요소들을 통합하려고 했던 어떠한 해석도 다소 설득력 없게 들릴 것이다. 이것은 그러한 해석이 반드시 딱딱해져서 논문으로 되어버리기 때문이 아니라 (비록 이 소설이나 다른 소설의 어떠한 해석에서도 경직성은 언제나 위험 요소이다), 근본적으로 『폭풍의 언덕』이 총괄적인 해석에 포함되지 않는 부인할 수 없이 강한 다루기 어려운 요소들을 가지고 있기 때문이다. 이 점에 있어서, 『폭풍의 언덕』은 『햄릿(Hamlet)』과 같은 특성을 지닌다.

critic n. 비평가, 평론가
counterpoint n. 대조[병치]적인 요소; 대위법
romantic a. 낭만적인; 공상적인
reading n. (상황 따위의) 해석, 판단; (연극 연출·음악 연주 등의) 해석; 연출[연주](법)
confirmation n. 확증, 확정; 확립
sophisticated a. 세련된; 복잡한, 정교한
authorial a. 저자의
heterogeneous a. 이질적인, 이류의
unconvincing a. 설득력 없는
recalcitrant a. 반항[저항]하는; 다루기 어려운
resist v. 저항[반항]하다

1	③	▶ 내용파악
		첫 번째 부분에서는 낭만적으로 읽는 것이 옳다는 것이 더 많은 확증을 얻는다고 했으므로, 첫 번째 부분과 대조가 되는 두 번째 부분은 그러한 확증을 덜 주는 부분일 것이다.

2	②	▶ 내용파악
		괄호 안에서 소설의 해석에서 경직성은 위험 요소라고 했으므로 저자는 소설을 해석함에 있어 완고한 태도를 취하는 것에 대해 좋지 않게 생각함을 알 수 있다. 따라서 ② '소설의 다양한 요소들을 분석할 때 완고한 태도를 취하지 말아야 한다'는 진술에 가장 잘 동의할 것이다.

inclusion n. 포함, 포괄; 함유물
all-encompassing a. 모든 것을 포함하는, 포괄적인
in this respect 이 점에 있어서

03 2019 중앙대

새로운 살인 추리소설의 가장 중요한 특징 중 하나는 소설이 독자들에게 부여하는 새로운 요구였는데, 그것은 독자들이 이야기를 만들고, 범인을 정하는 데 적극적인 역할을 해달라는 요구였다. 예전의 사형집행 설교문은 독자들이 설교문의 공식적인 확정적 진리(사형수의 죄상이 사실임)를 성직자적 권위에 입각해 받아들이기만을 요구했지만, 새로운 법정 소설은 사실상 독자들을 유죄판결 쪽이나 무죄판결 쪽에 표를 던져야 하는 <수령인>으로 대우해주었다.
유죄 판결을 받은 살인자의 사기번호 진술 옆의 여백에 "이 진술은 보편적으로 처음부터 끝까지 거짓말로 여겨짐"이라고 써넣는 익명의 독자는 독자로서의 그의 역할에 대한 이러한 기대에 잘 부응하고 있는 것이었다. 그러나 살인 추리소설은 독자들이 단순히 투표하는 것 이상을 하도록 요구했다. 살인 추리소설은 독자들로 하여금 증거를 꼼꼼하게 살피고, 사건의 단편들을 종합하고, 추적하고, 탐지하고, 조사하고 "진상을 밝히면서" 적극적으로 이야기를 만들게 했는데, 이는 사실상, 신과 같은 서술자(소설가)가 뒤로 물러난 후 사건의 주요 이야기를 만드는 책임을 독자들 스스로 떠맡게 한 것이었다.
이런 목적을 위해, 살인 추리소설은 독자들을 범죄 수사에 끌어들여, 주요 증거에 대한 시각적인 삽화와 범죄 현장에 대한 생생한 삽화를 제공했는데, 범죄현장 삽화에는 독자들이 3차원 공간에서 범죄를 재구성하도록 도와주는 지도인 건물의 정면도와 실내도, 그리고 살인자의 접근 방식(뒷 창문 또는 잠겨 있지 않은 문)에 특별히 주의를 기울이고, 때때로 점선으로 살인자의 경로를 추적하고, 피해자의 시신의 정확한 위치에 더욱 주목한 건물의 평면도가 있었다.

1	③	▶ 글의 요지
		이 글은 새로운 살인 추리소설의 특징을 다루고 있는데 독자들에게 이야기를 만드는 데 있어서 적극적인 역할을 해달라는 요구였다. 따라서 글의 요지로는 ③ '새로운 살인 추리소설을 읽는 독자들은 이야기를 기민하게 이해해야 한다'가 적절하다.

2	①	▶ 논지의 흐름상 적절하지 않은 어구 고르기
		첫 문장에서 독자는 이야기를 만드는 데 있어서 적극적인 역할을 하도록 요구받는다고 했는데, Ⓐ의 recipient(수령인, 수용자)는 적극적인 역할을 하는 사람이 아니므로 부적절하다. who 관계절에서 유무죄 판결에 표를 던진다고 했음을 고려하면, Ⓐ를 jurors(배심원)로 고치는 것이 문맥상 적절하다.

assign v. 할당하다; 부여하다
sermon n. 설교, 훈계
execution sermon 사형집행 설교문(17-18세기 뉴잉글랜드에서는 나중에 출판되어 대중에게 팔리기도 했음)
clerical a. 성직자의, 목사의
uncontestable a. 논쟁의 여지가 없는
effectively ad. 사실상, 실제로는
cast a vote 투표하다
conviction n. 유죄 선고[판결]
acquittal n. 무죄 선고
anonymous a. 익명의, 신원 불명의
margin n. (책 페이지의) 여백
exculpation n. 무죄로 함; 변명; 해명
sift through 꼼꼼하게 살펴 추려내다
piece something together (상황 이해를 위해 사실·세부 사항들을) 종합하다
fragment n. 조각, 파편
probe v. 엄밀히 조사하다
unveil v. (비밀을) 털어놓다, 밝히다
craft v. ~을 교묘하게[정성들여] 만들다
withdrawal n. 물러나기, 철수
providential a. 신의, 섭리의, 신의 뜻에 의한
illustration n. 삽화, 도해
facade n. 표면, 외관, 겉보기
assist v. 돕다, 거들다
dotted a. 점(선)이 있는

04 2020 한국외대

국제 공용어는 모국어가 다른 사람들의 의사소통 수단으로 사용되는 언어 또는 언어의 혼합이다. 국제 공용어는 또한 통상 언어, 접촉 언어, 그리고 세계 언어로도 알려져 있다. "국제 공용어로서의 영어"라는 용어는 서로 다른 모국어를 사용하는 사람들을 위한 일반적인 의사소통 수단으로서 영어를 가르치고 배우고 사용하는 것을 말한다. 영어의 지위는 대단해서 올림픽 스포츠, 국제 무역, 항공 교통 관제의 의사소통을 위한 국제 공용어로 채택되었다. 다른 언어들과는 달리, 영어는 5개 대륙 모두에 퍼져나갔고, 진정한 세계 언어가 되었다. 그러나 니콜라 오슬러(Nicholar Ostler)에 따르면, 우리는 교육을 통해 퍼지는 언어인 모국어와 채택을 통해 확산되는 언어인 국제 공용어 사이의 차이를 구별할 필요가 있다. 후자인 국제 공용어는 필요하기 때문에 의식적으로 배우는 언어이다. 모국어는 어쩔 수 없이 배우게 되는 언어이다. 영어가 지금 세계에 확산되고 있는 이유는 국제 공용어로서 영어가 가진 효용성 때문이다. 전 세계에서 사용되는 단순화된 영어인 글로비시(Globish)는 필요한 한 존재할 것이다. 그러나 이 언어는 모국어로 채택되고 있지 않기 때문에 전형적으로 사람들이 자녀들에게 말하는 데 쓰는 언어는 아니다. 이 언어는 언어의 장기적인 생존을 위한 가장 중요한 기반인 첫 단계에 효과적으로 도달하지 못하고 있다.

1 ②　▶ 글의 주제
　　　　이 글은 국제 공용어가 무엇인지 정의한 다음, 국제 공용어로서의 영어의 지위를 설명하고, 영어가 국제 공용어로서 사용되는 이유를 언급하고 있으므로 ②가 글의 주제로 적절하다.

2 ④　▶ 빈칸완성
　　　　빈칸 Ⓐ 앞의 since는 이유의 접속사이며, it은 전 세계에서 사용되는 영어의 단순화된 버전인 글로비시를 가리키는 대명사이다. 글로비시가 모국어로 채택되지 않는다고 했는데, 모국어는 사람들이 자녀들에게 하는 말이므로 ④가 정답이다. ① 자국 밖에서 ② 업무용으로 ③ 미국 대학에서

3 ③　▶ 내용파악
　　　　국제 공용어는 필요에 의해 의식적으로 배우는 언어라고 했으므로 부모님에게 무의식적으로 배우는 언어라고 볼 수 없다. 따라서 ③이 정답이다. 부모님에게 무의식적으로 배우는 언어는 모국어이다.

lingua franca 국제(공용)어
medium n. 매개, 수단
trade language 통상어(通商語)(주로 비즈니스에 쓰이는 혼성 공통어)
adopt v. 채택하다
draw a distinction between ~간에 구별을 짓다
recruitment n. 채용, 보충, 공급
utility n. 유익, 효용, 실리
long-term a. 장기적인
survival n. 살아남음, 생존

05 2017 단국대

영국 내과의사인 토머스 바우들러(Thomas Bowdler) 박사는 부모들이 자녀들에게 셰익스피어(Shakespeare)의 희곡을 읽어줘야 한다고 생각했다. 셰익스피어는 불후의 음유시인일지도 모르지만, 그의 희곡은 가족용으로 읽기에는 적절하지 않을지도 모르는 비속한 말과 선정적인 장면을 담고 있다. 그래서 1818년 바우들러는 셰익스피어 희곡의 가족판을 출간하기로 결정했다. 서문에서 바우들러는 '품위를 갖추어 가족에게 큰소리로 읽어줄 수 없는 모든 단어와 표현들'을 조심스럽게 편집했다고 썼다. 이에 격분한 비평가들은 바우들러를 비난했으며 저속한 것으로 여겨지는 책 또는 희곡 일부를 삭제하는 것을 말로 설명하기 위해 새로운 단어인 'bowdlerize(책이나 연극 등에서 불온한 부분을 삭제하다)'를 만들어 냈다. 흥미롭게도, 셰익스피어 작품의 불온 부분 삭제판은 상업적인 성공을 거둔 작품이 되었으며, 이에 따라 아마도 바우들러의 판단이 옳았음이 입증되었다. 불온 부분이 삭제된 책에 대한 논쟁은 토머스 바우들러로 끝나지 않았다. 다이앤 래비치(Diane Ravitch)는 그녀의 책인 『The Language Police』에서 미국 학생들이 여러 책에서, 심지어는 고전에서, 논란이 되는 내용을 삭제하거나 바꾸는 출판인들과 교과서 위원회에 의해 편집된 단조로운 교과서를 읽도록 강요받고 있다고 주장한다.

1 ②　▶ 동의어
　　　　suggestive scenes를 수식하는 관계대명사절에서 이것이 가족용 독서로 적절하지 않다고 했으므로, suggestive가 부정적인 의미로 쓰였음을 알 수 있다. suggestive에는 '선정

immortal a. 불후(不朽)의, 영원한
bard n. 음유시인
profanity n. 신성 모독, 불경; 불경스러운 언행
suggestive a. 연상시키는; 선정적인, 도발적인
preface n. 서문
with propriety 예절 바르게; 적당히
outraged a. 분노한, 격분한
coin v. (신어·신표현을) 만들어 내다
deletion n. 삭제(부분)
offensive a. 불쾌한; 저속한, 음란한
vindicate v. ~의 정당함을 입증하다
bland a. 특징 없는, 단조로운

적인', '도발적인'의 뜻이 있으므로 ② obscene(외설적인)이 정답이다. ① 가혹한 ③ 유익한 ④ 적절한

2 ①
▶ 내용파악
바우들러는 셰익스피어의 희곡이 가족용 독서로 적절하지 않은 비속한 말과 선정적인 장면을 담고 있다고 생각해서 가족들에게 읽어줄 수 없는 부분을 편집했다. 이에 격분한 비평가들이 "바우들러를 비난했으며 저속한 것으로 여겨지는 책 또는 희곡 일부를 삭제하는 것을 설명하기 위해 새로운 단어인 'bowdlerize'를 만들어 냈다."라고 했으므로, 이들은 ① '바우들러가 셰익스피어의 걸작을 편집해 훼손시킨 것'에 대해 격분했을 것이라고 볼 수 있다.

3 ①
▶ 빈칸완성
빈칸 앞에 있는 관계대명사 who의 선행사는 publishers and textbook committees인데, 이들은 자신들이 생각하기에 불온하다고 생각하는 부분을 삭제하거나 변경한 주체이므로, 이들이 손을 댄 자료들을 설명하는 표현으로는 ① controversial(논란이 되는)이 적절하다. ② 대조적인 ③ 변환된 ④ 조화된

06   2015 한양대

피진과 크리올은 언어를 공유하지 않는 사람들이 의사소통을 하려는 필요로 생겨난 산물이다. 의사소통의 목적을 위해 선택된 기존의 언어 또는 방언에서 피진이 시작하는 것이 아니라는 점에서, 피진과 크리올은 민족어나 국제어와 다르다. 그것은 오히려 두 언어의 특정한 결합이다. 로레토 토드(Loreto Todd)는 피진과 크리올에 관해 다음과 같이 말한다.
피진은 주변적인 언어로, 공통된 언어를 가지지 않은 사람들 사이의 어떤 제한적 의사소통의 필요를 충족시키기 위해 발생한다. 접촉의 초기 단계의 경우, 의사소통은 종종 세부적인 사고의 교환이 필요하지 않고 또 주로 한쪽 언어에서 독점적으로 가져온 소수의 어휘만으로 충분한 거래에 한정된다. 피진의 통사론적 구조는 접촉하고 있는 언어의 구조들보다 덜 복잡하고 덜 유연하며, 피진의 많은 특징들이 접촉하고 있는 언어들의 어법을 분명히 반영하고 있긴 하지만 나머지는 모두 피진 고유의 것들이다.
크리올은 피진이 한 언어 공동체의 모국어가 될 때 발생한다. 피진의 특성이었던 단순한 구조가 크리올 속으로 옮겨져 오지만, 하나의 모국어로서의 크리올은 총체적인 범위의 인간경험을 표현할 수 있어야 하므로 어휘 목록은 확장되고 빈번히 좀 더 정교한 통사론적 체계가 발전하게 된다.
크리올은 종종 '실제' 언어로 간주되지 않고 그 결과 열등한 것으로 간주되기 때문에, 예를 들어 불어와 영어 모두 피진의 산물일 수도 있다는 점, 즉 불어의 경우 갈리아 원주민들과 점령한 로마인들 사이의 접촉을 통해, 그리고 영어의 경우 앵글로-색슨 원주민들과 잉글랜드 동쪽 해안에 정착했던 덴마크 사람들 사이의 접촉을 통해 형성된 언어라는 점을 주목하는 것은 가치 있을 것이다.

1 ②
▶ 내용일치
두 언어가 접촉하는 초기 단계에는 "주로 한쪽 언어에서 독점적으로 가져온 소수의 어휘만으로 충분하다."라고 하였으므로, 피진은 주로 한쪽 언어에서 어휘를 차용하는 것으로 보아야 한다.

2 ①
▶ 내용추론
'불어와 영어 모두 피진의 산물이라는 점'이라는 지적에 주목한다. 이는 불어와 영어가 두 언어의 접촉에서 발생한 피진을 모태로 생겨난 결과물, 즉 크리올로서의 면모를 가졌다는 지적이다.

pidgin n. 피진어(어떤 언어의 제한된 어휘들이 토착 언어 어휘들과 결합되어 만들어진 단순한 형태의 혼성어; 서로 다른 언어를 쓰는 사람들의 의사소통 필요에 의해서 형성됨)
creole n. 크리올어(아주 초보적인 언어, 혹은 피진어가 노출된 아동들에게서 발달하는 언어로 피진어보다 더 정교화된 복잡한 언어)
outcome n. 결과, 결과물
dialect n. 방언, 사투리
marginal a. 미미한, 중요하지 않은; 주변부의
fulfil v. 실현하다; 충족시키다
arise v. 생기다, 발생하다
initial a. 처음의, 초기의
transaction n. 거래, 매매
exclusively ad. 배타적으로; 독점적으로
suffice v. 충분하다
syntactic a. 구문론적인, 통사론적인
feature n. 특색, 특징
usage n. 용법, 어법
lexicon n. 어휘, 어휘 목록
Gaul n. 골, 갈리아(고대 켈트 사람의 땅; 지금의 북이탈리아·프랑스·벨기에 등을 포함함)
Dane n. 덴마크 사람

07 2021 숭실대

『돈키호테(Don Quixote)』는 스페인 작가 미구엘 드 세르반테스(Miguel de Cervantes)가 2부작으로 나누어 출판한 소설로, 서양 문학에서 가장 널리 읽히는 고전 중의 하나다. 원래 문학적으로 인기를 오랫동안 끌어왔던 장르인 기사도 로맨스를 패러디한 것으로, 『돈키호테』는 그런 기사 이야기를 너무 탐독해서 정신 이상을 일으킨 나이 든 기사가 모험을 찾아 그의 늙은 애마인 로시난테(Rocinante)를 타고 수지타산에 빠른 종자(從者)인 산초 판사(Sanco Panza)와 함께 여행을 떠나며 일어나는 일을 사실적으로 묘사하고 있다. 널리 그리고 즉시 번역된(첫 번째 영어 번역본은 1612년에 나왔다) 그 소설은 계속해서 대성공을 이루었고 현대 소설의 원형으로 간주된다.

처음 출판되었을 때, 『돈키호테』는 일반적으로 코믹소설로 이해되었다. 프랑스 대혁명 이후, 『돈키호테』는 개인은 옳지만 사회는 매우 잘못되고 환멸을 느끼게 한다는 중심 윤리로 더 잘 알려졌다. 19세기에는 그 소설이 사회 논평으로 여겨졌지만, 어느 누구도 "세르반테스가 누구의 편인지"를 쉽게 알 수 없었다. 많은 비평가들은 이 작품을 돈키호테의 이상주의와 고귀함이 후기 기사도 세계에 의해 미친 것으로 간주되고 일반적인 현실에 의해 패배당하고 쓸모없게 되는 비극으로 보았다. 20세기에는 이미 그 소설은 현대 문학의 토대 중 하나로서의 표준적인 자리를 차지하게 되었다.

비판적인 논쟁의 수많은 비평을 낳은 데 더하여 『돈키호테』는 많은 매체에서 활동하는 예술가들에게 영감을 주었다. 유명한 각색 작품에는 1869년의 발레 작품, 1968년 브로드웨이에서 초연된 1965년 뮤지컬 작품인 『맨 오브 라만차(Man of La Mancha)』, 그리고 아서 힐러(Arthur Hiller)가 감독한 1972년 영화가 포함되었다. 또 다른 유명한 각색 영화는 테리 길리엄(Terry Gilliam) 감독이 세르반테스의 소설을 자유롭게 개작한 이야기인 『돈키호테를 죽인 사나이(The Man Who Killed Don Quixote)』(2018)가 있는데, 그 영화를 만들려는 거의 30년 동안의 그의 시도는 다양한 문제, 연기, 취소 등으로 인해 어려움에 봉착했고, 길리엄, 2002년 다큐멘터리 『Lost in La Mancha』에서 자세히 소개된 것처럼, 그 자신이 돈키호테 같은 비현설적인 인물로 변해버렸다.

1 ④ ▶ 지시대상
ⓐ, ⓑ, ⓒ는 세르반테스의 소설 『돈키호테』를 가리키지만, ⓓ는 2002년에 발표된 다큐멘터리이므로 ④가 정답이다.

2 ③ ▶ 내용파악
두 번째 단락에서 많은 비평가들은 돈키호테의 이상주의와 고귀함이 후기 기사도 세계에 의해 미친 것으로 간주된 비극으로 보았다고 했으므로 ③이 『돈키호테』에 대한 사실과 다르다.

3 ④ ▶ 내용일치
테리 길리엄은 세르반테스의 소설을 개작한 이야기인 『돈키호테를 죽인 사나이』의 감독이자, 2002년에 다큐멘터리 『Lost in La Mancha』에 출연한 사람이다. 따라서 ④가 글의 내용과 일치하지 않는다.

- **conceive** v. (생각·계획 등을) 마음속에 하다[품다]
- **vogue** n. 대(유행), 인기
- **befall** v. 일어나다
- **bemuse** v. ~을 멍하게 만들다; ~의 마음을 빼앗다
- **pragmatic** a. 실용적인, 현실적인
- **squire** n. 기사의 종자(從者)
- **set out** 출발하다, 여행을 시작하다
- **prototype** n. 원형(原型), 모형
- **interpret** v. 설명[해석]하다
- **ethic** n. 도덕, 윤리
- **disenchanting** a. 미몽에서 깨어나게 하는
- **insane** a. 정신 이상의, 미친
- **canonical** a. 정본에 속하는, 정규의, 표준[기본]적인
- **in addition to** ~에 더하여, ~일 뿐 아니라
- **spawn** v. (어떤 결과나 상황을) 낳다
- **adaptation** n. 개조; 개작, 번안(물), 각색 (작품)
- **retelling** n. 다시 만든[개작된] 이야기
- **beset** v. 뒤따르다, 괴롭히다
- **quixotic** a. 돈키호테식의; 공상적인, 비현실적인

08 2014 한국항공대

언어가 우리의 정신세계의 매우 지배적인 특징이어서 우리는 언어를 생각과 동일시하고 싶어진다. 일부 이론가들은 언어가 단지 생각을 표현하는 수단에 불과하다고까지 주장해왔다. 언어 상대성 가설은 언어가 생각의 본질을 형성한다고 주장한다. 벤자민 워프(Benjamin Whorf)가 이 견해를 지지했다. 가장 빈번히 인용되는 언어 상대성의 예시는 캐나다의 이뉴잇족(Inuit)에서 나타난다. 이뉴잇족의 언어에는 우리가 '눈(雪)'이라는 단어를 쓰는, 강설이라는 얼어붙은 흰 조각들을 의미하는 많은 다양한 용어들이 있다. 이뉴잇족이 눈에 대한 수많은 용어들을 가지고 있기 때문에, 벤자민 워프는 이뉴잇족이 영어 사용자보다 눈에 대해 다양하게 인식하고 생각한다고 여겼다. 벤자민 워프는 그의 관찰이 입증되지 않았다는 것으로 비난을 받아왔으며, 일부 대조군을 활용한 연구는 벤자민 워프의 가설에 의혹을 품어왔다. 엘리노어 로쉬(Eleanor Rosch)는 뉴기니(New Guinea)에 살고 있는 외딴 농경부족인 다니족(Dani)를 연구했다. 다니족에게는 대략 '어둠'과 '빛'을 의미하는 단 두 가지의 색상 용어 밖에 없다. 만일 벤자민 워프의 가설이 옳다면, 당신은 다니족이 색상의 다양한 음영

- **dominant** a. 지배적인, 주요한
- **feature** n. 특징, 특색
- **tempt** v. ~할 기분이 나게 하다
- **equate** v. 동일시하다, 동등하게 다루다
- **relativity** n. 관련성, 상대성
- **hypothesis** n. 가설, 가정
- **champion** v. 옹호하다, 지지하다
- **cite** v. 인용하다; 예로 들다
- **flake** n. (눈·구름·깃털 등의) 한 조각
- **precipitation** n. 강설(량), 강수(량)

들을 인지하고 배우는 데 문제가 있을 것으로 예상할 것이다. 그러나 로쉬의 실험에서, 모국어에 보다 많은 색상 용어를 가지고 있는 민족만큼 다니족도 색상의 음영들을 잘 익혔다. 보다 최근의 증거는 언어가 색상 인지처리에 영향을 줄지도 모른다는 점을 제시한다. 연구원들은 영국의 아이들과 힘바족(Himba)으로 알려진 나미비아(Namibia)의 소몰이 부족출신의 아프리카 아이들을 비교했다. 영국인들은 11개의 기본적인 색상 용어를 가지고 있지만, 외부세계와 대체적으로 고립된 힘바족에게는 색상 용어가 5개에 불과하다. 연구원들은 일련의 색칠된 타일들을 각각의 아이들에게 보여준 다음 줄지어 있는 22개의 다양한 색상들 중에서 그 색상을 고르도록 시켰다. 가장 나이 어린 아이들은 영국인과 힘바족 모두 색상의 이름을 거의 또는 전혀 알지 못해서 비슷한 색상들을 구별하지 못하는 경향이 있었다. 그러나 아이들이 커지면서 더 많은 색상 명칭들을 습득함에 따라, 점차 그들의 선택에 그들이 학습해온 색상 용어들이 반영되었다.

perceive v. 인지하다, 인식하다
anecdotal a. 입증되지 않은, 일화적인
cast doubt on ~에 의혹을 품다, 의문을 던지다
agricultural tribe 농경민족
roughly ad. 대략, 어림잡아
colored a. 채색된, 착색된
an array of 줄지어 있는
confuse v. 혼동하다, 구별하지 못하다

1 ③ ▶ 글의 주제
이 글에서는 "언어가 우리의 정신세계의 매우 지배적인 특징이어서 우리는 언어를 생각과 동일시하고 싶어진다."라는 언어 상대성 가설을 옹호한 벤자민 워프의 생각이 틀렸음을 여러 가지 예를 들어 설명하고 있다. 따라서 ③의 '언어와 생각 간의 동일화의 부당함'이 이 글의 전반적인 내용임을 알 수 있다.

2 ④ ▶ 내용일치
이 글에서 "언어 상대성 가설은 언어가 생각의 본질을 형성한다고 주장한다. 벤자민 워프가 이 견해를 지지했다."라고 했지만, 이 언어 상대성 가설은 가설일 뿐, 사실로 밝혀진 것이 아니다. 따라서 ④가 정답이다. ① "아이들이 커지면서 더 많은 색상 명칭들을 습득함에 따라, 점차 그들의 선택에 그들이 학습해온 색상 용어들이 반영되었다."라고 했으므로, 색상에 대한 언어를 배우는 것이, 색상에 대해 생각하고 표현하는 것에 영향을 주었다고 볼 수 있다. ② 이뉴잇족이 눈에 대한 다양한 용어를 가지고 있기 때문에, 벤자민 워프는 이뉴잇족이 영어를 쓰는 사람들보다 눈에 대해 다양하게 생각한다고 여겼다. ③ "보다 최근의 증거는 언어가 색상 인지처리에 영향을 줄지도 모른다는 것을 보여준다."라는 언급이 있으므로 옳은 진술이다.

3 ① ▶ 빈칸완성
벤자민의 가설은 "이뉴잇족이 눈에 관한 수많은 용어를 가지고 있기 때문에, 이뉴잇족은 영어 사용자보다 눈에 대해 다양하게 인지하고 생각한다."라는 것이다. 다니족에게는 '어둠'과 '빛'을 나타내는 두 개의 색상 용어 밖에 없다고 했으므로, 만약 벤자민의 가설이 옳다면 다니족은 색상을 인지하고 배우는 데 상대적으로 어려움이 있을 것이라고 추측할 수 있다. 따라서 ①이 빈칸에 가장 적절하다.

09 2021 인하대

몇 가지 기본적인 가정들인 널리 받아들여지고 있는 주장들로 시작해 보려고 한다. 첫째, 언어는 주로 말해졌으며 지금도 말해진다. 인간의 의사전달이 다중모드이고, 몸짓이 입으로 하는 말을 뒷받침할지도 모른다는 것은 물론 잘 알려져 있다. 수화(手話)는 오늘날 '완전한' 언어로 인정되지만, 수화의 그런 동작들이 언어의 초기 수십 년 사이에 완전히 성숙한 시스템으로 발달된 것 같지는 않다. <따라서 발성-청각 채널이 주된 것으로 대부분의 연구자들은 간주한다.>
둘째, 위치와 관련해서, 비록 정확한 위치는 한때 리프트 밸리로 생각되었고 지금도 여전히 논쟁 중이며 일부 아프리카 남부 지역이 조사되고 있지만, 아프리카가 인간 언어의 발생지로 널리 여겨지고 있다. 다원발생설이라는 개념은 현재 가능성이 없는 것으로 여겨지며, 중국과 같은 다른 가능한 발생지에 대한 주장들은 대부분 사라졌다.
셋째, 연대와 관련해서, 언어는 확실히 인류의 진화에 비해, 비교적 최근에 생겨난 것이다. 한때는 완전한 언어의 발생연대가 상당히 늦은 약 5만 년 전으로 추정되었다. 하지만 그 추정연대는 뒤로 (과거로) 조금씩 이동하고 있다. 점점 더 연구자들이 가능성 있는 조어(祖語: 원조언어)를 재구성하려고 노력하고는 있지만, 지금은 10만 년 전과 5만 년 전 사이의 어느 시점이 완전히 발달된 언어의 출현 시기와 관련한 그럴듯한 추정이다. 그 조어는 아마도 단계별로 출현했을 것인데, 그 중 가장 이른 단계는 수천 년 동안 존재했을지도 모른다.

assumption n. 가정
multi-modal a. 다중모드의
sign language 수어, 수화
fully-fledged a. 완전히 발달한
vocal-auditory a. 발성-청각의
with regard to ~와 관련해서는
Rift Valley (동아프리카의) 리프트 밸리
polygenesis n. 다원발생설
creep v. 조금씩 위치를 이동하다
plausible a. 그럴듯한
reconstruct v. 재현하다, 복원하다
proto-language n. 조어(祖語)
constituent n. 구성 성분[요소]

넷째, 인간의 언어와 동물의 의사소통의 관계는 더욱 더 분명해지고 있다. 인간의 언어가 동물의 의사소통과 이어져 있거나 단절되어 있는 정도가 널리 논의되어 왔다. 언어의 다양한 구성요소들이 개별적으로 평가될 필요가 있는데, 이는 청각 메커니즘은 동물의 의사소통과 겹치는 부분이 많고 뇌 배지(培地)와 발성 메커니즘은 동물의 의사소통과 거의 겹치지 않는 것과 같이 언어의 구성요소들마다 (동물의 의사소통과) 겹치는 정도가 서로 다르기 때문이다.

overlap n. (두 가지 활동의) 겹침
brain medium 뇌 배지(뇌에서 정보전달의 매개물질)
articulatory a. 발성의

1 ① ▶ **문장삽입**
제시문은 "따라서 발성-청각 채널이 주된 것으로 대부분의 연구자들은 간주한다."라는 뜻인데, 첫 단락에서 언어는 주로 말이라고 했고 말 이외에 몸짓은 말 언어를 뒷받침하는 부차적인 것이며 몸짓언어의 일종인 수화도 처음 단기간에 완성되어 주된 언어의 기능을 한 것이 아니라고 하여 말이 언어의 주된 모드임을 밝히고 있다. 제시문의 발성-청각 채널이 곧 말을 가리키므로 제시문이 Ⓐ에 들어가면 이러한 첫 단락의 내용을 결론짓게 되어 적절하다.

2 ① ▶ **내용일치**
"인간의 언어의 기원과 관련해 다원발생설이라는 개념은 현재 가능성이 없는 것으로 여겨지며, 중국과 같은 다른 가능한 발생지에 대한 주장들은 대부분 사라졌다."고 했으므로, ①이 정답이다.

10 2019 숭실대

『신흑인에 대한 이해(The New Negro: An Interpretation)』(1925)는 할렘 르네상스(Harlem Renaissance) 기간 동안 워싱턴 DC에 살며 하워드대학교에서 가르쳤던 알랜 로크(Alain Locke)가 편집한 아프리카와 아프리카계 미국 흑인의 예술과 문학에 대한 소설, 시, 에세이를 모은 문집이다. 급성장하는 신흑인 운동인 할렘 르네상스에서 나온 창조적인 노력의 집합체인 그 책은 문학 연구가들과 비평가들에 의해 이 운동의 완벽한 도서로 간주된다. 이 책에는 로크의 에세이 『신흑인』을 비롯하여 많은 아프리카계 미국인 작가들이 저술한 논픽션 에세이, 시, 소설 등이 실려 있었다.
『신흑인』에서는 아프리카계 미국인들이 사회적, 정치적, 예술적 변화를 어떻게 추구했는지 깊게 탐구한다. 그들의 사회적 지위를 받아들이는 대신에, 로크는 신흑인을 시민권을 지지하고 요구하는 것으로 생각했다. 또한, 그의 문집은 낡은 고정관념을 바꾸기 위해 노력했고 그 고정관념들을 단순화에 저항하는 흑인 정체성의 새로운 비전으로 대체하고자 했다. 그 문집 속에 수록된 에세이와 시는 실제의 사건과 경험을 반영한다. 그 문집은 백인 중산층과 같은 동등한 시민권을 갖길 원했던 중산층 아프리카계 미국인들의 목소리를 반영한다.
로크가 일반적으로 사용한 주제는 구흑인 대 신흑인의 개념이다. 로크에 따르면 구흑인의 개념은 그들이 창조한 것이 아니라 그들에게 부과된 고정관념과 견해의 산물이었다. 그들은 어쩔 수 없이 자신과 타인들의 행동의 그늘에서 살게 되었다. 신흑인은 현재 자신을 이해하는 흑인이다. 한때 그들은 새로운 역동성을 창조하고 신흑인의 탄생을 가능하게 했던 자기 존중과 자기 신뢰가 부족했다. 그들은 변화된 흑인이기도 한 현재의 흑인이 되었다. 로크는 흑인들이 공평한 경쟁의 장(場)을 만드는 데 영향을 주고 흑인들에 대한 시각을 넓히는 데 영향을 주었던 이주에 대해 이야기하는데, 흑인들이 미국 남부 주들을 떠나 그들이 새로 다시 출발할 수 있는 다른 지역으로 옮겨지기 때문이다. 어떤 의미에서 이주는 흑인들을 변화시켰고 그들을 결합시켰는데, 그들 모두가 세계 모든 지역, 모든 계층, 서로 다른 모든 배경 출신이었기 때문이다.

interpretation n. 해석, 설명
anthology n. (시)선집, 문집
edit v. (책을) 편집하다
Harlem Renaissance n. 할렘 르네상스(1920년대에 New York시의 Harlem에서 개화한 흑인 문학 및 흑인 음악 문화의 부흥)
collection n. (시·노래 등의) 모음집
burgeoning a. 급증하는; 급성장하는
definitive a. 최고의, 거의 완벽한
dive v. (활동·일·문제 따위에) 몰두하다
champion v. 지지하다, 옹호하다
stereotype n. 고정관념
shadow n. 어둠, 그늘
self-respect n. 자기 존중, 자존심
self-dependence n. 자기 의존, 독립독행
level the playing field 공평한 경쟁의 장을 만들다
fuse v. 융합[결합]되다[시키다]

1 ④ ▶ **빈칸완성**
주절에서 로크는 신흑인을 시민권을 지지하고 요구하는 것으로 보았다고 했는데, 이는 흑인들이 자신들의 지위를 받아들이는 것과 반대되므로 빈칸 Ⓐ에는 ④ Instead of가 적절하다. ① ~을 위해 ② ~의 경우에는 ③ ~에 비추어

2 ① ▶ **내용파악**
『The New Negro』는 아프리카와 아프리카계 미국 흑인의 예술과 문학에 대한 소설, 시, 에세이를 모은 문집이므로 ①이 사실이 아니다.

3 ②　▶ 내용파악

신흑인은 그들에게 부과된 고정관념에서 탈피하여 새로운 정체성을 찾고자 하였고, 자신을 이해하고자 했으며, 시민의 기본적인 권리를 요구하는 것을 특징으로 했다. 하지만 신흑인이 흑인 우월주의를 추구한 것은 아니므로 ②가 정답이다.

11 2022 홍익대

현대 언어 연구에서 담화 문제의 퇴조는 페르디낭 드 소쉬르(Ferdinand de Saussure)의 유명한 『일반 언어학 강의(Course in General Linguistics)』가 이뤄낸 엄청난 업적으로 인해 우리가 치러야 할 대가다. 그의 연구는 언어에서 '랑그(langue)'와 '파롤(parole)'을 근본적으로 구분하는 것에 의지하고 있다. '랑그'는 코드 혹은 코드들의 집합이며, 코드에 기초해서 특정 화자가 특정 메시지로서의 '파롤'을 만들어내는 것이다.

이 주된 이분법과 연결된 몇 가지 부수적인 구분이 있다. 메시지는 개별적이고, 그것의 코드는 집합적이다. 메시지와 코드는 같은 방식으로 시간에 속하지 않는다. 메시지는 시간의 통시적(通時的) 차원을 구성하는 사건들의 연속 중의 한 일시적인 사건인 반면, 코드는 동시적 요소들의 집합으로서의, 즉 공시적(共時的) 체계로서의 시간 안에 존재한다. 코드는 익명이며 의도된 것이 아니다. 이러한 의미에서 그것은 무의식적인데, 프로이트의 초(超)심리학에 따라 본능적 욕구와 충동이 무의식적이라는 의미에서 무의식적이 아니라, 비본능적인 구조적, 문화적 무의식이라는 의미에서 무의식적이다.

무엇보다도, 메시지는 임의적이고 우연적인 반면, 코드는 특정한 언어 공동체를 위해 체계적이고 강제적이다. 이 마지막의 대립은 코드가 과학적 조사에 알맞다는 점에 반영되어 있는데, 특히 음운체계, 어휘체계, 통사체계와 같은 개별 독립체들의 유한한 집합이 암시하는 유사 대수학적 수준의 결합 능력을 강조하는 "과학"이라는 단어의 의미에서 그러하다. '파롤'이 과학적으로 설명될 수 있다고 하더라도, 그것은 음향학, 생리학, 사회학, 의미 변화의 역사를 포함한 여러 과학들에 해당하여 그 영향을 받는 반면, '랑그'는 단 하나의 과학, 즉 언어의 공시적 체계에 대한 설명의 대상이다.

1 ③　▶ 글의 제목

'랑그'는 코드 혹은 코드의 집합이며 '파롤'은 랑그를 기초로 하여 화자가 특정 메시지를 생성해낸 결과물임을 주로 이야기하고 있으므로, 제목으로 ③이 적절하다.

2 ②　▶ 내용추론

랑그와 코드는 추상적이고 이론적(체계적)인 반면, 파롤과 메시지는 구체적이고 실제적(우연적)이어서, 랑그와 코드는 과학(언어학) 연구의 대상으로 삼기에 적합하지만 파롤과 메시지는 적합하지 않다. 그런데 첫 문장에 나온 담화는 랑그(코드)가 실생활 상황에서 실제로 사용되는 예들을 가리키는 것으로 파롤(메시지)에 해당한다. 따라서 소쉬르가 언어에 대한 과학적 연구를 위해 담화 개념을 버렸다(연구 대상에서 제외했다)고 한 ②를 추론할 수 있다. 저자는 이것을 과학적 연구를 위해 치러야 하는 대가로 보고 있다. ④ over time은 시간의 경과를 의미하여 동시적(공시적)이 아닌 통시적인 시간 개념이므로 랑그에 대한 진술에는 부적절하다.

3 ①　▶ 내용파악

파롤(메시지)은 코드의 개인적(개별적)이고 일시적인 한 예시이므로 ① atemporal(시간을 초월한)을 temporal(일시적인)로 고쳐야 한다.

---

withdrawal n. 철수; 철회
discourse n. 강연, 담화
contemporary a. 동시대의; 현대의
tremendous a. 굉장한; 엄청난
linguistics n. 언어학
fundamental a. 기초의, 근본적인
distinction n. 구별; 대조, 대비
langue n. 랑그(체계로서의 언어)
parole n. 파롤(구체적 언어 행위)
dichotomy n. 이분법
subsidiary a. 부차적인, 종속적인
temporal a. 일시적인
constitute v. ~을 구성하다
diachronic a. <언어학> 통시적(通時的)인(언어 사실을 사적(史的)으로 연구·기술하는 입장)
dimension n. 치수; 차원
contemporaneous a. 동시존재[발생]의
synchronic a. <언어학> 공시적(共時的)인(언어를 시대마다 구분하여 사적(史的) 배경을 배제하여 연구하는)
anonymous a. 익명의; 특징이 없는
drive n. 충동, 본능적 욕구
metapsychology n. 초(超)심리학
nonlibidinal a. 비본능적인
arbitrary a. 임의적인; 독단적인
contingent a. 우발적인, 우연의
compulsory a. 강제적인, 의무적인
opposition n. 반대; 대립
affinity n. 유사성; 좋아함, 애호
quasi-algebraic a. 유사 대수학적인
combinatory a. 결합하는, 결합성의
discrete a. 분리된; 구별된
entity n. 실재; 존재물; 통일체
phonological a. 음성학적인
lexical a. 사전의, 사전적인
syntactical a. 구문론적인
acoustics n. 음향학
physiology n. 생리학
sociology n. 사회학
semantic a. 의미론의

12 2017 가톨릭대

당신은 말하고 싶은 어떤 단어의 일부(예를 들면, 첫 글자)는 알고 있지만 그 단어 전체는 떠올릴 수 없었던 경험이 있는가? 이것은 '설단(舌端)'현상(어떤 사실을 알고 있기는 하지만 혀끝에서 뱅뱅 돌기만 할 뿐 말로 표현되지 않는 현상)으로 알려져 있다. 피험자가 원하는 단어에 가까이 갈 수 없을 때 이들이 하는 추측은 종종 우리의 정신 사전의 가능한 구조에 대한 정보를 제공한다.

설단현상으로 고생하는 사람들이 하는 추측은 단어 유형의 경계를 존중하는 대체단어들인 경향이 있다. 명사는 명사로 추측하고, 동사는 동사로 추측하는 식이다. 이것은 같은 문법적 부류(품사)의 단어들이 함께 저장된다는 것을 의미하며, 이것은 단어 연상 데이터 분석의 결과와 일치한다. 연구는 설단현상이 '욕조 효과'에 쉽게 영향을 받는다는 것을 보여주었다. 욕조 안에 있는 사람의 머리와 발은 잘 보이지만 몸통은 잘 보이지 않는 것과 같은 방식으로, 단어의 첫 부분과 마지막 부분이 가장 잘 기억된다. 예를 들면, 한 연구에서 피험자들이 단어의 첫 자와 마지막 자가 올바른 혹은 의도된 용어와 비슷했을 때 설단현상을 경험할 가능성이 가장 높다는 것을 확인했다. 예를 들면, 설단 상태에서 목표 단어가 'sextant(달과 별의 고도와 같은 각거리를 측정하는 데 사용되는 항법 기계)'이었다면, 'sextet'가 의미상 비슷한 'compass'보다 피험자들에 의해 잘못 '인식될' 가능성이 더 높았다. 사실, 설단현상의 오류 가운데 70퍼센트는 목표 단어와 소리가 비슷했지만, 의미가 비슷했던 것은 30퍼센트에 불과했다. 이것은 일단 피험자가 의미에 기초한 특정 단어를 염두에 두면, 그들은 의도한 단어와 <의미가 유사한 단어>를 잘못 생각해 맞는 단어로 인정해버릴 수 있다는 것을 보여준다. 따라서 의미와 음운체계 모두가 어휘 항목에 접근하여 만드는 데 역할을 한다. 의미를 아는 것이 피험자들로 하여금 올바른 어휘목록에 이르게 할 수도 있지만, 음운체계가 완전히 명시되지 않으면, 목표 단어와 음운적으로 비슷한 단어들이 잘못 만들어지거나 잘못 인식될지도 모른다.

1 ③ ▶ 글의 흐름상 적절하지 않은 표현 고르기
일단 의미에 기초해 특정 단어를 떠올린다고 했으므로 그런 다음은 소리가 유사한 단어를 생각해 맞추려 할 것이므로 ⓒ는 a semantic relative가 아니라 a phonological relative가 되어야 한다. 그다음 문장에서도 의미와 소리 모두가 어휘 항목에 접근하여 만드는 데 역할을 한다고 했다.

2 ② ▶ 빈칸완성
빈칸 앞뒤 문장이 인과 관계에 있는 것이 아니라 앞의 예와 같은 취지의 실험 결과를 더 정확한 수치로 제시하므로 '사실은'이라는 뜻의 ② In fact가 빈칸에 적절하다. ① 그러나 ③ 그 대신에 ④ 결과적으로

3 ② ▶ 내용일치
"설단현상이 '욕조 효과'에 쉽게 영향을 받는다는 것을 보여주었다. 욕조 안에 있는 사람의 머리와 발은 잘 보이지만 몸통은 잘 보이지 않는 것과 같은 방식으로, 단어의 첫 부분과 마지막 부분이 가장 잘 기억된다."라고 했으므로 욕조 효과는 설단현상에 대한 이해를 돕기 위해 언급된 것이다. 따라서 ②는 이 글의 내용과 다르다.

retrieve v. ~을 상기하다, 다시 생각해내다
tip-of-the-tongue phenomenon 설단현상
substitution n. 대리, 대용, 대체
substitute for ~을 대신하게 되다, 대신 쓰다
consistent with ~와 일치하는
visible a. 명백한, 분명한; 뚜렷한, 두드러진
angular distance 각(角)거리
semantically ad. 의미상; 의미론적으로
have in mind ~을 염두에 두다
trick into ~를 속여서 …하게 하다
phonology n. 음성학; (어떤 언어의) 음운 체계[조직]
play a part in 역(할)을 하다
lexical a. (한 언어의) 어휘의

13 2020 서강대

그림(Grimm) 형제가 1808년과 1810년 사이 어느 땐가에 도르첸 빌트(Dortchen Wild)가 들려준 "헨젤과 그레텔(Hansel and Gretel)"의 이야기를 처음 듣고서 1810년 웰렌베르크(Ölenberg) 원고에 "Das Brüderchen und das Schwesterchen(어린 남매)"이라는 제목으로 그 이야기를 썼다는 사실을 상기하자. 그것은 1812년 『Children and Household Tales』 초판에 그들이 발표했던 글에 비해 매우 짧았고 많이 달랐다. 최근 연구에서 게르하르트 노이만(Gerhard Neumann)은 "헨젤과 그레텔"을 동화 장르의 전형으로 간주하고서 고찰하고 있으며 헨젤과 그레텔이 집을 떠나면서 정신적인 사회화를 경험한다고 주장한다. 이러한 정신적인 사회화 과정을 통해 헨젤과 그레텔은 엄마와 집이 사랑스럽기도 하고 잔인하기도 하다는 사실을 깨달아야 하고 생존을 위해 이러한 양면성을 받아들이는 방법을 배워야 한다는 것이다. 그러나 노이만의 연구는 그 이야기의 텍스트 안에서 그리고 텍스트와 텍스트 사이에서 발전된 내용을 무시했고, 가난, 유기(遺棄), 가부장제와 같은 중요한

manuscript n. 원고; 사본, 필사본
edition n. (초판·재판의) 판(版), 간행
exemplary a. 모범적인; 본보기의; 전형적인
fairy tale 동화
undergo v. (영향·변화·검사 따위를) 받다, 입다; (시련 등을) 경험하다, 당하다
socialization n. 사회화
come to terms with (좋지 않은 일을) 받아들이는 법을 배우다

이슈들을 간과했다. 비판적으로 책을 읽으면서 가해자로서의 아빠의 역할을 최소화하고 아이들을 잡아먹고 싶어 하는 마녀와 '계모'를 동일선상에서 묘사하기 위해 그림 형제가 만든 텍스트의 변화에 초점을 맞춰야 한다. 47년 동안 그림 형제는 그 이야기를 계속해서 고쳐나갔고, 몇 가지 중요한 테마와 사건을 추가했다. 오늘날, 1857년 버전인 『Kinder- und Hausmärchen(아이들과 가정의 이야기)』이 가장 최종적인 "진본"으로 여겨지고 있다. 그러나 도르첸 빌트가 처음으로 들려줘서 그 내용을 받아 적어 그림 형제의 관점에서 옮겨지고 그런 다음 수없이 편집하고 수정한 텍스트가 어떻게 "진본"이나 "원전(原典)"으로 간주될 수 있는 것일까? 이 질문은 중요한 문제점, 즉 번역에 대한 우리의 인식 결여를 보여주고 있다. 번역은 구전 설화의 역사에 있어서 대단히 중요하다. 어떤 면에서, 번역이란 프로이드(Freud)가 "das Unheimliche", 즉 인생에서 겪는 기괴한 것이라 부르는 것을 극복함으로써, 낯선 것이 익숙해지게 되고 우리가 그것에 대해 편안함을 느끼도록 하는 것이다. 번역가는 "un-heimlich", 즉 편하게 느껴지지 않는 것을 택해서 그것을 "heimlich", 즉 편하게 느껴지는 무엇인가로 변형시킨다. 그 결과 우리는 만약 그렇지 않으면(번역에 의한 변형이 없으면) 우리가 이해할 수 없는 것들로부터 위협을 받지 않게 된다.

1 ④   ▶ 내용파악
"번역이란 프로이드가 인생에서 겪는 기괴한 것이라 부르는 것을 극복함으로써, 낯선 것이 익숙해지게 되고 우리가 그것에 대해 편안함을 느끼도록 하는 것이다."라는 내용을 통해 ④가 정답으로 적절함을 알 수 있다.

2 ④   ▶ 내용추론
"헨젤과 그레텔" 이야기에 대해 1810년, 1812년, 1857년 버전이 있음을 언급했으며, 또한 "47년 동안 그림 형제는 그 이야기를 계속해서 고쳐나갔고, 몇 가지 중요한 테마와 사건을 추가했다."고 했으므로, 19세기 전반기 동안 이 이야기에 대한 많은 개정판들이 존재했을 것이라 추론할 수 있다. ① 가장 진본으로 여겨지는 것은 1857년 판이다. ② 어머니(계모)를 아이를 잡아먹는 마녀로 그린 것은 도르첸 빌트가 들려준 이야기에 그림 형제가 변화를 준 결과이다. ③ 그의 연구는 오히려 가난과 유기와 가부장제 같은 중요한 이슈들을 간과했다.

ambivalence n. (애증 따위의) 반대 감정 병존, (상반되는) 감정의 교차; 양면 가치
disregard v. 무시하다; 경시하다
textual a. 본문의; 원문의
overlook v. 못 보고 넘어가다, 간과하다; (잘못된 것을) 못 본 체하다
abandonment n. 포기; 유기; 방종
patriarchy n. 가부장제
minimize v. 최소로 하다; 경시하다
victimizer n. 가해자, 희생시키는 사람
stepmother n. 계모, 의붓어머니
align v. 정렬시키다; 제휴하게 하다
witch n. 마녀
devour v. 게걸스럽게 먹다, 먹어치우다
motif n. 주제, 테마; 동기, 자극
incident n. 사건
definitive a. 결정적인; 명확한; 완성된
authentic a. 믿을만한, 확실한; 진정한, 진짜의
translate v. 번역하다; 쉬운 말로 다시 표현하다
perspective n. 시각, 전망, 견지
revise v. 개정하다; 수정하다, 교정하다
non-recognition n. 인지[인식]하지 않음
vital a. 절대로 필요한, 지극히 중요한
folk tale 설화, 전설
overcome v. 극복하다
uncanny a. 기묘한, 기분 나쁜; 초자연적인
homey a. 가정의; 마음 편한; 편안한, 아늑한
transform v. 변형시키다
threaten v. 협박하다, 위협하다

14   2018 단국대

A 단어는 종종 외연적 의미와 함축적 의미라는 두 가지 유형의 의미를 지닌다. 외연적 의미는 정서적 반응을 덧붙이지 않은 단어의 실제 사전적 정의를 가리킨다. 예를 들어, 만일 당신이 'aggressive'라는 단어를 (사전에서) 찾아본다면, 당신은 'aggressive'가 '정당한 이유 없이 공격적인', <'아주 우호적인'>, '정력적으로 활동적인', 그리고 '분명하게 단언적인'을 의미함을 알게 될 것이다. 만일 일종의 치명적인 질병의 치료법을 묘사하기 위해 사용된다면, 'aggressive'는 긍정적인 정서적 반응을 갖는다. 반대로, 만일 영업사원이 공격적이라고 당신의 친구가 불평한다면, 당신이 그 영업사원에 대해 생각하는 그림은 반드시 긍정적인 것은 아니다. 따라서 'aggressive'라는 단어는 그 단어가 쓰이는 상황에 따라 긍정적인 감정과 부정적인 감정을 모두 유발한다. 단어들에 대해 당신이 느끼는 함축적 의미는 당신의 추정 중 일부가 되어, 당신의 추론에 영향을 미친다.
B 작가들과 연설가들은 함축적인 언어를 의식적으로 사용하여 당신의 추론을 결정짓는다. 그들은 함축적인 언어를 사용할 때 보편적인 함축적 의미를 가진 단어들을 선택하여 사용한다. 따라서 그들은 그 선택된 단어에 당신이 특정한 방식으로 감정적 반응을 보일 것으로 기대한다. 예를 들어, 미술사 수업을 당신이 듣고 있다고 생각해 보자. 이 미술사 수업에서 강사는 인상파 화가인 클로드 모네(Claude Monet)의 후기 작품들 중 일부에 대해 토론하고 있다. 학생들이 그림을 형식과 양식으로 평가하는 법을 배우기를 강사는 원하기 때문에, 모네에 관한 의견을 포함시키는 것을 신중하게

denotation n. (언어의 문자 그대로의) 뜻, 외연적 의미, 명시적 의미
connotation n. 언외의 의미, 함축적 의미
unprovokedly ad. 정당한 이유 없이
offensive a. 모욕적인; 공격적인
amicable a. 우호적인
vigorously ad. 정력적으로, 힘차게
boldly ad. 대담하게; 분명히
assertive a. 단언하는, 단정적인
deadly a. 치명적인, 생명에 관계되는
not necessarily 반드시 ~인 것은 아니다
evoke v. (감정을) 유발하다
depending on ~에 따라

피한다. 그러나 모네의 후기 그림에 대해 논평할 때 그는 "명백하게도 무작위로 선택한 빨간색과 주황색은 모네가 똑같은 풍경을 그린 초기 그림에서 사용한 보다 차분한 파란색과 초록색에서 벗어난 것입니다."라고 말한다. (이때) 한 화가의 색상 선택을 가리키기 위해 사용된 'random'이라는 단어는 보다 부정적인 함축적 의미를 갖는다. 반면, 'serene'이라는 단어는 보다 긍정적인 함축적 의미를 갖는다. (따라서) 강사의 'random'과 'serene'이라는 단어 사용은 그가 모네의 후기 그림들에서는 초기 그림들에서 받았던 만큼의 감동을 받지 못하고 있음을 당신이 추론하도록 도와준다.

1 ④	▶ 내용파악	

①, ②, ③은 모두 aggressive가 '부정적인' 의미로 쓰인 반면, ④는 aggressive가 '적극적인'이라는 '긍정적인' 의미로 쓰였으므로, ④가 정답이다. "만일 일종의 치명적인 질병의 치료법을 묘사하기 위해 사용된다면, 'aggressive'는 긍정적인 정서적 반응을 갖는다."는 본문의 내용을 통해서도 확인할 수 있다.

2 ② ▶ 문맥상 적절하지 않은 단어 고르기

aggressive가 '공격적인', '적극적인', '단언적인'이라는 뜻으로는 쓰이지만, '우호적인'이라는 뜻으로는 쓰이지 않으므로, ②에서 amicable을 '공격적인'에 근접한 뜻인 hostile로 고쳐야 문맥상 어울리게 된다.

3 ② ▶ 빈칸완성

빈칸 (1) 앞에서는 강사가 '모네'에 관한 자신의 주관적 의견을 학생들에게 심어주는 행동을 '피하는' 모습을 이야기하고 있는 반면, 빈칸 (1) 다음에서는 '모네의 후기 그림'에 대해 강사가 'random(무작위)', 'departure(이탈)'와 같은 단어를 사용함으로써 자신의 주관적 의견을 학생들에게 심어주는 내용이 나온다. 빈칸 전후의 내용이 대조를 이루므로, 빈칸에는 역접의 접속부사인 ② However가 적절하다. ① 그러므로 ③ 그렇지 않으면 ④ 게다가

4 ③ ▶ 빈칸완성

강사가 모네의 초기 작품에 대해 사용한 serene은 긍정적인 함축적 의미를 가진 반면, 후기 작품에 대해 사용한 random은 부정적인 함축적 의미를 가졌다고 했다. 이를 통해 강사는 '모네의 초기 그림들에서 받았던 만큼의 감동을 후기 그림들로부터는 받지 못하고 있음'을 알 수 있다. 따라서 빈칸에는 ③이 적절하다.

context n. 문맥, 전후 관계; 상황
assumption n. 추측, 짐작
inference n. 추론
instructor n. 강사, 교사
impressionist n. 인상파 화가
random a. 무작위의, 임의의
departure n. 이탈
serene a. 고요한; 차분한
be diagnosed with ~라고 진단 받다

---

15 2016 홍익대

문학의 정의를 내리려는 시도는 지금껏 다양하게 있어 왔다. 예를 들어, 문학을 픽션의 의미에서 '상상의' 글, 즉 글자 그대로 사실이 아닌 글로 간주할 수도 있을 것이다. 그러나 사람들이 흔히 문학이라는 표제 아래에 포함시키는 것들을 잠깐만 살펴보면, 이것으로는 충분치 않다는 것을 알 수 있다. 17세기 영문학에는 셰익스피어, 웹스터, 마블, 밀턴이 포함되지만, 또 한편으로는 프랜시스 베이컨의 수필, 존 돈의 설교, 버니언의 영적인 자서전, 그리고 토마스 브라운 경이 쓴 모든 글까지 포함된다. 경우에 따라서는 홉스의 『리바이어던(Leviathan)』이나 클라렌든의 『혁명의 역사(History of the Rebellion)』도 포함하는 것으로 볼 수 있을 것이다. 프랑스의 17세기 문학에는 코르네유와 라신의 글과 함께, 라 로슈푸코의 격언집, 보쉬에의 장례식 연설, 부알로의 시에 대한 논문, 세비녜 부인이 딸에게 쓴 편지들, 그리고 데카르트와 파스칼의 철학서적도 포함된다. 19세기 영문학에는 대개 램(벤덤은 아니지만), 매컬리(그러나 마르크스는 아니고), 밀(그러나 다윈이나 허버트 스펜서는 아니고)이 포함된다.

그렇다면 '팩트(사실)'와 '픽션(허구)' 사이의 구별은 그다지 성공적이지 못한 것처럼 보이는데, 이는 특히 그러한 구별 자체가 종종 의심스러운 것이기 때문이다. 예를 들어, 우리가 '역사적' 진실과 '예술적' 진실을 서로 대립시키는 것이 초기 아이슬란드의 영웅전설에는 전혀 적용되지 않는다는 주장이 있어 왔다. 영국에서 16세기 말과 17세기 초에는, '소설(novel)'이라는 단어는 실제 일어난 사건과 허구의 사건에 두루 쓰였던 것으로 보이며, 심지어 뉴스 기사조차도 사실적이라고 거의 여겨지지 않았다. 소설과 뉴스 기사는 명백하게 사실적인 것도 아니었고 명백하게 허구적인 것도 아니었다. 그러므로 우리가 하는 것처럼 이 두 범주를 명확하게 구별하는 것은 당시에는 전혀 적용되지 않

various a. 가지각색의, 여러 가지의, 다양한
reflection n. 반사; 반영; 반성, 숙고, 심사
sermon n. 설교
autobiography n. 자서전
at a pinch 꼭 필요하면[해야 된다면]
encompass v. 둘러[에워]싸다; 포함하다
maxim n. 격언, 금언
funeral n. 장례식
treatise n. 논문, 보고서
get someone far 성공하게 하다, 성과를 거두게 하다
not least 특히
distinction n. 구별, 차별; 대조, 대비
opposition n. 반대, 저항
saga n. (영웅 등을 다룬) 북유럽의 전설; 무용담
factual a. 사실의, 사실에 입각한; 실제의
discrimination n. 구별, 식별; 차별, 차별대우

았다. 기번은 틀림없이 자신이 역사적 진실을 쓰고 있다고 생각했을 것이며, 아마 『창세기(Genesis)』의 저자도 마찬가지였을 것이다. 그러나 그들이 쓴 글을 지금 일부 사람들은 '사실'로 읽고 있고, 또 다른 사람들은 '허구'로 읽고 있다. 뉴먼은 확실히 자신의 신학적 묵상이 사실이라고 생각했지만, 많은 독자들에게 지금 그의 글은 '문학'이다. 게다가, '문학'이 '사실인' 글을 많이 포함하고 있다면, 그것은 또한 상당히 많은 허구를 배제하고 있기도 하다. 만화 『슈퍼맨(Superman)』과 밀즈 앤 분(Mills and Boon) 출판사의 소설들은 허구이지만 일반적으로 문학으로 간주되지 않으며, 위대한 문학으로 간주되지 않는 것은 확실하다. 만약 문학이 '창의적이거나', '상상력에 의한' 글이라면, 이것이 곧 역사, 철학, 자연과학은 창의적이지 않고 상상력에 의한 것이 아니라는 것을 의미할까? 틀림없이 그렇지 않다.

Genesis n. 창세기
theological a. 신학의, 성서에 기초한
meditation n. 명상; 묵상
exclude v. 제외하다, 배제하다
Mills and Boon 밀즈 앤 분(통속 연애 소설로 유명한 출판사)

1 ④ ▶ **내용파악**
본문은 '문학을 어떻게 정의할 수 있으며, 어떤 작품이 문학에 속하고 어떤 작품이 그렇지 않은가'에 대해 이야기하고 있는 내용이므로, 문학의 의미와 정의에 대한 글의 일부로 볼 수 있다.

2 ③ ▶ **내용추론**
"영국에서 16세기 말과 17세기 초에, '소설'이라는 단어는 실제 일어난 사건과 허구의 사건에 두루 쓰였던 것으로 보이며, 심지어 뉴스 기사도 사실적이라고 거의 여겨지지 않았다. 소설과 뉴스 기사는 명백하게 사실도 아니었고 명백하게 허구도 아니었다."라는 내용을 통해 ③의 진술을 추론할 수 있다.

3 ④ ▶ **내용파악**
본문에서는 허구의 내용이 아닌 '설교, 자서전, 편지, 격언집, 논문' 등도 문학의 범주에 속하는 반면, 만화 『슈퍼맨』과 밀즈 앤 분(Mills and Boon) 출판사의 소설들은 허구이지만 일반적으로 문학으로 간주되지 않음을 언급하고 있는데, 문학을 '허구의' 글로만 한정할 수 없는 이유는 이처럼 사실인 글들이 종종 문학으로 간주되고, 허구의 글들이 항상 문학에 포함되는 것은 아니기 때문이다.

05 철학·종교

01 2016 가톨릭대

기원전 5세기경, 그리스 철학자들은 파르메니데스(Parmenides)와 헤라클레이토스(Heraclitus)의 현격한 입장 차이를 극복하기 위해 노력했었다. 파르메니데스의 변하지 않는 존재의 사상과 헤라클레이토스의 영원한 생성(변화)의 개념을 조화시키기 위해서, 그리스 철학자들은 존재(the Being)는 몇 가지 불변하는 물질들에서 분명히 드러나며, 이런 물질들이 섞이고 떨어져 나가면서 세상의 변화를 초래한다고 추정했다. 이것이 눈에 띄지 않는 최소 물질단위인 원자의 개념을 낳았고, 이 원자의 개념은 데모크리토스(Democritus)의 철학에서 가장 명확하게 표현되었다. 그리스의 원자론자들은 정신과 물질을 명확하게 구분한 후에, 물질은 몇 가지 기본 구성요소로 형성된다고 생각했다. 이런 구성요소는 빈 공간에서 운동하는 순수하게 수동적이고 본질적으로 죽은 입자들이었다. 이 입자들의 운동 원인은 설명되지 않았지만, 그것은 정신에서 유래하여 물질과는 근본적으로 다르다고 추정되는 여러 외부적인 힘과 종종 연관 지어졌다. 뒤이은 여러 세기 동안, 이런 관념은 서양 사상의, 즉 정신과 물질, 육체와 영혼 사이의 이원론의, 본질적인 요소가 되었다.

| overcome v. 극복하다
| reconcile v. 화해시키다, (싸움·논쟁 따위를) 조정하다; 조화시키다
| manifest a. 명백한, 분명한
| invariable a. 변화하지 않는
| substance n. 물질
| separation n. 분리
| atomist n. 원자론자
| draw a line 구분하다
| intrinsically ad. 본질적으로
| external a. 외부의, 외관의
| dualism n. 이원론

1 ① ▶ 글의 주제
본문에서 서양 사상의 근간을 구성하는 '정신과 물질', '영혼과 육체'의 이원론적 세계의 기원을 설명하고 있다. 이원론적 세계관은 '변하지 않는 존재'를 설파했던 파르메니데스와 '영원한 생성'을 주장했던 헤라클레이토스의 서로 다른 철학에서 시작했다. 따라서 글의 주제로 적절한 것은 ① '서양 이원론의 기원'이다.

2 ② ▶ 내용일치
파르메니데스는 절대적이고 영원한 진리, 즉 로고스를 강조했던 반면, 헤라클레이토스는 만물은 변화 생성한다는 유물론적인 입장을 갖고 있었으므로, 둘 사이에는 서로 큰 차이가 있다. 따라서 본문의 내용과 일치하지 않는 것은 ②이다. 두 철학자의 입장을 조정하기 위해서 노력했던 사람들은 후대의 그리스 철학자들이었다.

02 2017 한성대

내려야 할 결정이 있을 때, 공리주의자들은 찬반양론의 목록을 만드는 것을 선호한다. 주요 도덕 이론들 중 하나인 공리주의는 무엇이 어떤 행동을 도덕적으로 옳은 것으로 혹은 그른 것으로 만드느냐를 규명하는 일에 있어 열쇠(핵심적 요소)는 그 행동의 결과라고 단정한다.
사람들의 의도가 좋은지 나쁜지는 (본 문제와) 관련 없다. 중요한 것은 그들의 행동의 결과가 좋은지 나쁜지의 여부다. 행복은 인간의 궁극적인 목표이고 가장 높은 도덕적 가치다. 따라서 한 행동 때문에 큰 불행이 있다면, 그 행동은 도덕적으로 잘못되었다고 말할 수 있다. 공리주의자들은 사람들이 행동을 취하기 전에 행동의 잠재적인 결과를 신중히 숙고해야 한다고 생각한다.
공리주의의 또 다른 문제점은 목적을 달성하기 위한 수단으로 다른 사람을 이용하고 많은 사람의 행복을 위해 소수의 행복을 희생시키는 것이 허용된다는 것이다.

| utilitarian n. 공리주의자
| pros and cons 찬반양론
| ethical a. 도덕상의, 윤리적인
| utilitarianism n. 공리주의
| morally ad. 도덕적으로
| intention n. 의사, 의도; 목적
| irrelevant a. 부적절한; 무관계한
| matter v. 중요하다
| ultimate a. 궁극적인; 근본적인
| weight v. 중시하다
| potential a. 잠재적인
| problematic a. 문제의, 문제가 있는[많은]
| sacrifice v. 희생하다, 희생시키다

1 ② ▶ 빈칸완성
"사람들의 의도가 중요한 것이 아니라, 중요한 것은 행동의 결과가 좋은지 나쁜지의 여부다."라고 했으므로, 공리주의는 "무엇이 어떤 행동을 도덕적으로 옳은 것으로 혹은 그른 것으로 만드느냐를 규명하는 데 중요한 것은 그 행동의 결과다."라고 단정적으로 주장할 것이다. 따라서 빈칸에는 '단정하다'는 뜻의 ② posits가 적절하다. ① 부인하다 ③ 의심하다 ④ 믿지 않다

2 ①　　▶ 내용일치
　　　　공리주의가 중시하는 것은 행동의 결과가 좋은지 나쁜지의 여부인데, 공리주의의 문제점이 마지막 단락에서 소개되고 있으므로 ①이 글의 내용과 일치한다.

3 ④　　▶ 내용일치
　　　　"공리주의자들은 사람들이 행동을 취하기 전에 행동의 잠재적인 결과를 신중히 숙고해야 한다고 생각한다."라고 했으므로 행동을 하고 나서 잠재적인 결과를 숙고하는 것이 아니라, 행동을 취하기 전에 결과를 숙고하는 것이다. 따라서 ④가 본문의 내용과 다르다.

03　2021 한국외대

17세기에 종교는 현세와 내세(來世) 모두에 있어서의 그리고 세상과 그 너머의 우주 안에서의 인간의 위치에 대해 논리적이고 편안한 설명을 제공해주었다. 엘리자베스 시대 우주론의 초석인 '존재의 대사슬(The Great Chain of Being)'은 그 미적(美的) 단순함과 완벽함으로 자연계의 모든 부분을 위계적 배치 안에서 설명할 수 있게 만드는 구조였다. 이 사슬은 신(神)을 맨 위에 놓고, 천사에서, 인간, 하등 동물, 그리고 마지막으로 무생물로 내려왔다. 인간의 위치를 환경과 관련하여 설명하는 방식으로 모든 것이 배열되었다. 운명예정설은, 존재의 대사슬과 마찬가지로, 17세기의 모든 개신교 종교의 교리였다. 내세에서의 인간의 위치도 태어날 때부터 예정되어 있었고, 그것을 바꾸기 위해 인간이 할 수 있는 일은 아무 것도 없었다. 다시 말해서, 아무리 많은 비행(非行)이나 선행(善行)도 사건의 예정된 과정을 변화시키지는 못할 것이었다.

accounting n. 회계; 설명
The Great Chain of Being 존재의 대사슬
cornerstone n. 주춧돌; (어떤 일의) 초석, 기반
cosmology n. 우주론
accountable a. 책임이 있는
in respect to ~에 관하여
predestination n. 운명예정설, 숙명
tenet n. 주의, 교리
afterlife n. 내세(來世)
foreordained a. 미리 정해진
exemplary a. 모범적인
hierarchical a. 계급[계층]에 따르는

1 ④　　▶ 빈칸완성
　　　　그다음 문장에서 '존재의 대사슬이 신을 맨 위에 놓고 그다음으로 천사, 인간, 하등 동물, 마지막으로 무생물이 맨 아래 위치하도록 모든 것을 위계적으로 배치하고 있음'을 설명하고 있으므로, Ⓐ에는 ④ '위계적 배치'가 적절하다. ① 거대한 주기 ② 종교적 사건 ③ 예정된 무질서

2 ②　　▶ 내용일치
　　　　17세기 개신교의 운명예정설에서는 "내세에서의 인간의 지위나 운명이 태어날 때부터 예정되어 있으며, 그것을 바꾸기 위해 인간이 할 수 있는 일은 아무 것도 없다."고 가르쳤다. 따라서 ②가 본문의 내용과 일치하지 않는다.

04　2020 숭실대

고대 그리스의 철학자인 플라톤(Platon)은 수학에서 윤리학 그리고 논리학에 이르기까지 모든 것에서 세상에 대해 우리가 생각하는 방식을 변화시키기 위해 많은 일을 했다. 그러나 아마도 철학에 대한 그의 가장 영향력 있는 공헌 중 하나는 이데아론(Theory of Forms: 형상이론)이었을 것이다. 기본적으로, 플라톤의 이데아론은 물리적인 세계가 실제로 '실재하는' 세계가 아니라고 주장한다. 그 대신 궁극적인 실재는 물리적인 세계 너머에 존재한다. 플라톤은 『국가론(The Republic)』이라고 부르는 가장 유명한 저서를 포함한 몇 가지 다른 담론에서 이러한 이론을 논한다. 플라톤은 이 이론의 일부를 그의 멘토인 소크라테스(Socrates)로부터 계승받았을 수도 있다.
플라톤의 철학은 물리적 영역과 정신적 영역, 두 영역이 있다고 주장한다. 물리적 영역은 매일 우리가 보고 상호작용하는 물질적인 것들이다. 이러한 물리적 영역은 우리가 모두 잘 알고 있다시피 변화하고 불완전하다. 그러나 정신적 영역은 물리적 영역 너머에 존재한다. 플라톤은 이 정신적 영역을 (관념의 영역 또는 이상의 영역이라고도 불리는) 이데아(형상)의 영역이라고 부른다. 플라톤의 이데아론은 물리적 영역이 이데아(형상) 영역에 존재하는 진정한 실재의 그림자 또는 이미지일 뿐이라고 주장한다.
플라톤에 따르면 이러한 이데아는 무엇인가? 이데아는 시간과 공간을 초월하는 추상적이고, 완벽하

form n. <철학> (내용·질에 대해) 형식; (F-) (플라톤 철학의) 이데아(= idea)
physical a. 물질의, 물질적인
dialogue n. 대화, 문답
inherit v. 물려받다
mentor n. 스승
imperfect a. 불완전한
shadow n. 그림자, 투영(投影)
abstract a. 추상적인
capitalize v. 대문자로 쓰다

며, 불변하는 개념이나 이상이다. 그것들은 이데아의 영역에 존재한다. 이데아는 추상적이지만, 그것이 이데아가 실재하지 않는다는 것을 의미하지는 않는다. 실제로 이데아는 어떤 개별적인 물체보다 더 '실재적'이다. 따라서 빨강, 둥긂, 아름다움, 정의 또는 선함과 같은 개념들은 이데아이다. (따라서 그것들은 일반적으로 대문자로 시작된다.) 빨간 책, 둥근 공, 아름다운 소녀, 정의로운 행동, 또는 선량한 사람과 같은 개별적인 사물들은 물리적 영역에 존재하고 단순히 이데아의 서로 다른 예에 불과하다.

1 ② ▶ **빈칸완성**
플라톤의 철학은 물리적 영역과 정신적 영역 두 영역이 있다고 했는데, 물리적 영역은 변화하고 불안정하다고 했다. 정신적 영역은 물리적 영역 너머에 존재하는데, 이 정신적 영역을 이데아의 영역이라고 부른다고 했다. (1) 앞에서 이데아가 불변의 개념이나 이상이라고 했으므로 이를 수식하는 that에는 변화와 불안정과 관계없는 시간과 공간을 초월한다는 ②가 빈칸에 적절하다.

2 ④ ▶ **문맥상 적절하지 않은 단어 고르기**
ⓓ 앞에서 실제로 이데아는 "어떤 개별적인 물체보다 더 '실재적'이다"라고 한 다음 역접의 접속사 But이 왔다. 그러나 ⓓ 다음에 언급된 이데아의 개념은 실재적인 것의 예이므로, 역접의 접속사 But이 아니라 순접의 접속사 So가 의미상 적절하다. 따라서 ④가 정답이다.

3 ① ▶ **내용일치**
고대 그리스의 철학자인 플라톤이 세상을 생각하는 방식을 바꾸기 위해 많은 일을 했음을 언급하면서, 그 예로 이데아론을 설명하고 있으므로, ①이 글의 내용과 일치한다. ③ physical과 spiritual을 서로 맞바꾸어야 한다. ④ 이데아론에서는 이데아의 세계가 실재 세계이고 이데아가 실재적인 것이다.

05 2016 서강대

마카리(Makari)의 대단히 매력적인 이야기는 르네 데카르트(René Descartes)에게서 시작된다. 그리스 철학이 그리스도교와 통합된 이후, 영혼은 '자연, 인간 그리고 하느님 사이를 통합하는 연결고리'로 간주되어왔다고 마카리는 쓰고 있다. 그러나 17세기에 이미, 그리스도교는 위기에 처해 있었고, 많은 사람들은 무형적인 영혼의 개념을 물질로 이루어진 것으로 점점 더 이해되고 있던 기계적 세계와 조화시키기가 어렵다고 여기게 되었다. 데카르트는 영혼의 개념을 '사고하는 존재'로 좁힘으로써 의심 많은 박물학자들의 요구를 충족시키고자 했지만 그것은 육체와는 분리된 것이었다. 그 프랑스의 철학자는 그리하여 불멸의 영혼에 대한 그리스도교 신앙에 새로운 생명력을 불어넣었다. 전체 범위의 반대 극단(데카르트와 정반대 쪽)에 토머스 홉스(Thomas Hobbes)가 있었는데, 그는 '비물질적 실체같은 것은 없다'고 생각했다. 영혼에 대한 그의 견해에 따르면, 영혼은 합리적이고 신을 닮은 어떤 것이라기보다는 '물질적이고, 질병에 걸리고, 오류를 범하기 쉬운' 존재였다. '사고하는 존재'의 본성에 대한 이처럼 본질적으로 다른 견해들은 엄청나게 큰 내포적 의미들을 가질 운명이었다. 그리고 그 견해들은 마카리의 담화가 단지 하나의 지적 운동(저술행위) 이상의 것으로서의 중요성을 지니고 있음을 보여줄 운명이었다. 인간은 불가피하게 갈등을 낳을 수밖에 없는 동물적 감정에 지배된다고 홉스가 결론을 내린 이후, 그가 제안한 해결책은 권력을 절대군주에게 넘겨주자는 것이었다.

1 ② ▶ **내용일치**
영혼에 대한 그리스도교적 이해에 대한 회의론이 심화되고, 인간에 대한 물질주의적 이해가 점점 더 깊어지는 17세기 이후의 서양철학을 언급하고 있으므로 ②가 정답이다. secular는 '종교와 무관한, 비종교적인'이라는 의미를 갖는다. ① 그리스도교는 위기에 처하였고, 많은 이들이 점점 더 물질적 세상을 이해하는 쪽으로 나아가고 있었다고 하였으므로 적절하지 않다. ③ 홉스는 동물적 감정과 그에 따른 갈등이 불가피한 인간세상의 질서회복을 위해 권력을 절대군주에게 넘겨주어야 한다고 하였으므로 적절하지 않다. ④ 데카르트는 비물질적인 존재로서의 영혼을 '사고하는 존재'로 축소함으로써 박물학자들

---

engaging a. 호감이 가는, 매력적인
merge with ~와 통합되다
reconcile v. 조화시키다, 화해시키다
incorporeal a. 무형의, 실체가 없는
skeptical a. 의심 많은, 회의적인
naturalist n. 박물학자, 동식물 연구자
immortal a. 죽지 않는, 불멸의
substance n. 물질; 실체
prone to ~에 취약한
monarch n. 군주, 제왕
chart v. (과정을) 기록하다
secular a. 현세의, 세속의; 종교에 관계하지 않는
demagoguery n. 민중 선동, 악선전
insignificance n. 하찮음, 무의미함
consistent with ~와 일치하는
extrapolate v. 추론하다
corroborate v. 확증하다, 입증하다
immaculate a. 티 없이 깔끔한, 깨끗한; 오류 없는
translate A into B A를 B로 바꾸다, 고치다, 변형하다
disparate a. 본질적으로 다른, 완전히 다른
monumental a. 기념비적인, 대단히 큰

의 요구를 충족시키고자 노력하였다고 했는데, 박물학자들이 기계적인 물질세계를 연구하는 사람들이므로 적절하지 않다.

2 ③ ▶ 빈칸완성

빈칸 다음 문장의 they는 ③의 The disparate views, 즉 데카르트와 홉스의 견해를 가리키며, 마카리의 담화가 이 두 견해의 상반된 면을 잘 다룸으로써 보통 이상으로 중요한 저술이 되었다고 언급하고 있다. 홉스가 절대군주론으로 기울어진 것도 인간 영혼에 대한 데카르트와 다른 그의 견해에서 비롯된 것이므로 이는 ③의 implications에 해당한다고 할 수 있다. 따라서 ③이 정답이다. 영혼에 대한 데카르트와 홉스의 견해가 대립되고 있음을 본문은 강조하고 있으므로 두 사상의 일치 또는 뒷받침 등을 언급하고 있는 ①, ②는 적절하지 않다. 앞에서 상반되는 두 견해를 균형 있게 진술하였으므로 빈칸 다음 문장의 they가 단순히 홉스의 견해나 진술만을 언급하는 것으로 보기에는 무리가 있다. 그러므로 홉스의 진술에 초점을 두고 있는 ④도 적절하지 않다.

3 ④ ▶ 빈칸완성

인간의 영혼에 대한 대립적인, 양극단에 해당하는 견해가 소개되고 있으므로 빈칸에 '범위, 영역'에 해당하는 표현이 들어가야 적절하다. ① 디아스포라(다른 나라에서 살며 일하기 위한 유대인들의 이동) ② 방어물 ③ 잊혀짐

posit v. 사실로 상정하다
gamut n. 전체 음계; 전 영역, 전반

06 2020 성균관대

종교는 사람들을 자극하여 이타주의적인 행동이나 무자비한 가혹 행위를 하게 할 수 있고, 경우에 따라 두 가지 결과를 모두 낳을 수도 있다. 이러한 모순을 분석하려는 생각을 카렌 암스트롱(Karen Armstrong)이 하게 되는 것은 당연한 일이다. 영국 태생의 전직 가톨릭 수녀였던 그녀는 가장 광범위한 종교사에 관한 책을 12권 이상 저술했으며, 신앙이 주장하는 바가 사실이든 아니든 신앙은 합법적인 인간 경험의 일부라는 자신의 견해를 설명했다. 암스트롱은 최근 작품인 『유혈의 들판(Fields of Blood)』에서 이미 나와 있는 기존의 많은 이론들에 또 다른 이론을 더하지는 않는다. 대신에, 그녀는 종교와 세계사에 대한 개관을 소개하면서, 세계 모든 신앙의 초기 발전을 약술한다. 이어서 거대한 필치와 수많은 (완전히 정확하지는 않지만) 세부 설명을 통해, 기독교적인 서양이 지난 500년 동안 세계에 미친 영향을 연구한다. 그녀가 어느 악마들과 싸우고 있는지 깨달을 때야 비로소 어떻게 이 모든 것이 일관성을 갖는지 명확해진다. 암스트롱은 어떤 것도 증명하려고 하지 않고, 몇 가지 것들의 오류를 입증하려고 한다. 그 몇 가지 중 첫째가 종교는 폭력의 불필요한 원인이어서, 종교를 없애면 평화가 증진될 것이라는 생각이다. 그리고 둘째가 이슬람교는 폭력을 부추기는 종교의 끔찍한 사례라는 견해다. 그녀의 세 번째 악마는 처음의 두 가지를 합친 것으로, "기독교적인" 서양이 이슬람 세계보다는 종교적 신념을 더 많이 버렸기 때문에, "기독교적인" 서양이 구제불능으로 폭력적인 이슬람교를 억눌러야 한다는 생각이다.

1 ⑤ ▶ 내용파악

셋째 문장 expounding 이하에서 '신앙이 주장하는 바가 사실이든 아니든 신앙은 합법적인 인간 경험의 일부'라고 했으므로 ⑤가 그녀가 주장하는 내용이다.

2 ④ ▶ 부분이해

밑줄 친 부분을 포함한 그녀의 세 번째 악마는 그녀가 맞서 싸우고 있는 잘못된 통념으로 그녀가 그 오류를 입증해 보이고자 하는 것이다. 따라서 that절 전체가 잘못된 생각인 것이다. shed가 여기서는 '버리다'는 뜻이고 baggage가 여기서는 faith(신앙)와는 다른, 고정된 신념의 뜻이다. 셋째는 첫째와 둘째의 결합인데 첫째 잘못된 생각의 설명에서 종교를 폭력의 불필요한 원인이라 했으므로 종교적인 신념을 많이 버릴수록 더욱 평화로운 것이 된다. 따라서 밑줄 친 내용은 ④를 의미한다.

inspire v. 영감을 주다, 고무하다
ruthless a. 무자비한, 잔인한
dissect v. 절단하다; 분석하다
expound v. 상술하다, 설명하다
on offer 팔려고 내놓은
overview n. 개관, 개요
sketch v. 개념을 말하다
stroke n. 일격; 발작; 한바탕의 일, 노력
cohere v. 결합하다, 논리 정연하다, 일치하다(with)
disprove v. 오류를 입증하다, 반박하다
gratuitous a. 불필요한, 쓸데없는
egregious a. 지독한, 어처구니없는; 악명 높은
bogeyman n. 귀신, 악귀; 고민거리
shed v. 버리다
baggage n. 여행용 수하물; 신념, 이론
incorrigible a. 고쳐지지 않는; 다루기 힘든
restrain v. 억제하다, 제한하다
authoritarian a. 권위주의적인, 독재적인

07　2018 한국항공대

『논고(Treatise)』의 첫머리에 언급된 흄(Hume) 철학의 가장 핵심적 원리 중 하나는 마음이 정신적 인식, 즉 마음에 존재하는 정신적 대상들로 구성되어 있으며, 그 정신적 대상들은 인상과 사상이라는 두 가지 범주로 나눌 수 있다는 것이 그의 생각이다. 흄의 『논고』는 그래서 다음과 같은 말로 시작한다. "인간의 마음의 모든 인식들은 분해되어 두 가지 다른 종류로 되는데, 나는 이를 인상 (IMPRESSIONS)과 사상(IDEAS)이라고 부르겠다." 흄은 "나는 이 구별을 설명하는 데 많은 말이 필요치 않다고 생각한다."라고 말하는데, 평론가들은 일반적으로 그것이 감정과 사고의 구별을 의미하는 것으로 받아들이고 있다. 논쟁의 여지가 있겠지만, 흄은 어떤 면에서 볼 때 그 차이를 정도의 문제로 간주하는 것 같은데, 그것은 그가 "인상"을 그것의 힘, 생기, 그리고 생동감에 기초해서 사상과 구별되는 것으로 보기 때문이다. 그러므로 사상은 약한 인상이다. 예를 들어, 뜨거운 냄비의 손잡이를 만져서 고통스러운 감각을 경험하는 것은 단순히 뜨거운 냄비를 만지는 생각보다 훨씬 강력하다. 흄에 따르면, 인상은 우리의 모든 사상의 원형적 형태를 의미하고, 그래서 돈 가렛(Don Garret)은 모든 사상은 궁극적으로 그 사상의 기원이 되는 그 어떤 원형적(원래의) 인상 ― 그것이 열정이든 감각이든 상관없이 ― 으로부터 복사되어 나온 것이라는 흄의 원리를 지칭하기 위해 "복사 원리"라는 용어를 만들어 냈다. 흄의 윤리학 저술들은 『논고』에서 시작되었다. 윤리에 대한 그의 관점은 "도덕적 결정이 도덕적 감정에 근거한다."는 것이다. 윤리적 행동을 통제하는 것이 지식이 아니라 감정이라는 것이다. 도덕의 이면에 이성이 있을 리 없다고 주장하면서 그는 다음과 같이 썼다. "도덕은 감정을 일으키고, 행동을 유발하거나 방지한다. 이 경우에 이성 그 자체는 완전히 무력하다. 그러므로 도덕의 규칙들은 우리의 이성이 내린 결론이 아니다." 도덕성에 관한 흄의 감정주의를 그의 친한 친구인 아담 스미스(Adam Smith)가 공유하였다. 그리고 흄과 스미스는 동시대에 그들보다 연장자였던 프란시스 허치슨(Francis Hutcheson)의 도덕적 성찰에 다 같이 영향을 받았다. 피터 싱어(Peter Singer)는 도덕은 이성적 근거를 갖지 못한다는 주장만으로도 흄이 "윤리학의 역사에서 한 자리를 차지하기에 충분할 것이다."라고 주장한다.

doctrine n. 원칙, 주의; 교리
resolve v. (분해하여) 변형시키다
commentator n. 해설자, 평론가
vivacity n. 생기, 활기
coin v. (신어·신표현을) 만들어 내다
passion n. (이성(理性)과 대비하여) 감정, 정감
sensation n. 느낌, 감각
sentiment n. 정서, 감정, 정감
impotent a. 무력한
sentimentalism n. 감상주의, 감정주의

1　②　▶ 빈칸완성
　　본문에서 흄은 인상(impressions)과 사상(ideas)을 '정도(degree)'의 차이에 따라 구별한다고 했다. 힘, 생기, 그리고 생동감이 강렬한 것이 인상(감정)이고, 그보다 힘, 생기, 생동감이 '약한 인상'이 곧 사상(이성)이라고 본 것이다. ① 윤리의 토대 ③ 도덕의 모방 ④ 강력한 이성

2　③　▶ 내용일치
　　인식의 본질, 인식 작용 및 인식의 대상 등을 논하는 철학 분야가 인식론(epistemology)인데, 본문에 따르면 흄은 『논고』에서 인식의 내용물을 인상(감정)과 사상(이성)으로 구별하고, 그들의 본질과 상관관계를 논하였으며, 그것들이 어떻게 도덕적 판단에 영향을 미치는지 논하고 있으므로, 인식론적 문제를 탐구하였다고 볼 수 있다.

08　2022 홍익대

비트겐슈타인(Wittgenstein)은 간단히 물었다. 언어란 무엇인가? 왜 그리고 어떻게 해서 사람이 내는 꽥꽥거리는 소리와 그들이 그리는 구부러진 선이 세상에 있는 온갖 것들을 떠올리게 하는 것인가? 영국의 철학자 앤서니 퀸튼(Anthony Quinton)은 비트겐슈타인의 직감을 아이작 뉴턴(Isaac Newton)경의 직감과 비교했는데, 뉴턴은 다른 사람들이 "원래 그런 것이다."라고 말하면서 충분히 만족하는 때에도 왜 돌이 땅에 떨어지는지를 애써 물었던 것이다.

비트겐슈타인의 대답은 언어의 그림 이론이었는데, 이는 말과 실제 세계 사이의 관계를 적절히 보여주는 것이었다. 그는 사람들이 가지고 있는 모든 의미 있는 생각은 그림의 배열이며, 이것은 '명제'로서 언어로 표현될 때에 다른 사람들에게 전달될 수 있다고 주장했다. 이것은 "고양이가 매트에 앉아있었다."라는 문장이 복잡한 문장들과 공통적으로 가지고 있는 것이다. 적어도 고양이 같은 유형의 사물의 경우에는 그것이 분명해 보일 지도 모른다. 그러나 비트겐슈타인은 새로운 장을 열고 있었다. 그 생각은 그가 자동차 충돌과 관련된 소송 사건에 대한 보고서를 읽을 때 떠올랐다. 변호사가 장난감 자동차와 인형을 사용해서 충돌사건을 설명했다는 것을 알게 된 그는 언어가 그림을 기

squawk n. 꽥꽥거리는 소리
squiggle n. 구부러진 선; 꼬부라져 읽기 어려운 글자
conjure up 상기시키다, 생각해내다
instinct n. 본능, 직감, 직관
content a. 만족하는, 불평 없는
demonstration n. 증명; 논증, 증거
arrangement n. 배열, 배치; 정돈
proposition n. 명제
tangible a. 실체적인; 유형의
feline n. 고양잇과 동물
obvious a. 명백한

반으로 한다는 점을 파악했다. 그는 이 관점을 주요 철학 문제에 적용했고, 철학은 대체로 세상에서 입증할 수 없고 따라서 그림으로 그려질 수 없는 것들을 논하기 때문에, 철학의 많은 명제들은 의미가 없다고 결론지었다. <다시 말해, 대부분의 철학은 '무의미하다'는 것이다.> 그는 언어를 사용하여 의미 있는 토론이 가능한 소수의 분야에 초점을 맞추는 것을 선호했다. 이를 통해 그는 "말할 수 없는 것에 대해서는 침묵해야 한다."라는 최종적이고도 결정적인 명제를 얻게 되었다.

break new ground 새 분야[신천지]를 개척하다, 새로운 일을 하다, 신기원을 열다
involve v. 수반하다, 포함하다
smash n. (차 따위의) 충돌
grasp v. 이해하다, 파악하다
pictorial a. 그림의, 그림으로 나타낸
definitive a. 결정적인
whereof ad. 그것에 관해
thereof ad. 거기서부터

1 ④ ▶ 문장삽입
주어진 문장은 "다시 말해, 대부분의 철학은 무의미하다."라는 의미인데, '다시 말해'에 유의하면 이 문장의 앞에 '철학의 무의미함'에 관한 내용이 있어야 한다. 따라서 "철학은 그림으로 그려질 수 없는 것들을 논하기 때문에, 철학의 많은 명제들은 의미가 없다고 결론지었다."는 내용 다음인 ⒟가 가장 적절한 위치다.

2 ① ▶ 내용파악
첫 번째 문단 후반부에서 '뉴턴이 다른 사람들이 당연하게 여기는 사실에 대해 질문을 던진 것'을 언급했는데, 뉴턴과 비트겐슈타인을 비교한 것은 이 점이 두 사람의 공통점이라는 것이므로 ①이 정답으로 적절하다.

3 ④ ▶ 내용파악
비트겐슈타인은 "사람들이 가지고 있는 모든 생각은 그림의 배열이며, 이것이 언어로 표현될 수 있을 때에 의미를 가진다."고 생각했는데, 이는 언어를 통해 그림처럼 묘사될 수 없는 것은 의미가 없다고 여겼다는 것이므로 ④가 정답으로 적절하다.

09 2018 한국항공대

하지만 그것은 너무 부정적으로 말하는 것입니다. 만약 제가 종교적 신앙을 보존하는 데 관심이 있다면, 저는 정확히 말해 진화 과학이 무신론적이라는 이유로 진화 과학의 긍정적인 힘을 무척 두려워할 것입니다. 생물학적 설계를 주장하는 모든 이론의 어려운 문제는 생물체들이 갖고 있는 통계학적으로 엄청나게 불가능해 보이는 점을 설명하는 것입니다. 좋은(선하신) 설계를 지지하는 쪽으로 작용하는 통계학적 불가능성, 바로 이것을 나타내는 또 다른 단어가 "복잡성"입니다. 단 하나뿐이고 모든 것이 이 하나로 환원되는 유일한 표준적인 창조론 주장은 통계학적 불가능성에서부터 전개되어 갑니다. 살아 있는 피조물은 너무나 복잡하여 우연히 생겨났을 수는 없고 그래서 그들을 설계한 자가 있었음에 틀림없다는 것입니다. 물론 이것은 제 발등을 찍는 주장입니다. 정말 복잡한 것을 설계할 수 있는 설계자 자신은 훨씬 더 복잡해야 합니다. 그리고 그것은 죄를 용서하고, 결혼을 축복하고, 기도를 들어주는 등, 그가 하기로 되어 있는 다른 일들에 관한 논의를 우리가 시작도 하기 전의 문제입니다. 복잡성은 생물학의 모든 이론이 해결해야 하는 문제이며, 훨씬 더 복잡한 어떤 행위자를 상정하여 문제를 복잡하게 만들기만 해서는 풀 수 없는 문제입니다. 다윈의 자연선택은 복잡성을 설명하는 문제를 오로지 단순성에 의해 해결하므로 놀랄 만큼 명쾌합니다. 본질적으로, 진화론은 점진적이고 단계적으로 증가하는 완만한 경사로를 제공하며 나아갑니다. 그러나 여기서 저는 다만 진화론의 그러한 명쾌함이 종교를 부식시킬 수 있다는 점을 지적하고 싶습니다. 진화론이 매우 명쾌하면서도, 인색할 정도로 간결하고, 강력하며, 경제적으로(능률적으로) 강력하기 때문입니다. 그것은 마치 아름다운 현수교처럼 탄탄한 근육질의 경제성을 지녔습니다. 신에 관한 이론은 단지 하나의 나쁜 이론에 그치지 않습니다. 원론적으로, 그것은 그것이 하도록 요구받은 일들을 해낼 능력이 없는 것으로 판명됩니다. 그래서 저는 전술과 진화론 진영으로 돌아가, (창조론에 대해) 평지풍파를 일으키는 것이 해야 할 옳은 일이라고 주장하고자 합니다. 진화론 진영과는 달리 제가 창조론을 공격하는 접근 방식은 종교 전반을 공격하는 것입니다.

improbability n. 사실 같지 않음, 있음직하지 않음
shoot oneself in the foot 제 발등을 찍다
postulate v. 상정하다, 가정하다
compound v. 복잡하게 하다; 악화시키다
stunningly ad. 놀랍도록
ramp n. 경사로
increment n. 증가
corrosive a. 부식시키는, 부식성의; 좀먹는, 유해한
parsimonious a. 인색한
sinewy a. 근육질의, 건장한
suspension bridge 현수교
lobby n. 압력 단체
tactic n. 전술
rock the boat 평지풍파를 일으키다

1 ④ ▶ 빈칸완성
종교적 신앙의 보존에 관심이 있으면 그 신앙을 해치는 세력을 두려워할 것인데, 여기서 필자가 두려워할 것이라 한 세력이 '진화 과학(evolutionary science)'이고 이것을 빈칸 앞의 it이 가리키므로 빈칸에는 신앙에 반하는 ④ atheistic(무신론적인)이 적절하다.
① 전능한 ② 암묵적인 ③ 비옥한

2 ①
▶ 글의 제목

필자는 "진화론의 강력함과 명쾌함이 종교를 부식시킬 수 있다."라고 하면서, 신에 관한 이론 및 종교 전반에 대한 공격을 감행하겠다고 말한다. 따라서 이 글의 제목은 '진화론 시대의 종교'라고 말할 수 있을 것이다.

---

10 2014 홍익대

다른 모든 학문들처럼, 철학은 그 무엇보다 지식을 목표로 삼는다. 철학이 지향하는 지식은 여러 과학들마다에 통일성과 체계성을 부여하는 종류의 지식이며, 우리의 신념, 편견, 확신의 근거에 대한 비판적인 검토의 결과로 나온 종류의 지식이다. 하지만 철학이 그것이 가진 문제점들에 명확한 해답을 제공하고자 한 시도에서 큰 성공을 거두었다고 주장할 수는 없다. 만약 수학자, 광물학자, 역사학자 혹은 그 밖의 다른 학자들에게 자신들의 과학을 통해 무슨 명확한 진리의 실체를 규명해냈는가 묻는다면, 그는 당신이 듣기를 원하는 만큼 길게 대답해줄 것이다. 하지만 동일한 질문을 철학자에게 하는 경우, 그는 만약 솔직한 사람이라면, 그의 학문이 다른 과학들에 의해 성취된 것과 같은 긍정적인 결과를 달성해내지 못했다고 인정할 수밖에 없을 것이다. 사실, 이것은 그 어떤 주제에 관한 명확한 지식이 생겨나게 되면, 곧 이 주제는 철학이라 불리지 않게 되며 별도의 과학이 된다는 사실에 의해 어느 정도 설명된다. 현재는 천문학에 속해 있는 천체에 관한 전반적인 연구는 한때 철학에 포함되어 있었다. 그래서 뉴턴(Newton)의 위대한 저작이 '자연 철학의 수학적 원리'라고 불렸던 것이다. 마찬가지로, 철학의 한 분야였던 인간의 정신에 관한 연구는 현재 철학과 분리되어 심리학이 되었다. 요컨대, 철학이 불확실하다는 것은 대부분 실제라기보다 겉보기에만 그런 것이다. 이미 명확한 해답이 가능한 문제들은 여러 과학에 들어가 있는 반면, 현재 명확한 해답을 줄 수 없는 문제들만이 남아 철학이라 불리는 잔존물을 형성하고 있다.

1 ① ▶ 글의 주제

학문을 통해 명확한 진리의 실체를 규명해 낸 다른 과학들과는 달리, 문제점들에 명확한 해답을 내놓지 못한 '철학'이라는 학문 분야에서 그 목표와 대상을 정하는 데 있어서의 어려움을 기술하고 있는 글이다.

2 ④ ▶ 동의어

candid는 '솔직한, 진솔한, 숨김없는'이라는 뜻이므로 ④ forthright가 동의어가 된다. ① 엄청난 ② 진실되지 못한 ③ 불만족한

3 ③ ▶ 지시대상

앞선 3개 문장의 내용, 즉, '다른 분야의 학자들과는 달리, 만약 철학자에게 진리의 실체를 규명했는가를 묻는 경우에는 긍정적인 결과를 이뤄내지 못했다고 인정할 수밖에 없는 상황'을 가리킨다. 따라서 이와 같은 의미의 ③이 정답이 된다.

4 ② ▶ 빈칸완성

과거에 철학에 속해있었지만, 현재 하나의 별도의 과학이 된 예를 이어서 들고 있다. 따라서 '이와 비슷하게, 마찬가지로'라는 의미의 ② Similarly가 빈칸에 가장 적절하다. ① 그에 반해서 ③ 그러므로 ④ 그럼에도 불구하고

philosophy n. 철학, 형이상학
aim v. 목표하다(at)
primarily ad. 첫째로, 처음으로; 원래, 본래
examination n. 조사, 검사; 검토
conviction n. 확신, 신념
prejudice n. 편견, 선입관
belief n. 믿음, 확신, 신념
maintain v. 지속하다, 계속하다; 단언하다
mathematician n. 수학자
mineralogist n. 광물학자
ascertain v. 확인하다, 확정하다; 규명하다
philosopher n. 철학자
candid a. 솔직한, 숨김없는
confess v. 자백하다, 고백하다, 실토하다
cease v. 그치다, 그만두다, 중지하다
separate a. 갈라진, 분리된; 개별적인, 단독의
astronomy n. 천문학
mathematical a. 수학의; 아주 정확한
to a great extent 대부분은, 크게
uncertainty n. 불확실성
residue n. 잔여, 나머지

---

11 2022 중앙대

종교를 사회구조와 물질세계에 뿌리를 두고 있는 현상으로 설명하는 것은 종교의 보다 더 영적이고 개인적인 기반을 찾으려는 사람들을 늘 만족시키지는 못한다. 수년 동안 철학자들과 사회과학자들은 다른 많은 요인들을 잔뜩 제시했고 그 중에는 자연의 힘에 대한 경외감, 죽음에 대한 공포, 꿈을 해석해야 할 필요, 자신의 부모를 죽이고 싶은 욕망에 대한 죄의식, 그리고 원죄 등을 요인으로 제시

factor n. 요인
subsistence n. 생계, 생존
in line with ~에 따라, ~에 의거하여
anthropologist n. 인류학자

했다. 일부 사회학자들은 자신의 감각의 한계를 피하고 자신의 삶의 의미가 일상 경험 너머에 있다고 느끼기 위한 초월의 필요성에 대해 이야기하기도 한다.

그러나 이러한 가능한 원천들은 신앙체계의 끝없는 다양성이나 시간 경과에 따른 신앙체계의 변화 방식을 설명할 수 없다. 이런 유형의 분석을 하려면 해당 집단의 특정 문화와 사회 구조를 살펴보아야 한다. 가령 채집 집단은 농업 부족집단과 다른 신앙체계를 발전시키는 경향이 있는가? 신앙의 기원이 인간 생존의 불확실성에 있다면 신앙 차이의 기반을 다양한 생존 방식에 있다고 볼 수 있을 것이다. 이러한 생각에 맞추어 마빈 해리스(Marvin Harris)라는 인류학자는 사람들이 숭배하는 종류의 신은 해당 사회 내 사회관계의 성격을 드러낸다고 말한다. 단순한 수렵 채집 집단에서 신들은 그들이 인도하는 사람들과 마찬가지로 기본적으로 평등주의 집단으로, 남녀 차이가 거의 없다. 이 신들은 집단을 창소하는 네 중요했지만 일상생활은 원수민들이나 더 낮은 등급의 신들에게 맡겨눈다. 반면에 농업 사회, 특히 중앙집권 국가 체제와 잘 정립된 사회 계급이 있는 농업 사회의 경우, 신들 자신이 고도로 계층화되어 있고 행동 및 도덕 기준에의 엄격한 복종을 주장한다.

중요한 의례 기능이 여성들에 의해 수행되었다는 증거도 있다. 가령 고대 유럽의 베스타 여신의 시중을 들던 처녀들, 영국의 옛 켈트 족 드루이드 여사제, 그리고 초기 로마사의 여성 컬트의 구성원들이 그 사례다. 고대 크레타 문명의 어머니 여신의 동상들, 그리고 석기 시대 터키에서 나온 벽화들은 여성들이 종교 의례뿐 아니라 사회 전체에서도 훨씬 더 중심적인 역할을 맡았다는 것을 시사한다. 실로 선사시대부터 현대 사회에 이르기까지 전 세계에 어머니 숭배가 널리 퍼져 있는 증거가 존재한다.

hunting band 사냥 집단
egalitarian a. 평등주의의
bunch n. 무리, 다발
stratify v. 계층화[서열화]하다
conduct n. 행동
ritual n. 의례, 의식
priestess n. 여사제
statue n. 동상, 석상
worship n. 숭배
contemporary a. 당대의, 현대의

1 ③ ▶ 글의 제목

"이런 유형의 분석을 하려면 해당 집단의 특정 문화와 사회 구조를 살펴보아야 한다."고 한 둘째 단락 둘째 문장이 글의 주제를 담은 문장이므로 ③이 글의 제목으로 적절하다. ① 여러 문화를 비교하는 관점이므로 글과 맞지 않고, ②와 ④의 여성에 대한 언급은 사회 문화적 특성의 일부에 해당하는 내용이므로 제목으로는 부적절하다.

2 ③ ▶ 내용추론

"단순한 수렵 채집 집단에서 신들은 평등주의 집단으로, 남녀 차이가 거의 없다(with little distinction between male and female)."고 했으므로 똑같이 성별에 따라 차이가 나지 않았다(were not distinctive in gender)고 한 ③을 추론할 수 있다. ① 인간의 초월 추구가 설명해줄 수 있는 것은 종교의 영적, 개인적 기반이다. ② Inter-societal이 아니라 Social이어야 한다. ④ 고대 그리스(Greek) 유물이 아니라 고대 크레타(Crete) 유물이어야 한다. 고대 크레타는 기원전 1100년 이전이고 고대 그리스는 기원전 500년~300년 정도다.

12 2021 홍익대

현상학이란 무엇인가? 그리고 왜 역사학자, 심리학자, 교육학자, 정치 경제학자뿐 아니라 인류학자도 현상학에 관심을 가져야 하는가? 철학 안에서 현상학은 그것을 연구하는 철학자들만큼이나 다양하다. 실제로, 현상학의 철학적 전통에 대한 입문서는 독자들에게 현상학이 "하나의 합의된 방법에 따르거나 하나의 이론적 전망이나 의식, 지식, 세계에 대한 한 부류의 고정된 테제를 받아들이는" 정도(程度)를 지나치게 과장하지 말라고 경고하는 것을 중요하게 여긴다. 이러한 다양성의 일부는 계속 현상학의 인류학적 이용의 특징이 되고 있다. 그러나 우리는 또한 현상학의 의미의 범위를 편의상 제한하자고 주장한다. 우리가 그렇게 하는 것은 현상학의 잠재적 적용 가능성을 넓혀서, 현상학을 인류학과 그 연관 학문 분야에 더 유용하게 만들기 위함이다. 역설처럼 보이는 것 — 즉, 그 사용 범위를 확장하기 위해 그 의미를 제한하는 것 — 은 사실상 현상학 자체의 가르침과 일치한다. (이해를 돕기 위한) 예비적인 목적을 위해, 우리는 현상학에 대한 쓸모 있고 편리한 정의를 이렇게 제공한다. 즉, 현상학은 인간이 어려서 물려받아 살아가는 사교적이고 물질적으로 결집된 이 세계를 인간이 어떻게 인식하고, 경험하고, 이해하는지에 대한 연구다.

현상학을 이렇게 규정지을 때, 인류학 속의 현상학은 모든 사회의 모든 남녀 그리고 아이와 관련된 인식과 경험의 이론이다. 그러한 것으로서 현상학은 인류학자가 드나드는 현장 연구 장소의 현지인에게뿐만 아니라, 모든 곳의 모든 사람처럼 인간과 비인간을 막론하고 의미 있는 타자(他者)에 둘러

phenomenology n. 현상학
practitioner n. 실천가
cohere v. 일관성이 있다; 논리 정연하다
argue for 찬성의견을 말하다
heuristic a. 스스로 발견하는; 발견적 학습의
applicability n. 적용성, 응용성
aligned a. 제휴된, 연관된
discipline n. 학문의 분야; 훈육
pertain v. 적합하다, 어울리다
universalistic a. 보편적인
determinedly ad. 완강히
set out 착수하다; 설명하다
temporal a. 일시적인; 시간의
cumulative a. 누적하는, 점증적인

싸여, 그들 나름의 지역적인 삶을 살아가는 철학자와 인류학자에게도 적절한 것이다. 그러므로 현상학은 확실히 보편주의적인 차원을 가지고 있다. 그러나 현상학은 또한 완강하게 특수주의적이기도 하다. 우리가 특권을 부여하는 현상학은 경험과 인식이 어떻게 사회적 실제적 참여를 통해 구성되는가를 보여주려고 한다. 사람들의 활동과 관심사에 대한 현상학적 설명에는, 시간적, 누적적 차원이 있으며, 이는 우리 몸에 거주하고(우리 안에 있으면서) 사람들의 행동과 관점을 어느 방향으로 나아가게 하는 지향성(指向性)이라는 현상학의 미묘한 어휘를 통해 가장 심오하게 드러난다.

orientation n. 지향성
come through 나타나다

1 ③ ▶ 글의 주제
이 글은 현상학의 기본적인 개념과 현상학에서 파생된 하나의 분과학문으로서 현상학적 인류학(인류학 속의 현상학), 즉 현상학의 인류학적 이용에 대해 개략적으로 설명하는 입문적인 글이다. 따라서 글의 주제로는 ③이 적절하다.

2 ② ▶ 내용일치
첫 단락 마지막 문장에서 현상학을 '세계를 인간이 어떻게 인식하고, 경험하고, 이해하는지에 대한 연구'라고 정의했으므로 ②가 옳은 진술이다. ① 현상학은 현상학을 연구하는 학자마다 다양하다. ③ 현상학은 현장 연구 장소의 현지인에게뿐만 아니라 철학자와 인류학자에게도 적절하다. ④ 현상학은 보편주의적인 차원을 가지면서도 특수주의적이기도 하다.

3 ① ▶ 내용파악
Ⓐ 앞 문장에서 현상학은 다양하다고 했으므로, 현상학 입문서가 독자에게 하는 경고는 현상학이 하나의 방법을 따르거나 하나의 전망이나 한 부류의 테제를 받아들이는 정도를 과장하라는 경고가 아니라 과장하지 말라는 경고일 것이다. 따라서 Ⓐ에 not이 들어가야 한다.

13 2014 아주대

비판적인 사상가들은 오류를 알아보는 법을 배운다. 대부분의 오류는 처음에는 타당해 보이지만 나중에는 모호한 가정과 부주의한 일반화에 기초한 것으로 밝혀지게 되는 일시적인 지름길이다. 흔한 논리적인 오류에는 인신공격의 오류, 순환논증의 오류, 주의분산의 오류, 흑백논리의 오류, 시류편승의 오류가 있다.
첫 번째, 인신공격의 오류는 논의 중인 주제에 집중하는 대신 상대방에 대한 개인적인 비난을 하는 것이다. 인신공격성 주장은 화자 혹은 필자가 상대방의 인성 혹은 (행위의) 동기에 대해 비난하는 경우 오명 씌우기 전술이 된다. 독설적인 수사법을 주로 사용하는 화자가 제안이 현실적인지 아닌지와 같은 실질적인 문제들을 잘 피해가는 것은 당연하다. <하지만 이러한 종류의 오류를 개인의 신뢰성과 관련된 문제와 혼동해서는 안 된다. 그러한 고려사항들이 논의 중인 문제와 연관된 것이라면, 자격 혹은 동기가 분명하지 않은 상대방에게 문제를 제기하는 것은 아주 합법적인 일이다.>
두 번째, 순환논증의 오류 — 질문에 대한 답변을 교묘하게 피하는 것이라고도 불리는 — 는 필자가 주장을 뒷받침하기보다 단지 그 주장을 다른 말로 바꿔 말할 때 발생한다. 다음의 잘못된 주장을 살펴보자. "국가에게 범죄자의 생명을 끝낼 권한은 없기 때문에 사형은 옳지 않은 것이다."라는 주장이다. 하지만 그것은 정확하게 사형이 의미하는 바로서, 사형은 국가에서 허가한 처형인 것이다.
세 번째, 주의분산의 오류는 관계없는 것들을 제기하여 청중의 관심을 주요 논점으로부터 다른 곳으로 전환시키는 것을 수반한다. 자신의 주장이 설득력이 약하다고 염려하는 사람들은 청중의 주의를 다른 곳으로 돌릴 수 있기를 바라며 감정에 치우치긴 하지만 (주제와) 관계없는 문제를 제기함으로써 주의분산의 오류를 사용할 수도 있다.
네 번째, 흑백논리의 오류는 한 사람이 오직 두 가지 선택사항 — 옳고 그름, 좋고 나쁨, 도덕적임과 부도덕함 등등 — 중에서 선택을 해야 한다는 것을 의미한다. 이것은 복잡한 문젯거리를 그럴듯한 말로 얼버무리고 그 대신에 상대방을 비난하는 또 다른 매우 단순화한 논법이다.
마지막으로, 시류편승의 오류는 어떠한 활동이나 결과는 그것이 인기 있는 것이기 때문에 할 만한 가치가 있다고 주장하는 것이다. 수백만 명의 사람들이 지적해왔듯, 인기가 반드시 우수성을 보장하는 것은 아니다.

critical a. 비판적인; 결정적인
recognize v. 인지하다, 알아보다
fallacy n. 그릇된 생각[믿음]
flashy a. 일시적으로 화려한; 한때 반짝하는; 불같은
shortcut n. 지름길; 손쉬운 방법
dubious a. 수상쩍은, 의심스러운; 모호한
assumption n. 가정, 가설, 억측
generalization n. 일반화, 보편화; 개괄
smear tactics (명예·평판 따위에) 오명 씌우기 전술
resort v. 의지하다, 호소하다
abusive a. 독설의; 모욕적인; 남용하는
rhetoric n. 수사법, 화려한 문체
relevant a. 관련된, 적절한
credibility n. 진실성, 신뢰성, 신용
legitimate a. 합법적인, 정당한
qualification n. 자격 증명; 능력
beg v. (문제·요점을) 회피하다, 답하지 않다
restate v. 다시 말하다, 바꿔 말하다
faulty a. 결점[결함]이 있는, 불완전한; 그릇된
distract v. (마음·주의를) 분산시키다, 딴 데로 돌리다
emotionally charged 감정이 북받친
reasoning n. 추론, 추리
gloss over ~을 감추다, 속이다

1 ③ ▶ 내용파악
대부분의 오류는 처음에는 타당해 보이지만 나중에는 모호한 가정과 부주의한 일반화에 기반을 둔 것으로 밝혀진다고 했으므로, 처음 겉보기에는 옳게 보이지만 실제로는 그렇지 않은 것 즉, 논리 정연한 주장에 대한 조잡한 모방품이라 할 수 있다. 따라서 ③이 정답이다.

2 ④ ▶ 동의어
sanction은 '인가[재가]하다'라는 의미의 동사이므로, '지지하다, 보증하다; 배서하다'라는 의미의 endorse가 동의어로 쓰일 수 있다. ① 벌하다, 응징하다 ② 이익이 되다, 이롭다 ③ 위반하다, 어기다 ⑤ 명명하다, 지명하다

3 ① ▶ 내용파악
법안의 내용에 관해서 논하고 있는 것이 아니라 법안에 반대하는 사람들에 대해 비판하고 있으므로 인신공격의 오류에 해당함을 알 수 있다.

4 ② ▶ 내용파악
raise taxes와 cost taxpayers more money는 동일한 의미다. 주장에 대한 이유를 들면서, 앞서 했던 주장을 단지 다른 말로 바꿔서 말하고 있으므로 순환논증의 오류에 해당함을 알 수 있다.

5 ② ▶ 문장삽입
이런 종류의 오류를 개인의 신뢰성과 관련된 문제와 혼동해서는 안 된다고 했으므로 '개인'과 관련된 오류 즉, 인신공격의 오류 다음에 올 내용이라 짐작할 수 있다. 따라서 Ⓑ에 들어가는 것이 가장 적절하다.

14 2013 숭실대

'샤먼(주술사)'이라는 단어는 시베리아의 한 종족인 에벤키 족(Evenki)으로부터 온 것이다. 그러나 샤먼은 지금의 런던, 보스턴, 그리고 많은 다른 서부 유럽의 도시들에 있는 샤먼의 중심지들을 포함하여 지구상 거의 모든 구석구석에서 발견된다. 샤먼은 보이지 않는 영혼이 우리가 있는 세상에 스며들고, 우리에게 행동하고, 우리의 운명을 좌우지한다고 믿는다. 의사, 성직자, 신비주의자, 심리학자, 마을의 어른들, 신탁을 행하는 사람, 그리고 시인들, 이들이 이 숨겨진 현실과의 교섭자로 지정된 사람들이며, 그들은 그들이 속한 사회에서 높은 지위를 차지한다.
샤머니즘의 정확한 정의는 없다. "복수형으로 '샤머니즘들'이라고 말하는 것이 더 나을 것입니다."라고 조지타운 대학의 인류학자인 마조리 맨델스탐 발처(Marjorie Mandelstam Balzer)는 말한다. 샤먼이 되는 길이 그 무엇보다 대단히 개인적인 것이기 때문에, 믿음, 관행, 그리고 의식은 사람에 따라 다르다고 그녀는 나에게 말했다. 그래도 유사성들은 존재한다. 황홀한 무아경이나 때때로 영혼의 여정이라 불리는 것이 특징적인 현상이다. 그러나 샤먼들이 그들의 기구나 영적 통찰력을 어떻게 이용하는가는, 의식(儀式)의 궁극적인 목적이 다를 수 있는 것처럼, 상당히 다르다. 많은 샤먼들이 홀로 일하는 반면, 다른 샤먼들은 노동조합 역할을 하는 큰 도시의 단체에 가입해 있다.
이슬람교가 우위를 차지하고 있는 중앙아시아 국가들의 대부분의 샤먼들은 그들 스스로를 독실한 무슬림으로 여긴다. 그리고 그들의 의식에는 수피즘의 신비한 전통들이 녹아있다. 순백색 덧옷으로 (자신들을) 감싸고, 그들은 그들의 의식을 무슬림 성지에서 행하며, 모든 의식은 코란에서 나온 광범위한 기도를 포함하고 있다. 시베리아와 몽고에서 샤머니즘은 현지 불교의 전통과 결합되는데, 너무 많은 것이 결합되었기 때문에 종종 어디가 샤머니즘이 끝나는 곳이고 어디서부터 불교가 시작되는지 말하는 것은 불가능하다.
샤머니즘의 인기가 높아지면서, 의식은 중요한 행사가 되었고, 심지어는 큰 사업이 되었다. 8월의 어느 날 시베리아에 위치한 러시아의 부랴티야 공화국(Republic of Buryatiya)의 햇볕 내리쬐는 목초지에서, 텡게리(Tengeri, 하늘의 영혼)라고 불리는 현지 샤먼 단체 소속의 대략 24명의 사람들이 남색 예복을 입고 탈리간(taligan)이라 불리는 에너지 넘치는 의식을 행했는데, 이는 근처 산의 성스러운 지점에 경의를 표하기 위해서였다. 샤머니즘은 영적 부활과 괜찮은 사업 그 이상을 상징하

unseen a. 눈에 보이지 않는
permeate v. 스며들다, 침투하다
by turns 차례로, 교대로
mystic n. 신비주의자
oracle n. 신탁
designated a. 지정된
exalted a. 높은, 고위층의; 고귀한
anthropologist n. 인류학자
ritual n. 의식절차, 의례
ecstatic a. 황홀해 하는, 열광하는
trance n. 무아지경
employ v. 고용하다, 쓰다
insight n. 통찰력, 이해
ultimate a. 궁극적인, 최후의, 최종의
trade union 노동조합
predominate v. 우세하다
devout a. 독실한
rite n. 의식, 의례
infuse v. 불어넣다, 스미다
Sufism n. 수피즘
swathe v. 감싸다, 뒤덮다
virginal a. 순결한, 무구한

다. 이것은 부랴티야 공화국의 원주민들 사이에서는 소련연방이 무너진 후에 일어난 문화 부흥의 촉매제이기도 하다. 세계에서 가장 깊은 담수호이자 시베리아에서 가장 신성한 장소 중 한곳인, 바이칼 호숫가에서는 민족자결권으로서의 샤머니즘, 즉 부랴트족을 위한 부랴트족의 의식을 목격할 수 있다.

1 ① ▶ 글의 제목
본문은 샤머니즘이 얼마나 널리 많이 퍼져있는지 설명하는 데 주력하고 있으며, 샤머니즘의 인기가 높아서 심지어 사업으로도 발전했다고 언급하고 있다. 그러므로 제목으로 ①이 가장 적절하다.

2 ② ▶ 내용파악
믿음, 관행 혹은 의식이 사람에 따라 다르고, 기구나 통찰력의 사용도 사람마다 다르다고 하였으므로 '개성'이 그 원인이다. ① 민족성 ③ 독실함 ④ 편재성

3 ① ▶ 내용일치
서양인이 샤머니즘에 끌리는 이유에 대해서는 언급한 바가 없으므로 ①은 사실이 아니다. ② 마지막 문단에서, 샤머니즘 의식이 행사, 나아가 사업으로 성장했다고 하였으므로 사실이다. ③ 부랴티야 공화국의 예를 보면 사실이다. ④ 두 번째 문단, 조지타운 대학의 인류학자에 따르면 사실이다.

smock n. 작업복, 덧옷; 기다란 셔츠
merge v. 합병하다, 합치다
sun-drenched a. 햇볕이 많이 내리쬐는
meadow n. 목초지
indigo n. 남색
robe n. 예복, 가운
sacred a. 성스러운, 종교적인
rebirth n. 부활, 거듭남
catalyst n. 촉매, 촉매제, 촉진제
revival n. 재생, 회복, 부활
observer n. 보는 사람, 목격자
self-determination n. 자발적 결정, 민족자결(권)

15 2019 한국항공대

칸트(Kant)는 행복을 극대화하고 미덕을 증진하는 것을 거부한다. 그 둘 중 어느 것도 인간의 자유를 존중하지 않는다고 그는 생각한다. 그러므로 칸트는 자유를 강력히 옹호하는 사람이다. 그러나 그가 제시하는 자유의 개념은 요구조건이 많다. 시장에서 물건을 사고팔면서 우리가 행하는 선택의 자유보다 훨씬 더 요구조건이 많다. 칸트에 따르면 우리가 흔히 시장의 자유 혹은 소비자의 선택이라고 생각하는 것은 단지 처음부터 우리가 선택하지 않은 욕망을 충족시키는 것과 관련된 것이기 때문에 진정한 자유가 아니다. 그러므로, 만약 우리가 자유를 행할 수 있으려면 우리에게 주어지거나 부과된 법칙에 따라서가 아니라, 우리가 스스로 부여한 법칙에 따라 행동할 수 있어야 한다. 그러나 그러한 법칙은 어디에서 나오는 것인가? 칸트의 답은 이성에서 나온다는 것이다. 우리는 감각이 전하는 쾌락과 고통에 지배를 받는 감각적 존재일 뿐만 아니라, 이성을 사용할 수 있는 이성적 존재이기도 하다. 만약 이성이 나의 의지를 결정한다면, 의지는 본성이나 성향이 명하는 바와 무관하게 선택할 수 있는 능력이 된다. (칸트가 이성이 언제나 의지를 지배한다고는 단언하지 않고 있음에 주목해야 한다. 그는 단지 우리가 스스로 부여한 법칙에 따라 자유로이 행동할 수 있는 한에서 이성이 의지를 지배할 수 있는 것이 틀림없다고 말하고 있을 뿐이다.) 물론, 칸트가 인간이 이성을 사용할 수 있다고 주장하는 첫 번째 철학자는 아니다. 그러나 그의 이성 개념은 그의 자유와 도덕 개념과 마찬가지로 특히 요구조건이 많다. 토머스 홉스(Thomas Hobbes)는 이성을 "욕망의 정찰병"이라고 불렀다. 데이비드 흄(David Hume)은 이성을 "정념의 노예"라고 불렀다. 공리주의자들에게 이성의 작용은 무슨 목적이 추구할 만한 가치가 있는지를 결정하는 것이 아니다. 이성이 하는 일은 우리가 우연히 갖게 되는 욕망을 충족시킴으로써 효용을 극대화하는 방법을 알아내는 것이다. 칸트는 이성의 이러한 종속적 역할을 거부한다. 그에게 있어, 이성은 정념의 노예에 불과한 것이 아니다. 만약 이성이 그런 정도에 불과하다면, 우리는 차라리 본능에 따라 살 때 더 행복해질 것이라고 칸트는 말한다. 칸트의 이성 개념, 즉 도덕과 관련된 실천 이성 개념은 도구적 이성이 아니라 "모든 경험적 목적과 무관하게 선험적으로 규정하는(법칙을 만드는) 순수 실천 이성"이다. 그러나 이성은 어떻게 이렇게 할 수 있는가? 칸트는 이성이 의지에게 명령할 수 있는 두 가지 방식을, 즉 서로 다른 두 가지 종류의 명령을 구별한다. 한 종류의 명령은 아마 가장 익숙한 종류의 명령으로, 가언(假言) 명령이다. 가언 명령은 도구적 이성을 사용한다. X를 원한다면 Y를 행하라는 식이다. 기업의 좋은 평판을 갖길 원한다면, 고객을 정직하게 대우하라는 것이다. 칸트는 항상 조건적인 가언 명령과 무조건적인 명령인, 정언(定言) 명령을 대조시킨다. "만약 그 행위가 다른 어떤 것을 위한 수단으로서만 선한 것이라면," "그 (행동을 하라는) 명령은 가언적이다. 만약 그 행위가 그 자체로 선한 것이라면, 그래서 이성과 저절로 일치하는 의지에 필연적인 것이라면, 그 명령은 정언적이다."라고 칸트는 썼다.

demanding a. 부담이 큰, 힘든
sentient a. 지각이 있는
dictate n. 명령, 요구, 규칙
assert v. 주장하다, 단언하다
insofar as ~하는 한에 있어서는
scout n. 정찰병, 척후병
utilitarian n. 공리주의자
subordinate a. 종속의
legislate v. 제정하다
a priori n. 선험적 명제
empirical a. 경험적인
imperative n. 명령
hypothetical a. 가설적인, 가언의
categorical a. 절대적인, 무조건적인
categorical imperative 정언 명령, 지상 명령
jargon n. 뜻을 알 수 없는 어려운 말
alleged a. (혐의로) 주장되는
emphatic a. 단호한, 강한
loophole n. 빠져나갈 구멍, 허점

"정언적"이라는 용어가 어렵게 느껴질지도 모르지만, 그것은 우리가 일상적으로 쓰는 그 용어의 용법에서 그리 멀지 않다. 칸트는 "정언적"이라는 용어를 무조건적이라는 의미로 쓴다. 그러므로 예를 들어, 어떤 정치인이 추문 혐의를 정언적으로 부인한다면, 그 부인은 단순히 단호한 것만이 아니라, 무조건적이다. 다시 말해 그 어떤 허점도, 예외도 없이 부인하는 것이다. 마찬가지로, 정언적 의무 혹은 정언적 권리란 상황과 무관하게 적용되는 의무 혹은 권리이다.

1 ①   ▶ **내용추론**

본문에서 필자는 "칸트는 이성의 이러한 종속적 역할을 거부한다. 그에게 있어, 이성은 정념의 노예에 불과한 것이 아니다."라고 하였고, "칸트의 이성 개념은 도덕과 관련된 실천 이성으로서, 도구적 이성이 아니다."라고 한 것에서 칸트와 대조되는 경험주의 철학자들에게 이성은 '도구적'인 것임을 알 수 있다.

2 ④   ▶ **내용일치**

본문에서 "만약 그 행위가 그 자체로 선한 것이라면, 그래서 이성과 저절로 일치하는 의지에 필연적인 것이라면, 그 명령은 정언적이다."라고 하였으므로 ④의 진술이 본문의 내용과 일치한다.

06 사회·정치

01 2016 한국외대

사랑이 오래 지속되는 것에 대한 낙관론이 오늘날과 같이 항상 있었던 것은 아니었다. 민주주의를 만들었고 독재자들에게 혹사당하는 것을 받아들이지 않았던 그리스 사람들에게, 사랑은 병들게 하는 경험이었고 따라서 되도록이면 짧은 것이 좋은 경험이었다. 그 후, 기사도적인 사랑(특히 중세 문학에서 이미 결혼한 귀부인에 대한 기사의 변함없는 사랑)이 유행하던 시기동안, 사랑은 부정한 것이었고 대개는 치명적이었다. 열정은 고통을 의미했지만 행복한 결말은 문화적 상상력 속에 아직 존재하지 않았다. 17세기까지 행복한 사랑이라는 혁신은 로맨스(연애)의 어휘집에 수록되지도 못했다. 가족이 오이디푸스적 긴장들의 온상이라기보다 주로 경제적인 생산단위였던 18세기 이전에는, 결혼은 가족들 간의 사업적인 합의였고, 결혼 당사자들은 그 문제에 대해 발언권이 거의 없었다. 일부 역사가들은 낭만적인 사랑이 실제로는 18세기 후반 — 이때에도 남편과 아내 사이의 애정은 의심스러운(있을 법하지 않은) 것으로 여겨졌지만 — 에야 비로소 소설을 읽는 새로운 유행과 더불어 시작된 하나의 학습된 행동이라고 생각한다. 물론 역사가들마다 의견이 다르긴 하다. 어떤 역사가들은 사랑의 이야기를 영원하고 변치 않는 정수라고 말하는 반면, 다른 역사가들은 질식할 것 같은 사회적 관례에 대한 진보적인 이야기라고 한다. 그러나 현대적인 사랑이 실제로 우리를 자유롭게 해주었는가? 그렇지는 않다. 우리는 사랑이 사라지면 실패자 같은 느낌이 든다.

optimism n. 낙관론
longevity n. 장수; 오래 지속됨
amenable a. 말을 잘 듣는; ~을 잘 받아들이는
push around 난폭하게 다루다, 괴롭히다
despot n. 전제 군주, 독재자
preferably ad. 오히려, 되도록이면
reign n. 치세, 통치[재위] 기간
courtly love 기사도적인 사랑
illicit a. 불법의, 부정한
fatal a. 치명적인
hothouse n. 온실; 중심지
Oedipal a. 오이디푸스 콤플렉스의
take off 급격히 인기를 얻다[유행하다]
affection n. 애정, 호의
stifling a. 숨 막힐 듯한, 질식할 것 같은; 답답한

1 ③ ▶ 글의 종류
이 글은 고대 그리스부터 현재까지의 사랑에 대한 사람들의 인식 변화를 소개하고 있다. 인간 사회와 인간의 사회적 행위(사랑)를 소개하는 글이므로, ③ '사회학'에서 지정된 글일 것이다.

2 ① ▶ 내용일치
"결혼은 가족들 간의 사업적인 합의였으며, 결혼 당사자들은 그 문제에 대해 발언권이 거의 없었다."라고 돼 있으므로, ①이 본문의 내용과 일치하지 않는 진술이다.

3 ① ▶ 글의 제목
사랑의 지속성에 대한 낙관론이 과거에는 없었다고 언급한 다음, 사랑을 부정하고, 사업적인 합의와 같이 여겨졌던 과거와 달리, 현대에 와서는 어떻게 낭만적인 것으로 변했는지를 설명하고 있다. 그런데 현대에서 사람들이 생각하는 사랑도 실제로 우리를 자유롭게 해주지 못했다고 했으므로, 사랑에 대한 사람들의 생각은 환상에 불과한 것으로 볼 수 있다. 따라서 이 글의 제목으로 적절한 것은 ①이다.

02 2020 한성대

ⓑ 미국은 이민자들의 나라다. 1840년대 이전에는 매년 약 6만 명의 이민자들이 도착했다. 1840년대와 1850년대에, 미국으로 오는 사람들의 수가 급격히 늘어났다. 이 시기에 3백만 명이 넘는 아일랜드인들과 독일인들이 대서양을 건너 미국으로 향했다.
ⓒ 대부분의 아일랜드 이민자들은 극도의 빈곤 속에서 살았다. 대부분이 보스턴과 뉴욕의 빈민가에 정착하여 보수가 낮은 일을 했다. 아일랜드 여자들이 부엌 하녀로 일했던 반면, 남자들은 위험한 일을 하는 저임금의 직업을 가졌다. 그와는 대조적으로, 대부분의 독일 이민자들은 아일랜드 이민자들에 비해 교육도 더 많이 받고 돈도 더 많이 가진 채로 왔다. 그들은 중서부에 땅을 살 수 있었다. 많은 사람들이 오하이오와 위스콘신 같은 주(州)에서 농부가 되었다.
ⓐ 1870년과 1900년 사이에 새로운 이민자들의 물결이 다시금 밀려왔다. 새로 온 사람들 중에는 중국인들이 많았는데, 그들은 대부분 남자였고 캘리포니아에 살았다. 그들 중 많은 사람들이 광산지대와 철도 건설 현장에서 일했고, 요리사, 세탁부, 하인과 같이 천한 직업에서 일했던 사람들도 있

immigrant n. (타국에서의) 이주자, 이민
newcomer n. 새로 온 사람; 초심자
minefield n. 탄광, 탄광지대
construction n. 건설, 건축
menial a. 천한, 비천한
laundryman n. 세탁업자, 세탁소 종업원
servant n. 하인; 부하
harsh a. 호된, 모진, 가혹한
racial prejudice 인종적 편견, 인종 차별
ban v. 금지하다

었다. 그러나 중국인들은 혹독한 인종 차별에 부딪혔다. 1882년, 미국 의회는 중국인 입국금지법을 통과시켜, 거의 모든 중국인들이 미국에 오지 못하게 만들었다.

1 ③ ▶ 문단배열
미국이 이민자들의 나라임을 이야기하면서 1840년대 이전과 1840~1850년대에 미국으로 많은 이민자들이 들어왔음을 언급한 B가 가장 먼저 와야 하고, B에서 이야기한 아일랜드와 독일의 이민자들에 대해 부연 설명하고 있는 C가 그 뒤에 와야 하며, 1870년과 1900년 사이에 들어온 새로운 이민자들에 관한 내용인 A가 마지막에 와야 한다.

2 ③ ▶ 내용일치
"1882년, 미국 의회는 중국인 입국금지법을 통과시켜, '거의 모든' 중국인들이 미국에 오지 못하게 만들었다."고 했으므로, ③이 옳지 않은 진술이다.

3 ② ▶ 빈칸완성
빈칸 전후로 아일랜드 이민자들과 독일 이민자들의 사회·경제적 상황이 대조를 이루고 있으므로, 빈칸에는 '이와는 대조적으로'라는 의미의 ②가 적절하다. ① 마찬가지로 ③ 결과적으로 ④ 그 자체로

extreme a. 극도의, 심한
settle v. 정착하다, 자리잡다, 살다
slum n. 빈민가
wage n. 임금

---

03 2018 서울여대

지난 15년 동안, 나의 조국은 엄청난 정치혁명을 겪었다. 조국의 근대적 창시자였던 무스타파 아타튀르크(Mustafa Ataturk)와 자신들을 동일시하는 기존의 세속적 엘리트 계층들을 종교적 보수주의자들이 대신하게 되었는데, 이들은 최근까지만 해도 대체로 권력을 갖고 있지 않았고 사회의 주변적인 사람들이었다. 이제 종교적 보수주의자들은 언론과 심지어 기업 분야의 상당 부분뿐만 아니라 국가의 거의 모든 기관을 지배하게 되었다.
이 정치혁명은 의도하지 않은 결과를 초래했다. 정치혁명은 이 종교적 보수주의자들의 표면적 도덕성을 시험하게 되었고, 그들은 낙제했다. 그들은 그 시험에서 너무나 끔찍할 정도로 낙제했기 때문에, 그것은 많은 종교인들이 즐겨 주장하는 것처럼 과연 종교성과 도덕성이 정말로 일치하는지에 대해 의문을 제기한다. 종교적 보수주의자들은 한때 그들이 부당하고 잔인하다고 비난했던 모든 것들을 결국은 그들도 했기 때문에 도덕적으로 실패했다. 수십 년 동안, 그들은 정실인사와 부패, 사법부를 무기로 삼은 것, 언론매체를 이용하여 정적을 악마로 만들고 위협을 가한 것 등의 이유로 세속적 엘리트 계층들을 비난했다.

1 ② ▶ 지시대상
종교적 보수주의자들이 비난하고 있는 for 이하의 행위를 하는 주체는 '세속적 엘리트 계층'인데, 밑줄 친 부분은 '이들의 정적'을 가리키므로, 결국 세속적 엘리트 계층의 반대편에 있는 '종교적 보수주의자들'을 가리키고 있음을 알 수 있다.

2 ③ ▶ 내용파악
두 번째 문장에서 새로운 정치 지도자들이 종교적 보수주의자들임을 알 수 있는데, 끝에서 두 번째 문장에서 "종교적 보수주의자들은 한때 그들이 부당하고 잔인하다고 비난했던 모든 것들을 결국은 그들도 했기 때문에 도덕적으로 실패했다."고 했으므로 ③이 정답이 된다.

go through 경험하다, 겪다
colossal a. 거대한; 어마어마한
secular a. 세속의, 비종교적인
identify with (본인·동일물임을) 확인하다; 동일시하다
founder n. 창립자, 설립자, 창시자
replace v. 제자리에 놓다, 되돌리다; 대신하다
conservative n. 보수주의자
marginalize v. ~을 무시하다; 사회 진보에서 처지게 하다; 사회의 주변적 지위로 내쫓다
dominate v. 지배하다, 통치하다, 위압하다
institution n. 기관, 협회; 시설; 제도
sector n. 분야, 영역
inadvertent a. 고의가 아닌, 우연의; 의도하지 않은
ostensible a. 외면의, 표면의, 겉치레의
religiosity n. 종교성, 독실함; 지나치게 종교적임
morality n. 도덕, 윤리
go hand in hand 관련되다, 함께 가다
condemn v. 비난하다, 나무라다; 규탄[매도]하다
unjust a. 부당한, 불공평한, 부정한
cruel a. 잔인한, 잔혹한, 무자비한
criticize v. 비판하다, 비난하다
nepotism n. 친족 등용, 족벌주의, 정실인사
corruption n. 타락, 부패
weaponize v. 무기화하다
judiciary n. 사법부, 사법제도
demonize v. 악마화하다
intimidate v. 위협하다, 협박하다
opponent n. 적, 상대

04 2017 숙명여대

사형제도에 대한 실질적인 반대는 사형수들의 목숨을 실제로 끊는 것에 대한 반대가 아니고, 목숨을 끊는 것을 그렇게도 오랫동안 미루는 우리 미국인의 잔인한 습관에 반대하는 것이다. 결국 우리 모두는 필경 머지않아 죽게 되어 있고, 살인자는 그런 슬픈 사실을 그의 철학(생각)의 초석(기본)으로 삼고 있는 사람으로 생각되어야 한다. 그러나 죽는 것과 죽음의 그림자 밑에서 몇 개월 그리고 심지어 몇 년 동안 있는 것은 상당히 다른 것이다. 분별 있는 사람이라면 그러한 최후를 선택하고 싶지 않을 것이다. 기도서의 내용에도 불구하고, 우리 모두는 종말(죽음)이 재빠르고 예상치 못하게 찾아오기를 갈망한다. 불행하게도, 불합리한 미국의 제도 아래에서 살인자는 그에게는 연이은 순간들이 온통 영원처럼 여겨지는 가운데 고문을 받고 있다. 몇 달 동안 그는 감옥에 있고 그의 변호인들은 영장, 금지 명령, 직무 집행 영장, 상고 등, 그들의 바보 같은 일을 낄낄대며 수행한다. 그의 돈(아니면 친구들의 돈)을 손에 넣기 위해 변호사들은 그에게 희망을 줘야 한다. 때때로 그들은 실제로 자신들의 그런 짓을 판사의 저능함이나 법률학적인 술책 탓으로 돌리며 변명한다. 그러나 이를테면, 살인자의 돈이 다 떨어지게 되면 그들은 마침내 포기한다. 그들의 의뢰인은 이제 밧줄이나 전기의자를 맞이할 처지다. 그러나 그는 밧줄이나 전기의자가 데려가기 전에 또 몇 달을 기다려야 한다.

1 ⑤ ▶ 빈칸완성
빈칸 앞에서 미국 사형제도에 대한 실질적인 반대가 사형수의 목숨을 끊는 것에 반대하는 것이 아니라 사형을 미루는 습관에 반대하는 것이라고 한 다음, 사형수이든 아니든 우리 모두가 필연적으로 맞이할 죽음(must die)에 대해 언급하고 있으므로, 빈칸에는 '결국'이라는 의미의 ⑤ After all이 적절하다. ① 그러므로 ② 그럼에도 불구하고 ③ 불행하게도 ④ 그러나

2 ③ ▶ 내용추론
"기도서의 내용에도 불구하고, 우리 모두는 종말(죽음)이 재빠르고 예상치 못하게 찾아오기를 갈망한다."라고 했으므로, 사람들은 갑작스럽고 예기치 않은 죽음을 원한다고 볼 수 있다. 따라서 ③이 정답이다.

3 ② ▶ 동의어
imbecility가 '저능', '우둔함'의 의미로 쓰였으므로, '어리석음'이라는 의미의 ② stupidity가 가장 가까운 의미의 표현이다. ① 부적절 ③ 지능 ④ 잘못 계산(판단)함 ⑤ 부패

4 ① ▶ 태도
이 글에서 미국의 사법제도는 사형수의 고통스런 심리상태를 전혀 고려하지 않고 오래 기다리게 하고 그 동안 변호사들의 배만 불리게 하는 모습으로 묘사되고 있다. 글 후반부에서 his lawyers carry on their idiotic buffoonery라고 한 것이나, In order to get his money they have to feed him with hope라고 한 것을 통해 저자는 변호사들의 비열한 짓을 빈정대는 냉소적인 어조로 설명하고 있음을 알 수 있으며, 이는 곧 미국의 사법제도를 그러한 태도로 바라보고 있음을 뜻한다. 그러므로 ① sarcastic이 정답으로 적절하다. 저자의 분노한 감정을 드러내고 있지는 않으므로, ②는 정답이 될 수 없다. ② 격노한 ③ 지원하는 ④ 동정적인 ⑤ 현학적인

---

capital punishment 사형
extermination n. 근절, 박멸, 몰살
condemned a. 유죄 선고를 받은; 사형수의
put off (시간·날짜를) 미루다[연기하다]
soon or late 조만간
cornerstone n. 토대, 기초, 초석
metaphysic n. 형이상학, 순수철학, 사유체계
shadow of death 죽음의 그림자
sane a. 제 정신의, (정신적으로) 온건한
long for 열망하다, 갈망하다
swift a. 빠른, 신속한; 순식간의
unexpected a. 예기치 않은, 예상 밖의
irrational a. 불합리한; 이성[분별]이 없는
torture v. 고문하다, 괴롭히다
eternity n. 영원, 무궁
idiotic a. 백치의; 천치의
buffoonery n. 저속한 익살[농담]
writ n. 영장
injunction n. 금지[강제] 명령; 이행 명령
mandamus n. 직무 집행 영장
appeal n. 항소, 상고
now and then 때때로, 가끔
imbecility n. 저능, 우둔
justify v. ~의 정당함을 증명하다, 변명하다
throw up one's hands 두 손 다 들다, 포기하다
fetch v. 가지고[데리고, 불러] 오다; (일격을) 가하다

---

05 2022 한양대

20세기 초, 다양한 학문 분야의 학자들은 서사적 이야기가 인간 사고와 동기 부여의 중심에 있다고 생각하기 시작했다. 사회 운동을 이해하려는 시도를 하면서 사회학자들은 서사적 이야기의 전파가 사회 변화의 중심에 있다고 생각하기 시작했다. 예를 들어, 백인 미국인들이 흑인 차별에 항의하는 시위에 동참했던 1960년대의 연좌 농성 운동을 연구했던 사회학자 프란체스카 폴레타(Francesca Polletta)는 참가 학생들이 그 시위들은 열병처럼 무계획적인 것이며, 몇 번이고 자발적으로 벌어진 것이라고 말한다고 보고하였다. 이러한 시위는 종종 "백인 전용"이라고 표시된 점심 카운터에서 서비스를 요구하는 흑인들에 관한 특정한 대중적 설화에 의해 유발되어 행해졌는데, 여기에는 흑인을 배제하는 것에 대해 도덕적 분노를 표출하던 젊은 백인 지지자들이 동참했다.

---

discipline n. (학문) 분야
narrative n. (사건·경험 따위를) 서술한 것, 이야기
contagion n. (감정이나 태도 등의 빠른) 전염[확산]
demonstration n. 시위
spontaneous a. 자발적인
accompany v. 동반하다
outrage n. 격분

연좌 농성 이야기는 1960년 그린즈버러 대학 학생 4명과 관련된 시위에 관한 한 편의 이야기에서 비롯되었다. 그 이야기는 흑인에게는 서빙이 되지 않는 점심 카운터에서 나가라는 명령을 <따랐던> 흑인 젊은이들을 중심으로 다루었다. 그 젊은이들은 레스토랑이 문을 닫을 때까지 서빙을 기다리며 참을성 있게 앉아 있었고, 다음 날에는 더 많은 젊은이들과 함께 돌아왔다. 이 이야기가 입소문을 타면서, 그리고 뉴스 매체들의 관심을 받으며 널리 퍼져 나갔고, 연좌 농성 시위는 미국 전역으로 확산하였다. 그 이야기의 확산이 완전히 무계획적이었던 것은 아니었다. 활동가들은 이 이야기를 널리 알리려 했다. 그러나 그들이 사회 운동을 전적으로 통제할 수는 없었고, 사회 운동은 주로 입소문에 의지했다. 1960년대에 신조어로 만들어진 연좌 농성(sit-in)이라는 단어는 정말로 크게 유행했다.

revolve around ~을 중심으로 다루다
viral a. (소식이) 빠르게 퍼지는
promulgate v. (사상·신조 등을) 널리 알리다; (법령·제도를) 반포[공포]하다
epidemic n. 전염병; 급속한 확산[유행]

1 ③ ▶ 글의 제목
   이 글은 미국의 1960년대 흑인 인권 운동의 한 부분이었던 연좌 농성의 기원을 이야기하면서 서사적 이야기의 전파가 사회 운동의 핵심에 있다는 견해를 소개하고 있다.

2 ④ ▶ 문맥상 적절하지 않은 표현 고르기
   레스토랑 카운터에서 연좌 농성을 벌였던 흑인 학생들은 흑인에게는 서빙이 되지 않으니 나가라는 명령을 '따랐던(obeyed)' 것이 아니라 '무시하며(ignored)' 가게 문을 닫을 때까지 계속 앉아 있었다.

06 2017 서강대

파시즘은 권력획득 투쟁에 몰두하는 동안, 인구 중 상당한 부분에게 호소력을 지녀야 한다. 독일과 이탈리아에서, 그것은 정통 사회주의 강령에 담긴 모든 반민족주의적 요소를 제거함으로써, 사회주의로부터 생겨났다. 파시즘은 사회주의로부터 경제계획과 국가권력 증대라는 이념을 물려받았지만, 그 계획이라는 것은 전체 세계의 이익이 아니라 한 국가에서 중상류 계급의 이익을 위한 것이었다. 그리고 파시즘은 임금소득자들과 중산층 가운데 인기 없는 부류의 사람들의 효율성을 증대시키기보다는 그들에 대한 억압을 증대시킴으로써 이러한 이익을 확보하고자 한다. 파시즘은 그것의 자선(시혜) 범위 밖에 존재하는 계급들에 대해서는 기껏해야 잘 굴러가는 교도소에서 발견될 법한 종류의 성공만을 성취할 뿐이다. 그 이상은 꿈도 꾸지 않는다.

Fascism n. 파시즘(일종의 우파 정치신념 체계로서 국가가 사회와 경제를 강력하게 통제하며 군대 등 무력에 의지해 일체의 정치적 비판과 저항을 억압하려는 정치이념)
appeal n. 호소; 간청, 애원
considerable a. 상당한
section n. 부분, 부문, 구획
arise v. 발생하다
socialism n. 사회주의
reject v. 거부[거절]하다
orthodox a. (특히 신앙·행동이) 정통의, 전통적인
programme n. (정당의) 강령, 정강(= program)
benevolence n. 자비심, 박애; 자선, 선행
entrepreneur n. 사업가, 기업가
clerk n. 점원, 직원, 사원
aristocrat n. 귀족
doctrine n. 교리; 신조; 정책

1 ④ ▶ 빈칸완성
   빈칸이 있는 문장에서 both of 이하는 efficiency와 oppression 모두에 공통으로 연결되는 구조이다. both of 다음의 '임금소득자들과 중산층 가운데 인기 없는 부류의 사람들'은 파시즘이 이익을 대변해주는 집단이 아니므로, '효율성 증대가 아니라 억압의 증대'라는 의미가 되도록 ④ 'not so much A as B(A가 아니라 B인)'가 적절하다. 문두에 언급된 파시즘이 확보하려고 하는 these interests는 중상류 계급의 이익이다.

2 ④ ▶ 부분이해
   파시즘의 경제정책은 중상류층의 계급적 이익을 옹호한다고 하였으므로, '그 자선(시혜) 범위에서 벗어나 있는 계급'으로는 ④가 적절하다.

3 ① ▶ 내용일치
   본문에서는 "파시즘은 정통 사회주의 강령에서 반민족주의적 요소는 모두 제거하였다."라고만 했다. 파시즘과 사회주의의 정통 신조에 민족주의가 포함되는지에 관해서는 언급하지 않았다. 따라서 ①이 옳지 않은 진술이다.

07 2019 숙명여대

21세기에 들어서 첫 10년 동안, 세계 사회는 엄청난 문제에 직면해 있다. 지구상에는 60억 명의 인구가 있으며, 예측가들은 2050년이 되면 세계 인구가 100억 명이 될 것으로 보고 있다. 그 100억 명의 사람들은 그들로 하여금 만족한 삶을 영위하게 해줄 음식, 주거지, 교육을 필요로 할 것이다. 20세기에는 여러 분야에서 큰 발전이 있었지만, 이런 발전이 대가 없이 이루어진 것은 아니었다. 예를 들면, 산성비는 우리의 식물과 야생 생물, 그리고 수많은 사람들의 몸을 오염시켰다. 전 세계 사람들은 협력하여 지구에 대한 체계적인 약탈(파괴)을 중단시킬 필요가 있다. 핵무기와 사제 폭발물과 같은 무기는 세계의 평화와 발전을 날마다 위협한다. 종교적 광신주의, 기아, 가난은 세계 곳곳에서 무모한 테러를 야기했다. 우리가 지금 전 인류의 생존을 위해 분투하고 있다고 말해도 과장된 표현이 아니다.

1 ③ ▶ 글의 제목
엄청난 문제에 직면해 있는 지구의 상황을 설명하는 글로, 지난 20세기에 인간은 여러 분야에서 큰 발전을 이루었지만, 이런 발전이 대가 없이 이루어지지 않았다고 한 다음 이에 대한 예를 들고 있다. 따라서 ③이 글의 제목으로 적절하다.

2 ④ ▶ 동의어
staggering은 '엄청난, 어마어마한'이라는 뜻이므로, ④ astounding이 대체어로 적절하다. ① 자극적인 ② 의심스러운 ③ 풍부한 ⑤ 정체된

3 ③ ▶ 내용일치
핵무기가 세계의 평화와 발전을 위협하고, 종교적 광신주의가 세계의 곳곳에서 무모한 테러를 야기했다고 한 다음 우리가 전 인류의 생존을 위해 분투하고 있다고 했다. 따라서 이러한 문제들은 쉽게 중단시킬 수 있는 것이라고 보기 어렵다. 그러므로 ③이 정답이다.

confront v. 직면하다, 맞서다
forecaster n. 예측자; (일기) 예보관
project v. 예상[추정]하다
shelter n. 주거지; 대피처
acid rain 산성비
pollute v. 오염시키다, 더럽히다
despoil v. 약탈하다, 빼앗다
improvised a. 즉흥[즉석]의, 임시변통의
explosive device 폭파 장치
desperate a. 필사적인, 무모한
overstatement n. 과장한 말, 허풍

08 2016 홍익대

그러나, 북부에 살고 있던 대부분의 유태인들은 지위가 너무나도 불안정했기 때문에 흑인들을 향해 일관되게 이타적인 행동을 할 수가 없었다. 대신에, 그들은 백인으로서의 자신들의 사회적 우위를 끊임없이 주장하면서도, 자신들의 지위에 문제가 되지 않을 때에는 흑인들에게 관심과 연민을 나타내기도 하는 등, 대체로 훨씬 더 양면적인 양상을 보였다. 주거지 분리 문제가 좋은 예가 된다. 유태인들은 뉴욕과 시카고의 동네 '보호' 협회를 지지했지만, 유태인 언론에서는 종종 그러한 움직임을 비판해야 마땅한 것으로 여겼다. 그러나 『American Hebrew』의 편집자들은 지위 의식이 강한 유태인들이 직면한 딜레마를 궁극적으로 이해하고 있었으며, 유태인들은 "자기들 동네가 아닌 다른 곳에서 흑인들이 발전하는" 한, 틀림없이 흑인들의 사회 발전, 교육, 자급자족을 도울 거라고 편집자들은 생각했다. 과도적인 동네에 사는 많은 유태인들은 거주 제한이라는 불편한 문제를 전적으로 회피하여, 흑인들에게 자신들의 집을 팔고 이사를 가는 쪽을 택했다. 이러한 방식으로, 그들은 자신들과 변하고 있는 동네 사이에 거리를 두고 싶은 한편 흑인들과의 분리 노력에 직접 가담하지 않고 싶은 모순적인 욕망을 충족시킬 수 있었다. 이런 이중적인 욕망은 1919년에 작용하고 있었는데, 그해에 시카고의 템플 이사야(Temple Isaiah)라는 동네의 주민들은 잠식해오고 있던 '흑인밀집지역'에서 딴 곳으로 옮겨가기로 투표로 결정했지만, 흑인들에게 팔지 말라는 하이드파크-켄우드 지역협회의 청원은 무시해버렸다.

1 ② ▶ 내용일치
본문에서의 주거 제한이란 흑인이 유태인 거주 지역에 같이 살지 못하도록 하는 것을 의미하므로, 이것은 이타적인 행동과는 전혀 무관한 것이다.

2 ④ ▶ 동의어
주어진 문장에서 but은 '~을 제외하고', '~외에는'이란 의미의 전치사로 쓰였으므로, except가 이와 같은 의미를 갖는 표현이다.

Jew n. 유태인
insecure a. 불안정한, 위험에 처한, 불안한
status n. 상태; 지위; 자격; 신분
altruistically ad. 이타적으로, 애타적으로
consistent a. (행동·신념 등이) 일치하는; (주의·언행 등이) 시종일관된, 견실한
ambivalent a. 반대 감정이 병존하는
assert v. 단언하다, 주장하다, 역설하다
superiority n. 우월, 우위, 탁월, 우수, 우세
sympathy n. 동정(심), 연민; 공감
residential a. 주거의, 주택에 알맞은; 거주에 적합한
segregation n. 분리, 격리
appropriate a. 적합한, 적절한
editor n. 편집자
dilemma n. 진퇴양난, 궁지, 딜레마
self-sufficiency n. 자급자족
transitional a. 변하는 시기의, 과도적인
restriction n. 제한, 한정, 구속
fulfill v. (약속·의무 등을) 이행하다, 다하다; (조건·요구 등을) 충족시키다
contradictory a. 모순된, 양립하지 않는

3 ④ ▶ 내용추론
유태인들은 흑인과 함께 미국사회에 포함되어 그들을 돕고 싶은 욕망과 자신들은 백인으로서 흑인들과 구별되고 싶은 욕망이 병존하는 상황에 처해 있었는데 이런 상황을 딜레마(dilemma)라고 했으므로 ④를 추론할 수 있다. ① 유태인들이 동네를 흑인으로부터 보호하려는, 즉 흑인이 들어오지 못하게 하려는 협회들을 지지하긴 했지만, 실제로는 흑인에게 집을 팔고 이사를 갔으므로 그 동네에 백인들만 있게 하지는 못했다. ② 첫 문장에서 "일관되게 이타적인 행동을 할 수가 없었다."라고 했다. ③ 둘째 문장과 셋째 문장에 따르면, 거주 문제는 유태인들의 양면성을 잘 보여주는 예이며, 거주 문제가 유태인들의 지위에 의문을 던진 것이 아니라 유태인들이 흑인들에게 관심과 연민을 나타내다가 흑인과 동일시되지 않는가 하는 스스로의 지위에 의문을 갖는 것이 흑인들과 같은 동네에 살지 않으려고 하는 거주 문제를 일으킨 것이다.

dual a. 둘의, 이중의
impulse n. 추진력; 충격, 자극; (마음의) 충동
encroach v. (서서히) 침입하다, 잠식[침해]하다
congregation n. 모임, 집회

09 2020 숙명여대

헌법을 제정한 사람들은 국민의 권리가 항상 안전하고, 중앙정부나 연방정부가 결코 너무 강력해지지 않게 하고 싶었다. 정부는 법을 만들고, 법을 집행하고, 법에 따라 재판을 하는 세 가지 주요 권한을 가져야 한다. 이 세 가지 기능이 한 사람의 손에 들어간다면, 그 사람이 그 권한을 국민보다는 개인의 이익을 위해 사용할 수 있다는 큰 위험이 있을 것이다. 이러한 가능성을 막기 위해 헌법은 정부를 삼부(三府)로 수립했다. 법률을 제정하는 입법부, 법을 집행하는 행정부, 그리고 헌법에 명시된 대로 국민의 권리를 보호하는 사법부가 그것이다. 이들 정부 삼부의 권한은 헌법에 자세하게 기술되어 있다. 삼부의 권한을 기술하는 이유는 어느 한 부가 다른 부들보다 강해지는 것을 막기 위해서였다. 정부의 각 부는 다른 부들과 연계된 조건에서만 기능을 수행할 수 있다. 이러한 제도는 삼부 간의 권력의 균형을 맞출 뿐만 아니라, 각각의 부가 다른 부들에 의해 견제될 수 있도록 한다. 이 제도는 국민의 권익이 언제나 세심하게 보호되고 있다는 것을 의미한다.

Constitution n. 헌법
make sure 확실하게 하다
legislature n. 입법부
executive n. 행정부
judiciary n. 사법부
function v. (제대로) 기능하다

1 ① ▶ 글의 제목
이 글은 권력의 집중을 막기 위한 삼권 분립 제도를 설명하면서, 그 제도의 목적이 삼부의 상호 견제와 권력의 균형을 통해 국민의 권익을 보호하기 위한 것임을 소개하고 있다. 따라서 제목으로는 ①이 적절하다.

2 ⑤ ▶ 빈칸완성
첫째 빈칸에는 make sure의 목적어가 되는 두 번째 명사절을 이끄는 접속사 that이 들어가는 것이 적절하다. 둘째 빈칸에는 prevent ~ from …ing의 전치사 from이 들어가야 한다.

3 ⑤ ▶ 문법적으로 옳지 않은 표현 고르기
ⓔ의 주어는 This system이므로, 단수 주어에 수를 일치시켜 provides가 되어야 한다.

10 2018 중앙대

누구든지 부당하게 투옥시켜버리는 정부 하에서, 정의로운 사람이 있을 진정한 장소는 감옥이다. 매사추세츠(Massachusetts) 주가 보다 자유롭고 덜 낙담한 사람들을 위해 오늘날 제공하는 적절한 장소, 유일한 장소는 감옥이다. 그들 스스로가 이미 자신의 원칙에 따라 추방된 자가 되었으므로 주에서는 자체의 법령으로 그들을 주에서 추방해 감옥에 가두어버린 것이다. 도주한 노예나 가석방된 멕시코인 죄수나 자기네 종족의 억울함을 호소하기 위해 온 인디언은 감옥 속에서, 다시 말하면 분리되어 있기는 하지만 보다 자유롭고 명예로운 곳, 매사추세츠 주가 주에 협력하지 않고 반대하는 사람들을 집어넣는 곳, 노예의 나라에서 자유인이 명예롭게 살 수 있는 유일한 집에서 원칙을 찾아야 할 것이다. 감옥 속에서는 그들의 영향력이 상실되고 그들의 목소리는 더 이상 정부를 괴롭히지 못하며 적으로서 감옥의 벽안에 있을 수는 없으리라 생각하는 사람들이 있다면, 그들은 진리가 오

fugitive n. 도망자
parole n. 가석방
plead the wrongs 유죄라고 답변하다, 잘못을 시인하다
afflict v. 괴롭히다
know by ~를 알고 있다
eloquently ad. 웅변으로, 설득력 있게
irresistible a. 저항할[억누를] 수 없는

류보다 얼마나 더 강한가를 모르며, 스스로 약간의 불의를 겪어본 사람이 얼마나 열렬하고 효과적으로 불의와 싸울 수 있는가를 모르는 것이다. 당신의 온몸으로 투표하라. 단지 한 장의 종잇조각이 아니라, 당신의 온전한 영향력을 내던져라. 소수가 무력한 것은 다수에 순응하고 있을 때이다. 그때는 이미 소수조차도 아니다. 하지만 소수가 온몸으로 막을 때, 그것은 거역할 수 없다. 만약 모든 의로운 이들을 투옥하든가, 전쟁과 노예제도를 포기하든가 양자택일의 선택밖에 없을 때, 주 정부는 주저 없이 어떤 하나를 선택할 것이다. 만약 천 명의 사람들이 올해 세금을 내지 않는다면 그것은 폭력적이고 유혈적인 수단은 아닐 것이다. 세금을 내어 주 정부로 하여금 폭력을 저지르고 무고한 피를 흘리게 만드는 것이 그런 수단일 것이니까. 사실, 이것이야말로, 만약 그런 혁명이 가능하다면, 평화적 혁명의 정의다. 만약 실제로 어떤 공무원이 내게 물었듯이, 세금 징수원이나 여타 공무원이 내게 "저는 어찌해야 합니까?"라고 묻는다면, "진정으로 뭔가 하기를 원한다면, 당신의 직책을 내려놓으시오."라고 답하리라. 국민이 충성을 거부하고, 공무원이 자신의 공직을 버릴 때, 그때 혁명은 완성된다.

clog v. 막다
hesitate v. 망설이다, 주저하다
allegiance n. 충성, 충실

1 ① ▶ 빈칸완성
필자는 정부의 불의한 탄압에 맞서 저항하다가 투옥된 '의로운' 사람들은 감옥에서도 ⓐ '낙담하거나 실망하지' 않고, 자유에 대한 의지를 더욱 불태우며 감옥 안에서도 효과적으로 싸운다고 하였다. 필자는 정부의 폭력과 유혈적 조치를 감소시키거나 포기시키기 위해 일반 시민이라면 세금을 내는 것을 거부하고, 공무원이라면 공직에서 물러나는 방법을 권하고 있으므로, 이는 ⓑ '비폭력적인, 평화적인' 방법이라고 말할 수 있다. ② 용기 있는 — 급진적인 ③ 완고한 — 호전적인 ④ 산만한 — 반항적인

2 ④ ▶ 내용일치
필자는 일반 국민들이 불의한 정부에 저항할 수 있는 가장 효과적인 방법들 중의 하나로 '징세에 저항하는 것'을 제시하고 있다.

11 2014 이화여대

10세기와 11세기의 남부 유럽 사회에서 여성들이 높은 위치에 있었다는 사실을 우리는 종종 깨닫지 못한다. 아내로서의 여성은 결혼지참금, 즉 *decimum*을 지급함으로써 보호받았다. 틀림없이, 이것의 목적은 버려지는 위험으로부터 아내를 보호하는 것이었다. 그러나 실제로 당시의 사회생활과 가족생활에 있어 그것의 기능은 훨씬 더 중요했다. *decimum*은 남편이 가진 총재산의 10분의 1을 아내가 받을 수 있는 권리였다. 아내는 남편이 하고자 하는 모든 거래에 대해 승낙을 유보할 수 있는 권리를 가지고 있었다. 그리고 이것은 단순히 권리에 그치는 것이 아니었다. 문헌기록들은 아내도 남편의 결정권과 똑같은 결정권을 갖고 있었다는 것을 보여준다.
여성들은 월권을 행사하려는 남편에 맞서서 자신들의 유산을 지킬 준비가 철저히 되어 있는 것처럼 보였다. 그리고 때로는 당당히 싸울 태도도 보여주었다. 바르셀로나에 살던 카탈로니아 여성인 마리아 비바스(Maria Vivas)의 경우가 딱 들어맞는 사례다. 살림하는 데 필요해서 그녀가 상속받은 밭을 팔기로 남편 미로(Miro)의 결정에 동의한 후에, 그녀는 보상을 해달라고 졸라댔다. 아무것도 받지 못했을 때, 그녀는 남편을 서기관에게 끌고 가서 미로의 개인 유산으로부터 토지의 일부를 그녀에게 할당한다는 계약서를 정식으로 쓰게 했다.

dowry n. 신부의 지참금
decimum n. <라틴어> 10번째, 10분의 1
desertion n. 버림, 유기, 도망
property n. 재산, 자산; 성질, 특성
consent n. 동의, 승낙
document n. 문서, 서류, 기록
inheritance n. 상속재산, 유산
exceed v. (수량·한도를) 넘다, 초과하다
household n. 가족, 세대
contract n. 계약, 약정; 계약서
duly ad. 정식으로, 정당하게; 지체 없이
assign v. 할당하다, 배당하다; 주다

1 ① ▶ 빈칸완성
아내에게는 남편의 재산 가운데 일부를 가질 수 있는 권리가 있었으므로, 자신의 몫에 영향을 미칠 수 있는 남편의 경제 행동에 영향력을 행사했을 것이다. 남편이 잘못된 거래나 계약을 하는 경우, 자신이 돈을 받지 못하게 될 수도 있기 때문이다. 따라서 첫 번째 빈칸에는 경제 행위와 관련된 transactions나 dealings가 가능하다. 한편, 두 번째 빈칸 뒤의 None being offered는 아내의 요구가 받아들여지지 않았다는 것을 의미하고, 아내는 그에 대해 강제로 재산 분할을 하도록 했다고 했으므로, 애초에 아내는 자신의 밭을 내놓은 것에 대해 반대급부나 보상을 요구했던 것으로 볼 수 있다. 그러므로 두 번째 빈칸에는 compensation만이 가능하다. 따라서 상기 두 조건을 모두 만족시키는 ①이 정답이다. ② 조약 — 협상 ③ 거래 — 법령 ④ 장사 — 청산 ⑤ 경매 — 면책

2 ⑤   ▶ 내용추론
본문에서는 10세기와 11세기 남부 유럽 사회에서 여성들이 누리고 있던 사회적 지위, 특히 아내가 경제적 측면에서 갖고 있던 힘에 대해 설명하고 있는데, 아내가 남편의 재산 일부에 대해 권리를 갖고 있었다거나, 경제 행위에 대해 결정권을 남편과 동등하게 행사했다는 내용이 있으므로, ⑤가 본문의 내용을 통해 유추할 수 있는 내용이다. ①, ② 결혼한 여성의 법적 지위가 미혼 여성이나 남편에 비해 높거나 낮았는지는 알 수 없다. ③ 땅에 국한되는 것이 아니라 모든 재산 가운데 10분의 1을 받을 수 있었다. ④ 장인이 아니라 아내 본인이 동의해야 했다.

3 ①   ▶ 빈칸완성
남편을 데려 가서 재산 분할에 대한 계약서를 썼다고 했으므로, 빈칸에 들어갈 직업은 계약서 작성과 관련된 것이어야 한다. 따라서 '서기관'이라는 의미의 ①이 적절하다. ② 땜장이 ③ 벽돌공 ④ 금속 세공인 ⑤ 대장장이

12   2019 성균관대

최근에 많은 요인들이 결합하여, 이 세계가 금권 정치가들과 과두제 집권층, 그리고 정경 유착한 정치인들에 의해 다수의 이익이 아니라 소수의 이익을 위하는 쪽으로 돌아간다는 인상을 자아내고 있었다.
2억 5천만 명에 달하는 사람들이 전 세계를 이동하고 있어서 우파 포퓰리스트 정치인들에게 그 어느 때보다 많은 공격 수단을 제공하는데, 그들은 정치적 엘리트들이 이민 관리에 실패함으로써 일자리와 임금, 사회적 결속이 위협받고 있다고 주장한다.
한편, 『포브스(Forbes)』지에 따르면 억만장자들의 수는 지난 20년 동안 다섯 배로 껑충 뛰어 2,200명을 넘어섰는데, 이는 세계화로 인해 기업가들이 이용할 수 있는 새로운 시장들이 개방되었고 이와 동시에, 자본과 자산, 수입을 세무당국으로부터 지키는 것이 가능해졌기 때문이다. 세계 최고 부자 8명이 가진 부(富)는 최빈곤층 35억 명이 가진 것과 같다. 금융 엘리트들이 벌어들인 돈은 무려 10조 파운드에 달한다.
그러나 포퓰리즘의 등장을 부분적으로나마 설명할지도 모르는 비경제적 요인들도 많이 있다. 엘리트들에 대한 문화적 반발, 우리 정치의 판을 새로 짜버린 기술 혁명, 이제는 서로 구별할 수 없는 좌우익 정당들의 기술 관료적 중도노선으로의 수렴 등이 그것이다.

a slew of 많은
plutocrat n. 금권 정치가, 부호
oligarch n. 과두제 집권층
semi-detached a. 한쪽 벽면이 옆집과 붙어 있는
ammunition n. 탄약; 공격 수단
populist n. 대중 인기에 영합하는 정치인
get a handle on ~을 관리하다
entrepreneur n. 기업가
tap v. 이용하다
backlash n. (사회 변화 등에 대한 대중의) 반발
convergence n. 집중, 수렴
indistinguishable a. 구별되지 않는

1 ④   ▶ 글의 제목
이 글은 현대에 들어 포퓰리즘이 등장하는 배경을 세계화에 따른 이민의 증가, 금권 정치를 뒷받침하는 거대 재벌의 등장, 정경 유착의 강화, 문화적 반발, 기술 혁명, 좌우익 정파들의 중도노선화 등으로 분석하고 있다.

2 ⑤   ▶ 내용파악
'좌우익 정당들이란 진보와 보수라는 이데올로기를 내세운 정당들인데, 이 정당들이 중도노선으로 수렴된다는 것은 정당들의 이데올로기적 대결은 없어지고 오로지 인기 대결만 있을 것임을 의미하므로 '이데올로기적 대결'은 적절하지 않다.

3 ③   ▶ 내용파악
두 번째 단락에서 우파 포퓰리스트 정치인들에 대해 언급하지만, 문제는 우파 포퓰리즘이 아니라 좌우파를 아우른 포퓰리즘에 대해 묻고 있다. 그런데 첫 번째 단락에 나온 금권 정치가, 과두제 집권층, 정경 유착한 정치인들의 이기적이고 부패한 정치행태가 포퓰리즘 대두의 배경이 된 것이므로 포퓰리즘은 ③의 '부패한 엘리트'에 대해 반대한다고 할 수 있다.

13 2015 서강대

그렇다면, 미국의 객관적인 모습은 심지어 개인과 군중의 형태적인 모습까지도 디즈니랜드 전역에서 그 자취를 찾아볼 수 있을지도 모른다. 미국의 모든 가치들이 이곳에서 축소 모형과 만화의 형태로 고양되어 있는데, 향유를 발라 보존되고 평화롭게 진정된 모습이다. 그래서 디즈니랜드에 대한 이념적 분석이 가능해진다. 즉 이곳은 미국식 생활방식을 요약해 놓은 곳이고, 미국적인 가치에 대해 극찬하는 곳이며, 모순된 현실을 이상화시켜 옮겨놓은 곳이다. 분명히 그러하다. 하지만 이 분석은 다른 무언가를 감추고 있으며, 그 감추는 "이념적" 담요가 3차 시뮬레이션(현실과 현실보다 더 현실 같은 가상현실이 구별할 수 없게 혼재된 과잉현실(hyperreality) 상태를 가리킴)을 덮어 가리는 데 확실히 이바지하고 있다. 그것은 곧 (어디에나 존재하는 완전한 형태의 사회가 바로 감옥이라는 사실을 감추기 위해 감옥이 존재하듯이) "현실" 국가가, "현실" 미국의 모든 것이, 바로 디즈니랜드라는 사실을 감추기 위해 디즈니랜드가 존재한다는 것이다. 사실은 디즈니랜드 이외의 나머지, 즉 로스앤젤레스의 모든 것과 로스앤젤레스를 둘러싼 미국이 더 이상 현실이 아니며 과잉현실 종류의 시뮬레이션의 세계인데도 불구하고 우리로 하여금 현실이라고 믿게 만들기 위해 디즈니랜드는 가상의 것이라는 인상을 주고 있는 것이다. 그것은 더 이상 현실을 거짓되게 표현하는 문제(이념의 문제)가 아니라 현실이 더 이상 현실이 아니라는 사실을 감추는 문제이며, 그래서 (현실이 아니다보니) 현실원칙(현실의 불만을 이성적으로 해결하는 원칙)을 적용하지 않아도 되게 하는 문제이다. 디즈니랜드라는 가상의 세계는 참도 거짓도 아니며 그것은 현실의 허구를 거꾸로 젊어지게 하기 위해 마련된 (노화) 억지 장치다. 그래서 이러한 가상의 세계에는 약함이 있고 유아로의 퇴보가 있다. 그 세계는 다른 어떤 곳에, 즉 "현실" 세계에 어른이 있다고 우리로 하여금 믿게 만들기 위해, 그리고 진짜 유치함이 어디에나, 특히 자신의 진짜 유치함에 대한 환상을 키우기(유치하지 않다고 착각하게 하기) 위해 그곳에 가서 어린아이 행동을 하는 그런 어른들 사이에, 있다는 사실을 감추기 위해 의도적으로 유아의 세계가 된 것이다.

objective a. 객관적인
morphology n. 형태적인 모습, 형태학
exalt v. (명예 따위를) 높이다; (신분 따위를) 올리다; 칭찬하다, 의기양양하게 하다
miniature n. 축소 모형
embalm v. (시체를) 방부 처리하다, 미라로 만들다; ~에 향기를 채우다
pacify v. 달래다, 진정시키다
panegyric n. 찬사, 과장된 칭찬의 말
transposition n. 치환, 전위(轉位)
contradictory a. 모순된, 양립하지 않는
conceal v. 숨기다, 감추다
banal a. 평범한, 진부한
omnipresence n. 편재, 어디에나 있음
rejuvenate v. 다시 젊어지게 하다, 활기 띠게 하다
debility n. (특히 육체적인) 약함; 쇠약, 무기력
degeneration n. 퇴보, 악화, 타락
childishness n. 어린아이 같음; 철없음
foster v. 촉진하다, 조장하다, 육성하다
illusion n. 환각, 착각, 환상

1 ② ▶ 빈칸완성
디즈니랜드를 통해서 실제 미국사회가 디즈니랜드와 같다는 것을 의미한다는 것과 마찬가지로, 감옥을 통해 실제 사회가 감옥과 같다는 것을 의미하는 비유법을 사용하고 있다. 그러므로 사회는 온전한 형태의 "감옥"이어야 논리에 맞는다. 따라서 정답은 '교도소의', '감금을 목적으로 한'이란 의미의 ②이다. ① 비참한 ③ 유약한 ④ 쾌활한

2 ③ ▶ 내용파악
과잉현실은 원본인 현실과 현실을 복제한 가상현실이 구별할 수 없게 같이 있는 것을 말하는데, ①과 ④는 원래의 곳이 아닌 곳에도 복제한 것이 있으며 ②는 현실(reality)을 원본으로 하여 만들어 낸 복제물인 프로그램이므로 과잉현실에 해당되지만, ③은 자연물이다. 따라서 ③이 정답이다.

3 ① ▶ 내용추론
글 마지막 부분에서 현실세계인 미국에는 어른다운 어른이 없고 모두 유치한 어른만 있다고 말하고 있을 뿐, 더 이상 성인기에 이를 수 없다는 말은 아니므로 ①은 추론할 수 없다. ② 끝에서 네 번째 문장에서 이념은 현실을 거짓되게 표현하는 것이라 했고 네 번째 문장의 '미국식 생활방식', '미국적인 가치', '모순된 현실'은 모두 일상생활이라 할 수 있다. ③ 환유어(metonym)는 부분(왕관)이 전체(왕)를 상징하여 나타낸 표현을 말하는데, 네 번째 문장에서 디즈니랜드를 '미국식 생활방식을 요약해놓은 곳'이라 했으므로, 부분인 디즈니랜드가 미국문화의 환유어라 할 수 있다. ④ 마지막 문장이 단서다.

4 ④ ▶ 빈칸완성
빈칸 앞의 in order to rejuvenate와 빈칸 뒤의 in order to make us believe that the adults are elsewhere, in the real world를 통해 빈칸에 '유아의'란 의미의 ④가 적절함을 알 수 있다. ① 반(反)이상향의 ② 단조로운 ③ 저속한

14　2021 숙명여대

남북전쟁 이전 남부의 위대한 정치인이었던 존 C. 캘훈(John C. Calhoun)은 소수가 다수의 뜻을 따르도록 강요하지 않고도 책임 있는 입헌 정부를 가질 수 있다고 생각했다. 그는 소수집단의 중요한 이익에 영향을 미치는 다수결에 대한 거부권을 그들에게 주는 것을 지지했다. 물론 이 해결책이 가진 문제점은 그것이 모든 중요한 문제들에 대해 정부를 비효율적으로 만들고 소수에게 다수의 뜻을 무효화하는 최고의 권력을 주게 된다는 것이다. 영국의 정치 사상가인 존 스튜어트 밀(John Stuart Mill)은 또 다른 해결책을 제안했는데, 이 해결책은 많은 나라의 선거 절차의 일부가 된 비례 대표제였다. 밀은 소수가 상당한 표를 얻으면서도 국가의 입법부에 어떠한 대표도 없는 것이 가능하다고 지적했다. 밀은 "소수대표제"가 다수결 원칙을 따라야 하며, 소수는 비록 최고의 권력은 아니지만 발언권을 가져야 한다고 생각했다. 그는 또한 "복수 투표" 제도를 제안했는데, 이는 고등 교육을 받은 사람 혹은 지식인들에게 더 많은 투표권을 주는 것이다. 비례 대표제가 다양한 정치적 신념에 보다 정의로운 대표성을 부여한다는 것은 의심의 여지가 없다. 그러나 그것은 정부를 불안정하게 만드는 경향이 있으며, 어떠한 단일 정당도 과반을 달성할 수 없는 결과를 낳게 된다. 나는 우리 모두가 다수가 특정한 인권을 앗아가는 것을 막아야 한다는 것에 동의한다고 생각한다. 또한 다수의 사람들이 소수집단에게 종교적 믿음, 정치적 신념, 삶의 방식을 강요하도록 허용해서도 안 된다.

statesman n. 정치인, 정치가
constitutional a. 합법의, 입헌의
submit v. 항복[굴복]하다, 따르게 하다
will n. 의지, 결의
veto power 거부권
majority decision 다수결
remedy n. 처리 방안, 해결[개선]책; 치료(약)
proportional representation 비례 대표제
a system of plural voting 복수 투표제
conviction n. (강한) 신념, 확신
impose v. 부과하다, 강요하다

1　④　▶ 내용파악
　존 스튜어트 밀이 제안한 비례 대표제는 많은 나라의 선거 절차의 일부가 되었다고 했고, "소수대표제"가 다수결 원칙을 따라야 하며 소수도 발언권을 가져야 한다고 생각했다. 그리고 복수 투표 제도를 제안했는데, 이는 고등 교육을 받은 사람 혹은 지식인들에게 더 많은 투표권을 주는 것이라고 했다. 비례 대표제를 수정했다는 내용은 본문에 언급되어 있지 않으므로 ④가 정답이다.

2　①　▶ 내용파악
　"비례 대표제가 다양한 정치적 신념에 보다 정의로운 대표성을 부여한다는 것은 의심의 여지가 없다. 그러나 그것은 정부를 불안정하게 만드는 경향이 있다."라고 했으므로 ①이 정답이다.

3　②　▶ 빈칸완성
　캘훈은 소수집단에게 다수결에 대한 거부권을 주는 것을 지지했다고 했는데, 이렇게 되면 소수집단의 이익에 반하는 다수의 뜻을 거부, 즉 '무효화'하려고 할 것이다. 따라서 ② nullification이 빈칸에 적절하다. ① 확인 ③ 옹호 ④ 설명, 해명 ⑤ 객관화

4　②　▶ 어법
　ⓑ 앞의 주격관계대명사 which의 선행사 majority decisions는 복수명사다. 따라서 ⓑ는 복수동사 affect가 되어야 한다.

15　2018 한국항공대

모든 사회는 상상의 계층 구조를 기반으로 하고 있지만, 반드시 동일한 계층 구조에 기반하고 있는 것은 아니다. 대부분의 경우 계층 구조는 일련의 우연적인 역사적 상황들의 결과로 생겨났고, 그런 다음 다양한 집단들이 계층 구조 속에 기득권들을 발전시킴에 따라 여러 세대에 걸쳐 영속화되고 다듬어졌다. 예를 들어, 많은 학자들은 힌두교의 카스트 제도가 인도-아리안 족이 약 3,000년 전에 인도 아대륙을 침략해 원주민들을 정복하면서 형성된 것이라고 추측한다. 그 침입자들은 계층화된 사회를 세웠는데, 자신들이 지도적 지위(사제와 전사)를 차지하고 원주민들은 종과 노예로 살도록 했다. 수적으로 열세였던 침입자들은 자신들의 특권적 상태와 고유한 정체성을 잃을까봐 두려워했다. 이러한 위험을 사전에 방지하기 위해, 그들은 주민들을 카스트로 나누었는데, 카스트별로 사회에서 특정 직업을 추구하거나 특정한 역할을 수행해야 했다. 각각의 카스트들은 서로 다른 법적 지위, 특권 및 의무를 가졌다. 카스트가 뒤섞이는 것 — 사회적 상호 작용, 결혼, 심지어 식사를 함께하는 것까지 — 은 금지되었다. 그리고 이러한 구분은 단지 법률적인 것이 아니라, 종교적 신화와 관습

hierarchy n. 계급[계층] 구조
perpetuate v. 영속화하다, 불멸[불후]하게 하다
refine v. 다듬다, 정제하다
vest v. 주다, 부여하다
vested interests 기득권
surmise v. 추정하다
subcontinent n. 아대륙
subjugate v. 지배하다, 복종[예속]시키다
stratify v. 계층화하다
privilege v. 특권[특전]을 주다 n. 특권

의 고유한 부분이 되었다. 통치자들은 카스트 제도가 우연한 역사적 발전이라기보다는 영원한 우주의 현실을 반영하는 것이라고 주장했다. 순결과 불순의 개념은 힌두교의 필수 요소였고 사회의 계층 구조를 지지하기 위해 활용되었다. 경건한 힌두교도는 다른 카스트 구성원과의 접촉은 개인적으로뿐만 아니라 사회 전체를 오염시킬 수 있으므로 혐오해야 한다고 배웠다. 그러한 생각은 힌두교도에게만 국한된 것은 아니다. 역사를 통틀어, 거의 모든 사회에서 오염과 순결의 개념은 사회적, 정치적 구별을 시행하는 데 주도적인 역할을 했으며 수많은 지배 계급들은 자신들의 특권을 유지하기 위해 이 개념을 이용해왔다. <그러나, 오염에 대한 두려움이 사제들과 왕족들이 지어낸 순전한 거짓말만은 아니다.> 그것은 아마도 사람들로 하여금 아픈 사람들 혹은 죽은 시체와 같은 잠재적인 질병 운반체들에 대해 본능적인 반발을 느끼도록 만드는 생물학적 생존 메커니즘에 뿌리를 두고 있는 것 같다. 여성, 유대인, 집시, 게이, 흑인 등 어떤 인간 집단을 고립시키려면 이 사람들이 오염의 근원이라는 사실을 모든 사람들에게 납득시키는 것이 가장 좋다.

forestall v. 미연에 방지하다
inherent a. 고유의, 본래의, 타고난, 내재적인
harness v. 이용하다
buttress v. 지지하다
pious a. 경건한, 독실한
abhor v. 몹시 싫어하다, 혐오[증오]하다
enforce v. 집행하다, 시행하다
exploit v. 이용하다, 활용하다; 개발하다
fabrication n. 꾸며낸 것, 거짓말, 날조
revulsion n. 혐오감, 역겨움
Roma n. 집시
accidental a. 우연한, 돌발적인
extant a. (문서·기록 따위가) 현존[잔존]하는
theological a. 신학(상)의, 신학적인

1 ② ▶ 빈칸완성
빈칸 앞에서 "모든 사회의 계층 구조가 반드시 동일한 것은 아니다."라고 하였는데, 동일하다면 거기에 필연성이 있겠지만 그렇지 않다는 것은 우연히 결정된 것임을 말한다. 그리고 빈칸 뒤 문장에서 "그런 다음 계층 구조가 여러 세대에 걸쳐 영속화되고 다듬어졌다."라고 한 것은 처음에는 계층 구조가 역사적으로 특정 세대에 생겨난 일시적인 것이었음을 암시한다. 따라서 빈칸에는 ②의 '우연적인 역사적 상황들'이 적절하다.

2 ④ ▶ 문장삽입
제시문의 내용은 '순결과 오염의 개념은 통치자들이 자신들의 지배를 용이하게 하기 위해 지어내어 이용하는 것'이라는 내용과 '순결과 오염의 개념은 실제로 있을 수 있는 생물학적 오염에 대한 두려움에 기반을 둔 생존 메커니즘'이라는 내용의 중간에 해당한다. 따라서 Ⓓ가 적절한 위치가 된다.

16 2022 성균관대

현재 스스로 민주주의 국가라고 여기는 곳들은 소수의 예외가 있지만 일반적으로 대의제 민주주의라고 알려진 과정에 의해 운영되고 있다. 그 수식하는 형용사(대의제)에 바짝 신경을 쓰고 생각해봐야 한다. 현대 민주주의의 출발점은 모든 분별 있는 성인이 공적인 일의 처리에 있어 동등한 발언권을 가질 권리가 있다는 믿음이다. 어떤 사람들은 다른 사람들보다 부유하고, 어떤 사람들은 더 총명하며, 어느 누구의 관심사도 다른 누군가의 관심사와 완전히 같지는 않다. 그러나 어떻게 통치되어야 하는지를 결정하는 데 있어서 모든 사람은 동등한 목소리를 낼 권리가 있다. 따라서 대부분의 민주주의에서 유권자들이 대통령을 선택하거나 대표를 선출된 의회에 보내는 선거에서 이 목소리가 몇 년에 한 번만 들린다는 사실과, 그 선거들 사이에, 최대 7년의 기간 동안 모든 결정을 내리는 것은 대통령과 국회의원인 반면, 민주주의에 속한 나머지 사람들은 자신과 무관한 승인에 대해 고개를 끄덕이거나 불만스러운 의견 차이에 대해 으르렁거리듯 말하면서 어느 정도 조용히 한쪽에 비켜서 있을 것으로 예상된다는 사실에는 뭔가 이상한 점이 있다. 이것은 시간제 민주주의이다.

몇몇 곳에는 민주주의를 시행하는 다른 방식이 존재하는데, 직접 민주주의라 불린다. 이런 직접적인 민주주의에서는, 선출된 대표들이 선거와 선거 사이의 기간 동안 자기 생각대로 하게 허용되지 않는다. 대부분의 사람들이 동의하지 않는 대표들의 어떤 결정을 취소하거나 때로는 대표들에게 원하지 않거나 생각지도 못했던 일을 하라고 주장함으로써 나머지 국민들은 언제든지 그들에게 잠자코 있으라고(직무를 정지하라고) 명할 수 있다. 이것이 행해지는 절차가 국민투표, 즉 국민 전체의 투표이다.

a handful of 소수의
representative a. 대표하는, 대리의
sit up 자세를 바로 하다[바로 앉다]
starting point 출발점
sane a. 제정신인, 분별 있는
be entitled to ~에 대한 권리가[자격이] 주어지다
odd a. 이상한, 특이한
parliamentarian n. 의회 의원
nod v. (고개를) 끄덕이다
irrelevant a. 무관한, 상관없는
growl v. 으르렁거리듯 말하다
straightforward a. 간단한, 복잡하지 않은; 직접의
call ~ to order ~에게 규칙을 지키도록[조용히 하라고] 명하다, 정숙히 할 것을 명하다
machinery n. 조직, 시스템, 기구; 복잡한 일련의 절차
referendum n. 국민 투표, 총선거

1 ⑤ ▶ 글의 제목
첫 번째 단락에서는 대의제 민주주의를 설명하고, 두 번째 단락에서는 직접 민주주의의 운영 과정에 대해서 설명하고 있으므로 ⑤가 글의 제목으로 적절하다.

2 ③ ▶ 내용파악
대의제 민주주의에서 유권자의 목소리는 대통령을 선택하거나 대표를 선출된 의회에 보

내는 선거에서만 들리고, 모든 결정을 내리는 것은 대통령과 국회의원이라고 했다. 따라서 필자가 대의제 민주주의를 시간제 민주주의라고 주장한 것은 사람들의 목소리, 즉 유권자의 목소리가 선거에서만 들리기 때문이므로 ③이 정답이다.

3 ③　　▶ 부분이해

left to one's own devices는 '제멋대로 하도록 허용된'이란 의미이므로 ③이 정답이다.

---

17 2014 고려대

사람들은 거지들과 보통의 "일하는" 사람들 사이에 어떤 본질적인 차이가 있다고 느끼는 것 같다. 거지들은 별개의 인종 — 범죄자와 같이 버림받은 자 취급을 받는다. 일하는 사람들은 "일을 하고", 거지들은 "일을 하지" 않는다. 그래서 거지들은 사회에 기생하는 존재들로, 본질적으로 무가치하다는 것이다. 거지는 벽돌공이나 문학 비평가가 자신의 생계비를 "버는 것"과는 달리, 자신의 생계비를 "버는 것"이 아니라고 여겨진다. 그는 사회의 군더더기에 불과하며, 우리가 인도적인 시대에 살고 있기에 용납되긴 하지만, 본질적으로 비천한 존재다. 그러나 주의 깊게 들여다본다면, 거지의 생계와 무수히 많은 훌륭한 사람들의 생계 사이에 본질적인 차이는 없다는 것을 알게 된다. 거지들은 일을 하지 않는다고들 하지만, 과연 일이란 무엇인가? 막일꾼은 곡괭이를 흔들며 일한다. 회계원은 숫자를 더하면서 일한다. 거지는 궂은 날씨에도 실외에 서서, 하지 정맥류와 만성 기관지염 등을 견디면서 일한다. 거지는 여느 다른 직업과 마찬가지로 하나의 직업이다. 물론, 전혀 쓸모가 없긴 하지만 말이다. 그러나, 쓸모없기는 다른 많은 평판 좋은 직업들도 마찬가지다. 그리고 하나의 사회적 유형으로서 거지는 수십 가지 다른 유형들과 견줄 만하다. 그는 대부분의 특허 의약품 판매상들에 비해 정직하고, 일요 신문 사주에 비해 고결한 편이며, 할부구입 호객꾼에 비해 상냥하다. 간단히 말해, 거지는 기생충이지만 상당히 무해한 기생충이다. 그는 자기의 지역사회로부터 그저 생계에 필요한 것 이상을 뜯어가는 일이 없으며, 우리의 윤리적 사고에 따라 그를 합리화시키자면, 그는 그것을 얻기 위해 거듭된 고통 속에서 대가를 치르고 있다. 나는 거지를 다른 사람들과 다른 부류로 분류할 만한 어떤 것, 혹은 대부분의 현대인들에게 그를 경멸할 권리를 부여할 만한 어떤 것이 있다고 생각하지 않는다.

1 ③　　▶ 부분이해

excrescence는 '군살, 군더더기'라는 뜻으로, 불필요한 존재를 의미한다. 따라서 '성가신 존재, 귀찮은 존재'를 뜻하는 nuisance가 의미상 가장 가깝다. ① 사회의 보루 ② 사회의 감시 ④ 사회의 중재자

2 ④　　▶ 빈칸완성

필자에 따르면, 거지는 이른바 다른 많은 평판 좋은 직업을 가진 대부분의 사람들에 비해 거의 피해를 끼치지 않는다. 따라서 보통 사람들에게 '그를 경멸할 권리는 없다'고 추론할 수 있다.

3 ④　　▶ 글의 제목

무가치한 존재, 사회의 군더더기, 사회에 기생하는 존재 취급을 받는 거지들도 분명히 대가를 치르면서 그들의 생계를 이어가고 있으며, 그들에 비해 보통 사람들이 가치적인 면에서나 도덕적인 면에서 우월할 것이 특별히 없다고 필자는 말한다. 그러므로, 필자는 거지들의 처지와 보통 사람들의 그것이 별반 다를 것 없다고 보는 것이다.

4 ①　　▶ 글의 어조

이 글은 표면적으로는 거지에 관한 이야기를 하고 있지만, "거지는 쓸모없긴 하지만, 쓸모없기는 다른 많은 평판 좋은 직업들도 마찬가지다."라든지, '대부분의 의약품 판매상들이 정직하지 못하고, 신문사 사주들이 고결하지 못하며, 할부판매자들은 정나미 떨어지는 사람들'이라는 등의 간접적 암시를 통해, 현대 사회에 존재하는 다양한 직업과 그 직업인들이 실제로 사회에 거지보다 더 큰 해악을 끼치고 있다고 비꼬고 있다. 따라서 이 글의 어조로는 ① ironic(비꼬는)이 적절하다. ② 도취감을 일으키는 ③ 고백적인 ④ 향수를 불러일으키는

---

essential a. 극히 중요한; 본질적인
outcast n. 버림받은 사람, 부랑자
parasite n. 기생동물
bricklayer n. 벽돌공
excrescence n. (군살·사마귀 등의) 이상 생성물; 무용지물
tolerate v. 용납하다, 용인하다
humane a. 인도적인
despicable a. 비루한, 천한
livelihood n. 생계, 생활
respectable a. 존경할만한, 훌륭한
navvy n. 인부, 막일꾼
swing v. 흔들다; 돌리다
pick n. 곡괭이
accountant n. 회계원, 회계사
varicose vein 하지 정맥류
bronchitis n. 기관지염
reputable a. 평판이 좋은; 훌륭한
patent medicine 특허 의약품
high-minded a. 고결한, 고매한, 고상한
proprietor n. 소유자, 경영자
amiable a. 쾌활한, 싹싹한, 정감 있는
hire-purchase n. 할부구입
tout n. 암표상; 호객꾼, 삐끼
extract v. 뽑다, 얻다, 추출하다
justify v. 옳음을 보여주다, 정당화하다
rationale n. 이론적 근거; 근본적 이유
immortalize v. 영원성을 부여하다, 불멸하게 하다
venerate v. 공경하다, 숭배하다
proselytize v. 개종시키다; 전향시키다
ignominy n. 불명예, 수치
ups and downs 곡절, 성쇠, 부침(浮沈)

18   2020 중앙대

B 정치적 안정을 정의하려는 시도는 정치와 정치 구조의 개념을 명확히 하는 것으로 시작해야 한다. 정치적 행위란 사회를 위한 결정을 내릴 권력을 분배하는 데 영향을 미치는 사회 구성원에 의한 어떤 행위를 말한다. 정치적 행위는 어디에나 존재한다. 사회 구성원들은 사회의 법에 복종하거나 불복종하여 권력 계층 체제를 지지하거나 훼손하는 한, 정치적으로 행동하게 된다. 법에 복종하는 것이 선거에서 경쟁하는 것만큼이나 정치적 행위가 된다.

A 왜냐하면, 의도했든 안 했든, 법에 대한 복종의 영향은 법은 어떤 것이어야 하며 법은 어떻게 집행되어야 하는가에 대해 결정하는 사람들의 권위를 지지하는 결과를 낳기 때문이다. 이 권위를 지지하는 것은 사회를 위한 결정을 내릴 권력을 분배하는 것의 양상들을 유지하는 데 도움을 주는 것이다. 마찬가지로, 모든 법 위반도 역시 정치적 행위가 되는데, 이는 모든 법 위반이 사실상 기존의 성립된 권위에 대한 저항이기 때문이다. 그것은 사회를 위한 결정을 내릴 권력을 분배하는 기존 패턴의 유지를 위협한다. 만약 법을 위반하는 사건이 계속해서 증가한다면, 정치적 권위는 결국 위축된다. 그것은 자명한 이치다.

C 우리는 분명 정치적인 특정한 행위를 정치적이지 않은 행위와 구별 짓는 통상적인 의미로 정치적이라는 것의 정의를 내리지 않았다. 또 그러한 정의는 내릴 생각도 없는데, 정치적이라는 것을 그런 식으로 기술하는 것은 오해를 불러일으키기 때문이다. 엄밀히 말해, 본질적으로 비정치적인 인간 행위는 없으며 심지어 머리를 길게 기르는 것만큼이나 단순한 행위조차도 본질적으로 비정치적인 행위인 것은 아니다. 이것이 사실인 이유는 어떤 행위의 "정치적임"은 그 행위에 내재된 속성이 아니라, 그 행위를 연구하는 맥락과 그 행위가 발생하는 맥락에 따라 정해지는 그 행위에 대한 특성 규정이기 때문이다.

D 예를 들어, 우리는 일반적으로 머리를 길게 기르는 것을 정치적 행위의 한 형태로 간주하지 않을 것이다. 그러나 청교도적인 독재자라면 이러한 행위를 타락한 것으로 판단하고 그에 따라 모든 사람들에게 머리를 짧게 자르라고 명령할지도 모른다. 그러한 포고령이 널리 강력하게 공표된 직후에, 그 독재자로부터 국가 기념식에 참석해달라는 초청을 받은 모든 사람들이 머리를 길게 기르고 온다고 가정해보라. 그런 경우에 우리는 이 사람들이 정치적 불복종이라는 매우 과감한 행동을 저지르고 있다는 결론을 당연히 내릴 것이다.

1 ② ▶ 단락배열
정치와 정치적 구조 개념에 기초한 정치적 안정에 대한 정의는 이 글의 주제문으로 시작하는 B가 제일 먼저 오고, B에서 법에의 복종과 불복종이 정치적 행위가 된다고 했는데 그 이유를 설명한 A가 온 다음, 지금까지 언급된 '정치적 행위'의 '정치적'이라는 특성이 행위의 본질적 속성이 아니라 맥락(상황)에 따라 정해지는 특성임을 말한 C가 온 다음, 그 이유를 머리를 길게 기르는 행위를 예로 들어 설명한 D가 오는 것이 논리적 흐름에 맞는 순서이다.

2 ④ ▶ 글의 주제
글의 첫째 문장 "정치적 안정을 정의하려는 시도는 정치와 정치 구조의 개념을 명확히 하는 것으로 시작해야 한다."에 이 글의 주제가 잘 드러나 있다.

---

obedience n. 복종, 순종
uphold v. (법·원칙 등을) 유지시키다, 지지하다
enforce v. 집행하다
ipso facto ad. 사실상
defiance n. 저항
incidence n. 발생 정도
atrophy n. 위축
axiomatic a. 자명한
clarify v. 분명하게 하다
ubiquitous a. 어디에나 존재하는, 편재하는
stratification n. 계층, 성층
demarcate v. 경계를 정하다, 구별 짓다
delineate v. 기술하다, 묘사하다
intrinsically ad. 본질적으로
puritanical a. 청교도적인
despot n. 독재자
decree n. 포고, 명령
legitimately ad. 합법적으로, 정당하게

---

19   2021 홍익대

1997년에 미국 의회가 연방법 위반 범죄 혐의로 기소되는 14세 이상의 청소년들은 성인으로서 재판을 받고 성인 교도소에 투옥되도록 하는 법을 통과시켰을 때, 그들은 미국 모든 주(州)들의 선례를 따르고 있었다.

하지만 형사사법제도상의 성인 연령을 낮추는 것이 엄청난 인기를 얻고 있음에도 불구하고, 그것이 범죄 발생을 낮추는 데 효과가 있다는 증거는 없다. 사실은, 아이러니하게도, 증거는 그 반대임을 보여주고 있다.

분명히, 석방되면 대중들이 결코 보호를 보장받을 수 없을 청소년 사이코패스 살인자들도 있다. 신문 헤드라인에 오를 만한 잔혹한 청소년 살인 사건은 매우 끔찍하지만, 중대한 청소년 범죄에서 극히 일부만을 차지한다. 성인 법정에서 재판을 받고 성인 교도소로 보내지는 청소년들 대부분은 살

require v. 요구하다, 규정하다
juvenile n. 청소년 a. 청소년의
charge v. 고발하다, 고소하다
try v. 재판하다
incarcerate v. 투옥하다, 감금하다
follow the lead 선례를 따르다
tremendous a. 무시무시한; 엄청난
lower v. 낮추다, 내리다

인보다 더 가벼운 범죄로 그곳에 보내지며 언젠가는 석방될 것이다.
지금까지 접할 수 있는 모든 연구는 성인 교도소로 보내지는 청소년들이 소년원에 남아 있는 청소년들보다 재범률이 더 높다는 사실을 보여준다. 그것은 성인 교도소에 보내지는 청소년들이 일단 석방되면 대중들을 위험하게 하고 훨씬 더 높은 비율로 다시 체포되는 경향이 있다는 것을 의미한다.
성인 교도소에서 복역한 청소년들이 석방될 때 소년원에서 복역한 청소년들보다 훨씬 더 위험한 이유는 자신들의 삶을 바꿀 수 있는 청소년들의 경우, 소년원에서 그들이 필요로 하는 생활 기술들을 습득할 가능성이 가장 높기 때문이다. 전부는 아니지만 대부분의 아이들에게, 아이들을 구하기 위해 세워진 소년원에서의 교육과 치료는 실제로 효과가 있다.
확실히, 사회복귀는 성공률이 100%는 아니며, 청소년이 사회복귀를 할 능력이 없거나 사회복귀에 마음을 열지 않는 그런 드문 경우에는 특히 그러하다. 내가 얘기를 나눴던 한 십대는 — 그 아이를 제시(Jesse)라고 부르겠다. — 일견 자녀 양육을 잘 해 보이는 이민 온 노동자 계급의 부모와 성공한 형제자매가 있는 좋은 가정을 버리고 학교에 다니지 않으면서 싸움과 범죄를 저지르는 사실상의 노숙자 생활을 선택했다. 그는 왜 자신이 불안정한 삶을 더 좋아했는지를 내게 분명하게 말하지 못했다.

1 ③ ▶ 내용추론
네 번째 문단의 "성인 교도소에 보내지는 청소년들이 소년원에 남아있는 청소년들보다 재범률이 더 높은데, 이것은 성인 교도소에 보내지는 청소년들이 석방되고 나서 대중들을 위험하게 할 가능성이 더 높다는 것을 의미한다."는 내용을 통해 ③을 추론할 수 있다.

2 ② ▶ 글의 목적
'청소년을 성인 법정에서 재판받게 하고 성인 교도소로 보내는 것이 재범률만 높일 뿐 청소년 범죄 감소에 그다지 도움이 되지 않음'을 이야기하고 있는 내용이므로, ②가 글의 목적으로 적절하다.

3 ① ▶ 내용파악
제시에 관한 내용은 "사회복귀는 성공률이 100%는 아니며, 청소년이 사회복귀를 할 능력이 없거나 사회복귀에 마음을 열지 않는 그런 드문 경우에는 특히 그러하다."라는 진술 뒤에 이어지고 있으므로, 제시는 사회복귀에 실패한 사례로 언급된 것이라 할 수 있다.

---

adulthood n. 성인, 성년
criminal justice system 형사 사법 제도
evidence n. 증거
crime n. 범죄
opposite a. 정반대의, 상반되는
psychopathic a. 정신병(성)의, 사이코패스적인
murderer n. 살인자, 살인범
release v. 방면하다, 석방하다
assure v. 보증하다, 보장하다; 납득시키다
nightmarish a. 악몽 같은
brutal a. 잔인한, 사나운
infinitesimal a. 극소의, 극미의
fraction n. 파편, 단편; 소량
lesser a. 적은 편의, 떨어지는 편의
homicide n. 살인
recidivism n. 상습적 범행, 재범
rate n. 비율
facilities n. 시설, 설비
endanger v. 위태롭게 하다, 위험에 빠뜨리다
rearrest v. 다시 체포하다
serve v. (임기·연한·형기 따위를) 채우다, 복무하다
counterpart n. 대응 관계에 있는 사람[것]
rehabilitation n. 사회복귀, 갱생
abandon v. 버리다, 버리고 떠나다
seemingly ad. 보기엔, 외관상
immigrant n. 이주자, 이민
sibling n. 형제, 자매
essentially ad. 본질적으로
articulate v. (생각·감정을) 분명히 표현하다[설명하다]
rootless a. 불안정한

---

20 2018 세종대

16세기에 토마스 모어(Thomas More)경은 자신의 책 『유토피아(Utopia)』에서 상상 속의 이상적인 사회를 묘사했다. 그가 묘사한 유토피아 사람들은 생명을 죽이는 행위와 결부되는 잔인함을 자유 시민들이 경험하기를 원하지 않았기 때문에 노예들만 동물을 죽일 수 있도록 했다. 현대의 도축장에서는 종종 불필요한 고통을 많이 겪게 하면서 가축들을 죽여 왔다. 동물들은 비참한 두려움과 고통으로 스트레스를 받아 왔다.
저명한 동물행동학자인 템플 그랜딘(Temple Grandin)은 도축장의 환경을 개선하고, (고통을 주지 않는 도축을 요구하는) 연방정부의 인도주의적 도축 법령에 대해 미국 정부에 자문을 제공하고, 미국 식용육 협회에 지침을 작성하는 일에 관한 유력한 권위자다. 그녀의 실용적 (도축장) 설계는 소가 일렬로 걷기 때문에 앞에 있는 소를 세 마리만 볼 수 있고, 소가 예기치 않은 것을 봄으로써 걸음을 멈추는 일이 없도록 통로가 180도로 굽어 있도록 도축장의 경사로를 설계하는 것이다. 높은 벽이 있고, 그림자나 시끄러운 소리가 없고, 폭력도 없고, 발밑이 미끄럽지 않은 경우, 동물들은 두려움 없이 앞으로 나아가고, 업계의 능률성도 향상된다. 많은 동물복지 옹호자들은 우리가 고기를 완전히 먹지 말아야 한다고 말하지만, 가축들은 인간의 목적을 위해 쓰이는 것이다. <그리고 그랜

slave n. 노예
cruelty n. 잔인함, 무자비함; 학대
slaughterhouse n. 도살장, 도축장
abject a. 비참한, 절망적인
renowned a. 유명한, 명성이 있는
guideline n. (보통 pl.) 지침
ramp n. (높이가 다른 두 도로나 건물의 사이를 연결하는) 경사로, 램프
cattle n. 소; 가축
single file (앞뒤) 한 줄로, 일렬종대로
slippage n. 미끄러짐
underfoot ad. 발밑에, 땅에

딘은 인간이 이 동물들에 대해 보살피는 역할을 인식해야 한다고 믿고 있다.>
동물 운동가들은 사람들에게 송아지 고기 업계의 잔혹한 환경에 대해서도 경고했다. 태어나는 순간 어미소를 뺏기게 되는 수컷 송아지는 혼자 작은 우리 속으로 넣어지며, 목에 사슬을 매기 때문에 걸을 수도 없다. 이 모두는 고기를 더 부드럽게 유지하기 위한 것이다. 철분과 섬유질이 부족하고 화학 물질, 항생제, 호르몬으로 가득 찬 유동식으로 기른 그 송아지들은 생후 4개월경에 실제로 도살장으로 끌려가게 된다. 영국에서는 그와 같은 환경이 현재 금지돼 있으며, 미국의 많은 소비자들과 요리사들은 이런 방식으로 기른 송아지 고기를 구입하거나 조리하는 것을 거부하고 있다.

소고기를 먹는 것에서 가금류의 고기를 먹는 것으로 바꾸는 경우도 마찬가지로 늘어나고 있다. 그러나 공장처럼 거대한 창고 속에 층층으로 된 철제 우리 안에 꼼짝달싹할 수 없게 갇혀 있는 병아리들에게도 항생제와 호르몬을 먹인다. 운송과 도축이 이뤄지는 환경은 종종 끔찍할 정도다. 그 결과, 소비자들은 "걱정 없는" 달걀과 "유기농" 닭만을 이용하는 매장에 관심을 갖게 되었다. 비용이 추가됨에도 불구하고, 동물을 그처럼 다루는 것에 대한 소비자들의 혐오와 식품 공급의 산업화(공장에서의 대량 생산화)에 대한 우려로 인해, 이러한 추세는 늘어나고 있다.

1 ③ ▶ 내용일치
그랜딘의 설계는 관련 업체의 능률성도 높일 수 있지만, 도축을 앞둔 소가 겪는 고통과 두려움의 시간을 줄여주기 위한 목적이 더 크다고 봐야 한다. 따라서 순전히 수익을 지향하는 목적만을 가진 것으로는 볼 수 없다.

2 ③ ▶ 내용추론
"비인간적인 방식으로 송아지 고기를 생산하는 관행에 대해, 많은 소비자들과 요리사들은 이런 방식으로 기른 송아지 고기를 구입하거나 조리하는 것을 거부하고 있고, 붉은 고기를 먹는 것에서 가금류의 고기를 먹는 것으로 바꾸는 경우도 마찬가지로 늘어나고 있다."고 했는데, 전자와 후자 모두 제품을 선택하고 구입하는 소비자의 힘을 이용하여 잘못된 관행을 바로잡고자 하는 노력들이므로, ③이 정답으로 가장 적절하다.

3 ② ▶ 동의어
deficient는 '불충분한', '부족한'이라는 의미이므로, '불충분한'이라는 의미의 insufficient가 적절하다. ① 견딜 수 없는 ③ 모양이 흉한 ④ 무능한

4 ② ▶ 글의 목적
본문은 '소의 사육과 도축이 비인간적으로 이루어지고 있고, 닭고기의 생산과정도 이와 크게 다르지 않음'을 이야기하고 있으므로, 글의 목적으로는 ②가 적절하다.

5 ② ▶ 문장삽입
주어진 문장은 "그리고 그랜딘은 인간이 이 동물들에 대해 보살피는 역할을 인식해야 한다고 믿고 있다."라는 의미이므로, 이 문장의 뒤에는 동물을 보살피려는 노력에 대한 구체적인 내용이 이어져야 한다. ⒝의 뒤에 위치한 두 문단에서 끔찍한 도축 환경을 개선시키려는 정부와 소비자들의 움직임에 대한 내용이 있으므로, ⒝에 주어진 문장이 들어가는 것이 적절하다.

livestock n. 가축
veal n. 송아지 고기
calf n. 송아지
pen n. 우리, 축사
liquid n. 액체, 유동체
deficient a. 모자라는, 불충분한, 결핍한
fiber n. 섬유, 섬유질
chemical n. 화학물질
antibiotic n. 항생물질
literally ad. 글자 그대로; 아주, 사실상
ban v. 금지하다, 금하다
consumer n. 소비자
chef n. 주방장, 요리사
switch n. 전환, 변경
poultry n. (식용의) 가금(家禽); 닭고기
confine v. 제한하다; 감금하다, 가둬넣다
transportation n. 수송, 운송
appalling a. 섬뜩하게 하는; 지독한, 형편없는
industrialization n. 산업화, 공업화

07 경제·경영

01 2014 경희대

보호무역주의는 국가가 자국의 산업이 다른 국가들에 의한 불공정 경쟁으로 피해를 입고 있다고 생각하는 경우에 사용된다. 보호무역주의는 방어적 조치이며, 대개 정치적인 동기를 갖고 있다. 그것은 단기적으로는 종종 효과를 볼 수 있다. 그러나 장기적으로는 대개 의도하는 바와 정반대의 효과를 낳는다. 그것은 그 국가와 그 국가가 보호하고자 하는 산업이 국제 시장에서 경쟁력이 떨어지도록 만들 수 있다. 국가는 자국의 무역을 보호하기 위한 다양한 방법들을 사용한다. 그 중 한 가지 방법은 관세를 법으로 정하여, 수입품에 세금을 부과하는 것이다. 이로 인해 수입된 제품은 가격이 즉시 오르게 되어, 국내에서 생산된 제품과 비교해 볼 때 경쟁력이 떨어지게 된다. 이것은 많은 제품을 수입하는 미국과 같은 국가에서 특히 좋은 효과를 거둔다. 가장 잘 알려져 있는 사례는 1930년에 만들어진 스무트-할리 관세법(Smoot-Hawley Tariff)이다. 그것은 처음에는 제1차 세계대전의 파괴 후에 농업을 강화하고 있던 유럽산 수입 농산품으로부터 농민들을 보호하려는 목적을 갖고 있었다. 그러나 법안이 의회를 통과했을 때는 이미, 더 많은 수입품에 관세가 부과되었다. 관세를 부과하는 경우 흔히 일어나듯이, 다른 국가들이 보복을 했다. 이러한 관세 전쟁은 세계 무역을 제한하였으며, 대공황이 가혹하게 오래 지속된 이유 가운데 하나였다.

1 ② ▶ 내용파악
본문의 세 번째 문장과 네 번째 문장에, "보호무역주의가 단기적으로는 종종 효과를 볼 수 있으나 장기적으로는 대개 의도하는 바와 정반대의 효과를 낳는다."고 돼 있다. 따라서 ②가 본문에서 언급하지 않은 내용이다.

2 ③ ▶ 빈칸완성
이어지는 문장 속의 '이러한 관세 전쟁'이라는 표현이 단서가 된다. 전쟁이란 쌍방 간에 이뤄지는 싸움이므로, 결국 한 국가가 자국의 산업보호를 위해 관세를 부과하는 경우 상대국 역시 관세를 부과함을 알 수 있다. 즉, 관세에 대해 관세로써 '보복'을 가하는 것이다. 그러므로 빈칸에 들어가기에 적절한 표현은 ③이다. ① 받아들이다 ② 줄어들다 ④ 혼동하다

trade protectionism 보호무역주의
unfair a. 불공정한, 불공평한
competition n. 경쟁; 경쟁자
defensive a. 방어적인; 수세의
measure n. 치수; 분량; 한도; 방책, 수단
motivate v. ~에게 동기를 주다, 자극하다
intention n. 의향, 의지; 목적, 의도
enact v. 법제화하다; 제정하다
tariff n. 관세, 관세표; 관세제도
agricultural a. 농업의
step up ~을 증가시키다[강화하다]
destruction n. 파괴; 파멸; 멸망
slap v. 집행하다; (벌금 따위를) 징수하다, 부과하다
restrict v. 제한하다, 한정하다; 금지하다
extend v. 늘이다, 연장하다; 연기하다
severity n. 엄격, 가혹; 엄중
the Great Depression 대공황

02 2015 한양대 에리카

직원들이 얼마나 업무수행을 잘 하고 있는가를 평가하는 것은 모든 조직의 인적자원관리에 있어서 핵심적인 부분이다. 대부분의 기업들은 1년에 1~2회에 걸쳐 업무수행평가를 실시한다. 널리 쓰이고 있는 방법들에는 정해진 목표와 직원들의 실제 성과를 비교하는 '목표관리제도', 함께 일하는 직원들이 서로를 평가하는 '동료평가', 고위간부에서 동료직원, 고객, 납품업체에 이르는 모든 사람들로부터 직원 평가가 이뤄지는 '360도 평가', 그리고 심지어 직원이 스스로를 평가하는 '자기평가' 등이 있다.
제대로 진행되는 경우, 상세한 업무수행평가는 여러 가지 이익을 가져다준다. 그것은 성공을 확인하고 보상하는 데 도움을 줘서, 직원들에게 보다 더 뛰어나고자 하는 동기를 부여해 준다. 그것은 실적을 바탕으로 한 임금 인상이나 승진을 결정하는 데 이용될 수 있으며, 개선하거나 보다 많은 훈련이 필요한 부분을 강조하는 데도 도움을 줄 수 있다. 적어도, 그것은 직원으로 하여금 회사가 필요로 하고 있는 것과 기대하고 있는 것을 보다 잘 이해할 수 있게 해준다.

1 ① ▶ 빈칸완성
Ⓐ의 경우, '함께 일하는 직원이 서로를 평가'하는 것이므로 동료평가라는 의미가 되도록 Peer-to-Peer가 적절하고, Ⓑ의 경우, 고위간부에서 동료직원, 고객, 납품업체에 이르는 '모든 사람들로부터 평가가 이뤄지는 것'이므로, 전방위 평가라는 의미가 되도록 360

assess v. (재산·수입 따위를) 평가하다, 사정하다; (사람·사물 따위의 가치를) 평가하다, 판단하다
human resource management 인적자원관리
appraisal n. 평가, 견적, 사정, 감정
evaluate v. 평가하다
detailed a. 상세한, 정밀한
raise n. 임금 인상, 가격 인상
promotion n. 승진, 진급
highlight v. 강조하다

Degree가 적절하다. ② 일방적인 — 전면적인 ③ 통신의 — 상의하달식의 ④ 상호적인 — 하의상달식의

2 ③   ▶ **내용일치**
업무수행평가가 잘 진행되는 경우, "성공을 확인하고 보상하는 데 도움을 줘서, 직원들에게 보다 더 뛰어나고자 하는 동기부여를 해 주고, 실적을 바탕으로 한 임금 인상이나 승진을 결정하는 데 이용될 수 있으며, 직원으로 하여금 회사가 필요로 하고 있는 것과 기대하고 있는 것을 보다 잘 이해할 수 있게 해 준다."라고 했다. 이는 곧 업무수행평가가 직원에게 많은 이점이 있음을 이야기하고 있는 것이므로, ③이 본문의 내용과 일치하는 진술이다.

03 2017 중앙대

경기주기의 한 국면으로 확장국면이 있다. 이 국면은 이중적이어서 회복과 번영이라는 두 측면을 갖고 있다. <확장국면을 촉발하는 것은 번영 그 자체가 아니라 번영에 대한 기대다.> 회복기에는 기존설비가 계속 확장되고, 새로운 생산설비가 생겨난다. 더 많은 사업체들이 생겨나며 기존의 사업체들은 확장된다. 다양한 분야에서의 발전이 이루어진다. 경제성장의 미래에 대한 낙관론이 점점 증폭된다. 많은 자본이 기계 산업 또는 중공업에 투자된다. 고용도 증대된다. 더 많은 원자재가 필요하게 된다. 경제의 한 부분이 발전하면서 다른 부분들에 영향을 미친다. 예를 들어, 자동차 산업에서의 대규모 성장은 철강, 유리, 고무산업의 확장을 가져온다. 도로도 필요하게 된다. 따라서 시멘트와 기계 산업이 활기를 띠게 된다. 노동력과 원자재에 대한 수요는 농민을 비롯해서 원자재를 공급하는 측과 노동자의 번영을 가져온다. 이는 다시 구매력과 사고 팔리는 상품 총량의 증대를 가져온다. 이런 식으로 번영이 전체 인구의 다양한 부분들로 확산된다. 이 번영은 분명한 종식도 없이 계속 상승과 상승을 거듭할 수 있다. 하지만 이 시기가 정점에 달하고 나선형의 상승을 멈추는 시기가 찾아온다. 이때가 바로 확장국면의 끝이다.

phase n. 단계, 국면
two-fold a. 이중적인
recovery n. 회복; 되찾음
prosperity n. 번영, 번창
facility n. (보통 pl.) 설비, 시설
optimism n. 낙관주의
raw material 원자재
volume n. 부피, 총량
diffuse v. 뿌리다; 확산하다, 보급시키다
segment n. 구획, 부분
apparent a. 분명한, 명백한; 외견상의
spiraling a. 상승하는
recession n. 경기후퇴

1 ①   ▶ **글의 흐름상 적합하지 않은 문장 고르기**
둘째 문장에서 "이 국면은 이중적이어서 회복과 번영이라는 두 측면을 갖고 있다."라고 하였고 Ⓐ 다음에서 '회복'과 관련된 설명과 '번영'과 관련된 내용이 이어지고 있다. 그런데 Ⓐ의 내용은 확장국면을 일으키는 원인에 관한 언급이므로 이 자리에 있기에는 적합하지 않다.

2 ②   ▶ **내용추론**
"경제의 한 부분이 발전하면서 다른 부분들에 영향을 미친다."고 함으로써, 확장국면의 이익이 한 부분에서 다른 부분으로 파급되는 현상을 설명하고 있다. ①, ③, ④는 본문에서 언급된 적 없으며 추론할 수 있는 근거도 없다.

04 2021 한국외대

'임베디드 마케팅(끼워 넣기 마케팅)'이라고도 불리는 '제품간접광고(PPL)'는 브랜드들이 제품을 다른 형태의 매체에 끼워 넣음으로써 그들의 목표 대상에게 다가가는 판매 전략이다. 브랜드의 제품이나 서비스를 이렇게 끼워 넣는 것은 영화나 TV와 같은 오락물에서 종종 발견된다. 대중매체에서 제품간접광고를 하는 예로, 당신이 보았던 영화를 생각해 보라. 만일 주연배우가 '코카콜라' 라벨이 분명하게 붙은 음료수를 마시거나 '삼성' 라벨이 분명하게 붙은 휴대폰을 사용하고 있다면, 이것은 제품간접광고에 해당한다. 대부분의 경우, 대형 브랜드들은 자사 브랜드가 영화에 들어가도록 거액을 지불했을 것이다. 제품간접광고의 비용이 높을 수도 있지만, 그에 대한 보상은 그 브랜드에게 훨씬 더 클 수 있다. 예를 들어, 허쉬(Hershey)는 영화 "E.T."에 자사의 초콜릿을 끼워 넣었더니 수익이 65%나 급상승했다. 제품간접광고는 수익을 증가시킬 뿐 아니라, 브랜드 인지도도 끌어올릴 수 있다. 『경영마케팅연구 저널』은 어떤 브랜드가 어떤 TV프로에서 광고되었을 때 그 브랜드가 그 프

product placement (영화·텔레비전 프로를 이용한) 제품간접광고(PPL)
merchandising n. 판매
strategy n. 전략
embed v. ~을 꽂아[끼워] 넣다
namely ad. 즉, 다시 말해
lead actor 주연배우
payout n. 보상
aside from ~뿐 아니라

로에 끼워 넣어진 것을 TV 시청자들 중 57.5%가 인지했다고 추정한다. 비록 이것이 즉각적인 매출로 이어지지는 않지만, 높아진 브랜드 인지도가 결국에는 당신의 사업에 이익을 가져다줄 것이다.

boost v. 끌어올리다
estimate v. 추정하다
translate v. ~로 변화하다

1 ①   ▶ 내용파악
본문에서 제품간접광고는 수익의 증가뿐 아니라, 브랜드 인지도도 끌어올릴 수 있다고 했으므로, ①이 정답이다.

2 ④   ▶ 빈칸완성
빈칸이 들어있는 주절 앞의 부사절에 양보의 접속사 even if가 왔으므로 부사절의 내용과 주절의 내용은 서로 대조를 이루어야 한다. 부사절에서, 높아진 브랜드 인지도가 즉각적인 매출로 이어지지는 않는다고 했으므로, 주절에는 즉각적인 것과 대조가 되는 '장기적으로는, 결국에는(in the long run)' 당신의 사업에 유익이 될 것이라고 해야 문맥상 적절하다. 따라서 빈칸에는 ④의 the long run이 적절하다. ① 창조적인 방식 ② 단기간 ③ 그 동안

05   2016 한양대

회사는 뛰어난 제품을 가지고 있고 당연히 소비자들이 이 제품을 그들이 구매할 수 있는 가장 좋은 제품이라고 생각해주기를 원한다. 그래서 마케팅 팀은 특징과 가격이라는 측면에서 왜 이 제품이 경쟁제품보다 더 우수한가를 보여주는 광고를 제작하며, 탄탄한 매출액으로 보상 받는다. 하지만 그런 성공을 누리는 대신, 그 회사는 많은 불평과 환불요청을 받기 시작한다. 분명, 그 전략이 역효과를 낳은 것이다. 그렇지만 왜일까? 비교를 통한 광고와 "우리 제품이 최고야!"라는 제품 포지셔닝(자사의 제품이나 상표를 표적시장 내 고객들에게 어떠한 것으로 알려야 할 것인가를 결정하는 활동)은 사람들이 완벽하지 않은 모든 것을 돈 낭비로 여기게 만드는, 최고지향 심리라고 알려진 것을 활성화시키는 것으로 드러났다. 우리 연구는 비록 일부 사람들은 천성적으로 '최고지향자'이고 다른 사람들은 "그 정도면 됐어."라는 말로 만족해하는 경향이 있지만, 그러한 태도들이 고정된 것은 아니라는 것을 알아냈다. 최고지향 심리는 사람들로 하여금 비교해보고 가장 좋은 것을 찾도록 부추기는 상황에 의해서 유발될 수 있다. 마케팅 메시지가 무심코 그것을 유발할 때, 그 결과는 구입 후의 후회이거나 약간의 실망에도 브랜드를 교체하는 것(다른 브랜드를 구입하는 것)일지 모른다.

naturally ad. 당연히, 물론
roll out 제작하다, 만들다
superior a. 우수한, 보다 나은, 뛰어난
robust a. 강력한, 풍부한
bask in (햇볕을) 쬐다; (은혜 등을) 입다, (관심·칭찬 등을) 누리다
complaint n. 불평, 불만
comparative a. 비교의, 비교에 의한
maximizer n. 최고지향자
by nature 선천[천성]적으로, 본래
inadvertently ad. 무심코, 우연히
induce v. 유도하다, 유발하다
contingent a. ~을 조건으로 하는, ~에 부수하는

1 ③   ▶ 빈칸완성
광고를 제작하여 높은 판매고로 보상 받는 것이 성공인데, 광고 후에 불만과 반품을 받게 되는 것은 실패이며, 광고 전략이 잘못된 것이다. 따라서 첫 번째 빈칸에는 failed나 recoiled나 backfired가 적절하다. 두 번째 빈칸의 경우에는, brand switching(브랜드를 교체하는 것)의 원인은 구입상품에 대한 실망일 것이므로, disappointment가 적절하다.
① 실패하다 — 역경 ② 반동하다 — 개선 ④ 몸부림치다 — 만족

2 ②   ▶ 내용일치
최고지향자들은 본인 스스로 비교하는 경향이 있다고 했지 타인까지 비교하도록 유도한다고 한 적은 없다. 따라서 ②는 글의 내용과 거리가 멀다.

06   2018 성균관대

아날로그 시대의 유익한 선례가 전혀 없는 기업 모델을 가지고 있는 소수의 막강한 거대 기업들의 부상은 자본주의 경제가 움직이는 방식을 재평가하게 하고 있다. 전 세계에서 가장 가치 있는 상위 7개 기업은 모두 기술 분야에 있다. 구글의 모기업인 알파벳(Alphabet)과 페이스북과 같은 거대 기업들은 3차원 공간에 존재하지 않는 상품을 전문으로 한다. 애플과 아마존은 상품의 콘셉트뿐만 아니라 실제 세계의 물건도 판매하지만, 이 기업들의 많은 자산과 시장에서의 우위는 디자인, 브랜드, 알고리즘과 같은 모호한 개념들을 바탕으로 만들어졌다.
부는 더 이상 공장, 송유관 또는 소매판매점에 있지 않다. 그들의 자본은 특정 분야에 고정되어 있지

a handful of 소수의
powerhouse n. 최강자, 최강 기구[단체, 기업]
instructive a. 교훈[교육]적인, 유익한
precedent n. 선례, 전례
reappraisal n. 재평가, 재검토
dimensional a. ~차수의; ~차원의

않다. 그것은 그 기업들을 규제하기 힘들게 하고 세금을 부과하기 어렵게 만든다. 이것들은 디지털 혁명보다 앞선 경제적 세계화의 패턴들이다. 예를 들면, 소프트웨어와 데이터와 같은 일부 무형 자본은 컴퓨터에 크게 의존하지만, 브랜드와 같은 다른 무형 자본은 그렇지 않다.

새로운 시대를 다르게 만드는 것은 가치가 유형 자본에서 분리되는 정도와 이에 상응하는 사회 경제적 결과다. 이것은 조너선 해스켈(Jonathan Haskell)과 스티언 웨스틀레이크(Stian Westlake)가 '자본이 없는 자본주의'라고 설명한 역동적 체제다. 그 제목의 그들의 책에서 저자들은 무형적인 것의 규모가 시장 경제라는 친숙한 메커니즘을 변형시키는 여러 방법을 조명한다.

1 ② ▶ 부분이해
현재 세계에서 가장 가치 있는 기업들은 유형 자본이 아닌 지식, 소프트웨어, 브랜드, 데이터와 같은 무형 자본의 토대 위에서 성장하고 있다고 했으므로, without capital이란 '무형 자본'을 의미한다고 볼 수 있다. 따라서 ②가 정답이다.

2 ③ ▶ 글의 제목
전 세계에서 가장 가치 있는 거대 기업들이 무형의 자본을 바탕으로 크게 성장하고 있음을 소개하고 있으므로, 글의 제목으로는 ③이 적절하다.

fortune n. 부(富); 자산
dominance n. 우세, 우위
pipeline n. 송유관; (상품 따위의) 유통[공급] 경로
retail outlet 소매판매점
anchor v. 정박시키다; ~에 단단히 기반을 두다
pre-date v. ~보다 먼저[앞서] 오다
intangible a. 실체가 없는, 무형의; 만질 수 없는 것, 실체 없는 것; (특히) 무형 자산
detach v. 떼어내다; 분리하다
tangible a. 만져서 알 수 있는; 분명히 실재하는[보이는], 유형의
corresponding a. 해당[상응]하는
illuminate v. (이해하기 쉽게) 밝히다[분명히 하다]
intangibility n. 만질 수 없음[없는 것], 무형의 것
deform v. 변형시키다

---

07 2020 한성대

주식회사에는 공개 주식회사와 비공개 주식회사가 있다. 공개 주식회사의 주식은 일반인이 살 수 있다. 이와는 대조적으로, 갈로 와인(Gallo Wine), 레비 스트라우스(Levi Strauss), 혹은 유나이티드 파슬 서비스(United Parcel Service) 등과 같은 비공개 주식회사의 주식은 소수의 사람들만이 소유하고 있으며 대개 일반인에게 팔지 않는다. 대주주는 가족 구성원이나 경영진일 수 있으며, 회사의 직원들일 수도 있다. <알려지지 않은 주식은 매수자를 끌어들이지 않는 경향이 있기 때문에, 대부분의 신생 주식회사들은 비공개 주식회사로 출발한다.>

주식회사는 몇 가지 장점이 있다. 가장 큰 장점은 유한책임이다. 투자자의 책임은 그들이 개인적으로 회사에 투자한 금액에 한정된다. 파산하는 경우에, 법원이 주식회사의 자산을 압류하여 매각할 수는 있지만 투자자의 개인 재산을 마음대로 처분하지는 못한다. 예를 들어, 만약 당신이 어떤 회사에 1,000달러를 투자했다가 그 회사가 파산한다면, 당신은 그 금액 이상을 잃을 수 없다. 다시 말해, 1,000달러가 당신이 지는 책임의 한도인 것이다. 또 다른 장점은 연속성이다. 주식회사는 소유주들의 생물학적 생명과 무관한 법적 생명(유효기간)이 있기 때문에, 적어도 이론상으로는, 영원히 존속할 수 있다. 예를 들어, 주식은 미래 세대에게 상속하는 것이 가능하다. 끝으로, 주식회사는 돈을 모으는 데 있어서 우위에 있다. 예를 들어, 더 많은 주식을 판매함으로써 투자자의 수와 자금의 양을 쉽게 늘릴 수 있다.

1 ② ▶ 문장삽입
주어진 문장은 "알려지지 않은 주식은 매수자를 끌어들이지 않는 경향이 있기 때문에, 대부분의 신생 주식회사들은 비공개 주식회사로 출발한다."라는 의미로, 비공개 주식회사에 대한 부연설명에 해당하므로 B에 들어가는 것이 적절하다.

2 ② ▶ 빈칸완성
소유주들의 생물학적 생명과 무관한 법적 생명(유효기간)이 정해져 있고 주식이 미래 세대에게 상속이 가능하다면, 주식회사는 현실에서는 어떨지 몰라도 '적어도 이론상으로는' 영원히 존속할 수 있는 것으로 볼 수 있다.

3 ③ ▶ 내용일치
주식회사는 소유주들의 생물학적 생명과 무관한 법적 생명(유효기간)이 있고 주식회사의 주식은 미래 세대에게 상속하는 것이 가능하므로 최초 투자자들이 사망한 후에도 존속할 수 있다.

corporation n. 법인; 주식회사
stock n. 주식
controlling stockholder 대주주
management group 경영진
liability n. 책임, 의무; 책임액수
investor n. 투자자
amount n. 총계, 총액
seize v. 빼앗다; 탈취하다
asset n. 자산, 재산; 이익
dispose of 처분하다, 팔아버리다, 버리다
possession n. 소유; (pl.) 재산
at will 뜻대로, 마음 내키는 대로
go bankrupt 파산하다
continuity n. 연속, 연속성
legal life 법정 유효기간
independent of ~에 관계없이
inherit v. (재산·권리 따위를) 상속하다, 물려받다
have the upper hand 이기다, 우세하다

08　2021 단국대

국가들마다 서로 다른 경제체제를 선택할지도 모르지만, 모든 국가들은 생산에 관심이 있다. 경제체제에 대한 모든 논의는 생산의 요소라고 설명되어 온 것들에 대한 이해를 필요로 한다. 모든 생산에는 자원, 노동, 자본, 그리고 경영이라는 네 가지 개별적인 요소가 수반된다.

자연이 제공하는 원료인 자원은 우리가 원하는 것들을 생산하는 데 반드시 필요하다. 일부 경제학자들은 이 요소를 토지라고 부르는 쪽을 선호한다. 땅 속의 광물, 숲, 폭포, 비옥한 토양은 모두 한 국가가 가진 자원의 예에 해당한다. 자원은 국가의 생산을 결정하는 데 있어 중요한 의미를 갖는데, 이는 자원이 점점 더 부족해지고 있기 때문에 특히 그러하다.

자원을 인간이 사용하기에 적합하도록 만들기 위해서는 가공을 해야 한다. 이것은 생산의 두 번째 요소인 노동에 의해 이루어진다. 생산을 결정하는 데는 기술과 노동량도 중요할 것이다. 인도는 미국보다 노동 인구가 두 배 이상 많지만, 미국 노동자의 기술이 더 뛰어나기 때문에 생산성은 훨씬 더 높다. 우수한 교육 덕분에 미국은 기계의 이용에 편승할 수 있었다.

생산의 세 번째 요소는 자본이다. 대부분의 사람들은 자본을 돈으로 생각한다. 경제학자에게 자본은 인간이 만든 모든 생산 수단이다. 다시 말해, 생산을 증진하는 데 사용된 모든 재화를 일컫는 것이다. 종종, 그것은 도구나 기계를 의미할 것이다. 그것은 또한 자동차의 생산에 사용되는 압연강판을 의미할 수도 있다. 만약 많은 자본을 숙련된 인력에 투입한다면 생산성을 엄청나게 증가시킬 수 있다.

1 ③　▶ 내용일치
보통 사람들은 자본을 돈으로 생각하지만, 경제학에서는 인간이 만든 모든 생산 수단을 자본으로 간주한다. 그러므로 ③이 옳지 않은 진술이다.

2 ②　▶ 빈칸완성
본문에서 설명하고 있는 자본은 생산의 4대 요소로서의 자본이며, 이것은 경제학 분야에서 다루는 내용이므로 ②가 적절하다. ① 심장병 전문의 ③ 환경보호론자 ④ 인류학자

3 ①　▶ 뒷내용 추론
생산의 네 가지 요소로 언급한 것 가운데 경영에 대한 내용이 없으므로, 다음 문단에서는 경영에 대한 설명이 이어질 것이다.

require v. 요구하다, 명하다; 필요로 하다
describe v. 묘사하다, 기술하다; 간주하다
ingredient n. 성분; 재료; 구성요소, 요인
involve v. 수반하다, 필요로 하다
factor n. 요인, 요소
capital n. 자본(금)
entrepreneurship n. 기업가 정신
material n. 재료, 물질, 원료
mineral n. 광물
fertile a. 비옥한, 기름진
soil n. 흙, 토양
determine v. 결정하다; 확정하다
particularly ad. 특히
scarce a. 부족한, 결핍한
adapt v. 적응시키다, 적합하게 하다
amount n. 총계, 총액; 양(量)
productivity n. 생산성
capitalize on ~을 이용하다, ~에 편승하다
instrument n. 기계, 기구, 도구
further v. 진전시키다, 조장하다, 촉진하다
tool n. 도구, 연장
rolled steel 압연강판, 압연강
skilled a. 숙련된, 능숙한
tremendously ad. 엄청나게, 굉장하게

09　2019 한양대

어떤 상품이 그 상품의 성공의 희생자가 될 수도 있다. 어떤 상품이 워낙 새롭거나, 워낙 혁신적이거나 마케팅이 워낙 잘 되어 시장과 소비자들의 마음을 지배해버릴 때, 그 상품의 상표명을 그 상품 자체와 연관 지어 생각하기가(상표명을 듣고 곧바로 상품을 떠올리기가) 쉬울 수 있다. 어떤 유형의 상품이 그 상품의 특정 버전을 나타내는 상표명으로 널리 알려지거나 언급되면, 그 상표명은 "일반명사화"의 희생자가 된다. 아스피린(아세틸살리실산), 에스컬레이터(움직이는 계단), 포고스틱(스카이콩콩)은 원래 상표명이었는데, 성공과 인기로 인해 그 이름이 너무나 일반적으로 그리고 광범위하게 사용되다 보니 애초의 발명가나 모기업은 그 등록 상표를 지킬 수 없게 되었거나, 심지어 한때 명확한 상표명이었던 용어로 표현되는 유사 상품들에 대해 경쟁적 우위를 상실하게 되었다. 신뢰받는 상표명으로서의 정체성을 상실한 하나의 용어가 영원히 일반 명사화된 상품으로 인식되는 데에는 한 번의 법원 결정이면 충분하다. 이런 일이 벌어지면, 회사는 소비자들의 의식 속에 있는 이윤 창출의 교두보 하나를 잃기 쉽다. 일반 명사화로 인한 수입원의 상실은 그런 일이 일어나지 않도록 막기 위해 회사가 많은 돈을 쓰는 것으로 더욱 심해진다. 법적 대응과 홍보 활동을 위해 수백만 달러를 썼음에도 불구하고, 킴벌리 클라크(Kimberly-Clark) 사(社)는 사람들이 모든 종류의 화장지를 크리넥스(Kleenex)라고 부르지 못하게 하기 위해 힘거운 싸움을 벌이고 있다.

1 ③　▶ 내용일치
'아스피린, 에스컬레이터 등은 원래 상표명이었다가 성공과 인기로 인해 그 이름이 일반적으로 그리고 광범위하게 사용되었다'는 진술에 비추어 볼 때, ③은 일치하지 않는다.

brand name 상표명
generic a. 통칭의
trademark n. 등록 상표
generic product 상표 없는 상품, 일반 명사화된 상품명(통칭되는 상품)
beachhead n. 상륙 거점, 해안 교두보
revenue n. 수입원, 수익
compound v. 더욱 심하게 하다
uphill battle 힘든 싸움

2 ① ▶ 빈칸완성
본문에서 '어떤 유형의 상품이 그 상품의 특정 버전을 나타내는 상표명으로 널리 알려지거나 언급되면, 그 상표명은 "일반 명사화"의 희생자가 된다', '경쟁적 우위를 상실하게 된다', '이윤 창출의 교두보 하나를 잃게 된다' 등의 내용을 바탕으로, '어떤 상품의 성공이 오히려 그 상품에 피해를 줄 수 있다'는 글 전체의 요지를 파악할 수 있는데, 그러한 의미가 빈칸에 들어가야 한다.

10 2018 인하대

많은 사업주들에게 있어서, 직원을 최대한 활용하는 것은 연중 끊이지 않는 문제다. 과수원 농사를 짓는 농부들의 경우, 아마도 "연중 끊이지 않는"은 잘못 쓰인 단어일지도 모른다. 일하는 사람들이 여름철 수확기에만 모습을 드러내기 때문이다.

과수원 농사는 과일을 따는 사람들에게 힘든 일이지만, 과수원 주인에게도 골칫거리인 것은 마찬가지다. 왜냐하면 주인은 최저임금법을 충족시키는 한편 느릿느릿 일하고 싶은 유혹이 드는 것도 이해할만한 산업(과수재배업)에서 일꾼들에게 동기도 부여할 수 있는 임금체계를 마련해야 하기 때문이다. 그리하여 좀처럼 있기 힘든 협력 관계가 영국의 대형 과수재배업체 주인과 경제학자 팀 사이에 형성됐다. 경제학자들은 임금, 작업장에서의 유대관계, 근로자의 생산성 사이의 연관성을 연구하기 위해 임금체계를 설계하고 시행했다.

경제학자들은 하급 관리자들에 대한 인센티브에 관심을 돌렸는데, 왜냐하면 그들은 그 자신들도 임시 이주 노동자들인 한편, 밭의 어느 줄에 어느 작업자들을 할당하는가와 같이 현장에서 이루어지는 결정에 대한 책임을 지고 있기 때문이다. 경제학자들은 관리자들이 친구들에게 가장 쉬운 줄을 할당함으로써 그들에게 호의를 베푸는 경향이 있음을 발견했다. 이것은 내부 사람들은 편히 살게 해주긴 했어도 생산적이지는 못했는데, 왜냐하면 과일을 따는 일을 함에 있어서 가장 효율적인 임무 할당 방법은 가장 일을 잘 하는 작업자들에게 가장 좋은 줄을 맡기는 것이기 때문이다. 경제학자들은 그에 대한 대응으로 관리자의 보수를 매일매일의 수확량과 연관시켰다. 그 결과, 관리자들은 자신들의 친구들 대신 가장 일을 잘 하는 작업자들을 선호하기 시작했고, 생산성은 20퍼센트 증가했다.

1 ③ ▶ 빈칸완성
"하급 관리자가 자신과 친분이 있는 작업자들을 편한 곳에 배치하는 관행에 대해 경제학자들은 생산량과 임금을 연동시킴으로써 관리자가 일을 잘 하는 사람들을 선호하게 만들었고, 그 결과 생산성이 향상되었다."는 내용이 이어지고 있으므로, Ⓐ, ⓒ, ⓓ는 이와 관련이 있으나, ⓑ는 관련이 없다.

2 ① ▶ 내용파악
하급 관리자가 자신과 친분이 있는 작업자들을 편한 곳에 배치하는 관행이 있어 생산성이 낮았는데, 하급 관리자의 임금을 그날그날의 생산량과 연동시킨 후에는 관리자가 일을 잘 하는 사람들을 선호하게 됐고, 그 결과 생산성이 향상되었다. 자신의 임금과 생산량이 무관할 때에는 관리자가 자신들과 친한 사람들을 편한 곳에서 일하게 했으나, 생산량이 임금에 영향을 미치게 된 후에는 친분보다는 실적을 우선하게 된 것이므로, 경제학자들이 실험한 임금체계는 '금전적 인센티브가 사회적 유대를 뛰어넘음'을 보여주고 있다고 할 수 있다.

---

get the most out of ~을 최대한 활용하다
perennial a. 연중 끊이지 않는; 계속 반복되는
harvest n. 수확, 추수
scheme n. 계획, 기획, 설계; 책략, 음모
satisfy v. 만족시키다, 충족시키다
minimum-wage a. 최저임금의
motivate v. ~에게 동기를 주다; 유발[유도]하다
slack v. (하는 일에) 해이해지다, 태만해지다
temptation n. 유혹
alliance n. 동맹, 협력, 제휴
administer v. 관리하다, 지배하다; (법령·의식을) 집행하다
nexus n. 관련, 유대, 관계
incentive n. 격려, 자극, 유인, 동기; (생산성 향상을 위한) 장려금
temporary a. 일시적인, 임시의
on-the-spot a. 즉석[즉결]의; 현장(現場)에서의
assign v. 할당하다, 배당하다; 지정하다
row n. 열, 줄, 횡렬; (극장 따위의) 좌석의 줄
insider n. 내부사람; 내막을 아는 사람, 소식통
efficient a. 능률적인, 효과적인
respond v. 응답하다, 대답하다; 반응하다
productivity n. 생산성

11 2020 홍익대

신자유주의 국가는 마땅히 개인의 강력한 사유재산권, 법치주의, 자유로이 기능하는 시장과 자유무역 제도를 지지한다. 이것들은 개인의 자유를 보장하기 위해 필수적인 것으로 여겨지는 제도적 장치다. 그러므로 국가는 어떤 대가를 치르더라도 이러한 자유를 지키기 위해 국가가 독점하고 있는 폭력수단을 사용해야 한다. 더 나아가, 자유시장과 자유무역이라는 이와 같은 제도적 틀 안에서 사업체나 기업(법적으로는 개인으로 간주됨)이 영업을 할 수 있는 자유는 근본적으로 좋은 것으로 간주된다. 민간 기업과 기업가적 진취성은 혁신과 부의 창출에 있어서 핵심적인 요소로 여겨진다. 지적재산권은 기술 변화를 촉진하기 위해 (예를 들어 특허를 통해) 보호된다.

신자유의자들은 자산의 사유화를 추구하는 데 특히 부단한 노력을 기울인다. 공유지를 사유시로 만드는 것과 사유재산권의 지정은 이른바 "공유지의 비극"을 막아내기 위한 최선의 방법으로 여겨진다. 이전에 국가가 운영하거나 규제한 부문은 민간 영역으로 이관하고 규제를 철폐해야 한다(국가의 그 어떤 간섭으로부터도 자유로워야 한다). 그들은 경쟁과 결합된 사유화와 규제철폐가 관료적 형식주의를 없애고, 효율성과 생산성을 높이고, 품질을 향상시키며, 직접적으로는 보다 값싼 상품과 서비스를 통해, 간접적으로는 세금부담의 완화를 통해 소비자들의 비용을 줄여준다고 주장하고 있다.

1 ① ▶ 내용일치
신자유주의 국가는 사유재산권, 법치주의, 자유무역 제도를 지지하며, 이것들이 개인의 자유를 보장하기 위해 필수적이라고 여기기 때문에 폭력을 써서라도 국가가 이러한 자유를 지켜야 한다는 입장에 있다. 따라서 ①이 정답으로 적절하다.

2 ④ ▶ 내용파악
신자유주의 국가는 사유재산권과 자유로운 시장을 신봉하는데, 이것들은 '사회적 정의와 재분배'와 상충된다. 따라서 ④가 정답이 된다.

3 ② ▶ 부분이해
"공유지를 사유지로 만드는 것과 사유재산권의 지정을 통해 '공유지의 비극'을 막아낼 수 있다."는 내용을 통해, "공유지의 비극"은 공공재가 함부로 쓰여서 그 원래의 취지에 맞는 결과를 가져오지 못하는 상황을 의미함을 추론할 수 있다. 실제로, 이것은 사전적으로도 '목초지, 어장과 같은 공동소유 자산의 활용을 둘러싸고 구성원들이 상호 협조와 타협이 없이 각자 개인 이익의 극대화만 추구할 경우, 공익이 훼손되고 궁극적으로 개개인의 이익 자체가 훼손되는 현상'을 의미한다.

neoliberal a. 신자유주의의 n. 신자유주의자
favor v. 호의를 보이다; 찬성하다, 지지하다
private property rights 사유재산권
institution n. 학회, 협회; 제도, 관례
arrangement n. 배열; 준비; 조절
guarantee v. 보증하다; 보장하다
monopoly n. 독점, 독점권
preserve v. 보전하다, 유지하다; 보존하다
by extension 더 나아가
entrepreneurial a. 실업가의, 기업가의
initiative n. 진취적 기상, 기업심
innovation n. 혁신
intellectual property right 지적재산권
patent n. 특허, 특허권
assiduous a. 근면한, 주도면밀한
privatization n. 민영화, 사유화
asset n. 자산, 재산
enclosure n. 울타리를 침(특히, 공유지를 사유지로 만들기 위해서); 인클로저(소작인이나 마을의 공유지를 회수 또는 매수하여 울타리를 둘러치고 목양지로 했던 일)
assignment n. 할당; 지정
regulate v. 통제하다; 조절하다
sphere n. (활동) 영역, (세력) 범위
deregulate v. (경제·가격 등의) 공적 규제를 해제하다
interference n. 방해, 훼방; 간섭
bureaucratic a. 관료정치의; 관료적인
red tape 관료적 형식주의
commodity n. 일용품, 필수품; 상품

12 2017 명지대

많은 사람들이 팀이나 대회 주최 측에는 돈을 지불하지 않고 스포츠의 유익을 누린다. 그들은 메이저리그 팀이 있는 도시에 살고 있다는 이유로 시민으로서 자부심을 느끼거나 그들의 국가대표 선수들이 올림픽에서 메달을 딸 때 국민적 자부심을 느낀다. 그들은 뉴욕 양키스가 메이저리그 월드시리즈에서 우승할 때 색종이가 뿌려지는 행진에 참여하려고 맨해튼 거리에서 줄을 서거나, 자기 도시가 올림픽 개최지가 된 것을 축하하려고 런던의 트라팔가 광장과 리우데자네이루의 해변을 가득 메운다.

이것은 스포츠를 지원하는 정부정책의 편익비용분석을 복잡하게 만든다. 원칙적으로, 티켓 구매와 유료 TV 채널 가입으로부터 얻는 유익을 평가하는 것은 쉬운 일이다. 예를 들어, 티켓 가격 및 매출에 관한 시장의 데이터는 수요함수, 소비자 잉여와 생산자 잉여를 산정할 수 있게 해준다. 이러한 방법들은 현시 선호 데이터를 사용하는데, 이런 이름이 붙여진 이유는 사람들의 티켓 구매가 사람들이 대체 상품 및 대체 서비스에 비해 스포츠를 얼마나 선호하는가를 드러내기 때문이다.

그러나 색종이가 뿌려지는 행진과 어젯밤 경기에 대한 사무실 대화를 다룰 시장은 전혀 없다. 어떤 리그나 팀도 국민적 자부심을 평가하거나 팬들이 ESPN.com에 나온 명장면들이나 지방 신문에 나온 자기 팀의 리그 순위를 확인하는 것을 얼마나 가치 있게 여기는가를 평가하는 통계자료를 수

bask in ~을 누리다
tickertape parade 색종이가 뿌려지는 행진
pack v. 가득 메우다
square n. 광장
demand function 수요함수
revealed preference 현시선호
alternative a. 대체의
statistics n. 통계자료
place value on ~에 가치를 두다, ~을 평가하다
in this respect 이런 점에서
non-excludable a. 배제 불가능한
scenic a. 경치의; 경치가 좋은

집하지는 않는다. 크롬프톤(Crompton)은 그러한 유익을 '심리적 소득'이라 부르며, 그러한 유익이 아마도 스포츠가 생산하는 가장 큰 무형의 유익일지도 모른다고 주장한다.

이런 점에서, 스포츠는 환경과 유사하다. 스포츠와 환경 모두 비경쟁적인, 비배타적인(보편적인) 공공재 성격의 중요한 유익을 만들어낸다. 많은 사람들이 아름다운 풍경, 멸종위기 동물의 생존, 그리고 청정한 공기와 같은 공공재를 중시한다는 것을 의심하는 사람은 아무도 없다. 그러나 아무도 그런 공공재를 구매하기 위해 동네 구멍가게에 가거나 온라인 판매업체에 접속할 필요는 없다. 바꾸어 말하면, 스포츠에서처럼, 많은 유익들은 평가하기 어려운데, 이는 수요와 소비자 잉여를 측정할 현시 선호 데이터가 없기 때문이다. 스포츠 경제학자들에게는 다행스럽게도, 환경경제학자들이 거래되지 않는 공공재의 유익을 평가하는 방법을 개발해놓았다.

vista n. 풍경; 전망, 앞날
endangered species 멸종위기 동식물
corner shop 동네 구멍가게
analogy n. 비유; 공통점
subsidization n. 보조금 지급
illustrate v. 설명하다, 예증하다

1 ① ▶ **빈칸완성**
빈칸 앞의 they는 such benefits(심리적 소득이라 불리는 유익)를 가리키는데, 심리적 소득은 정해진 형태가 있는 것이 아니므로, 빈칸에는 ①의 intangible(무형의)이 정답이다. ② 만연하는 ③ 화려한 ④ 즙이 많은

2 ③ ▶ **내용파악**
①은 첫 번째 단락의 세 번째 문장에서, ②는 두 번째 단락의 so called because 다음에서, ④는 마지막 단락의 첫 번째 문장에서 각각 확인할 수 있지만, ③은 세 번째 단락에서 "팬들이 ESPN.com에 나온 명장면이나 지방 신문에 나온 자기 팀의 리그 순위를 확인하는 것을 얼마나 가치 있게 여기는가"라고 했을 뿐, 팬들이 자기 팀의 리그 순위를 확인하는 구체적인 이유는 언급되지 않았으므로 ③이 정답이다.

3 ① ▶ **글의 목적**
이 글은 스포츠가 제공하는 무형의 유익에 어떤 것들이 있는가를 설명하고, 이런 유익을 크롬프톤은 심리적 소득이라 부르는데, 이런 유익은 현시 선호 데이터가 없어서 가치를 매기기 어렵지만 다행스럽게도 이와 유사한 공공재 성격의 환경 분야의 유익을 평가하는 방법을 환경경제학자들이 내놓았다고 했다. 즉 '심리적 소득'을 평가하는 방법을 환경 분야의 유익을 평가하는 방법에서 찾을 수 있을 것이라는 말이다. 따라서 이 글은 단순히 ④ 스포츠의 숨겨진(무형의) 유익을 예를 들어 설명하기 위한 글이 아니라 '심리적 소득'을 평가하는 방법에 대한 설명의 도입부로서 그 방법을 소개하기 위한 글이라 할 수 있으므로, ①이 정답이다.

13 2022 한양대

비트코인의 가치를 폄하하는 사람들은 그것이 단지 투기적 거품에 불과하다고 말한다. 전설적인 투자자 워렌 버핏(Warren Buffett)은 "이것은 도박의 도구"라고 말했다. 비판하는 사람들은 비트코인 이야기가 유명한 1630년대 네덜란드의 튤립 파동 이야기와 유사하다고 생각한다. 당시 투기꾼들은 튤립 알뿌리 가격을 집 한 채 값만큼 치솟게 했다. 다시 말해, 오늘날 비트코인이 가치 있는 것은 대중들의 흥분 때문이라는 말이다. 비트코인이 화려한 성공을 거두기 위해서는, 사람들이 비정상적 거래를 통해서라도 이를 구매하기 위해 행동에 나설 수 있을 만큼 충분히 비트코인 현상에 흥분해야만 했다.

비트코인 옹호자들에게 비트코인을 투기적 거품이라고 부르는 것은 궁극적인 모욕이다. 비트코인 지지자들은 비트코인에 대한 대중들의 지지는 다른 많은 것들에 대한 대중들의 지지와 근본적으로 다르지 않다고 종종 지적한다. 예를 들어, 금은 수천 년 동안 대중들의 마음속에 엄청난 가치를 지니고 있지만, 사람들이 돈으로 금이 아닌 다른 것을 사용하기 시작했더라면 대중들은 금에 거의 가치를 부여하지 않았을 수도 있다. 사람들은 주로 다른 이들이 금을 가치 있게 여기기 때문에 금을 가치 있게 여긴다. 또한, 이 거품은 오래 동안 지속될 수 있다는 지적도 나온다. 17세기 튤립 파동이 있은 지 한참이 지났지만, 희귀하고 아름다운 튤립은 그렇게 지극한 정도는 아니어도 여전히 매우 가치 있게 여겨졌다. 어느 정도 축소된 형태이지만 튤립 파동은 지금까지도 이어지고 있다. 비트코인도 이와 마찬가지로 될지 모른다.

detractor n. 가치를 깎아내리는[폄하하는] 사람
speculative a. 투기의
gambling n. 도박
tulip mania 튤립 파동
bulb n. 구근(球根), 알뿌리
spectacular a. 극적인, 화려한
advocate n. 옹호자
tremendous a. 엄청난, 굉장한
accord v. 부여하다

1 ③　▶ 어법상 적절하지 않은 표현 고르기
to 부정사의 의미상의 주어 앞에는 for를 써야 하므로 ⓒ는 For Bitcoin to achieve ~로 바꿔야 한다.

2 ②　▶ 내용일치
"사람들은 주로 다른 이들이 금을 가치 있게 여기기 때문에 금을 가치 있게 여긴다."고 하였으므로 ②가 본문의 내용과 일치한다.

14　2018 숭실대

토마스 피케티(Thomas Piketty)가 쓴『21세의 자본(Capital in the Twenty-first Century)』의 중심 주제는 불평등은 우연이 아니라, 오히려 자본주의의 특징이며, (이것은) 국가 개입주의를 통해서만 되돌릴 수 있다는 것이다. 따라서 그 책은 자본주의가 개혁되지 않는다면, 바로 그 민주 질서가 위협받게 될 것이라고 주장한다.

피케티는 자본 수익률(r)과 경제 성장률(g)을 결부시킨 공식에 자신의 주장의 근거를 두고 있는데, 자본 수익률(r)에는 이익, 배당금, 이자, 임대료 그리고 기타 자본 소득이 포함되며, 경제 성장률(g)은 소득이나 생산량으로 측정된다. 피케티는 성장률이 낮으면 부는 노동보다 자본 수익률에서 더 빨리 축적되는 경향이 있으며 상위 10%에서 1%에 이르는 사람들 사이에서 부가 더 많이 축적되어 불평등이 증가된다고 주장한다. 따라서 빈부의 갈라짐과 빈부격차의 증대를 야기하는 근본적인 요인은 불평등의 공식인 '$r > g$'로 요약될 수 있다. 그 동일한 공식의 관점에서 그는 상속 재산을 분석한다.

그 책은 불평등이 심화되는 추세가 1930년에서 1975년 사이에 특수한 상황 때문에 역전되었는데, 그 기간에는 두 차례의 세계대전, 대공황, 부채로 인한 경기침체 등이 많은 부를, 특히 엘리트들이 소유한 많은 부를 앗아갔다고 주장한다. 이러한 사건들은 특히 제2차 세계대전 이후에 정부들이 소득 재분배를 위한 조치를 취하도록 부추겼다. 그 당시의 전 세계적인 빠른 경제 성장은 세계 경제에서 상속된 부의 중요성을 줄이기 시작했다.

그 책은 오늘날 세계는 경제의 많은 부분이 상속된 부의 지배를 받는 '세습자본주의'로 되돌아가고 있으며, 부를 상속하는 이 경제 계층의 힘이 증가하고 있어 과두정치를 탄생시킬 우려가 있다고 주장한다. 피케티는 1800년대 초 영국과 프랑스에 존재했던 축적된 자본에 기초한 엄격한 계층 구조를 설명하기 위해 오노레 드 발자크(Honoré de Balzac), 제인 오스틴(Jane Austen)과 헨리 제임스(Henry James)의 소설들을 인용한다.

피케티는 80%에 달하는 누진소득세(과세표준이 커짐에 따라 세율이 점차 높아지는 소득세)와 함께, 2%의 연간 세계 누진부유세를 시행하면 불평등이 감소될 것이라는 의견을 내놓는다. 그러한 세금이 '정치적으로 불가능하다는 것'은 인정하지만 말이다.

inequality n. 불평등, 불균등
capitalism n. 자본주의
reverse v. 뒤집다, 바꿔 놓다
interventionism n. (정부의 자국 경제에 대한, 다른 나라 내정에 대한) 간섭주의[정책]
formula n. 공식
relate v. 관련시키다
rate of return 이익[수익]률
divergence n. 분기; 일탈; 상이; 발산
sum up 요약하다
inheritance n. 상속, 계승
patrimonial a. 세습 재산의; 조상 전래의, 세습의
oligarchy n. 과두 정치(국)
progressive tax 누진세
concede v. 인정하다, 수긍하다

1 ③　▶ 내용일치
피케티는『21세의 자본』에서 오늘날 세계는 세습자본주의로 되돌아가고 있으며, 이 세습자본주의에서는 경제의 많은 부분이 상속된 부의 지배를 받는다고 했다. 그 예로 부를 상속받는 경제 계층의 힘이 증가하고 있으며 과두정치를 탄생시킬 우려가 있다고 했으므로, 과두정치는 상속된 재산이 있다는 것을 전제로 한다고 볼 수 있다. 따라서 ③이 글의 내용과 일치하지 않는다.

2 ④　▶ 내용파악
네 번째 단락에서, 피케티는 세습자본주의를 비판하고 있다. 그는 "오늘날 세계는 세습자본주의로 되돌아가고 있으며, 세습자본주의에서는 경제의 많은 부분이 상속된 부의 지배를 받는다."라고 했으므로 세습자본주의는 불평등을 해소하기 위해 피케티가 제안한 것이 아니라, 불평등을 악화시키는 요인으로 언급한 것임을 알 수 있다. 따라서 ④가 정답이 된다.

15 2014 중앙대

어떤 제품을 경쟁관계에 있는 다른 제품과 구별시켜 주는 것은 무엇일까? 제품의 외양과 품질을 논외로 하면, 아마도 브랜드화가 판매대 위에 있는 어떤 상품을 다른 경쟁상품과 구별시켜 주는 가장 직접적인 방법일 것이다. 그 결과, 미국과 서구세계에서 판매되는 대부분의 제품에는 특정한 상품 이름과 제조장소, 제조회사를 나타내주는 증명서가 붙어있다.

미국 마케팅 협회에 따르면, 브랜드(상표)는 한 판매자나 일단의 판매자들의 상품이나 서비스를 식별해서 다른 경쟁업자들의 것과 구별하기 위한 목적으로 만들어진 어떤 이름, 용어, 기호, 상징이나 디자인, 혹은 이것들을 전부 다 결합한 것이다. 브랜드 이름은 브랜드 중에 음성으로 표현될 수 있는 부분이다. 트레이드마크(등록상표)는 배타적(독점적) 사용이 가능하기 때문에 법적으로 보호받는 브랜드나 브랜드의 일부다.

B 브랜드화는 특정 제조사의 제품을 식별하게 한다. 제품의 브랜드화를 통해 기업은 소비자가 특정 제품을 쉽게 알아보고 처음 구입한 후에 만족스러우면 또 다시 구입할 수 있게 한다.

C 그와 동시에, 브랜드화는 양날의 칼과 같다. 이전에 구입한 그 특정 브랜드 제품이 불만족스러웠다면, 그 제품이나 서비스를 쉽게 식별할 수 있음으로 해서 소비자는 다음번에 반복 구입을 피할 수 있다.

A 가장 중요하게도, 브랜드화는 소비자에게 제품의 일관성에 대한 신뢰감을 준다. 기업이 일관성 있는 제품을 만든다는 가정 하에, 브랜드화는 지금 구입하고 있는 상품이 전에 사용한 같은 브랜드의 제품과 품질과 성능 면에서 유사하다는 메시지를 전하는 데 도움을 준다.

예를 들면, 메이텍(Maytag) 세탁기는 오랜 기간 동안 많은 소비자들이 그 분야에서 가장 우수한 제품이라고 생각해왔다. 그래서 메이텍 사가 지어낸 "외로운 수리기사"라는 말이 있다. 잘 작동되고 오래 사용할 수 있는 제품이라는 이 이미지는 결코 우연히 생긴 것이 아니었다. 메이텍 사는 견고한 제품을 만듦과 동시에 제품에 대한 애프터서비스 또한 좋다는 확신을 심어주려 노력했다. 그 결과, 메이텍 세탁기를 갖고 있다가 새 세탁기가 필요하게 된 소비자들은 구입할 때 자주 메이텍을 "생각하곤" 했다. 본질적으로, 그러한 경우에 소비자는 브랜드 이름이 나타내는 제품의 일관성과 성능을 믿고 구입하는 것이다. 우리가 더 자주 구입하는 치약이나 세제 같은 제품의 경우, 브랜드의 식별이 지속적이고 빈번한 재구입을 촉진하는데, 이런 재구입이 소비자의 브랜드 충성도를 나타내주는 것이다.

set apart 따로 떼어 놓다, 따로 하다; 구별하다
aside prep. ~은 제쳐놓고; ~을 제외하고
branding n. 브랜드화(브랜드의 이미지, 느낌, 정체성을 소비자의 마음속에 심어주는 과정)
distinguish v. 구별하다, 분류하다
identification n. 신원 확인; 식별; 신원증명서
differentiate v. 구별하다
exclusive a. 독점적인; 배타적인
appropriation n. 전용, 사용(私用); 유용
convey v. 전달하다
dual-edged a. (칼의) 양날이 선
fable n. 우화, 꾸며낸 이야기 v. 지어내다
accident n. 사고, 재난; 우연한[불의의] 사건
more often than not 자주, 대개
in essence 사실, 본질적으로
bet on 가능성에 내기를 하다
detergent n. 세척제, 세제

1 ② ▶ 단락배열
B는 브랜드화의 장점을 설명하고, C는 '브랜드화는 양날의 칼과 같다'고 한 다음에 브랜드화의 단점을 지적하므로, B 다음에 C가 와야 한다. 한편, 마지막 단락의 메이텍 세탁기는 A에서 언급된 '브랜드화가 제품의 일관성에 대한 신뢰감을 주는' 예로 제시된 것이므로, A가 가장 끝에 와야 한다. 따라서 B — C — A의 순서가 적절하므로 ②가 정답이다.

2 ① ▶ 내용일치
본문에서 "브랜드화는 소비자가 특정 제품을 구입한 후에 그 제품이 만족스러우면 다시 구입하도록 만들지만, 만족하지 못하는 경우에는 다시 구입하지 않게 만들 수도 있다."고 했다. 따라서 ①이 본문의 내용과 일치한다.

16 2022 숭실대

스태그플레이션(stagflation)은 스태그네이션(stagnation)과 인플레이션(inflation)이라는 단어의 합성어이다. 스태그플레이션은 물가 상승(인플레이션)과 더불어 느린 성장과 높은 실업률(경기 침체)로 특징지어지는 경제 상태를 설명한다.

이 용어는 1965년 초 영국 보수당 정치인인 이안 매클로드(Ian Macleod)가 하원에서 한 연설에서 처음 등장했다. "우리는 현재 한쪽의 인플레이션만이나 다른 쪽의 스태그네이션만을 겪고 있는 것이 아니라 둘 모두가 함께 있어 양쪽 세계 모두의 최악을 겪고 있습니다. 우리는 일종의 '스태그플레이션' 상황을 겪고 있고 현대적 의미에서 역사가 실제로 만들어지고 있습니다."(현재의 스태그플레이션은 역사상 초유의 경험이라는 뜻)

combination n. 조합, 결합
stagnation n. 정체; 부진, 불경기
inflation n. 인플레이션, 통화 팽창; (물가 등의) 폭등
devastating a. 대단히 파괴적인
sustained a. 지속된, 한결같은, 일관된
in tandem with (~와) 동시에[나란히]
vice versa ad. 반대로; 역 또한 같음

<처음에 많은 경제학자들은 스태그플레이션이 불가능하다고 믿었다.> 결국, 실업률과 인플레이션율은 일반적으로 반대 방향으로 움직이는 것이다. 그러나 1970년대의 '대(大)인플레이션' 시대가 결국 증명했듯이, 스태그플레이션은 실재하며 경제에 치명적인 영향을 미칠 수 있다.

스태그플레이션과 인플레이션은 관련이 있지만, 그것들을 혼동해서는 안 된다. 인플레이션이라는 용어는 시간이 지남에 따라 경제에서 일부가 아닌 모든 재화 및 용역의 평균 가격 수준이 지속적으로 상승하는 것을 일컫는다. 인플레이션은 통화 공급량이 경제가 재화 및 용역을 생산할 수 있는 것보다 더 빠른 속도로 증가할 때 발생한다.

스태그플레이션은 느린 경제 성장과 높은 실업률과 함께 인플레이션이 존재할 때 발생한다. 일반적으로 이런 경제 상황들은 함께 발생하지 않는다. 실업률과 인플레이션은 반비례하는 경향이 있다. 따라서 실업률이 증가하면 인플레이션은 대개 감소하고 그 반대의 경우도 마찬가지이다. 물론 1970년대의 스태그플레이션이 보여주듯이, 이 관계가 항상 안정적이거나 예측할 수 있는 것은 아니다.

스태그플레이션은 경제 성장 둔화, 높은 실업률, 높은 물가 등 경제적 병폐의 더할 수 없이 나쁜 상황이다. 경제학자들이 일반적으로 동의하는 스태그플레이션의 두 가지 근본 원인은 공급 충격과 재정 및 통화정책이다. 가계의 경우, 스태그플레이션은 사람들이 더 적은 돈을 벌지만 음식과 의약품에서부터 주택과 소비재에 이르는 모든 것에 더 많은 돈을 소비한다는 것을 의미한다. 소비자 지출이 둔화되면서 기업 수익이 감소하여 경제에 미치는 전반적인 영향을 악화시킨다.

stable a. 안정된
predictable a. 예측할 수 있는
perfect storm (한꺼번에 여러 가지 안 좋은 일이 겹쳐) 더할 수 없이 나쁜 상황
root cause 근본 원인
household n. 가정, 가구

1 ② ▶ 문장삽입
주어진 문장에서 "경제학자들은 스태그플레이션이 불가능하다고 믿었다."고 했으므로, 스태그플레이션이 일어나기 어려운 이유와 관련된 내용이 주어진 문장 다음에 이어져야 한다. Ⓑ 다음에 높은 실업률을 의미하는) 스태그네이션과 (물가 상승을 의미하는) 인플레이션은 반대 방향으로 움직인다고 했으므로, 경제학자들이 스태그플레이션이 불가능하다고 생각한 이유가 될 것이다. 따라서 주어진 문장은 Ⓑ에 들어가야 적절하다.

2 ③ ▶ 내용일치
마지막 단락에서 "가계의 경우, 스태그플레이션은 사람들이 더 적은 돈을 벌지만 음식과 의약품에서부터 주택과 소비재에 이르는 모든 것에 더 많은 돈을 소비한다는 것을 의미한다."고 했으므로, 사람들이 더 적은 돈을 버는 것은 맞지만 지출은 늘어나게 되는 상황에 놓이게 되므로 ③이 글의 내용과 일치하지 않는다.

17 2018 한성대

경제의 미래 향방에 대한 예측은 경제학자들마다 크게 다르다. (경제학자들 중) 낙관주의자들은 경제가 이미 바닥을 쳤다고 말하지만, 비관주의자들은 더블딥 불황의 도래에 대해 경고한다. 경제학자들은 경제위기가 언제 끝날지를 적극적으로 예측할 수 있어야 하지만, 그런 예측은 쉬운 일이 아니다. 미국의 한 경제학자는 한때 "경제예측이 유일하게 할 줄 아는 것은 점성술이 훌륭해 보이도록 만드는 것이다."라고 말했다.

잘못된 예측은 틀림없이 실망스러운 일이지만, 일부 경제학자들은 전통적인 지표에서 탈피하여 전혀 관련 없는 분야에서 답을 찾으려고 노력한다. 유명한 경제학자인 로렌스 서머스(Lawrence Summers)는 미국경제가 하락하는 것이 멈췄다고 최근에 말했다. 그 증거로, 로렌스 서머스는 '경제불황'이라는 문구의 구글 검색 횟수를 지적했는데, 그 검색 횟수는 연초에 평소보다 4배나 급증했지만, 지금은 현저히 줄어들었다.

또 한 명의 유명한 경제학자인 앨런 그린스펀(Alan Greenspan)은 쓰레기 배출량, 세탁소 방문고객 수, 그리고 남성 속옷 매출을 조사해봤다고 한다. 앨런 그린스펀은 경제상황이 아주 좋을 때 가정에서 쓰레기를 더 많이 배출하게 되고, 더 많은 옷을 세탁소에 맡기게 되기 때문에 이런 조사를 실시했다고 한다. 반대로, 남성의 속옷 매출이 점점 줄어든다는 것은 경제상황이 갑자기 나빠졌다는 것을 의미한다.

optimist n. 낙관주의자
pessimist n. 비관주의자
double-dip n. 더블딥(경기침체 후 잠시 회복기를 보이다가 다시 침체에 빠지는 이중침체 현상)
recession n. 불황, 불경기
astrology n. 점성술, 점성학
respectable a. 존경할만한, 훌륭한
free fall 자유낙하(물체의 중력에 의한 낙하); (가치의) 급락
phrase n. 어구, 문구; 말
conspicuously ad. 눈에 띄게, 현저히
garbage n. 쓰레기
dwindle v. (점점) 줄어들다

1 ② ▶ 빈칸완성
낙관주의자들은 경제를 낙관하는 사람이므로, that절은 경제가 이제 오를 일만 남았다는

표현인 '바닥을 쳤다(hit the bottom)'는 뜻이 되어야 한다. 따라서 빈칸 Ⓐ에는 'bottom(바닥, 아래)'이 적절하다. 이와는 대조적으로, 비관주의자들은 경제를 비관하는 사람이므로, 더블딥 불황이 '닥쳐올' 것이라고 경고했다고 해야 한다. 따라서 빈칸 Ⓑ에는 'advent(도래)'가 적절하다. ① 정점 — 도래 ③ 바닥 — 끝 ④ 정점 — 끝

2 ② ▶ 부분이해
밑줄 친 ⓒ는 "경제예측이 유일하게 할 줄 아는 것은 점성술이 훌륭해 보이도록 만드는 것이다."라는 뜻으로, 과학적이지 않은 점성술을 오히려 돋보이게 만든다는 것은 경제예측이 그만큼이나 믿을 게 못된다는 뜻으로 받아들일 수 있다. 따라서 ②가 정답이다.

3 ① ▶ 빈칸완성
경제학자 로렌스 서머스는 미국경제가 하락하는 것이 멈추었다고 말했으며, 그 증거로 '경제불황'이라는 문구의 구글 검색 횟수를 지적했다고 했다. 따라서 미국경제의 하락이 멈추었다는 신호가 되려면, 경제의 하락을 나타내는 경제불황 검색 횟수가 과거에 크게 '치솟았다가' 지금은 현저히 '줄어들었다'는 내용이 되어야 한다. 따라서 빈칸 Ⓓ에는 soared, 빈칸 Ⓔ에는 dropped가 적절하다. ② 늘어나다 — 떨어지다 ③ 치솟다 — 만회하다 ④ 늘어나다 — 만회하다

4 ② ▶ 내용일치
"앨런 그린스펀은 경제상황이 아주 좋을 때는 가정에서 쓰레기를 더 많이 배출하게 되고, 더 많은 옷을 세탁소에 맡기게 되기 때문에, 이런 조사를 실시했다고 한다."라고 했으므로, ②에서 '경제위기일 때'(in an economic crisis)를 '경제상황이 좋을 때'로 고쳐야 적절하다.

18 2019 홍익대

패션 산업은 현대 시대의 산물이다. 19세기 중반 이전에는, 거의 모든 의류는 개인을 위해 손으로 만들어졌는데, 주로 가정에서 자가생산하거나 양장점과 양복점에서 주문 생산되었다. 이미 20세기 초에, 재봉틀과 같은 신기술의 등장, 전 세계적인 자본주의의 등장과 공장제 생산방식의 발달, 그리고 백화점과 같은 소매점의 급증으로, 의류는 점차 표준규격으로 대량 생산되고 정가에 팔리게 되었다. 패션 산업은 유럽과 미국에서 처음 발달되었지만, 의류는 종종 한 국가에서 디자인되고, 다른 국가에서 제조되며, 또 다른 국가에서 팔리게 되면서, 오늘날 패션 산업은 국제화되고 고도로 세계화된 산업이 되었다. <예를 들어, 미국의 패션 산업은 중국에서 섬유를 조달하고, 베트남에서 옷을 만들며, 이탈리아에서 마감처리하고, 미국의 창고로 옮겨져서 전 세계 소매점으로 유통된다.> 패션 산업은 오랫동안 미국에서 업체 수가 가장 많은 산업 중 하나였으며, 21세기에도 역시 그러하다. 그러나 생산이 점차 해외로, 특히 중국으로 이전함에 따라, (패션 산업에서) 고용이 상당히 감소했다. 패션 산업에 대한 데이터가 보통 개별 국가경제별로 보도되고 패션 산업의 많은 개별적인 영역별로 표현되기 때문에, 전 세계 섬유 및 의류 생산의 총 수치를 얻기는 어렵다. 그러나 어느 모로 보아도, 패션 산업은 이론의 여지없이 전 세계 경제 생산에서 상당한 부분을 차지한다. 패션 산업은 다음의 네 단계로 구성된다. 즉, 주로 섬유, 직물, 가죽, 모피인 원자재 생산과; 디자이너, 제조업체, 거래업체 등에 의한 패션 제품 생산과; 소매 판매와; 그리고 다양한 형태의 광고 및 선전으로 구성된다. 이러한 단계들은 개별적이면서도 상호의존적인 많은 영역으로 구성되는데, 이 모든 영역들에게는 패션 업계 참여자들로 하여금 수익을 내며 영업할 수 있게 해주는 조건하에 의복에 대한 소비 수요를 만족시킨다는 목적이 맡겨져 있다.

prior to ~전에
virtually all 거의 모든
on order (물건이) 주문중인, 발주가 끝난
dressmaker n. (여성복) 양장점
tailor n. (주로 신사복을 주문을 받아 만드는) 양복점
sewing machine 재봉틀
proliferation n. 확산, 급증
retail outlet 소매점
department store 백화점
mass-produce v. 대량 생산하다
fixed price 정가(定價)
source v. (부품·자료 따위를 ~에서) 조달하다
fabric n. 직물, 천
warehouse n. 창고
distribution n. 분배, 배급, 유통
aggregate a. 종합한, 총
textile n. 직물, 옷감
account for 차지하다
raw material 원료, 원자재
leather n. 가죽
fur n. 털, 모피
retail sale 소매
interdependent a. 서로 의지하는

1 ② ▶ 내용파악
본문에서 '재봉틀과 같은 신기술의 등장, 세계적인 자본주의의 등장, 공장제 생산방식의 발달, 소매점의 급증'으로 대량생산하게 되었다고 했으므로, ②가 정답이다.

2 ② ▶ 내용파악
패션 산업은 '원자재 생산 → 패션 제품 생산 → 소매 판매 → 광고 및 선전'이라는 네 단계를 거친다고 했다.

3 ③ ▶ 문장삽입

주어진 문장은 "예를 들어, 미국의 패션 산업은 중국에서 섬유를 조달하고, 베트남에서 옷을 만들며, 이탈리아에서 마감처리하고, 미국의 창고로 배송되어 전 세계 소매점으로 유통된다."라는 뜻으로, 원자재 조달, 제품 생산, 제품의 마감처리, 그리고 제품의 유통이 국가별로 나눠져 있음을 설명하는 예에 해당한다. 따라서 제품의 생산단계별로 다른 국가에서 행해지는 과정을 설명한 문장 다음인 ⓒ에 주어진 문장이 오는 것이 적절하다.

apparel n. 의류, 의복
outsource v. 외주제작하다

---

19 2015 숭실대

유한(有閑)계급은 산업공동체 안에서 살아가기보다는 산업공동체를 이용하여 살아간다. 유한계급이 산업과 맺는 관계는 생산적인 관계라기보다는 금전적인 관계다. 이 계급에 가입하기 위한 자격은 금전적인 적성들 ― 노력봉사보다는 금전의 취득에 적합한 적성들 ― 의 발휘를 통해 획득된다. 따라서 유한계급을 구성하는 인적자원은 지속적인 선택과정을 통해 정선되며, 이러한 선택과정은 부(富)의 추구에 적합한가를 바탕으로 하여 진행된다. 그러나 유한계급의 생활양식은 대부분 과거의 유산으로부터 온 것이며, 과거 야만시대의 습성과 이상을 상당 부분 구현한다. 고대적이고 야만적인 이런 생활양식이 다소 완화된 형태로 하류계급에도 부과된다. 이러한 생활과 관습의 틀이 이번에는 선택적으로 그리고 교육을 통해 작용하여 인적자원을 형성시키고, 그러한 작용은 주로 초기 야만시대 ― 용감하고 약탈적인 생활이 지배적인 시대 ― 에 속하는 특성, 습관, 이상을 보존하는 방향으로 이루어진다.

약탈시대의 인간을 특징짓는 그 고대의 인간 본성을 가장 직접적이고 명료하게 나타내는 것은 본연의 호전적인 성향이다. 약탈활동이 집단적으로 이루어지는 경우에 이러한 성향은 흔히 상무정신으로 불리는데, 최근 들어서는 애국심으로 불리기도 한다. 유럽의 문명국가들에서 세습적인 유한계급이 중산계급들보다 상무정신을 더 많이 물려받았다는 주장은 동의를 얻기 위해 새삼 강조할 필요가 없을 것이다. 사실 유한계급은 자긍심의 문제로서 다른 계급들과 차별화를 요구하는데, 확실히 그럴 만한 근거도 있다. 전쟁은 명예로운 것이며 호전적인 용맹성은 일반인들의 눈에는 뛰어나게 존경스럽다. 호전적인 용맹성에 대한 이런 예찬 자체가 전쟁 예찬자의 약탈기질을 가장 잘 보여주는 증거다. 전쟁에 대한 열광과 그 지표가 되는 약탈기질은 상류계급들 사이에, 그중에서도 특히 세습적인 유한계급 사이에, 가장 많이 팽배해 있다. 더욱이, 상류계급의 표면상 본격적인 직업은 통치하는 일이지만, 그 일도 또한 그 기원이나 발달내용 면에서는 약탈활동이다.

pecuniary a. 금전상의, 재정상의
acquisition n. 취득, 획득; 습득
serviceability n. 유용, 편리; 내구성
sift v. 체로 치다, 가려내다
scheme n. 계획, 책략; 조직; 도식; 개요
heritage n. 상속재산; 세습재산; 유산
embody v. 구현하다
archaic a. 고대의; 구식의
barbarian a. 야만인의, 미개인의
impose v. (의무 따위를) 부과하다; 강요[강제]하다
mitigation n. 완화, 경감
prowess n. 용감, 용감한 행위
predatory a. 약탈하는; 포식성의, 육식의
unequivocal a. 모호하지 않은, 명료한
propensity n. 경향, 성질
latterly ad. 최근, 요즘; 후기에
insistence n. 주장, 고집; 강요
assent n. 동의, 찬성, 인정
distinction n. 구별, 차별; 특성, 특질; 탁월성
eminently ad. 뛰어나게, 현저하게
honorific a. 존경의, 경의를 표하는
generality n. 일반적 원칙; 과반수; 일반성, 보편성
voucher n. 증인, 보증인; 증거; 영수증
index n. 보기, 색인; 표시, 지표
prevail v. 우세하다, 이기다; 널리 보급되다
occupation n. 직업; 점유; 점령

1 ① ▶ 글의 주제

유한계급의 성향과 생활양식, 특성 등에 대한 내용이므로, 이 글의 주제로는 ①의 '유한계급의 특징'이 적절하다.

2 ③ ▶ 내용파악

첫 번째 문단의 세 번째 문장에서, "유한계급에 가입하기 위한 자격은 금전적인 적성들 ― 노력봉사보다는 금전의 취득에 적합한 적성들 ― 의 발휘를 통해 획득된다."라고 했는데, 금전의 취득이란 곧 돈을 버는 것을 뜻한다고 볼 수 있으므로, ③이 정답이 된다.

3 ② ▶ 내용파악

호전적 성향은 약탈시대, 즉 초기 야만시대의 특징에 해당하므로, 유한계급에 속한 이들이 보이는 호전적인 태도를 이전 시대에 나타나지 않은 완전히 새로운 것으로 볼 수 없다. 그러므로 ②가 유한계급에 대해 사실이 아닌 진술이다.

20 2018 광운대

이메일은 비즈니스 세계에서 가장 일반적인 형태의 서면 통신이다. 이메일은 종종 사무용 통신문에 비해 격식을 덜 차리는 것으로 여겨지지만, 그럼에도 불구하고 어조와 구성에 있어서 전문적일 것을 요구하며, 당신이 친구나 가족에게 보내는 가벼운 메시지와는 확연히 다르다. 그러나 업무용 이메일은 단순히 컴퓨터를 통해 전송된 편지가 아니며, 반드시 이해하고 있어야 하는 나름의 양식을 갖추고 있다. 비즈니스 파트너에게 이메일을 보낼 때 기억해야 할 가장 중요한 사항들 중 하나는 간결해야 한다는 것이다. 많은 직업인들이 하루 종일 매우 많은 이메일을 받기 때문에 종종 각각의 서신을 다 읽어볼 수 있는 시간이 없다. 받는 사람은 수신되는 메시지 가운데 어떤 것이 가장 우선순위가 높은지를 검토해야 할지도 모르기 때문에, 제목의 내용을 신중하게 선택해야 하며, 제목을 이용하여 이메일을 보낸 목적을 분명하게 요약해야 한다. 회사의 외부로 보내지는 이메일 메시지는 보낸 사람의 성명과 기업명을 포함하는 마감 서명으로 끝나야 한다. 대부분의 이메일 프로그램은 마감 서명이 만들어져 모든 외부로 보내는 메시지에 자동적으로 첨부되도록 하는 옵션을 제공한다. '새 메시지' 페이지를 여는 대신 기존 메시지에 '회신' 옵션을 사용하는 것이 바람직한 업무 수행 방법이다. '회신'은 수신자에게 원본 메시지에 연결되는, 흔히 스레드라고 불리는, 링크와 하나의 메시지에 대해 여러 개의 회신이 쌓이는 경우에 따라가야 할 경로를 제공한다. 혹은, 수신되는 메시지가 길고 특정 항목만 응답이 필요한 경우, 보내는 사람은 관련 부분만 복사하여 '새 메시지'에 붙여 넣고 적절한 응답을 입력할 수도 있다.

1 ④ ▶ 내용파악
"비즈니스 파트너에게 이메일을 보낼 때 기억해야 할 가장 중요한 사항들 중 하나는 간결해야 한다는 것인데, 많은 직업인들이 하루 종일 매우 많은 이메일을 받음으로 인해 종종 각각의 서신을 다 읽어볼 수 있는 시간이 없기 때문이다."라는 내용이 있으므로, ④가 정답으로 적절하다.

2 ③ ▶ 부분이해
"'새 메시지' 페이지를 여는 대신 기존 메시지에 '회신' 옵션을 사용하는 것이 바람직하며, '회신'은 수신자에게 원본 메시지에 연결되는, 흔히 스레드라고 불리는, 링크와 하나의 메시지에 대해 여러 개의 회신이 쌓이는 경우에 따라가야 할 경로를 제공한다."라고 했으므로, ③이 부합되는 진술이다.

3 ③ ▶ 내용일치
"받는 사람이 수신의 우선순위를 검토할 수 있도록 보내는 사람은 제목을 이용하여 이메일을 보낸 목적을 분명하게 요약해야 한다."라고 했다. 즉 이메일의 제목에 목적을 요약해서 나타내야 하는 것이지, 직접적으로 중요도를 제목에 나타내라는 것이 아니다. 따라서 ③이 부합되지 않는 진술이다.

---

formal a. 격식을 차린, 정중한; 공식적인
tone n. 음질, 음색; 어조, 말씨
structure n. 구조, 구성; 체계
via prep. ~을 경유하여, ~을 거쳐
colleague n. 동료; 동업자
concise a. 간결한, 간명한
multitude n. 다수; 군중, 군집
thoroughly ad. 아주, 전적으로, 완전히, 철저히
correspondence n. 대응, 일치; 서신왕래, 편지
evaluate v. 평가하다
priority n. 우선사항; 우선, 우선권
summary n. 요약, 개요, 적요
signature n. 서명
affiliation n. 기업명, 기관명
append v. (서류 등을) 첨부하다; 추가[부가]하다
recipient n. 수령인
lengthy a. 너무 긴; 말이 많은, 장황한
response n. 응답, 대답
appropriate a. 적합한, 적절한

08 과학·기술

01 2021 국민대

퍼킨(Perkin), 노벨(Nobel), 플레밍(Fleming)은 운 좋은 사고(우연한 발견)로 혜택을 입었지만, 그들의 발견이 완전히 우연한 것은 아니었다. 그들의 발견은 우연한 사고의 현명한 이용을 의미하는 운 좋은 발견(serendipity)의 예이다. 운 좋은 발견은 엑스레이, 인슐린 그리고 DNA의 발견을 포함한 많은 중요한 과학적 업적을 이루는 데 큰 역할을 해왔다. 과학적 발견에서 운 좋은 발견이 제 역할을 하기 위해서는 연구자들이 예리하게 관찰하고 여러 가지 가능성을 열어두고 있어야 하며, 예상하지 못한 것에 대한 호기심을 가져야 한다. 퍼킨이 실험 후에 청소를 하다가 침전물의 색을 알아차리지 못했더라면, 그는 인공 염료를 발견하지 못했을 것이다. 그것은 부자가 아닌 일반인이 자주색 옷을 입을 수 있도록 저렴하게 제조될 수 있었던 최초의 인공염료였다. 노벨이 스스로에게 "콜로디온이 폭발물에 사용될 수 있을까?"라는 질문을 하지 않았더라면 그는 젤리그나이트를 발명하지 못했을 것이다. 플레밍이 그의 접시 중 하나에 핀 곰팡이에 대해 궁금하게 여기지 않았더라면, 그는 그렇게 많은 인간의 고통을 덜어준 항생제인 '페니실린'을 발견하지 못했을 것이다.

*collodion 콜로디온, 그 당시 상처에 바르는 일반적인 치료제
**gelignite 젤리그나이트, 다이너마이트보다 덜 위험한 최초의 폭약

serendipity n. 뜻밖의 재미[기쁨], 운 좋은 발견
fortuitous a. 뜻밖의; 우연한
observant a. 잘 지켜보고 있는, 조심성 있는, 빈틈없는
curious a. 호기심 있는
substance n. 물질; 실체
clean up 치우다, 청소하다
artificial dye 인공염료
explosive n. 폭발물, 폭약
mold n. 곰팡이
antibiotic n. 항생제
relieve v. 완화하다, 줄이다

1 ② ▶ 글의 제목
인공 염료를 발견한 퍼킨, 젤리그나이트(폭발물)를 발견한 노벨, 페니실린을 발견한 플레밍을 예로 들면서, 과학에서 운 좋은 발견이 많은 과학적 업적에 중요한 역할을 해왔다고 설명하는 글이므로 ②가 제목으로 적절하다.

2 ① ▶ 내용일치
노벨이 운 좋은 사고(우연한 발견)로 혜택을 입었지만, 그의 발견이 완전히 우연한 것은 아니었다고 했다. 과학에서 뜻밖의 발견을 위해서는 연구자들이 예리하게 관찰하고, 가능성을 열어두어야 하며, 예상치 못한 것에 대해 호기심을 가져야 한다고 했다. 노벨이 스스로에게 "콜로디온이 폭발물에 사용될 수 있을까?"라는 질문을 하지 않았더라면 그는 젤리그나이트를 발명하지 못했을 것이라고 했으므로, "노벨이 새로운 폭발물을 발명한 것은 순전히 우연이었다."라고 한 ①이 글의 내용과 일치하지 않는다.

02 2017 한국외대

블록체인(Blockchain)은 모든 인터넷 접속자가 살펴볼 수 있는 거대한 개방형 디지털 기록이다. 이 기록은 한 개인이나 기관이 아니라, 분산네트워크상의 대략 9,000여 대의 컴퓨터에 의해 관리되고 있다. 컴퓨터 소유주가 자원해서 자신의 컴퓨터를 네트워크에 포함시키는 이유는 컴퓨터의 사용대가로 종종 금전적 보상을 받기 때문이다. 기록된 모든 정보는 항구적이다. 정보를 변경할 수 없는 이유는 컴퓨터마다 기록을 복사하여 보관하기 때문이다. 당신이 이 시스템을 해킹하고자 한다면, 네트워크상의 모든 컴퓨터를 해킹해야 한다. 이런 시도가 여러 번 있었지만, 해킹은 지금까지 불가능한 것으로 입증되었다. 여러 컴퓨터의 전체 능력은 세계 최고의 슈퍼컴퓨터 500대를 합친 것 보다 더 크다. 그리고 2~3분에 한 번씩 새로운 정보를 기록에 추가할 수 있지만, 이것은 모든 컴퓨터가 승인할 때에, 즉 모든 컴퓨터에서 새로운 정보가 정확하고 만족스럽다고 판단할 때에만 그러하다. 모든 사람이 블록체인의 작동 방식을 알고는 있지만, 완전히 자동화되어 있기 때문에 아무도 그 작동 방식을 변경할 수는 없다.

Blockchain n. 블록체인(중앙관리 서버가 아니라 참여자들의 개인 장비에 분산 저장시켜 공동으로 관리하는 네트워크)
enormous a. 거대한, 막대한
approximately ad. 대략, 약
distributed a. 분포된; 광범위한; 분산된
volunteer v. 자원[자진]하다
in exchange for ~과 교환으로, ~대신에
permanent a. 영속하는, 영구적인
hack v. 자르다; 컴퓨터에 불법 침입하다
collective a. 집합적인; 집단의, 공통의, 공동의
combine v. 결합하다, 합동하다

1 ①	▶ 내용파악

블록체인은 중앙관리 서버가 아니라 분산네트워크로 구성되어 있어서 네트워크상의 모든 컴퓨터를 침입하지 않는 한 해킹이 불가능하다고 했다. 따라서 ①이 일치한다.

2 ②	▶ 빈칸완성

블록체인의 작동 방식을 변경할 수 없는 이유로는 '컴퓨터에 의해 완전히 자동적으로 이루어진다는 점'이 적절하다. ① 통제되지 않은 ③ 정기적으로 업데이트되는 ④ 자유롭게 접근할 수 있는

approval n. 승인; 찬성
delete v. 삭제하다

03 2013 성균관대

신선 야채를 보존 가능하고, 식용 가능한 사각형 모양으로 냉동시킨다는 생각이 처음 정착하게 된 것은 발명가 클래런스 버즈아이(Clarence Birdseye)가 특별히 저온에서 작동하는 고압, 급속 냉동 기법을 발명했던 1920년대였다. 급속 냉동이라는 부분이 그의 새로운 방법의 핵심이었다. 상대적으로 약간 더 높은 온도에서, 더 느리게 냉동시키게 되면 큰 얼음 결정이 식품 내부에 만들어져 섬유질과 세포 구조를 손상시키고 맛과 질감을 빼앗아간다. 버즈아이의 초고속, 초저온 냉동 기법은 오직 작은 결정만 만들어지도록 하여 식품의 비타민과 신선함을 더 많이 보존할 수 있었다. 그로부터 90여년이 흐른 지금까지 식품회사들은 품질 향상을 위해 몇 가지 추가적인 기법을 더해왔다. 예를 들어, 일부 과일과 채소들은 냉동 전에 껍질을 벗기거나 열처리를 하는데, 그렇게 하면 약간의 산화가 발생한다. 이것은 껍질 벗긴 사과나 바나나가 갈색으로 변하는 현상이다. 그러나 열처리를 하면 과일 속에 있으면서 색깔과 맛, 영양소를 급속히 떨어뜨리는 효소의 활동력이 사라진다. 더구나 열처리 과정은 식품의 섬유질을 농축시킴으로써 실제로 (섬유질을) 증가시키게 되는데, 이는 사람의 소화에 아주 유용하다.

preserved a. 보존된
edible a. 식용의, 식용에 적합한
rectangle n. 직사각형
hold n. 쥠; 지배력, 위력, 영향(력); 이해(력)
flash a. 돌발적인; (건조·냉동 등이) 순간적인
flash-freezing n. 급속 냉동
innovation n. 혁신, 쇄신; 새 제도; 새로 도입한 것
crystal n. 수정; 결정
fibrous a. 섬유질의; 섬유 모양의
cellular a. 세포로 된, 세포의
peel v. 껍질을 벗기다
blanch v. 희게 하다, 표백하다; (채소·고기 등을) 데치다, 더운 물에 담그다
oxidation n. 산화
deactivate v. 활동력을 잃게 하다; 비활성화시키다
blanching n. 데치기, 열처리
enzyme n. 효소
degrade v. 지위를 낮추다; 품질을 떨어뜨리다

1 ①	▶ 글의 제목

이 글은 1920년대 개발된 급속 냉동 기법의 발명 이후 열처리 등의 식품 보존을 위한 기술적인 발달을 언급하고 있다.

2 ②	▶ 내용일치

마지막 두 문장에서 냉동식품은 냉동 전의 열처리를 통해 영양소와 섬유질이 더 많이 보존됨을 알 수 있다. ① 냉동 속도가 느릴 때 섬유질이 손상되고 빠를 때 비타민이 더 많이 보존된다고 했다. ③ 비용이 더 많이 든다는 언급은 없다. ④ 껍질 벗기기를 더 선호한다는 언급은 없고 열처리를 하면 맛을 떨어뜨리는 효소의 활동력이 사라지므로 맛이 더 좋아진다. ⑤ 버즈아이의 냉동 기법은 식품의 비타민과 신선함을 더 많이 보존할 수 있다고 했다.

04 2017 한국항공대

빛의 광양자적(光量子的) 성질에 대한 추가적인 입증은 1923년에 아서 H. 콤프턴(Arthur H. Compton)이 행한 실험에서 이루어졌다. 그의 실험에서 콤프턴은 엑스레이 광선을 흑연 덩어리를 향해 쏘았다. 그는 투사된 엑스레이보다 산란된 엑스레이의 파장이 약간 더 길어지고, 따라서 산란된 광선의 에너지가 낮아졌다는 사실을 발견하였다. 에너지가 감소한 양은 엑스레이가 산란되는 각도에 따라 달라졌다. 산란된 엑스레이와 투사된 엑스레이 간의 파장 변화는 콤프턴 편이(偏移)라고 불린다. 이러한 효과를 설명하기 위해 콤프턴은 광양자가 하나의 입자처럼 움직인다면, 그것이 다른 입자와 부딪힐 때의 모습은 두 개의 당구공이 부딪힐 때와 비슷할 것이라고 가정하였다. 따라서 엑스레이 광양자는 측정 가능한 에너지와 운동량을 지니고 있으며, 이 두 특성(에너지와 운동량)은 충돌 시에 분명 보존될 것이라고 보았다. 투사된 광양자가 정지된 상태의 전자와 충돌하면 그 광양자는 에너지와 운동량의 일부를 그 전자에 전이시킨다.

justification n. 타당한[정당한] 이유; 정당성; 변명
photon n. 광자(光子), 광양자
wavelength n. 파장, 주파수
graphite n. 흑연
scatter v. (빛 등을) 확산시키다, 산란시키다
incident n. 사건 a. (빛 등이) 투사[입사]의
shift n. (파동의) 주파수의 편이(偏移)
collision n. 충돌
momentum n. 가속도; 운동량

1 ②	▶ 글의 제목
	이 글은 빛이 입자적인 성격을 가졌음을 보여주는 콤프턴의 실험과 그의 이론을 설명하고 있다. 따라서 ②가 제목으로 적절하다.

2 ①	▶ 내용파악
	본문에서 "투사된 엑스레이보다 산란된 엑스레이의 파장이 약간 더 길어져서 그 결과 산란된 광선의 에너지가 낮아진다."고 하였다.

3 ①	▶ 내용추론
	본문에서 "투사된 광양자가 정지된 상태의 전자와 충돌하면 그 광양자는 에너지와 운동량의 일부를 그 전자에 전이시킨다."고 하였으므로 투사된 광양자는 에너지의 일부를 잃게 될 것이다.

electron n. 전자
at rest 움직이지 않는
sequence n. 배열, 순서

05 2019 단국대

과학적인 관점, 즉 과학자들이 그들의 전문적인 능력으로 세계를 향해 택하는 태도를 채택함으로써 윤리가 상당히 큰 영향을 받을지도 모른다. 이 태도에는 진리를 높이(아마도 지나치게 높이) 존중하는 것과 정당성을 입증할 수 없는 결론에 이르기를 거부하는 것이 포함되는데, 이러한 거부는 종교의 차원에서는 불가지론으로 표현되는 것이다. 그리고 이와 함께 발견되는 것은 감정은 진리를 향한 길에 걸림돌이 된다는 이유로 가능한 마지막 순간까지 감정을 의도적으로 <해방>하는 것이다. 따라서 그 연구가 궁극적으로 촌충을 죽이고 장미를 번식시키는 결과를 초래하는 것이라 해도, 장미와 촌충은 같은 방법으로 연구되어야 하며 동일한 각도에서 보아야 한다. 그 밖에도 과학적인 관점은 과학의 미학적 이론을 특징짓는 특별한 형태의 아름다움을 즐기는 과학적 미학을 함양하는 것과 관련되어 있다. 선한 것과 아름다운 것 사이에서 친밀한 관계를 찾는 사람들은 과학자들만큼 영향력 있는 한 집단의 사람들이 특별한 종류의 아름다움을 추구하고 있다는 사실의 중요성을 깨닫게 될 것이다. 결국, 이와 같이 과학자가 인류의 지적 구조에 기여하고 있기 때문에, 전체적으로 과학자의 영향력은 필연적으로 국가, 인종, 계급의 한계를 초월하는 윤리 원칙과 실천을 위한 것이 될 것이다.

1 ②	▶ 빈칸완성
	과학자들의 역할의 중요성을 마지막 문장에서 결론짓고 있으므로 빈칸에는 ② Finally(결국)가 적절하다. ① 대신에 ③ 그럼에도 불구하고 ④ 흥미를 자아내어

2 ②	▶ 문맥상 적절하지 않은 어구 고르기
	과학자들이 택하는 태도에는 진실에 대한 높은 관심과 불가지론으로 표현되는 정당하지 못한 결론에 이르는 것을 거부하는 것이 포함된다고 했다. 따라서 감정이 진실을 향한 길의 방해가 된다면, 과학자들은 감정을 억제하려 할 것이므로 ⓑ는 문맥상 suppression이 되어야 한다.

3 ②	▶ 내용일치
	과학에는 특별한 형태의 아름다움을 즐기는 과학적 미학을 함양하는 것이 포함되어 있다고 했으므로, 과학은 미(美)에 대한 자체 개념이 있다고 볼 수 있다. 따라서 ②가 정답이다.

ethics n. 도덕 원리, 윤리
adoption n. 채용, 채택
unduly ad. 지나치게, 과도하게
regard n. 고려; 존경, 존중
unjustifiable a. 정당화할 수 없는, 정당성 없는
plane n. 수준, 레벨, 정도; 면
agnosticism n. 불가지론
emancipation n. 해방, 이탈, 벗어남
on the ground that ~라는 근거로
stumbling block 방해물, 장애물; 고민거리
tape-worm n. 촌충
rejoice v. 크게 기뻐하다
esthetic a. 미학의; 심미적인
intimate a. 친밀한, 친한
in favour of ~에 찬성[지지]하여, ~을 위하여
transcend v. 초월하다

06 2017 한국항공대

돌턴(Dalton)의 원자 개념은 데모크리토스(Democritus)의 그것보다 훨씬 자세하고 구체적이었다. 첫째 가설은 한 원소의 원자들은 다른 모든 원소들의 원자들과 다르다고 하는 것이다. 돌턴은 원자의 구조 또는 구성에 관해서는 기술하려 시도하지 않았다. 그러나 그는 수소원자와 산소원자가 다르다고 가정함으로써 수소와 산소 같은 원소들이 보여주는 서로 다른 특성들을 설명할 수 있다는

atom n. 원자
detailed a. 상세한
specific a. 구체적인, 명확한; 특정한; 특유한
hypothesis n. 가설, 가정

점을 알아차렸다. 둘째 가설은, 특정한 화합물을 형성하기 위해서는 적절한 종류의 원소의 원자뿐 아니라 특정한 수의 원자들도 필요하다고 말한다. 돌턴의 둘째 가설은 또 다른 중요 법칙인 배수 비례의 법칙을 뒷받침해준다. 이 법칙에 따르면 두 원소가 결합해 한 가지 이상의 화합물을 형성할 경우, 다른 원소의 일정량과 결합하는 한 원소의 양은 간단한 정수비를 나타낸다. 돌턴의 이론은 배수 비례의 법칙을 아주 간단히 설명한다. 화합물마다 결합하는 각 종류의 원자들의 수가 다르다는 것이다. 예를 들어, 탄소는 산소와 결합하여 일산화탄소, 이산화탄소라는 안정된 두 개의 화합물을 형성한다. 돌턴의 원자이론에 입각해, 우리는 어떤 원소의 원자를 화학 결합을 시작할 수 있는 그 원소의 기본 단위라고 정의할 수 있다. 돌턴은 원자가 아주 작고 나눌 수 없는 것이라고 상상하였다. 그러나 1850년대에 시작되고 20세기까지 이어진 일련의 연구들을 통해 원자도 실제로는 내부적인 구조를 지녔음이 분명히 입증되었다.

element n. 원소
structure n. 구조, 구성; 체계
composition n. 구성
property n. 성질, 특징, 속성
assume v. 가정하다, 추정하다
compound n. 복합물, 화합물
law of multiple proportion 배수 비례의 법칙
whole number 정수(整數)
namely ad. 즉, 다시 말해
enter into 시작하다, ~에 들어가다, ~에 관여하다
combination n. 조합, 결합
indivisible a. 나눌 수 없는, 불가분의
investigation n. 조사, 연구, 수사
extend v. 미치다, 퍼지다; 계속되다
formulate v. 만들어내다, 표현하다

1 ① ▶ 글의 주제
이 글은 돌턴의 원자이론을 소개하고, 그것이 갖는 과학적 설명력을 강조하고 있다.

2 ③ ▶ 내용일치
본문에서 "특정한 화합물을 형성하기 위해서는 적절한 종류의 원소의 원자뿐 아니라 특정한 수의 원자들도 필요하다."고 하였으므로 ③이 일치하는 진술이다.

07 2022 한국외대

'메타버스(metaverse)'라는 단어는 닐 스티븐슨(Neal Stephenson)이 1992년에 발표한 반이상향적인 하이테크 공상 과학 소설인 『스노 크래시(Snow Crash)』에서 종종 기원을 찾을 수 있으며, 많은 사람들은 어니스트 클라인(Ernest Cline)의 2011년 소설 『레디 플레이어 원(Ready Player One)』의 중심에서 펼쳐지는 눈부신 경험의 미로에서 보다 최근의 영감을 찾아낸다. 그러나 메타버스는 공상 과학적인 것이 전혀 아니다. 그것은 심지어 새로운 것도 아니다. 온라인 커뮤니티는 1980년대 중반부터 존재해 왔으며, 1990년대에는 채팅방, AOL 인스턴트 메신저, 최초의 소셜 미디어 사이트와 함께 성장했다. 게임 "월드 오브 워크래프트"는 2000년대 초 수백만 명의 사람들에게 지속적인 사회의 장이 됐고 커뮤니티가 게임 안팎에서 계속해서 생겨났다. 현재, "포트나이트(Fortnite)"에 로그인하고, 콘솔 플랫폼을 통해 친구들과 채팅에 참여하고, 그들과 게임을 시작하는 것은, 특히 젊은 세대들에게 대부분의 물리적 상호작용만큼이나 사회적인 경험이다. 가상현실(VR)이나 증강현실(AR)에서든 단순히 화면에서든, 메타버스의 약속은 부(富), 사회화, 생산성, 쇼핑 및 엔테테인먼트에 있어서 우리의 디지털 삶과 물리적 삶을 더 많이 겹치게 해주겠다는 것이다. 이런 두 세상은 이미 섞여 있으므로 헤드폰이 필요하지 않다. 위치 정보를 통해 자동차가 얼마나 멀리 떨어져 있는지를 당신에게 알려주는 우버(Uber) 앱을 생각해 보라. 넷플릭스(Netflix)가 이전에 시청한 콘텐츠를 판단하여 추천하는 방법에 대해 생각해 보라. 메타버스는, 그 핵심적인 면에서, 현재의 인터넷이 진화한 것이다.

trace v. 추적하다; ~의 유래[기원]를 조사하다
dystopic a. 반이상향의
cyberpunk n. 하이테크 공상 과학 소설
dazzling a. 눈부신, 휘황찬란한; 현혹적인
warren n. 굴밀 주거, 많은 사람이 살고 있는 건물[지역], 복잡한 미로
sprout v. 생기다, 나타나다
log onto ~에 접속하다
launch into ~을 시작하다
overlap n. 공통부분, 겹침
interweave v. 혼합하다, 섞다
gauge v. 판단하다, 측정하다

1 ③ ▶ 글의 제목
메타버스라는 단어의 기원과 함께 메타버스가 1980년대부터 존재해왔으며 우리의 삶을 변화시켜왔음을 설명하는 글이므로 ③이 제목으로 적절하다. 메타버스는 새로운 것이 아니며, 우리의 삶을 변화시켜왔으므로 ④는 정답이 될 수 없다.

2 ③ ▶ 내용일치
"메타버스의 약속은 부(富), 사회화, 생산성, 쇼핑 및 엔테테인먼트에 있어서 우리의 디지털 삶과 물리적 삶을 더 많이 겹치게 해주겠다는 것이다."라고 했으므로 ③이 정답이다.

3 ② ▶ 빈칸완성
위치 정보를 통해 자동차가 얼마나 멀리 떨어져 있는지를 당신에게 알려주는 우버와 추천 콘텐츠를 제공하는 넷플릭스의 기술의 핵심에는 메타버스가 있다고 했는데, 이는 인터넷 기술이 '진화[발전]하여' 가능하게 된 것이다. 따라서 ② evolution이 빈칸에 적절하다. ① 쇠퇴 ③ 축약 ④ 조작

08　2018 인하대

열은 어디에나 있다. 그것은 원초적인 에너지이며, 결국 본질적으로 운동 중인 물질이다. 우리 자신을 비롯한 우리 주위 모든 것들의 기본 구성요소인 원자와 분자는 끊임없이 그리고 무작위로 운동하고 있으며, 원자와 분자가 운동하는 속도가 빠를수록 그것들이 구성하고 있는 물질은 그만큼 더 따뜻하다. 이 세상의 모든 사물은 — 아무리 차갑게 보일지라도 — 어느 정도의 열을 가지고 있다. 주전자에 담긴 얼음물조차도 그 안에서는 매우 많은 분자의 운동이 이루어지고 있어서, 그 표면에 잉크 한 방울을 살짝 떨어뜨려 놓으면 몇 시간 안에 얼음물 전체에 균일하게 확산된다. 사실, 만약 당신이 1월에 한 개의 눈 덮인 스키 슬로프가 가지고 있는 모든 열에너지를 추출하고 저장할 수 있다면, 그 에너지로 며칠 동안 당신의 집을 데울 수 있을 것이다. 과학자들은 적어도 이론상으로는 (분자의) 모든 운동이 — 따라서 모든 열이 — 존재하지 않게 되는 절대온도 0도라는 지점이 존재한다고 확정지었다. 그러나 그것은 도달이 불가능할 정도로 차가운 온도인 화씨 영하 460도이다.

열은 온도를 일정하게 유지하는 경향이 있는 어느 방향으로든 항상 이동한다. 즉, 열에너지가 높고 상대적으로 따뜻한 곳에서 더 차가운 곳으로 이동하는 것이다. 한 곳에 충분한 열을 모으면, 원자들과 분자들 사이의 인력을 극복하여 고체에서 액체로 혹은 액체에서 기체로 상태를 변화시킬 수 있을지도 모른다. 그러한 변화를 위해서는 잠열(潛熱)이라 불리는 추가적인 에너지를 필요로 하는데, 잠열이란 물질의 온도를 상승시키지는 않고 오직 상태를 변화시키는 데만 필요한 추가적인 에너지를 말한다. 따라서, 물 1쿼트의 온도를 화씨 85도(액체)에서 화씨 95도(액체)로 올리는 데보다 화씨 210도(액체)에서 화씨 220도(기체)로 올리는 데 더 많은 에너지가 필요하다.

1 ④　▶ 내용일치
"만약 당신이 1월에 한 개의 눈 덮인 스키 슬로프가 가지고 있는 모든 열에너지를 추출하고 저장할 수 있다면, 그 에너지로 며칠 동안 당신의 집을 데울 수 있을 것이다."라고 했으므로, 겨울철의 스키 슬로프에조차도 상당한 양의 열에너지가 있음을 알 수 있다. 따라서 ④가 옳지 않은 진술이다.

2 ①　▶ 빈칸완성
두 번째 문단 중반부에서 "고체에서 액체 또는 액체에서 기체로 상태를 변화시키기 위해서는 잠열(潛熱)이라 불리는 추가적인 에너지를 필요로 한다."라고 했는데, 이는 동일한 온도만큼의 변화라 하더라도 상태의 변화를 동반하는 경우에는 더 많은 에너지를 필요로 한다는 것이므로, 빈칸에는 ①이 적절하다.

---

boil down to 결국 ~이 되다, 핵심[본질]이 ~이다
atom n. 원자
molecule n. 분자
constantly ad. 변함없이, 항상
randomly ad. 임의로, 무작위로
substance n. 물질, 물체
object n. 물체, 물건; 대상
frigid a. 추운, 극한의
contain v. 담고 있다, 내포하다, 포함하다
jug n. (주둥이가 넓은) 주전자, (손잡이가 달린) 항아리
harbor v. 피난처[은신처]를 제공하다; 감추다
diffuse v. 흩뜨리다; (빛·열 따위를) 발산하다
evenly ad. 평평[평탄]하게; 고르게, 균일하게
extract v. 뽑아내다; 추출하다
thermal a. 열의, 열량의, 온도의
determine v. 결정하다, 조건 짓다
absolute a. 절대적인; 순진한
unattainably ad. 도달[달성]할 수 없게
equalize v. 같게 하다, 동등하게 하다
temperature n. 온도, 기온
latent a. 숨어 있는, 잠재적인
consequently ad. 따라서, 그 결과로서
quart n. 쿼트(1/4갤런의 액량 단위)

09　2022 단국대

과학자는 어떤 통찰력으로 자연을 들여다보려고 하는가? 그 통찰력은 정말로 상상력이 풍부하거나 창조적이라고 간주될 수 있을까? 문학인에게 그런 질문은 그저 어리석게 보일지도 모른다. 그는 과학이 사실들을 모아놓은 거대한 집합체라고 배웠다. 그리고 만일 이것이 사실이라면, 그러면 과학자들이 해야 하는 유일한 관찰은 사실들을 관찰하는 것뿐이라고 문학인은 생각한다. 그는 그들, 즉 중립적인 과학 전문가들이 아침에 중립적이고 노출되지 않은 상태에서 우주 속으로 일하러 나가는 모습을 상상한다. 그런 다음 그들은 사진 감광판처럼 자신을 노출시킨다. 그리고 나서 그들은 암실이나 실험실에서 영상을 현상하며, 갑작스러우면서도 놀랍게도 그 영상이 대문자로 인쇄되어 새로운 원자 에너지 공식으로 나타나게 된다.

발자크(Balzac)와 졸라(Zola)의 작품을 읽은 사람들은 이 작가들이 자신들은 사실을 기록하는 사람에 지나지 않는다고 주장하는 것에 현혹되지 않는다. 크리스토퍼 이셔우드(Christopher Isherwood)의 독자들은 그가 "나는 카메라다."라고 쓸 때 문자 그대로 받아들이지 않는다. 그러나 그 동일한 독자들은 자연의 사실을 어떤 기계적인 과정에 의해 확정짓는 이 어리석은 과학자상을 학창 시절부터 진지하게 지니고 있다. 모든 사람들 중에서 한 역사가가 나에게 과학은 사실의 집합체라고 말한 적이 있는데, 그의 목소리에는 한 서류 캐비닛이 다른 서류 캐비닛을 비난하는 아이러니한 삐걱거림조차 담겨있지 않았다.

이 역사가는 과학적 발견의 시작을 연구한 적이 있었을 리 없어 보인다. 과학혁명은 1543년 코페르니쿠스(Copernicus)에게 아마도 임종 때에 그가 약 12년 전에 완성한 책의 첫 인쇄본이 전해졌

---

insight n. 통찰력
imaginative a. 상상력이 풍부한
silly a. 어리석은
colorless a. 무색의; 공평한, 중립의
neutral a. 중립적인, 공평한
professional n. 전문가
plate n. <사진> 감광판
dark room 암실
develop v. (필름을) 현상하다
startlingly ad. 놀랄 만큼
formula n. 공식
atomic energy 원자 에너지, 원자력
literally ad. 문자 그대로
solemnly ad. 엄숙하게, 진지하게
rasp n. 거친 소리; 안달, 초조

을 때 시작된 것으로 간주될 수 있다. 이 책의 주제는 지구가 태양 주위를 돈다는 것이다. 코페르니쿠스는 언제 밖으로 나가서 카메라로 이 사실을 기록했는가? 자연의 어떤 모습이 그의 터무니없는 추측을 불러일으켰는가? 그리고 어떤 특별한 의미에서 이 추측이 사실의 중립적 기록이라고 불릴 수 있는가?

reprove v. 꾸짖다, 비난하다
deathbed n. 임종
thesis n. 논제, 주제
outrageous a. 터무니없는

1 ② ▶ 지시대상
바로 앞에서 발자크와 졸라의 작품을 읽은 사람들을 예로 들어 이야기하고 있으므로 사실을 기록하는 사람은 Balzac and Zola이다.

2 ④ ▶ 내용일치
마지막 단락에서 과학혁명은 1543년 코페르니쿠스에게 그가 약 12년 전에 완성한 책의 첫 인쇄본이 전해졌을 때 시작된 것으로 간주될 수 있다고 했는데, 이어진 수사의문문에서 이 책은 자연에 대한 사실을 기록한 것이 아니라고 했다. 따라서 ④가 본문의 내용과 다르다.

3 ③ ▶ 빈칸완성
과학은 사진 감광판이 영상을 담는 것처럼 사실을 있는 그대로 기록하는 것이 아니라는 것이 이 글의 주장인데 그런 기록은 본문에서 언급된 the colorless professionals of science, in a neutral, unexposed state 등에 비춰 볼 때 중립적인 기록이라 할 수 있다. 따라서 빈칸에는 '중립적인'의 의미의 neutral이 적절하다. ① 치우친, 편향된 ② 치우친, 편견을 가진 ④ 완전한

10 2019 홍익대

포스트휴먼 주체는 이질적인 구성요소를 한데 모은 결합물로, 그 경계가 계속 구성되고 재구성되는 물질-정보적 실체다. 포스트휴먼 정권의 전형적인 시민인 6백만 달러의 사나이를 예로 들어보자. 그의 이름이 암시하듯이, 자신의 신체 부분들은 정말로 자신이 소유하고 있지만, 엄밀하게 말해 그 부분들이 구입됐기 때문에 소유하고 있는 것이지, (사고 파는) 시장관계가 있기 전에 이미 자연적으로 소유한 상태에 있기 때문은 아니다. 마찬가지로, 자신에게 속하고 다른 사람들의 의지와 분명히 구별되는 작인(作因)이나 욕망이나 의지가 있다는 추정은 포스트휴먼에게는 힘을 잃게 되는데, 이는 포스트휴먼의 집단적인 이질적 속성이 인식이 각기 다른 여러 부분들에 분산되어 일어남을 암시하기 때문이다. 포스트휴먼의 분산된 인식이 어떻게 개별적 작인(作因)을 복잡하게 만드는지 이해하기 위해서는 프로그램화 되어있는 로보캅의 지령을 방해하는 로보캅의 메모리 플래시를 떠올려 보기만 하면 된다. 만일 인간의 본질이 다른 사람의 의지로부터 자유라면, 포스트휴먼은 '포스트'인데, 그 이유는 포스트휴먼이 반드시 자유롭지 않기 때문이 아니라 타인의 의지와 분명히 구분될 수 있는 자신의 의지를 확인할 수 있는 선험적인 방법이 없기 때문이다. 이런 예들은 포스트휴먼의 인공두뇌학적 측면을 보여주지만, 포스트휴먼의 구성은 그 주체가 반드시 말 그대로 사이보그이기를 요구하지는 않는다는 것을 인식하는 것이 중요하다. 개입이 신체에 이뤄졌든 아니든, 인지 과학과 인공 생명과 같은 분야에서 나오는 새로운 주체성 모델은 생물학적으로 바뀌지 않은 '호모 사피엔스'조차도 포스트휴먼으로 간주된다는 것을 암시한다. 포스트휴먼을 정의하는 특징들은 주체성의 구성과 관련된 것이지 비생물학적인 구성요소의 존재와 관련된 것은 아니다.

posthuman n. 포스트휴먼(로봇 공학 및 다른 기술로 유전적 구조를 조작하고 자기의 몸을 확대·증대하여 인간에서 진화한 상상의 인류)
subject n. 주제, 논제
amalgam n. 아말감(수은과 다른 금속과의 합금); 혼합물, 결합물
heterogeneous a. 이종의, 이질적인
entity n. 독립체; 본질, 실체
undergo v. 경험하다, 겪다
paradigmatic a. 모범의, 전형적인
regime n. 정권; 제도, 체제
presumption n. 추정, 가정
agency n. 작용, 힘, 작인(作因)
will n. 의지
undercut v. 효력을 약화시키다
distributed cognition 분산 인식
disparate a. 이질적인, 서로 전혀 다른
recall v. 기억해내다, 상기하다
directive n. 지시, 지령
essence n. 본질
a priori a. 연역적인; (실험·경험이 아닌 가설·이론에 기초해서) 선험적인
foreground v. ~을 중시하다
cybernetic a. 인공두뇌의
literal a. 글자그대로의

1 ④ ▶ 내용파악
생물학적으로 '바뀌지 않은' 호모 사피엔스조차도 포스트휴먼으로 간주된다는 것을 암시한다고 했으므로, ④는 포스트휴먼의 특징으로 적절하지 않다. ① 포스트휴먼 주체는 '이질적인 구성요소를 한데 모은 결합물'이라고 했다. ② 포스트휴먼의 집단적인 이질적 속성이 '분산 인식'을 암시해준다고 했다. ③ '새로운 주체성 모델'이 생물학적으로 바뀌지 않은 호모 사피엔스조차도 포스트휴먼으로 간주된다는 것을 암시해준다고 했다.

2 ③ ▶ 내용추론
"새로운 주체성 모델은 생물학적으로 바뀌지 않은 호모 사피엔스조차도 포스트휴먼으로 간주된다."는 내용에서 호모 사피엔스는 곧 비인공적인 것이니까, ③이 정답임을 알 수

있다. ① 자신에게 속하고 다른 사람들의 의지와 분명히 구별되는 작인(作因)이나 욕망이나 의지가 있다는 추정은 포스트휴먼 이전의 휴먼(인본주의적) 추정인데 이것이 포스트휴먼에게는 힘을 잃게 된다고 했다. ② '개입이 신체에 이뤄지든 아니든'이라고 한 것에서 포스트휴먼에서의 개입에 비신체적 개입도 있음을 알 수 있다. ④ 포스트휴먼은 호모 사피엔스의 생물학적인 측면도 포함한다.

intervention n. 개입, 조정, 중재
subjectivity n. 주관성
count v. 중요하다
hybrid n. 잡종; 혼합물
give way to (특히 감정에) 못 이기다[무너지다]
put an emphasis on ~를 강조하다

3 ② ▶ 내용파악
"포스트휴먼의 분산된 인식이 어떻게 개별적 작인(作因)을 복잡하게 만드는지 이해하기 위해서는 프로그램화 되어있는 로보캅의 지령을 방해하는 로보캅의 메모리 플래시를 떠올려 보기만 하면 된다."라고 본문에서 언급했으므로, 로보캅을 언급한 이유로 ②가 적절하다.

11 2015 한성대

현재 우리가 물체의 운동에 대해 가지고 있는 개념은 갈릴레오(Galileo)와 뉴턴(Newton)까지 거슬러 올라간다. 갈릴레오와 뉴턴 이전의 사람들은 물체의 자연적인 상태는 정지 상태에 있는 것이며 힘 또는 자극에 의해서만 움직인다고 말한 아리스토텔레스(Aristotle)를 믿었다. 그것은 무거운 물체가 가벼운 물체보다 더 빠르게 떨어진다는 것을 뜻하는데, 왜냐하면 지구를 향해 무거운 물체의 인력이 더 강하게 작용하고 있을 것이기 때문이다.
아리스토텔레스의 전통에서는 또한 사람은 우주를 관장하는 모든 법칙들을 생각만으로도 이해할 수 있으며 관찰에 의해 확인할 필요는 없다고 주장했다. 그래서 갈릴레오가 등장하기까지는 실제로 다른 무게를 가진 물체가 다른 속도로 떨어지는지에 대해 아무도 확인하려 하지 않았다. 갈릴레오는 기울어진 피사의 사탑에서 물체를 떨어뜨려서 아리스토텔레스의 생각이 잘못되었다는 것을 입증하였다고 한다. 그 이야기는 거의 확실히 사실이 아니지만, 갈릴레오는 이와 비슷한 실험을 실제로 했다. 그는 다른 무게를 가진 공을 완만한 경사면 아래로 굴렸다. 이 상황은 무거운 물체를 수직으로 떨어뜨리는 것과 비슷하지만, 속도가 더 늦기 때문에 관찰하기가 더 쉽다. 갈릴레오의 측정은 모든 물체가 그 무게에 상관없이 같은 비율로 속도가 증가한다는 것을 보여주었다.

date back to ~까지 거슬러 올라가다
at rest 움직이지 않는
impulse n. 충격; 자극
work out 이해하다
govern v. 통치하다, 지배하다, 관리하다
observation n. 관찰, 주목, 주시
bother v. 근심하다, 귀찮게 하다
demonstrate v. 논증하다, 입증하다, 증명하다
lean v. 기울다, 경사지다
equivalent a. 동등한, 맞먹는
slope n. 경사면, 비탈
vertically ad. 수직으로
measurement n. 측정, 측량

1 ④ ▶ 지시대상
첫 번째 문장에서 물체의 운동에 대한 현재의 생각은 갈릴레오와 뉴턴까지 거슬러 올라간다고 한 다음 그 이전의 사람들은 아리스토텔레스를 믿었다고 했으므로 ④가 가리키는 것은 Galileo and Newton이다.

2 ③ ▶ 빈칸완성
빈칸 뒤의 because절에서 '지구를 향해 무거운 물체의 인력이 더 강하게 작용하고 있을 것임'을 언급했으므로, 무거운 물체가 가벼운 물체보다 더 빠르게 떨어진다고 볼 수 있다. 따라서 빈칸에는 ③이 적절하다.

3 ① ▶ 내용추론
낙하 속도가 무게에 따라 다르다고 주장한 아리스토텔레스와 달리 갈릴레오는 낙하 속도가 무게에 상관없다는 것을 실험을 통해 증명했으므로, 모든 물체는 공기의 저항이 없다면 동일한 속도로 떨어진다고 추론할 수 있다. 따라서 ①이 정답이다.

4 ② ▶ 내용일치
두 번째 단락 두 번째 문장에서 "갈릴레오가 등장하기까지는 실제로 다른 무게를 가진 물체가 다른 속도로 떨어지는지에 대해 아무도 확인하려 하지 않았다."라고 했으므로 갈릴레오가 그런 확인을 시도한 첫 번째 사람이라 할 수 있다. 따라서 ②가 사실인 진술이다. ① 아리스토텔레스의 생각을 실험을 통해 반박한 사람은 뉴턴이 아니라 갈릴레오였다. ③ 첫 번째 단락 첫 번째 문장에서 물체의 운동에 관한 현재의 생각은 갈릴레오와 뉴턴까지 거슬러 올라간다(부터 시작되었다)고 했으므로 그 이전의 아리스토텔레스의 생각은 지금은 받아들여지지 않는 것이다. ④ 갈릴레오는 실험을 통해 물체의 무게가 다르더라도 같은 속도로 떨어진다고 했으므로 사실이 아니다.

12 2014 중앙대

무어의 법칙은 1965년 고든 무어(Gordon Moore)가 쓴 4페이지짜리 잡지 기사에서 시작되었는데, 당시 무어는 페어차일드(Fairchild) 반도체 회사에 근무하고 있었으며 나중에는 인텔(Intel)사의 공동 창업자 가운데 한 명이 된다. 그 기사에서 무어는 하나의 집적회로를 구성하는 부품의 숫자는 당시 대략 26이었던 데에서 그 후 10년 안에 대략 216으로 늘어날 것으로, 다시 말해 집적회로 구성 요소의 숫자가 매년 두 배씩 증가할 것으로 예측했다. 무어는 네 가지 경험적 데이터 포인트와 한 가지 빈(null) 데이터 포인트를 기초로 하여 이런 예측을 했는데, 이 예측은 연도를 나타내는 눈금을 가로축으로, 하나의 칩에 들어가는 구성부품의 수의 로그값을 세로축으로 했을 때, 그 해당하는 점들을 그래프에 직선으로 이은 것과 맞아 떨어졌다. 나중에 인텔사는 무어의 법칙을 수정해서 "한 개의 칩에 들어가는 트랜지스터의 수는 2년마다 대략 두 배로 증가한다."라고 했다.

무어의 법칙은 지난 50년간 우리 세계에 일어난 정보기술혁명의 근본적인 원동력으로 간주되어 마땅하다. 트랜지스터의 숫자를 그토록 자주 두 배로 늘리는 것은 때때로 같은 가격에 컴퓨터의 성능을 두 배로 향상시켰으며, 일반적으로 시계처럼 정확한 스케줄에 따라 컴퓨터를 가능한 모든 면에서 두 배만큼 향상시켰다.

그러나 왜 그렇게 되었을까? 자동차는 무어의 법칙을 따르지 않았다. 배터리도, 의류도, 식량생산도, 정치 담론의 수준도 무어의 법칙을 따르지 않았다. 정치 담론의 수준을 제외한 모든 것들은 무어의 법칙으로 인해 명백히 향상되었지만, 그 어떤 것도 똑같이 기하급수적으로 끊임없이 향상되지는 않았다. 무엇이 무어의 법칙을 가능하게 만드는가에 대한 가장 명쾌한 설명은, 디지털 논리는 전적으로 추상작용 — 사실, 1비트 추상작용, 즉 질문에 대한 예/아니오의 답변 — 에 관한 것이며 추상작용은 물리적 용량과는 무관하다는 것이다.

전적으로 빨간색의 모래와 녹색의 모래 더미로 이루어져 있는 세계에서, 더미의 크기는 아무 상관이 없다. 어떤 한 더미가 빨간색이거나 녹색이고 그 더미의 반을 덜어낼 수 있다고 하면, 그래도 여전히 그 더미는 빨간색 모래 더미이거나 녹색 모래 더미다. 그리고 일정 속도로 반복해서 반으로 나누면 2배수가 된다. 바로 이것이 무어의 법칙이 디지털 기술에만 유효하고 물리적 힘을 필요로 하는 다른 기술 분야에는 적용되지 않는 이유다. 디지털 기술은 물리학을 이용하여 추상작용을 유지하기만 하고 그 이상은 하지 않는다.

1 ③ ▶ 글의 제목
이 글에서는 디지털 기술(컴퓨터 성능)이 기하급수적으로 향상된다는 무어의 법칙에 대해 설명하고 있으므로, 글의 제목으로는 ③이 적절하다.

2 ④ ▶ 내용일치
무어의 법칙은 추상작용의 디지털 논리에 근거하기 때문에, 물리적인 힘을 요하는 자동차 산업에는 적용될 수 없다. 따라서 ④는 더 많은 디지털 기술을 필요로 하기 때문이 아니라, 물리적 힘을 필요로 하기 때문이라 해야 한다.

originate v. 기원하다, 시작하다; 창설하다
semiconductor n. 반도체
integrated circuit 집적회로
empirical a. 경험에 의한, 사실에 의한
plot v. 계획하다, 획책하다; 곡선으로 나타내다, 그래프로 계산하다
amend v. 개정하다, 수정하다
rightly ad. 올바르게, 틀림없이, 당연히
factor n. 요소, 요인; 인수
by a factor of ~배만큼
all but 사실상, 거의
demonstrably ad. 명백하게
relentless a. 사정없는, 가혹한, 가차 없는; 완고한
exponential a. 지수적인
elegant a. 기품 있는, 품위 있는; 정밀한
independent a. 독립한, 별개의, 자주적인
halve v. 양분하다, 반분하다

13 2020 한성대

컴퓨터 기술의 발달로 과학자들은 인공지능(AI) 분야에서 엄청난 발전을 이뤄냈지만, 시뮬레이션을 통해 인간의 뇌를 재현하는 것은 여전히 어려운 일이다. 사람들은 인간처럼 행동하는 기계는 겉모습도 인간처럼 보일 것을 기대한다. 예를 들어, 혼다(Honda)는 2000년에 130cm의 휴머노이드 로봇인 ASIMO를 공개했다. Advanced Step in Innovative Mobility(새로운 시대로 진화한 혁신적인 이동성)를 의미하는 ASIMO는 이동하는 데 어려움을 겪는 사람이 일상 업무를 할 수 있도록 도움을 주기 위해 만들어졌다. ASIMO는 걸을 수 있고, 계단처럼 고르지 않은 지형을 다닐 수 있으며, 최고 시속 6km까지 낼 수 있다. 그 로봇은 두 대의 카메라 "눈"을 이용하여 방향과 거리를 측정하고, 사람의 몸짓에 반응하며, 최대 10명까지 인식하고 이름을 옳게 말할 수 있도록 프로그램화되어 있다. <과학에 대한 관심을 고취시키기 위해, ASIMO는 종종 대중 앞에 모습을 드러내서 안무를 선보이고 음성 명령에 대한 이해를 보여준다.>

하지만, 인간의 특성을 가질 수 있는 기계를 설계하게 될 거라는 전망은 또한 많은 두려움과 불안을 초래했다. 1968년, 필립 딕(Phillip K. Dick)이 쓴 『Do Androids Dream of Electric Sheep?』라는

computing n. 컴퓨터 사용; 계산
vast a. 광대한, 거대한
advancement n. 전진; 진보, 발달
simulate v. 모의실험하다, 흉내 내다
unattainable a. 도달하기 어려운
humanoid robot 휴머노이드 로봇(머리, 몸통, 팔다리와 같은 인간의 신체와 유사한 형태를 지닌 로봇)
stand for ~을 나타내다, 뜻하다
terrain n. 지대, 지역; 지형
determine v. 결정하다; 측정하다
prospect n. 예상, 기대; (장래의) 가망

제목의 반(反) 이상향적인 소설에서, 안드로이드는 인간의 모습을 하고 있고 인간의 기억 능력을 이식받았지만, 다른 사람들의 감정을 전혀 이해하지 못한다. 그들은 인간을 대신해서 힘들거나 위험한 일을 해야 한다. 이 안드로이드들 가운데 여섯 대가 반란을 일으키기 시작할 때, 현상금 사냥꾼에게 그들을 추적하여 파괴하도록 요청한다. 이 소설은 "인간과 기계를 구별하는 것은 무엇인가?" 그리고 "스스로를 인간이라고 생각하는 기계를 파괴하는 것이 과연 도덕적인가?"라는 질문을 던지고 있다.

possess v. 소유하다, 가지고 있다
dystopian a. 암흑향(暗黑鄕)의, 반(反)이상향적인
entitle v. ~에 제목을 붙이다, ~에게 명칭을 부여하다
android n. 인조로봇, 안드로이드
implant v. (마음에) 심다, 주입시키다, 이식하다
rebellion n. 반란, 폭동
bounty hunter 현상금 사냥꾼
distinguish v. 구별하다, 분별하다
moral a. 도덕적인, 윤리적인

1 ④ ▶ **문장삽입**
주어진 문장은 "과학에 대한 관심을 고취시키기 위해, ASIMO는 종종 대중 앞에 모습을 드러내서 안무를 선보이고 음성 명령에 대한 이해를 보여준다."라는 의미인데, 이러한 내용은 ASIMO를 소개하는 내용 이후에 나와야 하므로 오직 D에만 들어갈 수 있다.

2 ④ ▶ **부분이해**
but 앞의 '인간의 모습을 하고 있고 인간처럼 기억할 수 있는 것'은 인간과 안드로이드의 공통점으로 볼 수 있으므로, but 이하의 ④는 인간과 안드로이드의 다른 점, 즉 인간을 안드로이드와 구별시켜 주는 점이라 할 수 있다.

3 ① ▶ **내용일치**
"사람들은 인간처럼 행동하는 기계는 겉모습도 인간처럼 보일 것을 기대한다."고 했으므로, ①이 정답으로 적절하다. ③ 기억이 아니라 다른 사람의 감정을 이해할 수 있는 능력이 결성석인 요소다.

4 ③ ▶ **빈칸에 들어가기에 적절하지 않은 표현 고르기**
안드로이드는 인간의 모습을 하고 있고 인간의 기억 능력을 갖고 있으므로, 안드로이드에게 인간이 하기 힘들고 위험한 일을 인간을 '대신해서' 하도록 할 것이다. ①, ②, ④는 모두 '~을 대신하여'라는 의미를 갖고 있어서 빈칸에 들어갈 수 있지만, ③은 '~을 바라면서'라는 의미이므로 빈칸에 들어가기에 적절하지 않다.

14 2016 홍익대

아인슈타인(Einstein)을 10년 동안 괴롭혔던 역설은 이것이었다. 1800년대 중반에 영국의 물리학자 마이클 패러데이(Michael Faraday)의 실험 연구를 면밀히 살펴본 후에, 스코틀랜드의 물리학자 제임스 클럭 맥스웰(James Clerk Maxwell)은 전기와 자기를 전자기장 이론체계 속에서 하나로 통합하는 데 성공했다. 만약, 당신이 심한 폭풍우가 몰아치기 직전에 산꼭대기에 오른 적이 있거나 밴더 그라프 발전기 근처에 서 있어 본 적이 있다면, 직접 느꼈기 때문에 전자기장이 무엇인지를 마음속으로 알고 있을 것이다. 이런 경험이 없다면, 전자기장이란 어떤 한 공간영역을 지나가며 스며드는 전자기력선의 흐름이라고 이해하면 된다. 예를 들어, 자석 주위에 쇳가루를 뿌리면, 눈에 보이지 않는 자기력선을 그 쇳가루가 질서정연한 모양으로 그려낸다. 특히 건조한 날에 털 스웨터를 벗을 때 탁탁거리는 소리를 들으면서 한두 번 순간적인 충격을 느낀다면, 스웨터 속의 섬유가 쓸어 모은 전하가 만들어낸 전기력선이 존재한다는 증거를 직접 보고 있는 것이다. 맥스웰의 이론은 이것들과 그 밖의 모든 전기적, 자기적 현상을 하나의 수학적 이론체계 속에 통합시키는 것에 그치지 않고, 전자기적 파동은 변하지 않는 일정한 속도로 이동한다는 사실도 — 매우 우연히 — 보여주었는데, 이 속도는 알고 보니 빛의 속도와 같은 속도다. 맥스웰은 이것으로부터, 가시광선 자체도 특별한 종류의 전자기파에 불과하다는 사실을 깨닫게 되었는데, 이것은 지금 망막 속의 화학물질과 상호작용하여 눈에 보이게 된다고 이해되고 있는 파동이다. 게다가 (그리고 이 점이 중요한데) 맥스웰의 이론은 또한 모든 종류의 전자기파들 — 가시광선도 포함되는데 — 이 순회 여행자의 전형으로 결코 멈추거나 느려지는 일 없이 '영원히' 빛의 속도로 나아간다는 사실을 입증했다.

여기까지는 모든 것이 잘 되고 있지만 이제 마침내 우리는 질문을 던지게 된다. 만약 우리가 빛과 동일한 속도로 빛을 쫓아간다면 무슨 일이 벌어질까? 뉴턴의 운동법칙에 기초하여 직관적으로 생각해보면, 우리는 빛을 따라잡게 될 것이고, 그 결과 빛은 정지해있는 것처럼 보일 것이다. 다시 말해, 빛이 가만히 멈춰 서있을 것이다. 그러나 맥스웰의 이론과 모든 믿을 만한 관찰들에 의하면, '정지된

paradox n. 역설, 패러독스
physicist n. 물리학자
magnetism n. 자기(磁氣); 자력
succeed in ~에 성공하다
framework n. 뼈대, 기초구조; 체제
electromagnetic field 전자기장
generator n. 발전기
visceral a. 내장의; 마음속에서 느끼는; 본능적인
permeate v. 스며들다, 침투하다
filling n. (치아에 생긴 구멍에 박는) 봉; (파이 등 음식의) 소; (베개 등의) 속
magnet n. 자석
invisible a. 눈에 보이지 않는
momentary a. 순간의, 찰나의
fiber n. 섬유, 실; 소질, 기질
phenomenon n. 현상
interact v. 상호작용하다, 서로 영향을 주다
chemical n. 화학제품, 화학약품
retina n. (눈의) 망막

빛'과 같은 그런 것은 전혀 없다. 아무도 정지된 빛 덩어리를 손바닥 안에 쥐어 본 적이 없다. 그래서 (아인슈타인을 괴롭힌) 문제가 발생한 것이다. 다행스럽게도, 아인슈타인은 당시 세계 유수의 많은 물리학자들이 이 문제로 골머리를 앓고 있다는 (그리고 잘못된 길로 가고 있다는) 사실을 모른 채, 맥스웰과 뉴턴의 역설에 대해 대체로 순전히 자신만의 생각으로 심사숙고했다.

crucial a. 결정적인, 중대한
epitome n. 개략, 요약; 발췌; 전형
peripatetic a. 걸어서 돌아다니는, 순회하는
intuitive a. 직관적인
stationary a. 움직이지 않는
pristine a. 원래의, 옛날의, 원시시대의; 청결한

1 ④ ▶ 내용파악
첫 번째 문단 세 번째 문장 이하에서 예를 들고 있는데, ④는 여기에 해당되지 않는다.

2 ② ▶ 내용파악
아인슈타인이 직면한 문제는 두 번째 문단에서 이야기하고 있으며, 첫 번째 문단은 이것을 설명하기 위한 과학적 배경에 해당한다. 두 번째 문단의 "만약 우리가 빛과 동일한 속도로 빛을 쫓아간다면 무슨 일이 벌어질까? 뉴턴의 운동법칙에 기초하여 생각해보면, 우리는 빛을 따라잡게 될 것이고, 그 결과 빛은 정지해있는 것처럼 보일 것이다. 그러나 맥스웰의 이론과 모든 믿을 만한 관찰들에 의하면, '정지된 빛'과 같은 그런 것은 없다. 그래서 문제가 발생한 것이다."가 아인슈타인이 직면한 문제에 해당하므로, ②가 정답이 된다.

3 ① ▶ 내용추론
맥스웰은 전기와 자기를 전자기장 이론으로 통합했고 뉴턴은 운동법칙을 정립했을 뿐이므로 이들이 후대에 아인슈타인이 직면한 역설적인 문제를 인식했다고는 말할 수 없다. 따라서 ①은 추론할 수 없다. ③ 맥스웰 이론은 빛이 정지해있을 수 없음을 말하고 뉴턴 이론은 빛의 속도로 빛을 따라가면 빛이 정지해 보여야 함을 말한다. ④ 전자는 자기현상, 후자는 전기현상인데, 전자기장 이론이 이 둘을 통합한 이론이므로 둘 모두를 설명할 수 있다.

15 2021 아주대

Ⓐ 당신이 마지막으로 본 상업광고에 대해 어떻게 생각하는가? 재미있었는가? 혼란스러웠는가? 당신은 그 상품을 구매하고 싶었나? 당신이 어떤 느낌이었는지 당신은 확실히 기억하거나 알지 못하지만, 점점 더 컴퓨터 시스템은 알고 있다. 새로운 인공지능(AI) 기술은 인간의 감정을 학습하고 인식하고 있으며, 마케팅 광고에서부터 건강관리에 이르기까지 모든 것들을 향상시키기 위해 그 (인간감정에 대한) 지식을 활용하고 있다.
Ⓑ 이 기술은 "감정 AI"라 불린다. 감정 AI는 (컴퓨터 시스템이 인간의 사고방식을 복제하는 것을 칭하는 광의의 용어인) 인공지능에 속하는 한 하부영역인데, 인간의 감정을 측정하고, 이해하고, 시뮬레이션하며, 인간의 감정에 반응한다. 그것은 정서적 컴퓨팅 또는 인공 정서 지능이라고도 알려져 있다. 이 분야의 시작은 적어도 MIT의 미디어 연구소 교수인 로잘린드 피카드(Rosalind Picard)가 『감성 컴퓨팅(Affective Computing)』을 출간했던 1995년까지 거슬러 올라간다. MIT 미디어 연구소의 감성 컴퓨팅 그룹의 연구원 하비에르 에르난데스(Javier Hernandez)는 감정 AI는 인간과 컴퓨터 간에 훨씬 더 자연스러운 상호작용을 허용하는 도구라 설명한다. <"당신이 다른 사람들과 상호작용하는 방식을 생각해보세요. 당신은 상대방의 얼굴을 보고, 그들의 몸을 바라보며, 그에 따라 당신의 상호작용을 변화시킵니다."라고 에르난데스는 말했다. "당신의 감정 상태를 모른다면, 당신이 어떻게 감정을 느끼는지 알지 못한다면, 그리고 당신이 특정한 내용에 대해 어떻게 반응할지 모른다면, [컴퓨터가] 어떻게 효과적으로 정보를 소통할 수 있겠습니까?">
Ⓒ 현재로서는 감정을 읽는 데 인간이 우세하겠지만, 컴퓨터 시스템들은 나름의 장점을 활용하면서 점점 더 강력해지고 있다. MIT 슬론(Sloan)의 에릭 브린졸프슨(Erik Brynjolfsson) 교수는 컴퓨터 시스템들은 대량의 데이터를 분석하는 데 매우 뛰어나다고 설명했다. 그들은 목소리의 억양에 주목해 그 억양이 스트레스나 분노와 상관관계가 있을 때를 알아차리기 시작하고 있다. 컴퓨터 시스템들은 이미지를 분석하여 인간이 알아차리기에는 너무 빠른 사람 얼굴의 미세 표정들 속에서 미묘한 감정까지 포착할 수 있다.
Ⓓ "인간의 뇌에는 사회적 상호작용을 위한 수많은 뉴런들이 있습니다. 우리는 이러한 사회성 기술들 중 일부를 갖고 태어나고, 또 다른 것들은 태어난 뒤에 학습합니다. 인간의 분석적 뇌뿐만 아니라, 사회적 뇌와도 연결하기 위해 기술을 사용하는 것이 타당합니다."라고 브린졸프슨은 말했다.

commercial a. 상업의 n. 광고
healthcare n. 건강관리
refer to A as B A를 B라고 언급하다
subset n. 부분 집합
replicate v. 모사[복제]하다
simulate v. 모의실험하다; 흉내 내다
affective a. 정서적인
have the upper hand 우세하다, 우위를 점하다
gain ground 더 강력해지다
inflection n. 굴절; 억양; 어조
correlate v. 연관성이 있다
subtlety n. 미묘함
micro-expression n. 숨기고 있는 감정을 드러내는 미세한 표정
neuron n. 뉴런, 신경세포
analytic a. 분석적인, 해석적인

"우리가 말을 이해하듯이 컴퓨터도 말로 의사소통할 수 있습니다. 인간은 유머나 다른 종류의 감정들도 이해하고 소통하는데, 그런 언어 즉 감정의 언어를 구사할 수 있는 컴퓨터들이 인간과 더욱 개선되고, 더욱 효과적인 의사소통을 해나가고 있습니다. 멋지게도 우리는 꽤 많은 발전을 이룩했습니다. 그것은 20년 또는 30년 전에는 선택사항이 아니었는데, 지금은 그게 우리 눈앞에 놓여 있습니다."

1 ⑤   ▶ **글의 제목**
이 글은 최신 인공지능 기술의 한 분야인 인공 정서 지능의 발전을 소개하고 있는 글이다. 제목에는 반드시 주제(또는 핵심소재)가 직간접적으로 포함되어야 한다. 정답을 제외한 모든 오답들이 본문의 내용을 조금씩 담고 있지만, 모두 주제는 빠져 있다. 구체적으로 ①은 '감정의 언어'가 인간의 것을 가리키는지, 인공지능의 그것을 가리키는지 불분명하다. ②는 B 단락 첫 문장에서 이 기술(새로운 인공지능 기술)은 "감정 AI"라 불린다고 했지만 제목을 이렇게 하면 그것이 감정 AI(인공 정서 지능)인지 알 수 없다. ③은 본문에서는 '인간과 컴퓨터 간의 좀 더 자연스러운 상호작용'을 가능하게 하는 것이 인공 정서 지능이라고 소개되었는데, 그런 상호작용 자체가 인공 정서 지능인 것은 아니다. ④는 감정의 언어를 구사할 수 있는 컴퓨터들이 인간과 할 수 있는 것을 말할 뿐 인공 정서 지능은 아니다.

2 ①   ▶ **내용파악**
A 단락에서 '감정 AI는 마케팅 광고에서부터 건강관리에 이르기까지 모든 것들을 향상시키기 위해 개발되었다'고 밝히고 있다. ①에서 언급한 '인간과 컴퓨터 간의 좀 더 정서적인 상호작용'은 감정 AI의 개발 목적이 아니라 개발의 결과로 가능해진 것에 해당한다.

3 ②   ▶ **문장삽입**
주어진 문장은 인간과 컴퓨터 간의 의사소통의 기본적인 원리를 유추적으로(analogical) 상술하고 있다. 앞서 연구원 하비에르 에르난데스가 말한 '인간과 컴퓨터 간에 훨씬 더 자연스러운 상호작용을 허용하는 도구'를 에르난데스 자신이 구체화하여 설명하는 문장이므로 ❷에 들어가는 것이 가장 적절하다.

4 ②   ▶ **내용일치**
C 단락에서 '현재로서는 감정을 읽는 데 인간이 우세하다'고 하였으므로 ①은 일치하지 않는다. C 단락에서 '컴퓨터 시스템들은 대량의 데이터들을 분석하는 데 매우 뛰어나다'고 하였으므로 ②가 본문의 내용에 일치한다. B 단락에서 '감정 AI는 인공지능에 속하는 한 영역이다'고 하였으므로 ③은 일치하지 않는다. C 단락에 따르면 인공지능 컴퓨터는 인간의 목소리와 감정의 상관관계나 이미지를 분석하여 인간의 감정을 읽어내는 것이지, 인간의 뇌 기능 속 사회적 상호작용을 복제하는 것은 아니므로 ④는 일치하지 않는다. B 단락에 따르면 감성 컴퓨팅은 감정 AI의 다른 이름이므로 ⑤는 일치하지 않는다.

09 우주·지구

01   2016 한국항공대

1967년에 케임브리지(Cambridge) 대학의 연구생인 조슬린 벨 버넬(Jocelyn Bell-Burnell)이 하늘에서 규칙적인 전파의 파동을 방출하는 물체들을 발견함으로 인해, 블랙홀의 존재를 규명하려는 연구는 더욱 촉진되었다. 처음에 벨과 그녀의 지도 교수인 안토니 휴이시(Antony Hewish)는 자신들이 은하계에 있는 외계 문명과 접촉했을지도 모른다고 생각했다. 그러나 결국, 그들은 펄서(전파를 방출하고 있는 작은 천체)라는 이름이 붙은 이들 물체들이 실제로는 중력장과 주변물질 간의 복잡한 상호작용으로 인해 전파의 파동을 방출하면서 회전하고 있는 중성자별이라는 보다 덜 공상적인 결론을 내렸다. 이것은 우주 서부극(공상과학소설의 하위 장르) 작가들에게는 좋지 않은 소식이었지만, 당시에 블랙홀의 존재를 믿고 있었던 우리 같은 소수의 사람들에게는 매우 희망적인 소식이었다. 그것은 중성자별이 존재한다는 것을 보여주는 최초의 결정적인 증거였기 때문이다. 중성자별은 반지름이 약 10마일인데, 이것은 별이 블랙홀이 되는 임계 반지름의 몇 배에 불과한 것이다. 설령 어떤 별이 그렇게 작은 크기로 붕괴할 수 있다 하더라도, 다른 별들이 훨씬 더 작은 크기로 붕괴해서 블랙홀이 될 수 있다고 예상하는 것은 사리에 맞지 않다. 어떠한 빛도 방출하지 않는다는 의미를 가진 블랙홀을 어떻게 우리가 발견하기를 바랄 수 있을 것인가? 그것은 마치 지하 석탄 저장고에서 검은 고양이를 찾는 것과 같을지도 모른다. 다행히, (블랙홀을 발견할 수 있는) 한 가지 방법은 있다. 존 미셸(John Michell)이 1783년에 그의 선구적인 논문에서 지적했듯이, 블랙홀은 인근의 물체들에 중력을 끊임없이 가하고 있다.

1 ③   ▶ 글의 주제
    본문에서 "1967년에 하늘에서 규칙적인 전파의 파동을 방출하는 물체들을 발견함으로 인해 블랙홀의 존재를 규명하려는 연구가 더욱 촉진되었다."라고 했으며, 이 물체의 발견이 "그 당시 블랙홀의 존재를 믿었던 우리 같은 소수의 사람들에게는 매우 희망적인 소식이었다."라고 언급한 다음, (블랙홀을 발견하는) 한 가지 방법이 있다고 글을 마무리하고 있으므로, 글의 주제로는 ③의 '블랙홀의 발견'이 적절하다.

2 ①   ▶ 빈칸완성
    빈칸 앞에서 "어떠한 빛도 방출하지 않는 블랙홀을 어떻게 우리가 발견하기를 바랄 수 있을 것인가?"라고 했는데, 이것은 새까만 장소에서 검은 물체를 찾는 것에 비유할 수 있을 것이므로, 빈칸에는 ①이 적절하다.

3 ④   ▶ 내용일치
    마지막 문장에서 "블랙홀은 인근의 물체들에 중력을 끊임없이 가하고 있다."라고 했으므로 ④가 사실이다.

encouragement n. 격려, 고무
emit v. (액체·빛·열·냄새 등을) 내뿜다, 방출하다
pulse n. 파동, 진동
radio wave 전파
supervisor n. 관리자, 감독자; 지도 교수
alien a. 외계의
civilization n. 문명
galaxy n. 은하; 은하계
neutron n. 중성자
magnetic field 자기장
radius n. 반지름, 반경
critical a. (분량·상태 등이) 임계의
detect v. 탐지하다, 발견하다
pioneering a. 선구적인, 개척의
exert v. (힘·능력 등을) 쓰다; (영향 등을) 미치다
gravitational force 중력
legacy n. 유산
latent a. 잠재적인, 숨어있는
coal cellar 지하 석탄 저장고
inflated a. 부푼
balloon n. 풍선
triangular-shaped a. 삼각형 모양의
concave lens 오목렌즈
telescope n. 망원경
exercise v. 발휘하다, 행사하다

02   2015 한양대

과학자들은 오랫동안 지구 기후의 점진적인 변화로 인해 공룡들이 멸종했다고 믿어 왔다. 그러나 1979년, 버클리(Berkeley) 연구진은 공룡이 사라지던 시기의 점토층의 이리듐 수치가 인접한 점토층에 있는 이리듐 수치보다 약 30배나 더 높은 것을 이탈리아에서 발견하였다. 이리듐은 시간이 경과하면서 매우 고르게 쌓이고 또 본래 외계에서 유래한 것이기 때문에, 그 연구원들은 이 점토층의 이리듐 수치가 높은 것은 분명 갑작스럽게 발생한 파국적인 사건에서 초래되었음이 틀림없다고 결론을 내렸다. 그 사건의 정확한 본질에 관해서 과학자들의 의견이 엇갈린다. 어떤 별의 폭발이 이러한 침적(沈積)을 유발했을 가능성은 특정 방사성 동위원소들이 그 점토에서 거의 발견되지 않았기 때문에 무시되어 왔다. 만약 그 물질이 태양계 내부에서 생긴 것이라면, 틀림없이 지구 전체에 걸

gradual a. 점진적인
layer n. 층
clay n. 점토, 찰흙
iridium n. 이리듐
adjacent a. 접근한, 인접한, 부근의
stratum n. (암석 등의) 층, 지층, 단층
settle v. (떨어져) 내리다, 가라앉다; 안정시키다

쳐 이리듐 수치가 높은 물질을 퍼트릴 만큼 커다란 천체와 지구가 충돌했을 것이다. 그런 거대한 물체와 충돌했다는 지질학적 증거는 없지만, 그리브(Grieve)는 대기권에서 폭발이 있은 뒤 낙진의 형태로 가라앉아 그 점토층들이 형성되었을 수도 있다고 주장한다. 카이트(Kyte)는 지구의 중력장에 의해 붕괴된 혜성 하나가 커다란 분화구는 만들지 않고 수없이 많은 파편들만 떨어져 내리게 했을 수 있다고 주장한다. 버클리 연구진은 소행성 하나가 지구의 바다에 떨어졌을지도 모른다고 주장한다. 그 사건의 유형이 무엇이건 간에, 버클리 연구진은 그 사건으로 인해 거대한 먼지 구름이 성층권에 떠 있게 됨으로써 지구 전체의 생태계가 붕괴되었다고 주장한다. 태양광선의 차단은 광합성을 방해하였을 것이므로 그 충돌의 영향은 점점 더 커지면서 결국에는 지구 전체의 먹이사슬의 토대를 크게 와해시켰을 것이다.

1 ② ▶ 저자의 의도
공룡의 멸종 원인을 연구하던 버클리 연구진들의 발견을 소개하고 그 의미를 다루고 있는 글이다. 공룡이 멸종되던 시기의 점토층의 이리듐 수치가 주변보다 30배나 높았다는 발견은 그 이리듐의 기원이 본래 우주이므로 외계 천체와 지구 사이의 어떤 파국적 사건을 암시하는 것으로 과학자들은 보고 있다. 다만 그 사건이 무엇이었느냐에 대해서는 의견이 분분한 것이다.

2 ① ▶ 내용파악
파국적 사건으로 인해 태양광선이 차단되어 광합성이 방해를 받았을 것이라는 것이 버클리 연구진의 주장이다. 만약 그 주장이 옳다면, 그 사건 이후 식물들이 대량으로 사멸했을 것이므로, '해당 점토층 위의 쌓인 층에서 식물화석의 수가 감소한 것'은 버클리 연구진의 주장을 뒷받침하는 근거가 될 수 있다.

evenly ad. 고르게, 균등하게
extraterrestrial a. 외계의, 우주에서 온
stellar a. 별의; 뛰어난
deposition n. 퇴적; 침적
discount v. (무가치한 것으로) 치부하다, 무시하다
radioactive a. 방사성의
isotope n. 동위원소
originate v. 비롯되다, 유래하다
collide v. 충돌하다, 부딪치다
astral a. 별의
geological a. 지질학의
fallout n. 낙진; (방사성 물질 등의) 강하
assert v. 주장하다, 단언하다
comet n. 혜성
gravitational a. 중력의
deluge n. 폭우, 호우; 쇄도, 폭주
crater n. 분화구, 큰 구멍
asteroid n. 소행성
suspend v. (먼지·미립자 등을) 떠있게 하다, 부유시키다
stratosphere n. 성층권
blockage n. 막는 것; 장애, 차단
impede v. 지연시키다, 방해하다
photosynthesis n. 광합성
rebut v. 논박[반박]하다
assess v. 평가하다, 사정하다
elevate v. 높이다, 증가시키다
consensus n. 의견 일치, 합의

03 2018 한국항공대

1920년대까지 모든 사람들은 우주가 본질적으로 정적이고 시간이 지나도 불변이라고 생각했습니다. 그러다가 우주가 팽창하고 있다는 것이 발견되었습니다. 먼 은하들이 우리에게서 멀어지고 있었습니다. 이것은 과거에는 그 은하들이 서로 더 가까이 있었던 것이 틀림없다는 것을 의미했습니다. 지금의 사실로 과거를 추정해 볼 때, 우리 모두는 약 150억 년 전에는 서로 한 데 엉겨 붙어 있었음을 알게 됩니다. 이것이 바로 우주의 시작, 빅뱅이었습니다. 그러나 빅뱅 전에는 그 무엇이라도 있었나요? 아무 것도 없었다면, 우주를 창조한(있게 한) 것은 무엇일까요? 우주는 왜 다름 아닌 빅뱅에서 나오는 방식으로 나오게 된 걸까요? 우리는 우주 이론이 두 부분으로 나뉠 수 있다고 생각했습니다. 첫째, 단번에 모든 공간 전체를 차지한 우주의 상태를 고려해 보았을 때, 맥스웰(Maxwell) 방정식이나 일반 상대성 이론과 같이 우주의 진화를 (미리) 결정짓는 법칙들이 있었습니다. 둘째, 우주의 초기 상태에 대해서는 질문 자체가 없었습니다. 우리는 첫 부분에 관해서는 좋은 진전을 이루어서, 이제는 가장 극단적인 상황을 제외한 모든 상황에서의 진화의 법칙들에 대해 알고 있습니다만, 우주의 초기 조건(상태)에 대해서는 최근까지도 거의 알지 못했습니다. 그러나 이처럼 진화의 법칙과 초기 조건으로 구분하는 것은 시간과 공간이 서로 분리되어 있고 서로 다른 것이라는 것에 의존해(기초해) 있습니다. 극단적인 상황에서는, 일반 상대성 이론과 양자 이론은 시간이 또 다른 차원의 공간처럼 행동하도록 허용합니다. 이렇게 되면 시간과 공간의 차이는 없어지고, 진화의 법칙이 초기 상태도 결정할 수 있다는 의미입니다. 우주가 무(無)에서 자연발생적으로 창조될(생겨날) 수 있다는 것입니다. 더구나, 우리는 우주가 다양한 상태에서 만들어졌을 확률까지 계산할 수 있습

static a. 정적인, 고정된
unchanging a. 불변의, 항상 일정한
distant a. 먼, 떨어져 있는
extrapolate v. 추론[추정]하다
be on top of each other 한데 엉겨 붙어 있다, 차곡차곡 쌓여있다
equation n. 방정식, 화학식
initial a. 처음의, 최초의, 초기의
all but 거의, ~외에 모두
quantum theory 양자론, 양자이론
spontaneously ad. 자발적으로, 자연스럽게
cosmic microwave background 우주 마이크로파 배경(관측 가능한 우주를 가득 채우고 있는 마이크로파 열복사)
imprint n. 자국, 흔적

니다. 이러한 예측들은 매우 초기의 우주가 남긴 흔적인 우주 마이크로파 배경을 더블유맵(WMAP) 위성이 관측한 결과들과 아주 잘 일치합니다. 우리는 창조의 비밀을 풀었다고 생각합니다. 어쩌면 우리는 우주에 대하여 특허를 받아 모든 사람들에게 그들의 (우주에서의) 생존에 대한 사용료를 부과해야 할지도 모르겠습니다.

patent v. 특허를 받다
royalty n. 사용료, 특허권

1 ② ▶ 빈칸완성
시간과 공간을 서로 다른 것으로 이해하는 전통적 사고로는 빅뱅 이전의 상황(우주의 초기 조건)을 알 수 없었다. 하지만, 시간이 또 다른 차원의 공간이라고 본다면, 즉 시간과 공간의 차이가 사라질 수 있다고 본다면 "우주 진화의 법칙이 우주의 초기 상태도 결정할 수 있다."고 하였다. 따라서, 빈칸에는 '우주 초기 상태의 비밀' 혹은 '창조의 비밀'이라는 표현이 들어가야 한다.

2 ③ ▶ 내용일치
"극단적인 상황에서는 시간은 또 다른 차원의 공간처럼 행동한다." 그리하여 "시간과 공간의 차이가 없어진다."고 하였으므로, ③이 일치하는 진술이다. 한편, 끝에서 세 번째 문장에 언급된 더블유맵(WMAP) 위성이 관찰한 우주 마이크로파 배경은 초기의 우주가 남긴 흔적인데, 이것을 관찰한 결과에서 그 초기의 시점도 추정할 수 있을 것이므로 "우주의 나이 계산은 경험적 관찰에 의해 뒷받침되지 않는다."고 한 ④는 사실이 아니다.

04 2016 경기대

조수(潮水)는 현저한 역설을 보여주는데, 그 역설의 핵심은 다음과 같다. 조수를 움직이게 하는 힘은 우주적인 것이라서, 완전히 지구 밖에 있으면서 지구의 전 지역에 골고루 똑같이 영향을 미치고 있을 것인데 반해, 어떤 특정 장소에서 갖는 조수의 성질은 지역적인 문제여서, 지리적으로 아주 짧은 거리 내에서도 차이가 매우 크다. 해변에서 긴 여름휴가를 보낸다면, 우리가 있는 작은 만(灣)의 조수는 해안을 따라 위쪽으로 20마일 떨어져 있는 친구가 있는 곳의 조수와 매우 다르게 작용하며, 우리가 또 다른 어떤 지역에서 알고 있었을 수 있는 것과도 상당히 다르다는 것을 알게 될 것이다. 만약 우리가 낸터킷(Nantucket) 섬에서 여름을 보내고 있다면, 보트를 젓거나 수영을 할 때 조수의 영향을 거의 받지 않을 것이다. 왜냐하면, 만조와 간조 사이의 범위(변화폭)가 1~2피트에 불과하기 때문이다. 그러나 펀디(Fundy) 만의 위쪽 지역에서 휴가를 보내기로 한다면, 40~50피트에 달하는 조수간만의 차에 적응해야 한다. 두 곳 모두 메인(Maine) 만이라는 같은 수역(水域)에 속해 있는데도 말이다. 혹은 만약 우리가 휴가를 체사피크(Chesapeake) 만에서 보낸다면, 만조 시간이 같은 만의 해안에 위치한 다른 장소와 날마다 12시간이나 차이가 난다는 사실을 알게 될 것이다.

tide n. 조수, 조류
striking a. 현저한, 두드러진
essence n. 본질, 핵심
set ~ in motion ~에 시동을 걸다, ~을 움직이게 하다
cosmic a. 우주의; 질서 있는, 정연한
presumably ad. 추측상, 아마도
impartially ad. 공평하게, 편견 없이
globe n. 공, 구체(球體); 지구, 세계
geographic a. 지리학의, 지리적인
cove n. 후미, 작은 만(灣); 한 구석; 협곡
behave v. 행동[처신]하다; 움직이다
locality n. 위치, 장소, 소재
disturb v. 방해하다; 불안하게 하다; (행위·상태를) 저해하다, 막다
vacation v. 휴가를 얻다, 휴가를 보내다
vary v. 다르다, 차이가 있다; 변하다, 바뀌다

1 ② ▶ 글의 제목
첫 번째 문장에 "조수의 성질은 지역적인 문제여서, 지리적으로 아주 짧은 거리 내에서도 차이가 매우 크다."라는 내용이 있는데, 두 번째 문장 이하 전체에서 "거의 같은 장소에서도 조수간만의 차이가 달리 나타난다."는 사실을 구체적으로 예를 들면서 설명하고 있으므로, 글의 제목으로는 ②가 가장 적절하다.

2 ③ ▶ 빈칸완성
to 이하에서 언급하고 있는 '40~50피트에 달하는 조수간만의 차이'는 다른 곳과 확연한 차이를 보이는 환경조건이므로, 이곳에 휴가를 가는 사람들은 이런 환경에 '적응해야' 할 것이다. 그러므로 '적응시키다'라는 의미의 accommodate가 빈칸에 적절하다. ① 명시하다 ② 딴 데로 돌리다; 즐겁게 하다 ④ 퇴거시키다

3 ③ ▶ 내용일치
네 번째 문장의 although 이하에서 '낸터킷 섬과 펀디 만의 위쪽 지역이 모두 메인 만에 속한 지역임'을 밝히고 있다. 따라서 ③이 적절하다. ① 조수를 움직이게 하는 우주적인 힘은 지구의 전 지역에 골고루 똑같이 영향을 미치고 있다. ② 낸터킷 섬의 조수간만의 차는 1~2피트에 불과하다. ④ 체사피크 만은 위치에 따라 만조 시간의 차이가 12시간에 이른다.

05 2019 한국공학대

B 지하 깊숙한 곳에 많은 양의 물이 침전돼 있다. 이러한 지하 저수지들은 사막을 포함한 모든 종류의 환경에서 발견될 수 있다. 지하수의 총량은 모든 호수와 강을 합친 것보다 훨씬 많다. 지하에 존재하는 대부분의 물은 물을 저장할 수 있는 다공성 암석층인 대수층에서 발견된다. 과학자들은 대수층을 두 가지 유형으로 분류했는데 비피압(非被壓) 대수층(unconfined aquifer)과 피압(被壓) 대수층(confined aquifer)이 그것이다. 비피압 대수층은 투과성 물질의 층 아래에 있다. 결과적으로, 비피압 대수층은 지표면으로부터 물을 쉽게 받을 수 있고, 지하수면은 물이 재충전되는 속도에 따라 위 아래로 오르내린다.

A 일반적으로 비피압 대수층 아래에는 피압 대수층이 있으며 이 대수층은 돌과 점토로 이루어진 불투수층(不透水層)으로 덮여있다. 따라서 비피압 상태에 있어서 물의 재충전을 허용하는 지하수도 일부 있긴 하지만, 대부분의 지하수는 여전히 큰 압력을 받고 있는(피압) 상태에 있다. 만약 바위를 뚫어 우물을 파면, 지하수는 지표면으로 올라올 것이다.

C 피압 대수층과 비피압 대수층은 지하수로 다시 채워진다. 그러나 피압 대수충과 비피압 대수층에 지하수가 채워지는 속도는 다르다. 대부분의 지하수는 비가 땅을 투과해 들어간 결과물이다. 이 물은 대수층에 도달할 때까지 점점 더 낮은 층으로 조금씩 흘러들어갈 것이다. 피압 대수층은 비피압 대수층보다 더 느린 속도로 물이 채워진다. 이것은 주로 물이 피압 대수층으로 들어가기가 더 어렵기 때문이다. 열대 지방에서는 물의 재충전이 우기(雨期) 동안 발생하며, 더 온화한 지역에서는 겨울 동안 이뤄진다.

1 ② ▶ 단락배열
'지표면 아래에는 대수층이 존재하며, 이 대수층은 두 가지 유형(비피압 대수층, 피압 대수층)으로 분류된다'고 설명한 B가 첫 단락으로 적절하며, B의 마지막 부분에서 비피압 대수층에 대해서 설명하고 있으므로, 그다음에는 피압 대수층에 대한 설명인 A가 와야 한다. 그리고 피압 대수층과 비피압 대수층의 차이점을 설명한 C로 글이 마무리되어야 한다.

2 ④ ▶ 내용파악
A 단락에서 피압 대수층은 높은 압력을 받고 있다고 했으므로 ④가 정답이다.

3 ③ ▶ 글의 제목
이 글에서는 '피압 대수층과 비피압 대수층의 차이, 그리고 각각의 대수층에서 어떤 방식으로 지하수가 채워지는지'에 대해 주로 설명하고 있다. 따라서 ③이 제목으로 적절하다.

---

unconfined a. 제한을 받지 않는, 무한정의
aquifer n. 대수층(帶水層: 지하수를 품고 있는 지층)
impermeable a. 통과시키지 않는, 불침투성의
well n. 우물; (유전 등의) 정(井)
groundwater n. 지하수
drill v. (드릴로) 구멍을 뚫다
deposit n. 퇴적물, 침적물, 침전물
reservoir n. 저수지, 급수장
sum n. 합계, 총계
porous a. (구멍이 많은) 다공성[투과성]의
store v. 저장하다, 보관하다
permeable a. 침투[투과]할 수 있는, 투과성의
water table 지하수면
fluctuate v. 변동[등락]을 거듭하다
refill v. 다시 채우다, 리필하다
penetrate v. 관통하다, 꿰뚫다, 투과하다
trickle down (조금씩) 흘러내리다

---

06 2019 세종대

NASA의 인사이트(InSight) 우주선은 태양계를 가로질러 3억 마일을 여행한 후, 화성의 하늘을 내려와 엘리시움 평원(Elysium Planitia)의 매끄러운 표면에 안전하게 착륙했다. <그 항공우주국의 탐사로봇들과는 달리, 인사이트는 오직 한 장소에서 행성 전체를 연구하도록 설계된 착륙선이다.> 이 착륙선은 로봇 팔을 이용하여 가장 먼저 화성 표면에 고감도 지진계를 설치할 것이며, 거기서 지진계는 운석 충돌과 화성 지진을 감지하기 위해 귀 기울일 것이다. 이 사건들(운석 충돌과 화성 지진)에서 발생하는 지진파를 통해 과학자들은 화성의 내부 구조를 보다 분명하게 알게 될 것이다. 인사이트는 그런 다음 열(熱) 탐지장치를 내보낼 것인데, 이것은 스스로 땅을 두드려 땅속으로 들어가는 16인치 못 모양의 장비로, 몇 주간의 과정을 걸쳐 16피트 깊이까지 땅을 파 내려갈 것이다. 이 기구는 화성의 내부로부터 얼마나 많은 열이 빠져나가는지를 측정하게 되는데, 이를 통해 화성의 내부에 열을 발생시키는 방사성 원소가 얼마나 있는지와 현재 화성의 지질학적 활동이 얼마나 활발하게 진행 중인지를 알 수 있게 될 것이다. 또한 그 우주선의 지붕 위에는 RISE라고 불리는 X-밴드 안테나가 두 개 있으며, 이것이 세 번째 기구를 구성한다. RISE의 무선 신호는 화성 궤도의 불안정한 흔들림을 추적하는 데 사용될 것이다. 이것은 과학자들이 화성의 중심핵의 크기와 상태를 이해하는 데 도움을 줄 것이다. 이 실험들이 모두 합하여 화성을 파헤쳐 과학자들이 수십 년 동안 찾아온 화성의 비밀을 밝혀낼 것이다.

---

the solar system 태양계
descend v. 내려가다, 내려오다
touch down (우주선·비행기 등이) 착륙하다
lander n. (달 표면 등에서의) 착륙선
install v. 설치하다, 가설하다, 장치하다
seismometer n. 지진계
Martian a. 화성의
meteorite n. 운석, 유성
impact n. 충돌; 충격
Marsquake n. 화성의 지진
seismic wave 지진파
planet n. 행성
structure n. 구조
release v. 방출하다, 투하다

1	③	▶ 글의 목적	

두 번째 문단 전반에 걸쳐 '인사이트가 화성에서 수행하게 될 실험과 그 목적'을 설명하고 있으므로, ③이 정답으로 적절하다.

2 ① ▶ 문장삽입

주어진 문장은 "그 항공우주국의 탐사로봇들과는 달리, 인사이트는 오직 한 장소에서 행성 전체를 연구하도록 설계된 착륙선이다."라는 의미다. '그 항공우주국'은 NASA를 가리키므로, 주어진 문장은 NASA가 언급된 내용 뒤에 와야 하므로 Ⓐ가 적절한 위치가 된다.

3 ② ▶ 빈칸완성

'땅 속에서 빠져나가는 열을 조사하는 것'과 가장 관련이 깊은 분야는 '지질학'일 것이므로, 빈칸에는 '지질학적으로'라는 뜻의 ②가 적절하다. ① 천문학적으로 ③ 기하학적으로 ④ 우주비행학적으로

4 ④ ▶ 내용일치

'인사이트는 못 모양의 열(熱) 탐지장치를 이용하여 화성의 내부로부터 얼마나 많은 열이 빠져나가는지를 측정하게 될 것'이라 했으므로, ④가 옳은 진술이다. ① 본문의 내용을 통해서는 알 수 없다. ② RISE라고 불리는 X-밴드 안테나 두 개가 설치돼 있다. ③ RISE에서 나오는 무선신호가 화성 궤도의 흔들림을 추적하는 데 사용될 것이다.

probe n. 무인 우주탐사선, 탐사용 로켓, 탐사기
burrow v. 굴을 파다
instrument n. 기계, 기구, 도구
reveal v. (알려지지 않은 것을) 드러내다; 알리다
amount n. 총계, 총액; 양(量)
radioactive a. 방사성의, 방사능의
element n. 요소; 원소
contain v. 내포하다, 포함하다
wobble n. 비틀거림, 흔들림, 동요
orbit n. 궤도
core n. 핵심; 중심
crack v. (호두 따위를) 까다; 부수다; ~의 비밀을 밝히다
spill v. (액체 따위를) 엎지르다; (정보·비밀을) 누설하다

07 2022 단국대

지구는 어떤 물질로 구성되어 있으며, 이 물질들은 어떤 방식으로 배열되어 있는가? 이는 지질학이 몰두한 첫 번째 연구인데, 지질학은 지구를 뜻하는 그리스어 'ge'와 담론을 뜻하는 그리스어 'logos'에서 이름을 딴 과학이다. 경험해보기 전에는 우리는 이런 종류의 조사가 오로지 광물계, 그리고 지표면이나 지표면 아래 여러 깊은 곳에 있는 다양한 바위, 토양, 금속과 관련이 있을 것이라고 상상했을지도 모른다. 그러나, 그러한 연구를 수행하면서, 우리는 곧 지표면과 내부의 이전 상태에서 일어난 연속적인 변화와 이러한 변화를 일으킨 원인을 고려하게 되었다. 그리고 훨씬 더 특이하고 예기치 못하게, 우리는 곧 생물 창조의 역사, 즉 과거의 여러 시기에 지구에 살았던 동식물의 다양한 종의 역사에 대한 연구를 시작하게 되었다.

모든 사람들은 지구의 단단한 부분이 점토, 백악, 모래, 석회암, 석탄, 점판암, 화강암 등과 같은 서로 다른 물질들로 이루어져 있다는 것을 알고 있다. 그러나 관찰해보기 전에는, 이 모든 것이 처음부터 지금 우리가 그것들을 보고 있는 상태로 남아있었다고, 즉 현재의 형태와 현재의 위치에서 만들어졌다고 일반적으로 여겨진다. 지질학자는 곧 이와 다른 결론에 도달하는데, 지구의 바깥 부분들이 태초에 우리가 지금 그것들을 보고 있는 상태로 모두 만들어졌던 것도 아니며, 순식간에 만들어졌던 것도 아니라는 증거를 발견했기 때문이다. 반대로, 지질학자는 그것들이 매우 다양한 상황에서 연이는 여러 시기에 걸쳐 점차적으로 실제의 형태와 상태를 갖게 되었다는 것을 보여줄 수 있는데, 그 각 시기 동안 각기 다른 종족의 생물이 땅과 물에서 번성했으며, 이 생물들의 유해가 지금도 여전히 지구의 지각에 묻혀 있다.

1 ④ ▶ 글의 구성방식

지질학의 뜻이 무엇인지 그리고 지질학자가 무엇을 연구하는지 정의하고 있다. 따라서 ④ definition이 적절하다.

2 ④ ▶ 동의어

configuration은 '형상, 형태'의 의미이므로 동의어로는 ④ shape가 적절하다. ① 수로; 경로 ② 탄도, 궤적 ③ 변화; 돌연변이

3 ② ▶ 내용일치

지질학은 처음에는 광물에 대한 연구로 생각되었지만, 연구를 수행하면서 생물 창조의 역사, 즉 과거의 여러 시기에 지구에 살았던 동식물의 다양한 종의 역사에 대한 연구를 시작하게 되었다고 했다. 따라서 ②가 본문의 내용과 일치한다.

be composed of ~로 구성되어 있다
geology n. 지질학
inquiry n. 연구, 탐구; 조사
derive v. 끌어내다; ~에서 파생하다
discourse n. 담론, 담화
exclusively ad. 배타[독점]적으로; 오로지
pursue v. 뒤쫓다; 추구하다; (일·연구 등을) 수행하다
successive a. 연속적인, 잇따른
give rise to ~을 일으키다, 낳다
inhabit v. 살다, 거주하다, 서식하다
distinct a. 별개의, 다른
consist of ~으로 구성되다
geologist n. 지질학자
discover v. 발견하다
proof n. 증거; 증명
external a. 외부의, 밖의
flourish v. 번영하다, 번성하다
remains n. 유해
crust n. 지각

08 2020 이화여대

오늘날 대부분의 천문학 데이터는 전 세계 약 1만 명의 천문학 전문가들이 평생 동안 평가할 수 있는 것보다 훨씬 더 많은 정보를 모으는 로봇 시스템을 통해 자동으로 수집되고 있다. 그러나 아마추어 천문학자들도 100만 명이 넘으며, 그들은 이제 그 활동에 참여하여 실질적인 기여를 할 수 있는 방법을 가지고 있다.

A 2007년, 한 무리의 천문학자들이 갤럭시 주(Galaxy Zoo)라 불리는 웹 기반 응용 프로그램을 작성했는데, 이 프로그램은 Sloan Digital Sky Survey가 수집한 천문학 정보의 데이터베이스를 위한 게임처럼 창의력 있는 사용자 인터페이스를 만들어냈다. (이것을 통해) 컴퓨터가 아직 그리 능숙하지 않은 특정 종류의 은하 분류를 사람들이 시각을 통해 할 수 있는 것으로 드러났다. 그래서 이 프로젝트는 일반인들이 분류 작업에 재미있게 참여하도록 만들었고, 이것은 또한 나선은하가 시계방향으로 회전하는 경향이 있다는 이론의 진위를 천문학자들이 검증하는 데도 도움을 주었다.

C 갤럭시 주는 로봇 망원경으로 찍은 100만 개의 은하 영상물로 이뤄진 데이터 세트에서 시작되었다. 참가자들은 영상을 보고 나서 그 은하들을 "오른쪽으로 도는 것"(시계방향으로 회전한다는 뜻) 혹은 "왼쪽으로 도는 것"(시계 반대 방향으로 회전한다는 뜻)으로 분류했다. 은하의 수가 너무나 많기 때문에, 연구팀은 그 사이트를 방문하는 사람들이 작업을 모두 마치는 데는 적어도 2년이 걸릴 거라 생각했다. 그러나 그 사이트는 시작한 지 24시간 만에 시간당 7만 건의 분류 결과를 받고 있었고, 그 프로젝트는 첫해에 거의 15만 명으로부터 5,000만 건 이상의 분류 결과를 받았다. 그러한 노력의 결과 대부분의 나선은하가 오른쪽으로 돈다는 생각을 반박할 수 있게 되었다. 오른쪽으로 도는 것은 절반밖에 되지 않는다는 사실이 드러났던 것이다. 더욱 놀랍게도, 이 프로젝트에 참여한 한 네덜란드인 교사는 천문학자들을 당황하게 만든 기묘한 은하를 발견하여 결국 허블 망원경이 그 은하를 주목하도록 만들기도 했다.

E 2008년, 마이크로소프트는 WorldWide Telescope(WWT) 프로그램을 도입하여 천문학자와 일반인이 하늘, 행성, 은하에 대한 양방향 3차원 영상을 접할 수 있게 해주었다. 방문자들은 표준 브라우저를 통해 영상을 볼 수 있으며, 천문학 전문가들이 사용하는 것과 똑같은 데이터를 시각화할 수 있다. WWT는 갤럭시 주의 분류 결과와 그 밖의 것들을 통합한다. WWT와 같은 시각화 도구들은 때때로 일반 시민들의 도움을 받아, 과학자들이 데이터로부터 식견을 얻을 수 있는 능력을 실제로 변화시킬 수 있다.

1 ④ ▶ 문단 나누기
A까지는 '천문학 데이터 수집에 아마추어 천문학자들도 참여할 수 있다'는 내용이고, A부터 C까지는 '아마추어 천문학자가 참여한 갤럭시 주 프로그램과 그 참여내용'을 간략하게 소개하고 있으며, C부터 E까지는 갤럭시 주 프로그램의 진행 과정과 성과를 구체적으로 이야기하고 있고, E 이하에서는 마이크로소프트의 WWT 프로그램과 이러한 도구들이 갖는 의미에 대해 말하고 있다.

2 ③ ▶ 내용추론
"시각적인 은하 분류에 대해 컴퓨터가 아직 그리 능숙하지 않다."라고 했을 뿐, 사람과의 비교를 통해 그 우열을 직접적으로 언급하진 않았다. 그러므로 ③이 정답으로 적절하다.

---

astronomy n. 천문학
roughly ad. 대략적으로
evaluate v. 평가하다
get in on ~에 참여하다
contribution n. 기여, 공헌
galaxy n. 은하, 은하수
classification n. 분류
visually ad. 시각적으로, 눈에 보이도록
participate in ~에 참여하다
spiral galaxy 나선은하
rotate v. 회전하다
clockwise ad. 시계 바늘 방향으로 도는
launch v. (사업 따위에) 손을 대다, 나서다, 착수하다
right-handed a. 오른손잡이의; 오른쪽으로 도는, 시계 바늘 방향의
left-handed a. 왼손잡이의; 왼쪽으로 도는, 시계 바늘 반대 방향의
counterclockwise a. 시계 바늘 반대 방향의
refute v. 반박하다
baffle v. 좌절시키다; 당황하게 하다
end up ~ing 결국 ~하게 되다
introduce v. 소개하다; 도입하다
access n. 접근, 면접, 출입
interactive a. 상호작용하는; 양방향의
incorporate v. 통합하다
transform v. 변형시키다, 바꾸다
insight n. 통찰력

---

09 2021 가톨릭대

지구의 운동은 두 가지 요소로 이루어져 있다. 지구는 지구가 돌고 있는 가상의 선인 축을 중심으로 '자전하고', 궤도를 그리며 태양 주위를 '공전한다.' 지구의 자전에 관해서는 많은 증거와 주장이 있다. 태양, 행성, 항성은 지구가 자전하기 때문에 동쪽에서 뜨고 서쪽에서 진다. 또한 북반구에서 관찰하는 사람들은 북쪽에 있는 별들이 북극성을 중심으로 원을 그리며 시계 반대방향으로 움직이는 것을 볼 수 있다. 그러나 이러한 관찰은 자전하는 지구에 의해서뿐만 아니라 지구는 정지해있고 하늘이 움직이는 것에 의해서도 설명될 수 있다. 따라서 우리는 다음과 같은 더욱 강력한 주장이 필요하다.

우선, 지구는 정확한 구(救)의 형태가 아니다. 적도에서 지구를 통과하는 거리는 12,756km이지만 한 극에서 다른 극까지의 거리는 12,713km에 불과하다. 그래서 지구는 불룩한 모양이고, 과학자

component n. 성분, 구성 요소
rotate v. (축을 중심으로 하여) 회전[순환]하다
axis n. (중심) 축
revolve v. 회전하다; (천체가) 공전(公轉)하다
orbit n. 궤도
counterclockwise ad. 반시계 방향으로
North Star (the ~) 북극성(= Polaris)
stationary a. 움직이지 않는, 정지된

들은 움직이는 물질이 같은 방향으로 계속 움직이려고 하는 경향인 '관성'의 개념을 사용하여 그것을 설명한다. 행성을 구성하는 물질이 행성의 중력에 의해 제자리에 고정되어 있지 않는다면, 그것은 회전하는 바퀴에서 진흙이 떨어져 나가는 것처럼 회전하는 행성으로부터 떨어져 나갈 것이다. 지구의 표면은 적도에서 가장 빠르게 움직이며, 적도에서 지구표면의 물질이 안쪽으로 향하는 중력의 힘에 맞서 밖으로 돌출된다. 그래서 결과적으로 적도 부분이 불룩해진다.

또 다른 증거는 지구의 바람 패턴에서 나온다. 만약 지구가 회전하지 않고 동일한 대기 열 분포를 유지한다면 바람의 패턴은 훨씬 더 단순할 것이다. 적도에서 가열된 공기는 극지방을 향해 움직일 것이고, 더 높은 위도의 찬 공기는 적도를 향해 다시 이동할 것이다. 그 이동은 남북으로만 향할 것이다. 그러나 우리는 지구의 회전이 바람의 방향을 바꾸기 때문에 실제로 굽은 바람의 패턴을 관찰할 수 있다.

마지막으로, 우리는 지구가 회전하고 있다는 것을 직접 관찰함으로써 알고 있다. 달에 착륙한 우주비행사들은 매일 24시간 만에 지구의 전체 표면을 보았다. 달은 매일 한 번씩 지구 주위를 공전하지 않는다. 따라서 지구가 자전하고 있음에 틀림없다.

1 ① ▶ 빈칸완성
두 번째 문단부터 네 번째 문단까지는 모두 지구의 자전을 입증하고 있는 사실들에 관한 내용이므로, ①이 빈칸에 적절하다.

2 ② ▶ 글의 제목
지구의 모양, 지구 바람의 패턴, 직접적인 관찰을 증거로 지구가 자전하고 있음을 설명하는 글이므로, ②가 제목으로 적절하다.

3 ② ▶ 내용파악
세 번째 단락에서 지구가 자전하는 증거로 지구 바람의 패턴을 들고 있는데, 지구의 자전이 바람의 방향을 바꾸기 때문에 굽은 바람의 패턴을 관찰할 수 있다고 했으므로 ②가 정답이다.

spherical a. 구 모양의, 구체의
pole n. (지구의) 극
bulging a. 볼록한, 돌출한
inertia n. <물리> 관성
gravity n. (지구) 중력
equator n. (지구의) 적도
retain v. 유지[보유]하다
distribution n. 분배 (방식), 분포
latitude n. 위도; 지역, 지방
deflect v. 방향을 바꾸다[바꾸게 하다]

---

10 2016 명지대

1920년 4월, 할로 섀플리(Harlow Shapley)와 히버 커티스(Heber Curtis)는 워싱턴 D.C.에 있는 스미스소니언(Smithonian) 자연사박물관의 대강당에서 우주의 크기에 대해 논쟁을 벌였다. 이 논쟁에서 커티스는 우주가 많은 별개의 '섬 우주들'로 구성되어 있으며, 소위 나선성운들은 우리 은하계 밖에 멀리 떨어져 있는 별들의 체계라고 주장했다. (반면에) 섀플리는 나선성운들이 은하계에 있는 가스구름에 불과하다고 주장했다. 섀플리는 태양의 위치를 은하계의 ─ 그의 주장에 따르면 전체 우주의 ─ 가장자리 근처에 두었다. 반면 커티스는 태양이 은하계의 중심 부근에 있다고 믿었다. 커티스는 우주의 크기가 크다는 것에 대해서는 옳았지만, 은하계에서 태양의 위치에 대해서는 틀렸던 반면, 섀플리는 우주의 크기가 보다 작다는 것에 대해서는 틀렸지만 은하계에서의 태양의 위치에 대해서는 옳았다.

은하계 밖의 거리 측정법들이 많이 출현함에 따라, 우주 팽창률인 '허블 상수(Hubble Constant)'와 관련해 새로운 주장들이 봇물 터지듯이 쏟아져 나왔다. 일단의 천문학자들은 1996년에 두 번째 대논쟁을 벌였다. 우주의 나이와 크기는 당연히 서로 관련돼 있으며, 우주의 나이와 크기 모두 결정적으로 허블 상수에 달려있다. 섀플리와 커티스가 사용한 바로 그 대강당에서, 은하계를 연구하는 시드니 반 덴 버그(Sidney van den Bergh)와 구스타프 타만(Gustav Tammann)은 이 문제를 놓고 논쟁을 벌였다. 반 덴 버그는 허블 상수의 높은 값을 뒷받침하는 증거를 제시하며, 우주의 젊은 나이와 그에 따른 우주의 작은 크기를 주장했다. (반면) 타만은 보다 나이가 들고 보다 규모가 큰 우주를 나타내는 허블 상수의 낮은 값을 주장했다. 반 덴 버그와 구스타프 타만 모두 상대진영의 천문학자들을 설득시키는 데 성공하지 못했다.

그럼에도 불구하고, 천문학자들은 무엇이 확실히 사실인가에 대한 한계를 둘 수는 있다. 천문학자들은 고배율의 망원경을 이용하여 100억~120억 광년 떨어진 은하계들을 본다. 1광년은 약 10조 킬로미터이므로, 가시성의 '지평'은 지름이 약 240억 광년이다. 그러나 이 지름은 우리가 볼 때 그런 것이다. 멀리 떨어진 은하계들에서 본 지평은 어떠한가? 우주가 우리가 볼 수 있는 부분보다 훨

auditorium n. 강당, 대강의실, 회관
cosmos n. 우주
spiral a. 나선의, 나선형의
nebula n. 성운
the milky way 은하계, 은하
the way out 출구; 해결수단, 타개책
edge n. 가장자리, 끝, 모서리; 경계
advent n. 도래, 출현
extragalactic a. 은하계 밖의
measurement n. 측정; 측정법, 측량법
erupt v. (봇물 터지듯이) 쏟아져 나오다
constant n. 상수, 정수
astronomer n. 천문학자
telescope n. 망원경
light year 광년
horizon n. 지평선, 수평선; <천문> 지평(地平)
diameter n. 지름, 직경
viewpoint n. 입장
in the event that ~일 경우에는
hypothesis n. 가설

씬 클 수 있다. 있을 법하게도 MIT의 앨런 구스(Alan Guth)가 제시한 팽창가설이 옳은 것으로 밝혀질 경우에는 이것이 사실일 것이다. 이 (팽창)가설은 극도로 나이 어린 우주가 한순간에 너무나도 큰 고도증대를 경험하다 보니 우주가 원자보다 작은 입자 크기에서 순식간에 소프트볼 크기로 부풀었다는 것을 말한다. 만일 팽창이 일어났다면, 그러면 우주는 우리가 예상하는 것보다 훨씬 규모가 클지도 모른다.

여기서 불가사의해진다. 만일 팽창이 일어났다면, 그러면 가시적인 지평 너머 많은 곳에서 팽창이 일어났을지도 모른다. 만일 이것이 사실이라면, 그러면 다른 우주들이 우리의 탐지능력 너머에(우리가 탐지할 수 없는 곳에) 존재할지도 모른다. 과학은 이런 질문에 대해 답변을 못 하겠다고 한다. 정의상(자명한 일로서), 과학은 시험 가능한 생각들을 만들어내고 실험하는 것에 관한 것이기 때문이다. 지금으로서는, 우리가 지름이 적어도 1500억 조 마일이나 되는 우주에 산다는 것을 아는 것은 경이로운 일이다.

1 ①   ▶ 빈칸완성

빈칸 앞에서 "우주가 우리가 볼 수 있는 부분보다 클 수 있다."라고 했으며, "팽창가설은 극도로 나이 어린 우주가 한순간에 너무나도 큰 고도증대를 경험하다 보니 우주가 원자보다 작은 입자 크기에서 순식간에 소프트볼 크기로 부풀었다는 것을 말한다."라고 했으므로 빈칸에도 우주의 크기가 생각보다 크다는 것과 관련된 내용이 와야 적절하다. 따라서 ①의 "그것(우주)은 우리가 예상하는 것보다 훨씬 규모가 클지도 모른다."가 정답이다.

2 ③   ▶ 글의 요지

은하계 밖의 거리 측정법들이 많이 출현했음에도 불구하고, 1996년 시드니 반 덴 버그와 구스타프 타만이 우주의 규모를 두고 두 번째로 대논쟁을 벌였지만, 상대진영의 천문학자들을 설득시키는 데 성공하지 못했다고 했다. 따라서 이에 대해 아직 결론이 나지 못했음을 알 수 있으므로, 글의 요지로는 ③의 "과학적 발전에도 불구하고, 우리가 살고 있는 우주의 크기는 여전히 미스터리로 남아있다."가 적절하다.

3 ④   ▶ 내용일치

마지막 단락 둘째 문장에서 "다른 우주들이 우리가 탐지할 수 없는 곳에 존재할지도 모른다."라고 언급하고, 이어서 과학이 이런 질문에 대해 답변을 안 하는 이유로 "과학은 시험 가능한 생각들을 만들어내고 실험하는 것에 관한 것이기 때문이다."라고 했으므로 "실험에 근거해서 다른 우주의 존재를 확정적으로 인정한다."는 취지의 ④는 본문과 일치하지 않는 진술이다.

---

put forth 내다, 제출하다
hypergrowth n. 고도성장, 급성장
balloon v. 부풀다, 커지다
subatomic a. 원자보다 작은
in an instant 눈 깜짝할 사이에, 순식간에
detect v. 탐지하다, 발견하다
beg off ~을 못하겠다고 하다, ~을 면제되게 하다
wondrous a. 경이로운, 감탄스러운
all bets are off (모든) 계획이 무효가 되다, 모두 백지화되다
reassess v. 재평가하다, 재검토하다
contend with ~와 싸우다, 씨름하다
validation n. 확인, 비준
idle speculation 공상
cosmology n. 우주론

10 환경·기상

01 2020 경기대

새는 어디에나 있다. 우리는 새가 우리 머리 위를 날아다니거나 우리의 뒷마당을 뛰어다니는 것을 매일 본다. 그러나 과학자들은 새의 개체수가 특히 북미에서 급격히 감소하고 있다고 말한다. 1970년 이후로 북미 대륙 전체 새의 개체들 중 약 29%가 없어졌다. 더욱이 참새와 찌르레기 같이 흔한 새의 종(種)이 놀라운 속도로, 희귀한 조류의 종보다 훨씬 더 빨리 사라지고 있는 것으로 밝혀졌다. 새로운 연구에 따르면, 거의 모든 새의 집단들이 위기에 직면해 있다고 한다. 초원에 사는 새의 경우, 53%가 감소하여 감소폭이 가장 컸다. 숲에 사는 새들은 초원에 사는 새들보다 개체수가 더 많긴 하지만 역시 빠른 속도로 사라지고 있다. 사라진 새의 수가 10억 마리에 이른다. 북반구 전체를 이동하는 물새들도 뚜렷하고 일관된 개체수 감소세를 보이고 있다. 이들의 총 개체수는 지난 50년 동안 37%나 감소했다. 종종 다른 환경에 적응할 수 있는 외래 침입종도 이 운명에서 벗어나지 못했다. 새는 생태계의 전반적인 건강을 반영할 수 있는 지표 동물이기 때문에, 과학자들은 이 같은 엄청난 개체수 감소를 북미 생태계의 전반적인 상태에 대한 경고로 받아들여야 한다고 말한다.

1 ④ ▶ 빈칸완성
빈칸 뒤 문장의 내용은 빈칸 앞 문장의 내용, 즉 "북미의 새 개체수가 급감하고 있다."는 내용을 구체적으로 부연해서 설명하고 있다. 따라서 빈칸에는 첨언, 부연설명의 역할을 하는 표현이 필요하므로, '더욱이'라는 의미의 ④가 적절하다. ① 마침내 ② 따라서 ③ 그러나

2 ③ ▶ 내용파악
"초원에 사는 새의 경우, 53%가 감소하여 감소폭이 가장 컸다."고 했으므로, ③이 정답으로 적절하다.

3 ① ▶ 내용추론
"새는 생태계의 전반적인 건강을 반영할 수 있는 지표 동물이기 때문에 새의 엄청난 개체수 감소를 북미 생태계의 전반적인 상태에 대한 경고로 받아들여야 한다."고 했는데, 이는 "새가 위태로운 상황에 처해 있다는 것은 다른 동물도 마찬가지로 위태로운 상황에 있다는 것을 보여준다."는 것이다. 그러므로 ①이 정답으로 적절하다.

hop v. 뛰다, (새 따위가 발을 모으고) 깡충 뛰다
backyard n. 뒷뜰
continent n. 대륙
sparrow n. 참새
blackbird n. 찌르레기
alarming a. 놀라운
grassland n. 목초지, 초원
dwell v. 살다, 거주하다
outnumber v. ~보다 수가 많다, ~보다 수적으로 우세하다, 수로 압도하다
shorebird n. 강변·바닷가에 사는 새(도요새·물떼새류)
migrate v. 이주하다; (새나 물고기 등이) 이동하다
hemisphere n. (지구·천체의) 반구(半球)
sharp a. 명확한, 뚜렷한
invasive species 침입종, 외래유입종
adapt v. (환경 등에) 순응하다
indicator animal 지표동물(환경조건을 나타내는 지표가 되는 동물)
reflect v. 반영하다; 반사하다
ecosystem n. 생태계
overall a. 종합적인, 일반적인
massive a. 대량의, 대규모의

02 2017 단국대

현대적인 기상 예보 방법들은 단기간의 날씨를 확정짓는 것과 관련해서는 꽤 정확하지만, 예보가 길어질수록 그 예보가 틀릴 확률은 더 높아진다. 수학적으로 계산하여 기상 상태를 확인하는 현재의 방법은 날씨의 급변하는 성질 때문에 정확한 예측이 약 5일 앞서 하는 것으로 제한된다. 기상학자들은 컴퓨터 데이터 수집 방식의 결과를 현재 일어나고 있는 실제 기상 조건과 합친다. 다양한 고도에서의 온도, 이슬점, 바람과 관련한 현재의 정보가 전 세계에서 온 종일 모아져서 여러 단서들을 제공하고 이 단서들을 과거의 상황에 근거한 컴퓨터 모형과 비교하여 개연성 있는 기후 패턴을 제시하게 된다. <그러나 기상 관측법의 과학과 방법론이 향상되었음에도 불구하고, 대기와 날씨가 관련된 움직임을 이해하는 데는 여전히 큰 격차가 있다.> 결과적으로 다양한 기상 조건을 보아왔고 그러한 기상 조건이 가져올 변화와 추이에 대해 잘 알고 있는 경험 많은 기상학자가 컴퓨터에서 생성된 모형 못지않게 미래의 기상 상태를 정확히 예측할 수 있다.

1 ④ ▶ 동의어
level은 '수준', '정도', '높이', '고도' 등의 뜻으로 사용되는 다의어다. 정확한 날씨를 예측

forecasting n. 예측, 예상; (일기) 예보
accurate a. 정확한; 정밀한
short-range a. 단기의
predication n. 단정, 단언
mathematically ad. 수학적으로, 아주 정확히
calculate v. 계산하다, 산정하다
confine v. 제한하다, 국한하다
in advance (~보다) 미리[앞서]; 사전에
chaotic a. 무질서한, 혼란한
meteorologist n. 기상학자
dew point 이슬점

하기 위해서는 다양한 고도에서 정보가 모아질 것이므로 ④ elevations가 밑줄 친 levels 와 의미가 가장 유사하다. 참고로 at various levels는 수직적으로 모든 곳을 가리키고 all around the world는 수평적으로 모든 곳을 가리켜서 결국 지상의 모든 곳을 포함하게 된다. ① 변화 ② 온도 ③ 속도

2 ④ ▶ 문장삽입
주어진 문장은 "그러나 기상 관측법의 과학과 방법론이 향상되었음에도 불구하고, 대기와 날씨가 관련된 움직임을 이해하는 데는 여전히 큰 격차가 있다."의 뜻으로, 현재의 과학적 기상 관측법이 여전히 정확한 기상 예보를 하기에는 한계가 있음을 내포하고 있다. 한편, As a result 이하의 내용은 "컴퓨터에서 생성된 모형을 바탕으로 하는 기상 예측이 노련한 기상학자가 경험을 바탕으로 하는 기상 예측과 별반 차이가 없다."는 것으로, 주어진 문장과 마찬가지로 과학적 예측방법의 한계에 관한 내용이므로, 주어진 문장은 As a result의 앞에 오는 것이 적절하다. 따라서 ⓓ에 위치하는 것이 적절하다.

3 ① ▶ 내용일치
본문은 컴퓨터를 이용한 기상 예측의 한계에 대한 내용이므로 ①이 일치하지 않는 진술이다.

03 2019 경기대

자연은 질병, 날씨, 기근을 통해 여러 가지 방법으로 인간에게 도전한다. 해안 지역에 사는 사람들에게는, 파멸적인 파괴를 가져올 수 있는 흔치 않은 현상이 쓰나미다. 쓰나미는 충격적인 동요에 의해 수역(바다)에서 생성되는 일련의 파도다. 지진, 산사태, 화산 분출, 폭발, 그리고 심지어 운석의 충돌도 쓰나미를 일으킬 수 있다. 바다에서 시작된 쓰나미는 서서히 육지로 접근하면서 바닥의 마찰과 물결의 거친 몰아침으로 인해 높이는 높아지고 에너지는 줄어들게 된다. 그럼에도 불구하고, 다른 파도와 마찬가지로 쓰나미도 해안으로 밀려들 때 엄청난 에너지를 쏟아낸다. 쓰나미는 침식하는 힘이 매우 강해서, 해변에서 모래를 쓸어내고, 나무들의 밑을 파서 약화시키며, 내륙으로 수백 미터까지 물에 잠기게 한다. 쓰나미는 자동차, 집, 초목, 그리고 충돌하는 무엇이든 쉽게 파괴할 수 있다. 쓰나미에 의한 파괴를 최소화하기 위해, 과학자들은 더 정확하고 더 빨리 쓰나미를 예측하려고 끊임없이 노력하고 있다. 많은 요인들이 합쳐져서 생명을 위협하는 쓰나미가 발생하기 때문에, 이것을 예측하기는 쉽지 않다. 그럼에도 불구하고, 기상학자들은 쓰나미의 움직임을 연구하고 예측하는 일을 끈기 있게 계속하고 있다.

1 ③ ▶ 내용파악
첫 번째 문장의 질병, 날씨, 기근 등은 모두 인간을 어려움에 처하게 만드는 자연현상 혹은 자연력(自然力)에 해당하므로, ③이 정답으로 적절하다.

2 ① ▶ 동의어
unleash가 '붙들고 있던 것을 놓아주다, 해방하다'라는 의미로 쓰였으므로, '풀어놓다, 방출하다'라는 뜻을 가진 ① release가 동의어로 적절하다. ② 소비하다 ③ 포함하다 ④ 떠받치다

3 ② ▶ 빈칸완성
빈칸 뒤의 this는 "쓰나미를 발생시키는 요인이 많기 때문에, 쓰나미의 예측이 쉽지 않다."는 앞 문장의 내용을 가리키고, 주절의 내용은 "기상학자들이 쓰나미의 움직임을 연구하고 예측하는 일을 끈기 있게 계속하고 있다."는 것이다. 빈칸 전후의 문장이 대조를 이루므로, 빈칸에는 양보의 의미를 가진 전치사가 들어가야 한다. 따라서 '~에도 불구하고'라는 뜻의 ② Despite가 정답이 된다. ① ~와 조화하여 ③ ~와 반대로 ④ ~와 비교하면

4 ③ ▶ 내용파악
본문에서는 "쓰나미가 엄청난 에너지를 가진 채 해안 지역에 밀려들어 이곳에 큰 피해를 줄 수 있다."는 내용을 주로 이야기하고 있으므로, ③이 정답으로 적절하다.

---

famine n. 기근; 굶주림, 배고픔, 기아(饑餓)
catastrophic a. 큰 재앙의; 파멸의, 비극적인
destruction n. 파괴, 파멸
generate v. 산출하다; (전기·열 등을) 발생시키다; (결과·상태 등을) 야기하다, 초래하다
impulsive a. 충동적인; 추진적인
disturbance n. 소동; 방해, 교란; 외란
landslide n. 산사태
volcanic a. 화산의, 화산성의, 화산작용에 의한
eruption n. (화산의) 폭발, 분화; (용암·간헐천의) 분출
meteorite n. 운석
friction n. 마찰
turbulence n. (바람·물결 등의) 거칠게 몰아침
tremendous a. 무서운; 굉장한, 엄청난
plunge v. 뛰어들다, 돌입하다; 돌진하다
erosion n. 부식, 침식
potential n. 잠재력; 가능성
strip v. 벗기다; ~로부터 빼앗다[제거하다]
undermine v. ~의 밑을 파다; (명성 따위를) 음험한 수단으로 훼손하다
flood v. 범람시키다, 물에 잠기게 하다
collide with ~와 충돌하다
minimize v. 최소화하다
devastation n. 황폐하게 함; 유린
foresee v. 예견하다, 앞일을 내다보다
meteorology n. 기상학
persevere v. 인내하며 계속하다, 인내심을 갖고 하다

04 2021 성균관대

우리 모두는 믿을만한 에너지원을 영원히 이용 가능하리라 생각하게 되었다. 우리는 언제 어디서든지 원하는 곳으로 차를 몰고 간다. 계기판의 연료탱크 눈금이 내려가면, 그냥 가장 가까운 주유소에 차를 댄다. 집에서는, 실내온도를 바꾸거나 음식 준비를 해야 할 때마다 가장 가까이 있는 전자 제품을 켜기만 하면 된다. 이렇게 아무런 생각 없이 이용하는 모든 에너지의 원천은 무엇인가? 세계 대부분에서 에너지는 석탄, 천연가스, 석유와 같은 화석연료를 태워서 만들어진다. 문제는 이런 자원이 유한하다는 것이다. 현재의 사용률로 사용하면, 2080년 이전에 세계의 석유 공급은 거의 다 없어질 것이다.

C 이 세계적인 문제에 대한 최선의 해결책은 미래의 필요를 충족시키기 위한 대체 에너지원을 찾는 것이다. 현재 화석연료를 대체하는 최고의 대안은 핵융합과 태양 에너지이다. 핵융합은 엄청난 에너지를 방출하는 핵반응이다. 사실상 오염도 없어서 아마도 장기적으로는 최고의 선택일 수 있다. 그러나 유감스럽게도, 이용 가능하려면 적어도 20년은 더 있어야 한다. 다른 가능한 에너지원인 태양열은 핵을 제외한 지구의 모든 에너지의 원천이다. 태양 에너지에 대해 생각할 때 사람들은 일반적으로 개별 주택 소유자들이 태양력을 이용하여 물을 데우고 건물 난방을 할 수 있는 많은 방식에 대해 생각한다. 하지만 태양 에너지는 전기를 생산하고 자동차 연료를 정제하는 데도 이용할 수 있다.

F 21세기에 충분한 에너지원을 확보하기 위해서는 개발을 추구하고 대체 에너지원 사용을 세계적으로 독려해야 한다는 것이 명백하다. 만약 우리가 이 문제를 무시하면, 우리 아이들은 어떻게 될까? 2050년에 그들의 삶은 어떠할까?

pull into 차를 세우다
appliance n. 가전제품
fossil fuel 화석연료
meet v. 충족시키다
fusion n. 핵융합
nuclear reaction 핵반응
enormous a. 막대한
utilize v. 활용하다
generate v. (전기·열 등을) 발생시키다
purify v. 정화하다, 정제하다
what become of ~이 어떻게 되다

1 ⑤ ▶ 단락 나누기
'문제 제기 → 해결방안 제시 → 결론'으로 이어지는 구성이다. 처음부터 C까지가 '문제 제기'이고, C부터 F까지가 '해결방안 제시'이며, F 이하가 결론인 셈이다. 따라서 ⑤가 정답이다.

2 ② ▶ 빈칸완성
Ⓐ가 들어있는 문장은 '문제는 ~'으로 시작하는데, 다음 문장에서 "2080년 이전에 석유 자원은 고갈될 것이다."라고 했으므로, 문제는 에너지원의 '유한성'이다. 따라서 빈칸에는 '한정되어 있는', '유한한'이라는 뜻의 ②가 적절하다. ① 인공적인 ③ 오염된 ④ 위험한 ⑤ 쓸모없는

3 ④ ▶ 글의 요지
이 글은 화석연료를 대체하는 새로운 에너지원을 찾는 것이 필요하다는 내용이므로 ④가 글의 요지로 적절하다.

05 2022 서울여대

웨섹스 고고학(Wessex Archaeology, 고고학 및 유산 서비스 제공 회사)에 따르면 약 18,000년 전, 오늘날 영국의 대부분은 빙하기에 들어있었다. 이 빙하기는 약 12,000년 전까지 수천 년 동안 지속되었는데 그때는 온난해지는 기후로 인해 얼음으로 뒤덮인 지역이 없어진 후였다. 『내셔널 지오그래픽(National Geographic)』에 따르면, 그 여파로 오늘날 북해와 영국 해협인 지역은 풀이 무성한 습지, 숲이 우거진 계곡 및 늪으로 가득 차 있었다고 한다. 도거랜드(Doggerland)로 알려진 이 지역은 영국과 유럽 본토를 연결했으며 18,000평방마일이 넘는 면적에 걸쳐 있었다.

영국의 유럽 대륙과의 연결이 끝나기 시작한 것은 약 8,200년 전 거대한 쓰나미가 도거랜드를 강타했을 때부터였다. 『Nature Climate Change』 저널에 발표된 연구에 따르면, 노르웨이 연안 앞바다에서 스토레가 슬라이드(Storegga Slide)로 알려진 거대한 수중 산사태가 일어나 720입방 마일 이상의 물질을 물속으로 이동시켰다고 한다. 이것은 전 세계의 모든 강에서 나오는 연간 침전물의 300배에 달하는 양이다.

『해양 석유 지질학(Marine and Petroleum Geology)』 저널에 따르면, 스토레가 슬라이드는 노르웨이 전역에서 퇴빙 시기 이후 이어진 지진 활동에 의해 촉발되었을 가능성이 높다고 한다. (수중

archaeology n. 고고학
glaciation n. 빙하 작용; 빙결(氷結)
expanse n. 넓게 트인 지역
bring to an end ~을 끝내다, 마치다
grassy a. 풀이 무성한
marshland n. 습지대
swamp n. 늪, 습지
massive a. 거대한, 엄청나게 큰
landslide n. 산사태
sediment n. 침전물, 퇴적물
seismic a. 지진의, 지진에 의한
deglaciation n. (빙하의) 퇴빙(退氷)

산사태에 의한 물의 빠른 움직임과 위치이동은 쓰나미를 일으키기에 충분한 에너지를 발생시켰다. 『Nature Climate Change』에 따르면 이 거대한 파도는 66피트 높이까지 치솟았을 것이라고 한다. 쓰나미가 도거랜드를 집어삼켰다. BBC에 따르면 쓰나미는 영국 북동쪽을 덮쳐 밀고 들어와 내륙으로 25마일을 이동하여 영국을 새로 형성된 섬으로 만들었다고 한다.

displacement n. (장소를) 바꾸어 놓기
swallow up 삼키다, 빨아들이다

1 ② ▶ 글의 주제
수천 년 동안 지속된 빙하기로 영국 해협은 유럽 본토와 연결되어 있었는데, 쓰나미가 도거랜드를 집어삼켜 영국과 유럽 본토를 연결하는 지대가 사라졌음을 설명하고 있으므로 ②가 정답이다.

2 ② ▶ 내용일치
"(수중) 산사태에 의한 물의 빠른 움직임과 위치이동은 쓰나미를 일으키기에 충분한 에너지를 발생시켰다."고 했으므로 ②가 정답이다. ① 수천 년 계속되었다. ③ 약 8,200년 전은 수중 산사태와 쓰나미로 인해 영국이 유럽본토와 분리되기 시작한 때이다. ④ 쓰나미가 밀어닥친 곳은 영국 북동부였고 그때 도거랜드가 형성된 것이 아니라 물에 잠겼다.

06   2020 한성대

(환경파괴 없이) 지속가능한 생활은 사용하는 것을 최대한 재활용함으로써 천연자원의 수요를 줄이려는 관행에 관한 것이다. 때때로 그것은 지속가능성을 촉진하지 않는 관행을 이용하여 만든 제품을 소비하지 않는다는 뜻일 수도 있고, 때로는 생명의 순환에서 여러분들이 적극적인 역할을 보다 많이 시작할 수 있도록 행동을 바꾸는 것을 의미하기도 한다.
사람들은 지구온난화, 기후변화, 오존층의 고갈, 자원 고갈이 실재하는 것이며 그것들이 인간과 동물의 생활에 미치는 영향은 재앙에 가까운 것임을 알고 있다. 지금은 개개인이 자신들의 생활방식을 바꿈으로써 지속가능한 생활을 할 수 있도록 행동을 취해야 할 때다. 예를 들어, 대중교통을 더 자주 이용하고, 에너지 소비를 줄이고, 보다 환경친화적이 되는 것과 같은 기본적인 조치는 여러분들이 환경에 미치는 영향을 최소화하고, 지구를 안전하고 깨끗한 곳으로 만드는 데 큰 도움이 될 수 있다.

sustainable a. 유지[계속]할 수 있는; (자원 이용이) 환경이 파괴되지 않고 계속될 수 있는
ensure v. 책임지다, 보장[보증]하다, (성공 등을) 확실하게 하다
to the best of one's ability 최선을 다해, 힘닿는 데까지
promote v. 진전시키다, 조장하다
sustainability n. 지속가능성; 환경 파괴 없이 지속될 수 있음
alter v. (모양·성질 등을) 바꾸다, 변경하다
depletion n. 고갈, 소모
ozone layer 오존층
resource n. 자원, 재원
catastrophic a. 대변동[큰 재앙]의; 파멸의, 비극적인
adopt v. (의견·방침·조처 따위를) 채용[채택]하다
public transportation 공공 운송기관, 대중교통
consumption n. 소비; 소모
eco-friendly a. 환경친화적인
go a long way 큰 도움이 되다, 기여하다
minimize v. 최소로 하다

1 ② ▶ 내용일치
지속가능한 생활은 재활용을 최대한으로 함으로써 천연자원의 수요를 줄이는 것이 포함된다고 했다. 그러므로 ②가 옳지 않은 진술이다.

2 ④ ▶ 내용추론
세계 이곳저곳을 돌아다니는 활동은 필연적으로 자원과 에너지의 소비를 초래하므로, 환경에 부정적인 영향을 끼칠 것이다. 따라서 ④가 추론할 수 없는 진술이다.

3 ③ ▶ 빈칸완성
빈칸 Ⓐ 다음의 제품이 지속가능성을 저해하는 제품이어서 지속가능한 생활을 위해서는 이런 제품을 소비하지 말아야 할 것이므로 빈칸 Ⓐ에는 consume이 적절하며, 지구온난화, 기후변화, 오존층의 고갈, 자원 고갈 등은 인간의 생활에 큰 '영향'을 끼치므로, 빈칸 Ⓑ에는 impact가 들어간다. ① 소비하다 — 계약 ② 상담하다 — 계약 ④ 상담하다 — 영향

4 ④ ▶ 글의 제목
지속가능한 생활의 의미와 실천방법에 대해 이야기하고 있는 내용이므로, 제목으로는 ④가 적절하다.

07　2019 숭실대

　환경보호론자들은 깨끗한 석탄은 근거 없는 믿음이라고 말한다. 물론 그것은 맞는 말이다. 지하에 매장된 석탄을 캐기 위해 애팔래치아산맥 전체의 봉우리를 허물어 계곡으로 만들고 개울에는 주황색 빛을 띠는 산성수(酸性水)가 흐르는 웨스트버지니아를 한번 보라. 아니면 요즘 공기가 공항의 흡연실보다 종종 더 탁한 베이징 시내를 살펴보라. 주로 석탄 연소에서 비롯된 중국의 대기 오염은 매년 백만 명 이상의 사람들의 조기 사망의 원인으로 여겨지고 있다. 그것은 중국이나 다른 곳에서 광산 사고로 죽는 그 수천 명의 사람들보다 더 많은 것이다.
　이러한 문제들은 새로운 것이 아니다. 웨일즈와 노섬벌랜드에서 나온 석탄이 영국에서 산업혁명의 첫 번째 불을 밝혔던 17세기 후반에, 영국의 작가인 존 이블린(John Evelyn)은 런던을 가득 메운 자욱한 연기의 '악취와 어둠'에 대해 이미 불만을 터뜨리고 있었다. 3세기가 지난 1952년 12월, 석탄으로 가득한 두꺼운 층을 이룬 스모그가 런던에 내려와 긴 주말 연휴 동안 머물러 있었는데, 이로 인해 호흡기 질환이 급속히 확산되었고 그 후 몇 달 사이에 12,000명이나 되는 사람들이 사망했다. 경제학자들의 완곡한 표현을 사용하자면, 석탄은 외부적인 것들로 가득한데, 그것은 곧 석탄이 사회에 부과하는 막대한 비용들을 말한다. 석탄은 우리가 사용하는 가장 더럽고, 가장 치명적인 에너지원이다. 그러나 대부분의 기준에서 볼 때 석탄은 또한 가장 저렴한 에너지원이며 우리는 석탄에 의존하고 있다. 따라서 오늘날 가장 큰 문제는 석탄이 과연 '깨끗해질 수' 있느냐가 아니다. 석탄은 깨끗해질 수 없다. 문제는 석탄이 국지적 재난뿐 아니라 지구의 급격한 기후변화를 방지할 수 있을 만큼 깨끗해질 수 있느냐 하는 것이다.
　2012년에 세계는 기록적인 345억 미터 톤의 이산화탄소를 화석연료에서 배출했다. 석탄은 대기 오염에 가장 큰 원인을 제공했다. 저렴한 천연가스가 최근 미국의 석탄 수요를 감소시키고 있지만, 다른 곳, 특히 중국에서는 석탄의 수요가 급증하고 있다. 향후 이십 년 동안 전 세계 수억 명의 사람들이 처음으로 전기를 공급받을 것이며 현재의 추세가 계속된다면 대부분은 석탄으로 생산되는 에너지를 사용할 것이다. 대체에너지원과 환경보존에 대한 가장 강력한 압박조차도 석탄을 대체할 수 없을 것이다. 적어도 지금 당장은 대체할 수 없을 것이다.

environmentalist n. 환경(보호)론자
underneath ad. 아래에, 하부(下部)에
stream n. 개울, 시내
acidic a. 산성의
thick a. 탁한, 흐린, 투명하지 않은
stink n. 악취, 고약한 냄새
wreath v. 둘러[에워]싸다
-laden a. (형용사를 형성하여) ~이 가득한
linger v. 오래 머물다
long weekend 긴 주말 연휴(주말에 더해 금요일이나 월요일이 휴일이 되는 경우)
respiratory a. 호흡의, 호흡 기관의
ailment n. 질병
ensuing a. 다음의, 뒤이은
euphemism n. 완곡어
externality n. 외부 효과
emit v. (빛·열·가스·소리 등을) 내다[내뿜다]
metric a. 미터(법)의
contributor n. 원인 제공자
surge v. 급등[급증]하다
aggressive a. 공격적인, 대단히 적극적인

1 ①　▶ 빈칸완성
　빈칸 Ⓐ 다음에는 석탄의 채굴로 인하여 발생된 자연 경관 손상, 대기 오염 등을 들고 있는데, 이는 석탄의 연소로 인한 악영향이므로, 환경학자들은 석탄의 단점을 지적할 것이다. 따라서 '깨끗한 석탄은 존재하지 않는다'는 의미의 ①이 빈칸에 적절하다.

2 ③　▶ 부분이해
　externalities(외부적인 것들)가 대시 다음의 the heavy costs와 동격을 이루어, Ⓑ 다음에는 석탄이 사회에 부과하는 막대한 비용들에 대한 설명이 이어지고 있다. 더럽지만 가장 저렴하기 때문에 의존할 수밖에 없는 석탄으로 인하여 국지적 재난뿐 아니라 지구의 급격한 기후변화가 일어나고 있는 것이다. 따라서 Ⓑ externalities가 의미하는 것은 ③의 '사회가 지불해야 하는 간접비용'이라고 볼 수 있다.

3 ④　▶ 내용일치
　마지막 단락에서 "미국의 경우는 저렴한 천연가스가 석탄의 수요를 감소시키고 있지만, 중국은 이와 달리 석탄의 수요가 급증하고 있다."고 했으므로 ④가 정답이다.

08 2016 아주대

Ⓐ 대기는 다섯 개의 층으로 나뉜다. 대기는 지표 부근에서 가장 밀집하며, 고도가 높아져 결국 우주공간과 합쳐질 때까지 점점 희박해진다. 오존은 지구 대기의 서로 다른 두 곳, 즉 대류권과 성층권에서 발견된다. 전자(前者)는 지상에 있는 오존으로, 인간의 건강이상 유발물질이며 스모그의 성분이다. 반면에, 후자(後者)는 대기 중에 있는 오존의 대부분을 차지하는 것으로, 태양 자외선을 흡수할 때 인간의 건강을 보호하는데, 그 흡수가 자외선이 지구 표면에 도달해서 생물에게 생물학적으로 위험한 자외선으로 인한 해를 입히는 것을 막아준다.

Ⓑ '오존구멍'이라는 말은 이러한 보호 역할을 하는 성층권의 오존층이 극지방에서 최근 들어 고갈된 것을 가리킨다. 오존구멍 아래에서 살고 있는 사람들과 동식물은 지금 지표면에 도달하는 태양 방사선으로 인해 손상을 입고 있는데, 그것은 눈 손상에서 피부암에 이르는 건강상의 문제를 일으킨다.

Ⓒ 과학자들은 하층부 성층권에서 오존이 엷어지고 있으며, 남극지방에서 봄철에 ― 오존구멍으로 알려져 있는 ― 특히 급격한 오존 감소가 진행되고 있다는 사실을 발견했다. 이것은 프레온 가스(CFC)라는 이름의 오존을 고갈시키는 화학물질의 농도가 성층권에서 높아졌기 때문인데, 프레온 가스는 수십 년에서 길게는 100년 넘게 대기에 남아 있게 된다. 극지방의 봄에 태양이 다시 나오면, 얼음 입자가 녹으면서 오존을 고갈시키는 분자를 방출하며, 이번에는 또한 이것이 자외선을 흡수하는 오존 안의 분자 결합을 깨뜨리는 궂은일을 하게 된다.

Ⓓ 그러나 오존구멍은 지구온난화에 이르는 메커니즘(과정)이 아니다. 자외선은 태양 에너지의 1%도 채 되지 않아서, 인간의 활동으로부터 생기는 과도한 열의 원인이 되기에 충분하지 않다. 지구온난화의 주된 원인은 전기를 생산하거나 자동차를 운행하기 위해 석탄이나 석유를 태울 때 과도한 탄소를 대기 중에 배출하는 것이다. 이 가스들은 담요처럼 지구 주위로 확산되어서, 그렇지 않으면 우주공간으로 퍼져나갈 태양열을 붙잡고 있게 된다.

Ⓔ 그러나 이러한 환경 문제는 둘 다 공통의 원인을 갖고 있다. 그것은 곧 가스를 대기 중으로 방출하여 대기를 변화시키는 인간의 활동이다. 오존 고갈은 ― 이전에 에어로졸 스프레이 캔이나 냉각제에서 발견되던 ― 프레온 가스가 대기 중으로 방출될 때 일어난다. 이 가스들은 몇몇 화학반응을 거쳐 오존 분자를 분해시키며, 결국 오존이 가진 자외선 흡수 능력을 떨어뜨리게 된다. <지구의 대기는 하나로 연결돼 있기 때문에, 이와 다른 몇 가지 방식으로 오존 고갈과 지구온난화가 연관되어 있다고 해도 그리 놀라운 일은 아니다. 예를 들어, 증거에 의하면, 기후변화가 보호 역할의 오존층을 엷어지게 만드는 원인일 수도 있다.>

atmosphere	n.	대기; 분위기, 주위의 상황
merge	v.	융합되다, 합쳐지다; 합병하다
troposphere	n.	대류권
stratosphere	n.	성층권
irritant	n.	자극제
radiation	n.	(빛·열 등의) 방사; 복사에너지
organism	n.	유기체; 생물
depletion	n.	고갈, 소모
concentration	n.	집중, 전념; 농도; 농축
chlorofluorocarbon	n.	프레온 가스
particle	n.	미립자, 분자, 극히 작은 조각
molecule	n.	분자
ultraviolet	n.	자외선
carbon	n.	탄소
generate	v.	발생시키다; 산출하다
blanket	n.	담요
refrigerant	n.	냉각제, 해열제
chemical reaction		화학반응

1 ④ ▶ 내용파악

문단 Ⓓ의 첫 문장에서 "오존구멍은 지구온난화에 이르는 메커니즘(과정)이 아니다."라고 진술하였으므로 이 글이 ④에 대해서는 답하지 않고 있다고 말할 수 있다. ①은 문단 Ⓑ의 첫 문장에서, ②는 문단 Ⓒ의 둘째 문장에서, ③은 문단 Ⓑ의 둘째 문장에서, ⑤는 문단 Ⓔ에 이어질 2번 문제에서 제시된 글의 마지막 문장에서 각각 답하고 있다.

2 ⑤ ▶ 문장삽입

문단 Ⓔ 첫 문장의 두 가지 환경 문제는 '오존구멍'과 '지구온난화'인데 이 둘 모두의 원인은 인간 활동이 배출하는 프레온 가스라고 했다. 이 가스들이 오존구멍을 일으키는 것은 문단 Ⓔ에서, 지구온난화를 일으키는 것은 문단 Ⓓ에서 각각 언급되었다. 그런데 두 환경 문제 상호 간의 관계에 있어 오존구멍이 지구온난화의 원인일 가능성은 문단 Ⓓ에서 부인되었다. 따라서 이와는 다른 방식으로 관계되어 있을 가능성, 즉 지구온난화(기후변화)가 오존구멍(오존층 고갈)의 원인일 가능성을 언급한 제시문은 전체 글을 마무리하는 문단 Ⓔ 끝에 들어가는 것이 가장 적절하다.

3 ① ▶ 내용일치

'오존구멍'을 정의하는 문단 Ⓑ에서 분명히 '성층권의 오존층의 고갈'이라고 했으며 문단 Ⓒ에서도 하층부 성층권에서 오존층이 엷어지고 있다고 했으므로 ①의 '대류권의 오존구멍'은 사실과 다르다. troposphere를 stratosphere로 고쳐야 한다. 문단 Ⓒ에서는 '극지방의 봄에 태양이 다시 나오면, 얼음 입자가 녹으면서 ~'라고 하여 태양열이 얼음입자를 녹이는 것으로 언급되었지만 결국은 열로 인해 얼음이 녹는 것이므로 "지구온난화로 인해 얼음입자가 녹아 거기서 오존을 고갈시키는 분자가 방출된다."라고 한 ②는 사실이다.

09 2022 중앙대

수은 오염은 전 지구적인 문제다. 금 채굴, 석탄 연소, 또 다른 산업 공정에서 나오는 수은 배출물은 대기 중에서 돌아다니다가 결국 비나 눈과 섞여 땅으로 떨어진다. 수은이라는 독극물은 물고기와 그걸 먹는 인간에게 들어가, 자궁에서 수은에 노출된 아이들의 발달 중인 신경계에 손상을 입혀 기억과 언어에 문제를 일으킬 수 있다.

수은이 습지나 호수의 퇴적층에 가라앉으면 미생물이 그 금속성 원소(수은)를 메틸수은이라는 위험한 화합물로 바꾸고, 이 물질은 먹이사슬에 쌓인다. 크고 육식성인 물고기일수록 몸속에 쌓인 메틸수은의 농도가 가장 높다. 공중보건기관들은 많은 호수에서 이러한 물고기를 정기적으로 테스트하고 때로는 이런 생선의 소비를 줄이라고 경고하기도 한다.

B 1980년 이후 대기 오염을 통제하려는 규제들이 북미와 유럽의 수은 배출량을 점차 낮추었지만 다른 곳의 수은 원천들은 계속 늘고 있다. 특히 라틴아메리카의 소규모 금광과 아시아의 석탄 발전소에서 상황이 심각하다. 2013년, 각국은 수은에 관한 미나마타 협약이라는 국제 협약에 합의했다. 협약 조인국은 전구와 배터리 같은 상품에 수은을 금지해야 하고 산업 수은 배출량도 감소시켜야 한다.

C 하지만 이러한 조치들이 얼마나 빨리 효과를 낼까? 이 질문에 대한 대답을 막는 한 가지 장애물은 생태계에서 기능하는 수은의 복잡한 작용이었으며, 이로 인해 생선 내의 수은 농도감소분 중 어느 정도가 영양분 과다와 침입종들 그리고 또 다른 생태적 변화와 같은 요인이 아니라 정말 대기 오염 감소로 인한 것인지 파악하기가 어렵게 된다.

A 명확한 파악을 위해 대규모 연구 프로젝트가 2001년에 일종의 화학 추적자인 수은의 농축 안정 동위원소를 사용하여 실험을 시작했다. 이러한 농축된 형태의 수은 원소는 화학적으로는 일반 수은과 동일한 방식으로 작용하지만 환경에서는 일반 수은과 구별된다. 7년 동안 연구자들은 수은 동위원소를 Lake 658의 물에 추가했는데, Lake 658은 58개 호수와 분수계를 과학 연구용으로 따로 보존한 실험용 호수 유역이라는, 멀리 떨어진 캐나다 연구 기지의 일부. 연구자들은 또한 서로 다른 동위원소를 비행기에서 주변 습지와 고지대로 살포해 호수 속으로 어떻게 이동하는지 연구했다. 실험이 시작된 직후, 동위원소 표를 붙인 메틸수은이 동물성 플랑크톤 같이 호수에 서식하는 무척추동물 내부에 축적되기 시작했다. 메틸수은은 동물성 플랑크톤을 먹는 옐로퍼치와 또 다른 작은 물고기 속에서도 수치가 상승했으며, 작은 물고기를 먹는 강꼬치고기 같은 큰 물고기에서도 약 40% 상승했다. 실험 첫 7년이 지나고 연구자들은 동위원소 수은을 추가하기를 중단하고 호수에 사는 동물들의 농도를 계속 점검했다. 그 후 8년의 연구 기간 동안 동위원소 수은의 농도는 작은 물고기에서 최대 91%까지 떨어졌다. 농도는 더 큰 물고기 개체군에서도 떨어졌다. 주변의 땅에 추가된 수은의 소량만 물고기에게서 발견되었고 이 수치도 급속히 떨어졌다.

특정 호수에 가져다준 정확한 이익은 예측하기 어려울 것이라고 연구자들은 말한다. 그 이유는 주변 분수계의 규모와 메틸화 비율 같은 지역적 조건이 물고기 속에 쌓이는 수은 수치에 영향을 끼치기 때문이라는 것이다. 그리고 모든 대기 중의 배출량이 멈춘다 해도 일부 수은 — 과거 대기오염의 유산 — 은 계속해서 주변 분수계에서 호수로 들어갈 것이다.

1 ② ▶ 단락배열
수은을 감소시키기 위한 조치의 내용인 B가 먼저 오고, 이 조치들의 효력에 대한 질문인 C가 그다음에 오고, 효력을 알아보는 실험을 다루는 A가 그다음으로 와야 한다.

2 ③ ▶ 글의 요지
C 단락에서 던진 질문이 수은 감소 조치의 효력이 얼마나 되는가 하는 것이었고 그것을 알아보는 실험 '결과'가 주제인 글이므로, '실험 결과 수은 오염을 줄여 환경이 회복되었다'는 내용의 ③이 글의 요지로 적절하다.

---

mercury n. 수은
emission n. 방출, 방출물
gold mining 금 채굴
poison n. 독, 독약
make one's way to ~로 들어가다
womb n. 자궁
wetland n. (보통 pl.) 습지
sediment n. 퇴적물, 침전물
microbe n. 미생물
food web 먹이사슬
predatory a. 포식성의, 육식의
isotope n. 동위원소
watershed n. 강의 분수계(강이 서로 갈라지는 지점)
spray v. 뿌리다, 살포하다
treaty n. 조약, 협정
hurdle n. 장애물
complicated a. 복잡한
concentration n. 농도
ecological a. 생태계의
invertebrate n. 무척추동물

10 2021 아주대

A 마인츠(Mainz)에 있는 요하네스 구텐베르크 대학(JGU) 지구과학 연구소의 마이클 디닝거(Michael Deininger) 박사는 약 1만 년 전에 현재의 간빙기가 시작된 이래 지역적 기후 체계가 어떻게 변해왔는지, 그리고 그로부터 어떤 결론을 도출해낼 수 있는지를 연구했다. <이렇게 하기 위해 그 고생대기후학자는 다양한 기후 기록 보관소에 기록된 강우 시계열(時系列) 데이터를 살펴보았다.> "우리는 아프리카와 남아메리카 몬순 지역의 여름철 강우량을 정확하게 재구성해내고 이 데이터를 북반구 중위도 지역의 강우량 변화와 비교해서 이것을 기온 변화와 연관시킬 수 있었습니다."라고 디닝거는 설명했다. 이 연구에는 호주, 브라질, 멕시코, 아일랜드, 오스트리아 및 남아프리카의 과학자들도 참여하였다.

B 태양 복사의 분포가 다름으로 인해 극지방보다는 적도에서 지구가 더 가열되므로 기온 기울기가 발생하는데, 간단히 말해 이것이 대기 순환으로 하여금 에너지를 극지방으로 이동시키게 만든다. 태양 복사와 관련된 이러한 기온 차이에 생긴 변화는 대기의 순환에 영향을 미치고, 이는 다시 지역적 강수 패턴에 영향을 미치게 된다.

C 이번 새로운 연구는 지난 1만 년 동안 북위도(북반구) 지역과 아프리카, 남아메리카의 지역적 강우량의 변화는 다소 동시에 발생했음을 보여준다. "이러한 지역적 기후 편차는 연관되어 있고, 그 편차는 주로 태양 복사 변화 및 그와 연관된 열대 지방과 극지방 간의 기온 차이로 인해 생긴 것이라고 우리는 주장합니다."라고 디닝거는 말했다.

D 연구에 참여한 연구원들은 미래에 유익을 주기 위해 과거로부터 배우는 것이 가능한가라는 질문에 특별히 관심을 가졌다. 현재의 지구 온난화, 특히 북극의 온난화가 현저하다는 사실로 인해 적도와 극지방 간의 기온 기울기는 감소하고 있다. 이는 북반구 중위도의 편서풍을 약화시켜, 남아메리카의 몬순은 약해지고 아프리카의 몬순은 강해지는 반면, 남동부 아프리카 여름 강우 지역의 강우량은 줄어드는 결과가 생길 수 있다. 이것의 결과로 지역적 강우 패턴이 바뀌고 잠재적으로 어떤 지역에서는 가뭄이, 다른 지역에서는 홍수가 생길 수 있다. "다가오는 미래에, 우리는 기온 기울기의 변화가 우리 기후 체계를 제어하는 데 있어서의 근본적인 역할을 제대로 알 필요가 있습니다."라고 디닝거 박사는 결론지었다.

---

geoscience n. 지구과학
interglacial a. 빙하 시대 중간의, 간빙기의
precipitation n. 강수, 강수량
paleoclimatologist n. 고생대기후학자
rainfall time series 강우 시계열(時系列)
monsoon n. (여름철의) 우기(장마)
latitude n. 위도
archive n. 기록 보관소
solar radiation 태양 복사
gradient n. 변화도; 경사도
temperature gradient 기온 경도, 온도 기울기
synchronous a. 동시에 발생하는
variation n. 변화
alteration n. 변화, 변경
tropic n. 열대 지방
westerly wind 편서풍
hemisphere n. 반구

---

1 ⑤   ▶ 글의 제목
이 글의 요지는 C 단락에 요약되어 있다. ③과 ④는 이 글의 핵심 소재이기는 하지만, 그것이 '기후 변화' 또는 '강수 변화'와 어떤 관계에 있는지 담고 있지 못하므로 제목이 되기에는 부족하다.

2 ④   ▶ 문법적으로 옳지 않은 표현 고르기
접속사 없이 동사가 병렬될 수 없으므로 ⓓ는 분사구문이 되어야 한다. ⓓ를 potentially causing droughts로 고쳐야 문법적으로 적절하다.

3 ①   ▶ 문장삽입
주어진 문장에 나온 this가 ❶ 앞의 마이클 디닝거 박사가 두 가지 사항을 연구한 것을 가리키고, '그 고생대기후학자'가 마이클 디닝거 박사를 가리키며, 살펴본 데이터를 어떻게 이용했는지가 ❶ 다음의 인용문에서 설명되므로, 주어진 문장은 ❶에 들어가는 것이 적절하다.

4 ④   ▶ 내용일치
C 단락에서 "이번 새로운 연구는 지난 1만 년 동안 북위도 지역과 아프리카, 남아메리카의 지역적 강우 변화는 다소 동시에 발생했음을 보여준다."라고 하였으므로 ④는 글의 내용과 일치하지 않는다.

11 의학·건강

01 2014 한양대

몸무게가 반복적으로 늘었다 줄었다 하는 사람들은 영구적이고 장기적인 신진대사의 변화를 얻게 된다. 그들의 신진대사는 느려지며, 따라서 다른 사람들보다 음식의 에너지를 덜 소모한다. 결과적으로 음식 속에 들어 있는 잉여 에너지는 지방으로 저장된다. 이것이 벼락치기 다이어트가 문제를 오히려 커지게 한다는 것을 의미한다. 쥐에 대한 실험 결과, 먹을 것을 과도하게 많이 주는 것과 과도하게 적게 주는 것을 번갈아 하면 신진대사율이 더 낮아진다는 사실이 드러났다. 더 낮은 신진대사율은 쥐가 평소에 필요했을 것보다 더 적은 양의 음식으로도 보다 쉽게 몸무게가 늘어나게 했다. 나아가, 고등학교 레슬링 선수들을 대상으로 한 연구에 따르면, 그들 가운데 일부는 레슬링 시즌에 10번이나 자주 몸무게를 뺐다가 다시 늘린 것으로 드러났다. 비시즌 기간에는 몸무게가 변하지 않았던 사람들만큼 뚱뚱하지 않았으나, 그들의 신진대사율은 매우 낮았다. 그것이 의미하는 바는 벼락치기로 다이어트를 하고서 다시 몸무게가 늘어나는 사람들은 몸무게를 줄이는 데 점점 더 많은 어려움을 겪을 가능성이 크다는 것이다.

1 ④ ▶ 빈칸완성
쥐에 대한 실험 결과와 레슬링 선수들을 대상으로 한 연구 결과가 보여주는 것은 "체중의 변화나 음식량의 변화를 자주 겪는 경우 신진대가가 느려진다."는 사실이다. 두 번째 문장에서 신진대사가 느려지면, 에너지를 덜 소모하게 된다고 했으므로, 벼락치기 다이어트를 한 후 다시 몸무게가 늘어나면, 그 사람의 몸은 신진대사율이 낮아 에너지를 덜 소모하게 된 상태이므로, 살을 빼는 것이 더 어려워질 것이라 추론할 수 있다. 살을 빼는 것은 에너지를 소모하여 얻는 결과이기 때문이다.

2 ③ ▶ 내용일치
마지막 문장에서 "신진대사율이 낮으면 다이어트 이후에 다시 몸무게가 늘어나는 사람들이 몸무게를 줄이는 데 애를 먹는다."고 했으므로, 신진대사율은 체중조절과 밀접한 관련이 있다고 볼 수 있다. ② 벼락치기 다이어트를 한 후에 다시 살이 찌면, 그 후에 체중감량을 하는 것은 더욱 더 힘들어진다는 것이 본문의 내용이므로, 운동선수들에게 벼락치기 다이어트를 권할 것은 못 된다. ④ "쥐에 대한 실험 결과, 먹을 것을 과도하게 많이 주는 것과 과도하게 적게 주는 것을 번갈아 하면 신진대사율이 더 낮아진다는 사실이 드러났다."고 돼 있으므로 옳지 않은 진술이다.

repeatedly ad. 되풀이하여
acquire v. 획득하다; 몸에 익히다
permanent a. 영구한, 영속하는; 불변의
long-term a. 장기적인
metabolism n. 물질대사, 신진대사
consume v. 소비하다; 소모하다
excess n. 과다, 과잉; 초과
crash a. 단숨에 해내는; (수업 등이) 벼락치기의
self-defeating a. (문제를 해결하기는커녕) 문제를 오히려 키우는; 자멸적인
alternate v. 번갈아[교대로] 하다
underfeed v. ~에 대하여 충분한 음식[연료]을 주지 않다; 감식하다
overfeed v. 너무 많이 먹이다[주다]; 너무 먹다
substantially ad. 대체로; 사실상; 충분히
implication n. 내포, 함축; 암시

02 2015 성균관대

외상 후 스트레스 장애에 대한 가장 일반적인 치료는 노출 치료법으로 알려져 있다. 이러한 치료법에서는 환자들에게 정신적 외상을 초래한 광경 및 소리를 상상하도록 하고 난 후에, 그러한 기억들을 대면하도록 도와준다. 이는 종종 효과가 있다. 그러나 항상 그렇지만은 않다. 또한 우선은 군대가 그러한 병에 걸리지 않는 것이 확실히 더 나을 것이다. 이러한 점을 염두에 두고서, 스킵 리조(Skip Rizzo) 박사의 지휘 아래 엔지니어들과 컴퓨터 관련 과학자들 및 심리학자들이 심리적 백신 접종 같은 것을 제시하고 있다. 리조 박사는 전쟁터에 가기 전에 군인들에게 전쟁의 공포를 미리 제공함으로써 군인들이 전투지에서 목격할 수 있는 상황들에 면역이 되기를 기대한다. 이런 아이디어는 가상현실을 이용하여 노출 치료법을 돕는 리조 박사의 연구에서 생겨났다. 그러한 가상현실은 전쟁터의 광경, 소리, 진동, 그리고 심지어 냄새조차 안전한 진료소 안에서 재현될 수 있도록 해주며, 시행 결과는 가상현실이 표준 노출 치료법에 반응하지 않는 환자들을 도와줄 수 있음을 시사하고 있다. 모의실험이 성공을 거두면서, 리조 박사는 실제 전투에 앞서서 유사한 상황을 경험하는 경우, 기존의 훈련이 군대를 육체적으로 준비시키는 것처럼 군대를 정신적으로 준비시킬 수 있지 않을까

traumatic a. 대단히 충격적인, 정신적 외상(外傷)의
exposure n. 노출; 폭로
afflict v. 괴롭히다, 피해를 입다
sight n. 시력, 시야; 광경
traumatize v. 외상을 입히다, 정신적 충격을 주다
confront v. 직면하다, 마주보다; 맞서다
undoubtedly ad. 틀림없이, 명백히
troop n. 무리, 군대
in the first place 우선, 첫째로
vaccination n. 백신 접종
inure v. 익숙케 하다, 단련하다

궁금히 여기게 되었다. 리조 박사의 예비적 실험 결과는 그럴 수도 있음을 시사하고 있다.

1 ② ▶ 빈칸완성
빈칸을 포함한 문장은 앞 문장의 내용을 부연 설명하고 있다. 앞 문장에서는 '심리적 백신 접종'을 언급하고 있는데, 백신이란 약하게 만든 병균을 주입하여 인체가 면역을 갖도록 하는 것이므로, 심리적 백신 접종은 공포 등을 미리 경험하게 하여 이에 대해 내성을 갖게 하는 것을 의미할 것이다. 따라서 빈칸에는 이와 관련된 ②가 들어가는 것이 적절하다. ①은 미리 경험하게 하는 것과 관련이 없으며, ③은 육체적이 아니라 정신적으로 준비시키는 것이므로 정답이 될 수 없다.

2 ① ▶ 내용파악
여덟 번째 문장(The idea of doing this ~ with exposure-based therapy)의 내용을 통해, 리조 박사의 치료 방법이 노출 치료법과 완전히 별개의 것이 아님을 알 수 있다.

squaddie n. 신병, 병사
witness v. 목격하다, 증언하다; 입증하다
virtual a. 가상의, 실질적인
vibration n. 진동, 동요
recreate v. 재현하다, 다시 만들다; 기분 전환을 시키다
trial n. 재판; 시험, 실험
standard a. 표준의; 보통의, 일반적인
simulation n. 모의실험; 가장, 겉치레
regime n. 정권, 체제; (행위의) 상황
preliminary a. 예비의, 서두의

03 2022 인하대

건강하게 먹기 위한 핵심 전략은 상당한 양의 영양소를 제공하지만 칼로리는 적은 음식을 선택하는 것이다. 특정 음식이 칼로리 대비 영양소 비율이 높으면, 그것이 고영양(영양소고밀도) 음식이다. 식품의 영양소밀도를 결정하는 과정은 1인분의 포장 라벨에 기재된 8가지 필수 영양소의 권장 식이 허용량의 백분율을 더하여 1인분의 식사 당 칼로리 수로 나누는 방식으로 이뤄진다. <영양소밀도라고 하는 이 비율은 음식의 영양적인 질을 판단하기 위한 양적인 기초를 제공한다.> 점수가 높을수록 음식의 영양적인 질(영양소밀도)이 높다. 만약 두 음식이 1인분 당 같은 칼로리를 가지고 있지만 한 음식이 더 많은 영양소를 가지고 있다면, 그것은 더 고영양인(더 영양소고밀도인) 음식이다. 영양소밀도의 개념은 건강을 의식하고 체중을 신경 쓰는 사람에게 정보에 근거한 선택을 할 수 있도록 도움을 줄 수 있다. 이용 가능한 음식의 수와 그 음식에 딸려 있는 약속과 설명이 주어져 있을 때 사람들은 음식을 평가할 방법이 필요하다. 영양소밀도는 소비자들이 음식을 고르는 데 사용할 수 있는 방법 중 하나이다.

1 ③ ▶ 문장삽입
주어진 문장에서 영양소밀도인 This ratio가 음식의 영양적인 질을 판단하기 위한 기초를 제공한다고 했는데, ⓒ 다음 문장에서 이 비율의 점수가 높을수록 음식의 영양적인 질(영양소밀도)이 높다고 했으므로 주어진 문장은 ⓒ에 삽입되어야 한다.

2 ① ▶ 글의 주제
영양소밀도의 개념과 건강한 음식을 먹는 데 도움이 되는 정보인 영양소밀도를 통해 사람들이 이에 근거해서 영양소가 풍부한 음식을 고를 수 있다고 했으므로 ①이 글의 주제로 적절하다.

strategy n. 전략
nutrient n. 영양소
nutrient density 영양소밀도
dietary allowance 식이 허용량
health-conscious a. (자기의) 건강을 의식하는
weight-conscious a. 체중을 의식하는
evaluate v. 평가하다

04 2020 한국외대

사람의 걸음걸이 방식의 미묘한 변화는 인지 저하의 초기 경고 징후이자 정밀(첨단)검사가 필요하다는 신호일 수 있다. 연구 결과는 신체적 증상과 알츠하이머병의 연관성을 처음으로 밝혀낸 것인데, 지금까지는 알츠하이머병을 진단하려면 의사들이 인지능력에 초점을 맞추고 장기간 신경 검사를 실시해야 했다. 걸음걸이의 퇴보와 또 다른 변화들을 조사하는 것은 고가의 첨단 기술이 필요 없고 검사에 많은 시간을 요하지 않기 때문에 이상적인 방법이다. 미국에서 알츠하이머병을 앓는 사람은 대부분 노인들로, 그 수가 540만 명에 이르는데, 베이비부머 세대가 노인이 되는 2050년에는 1,600만 명으로 급증할 것으로 예상된다. 사람이 걷기 위해서는 뇌의 여러 부위들이 완벽하고 동시에 통합적인 작용을 해야 한다. 그런데 이런 뇌의 여러 부위 사이의 신경 회로를 알츠하이머병이 방해하기 때문에 걸음걸이에 변화가 일어나는 것이다. 메이오클리닉(Mayo Clinic)에서는 연구

sign n. 기호, 표시; 징후
finding n. (종종 pl.) (조사·연구 등의) 결과, 결론; 소견
symptom n. 징후, <병리> 증상
diagnosis n. 진찰, 진단
deterioration n. 악화, 저하된 상태
gait n. 걸음걸이, 보조
baby boomer 베이비부머 세대(미국의 경우에는 1946년부터 1964년 사이에 태어난 사람들을 뜻함)

원들이 1,340명 이상의 참가자들을 대상으로 15개월 간격으로 두 번 혹은 그 이상 방문하여 전산화된 보행측정기를 통해 걸음걸이의 보폭과 속도를 측정했다. 그들은 속도가 느려지고 보폭이 짧아진 연구 참가자들의 인지능력, 기억, 그리고 수행 기능이 (그렇지 않은 참가자들에 비해) 상당히 크게 나빠졌음을 발견했다.

spike v. 급증하다
multiple a. 다수의, 다양한
circuitry n. 전기 회로, 신경 회로
stride length 보폭
executive function 집행 기능(다른 인지적 기능을 통제하는 심리적 기능으로 계획하고 행동의 개시와 종료 등을 모두 포함)

1 ④ ▶ 글의 제목
걸음걸이 같은 신체 동작은 여러 뇌신경 회로가 무리 없이 통합 작용하는 결과물이다. 따라서 걸음걸이의 변화는 기능 저하는 뇌신경 회로의 문제이고 또한 알츠하이머병의 전조일 수 있다고 지적하고 있다. 그러므로 글의 제목으로 적절한 것은 ④이다.

2 ① ▶ 빈칸완성
because절에서 '고가의 첨단기술이 필요 없고 검사에 많은 시간을 요하지 않기 때문에'라고 했으므로 ④에 적절한 것은 ideal이나 preferred이고, 뇌의 여러 부위들이 작용하여 걸음이라는 하나의 동작을 유발하려면 그 여러 부위가 서로 어긋나지 않게 완벽하게 그리고 동시에 작용해야 할 것이다. 따라서 ⑧에는 simultaneous가 적절하다. ② 도전적인 — 즉각의 ③ 선호하는 — 정지된 ④ 정확한 — 간헐적인

05 2018 인하대

뼈는 나이가 들수록 나빠지기 때문에, 우리가 늙어가면서 골절의 위험을 낮추기 위해 칼슘을 더 많이 섭취하는 것은 이치에 맞는 일이다. 하지만 얼마나 많이 섭취해야 충분할까?
스웨덴 연구원들의 보고서에 따르면, 50세 이상의 여성의 경우, 골절 예방에 이상적인 하루 칼슘 섭취량은 700~900mg이다. 그보다 높은 수준의 칼슘 섭취는 골절 위험의 예방에 추가적인 영향을 미치지 않았다. 연구원들은 6만 명 이상의 여성들을 대상으로 연구를 실시했는데, 그 여성들은 19년에 걸쳐 자신들의 골절 발생률뿐만 아니라 식사와 영양보충제를 통한 칼슘 섭취량을 보고했다. 하루에 750mg 미만의 칼슘을 섭취한 여성들은 하루에 약 900mg을 섭취한 여성들보다 골절 위험이 26% 높았지만, 그 이상을 — 최대 하루에 1,185mg — 섭취한 여성들은 900mg을 섭취한 여성들에 비해 골절 위험을 추가적으로 더 낮추지는 못했다.
그러한 연구 결과는 미국 식단지침에 따른 50세 이상 여성들의 칼슘 권장 섭취량 — 하루 1,200mg — 이 지나치게 높은 것일 수도 있음을 시사한다. 칼슘이 뼈의 건강을 증진시키는 데 도움이 되지 않는다는 것이 아니다. 임계치를 초과하는 경우에는 효과를 더 발생시키지 않을 수도 있다는 것이다.

deteriorate v. (질·가치가) 떨어지다, 악화하다
lower v. 낮추다, 낮게 하다
fracture n. 분쇄, 분열; 골절
ideal a. 이상적인
prevent v. 막다, 방해하다; 예방하다
additional a. 부가적인, 추가적인
impact n. 충돌, 충격; 영향
dietary a. 식사의, 음식의; 규정식의, 식이 요법의
supplementary a. 보충의, 추가의
intake n. 흡입량, 섭취량
consume v. 소비하다, 소모하다; 먹다, 마시다
finding n. (종종 pl.) (조사·연구 등의) 결과, 결론; 소견
promote v. 진전[진척]시키다, 조장[증진]하다
exceed v. (수량·정도·한도를) 넘다, 초과하다
threshold n. 문지방; 시초, 출발점; 한계, 임계치
benefit n. 이익, 이득

1 ② ▶ 내용파악
보고서의 내용은 "50세 이상의 여성의 경우, 골절 예방에 이상적인 하루 칼슘 섭취량은 700~900mg이며, 그보다 더 많이 칼슘을 섭취하더라도 골절 예방에 더 많은 도움을 얻지는 못한다."는 것이다. 그러므로 ②가 이 내용과 일치하는 진술이다. ① 효과가 없어지는 게 아니라 일정 수준 이상의 효과를 기대하긴 어렵다는 것이다. ③ 임계치 이상으로 섭취하는 칼슘은 골절 위험을 낮추는 효과를 내지 못한다. ④ 나이가 들수록 뼈가 나빠진다고 했으므로, 그 반대일 것이다. ⑤ 본문의 내용을 통해서는 알 수 없다.

2 ③ ▶ 지시대상
"하루에 750mg 미만의 칼슘을 섭취한 여성들은 하루에 약 900mg을 섭취한 여성들보다 골절 위험이 26% 높았지만, 그 이상을 섭취한 여성들은 900mg을 섭취한 사람들에 비해 골절 위험을 추가적으로 더 낮추지는 못했다."고 했다. 따라서 900mg이 칼슘 섭취를 통해 골절 위험을 낮추는 효과를 낼 수 있는 최대섭취량, 즉 임계점(threshold)이다.

06 2016 국민대

한때는 유아기에 가졌던 호기심의 영역이었던, "왜 우리는 우리 자신을 간지럽게 할 수 없을까?"라는 질문이 지금 신경과학자들의 관심을 불러일으키고 있다. 신경과학자들의 관심을 이해하기 위해서는, 이것을 고려해야 한다. 당신의 몸이 움직일 때마다, 그 몸의 움직임은 당신을 모든 방식으로 잠재적으로 혼란시킬 수 있는 감각들을 만들어낸다는 것이다. 당신의 한 손이 당신의 다리를 스칠 때마다, 누군가가 당신을 어루만지거나 공격하고 있다고 당신이 생각할 경우에 나타나는 혼란을 상상해 보라. 당신의 움직임과 다른 사람들의 움직임을 구분할 수 있는 것은 우리의 자아의식과 행위의식의 중추적인 부분이다.

이 질문("왜 우리는 우리 자신을 간지럽게 할 수 없을까?")에 대한 답을 찾기 위해, 사라 제인 블랙모어(Sarah-Jayne Blackmore)는 그녀의 동료들이 피실험자들의 손바닥을 간지럽게 했을 때와 피실험자들이 스스로를 간지럽게 했을 때의 피실험자들의 뇌를 (각각) 단층촬영 해보았다. 그 결과 일어난 뇌 활동으로부터, 우리가 팔다리를 움직일 때마다, 소뇌가 신체 동작을 정확하게 예측한 다음, 촉각이 처리되는 곳인 체감각 피질에서의 활동을 둔화시키는 또 다른 그림자 신호를 보낸다고 그녀는 결론 내렸다. 그 결과, 우리는 우리 자신을 간지럽게 할 때 다른 사람들이 우리를 간지럽게 할 때와 똑같은 강도로 감각을 느끼지 않으며, 그래서 차분하게 있는 것이다.

domain n. 영역, 분야
curiosity n. 호기심; 진기한 것
tickle v. 간질이다; 기쁘게[즐겁게] 하다
neuroscientist n. 신경과학자
brush v. 스치다, 지나가면서 가볍게 닿다
fondle v. 어루만지다
attack v. 공격하다
agency n. 힘, 작용
scan v. 조영하다, 단층촬영하다
palm n. 손바닥
limb n. 손발, 수족, 팔, 다리
cerebellum n. 소뇌
precise a. 정확한, 정밀한
damp down 둔화시키다
somatosensory a. 체감각의
cortex n. 피질
tactile a. 촉각의

1 ④ ▶ 글의 주제
"왜 우리는 우리 자신을 간지럽게 할 수 없을까?"에 대한 답을 찾기 위해, 사라 제인 블랙모어가 실험을 했는데, 그 결과 우리 자신을 간지럽게 할 때 우리의 뇌는 다른 사람들이 우리를 간지럽게 할 때 우리가 느끼는 감각과 똑같은 강도로 감각을 느끼지 않기 때문에, 차분하게 있게 된다고 했다. 이 글은 '간지럽게 하는 실험을 통해 자신과 타인을 구별하는 뇌의 작용을 알아본 것'이 주된 내용이므로, ④가 글의 주제로 적절하다.

2 ① ▶ 빈칸완성
맨 마지막 문장의 that절의 내용(when we ~ someone else)은 앞 문장에서 설명된 '우리가 우리의 팔다리를 움직일 때는 소뇌가 신체 동작을 정확하게 예측하여 그림자 신호를 체감각 피질로 보내어 그곳에서의 촉각처리 활동을 둔화시킨다는 것'의 결과에 해당하므로 빈칸에는 ①의 result(결과)가 정답이다. ② 이유 ③ 증거 ④ 예측

3 ④ ▶ 내용일치
"우리의 소뇌가 신체 동작(스스로를 간지럽게 함)을 정확하게 '예측'한 다음, 촉각이 처리되는 체감각 피질에서의 활동을 둔화시키는 또 다른 그림자 신호를 보낸다."라고 하였으며, 그 결과 "우리가 우리 자신을 간지럽게 할 때는 다른 사람들이 우리를 간지럽게 할 때와 똑같은 강도로 감각을 느끼지 않기 때문에, 우리가 차분하게 있게 된다."라고 했으므로 ④가 정답이다.

07 2019 서울여대

우리는 무엇을 먹으면 안 되고, 무엇을 먹으면 나중에 후회할 것이고, 유해한 음식, 구미가 당기는데 위험한 음식, 건강에 해로운 음식은 무엇 무엇인지 등, 음식에 대해 부정적으로 이야기한다. 그것은 '나쁜 음식'을 과도하게 탐닉하는 것이 미칠 수 있는 영향보다 더 은밀하게 영향을 미친다. 음식에 대해 전전긍긍함으로써, 우리는 (식사라는) 편안하고 즐거울 일을 두려움과 걱정의 원천으로 만들어 버린다. 그리고 우리가 특정 음식을 피할 때, 우리는 대개 그것에 대한 보상으로 다른 음식들을 과도하게 섭취한다. 이 모든 일은 과학을 가장하여 일어난다. 그러나 음식 공포의 이면에 대한 연구를 좀 더 자세히 살펴보면, 우리가 가장 악마 취급한 음식들 중 많은 것이 실제로는 우리에게 좋은 것으로 밝혀진다. 소금을 예로 들어보자. 만일 고혈압이 있는 사람들이 많은 양의 소금을 섭취한다면, 소금이 심장마비 같은 심혈관 질환을 일으킬 수 있다는 것은 사실이다. 소금이 가공 음식에 과도하게 사용된다는 것 또한 사실이다. 그러나 평균적인 미국인은 하루에 나트륨을 불과 3그램 남짓 먹는데, 이 정도는 사실 건강에 딱 좋은 수준이다. 소금을 너무 적게 먹는 것은 소금을 너무 많이 먹는 것만큼 위험할지도 모른다. 이것은 고혈압이 아닌 대다수의 사람들에게 특히 사실이다. 이런

tempting a. 솔깃한, 구미가 당기는
unhealthy a. 건강에 해로운
insidious a. 방심할 수 없는; 은밀히 퍼지는
overindulgent a. 지나치게 탐닉하는
fret about 전전긍긍하다
occasion n. 의식, 행사
under the guise of ~을 가장하여; ~라는 명목으로
demonize v. 악마로 만들다, 악마취급을 하다
cardiovascular a. 심혈관의
heart attack 심장마비, 심근경색
sodium n. 나트륨

사실에 개의치 않고 전문가들은 소금을 보다 적게 먹을 것을 계속해서 권고하고 있다. 특정 음식을 피할 것을 권고하는 많은 의사들과 영양사들 중에는 그 음식이 얼마나 위험한지를 제대로 설명하지 못하는 사람이 많다. 몇몇 연구에서는, 가공한 붉은 육류를 많이 먹는 것은 암 발병의 위험이 상대적으로 증가하는 것과 연관 있는 것으로 드러난다. 그러나 절대적 위험은 종종 아주 미미한 수준이다.

sweet spot (야구의 배트 등에서) 공이 가장 잘 맞는 장소; 안성맞춤인 상황
nutritionist n. 영양학자, 영양사
relative risk 상대위험도

1 ① ▶ 부분이해
Ⓐ의 The effects는 우리가 음식에 대해 부정적으로 이야기하는 것이 미치는 영향을 가리키는데, 특히 Ⓐ 다음에서 음식에 대해 전전긍긍함으로써 생기는 결과에 대해 이야기하고 있으므로, ①의 '음식에 대한 두려움이 미치는 영향'이 정답이다.

2 ④ ▶ 내용파악
Ⓑ는 소금을 적게 먹을 것을 계속해서 권고하는 전문가를 가리키는데, 저자는 "소금을 너무 적게 먹는 것은 소금을 너무 많이 먹는 것만큼 위험할지도 모른다. 이것은 고혈압이 아닌 대다수의 사람들에게 특히 사실이다."라고 말하여 소금을 너무 적게 먹는 것에 '부정적'임을 알 수 있다. Ⓒ는 특정 음식을 피할 것을 권고하는 의사 및 영양사들을 가리키는데, 그다음에서 그들은 특정 음식 기피가 갖는 위험성을 제대로 설명하지 못한다고 했으므로, 저자는 이들의 의견에 모두 '부정적'임을 알 수 있다. 따라서 ④가 정답이다.

08 2022 단국대

대기 오염에 노출됨으로 인해 가벼운 두통에서 심각한 인지 장애에 이르는 건강 문제가 발생할 수 있다. 오염물질이 건강에 영향을 미치는 정도는 오염물질에 대해 사람이 근접한 정도, 오염물질에 노출된 사람의 나이, 노출 기간 등의 많은 요인에 의해 좌우된다. 오염물질에 대한 반응은 사람마다 다르지만, 좋지 못한 건강의 패턴 — 특히 가정에서 가족 전체가, 혹은 사무실 건물에서 여러 명의 근로자가, 경험했을 때 — 은 병을 진단하고 문제를 해결하는 데 도움이 될 수 있다. 그러나 (많은 직장인이나 주민이 두통이나 인후통과 같은 증상을 많이 이야기하지만 신체적인 원인을 찾지 못하는) "새 건물 증후군" 현상은 진단이 항상 쉽지만은 않고 심지어는 가능하지도 않음을 보여준다.
미국 의학 협회가 진단적 평가를 위해 설정한 범주에 따르면, 실내에 있는 대기오염물질은 연소 생성물, 생물학적 오염물질, 휘발성 유기 화합물, 중금속 등으로 분류될 수 있다. 이러한 범주들은 몇 가지 기준에 따라 추가로 분류될 수 있다. 예를 들어, 생물학적 오염물질은 그 질병이 현저하게 불편함을 주는지의 여부와 관계없이, 질병을 일으킬 가능성인 병원성(病原性)에 따라 분류할 수 있다.

cognitive a. 인식의
impairment n. 장애
exposure n. 노출
pollutant n. 오염물질
proximity n. 근접, 가까움
duration n. 지속
diagnose v. 진단하다
resolve v. (문제·곤란 따위를) 풀다, 해결하다
sick building syndrome 새 건물 증후군(건물 속의 오염된 공기·화학 물질 등으로 인해 그 속에서 생활하는 사람들이 피로, 두통, 눈 따가움, 호흡 곤란 등을 겪는 것)
resident n. 거주자
symptom n. 징후, 조짐; 증상
sore throat 인후염
combustion n. 연소
volatile a. 휘발성의
organic a. 유기체의, 유기물의
compound n. 혼합물, 화합물
pathogenicity n. (미생물이 질병을 유발하는) 병원성(病原性)

1 ② ▶ 내용파악
미국 의학 협회는 실내에 있는 대기오염 물질을 연소 생성물, 생물학적 오염물질, 휘발성 유기 화합물, 중금속 등으로 분류하는데, ①은 연소 생성물에, ③은 생물학적 오염물질에, ④는 중금속에 각각 포함된다. 따라서 ②가 정답이 된다. 휘발성 유기 화합물은 상온에서 쉽게 기화하여 대기를 오염시키는 벤젠, 톨루엔, 포름알데히드 등을 말하며 유기 엽산은 비타민의 일종인 영양소이다.

2 ④ ▶ 내용파악
본문의 두 번째 문장에서 오염물질에 대해 사람이 근접한 정도, 오염물질에 노출된 사람의 나이, 노출 기간 등의 요인을 언급했다. ④는 여기에 해당되지 않는다.

09 2020 인하대

유럽은 이미 많은 심각한 질병의 창궐을 경험했었지만 가장 파괴적인 것은 14세기 중엽에 발생했으며, 이로 인해 유럽 대륙 인구의 1/3~1/2이 목숨을 잃었다. 흑사병으로 알려져 있는 그 전염병은 중앙아시아로부터 유럽으로 퍼졌을지도 모른다. 그 질병의 원인은 설치류에 기생하는 벼룩이 옮기는 박테리아인 "페스트균(Yersinis pestis)"이었던 것으로 널리 알려져 있지만, 여러 이론들이 분분하다. 그 전염병은 목, 사타구니, 겨드랑이의 림프선종, 즉, 부종(浮腫)을 특징으로 하는 림프절 페스트, 폐를 감염시키는 폐 페스트, 혈액이 오염되는 패혈성 페스트의 3가지 변종이 있다. 페스트는 1347년에 콘스탄티노플을 통해 전해졌으며 1348년과 1349년 동안 유럽 대부분의 지역에 도달했다. 그것은 광범위한 두려움과 공포를 야기했고, 그것의 확산을 막으려는 시도는 대부분 아무 소용이 없었다. 1350년 무렵, 흑사병은 대체로 자연히 끝났지만, 2,500만~5,000만 명의 유럽인들이 사망한 데 따른 갑작스러운 노동력의 부족은 중대한 사회변화의 원인이 됐을지도 모른다. 농민들은 자신들의 수가 줄어듦으로 인해 자신들이 하는 일에 대한 수요가 훨씬 더 커졌다는 사실을 알게 되었는데, 이는 농민들의 생활 여건과 법적 권리가 크게 향상되었다는 것을 의미했다.

1 ① ▶ 빈칸완성
바로 앞에서 '2,500만~5,000만 명이 사망했다'고 했으므로, 노동력이 '부족'하게 됐을 것임을 알 수 있다. ② 통합 ③ 분할 ④ 풍부 ⑤ 다각화

2 ② ▶ 내용일치
1350년 무렵, 흑사병은 대체로 자연히 끝났다고 했으므로 흑사병이 절정에 달했다고 한 ②가 옳지 않은 진술이다. ③ 본문에서는 페스트의 증상이 아니라 페스트에 3가지 변종이 있다고 했지만, 페스트의 종류에 따라 증상도 크게 세 가지 범주로 나눌 수 있을 것이므로 옳은 진술이다.

outbreak n. (전쟁·유행병 등의) 발발, 돌발, 창궐
continent n. 대륙, 육지; 유럽대륙
Black Death 흑사병
plague n. 전염병; 흑사병, 페스트; 재앙
abound v. (동물·물건·문제 등이) 많이 있다; (장소 등이 ~로) 그득하다
Yersinis pestis 페스트균
flea n. 벼룩
rodent n. 설치류 (동물)
infection n. 전염, 감염; 전염병
variant n. 변체, 변형, 변종
bubonic a. 서혜 임파선종의, 림프절의
bubo n. (특히 살·겨드랑이 밑의) 림프선종(腫)
swelling n. 부어오름, 종창
groin n. 서혜부, 사타구니
armpit n. 겨드랑이
pneumonic a. 폐의
infect v. 감염시키다
lung n. 허파, 폐
septicemic a. 패혈증의
transmit v. (병을) 옮기다, 전염시키다
via prep. ~을 경유하여
run its course 자연히 끝나다(= come to a natural end)
contribute to 기여[기부]하다; ~의 원인이 되다
profound a. 깊은; 뜻 깊은, 심원한
peasantry n. 농민; 소작농
demand n. 요구, 청구; 수요; 판로

10 2017 한국외대

충분히 달리는 것은 최소한 일시적으로나마 당신을 완전히 새로운 사람으로 변화시킬 수 있다. 현재 신경발생 분야에서 이루어지고 있는 연구에서는 이것이 사실인 이유에 대해 설명하기 위해 노력해왔다. 최근까지, 지배적인 이론은 뇌 속의 뉴런의 수는 한정되어 있어서 성인이 된 후에는 더 이상 뉴런이 생기지 않는다는 것이었다. 그러나 여러 연구들은 뉴런이 일생 동안 생산될 수 있지만, 단 하나의 조건인 격렬한 운동을 한다는 조건에서만 생산될 수 있다는 것을 보여주었다. 더구나, 뇌 세포가 새로 생산되는 곳은 두뇌에서 학습과 기억과 관계된 영역인 해마 안쪽이다. 따라서 당신이 땀을 흘릴 정도로 30분에서 40분 동안 충분히 운동을 한다면, 기억과 관련된 뇌 영역이 발달할 것이다. 게다가, 이와 동일한 양의 운동은 대뇌 앞부분에 위치한 실행 네트워크 체계인 전두엽에서 뇌 발달이 일어나게 한다. 대뇌의 이 영역은 목표 설정, 계획, 집중력, 시간 관리와 연관되어 있다. 더구나 전두엽은 감정 조절과 연관되어 있다. 그래서 오랜 시간 동안 달리기를 한 사람들은 좋은 기분을 느낀다. 따라서 약이 아닌 달리기가 우울증 또는 불안 장애가 있는 사람들을 위한 최고의 명약일지도 모른다. 마지막으로, 달리기 운동을 하는 사람들은 운동을 하면서 거의 항상 마음을 자유롭게 내버려 둔다. 이러한 공상은 창조성과 문제 해결 능력에 긍정적인 영향을 미친다.

transform v. 바꾸어 놓다, 변형시키다, 변화시키다
temporarily ad. 일시적으로, 임시로
brand-new a. 아주 새로운, 신품의
neurogenesis n. 신경발생
account for ~을 설명하다
prevailing a. 우세한, 지배적인
finite a. 한정된, 유한의
adulthood n. 성인(임), 성년, 성인기
hippocampus n. (대뇌 측두엽의) 해마
sweat v. 땀을 흘리다
frontal lobe (대뇌의) 전두엽
goal-setting n. 목표 설정

1 ③ ▶ 빈칸완성
ⓐ 앞에서 뉴런의 수가 한정되어 있어서 성인이 된 후에는 더 이상 뉴런이 생기지 않는다는 이론에 관해서 설명한 다음, 빈칸 다음에 뉴런이 격렬한 운동을 통해서 일생 동안 생길 수 있다는 연구를 소개하고 있으므로, 이 두 문장의 내용은 서로 대조를 이룬다. 따라서 ⓐ에는 However가 적절하다. 그리고 ⓑ 이하는 이렇게 새로 생긴 뉴런이 위치하는 장소에 대해서 부연하여 설명하므로, ⓑ에는 Furthermore가 적절하다. 한편, ⓒ 앞의 "오랜 시간 동안 달리기를 한 사람들은 좋은 기분을 느낀다."는 것과 ⓒ 뒤의 "달리기가 우울증 또는 불안 장애가 있는 사람들을 위한 최고의 명약일지도 모른다."는 내용은 원인과 결과의 관계에 있으므로, ⓒ에는 인과관계를 나타내는 접속부사 Therefore가 적절하다. 따라서 ③이 정답이다.

2 ① ▶ 내용파악
격렬한 운동을 하는 경우, 학습과 기억과 관계된 대뇌 영역인 해마의 뉴런의 수가 증가하여, 집중력이 향상되고 창조성과 문제 해결 능력에 긍정적인 영향을 준다고는 했지만, 근육의 조정력에 대해서는 언급되지 않았으므로 ①이 정답이다.

3 ② ▶ 내용일치
글의 중간 부분에서 "이와 동일한 양의 운동은 전두엽에서 뇌 발달이 일어나게 한다. 대뇌의 이 영역은 목표 설정, 계획, 집중력, 시간 관리와 연관되어 있다."라고 했고, 마지막 부분에서 "달리기 운동을 하는 사람들은 운동하면서 거의 항상 마음을 자유롭게 내버려 둔다. 이러한 공상은 창조성과 문제 해결 능력에 긍정적인 영향을 준다."라고 했으므로, ②가 이 글의 내용과 일치한다. 참고로 감정 조절을 담당하는 영역은 전두엽이며, 해마는 학습과 기억과 관련되어 있으므로 ③은 정답이 될 수 없다.

pharmaceutical n. 약, 제약
wander v. (정처 없이) 돌아다니다, 헤매다; (마음·생각·소원 등이) 종잡지 못하게 되다
daydreaming n. 백일몽, 공상

11 2019 덕성여대

에볼라(Ebola) 바이러스는 치료하지 않으면 종종 치명적일 정도로 심각한 급성 질병을 일으킨다. 에볼라 출혈열(EVD)은 1976년에 2건이 동시에 발생하면서 처음으로 모습을 드러냈는데, 하나는 수단의 은자라(Nzara)에서, 나머지 하나는 콩고민주공화국의 얌부쿠(Yambuku)에서 발생했다. 후자는 에볼라 강 근처의 마을에서 발생했는데, 에볼라 출혈열이라는 이름은 여기에서 따온 것이다. 에볼라는 병 들거나 죽은 채로 발견된 과일박쥐, 원숭이, 호저(豪猪) 같은 감염된 동물의 혈액, 분비물, 장기 또는 기타 체액을 가깝게 접촉함으로써 사람들 속으로 들어오게 된다.
그런 다음 에볼라는 감염된 사람들의 혈액, 분비물, 장기 또는 기타 체액과의 직접 접촉, 그리고 이러한 체액에 오염된 표면과 물질과의 직접 접촉을 거쳐 사람과 사람 사이의 전염을 통해 확산된다. 의료계 종사자들은 의심되거나 확인된 EVD 환자들을 치료하면서 자주 감염됐다. 이는 감염 관리를 위한 예방 조치가 엄격하게 시행되지 않는 상황에서 환자와 가까이 접촉함으로써 발생한 것이다. 사람들은 그들의 혈액, 그리고 정액과 모유를 비롯한 체액에 바이러스가 들어 있는 한, 여전히 다른 사람에게 전염시킬 수 있다.

1 ② ▶ 부분이해
simultaneous는 '동시의', '동시에 발생하는'이라는 뜻이므로, '두 지역에서 에볼라 바이러스가 같은 시기에 발생했다'는 것을 말하고 있다.

2 ④ ▶ 내용파악
두 번째 문단에서 에볼라의 전염 경로와 전염성을 설명하면서 감염을 예방하기 위한 조치가 반드시 필요함을 이야기하고 있다. 그러므로 ④가 정답으로 적절하다. ① 1976년에 처음 발생했다. ② 감염된 사람들의 혈액과 체액 등에 오염된 표면과 물질과 접촉한 경우에도 감염된다. ③ 의심되거나 확인된 EVD 환자들을 치료하는 과정에서 자주 감염됐다고 했지만, 에볼라 바이러스 환자들을 돌보는 의료 종사자가 없는 것은 아니다.

acute a. 날카로운, 뾰족한; 빈틈없는; 급성의
simultaneous a. 동시의, 동시에 일어나는
outbreak n. (소동·전쟁·유행병 따위의) 발발, 창궐
the latter (둘 중의) 후자(後者)
introduce v. 안으로 들이다; 받아들이다; 소개하다
contact n. 접촉
secretion n. 분비, 분비물
organ n. (생물의) 기관, 장기(臟器)
fluid n. 유동체, 유체
infect v. 감염시키다, 전염시키다
fruit bat 큰박쥐, 과일박쥐
porcupine n. <동물> 호저(豪猪)
spread v. 퍼지다, 번지다, 전해지다
transmission n. 전달, 매개, 전염
via prep. ~을 경유하여, ~을 거쳐
contaminate v. (접촉하여) 더럽히다, 오염하다
suspect v. 의심하다
confirm v. 확증하다, 확인하다
precaution n. 조심, 경계; 예방책
strictly ad. 엄격하게
infectious a. 전염성의
semen n. 정액
contain v. (속에) 담고 있다, 포함하다

12 2014 한국항공대

우리는 일반적으로 과도하게 숨을 쉬거나 과도하게 술을 마시거나 과도하게 성생활을 하지는 않는다. 그렇다면 왜 우리는 과식을 하는가? 과식을 하는 데는 적어도 세 가지 이유가 있다. 첫째, 생화학적 이상이 과식을 야기할 수 있다. 예를 들어, 비만인 사람들은 종종 지방억제호르몬에 저항력이 있는데, 바꾸어 말하면 비만인 사람들의 두뇌는 공복감을 차단하는 화학적인 메시지에 반응하지 않는다는 것이며, 그래서 지방억제호르몬 주사도 비만인 사람들에게 도움을 주지 못한다. 그러한 사람들에게 먹고자 하는 욕구는 믿을 수 없을 만큼 강렬해서, 우리가 숨 쉬는 것을 그냥 멈추기로 할 수 없는 것과 마찬가지로 그들은 먹는 것을 그냥 멈추어버릴 수 없는 것이다. 둘째, 우리는 실제로 배가 고프지 않을 때도 종종 먹는다. 예를 들어, 우리는 슬픔이나 걱정과 같은 부정적인 감정을 완화시키기 위해 먹을지도 모르고, 습관적으로 먹을지도 모르며("나는 항상 밤에 아이스크림을 먹어."), 그리고 사회적 의무 때문에 먹을지도 모른다("다른 사람들이 모두 후식을 주문하고 있네."). 셋째, 본성적으로 우리는 과식하도록 되어 있다. 우리의 진화 역사 대부분에 있어, 우리의 선조들이 직면한 음식과 관련된 주요 문제는 굶주림이었고, 우리는 굶주림을 피하기 위해 두 가지 전략을 이끌어 냈다. 첫째, 우리는 한 입에 많은 양의 에너지를 제공하는 음식, 다시 말해 열량이 풍부한 음식에 강한 매력을 느끼게 되었는데, 바로 이런 이유로 우리 대부분은 셀러리와 물보다 햄버거와 밀크셰이크를 더 선호한다. 둘째, 우리는 여분의 식품 열량을 지방 형태로 저장하는 능력을 발달시켰는데, 이것이 우리로 하여금 음식이 풍부할 때 우리가 필요한 양보다 더 많이 먹고 음식이 부족할 때 우리가 비축해 놓은 영양분에 의존할 수 있게 해주었다.

1 ① ▶ 뒷내용 추론
마지막 문장에서 "우리는 여분의 식품 열량을 지방 형태로 저장할 능력을 발달시켰는데, 이것이 우리로 하여금 음식이 풍부할 때 필요한 양보다 더 많이 먹고 음식이 부족할 때에 비축해 놓은 영양분에 의존할 수 있게 해주었다."라고 하였다. 이것은 음식이 부족할 때에 대비할 수 있게 우리의 몸이 맞춰져 있다는 의미이다. 따라서 다음에 올 문장으로 "우리는 음식이 일반적으로 저칼로리이고 부족한 세상에 적합하도록 훌륭하게 맞춰져 있다."는 ①이 적절하다.

2 ② ▶ 빈칸완성
"다른 사람들 모두가 후식을 주문하고 있다."라고 했는데, 이는 사회 구성원들 모두의 행동에 자신도 따라야 한다는 '사회적 의무'에 해당한다. ① 철저한 순응 ③ 합리적 순응 ④ 사회적 격차

3 ④ ▶ 내용일치
본문에 "지방억제호르몬 주사도 비만인 사람들에게 도움을 주지 못한다."라는 언급이 있는데, 이것은 지방억제호르몬 주사가 비만인 사람들이 계속 먹는 것을 막지 못한다는 뜻이지, 저장된 지방을 소비하지 않게 하는 것과는 상관이 없으므로 ④가 정답이다. ① "진화 역사 대부분에 있어, 선조들이 직면했던 굶주림을 피하기 위해 열량이 풍부한 음식에 강한 매력을 느끼게 되었고, 여분의 식품 열량을 지방 형태로 저장할 능력을 개발했다."는 언급을 통해 음식을 많이 먹도록 진화되어 왔다는 사실을 알 수 있다. ② "나는 항상 밤에 아이스크림을 먹어."라는 언급과 같이 우리는 습관적으로 먹을지도 모른다고 했다. ③ 우리가 정말로 배가 고프지 않을 때도 종종 먹는 경우가 있다고 했는데 그 예로 "우리는 슬픔이나 걱정과 같은 부정적인 감정을 완화시키기 위해 먹을지도 모른다."라는 언급이 있다.

overdrink v. 과음하다
biochemical a. 생화학적인
abnormality n. 기형; 이상
obese a. 비만인, 비대한
leptin n. 렙틴(체내 지방 억제 물질)
resistant a. 저항력이 있는, 견디는
shut off ~을 세우다, 정지시키다
urge n. 충동, 욕구
incredibly ad. 믿을 수 없을 만큼, 엄청나게
compelling a. 강렬한; 억누를 수 없는
not A any more than B B가 아니듯 A도 아니다
(= no more A than B)
evolutionary a. 진화의, 진화론적인
ancestor n. 조상, 선조
bite n. 한 입; 한 입의 분량; 소량의 식사
store v. 저장하다, 보관하다
excess a. 여분의, 초과의
plentiful a. 풍부한, 많은
live off ~에 의지해서 살다, ~에 의존하다
reserve n. 비축량, 비축물
scarce a. 부족한, 모자라는

13 2021 중앙대

면역학이란 감염에 대한 신체의 방어를 연구하는 학문이다. 우리는 미생물에 지속적으로 노출되고 있으며 이 미생물 중 많은 것들이 질병을 일으키지만, 질병에 걸리는 일은 매우 드물다. 몸은 어떻게 스스로를 방어하는 것일까? 감염이 발생하면 몸은 침입자를 어떻게 제거하여 자신을 치유할까? 왜 우리는 한 번 맞서 싸우고 극복한 수많은 감염 질환에 지속적인 면역력을 갖게 되는 걸까? 이것들이 면역학에서 다루는 질문들이며, 우리는 세포와 분자 수준에서 감염에 대한 우리 몸의 방어를 이해

immunology n. 면역학
defense n. 방어
infection n. 감염
microorganism n. 미생물

하기 위해 면역학을 연구한다.
B 과학으로서의 면역학은 대개 18세기 후반 에드워드 제너(Edward Jenner)의 연구로 인해 그에 게서 시작된 것으로 간주된다. 면역이라는 개념 — 즉, 질병에서 살아남으면 나중에 더 큰 보호를 제공받는다는 개념 — 은 고대 그리스 때부터 알려져 있었다. 종두법 — 즉, 천연두 농포(膿疱) 물질을 흡입하거나 피부의 상처로 옮기는 것 — 은 최소한 1400년대부터 중동과 중국에서 천연두를 막는 보호책으로 실행되어왔고 제너도 알고 있었다.
A 제너는 우두, 즉 종두증이라는 비교적 가벼운 질병이 치명적인 천연두에 대한 보호책을 주는 것 같다는 사실을 관찰했고, 1796년에 우두로 접종을 하면 접종을 받은 사람이 천연두에 걸리지 않는다는 것을 입증해보였다. 그의 과학적 증거는 예방접종자를 접종 2개월 후 감염성 있는 천연두 물질에 일부러 노출시키는 방법에 의지했다. 이 과학적 검증이 제너의 독창적인 공헌이었다.
C 제너는 이 과정을 백신접종이라 불렀다. 이 용어는 건강한 사람들에게 질병인자를 약화시켜 접종함으로써 해당 질환으로부터 보호를 제공하는 방법을 기술할 때 여전히 쓰이고 있다. 제너의 과감한 실험은 성공을 거두었으나 천연두 백신접종이 보편화되는 데는 거의 200년이 걸렸다. 이러한 발전으로 인해 세계보건기구는 1979년에 천연두 근절을 선언할 수 있었는데, 이는 필시 현대의학의 가장 위대한 승리라고 할 수 있다.

immunity n. 면역
cellular a. 세포의
molecular a. 분자의
cowpox n. 우두
confer v. 제공하다
recipient n. 받은 사람, 수혜자
inoculate v. 접종하다
smallpox n. 천연두
pustule n. 농포
variolation n. 종두법
eradicate v. 근절하다

1 ① ▶ 단락배열
첫 문단이 면역학 일반에 대한 소개, 그다음이 B 문단의 면역학의 탄생 이야기, 그다음이 제너의 백신 접종 관련 역사인 A, 그다음이 제너의 백신접종의 의의인 C가 되는 것이 가장 자연스러운 순서다.

2 ④ ▶ 내용일치
B 문단 마지막에 "Variolation ~ that disease and was known to Jenner."라고 되어 있으므로 ④가 본문의 내용과 일치한다. ① 종두법을 알고 있었으므로 천연두 농포의 존재도 알고 있었다. ② 더 약한 질병인 우두로 접종을 하면 접종을 받은 사람이 더 큰 질병인 천연두에 걸리지 않는다는 것을 입증해보였다고 했는데, 우두 접종이 종두법이다. ③ 백신 접종은 천연두를 막기 위한 것이다.

14 2019 국민대

건강하게 오래 사는 데 도움이 될 만한 몇 가지 팁이 있다. 가장 먼저, 다이어트를 들 수 있다. 체중 감량은 아마도 혈압을 낮추고 혈당 수치가 좋아지는 것과 같은 많은 긍정적인 변화를 가져올 것이다. 그러나 일부 전문가들은 금식이 또한 우리 몸으로 하여금 스트레스에 내성을 많이 갖게 만들며, 이는 세포 수준에서 유익한 효과를 나타낼 수 있다고 추측한다. 한 전문가는 "다이어트가 노화와 노화로 인한 질병을 지연시키기 위한 가장 강력한 개입이다."라고 말한다.
지난 2년 동안, 과학자들은 하루 종일 앉아 있는 것과 같이 몸을 많이 움직이지 않는 행동이 조기 사망의 위험 요인이라는 것을 보여주었다. 그들은 앉아서 보내는 시간이 제2형 당뇨병과 비알코올성 지방간 질환의 위험 증가와 관련돼 있다는 사실을 발견했다. 너무 많이 앉아 있는 것이 끼치는 온갖 나쁜 영향들을 운동을 해서 모두 없앨 수는 없다. 그러나 좋은 소식은 가만히 앉아 있는 것을 제외하면 무엇을 하든 — 심지어 몸을 꼼지락대는 것도 가치 있다 — 보탬이 될 수 있다는 것이다. 신체 활동을 가장 적게 기록한 사람들은 향후 10년 안에 심장질환이 발생할 위험이 가장 높았는데, 이것은 충격적이지 않다. 그러나 과학자들에게 놀라웠던 사실은 낮 동안 조금만 더 움직여도 — 집안 여기저기서 허드렛일을 하는 것과 같이 — 심장 질환의 위험을 줄이기에 충분했다는 점이다.
이제는 우리의 감정이 우리 몸의 상태에 영향을 미친다는 것을 과학자들은 분명하게 받아들이고 있다. 연구 결과들은 분노와 스트레스가 아드레날린과 같은 스트레스 호르몬을 우리 혈액에 방출시킬 수 있다는 것을 오랫동안 보여주었는데, 이렇게 되면 심장은 더 빠르게 강하게 뛰게 된다. 스트레스는 심지어 우리 뇌가 알츠하이머병에 얼마나 잘 대항하는지에도 영향을 미칠지 모른다. 과학자들은 젊었을 때 노화에 대해 더 부정적인 태도를 갖고 있던 사람들의 경우 해마의 크기가 더 작아져 있었다는 사실을 발견했는데, 해마는 뇌의 일부분으로, 이것의 크기가 작아지는 것은 알츠하이머병과 관련이 있다. 노화에 관해 우리가 어떻게 생각하는가가 우리가 어떻게 늙어가는가에 영향을 끼칠 수 있다는 연구 결과가 나온 것은 이번이 처음이 아니다.

pro tip 유용한 팁
positive a. 확신하는; 단정적인; 확실한; 긍정적인
expert n. 전문가
speculate v. 추측하다, 억측하다; 투기하다
fasting n. 단식, 금식
resistant a. 저항하는; 견디는, 내성이 있는
beneficial a. 유익한, 이익을 가져오는
intervention n. 조정, 중재, 간섭, 개입
risk factor 위험요인
fidget v. 안절부절 못하다; 꼼지락거리다
add up 조금씩 보태어 많아지다
log v. 일지에 기록하다; (특정 거리나 시간을) 항해[운항, 비행]하다
chore n. 지루한 일; (pl.) (일상의) 잡일, 허드렛일
affect v. 영향을 미치다, 악영향을 끼치다
trigger v. (일련의 사건·반응 등을) 일으키다, 유발하다
negative a. 부정적인; 소극적인
hippocampus n. (대뇌 측두엽의) 해마

1 ③ ▶ 빈칸완성

빈칸에 들어갈 행동과 관련하여, 바로 뒤에서 '하루 종일 앉아 있는 것'을 예로 들고 있으므로, 이와 유사하거나 관련 있는 표현이 빈칸에 들어가야 한다. 따라서 '앉은 채 있는, 몸을 많이 움직이지 않는'이란 의미의 ③ sedentary가 정답으로 적절하다. ① 활동적인 ② 갑작스러운, 무뚝뚝한 ④ 큰 소리로 외치는, 소란스러운

2 ② ▶ 내용파악

첫 번째 문단에서 ③을, 두 번째 문단에서 ①을, 세 번째 문단에서 ④를 각각 언급하고 있다. 운동을 과도하게 할 것을 권하고 있지는 않으므로, ②가 본문에서 언급하지 않은 내용이다.

3 ① ▶ 빈칸완성

빈칸을 포함하고 있는 문장의 바로 앞에, "젊었을 때 노화에 대해 더 부정적인 태도를 갖고 있던 사람들의 경우 알츠하이머병에 걸릴 가능성이 더 높은 상태에 있었다."는 내용이 있으며, 병에 걸리는 것은 삶의 질이 나빠지는 것으로 볼 수 있다. 빈칸을 포함하고 있는 문장은 이 점을 재확인하는 역할을 하므로, 빈칸에는 이러한 내용과 가장 가까운 의미인 ①이 들어가는 것이 적절하다.

15 2013 동덕여대

인간의 귀는 청각기관과 균형기관을 가지고 있다. 두 기관 모두 유동체로 채워진 관을 포함하는데, 그 관들은 움직이는 유동체가 털을 자극할 때 전기화학적 자극을 생성하는 유모세포(털 세포)를 가지고 있다.

귀는 외이, 중이, 그리고 내이 세 부분으로 나눌 수 있다. 외이는 음파를 모은 후, 이를 외이와 중이를 구분 짓는 고막으로 전달한다. 중이는 소리 진동을 세 개의 작은 뼈를 통해 내이로 전달한다. 내이는 소리나 진동에 반응하는 유동체를 가지고 있는 여러 관들이 망처럼 얽혀있는 곳이다.

청각기능을 수행하기 위해서, 귀는 공기 중에 떠돌아다니는 기압파 에너지를 신경 자극으로 전환시키고, 이 자극을 뇌는 소리로써 받아들인다. 말하고 있는 사람의 성대와 같이 진동하는 물체는 주변 공기에 파동을 만들어 낸다. 이 파동은 고막으로 하여금 같은 진동수로 진동하도록 만든다. 중이의 세 개의 뼈는 이 진동을 증폭시키고 청각기관인 달팽이관 표면에 있는 막인 난원창으로 전송한다. 난원창의 진동은 달팽이관 안에 있는 유동체에 압력 주파를 생성한다. 달팽이관의 유모세포들은 진동하는 유동체의 에너지를 자극으로 전환시키고, 이 자극은 청각 신경을 따라 뇌로 전달된다.

균형기관 역시 내이에 위치해 있다. 몸의 자세에 관련된 감각들은 소리에 대한 감각들과 비슷한 방식으로 만들어진다. 내이의 유모세포들은 중력과 움직임에 따라 달라지는 머리의 위치 변화에 반응한다. 중력은 항상 털들을 잡아당겨서 끊임없는 일련의 자극들을 뇌로 보낸다. 우리가 머리를 앞으로 숙일 때와 같이 머리의 위치를 바꾸면, 유모세포에 있는 힘은 신경 자극의 생산량에 변화를 준다. 그러면 뇌는 이 변화들을 해석하여 머리의 새로운 위치를 알아낸다.

1 ② ▶ 내용추론

본문 세 번째 단락에서 신경 자극은 귀의 여러 기관을 거쳐 마지막에는 청각신경을 따라 뇌로 전달된다고 하였다. 또 네 번째 단락을 살펴보면 몸 일부의 위치가 바뀔 때 신경 자극 생산량이 바뀌고, 이 변화는 뇌로 전달되어 뇌가 위치 변화를 인식하게 된다고 설명하고 있다. 그러므로 두 기관 모두 생성된 신경 자극을 뇌로 보낸다는 사실을 언급한 ②가 정답으로 가장 적절하다. ① 본문에서 언급하지 않은 내용이다. ③ 유동체에 관한 부분은 있지만 그 양에 관해서는 본문에서 설명하고 있지 않으므로 적절하지 않다. ④ 청각기관에 관해서는 세 번째 단락에서, 외부의 소리가 귀 전체를 거쳐 뇌에 도달하는 과정을 설명해주고 있다. 한편 네 번째 단락 첫 문장에서 균형기관은 내이에 있다고 하였으므로 적절하지 않다.

2 ① ▶ 내용파악

청각에 포함되는 것은 성대의 움직임이 아니라 성대의 떨림으로 인한 주변 공기의 파동이다. 본문 세 번째 단락 처음 세 문장을 보면 이를 알 수 있다. 그러므로 ①이 가장 적절

---

organ n. 기관(器官), 장기
fluid-filled a. 액체로 가득 찬[채워진]
electrochemical a. 전기화학의
impulse n. 충동; 충격, 자극
stimulate v. 자극하다, 격려하다; 고무하다
eardrum n. 고막
vibration n. 떨림, 진동
convert v. 전환시키다; 개조하다
nerve n. 신경
perceive v. 감지하다, 인지하다
vocal cord 성대
frequency n. 빈도; 진동수; 주파수
amplify v. 증폭시키다
transmit v. 전송하다; 전염시키다; (열·전기·소리 등을) 전도시키다
oval a. 계란형의, 타원형의
oval window (중이의) 난원창(卵圓窓)
membrane n. (인체 피부 혹은 조직의) 막
cochlea n. 달팽이관
auditory a. 청각의
gravity n. 중력
determine v. 알아내다, 밝히다; 결정하다

하다. ①은 speaking과 관련 있다.

3 ④ ▶ 내용추론
두 번째 단락에서 내이는 유동체를 가지고 있는 여러 개의 관들로 이루어져 있다고 했다. 세 번째 단락에서는 난원창의 진동은 달팽이관 안에 있는 유동체에 영향을 준다고 하였다. 이를 바탕으로 달팽이관 안에 유동체가 있다는 것이고, 결국에는 달팽이관은 내이에 있다는 사실을 알 수 있다. 그러므로 ④가 적절하다.

4 ① ▶ 내용추론
본문 네 번째 단락에서, 몸의 위치 변화에 관해 뇌로 자극을 보내는 유모세포들이 중력과 움직임에 반응한다고 하였다. 그러므로 중력이 중요한 역할을 한다는 ①이 적절하다.

16 2019 한성대

당신이 나이를 먹으면, 연성섬유종(쥐젖)이라고 불리는 작은 혹이 당신의 몸에 나타나기 시작할지도 모른다. 연성섬유종의 밑 부분은 얇고 위쪽으로 갈수록 넓어지기 때문에 연성섬유종을 식별할 수 있을 것이다. 그것들은 암성(癌性) 사마귀와 같이 아프거나 위험하지는 않지만, 당신이 연성섬유종을 제거하길 원하는 데는 매우 합당한 이유가 있다. 사람들은 온갖 종류의 무분별한 방법을 사용하여 혼자 연성섬유종을 제거하려고 한다고 피부과 의사인 로시(Rossi) 박사는 말한다. 그는 사람들이 연성섬유종 주위를 실로 묶고, 태우고, 손가락으로 뽑으려고 하며, 심지어 연성섬유종을 책으로 세게 치기도 한다는 말을 들어왔다. 반면에, 피부과 의사는 연성섬유종을 빠르고 깨끗하게 제거할 수 있다.
우선 첫째로 피부과 의사들은 살균 기기를 가지고 있지만, 당신이 갖고 있는 기기를 사용하는 것은 감염을 일으킬 수 있다. 또한 피부과 의사들은 국소마취를 하고 지혈을 해주는 비품들이 있지만, 당신이 집에서 하는 방법으로는 감당하지 못할 정도로 출혈이 일어날 수도 있다. 심지어 연성섬유종을 녹여 없앤다고 하는 병원약도 좋지 않은 것일 수 있다고 로시 박사는 말한다. "당신은 피부에 화상을 입거나 상처를 남길 수 있고 의도하지 않은 결과를 낳을 수도 있습니다."라고 그는 말한다.
그러나 당신이 전문가에게 진찰을 받아야하는 더 중요한 이유가 있다. 피부과 의사가 혹을 제거한 후에 그들은 그 혹을 현미경으로 자세히 살펴볼 것이다. "연성섬유종처럼 보이지만, 암인 경우가 있습니다."라고 로시 박사는 말한다. 그렇다고 연성섬유종을 발견하면 겁을 먹어야한다는 의미는 아니다. <대부분의 연성섬유종은 양성(良性)이지만, 당신이 물어보기 전까지는 확실히 알 수 없을 것이다.> 이 뿐만 아니라 연성섬유종을 검사하는 것은 의사로 하여금 당신의 몸의 나머지 부분을 검사하여 피부암과 비정형 종양 혹은 악성 종양이 있는지 확인하게 할 수 있는 '좋은 구실'이기도 하다고 로시 박사는 말한다.

1 ① ▶ 글의 제목
나이가 들면서 몸에 생기는 작은 혹인 연성섬유종에 대해 설명하는 글이다. 필자는 사람들이 연성섬유종을 무분별하게 제거한다고 언급하면서, 혹시 생길 수도 있는 감염이나 출혈을 방지하고, 연성섬유종이 피부암이나 악성 종양일 수도 있으므로 피부과 전문의의 도움을 받아야 한다고 말하고 있다. 따라서 ①의 '연성섬유종을 해결하는 방법'이 글의 제목으로 적절하다.

2 ③ ▶ 내용일치
대부분의 연성섬유종이 양성이라고 했으므로 악성이라고 한 ③이 글의 내용과 일치하지 않는다.

3 ④ ▶ 문장삽입
제시문의 Most는 skin tags(연성섬유종)를 가리키는 대명사다. 제시문은 "대부분의 연성섬유종은 양성이지만, 당신이 물어보기 전까지는 확실히 알 수 없을 것이다."라는 의미이므로, 제시문 앞부분에는 연성섬유종을 확인하더라도 겁을 먹을 필요가 없다는 내용이 있어야 하며, 제시문 뒷부분에는 연성섬유종이 양성인지 악성인지 확인하는 것과 관련된 내용이 있어야 적절하다. 따라서 D에 제시문이 들어가야 한다.

---

growth n. 종양, 혹
skin tag 연성 섬유종(쥐젖)
pop up 튀어나오다[오르다], 불쑥 나타나다
cancerous a. 암의; 암에 걸린
mole n. (피부 위에 작게 돋은 진갈색) 점, 사마귀
dermatologic a. 피부(皮膚)의
slam v. 내동댕이치다, 쳐서 맞히다
snip v. 싹둑 자르다, 가위로 자르다
sterile a. 살균한, 소독한
dissolve v. 녹이다, 용해시키다; 사라지다
under a microscope 현미경으로, 꼼꼼하게
freak out 자제력을 잃다

4 ①　▶ 빈칸완성
연성섬유종이 양성인지 악성인지를 확실하게 진단을 받기 위해서는 검진을 권유하고 있으므로, 연성섬유종을 전문의에게 확인받는 것은 몸의 다른 곳에는 이상이 없는지, 즉 전반적인 건강을 확인할 수 있는 '좋은 구실' 혹은 '계기'가 될 것이다. 따라서 ①이 빈칸에 적절하다. 나머지 보기는 모두 부정적인 의미를 가지고 있으므로 검진을 권하는 내용과는 어울리지 않는다. ② 위험한 과정 ③ 쓸모없는 방법 ④ 필요악

17　2017 가톨릭대

우리가 빵 한 조각을 소화할 때, 탄수화물은 단당으로 분해하고 단백질은 아미노산으로 분해한다. 이와 동시에, 우리는 또한 피부, 근육, 뼈의 단백질을 분해하고 재구성한다. 모든 유기체들은 계속해서 고분자를 분해하고 구성요소들을 재사용한다.

유기체들은 쉽게 고분자를 결합하고 분해해야 한다. 고분자를 함께 묶는 결합은 고분자들이 서로 떨어지지 않을 만큼 충분히 강해야 한다. 그러나 그 결합이 유기체가 필요할 경우에도 쉽게 서로 분리할 수 없을 정도로 너무 강해서는 안 된다. 아이들의 팝 구슬(가운데 구멍이 있어 끈으로 서로를 연결시킬 수 있는 구슬)과 레고 블록과 같이 생명의 구성요소는 쉽게 결합되고 쉽게 분리된다.

놀랍게도, 모든 생물학적인 구성요소들은 같은 방식으로 함께 결합한다. 모든 주요 고분자들의 구성요소는 같은 간단한 화학 반응에 의해 결합한다. 모든 경우에, 효소(화학적인 결합을 만들고 끊는 것을 돕는 분자)는 구성요소 쌍들 사이에서 두 개의 수소 원자와 한 개의 산소 원자를 제거하고 결합을 한다. 한 개의 물 분자에 해당하는 두 개의 수소와 한 개의 산소를 제거하는 것은 탈수소 응축 반응이라고 불리는데, 하나의 물 분자가 제거되기 때문이다.

고분자를 분리하기 위해, 유기체들은 탈수소 응축 반응을 역으로 행하여, 각 쌍의 구성요소에 물 분자 하나를 더한다. 효소는 물 분자를 첨가함으로써 고분자에서 각각의 작은 분자를 분리하는데, 이 과정은 가수분해로 불린다. (그리스어로 hydro는 물이며, lysis는 분해를 의미한다)

모든 구성요소들은 비슷한 탈수소 응축 반응에 의해 결합됨에도 불구하고, 형성되는 정확한 결합은 각각의 경우에 서로 다르다. 예를 들면, 당은 글리코시드 결합을 형성하고, 아미노산은 펩티드 결합을 형성한다.

digest v. 소화하다; 요약하다
carbohydrate n. 탄수화물
simple sugar 단당(糖)
protein n. 단백질
amino acid 아미노산
macromolecule n. 거대 분자, 고분자
assemble v. 모으다, 집합시키다
disassemble v. 분해[해체]하다
bond n. 묶는[매는] 것; 유대; 결합력
bead n. 구슬, 염주알
building block (복잡한 것을 구성하는) 기초 단위, 구성물, 구성요소
enzyme n. 효소(酵素)
molecule n. 분자
hydrogen n. 수소
oxygen n. 산소
equivalent n. 동등한 것, 등가[등량]물
dehydration n. 탈수(증)
condensation n. 농축, 응결, 응축
reverse v. 반대로[거꾸로] 하다, 바꾸다
detach v. 떼어내다, 분리하다
hydrolysis n. 가수분해

1 ④　▶ 글의 주제
이 글은 효소에 의해 생명의 구성요소들이 서로 결합되어 고분자를 이루고, 효소에 의해 고분자가 작은 분자로 분해되는 메커니즘을 중점적으로 설명하고 있으므로 ④가 주제로 적절하다.

2 ①　▶ 내용파악
세 번째 단락에서 화학적인 결합을 돕고 분해하는 효소는 "구성요소 쌍들 사이에서 두 개의 수소 원자와 한 개의 산소 원자를 제거하고 결합을 한다."라고 했으므로 물 분자에 상당하는 것을 제거함으로써 구성요소를 연결할 수 있다. 따라서 첫 번째 빈칸에는 taking away가 적절하다. 네 번째 단락에서는 물 분자를 더함으로써 고분자에서 작은 분자를 분리해낸다고 했으므로, 두 번째 빈칸에는 'break A into B(A를 B로 나누다)' 구문을 활용하여 긴 사슬에서 두 개의 단일 구성요소로 나눈다는 뜻이 되도록 하면 된다.

3 ②　▶ 내용일치
두 번째 단락에서 "고분자들이 서로 떨어지지 않을 만큼 고분자를 함께 묶는 결합은 충분히 강해야 한다. 그러나 그 결합이 유기체가 필요할 경우에도 쉽게 서로 분리할 수 없을 정도로 너무 강해서는 안 된다."라고 했으므로 필요할 경우 고분자의 결합은 서로 분리될 수 있다고 볼 수 있다. 따라서 ②가 글의 내용과 일치하지 않는다. ③, ④는 끝에서 두 번째 문장이 단서가 된다.

18 2015 숭실대

수백 년 동안 사람들은 뇌의 작동 원리에 흥미를 가져왔는데, 언어에 대한 연구는 이 복잡한 인체기관을 깊이 이해할 수 있는 유일무이한 기회를 제공해 준다. 초기 이집트인들은 뇌가 아니라 심장이 지적활동의 중심이라고 관행적으로 여겨왔었는데, 그 이후로 우리는 큰 진전을 이뤄냈다. 프란츠 요제프 갈(Franz Joseph Gall)이 뇌의 특정 영역이 특정 행동을 담당한다는 의견을 제시했던 19세기 초 이후에도 우리는 또한 발전을 이루어왔다. 뇌의 영역별 기능에 대한 이러한 생각은 오늘날에도 여전히 쓸모가 있지만, 갈의 연구는 (매우 비과학적인) 골상학 이론을 이끌어냈는데, 골상학이란 성격의 특징들과 두개골이 융기한 형태 사이의 연관성을 조사하는 것이다. 지금은 뇌파검사(EEG), 양전자 방사 단층촬영(PET), 기능성 자기공명영상(fMRI)을 이용해, 우리는 매우 큰 성과를 얻게 되었다! 뇌의 외상(外傷)에 의해 발생한 언어장애는 뇌를 이해할 수 있게 하는 많은 정보를 제공해주며, 동시에 인간 언어의 선천적 측면에 대한 우리의 지식을 넓혀준다.

뇌, 그중에서도 특히 좌반구에 위치한 전두엽이 손상된 사람들은 특정 종류의 언어장애 혹은 언어 결손을 전형적으로 경험한다. 실어증이라 불리는 이와 같은 언어 관련 장애와 결손 증상은 우리에게 뇌에서 언어를 주로 담당하고 있는 것처럼 보이는 영역을 알 수 있게 해준다. 두 가지 유형의 주요 언어 장애는 브로카 실어증과 베르니케 실어증인데, 브로카 실어증은 1860년대에 최초로 그것에 대해 설명했던 프랑스인 의사 폴 브로카(Paul Broca)의 이름을 따서 붙여진 실어증이고 베르니케 실어증은 1870년대에 처음으로 이런 종류의 언어결손을 설명했던 독일인 의사 칼 베르니케(Karl Wernicke)의 이름을 따서 명명된 실어증이다. 그들의 연구 덕분에 신경과학이라는 새로운 분야가 생겨나게 되었다. 실서증(失書症), 실독증(失讀症), 건망성 실어증을 비롯해, 여러 가지 실어증이 많이 있다.

브로카 실어증과 베르니케 실어증 모두 언어가 다른 인지 능력과 분리돼 있다는 증거를 제공해주는데, 왜냐하면 이런 언어장애를 가진 사람들이 언어와 밀접한 연관이 없는 다른 기능들은 제어할 수 있기 때문이다. 그들은 비언어적 지능검사에서 좋은 점수를 받으며, 시계를 맞추고, 지도를 읽고, 물건을 만들고, 지시를 따르는 일을 할 수 있는데, 이것은 적어도 어떤 점에 있어서는, 언어 능력과 다른 인지 능력이 분리되어 있음을 시사하고 있는 것이다.

1 ④ ▶ 빈칸완성
비언어적 지능검사에서 좋은 점수를 받고, 시계를 맞추고, 지도를 읽고, 물건을 만들고, 지시를 따르는 일 등을 하는 데 있어서 인지 능력이 필요하다. 그런데, 언어장애를 가진 사람들이 이런 일을 해낸다는 것은 결국 '언어 능력과 언어 외의 다른 인지 능력은 서로 별개의 영역임을 의미하는 것'으로 볼 수 있다.

2 ③ ▶ 내용파악
폴 브로카는 프랑스인 의사였고, 칼 베르니케는 독일인 의사였다. 그러므로 ③이 본문의 내용과 일치한다.

3 ② ▶ 내용일치
골상학을 매우 '비과학적인' 이론으로 설명하고 있으므로, ②가 사실이 아닌 진술이다.

come a long way (사람·일이) 크게 발전[진보]하다; 기운을 차리다, 회복하다, 출세하다
localization n. 지방화, 국부화; 국한
phrenology n. 골상학
bump n. 충돌; (두개골의) 융기
skull n. 두개골, 두뇌
electroencephalography n. 뇌파검사
positron emission tomography 양전자 방사 단층촬영
trauma n. 외상(外傷), 정신적 외상, 마음의 상처
innateness n. 타고남, 천부적임; 본질적임
frontal lobe 전두엽
hemisphere n. (지구·천체의) 반구; <해부> 뇌반구
deficit n. 결손, 적자, 부족; 부족액
aphasia n. 실어증
insight n. 통찰, 간파; 통찰력
neuroscience n. 신경과학
agraphia n. 실서증(失書症)(대뇌 장애로 글을 쓸 수 없는 병)
alexia n. 독서 불능증, 실독증(失讀症)
anomia n. 건망성 실어증
separation n. 분리
cognitive a. 인식의, 인식력이 있는
faculty n. 능력, 재능; 기능
nonverbal a. 말에 의하지 않는, 비언어적인

19 2021 동국대

A 스페인 독감은 1918년 독감 대유행으로도 알려져 있는데, 현대사에서 치명적인 대유행병이었다. 스페인 독감은 1918~1919년 기간 동안 전 세계로 퍼졌다. 스페인 독감 바이러스는 5억 명을 감염시켰는데, 이는 당시 세계 인구의 대략 1/3 수이다. 사망자 수는 전 세계적으로 최소 5천만 명, 많게는 1억 명에 달하는 것으로 추정되었다. 이것이 스페인 독감을 인류 역사상 가장 심각한 세계적인 유행병으로 만들어주었다.

B 스페인 독감의 발병은 조류에 기원을 둔 유전자가 들어있는 H1N1 바이러스가 원인이었다. 현재 역사학자들은 이 바이러스가 퍼지는 데 제1차 세계대전이 부분적인 원인이었을 수 있다고 믿고 있다. 비위생적인 환경과 영양실조도 면역체계를 약화시킨 원인이었을지도 모른다. 예를 들어, 세계적인 유행병 기간 동안 나온 의학저널들을 2007년에 분석한 결과 그 바이러스 전염병이 이전의 독

flu n. 독감
pandemic n. 전 세계적인 유행병
deadly a. 치명적인
death toll 사망자 수
avian a. 새의, 조류의
hygiene n. 위생, 청결
malnourishment n. 영양실조
immune system 면역체계

감 종류들과 마찬가지로 공격적이지 않았던 것으로 밝혀졌다. 그 대신, 영양실조, 과밀한 의료 수용소 및 병원, 그리고 비위생적인 환경이 최근의 전쟁으로 인해 모두 악화되어, 세균의 중복감염을 촉진시켰다.

C 그 바이러스의 기원에 대해서는 의견이 일치하지 않는다. 1918년의 독감은 유럽, 미국, 그리고 아시아 일부 지역에서 처음 목격된 이후, 빠른 속도로 전 세계로 퍼졌다. 그 세계적인 유행병을 스페인 독감이라고 했던 주된 이유는 바로 검열이었던 것으로 여겨진다. (군인들의) 사기를 유지시키기 위해, 제1차 세계대전의 검열관들은 독일, 영국, 프랑스, 그리고 미국에서 그 질병의 발병과 사망자 수에 대한 초기 보도를 최소화시켰다. 그러나 중립국이었던 스페인에서는 신문들이 스페인의 왕이었던 알폰소(Alfonso) 13세의 중대한 발병과 같은, 그 유행병의 결과를 자유롭게 보도했고, 이런 이야기들로 인해 스페인이 유행병에 특별히 큰 타격을 받은 국가라는 잘못된 인상이 심어졌다. 이것이 '스페인 독감'이라는 이름을 발생시켰다. 역사 및 역학 자료는 그 세계적인 유행병의 지리적 기원을 확실히 규명하는 데 충분하지 않으며, 그래서 그 유행병의 위치에 대해 다양한 의견이 있다.

D 스페인 독감이 발생한지 거의 한 세기가 지나, 세계보건기구(WHO)는 과학자, 국가당국, 그리고 언론에게 새로운 인간 전염병의 이름을 지을 때 모범 관행들을 따라 지어서 국가, 경제, 그리고 국민들에게 미치는 불필요한 부정적인 영향을 최소화하도록 해달라고 요청했다. 이 바이러스를 가리키는 보다 현대적인 용어에는 '1918 influenza pandemic'이나, '1918 flu pandemic', 또는 이것들에서 변형된 용어들이 있다.

1 ② ▶ 내용파악
스페인 독감이 발생한지 거의 한 세기가 지나 세계보건기구가 전염병의 이름을 지을 때 모범 관행을 따라 지어서 국가, 경제, 그리고 국민에게 미치는 부정적인 영향을 최소화하도록 해달라고 요청했다고 한 다음, '1918년 독감 대유행'을 예로 들었다. 따라서 '1918년 독감 대유행'은 스페인 독감이라는 원래 이름의 부정적인 영향을 '줄이기' 위해 한 세기가 지난 나중에 만들어진 것으로 볼 수 있다. 그러므로 ②가 정답으로 적절하다.

2 ④ ▶ 단락의 주제
단락 B에서는 스페인 독감의 발병 원인이 무엇인지에 대해 H1N1 바이러스, 제1차 세계대전, 비위생적인 환경, 영양실조 등을 이야기하고 있으므로, 단락 B의 주제로는 ④가 적절하다.

3 ③ ▶ 단락의 주제
단락 C는 첫 문장에서 '이 바이러스의 기원에 대해서는 의견이 일치되지 않는다'고 한 다음, 유럽, 미국, 아시아 일부 지역에서 처음 목격된 후 확산되었다고 했고 그다음은 스페인이 이 바이러스의 기원으로 잘못 알려지게 된 경위를 설명하고 마지막 문장에서는 자료가 적합하지 않아 이 유행병의 지리적 기원을 확실히 규명할 수 없어서 다양한 의견이 있다고 설명하고 있다. 그러므로 1918년 독감 대유행의 지리적 기원을 묻는 ③이 단락 C의 주제로 적절하다.

no more A than B B가 아닌 것과 같이 A도 아니다
strain n. 변종; 종류
exacerbate v. (병 등을) 악화시키다
censorship n. 검열 (제도)
morale n. 사기, 의욕
censor n. 검열관
mortality n. 사망자 수, 사망률
grave a. 중대한; 심각한
hard-hit a. 큰 타격을 입은
give rise to ~이 생기게 하다
epidemiological a. 전염병학의, 역학의
call on ~을 요청하다

20 2015 중앙대

암 유전학자 보겔스타인(Vogelstein)과 응용수학자 크리스티안 토마세티(Cristian Tomasetti)는 연구 논문에서 암의 발병을 설명할 수 있는 수학적 공식을 발표했는데, 그 원리는 다음과 같다. 어떤 장기 속에 있는 세포의 숫자를 헤아린 후에, 그중에서 오래된 줄기세포가 몇 퍼센트인지를 확인하고, 그 줄기세포가 몇 번 분열하는가를 측정하는 것이다. 분열이 일어날 때마다, 딸세포에서 암을 유발하는 돌연변이가 발생할 위험이 있다. 그래서 토마세티와 보겔스타인은 줄기세포 분열이 가장 많은 횟수로 일어나는 조직이 암에 가장 취약하다고 판단했다. <암이 무작위적으로 발생하는 면은 놀라울 정도지만, 현장의 과학자들 또한 긍정적인 측면을 발견하고 있다.> 그 숫자를 계산해서 그것을 실제 암 관련 통계자료와 비교한 후에, 토마세티는 이 이론을 통해 모든 암의 2/3를 설명할 수 있다고 결론을 내렸다.

"진화의 수학을 이용하면, 그 질병을 명확하게 이해할 수 있습니다. 그것은 분열해야 할 필요가 있는 세포를 가진 동물이 가진 근원적인 위험입니다."라고 토마세티와 보걸스타인과 함께 공동연구를

geneticist n. 유전학자
applied a. 적용된, 응용된
mathematician n. 수학자
put forth 발표하다
formula n. 공식, 식; 방식; 방법
genesis n. 기원, 발생
stem cell 줄기세포
baseline a. 기본적인
mutation n. 돌연변이
crunch v. 아작아작 씹다; 처리하다

해왔던 노웍(Nowak)은 말한다. 이런 생각은 보겔스타인의 연구실에서 가졌던 두 사람의 주간 아이디어 회합에서 떠올랐다. 그들은 얼마나 많은 암이 환경적인 요인들에 의해 발병하고, 얼마나 많은 암이 유전적인 요인들에 의해 발병하는가라는 오래된 질문으로 돌아갔다. 그 문제를 해결하기 위해서 토마세티는 "우선 먼저 어느 만큼이 운에 의한 것인지를 이해하고, 그 만큼을 전체 정황에서 빼야겠다."라고 판단했다.

토마세티에 따르면, "우연"이라는 것은 유해한 유전자 혹은 흡연이나 방사능 노출과 같은 환경적인 요인들의 영향은 배제한 가운데, 매번의 세포분열이 나타내는 확률을 의미했다. 그가 줄기세포에 가장 큰 관심을 가졌던 이유는 줄기세포는 계속 지속되기 때문인데, 줄기세포가 계속 지속된다는 것은 줄기세포에서의 돌연변이가 보다 빨리 죽는 세포에서의 돌연변이보다 문제를 유발할 가능성이 더 크다는 뜻이다. 토마세티는 논문들을 검색해서 각각의 세포조직 안에 있는 줄기세포 "구획"의 크기와 같이 그가 필요로 하던 수치를 찾았다. 31개의 서로 다른 장기 안에서 평생 동안의 줄기세포 분열 횟수를 평생 동안의 암 발병 위험에 견주어 계산해보니 상관관계가 밝혀졌다. 세포분열의 횟수가 증가할수록, 암 발병의 위험도 증가했던 것이다.

예를 들어, 대장암은 소장(小腸)에서 처음 뻗어나가는 부분인 십이지장의 암보다 훨씬 더 빈번하게 발생한다. 이것은 장(腸) 전체를 위험하게 하는 돌연변이 유전자를 갖고 있는 사람들에게조차 사실이다. 토마세티는 평생 동안 십이지장에서 약 10^{10}번의 줄기세포 분열이 일어나는데 반해, 대장에서는 줄기세포 분열횟수가 약 10^{12}번이라는 사실을 발견했다. 이와는 대조적으로, 쥐의 경우에는 대장에서보다 소장에서 줄기세포의 분열이 더 많이 발생하고, 암도 더 많이 발생한다. 돌연변이와 암의 관계가 반드시 직접적이라고 할 수는 없다. "암은 단순히 돌연변이가 일어나느냐 아니냐의 문제가 아닐지도 모릅니다."라고 장기간 암을 연구해 온 브루스 폰더(Bruce Ponder)는 말한다.

statistics n. 통계자료
brainstorming n. 브레인스토밍, 회의에서 모두가 차례로 아이디어를 제출하여 그중에서 최선책을 결정하는 방법
factor n. 요인, 인자, 요소
genetics n. 유전학
out of the picture 관계가 없는; 사실을 잘 모르는; 중요하지 않은
deleterious a. 해로운, 유해한
exposure n. 노출; 발각; 탄로
radiation n. 방사선; (열·에너지 등의) 복사
literature n. 문학; 문헌, 보고서, 논문
correlation n. 상호관계, 상관관계
colon n. 결장(結腸), 대장 전체
duodenum n. 십이지장
small intestine 소장(小腸)
direct a. 직접적인

1 ② ▶ 글의 흐름상 적절하지 않은 문장 고르기
ⓑ는 '암의 무작위적 발생'과 관련한 내용이므로, ⓑ 전후의 "토마세티와 보겔스타인은 줄기세포 분열의 횟수가 많은 경우 암에 걸릴 확률이 높다는 이론을 세웠으며, 관련 수치를 여러 자료와 대조하여 상당히 신뢰할 만한 이론임을 확인했다."라는 내용과 무관하다.

2 ③ ▶ 내용추론
세 번째 문단의 "오래 지속되는 줄기세포에서의 돌연변이가 보다 빨리 죽는 세포에서의 돌연변이보다 문제를 유발할 가능성이 더 크다."라는 내용을 통해, 수명이 짧은 세포는 암을 유발하는 돌연변이를 줄기세포보다 더 적게 초래한다고 유추할 수 있다. 따라서 ③이 적절하다.

3 ① ▶ 글의 제목
본문은 줄기세포 분열 횟수와 암의 발병 위험의 관계를 진화의 수학을 이용해 살펴본 연구에 대한 글이다. 따라서 ①의 '암이 발생되는 이유를 설명하는 간단한 수학'이 제목으로 가장 적절하다.

12 생물학·생명과학

01 2022 세종대

동물들 사이의 모든 관계가 포식 관계인 것은 아니다. 일부 관계는 상리공생(相利共生)의 관계인데, 이는 관계를 맺은 두 생물 모두가 서로에게서 이익을 얻는다는 것을 의미한다. 예를 들어, 꽃의 화밀(花蜜)을 먹는 곤충들은 또한 꽃에게 도움을 준다. 꽃의 꽃가루는 곤충들이 (화밀을) 먹는 동안 그 곤충들에게 달라붙고, 그런 다음 곤충들이 다른 꽃으로 날아갈 때 꽃가루가 떨어지게 된다.

일부 관계는 기생(寄生) 관계인데, 이는 한 생물이 이익을 얻는 반면 다른 생물은 고통을 겪는다는 것을 의미한다. 개의 몸 위에 있는 벼룩에 대해 생각해 보라. 벼룩은 개를 물어서 개의 피에서 에너지를 얻으며, 그 대신 그 불쌍한 개는 가렵고 부풀어 오른 자국과 그 밖의 다른 가능한 질병들을 얻게 된다. 이런 종류의 관계에서, 벼룩은 기생생물, 개는 숙주라고 불린다. <촌충, 진드기, 그리고 이는 기생생물의 다른 예들이다.>

일부 관계는 편리공생(片利共生) 관계를 보여주는데, 이는 한 생물이 도움을 받는 반면 나머지 한 생물은 도움을 받지도 않고 해를 입지도 않는다는 것을 의미한다. 편리공생의 좋은 예는 빨판상어와 고래의 관계다. 빨판상어는 머리 꼭대기에 빨판이 있는데, 이 빨판은 고래의 윗면이나 입이나 아랫면에 달라붙게 된다. 이렇게 달라붙음으로써 빨판상어는 더 손쉽게 돌아다닐 수 있으며 고래로부터 떨어지는 부스러기들을 먹을 수 있다. 고래는 전혀 해를 입지 않은 채 있게 된다.

predatory a. 포식성의; 약탈하는
mutualistic a. 상리 공생(相利共生)의
organism n. 생물, 유기체
benefit v. ~에게 이롭다; 이익이 되다
nectar n. 과즙; 화밀(花蜜)
pollen n. 꽃가루
stick v. 달라붙다
parasitic a. 기생하는, 기생적인
flea n. 벼룩
itchy a. 가려운
welt n. (맞거나 쓸려서 피부가) 부푼[부은] 자국
parasite n. 기생충, 기생생물
host n. 숙주
commensalism n. 편리공생(片利共生)
remora n. 빨판상어
sucker n. 흡반(吸盤), 빨판
attach v. 부착하다
debris n. 부스러기, 파편

1 ① ▶ 빈칸완성
빨판상어와 고래는 편리공생 관계인데, 편리공생은 '한 생물이 도움을 받는 반면 나머지 한 생물은 도움을 받지도 않고 해를 입지도 않는 관계'이다. 그런데 앞에서 빨판상어가 얻는 이익에 대해 언급했으므로, 고래는 아무런 도움도 받지 않고 해도 입지 않을 것이다. 따라서 빈칸에는 '해를 입지 않은'의 의미인 ① unharmed가 적절하다. ② 위험한 ③ 보통의 ④ 유익한

2 ③ ▶ 문장삽입
주어진 문장은 "촌충, 진드기, 그리고 이는 기생생물의 다른 예들이다."라는 의미이므로, 기생생물의 예에 해당하는 것을 언급한 부분 다음에 와야 한다. 따라서 벼룩이 기생생물에 속함을 언급한 다음인 ⓒ에 들어가는 것이 적절하다.

3 ④ ▶ 내용일치
벼룩의 숙주인 개가 '가렵고 부풀어 오른 자국과 그 밖의 다른 가능한 질병들을 얻게 된다'고 했으므로, ④가 본문의 내용과 일치하는 진술이다. ③ 본문 내용에 국한해 볼 때, 기생관계에서 숙주인 생물과 편리공생관계에서 도움도 해도 받지 않는 생물은 생존을 위해 다른 생물에 의존하지 않는다.

02 2018 한국외대

잡아먹히는 것을 피하기 위해 무당벌레와 그 밖의 다른 곤충들은 밝은 색채와 무늬를 발달시켜 왔는데, 이것은 포식자들에게 그들이 맛이 매우 좋지 않거나 독이 있다고 알려주는 역할을 한다. 그러나 모든 새가 먼저 이 곤충들 중 하나를 먹어 봐서 그것들이 먹을 수 없다는 것을 깨달아야 한다면, 그 곤충들은 경고색이 진화하기도 전에 남아나지 않게 될 것이다. 지금, 과학자들은 새가 하는 약간의 사회적 학습이 곤충들을 이런 곤경에서 구해준다고 보고하고 있다. 과학자들은 검은색 정사각형이 찍혀 있는 흰 종이 통을 열고 있는 박새를 촬영했다. 통 안에는 쓴맛의 액체로 젖어 있는 아몬드 몇 개가 들어 있었다. 박새는 아몬드를 쪼아 보고는 거의 즉시 아몬드를 떨어뜨렸고, 머리를 흔들면서 부리를 거듭해서 횃대에다 문질러댔는데, 박새는 이런 행동을 통해 그것이 먹을 수 없는 것임을

ladybug n. 무당벌레
evolve v. 발전하다, 진화하다
predator n. 약탈자, 육식동물
foul a. 더러운, 불결한; 불쾌한
toxic a. 유독한
inedible a. 먹을 수 없는, 못 먹는, 식용에 적합하지 않은
vanish v. 사라지다
great tit 박새

말해준다. 이후에 연구원들은 15마리의 다른 박새들에게 그 영상을 보여주었다. 나중에 이 새들이 검은색 정사각형 혹은 검은색 십자 표시가 찍혀 있는 종이 통이 들어 있는 사육장에서 먹을 것을 찾아 돌아다녔을 때, 영상을 봤었던 박새들은 영상을 보지 않았던 새들보다 정사각형이 찍혀 있는 종이 통을 고를 확률이 32% 더 적었다. 물론, 야생에 있는 새들이 영상을 보고서 먹을 수 없는 것을 알게 되지는 않는다. 그러나 다른 연구들은 새들이 분명히 서로를 지켜본다는 사실을 보여주었다. 이러한 사실로부터 우리는 다른 새가 "우웩!"이라고 말할 때 그들이 분명히 주의를 기울이고 있다고 확실하게 주장할 수 있다.

packet n. (종이나 마분지로 된 상품 포장용) 통; 묶음
square n. 정사각형; 광장
soak v. 적시다, 담그다
instantly ad. 당장에, 즉각, 즉시
beak n. (새의) 부리
perch n. (새의) 횃대
forage v. (식량을) 찾아 돌아다니다; 약탈하다
aviary n. (큰) 새장
claim v. 요구하다, 청구하다; 주장하다

1 ④   ▶ **글의 제목**
위 글은 "새는 어떤 곤충이 먹어도 되는 것인지의 여부를 사회적 학습을 통해, 즉, 다른 새가 그것을 먹고서 어떤 반응을 보이는지에 주목함으로써 판단한다."는 내용을 담고 있다. 그러므로 이 글의 제목으로는 ④가 적절하다.

2 ③   ▶ **부분이해**
밑줄 친 부분을 앞부분의 내용과 결부해서 파악하면, "새들이 어떤 곤충이 먹을 수 있는 것인지 아닌지를 직접 먹어봐서 알아야 한다면 곤충이 남아나지 않게 되겠지만, 새들은 이와 관련된 판단을 사회적 학습을 통해 하기 때문에 곤충이 살아남을 수 있게 된다."는 것이다. 그러므로 ③이 정답이 된다.

3 ①   ▶ **빈칸완성**
앞 문장의 "야생의 새들이 서로를 지켜본다."는 것은 문맥상 "새들은 어떤 곤충이 먹을 수 있는 것인지의 여부를 다른 새의 행동을 통해 판단한다."는 것을 의미한다. 그러므로 새들은 다른 새들이 '불쾌하거나 역한' 반응을 보이는 경우에 주의를 기울일 것이라 할 수 있다. yuck은 "웩"이라는 '구토, 혐오, 불쾌' 등을 나타내는 감탄사이고, yummy는 '맛있는(형용사)'이나 '맛있는 것(명사)'의 뜻이다.

03 2021 광운대

수십 년 동안의 연구는 신경전달물질인 도파민이 우리가 시간을 인식하는 방식에 중요한 역할을 하고 있음을 시사한다. 일부 연구들에서는 도파민이 늘어나면 동물의 생체시계가 빨라져서 생체시계가 시간의 흐름을 과대평가하게 된다는 것을 발견했고, 다른 연구들에서는 도파민이 사건을 압축시켜 그 사건들이 더 짧은 시간에 일어난 것처럼 보이게 한다는 것을 발견했으며, 또 다른 연구들에서는 상황에 따라 두 가지 효과를 모두 발견했다. 시간 인식과 도파민의 연관성은 흥미로운데, 그 이유의 일부는 신경전달물질이 보상과 강화의 학습과정에 일정 역할을 하는 것으로 더 잘 알려져 있기 때문이다. 예를 들어, ─ 예측 오류라고 알려진 것에서 ─ 우리가 예상치 못한 보상을 받았을 경우, 우리는 그 화학물질(도파민)의 급증을 경험하게 되고, 이러한 상황은 미래에도 그러한 행동을 계속 추구하도록 우리에게 가르친다. 도파민이 시간 인식과 학습 과정 모두에 매우 중요한 것은 우연의 일치 이상일 것이다. 필로폰 같은 약물과 파킨슨병 같은 신경질환은 두 과정을 모두 바꾸며 또한 도파민에도 변화를 가져온다. 그리고 행동과 그 결과를 연관 짓는 것인 학습 그 자체는 한 사건을 시간이 지난 후의 다른 사건과 연결시키는 것을 필요로 한다. "실제로, 강화 학습 알고리즘의 핵심에는 시간에 대한 정보가 있습니다."라고 한 신경과학자는 말했다.

neurotransmitter n. 신경전달물질
dopamine n. 도파민(부신에서 만들어지는 뇌에 필요한 호르몬)
critical a. 결정적인, 중대한
perceive v. 감지하다, 인식하다
internal clock 내부시계, 생체시계
passage n. 통행, 통과; 경과
compress v. 압축하다
fleeting a. 질주하는; 빨리 지나가는
uncover v. (비밀 등을) 알아내다
context n. 문맥; (사건 등에 대한) 경위, 배경; 상황
association n. 연합, 관련; 결합
perception n. 지각작용; 인식
intriguing a. 음모를 꾸미는; 흥미를 자아내는
reward n. 보상, 포상
reinforcement n. 강화, 보강
process n. 진행, 경과, 과정
prediction n. 예측, 예언
chemical n. 화학제품, 화학물질
pursue v. 추적하다; 추구하다
coincidence n. (우연의) 일치; 동시발생

1 ⑤   ▶ **빈칸완성**
생체시계가 빨라지면 물리적인 시간이 흐른 것보다 더 많은 시간이 흘러갔다고 인식할 것인데 이것은 시간의 흐름을 '과대평가'하는 것이다. ① 예측하도록 ② 종결하도록 ③ 작게 하도록 ④ 기억하도록

2 ④   ▶ **빈칸완성**
마지막 문장의 인용문은 바로 앞 문장에 대한 부연설명에 해당한다. 앞에서 "행동과 그 결과를 연관 짓는 것인 학습은 한 사건을 시간이 지난 후의 다른 사건과 연결시키는 것을 필요로 한다."고 했는데, 이것은 '시간과 관련된' 것이므로, 빈칸에는 ④가 적절하다. ① 예측 오류 ② 파킨슨병 ③ 학습 과정 ⑤ 신경과학의 연구

3 ④ ▶ 내용일치
"우리가 예상치 못한 보상을 받았을 경우, 우리는 그 화학물질(도파민)의 급증을 경험하게 되고, 이러한 상황은 미래에도 그러한 행동을 계속 추구하도록 우리에게 가르친다."는 내용과 ④의 진술이 일치한다.

fundamental a. 근본적인, 중요한
methamphetamine n. 메탐페타민, 필로폰
neurological a. 신경학상의
disorder n. 무질서; 장애, 질환
alter v. 바꾸다, 변경하다
involve v. 수반하다
outcome n. 결과, 과정
algorithm n. 알고리즘, 연산(방식)
neuroscientist n. 신경과학자

04 2019 한국항공대

『이기적 유전자(The Selfish Gene)』가 출간되고 나서 12년 사이에 그 핵심적 메시지는 오늘날 교과서적 정설이 되었다. 이는 참으로 역설적이지만, 드러나지 않게 역설적이다. 이 책은 출간 당시 혁명적이라고 매도당한 후 꾸준히 전향자들을 얻다가 결국 정설이 됨으로써 우리가 왜 그렇게 호들갑을 떨었는가 하고 의아해 하게 되는 그런 부류의 책은 아니다. 아니 정반대이다. 애초부터 논평들은 흡족할 만큼 우호적이었으며, 논란을 불러일으킬 책처럼 여겨지지 않았다. 이 책의 호전적인 평판이 부각되다가 마침내 급진적 극단주의의 저술로 널리 인식되기까지는 꽤 많은 세월이 흘러야 했다. 그러나 이 책의 극단주의의 평판이 점점 높아져온 바로 그 여러 해 동안에, 책의 실질적인 내용은 점점 덜 극단적인 것으로, 그리고 점점 더 일반적으로 통용되는 것으로 여겨졌다. 이기적 유전자 이론은 다윈의 이론이지만, 다윈의 이론을, 다윈이 그 방법을 선택하지는 않았지만, 내가 생각하고 싶은 바로는, 그 방법의 적합성을 그도 즉시 인정하고 기뻐했을 그런 방법으로 표현한 것이다. 이 이론은 사실상 정통 신(新)다윈주의(Neo-Darwinism)의 논리적 결과물이지만 그것이 새로운 모습으로 표현된 것이다. 이 이론은 개별적 생물에 초점을 맞추기보다, 자연을 유전자적 시각에서 바라본다. 나는 이것을 『확장된 표현형(The Extended Phenotype)』의 서두에서 네커의 정육면체(Necker cube)라는 은유를 이용해 설명했다. 이것은 종이 위에 그려진 2차원 패턴이지만 투명한 3차원 정육면체로 인식된다. 그것을 2~3초간 응시하면 다른 쪽 방향에서 보는 모습으로 바뀐다. 계속 응시하면 다시 뒤집히면서 원래의 정육면체로 돌아간다. 2개의 정육면체 모두가 망막에 맺힌 2차원 데이터와 똑같이 양립 가능하므로, 뇌는 기꺼이 그 둘을 번갈아 인식하게 된다. 둘 중 어느 것도 더 옳지 않다(둘 다 똑같이 옳다). 내가 주장한 바는 자연선택을 바라보는 데 유전자적 관점과 개체적 관점이라는 두 가지 방식이 있다는 것이었다. 제대로 이해한다면, 그 둘은 동일한 진리에 대한 두 가지 관점으로 동등한 것이다. 당신은 한 관점에서 다른 관점으로 뒤집을 수 있지만, 그래도 여전히 같은 신다윈주의일 것이다.

orthodoxy n. 정설, 통설
paradoxical a. 역설적인
revile v. 욕하다; 매도하다
convert n. 개종자, 전향자
fuss n. 호들갑, 야단법석
gratifyingly ad. 기쁘게도
contentiousness n. 호전적임, 논쟁적임
extremism n. 극단론, 과격주의
escalate v. 악화시키다
outgrowth n. 결과물
phenotype n. 표현형
flip v. 홱 뒤집다
compatible a. 호환되는, 양립 가능한
retina n. 망막
alternate v. 번갈아 나오게 하다
equivalent a. 동등한, 상응하는

1 ① ▶ 내용파악
필자는 자신의 이기적 유전자 이론이 바라보는 시각이 다를 뿐 여전히 신다윈주의이고, 그와 다른 이론은 아니라고 말하고 있다.

2 ④ ▶ 내용추론
네커의 정육면체는 동일한 사실(혹은 대상)을 바라보는 관점이 여러 개일 수 있다는 것을 시사하는 사례로서 필자가 제시한 것이다.

05 2017 중앙대

1890년대 후반에, 두 명의 독일 심리학자 게오르크 뮐러(Georg Müller)와 알폰소 필체커(Alfons Pilzecker)는 뇌 속에서 기억이 고정되기 위해서는, 즉 '강화되기' 위해서는 한 시간 정도가 걸린다는 사실을 발견했다. 후속연구들을 통해 단기기억과 장기기억이 존재한다는 점이 확인되었고, 단기기억이 장기기억으로 전환되는 강화단계가 중요하다는 증거가 추가적으로 확인되었다. 1960년대에, 펜실베이니아 대학의 신경학자 루이 플렉스너(Louis Flexner)는 매우 흥미로운 발견을 했다. 생쥐에게 세포의 단백질 생성을 방해하는 항생제를 주입하였더니, 그 동물들이 장기기억은 형성하지 못하지만 단기기억은 여전히 저장할 수 있다는 것을 알게 되었다. 그것이 함축하고 있는 의미는 분명했다. 장기기억은 단기기억보다 더 강력한 형태의 기억에 불과한 것이 아니라는 것이었다. <그 두 유형의 기억에는 서로 다른 생물학적 과정이 수반된다.> 장기기억을 저장하려면 새로운 단백질의 합성이 필요하다. 단기기억의 저장은 그렇지 않다. 좀 더 최근의 연구는 단기기억과 장기기억의 물리적 작용이라는 문제에 관심을 돌렸다. 그 결과, 어떤 경험을 더 많이 반복할수록 그 경험에 대한 기억은 더 오래 지속된다는 사실이 입증되었다. 반복이 강화를 촉진하는 것이다. 특히, 반복이 신경신호에 미치는 생리적 영향을 조사한 연구자들은 놀라운 사실을 발견하였다. 신경세포 접합부의 신경전달물질 농도가 변화하여 신경세포 간의 기존 연결 강도가 변화했을 뿐 아니라, 신경세포들이 완전히 새로운 신경세포 접합부 말단들을 생성시키는 것이었다. 달리 말해, 장기기억의 생성은 생화학적 변화뿐만 아니라 해부학적 변화까지 수반하는 것이다. 이는 기억강화에 왜 새로운 단백질이 필요한지를 설명해준다. 단백질은 세포의 구조적 변화를 발생시키는 데 필수적인 역할을 수행한다.

consolidate v. 강화하다, 통합하다
subsequent a. 그다음의, 후속의
neurologist n. 신경학자
intriguing a. 흥미[호기심]를 자아내는, 아주 흥미로운
inject v. 주사하다, 주입하다
antibiotic n. 항생제
implication n. 함축, 암시; 함축적 의미
synthesis n. 종합, 통합; 합성
demonstrate v. 입증하다, 증명하다
physiological a. 생리학(상)의, 생리적인
neurotransmitter n. 신경전달물질
concentration n. 집중; 농도
synapse n. 신경세포 접합부, 시냅스
neuron n. 뉴런, 신경세포
terminal n. 말단, 맨 끝
anatomical a. 해부학상의
entail v. 수반하다

1 ①   ▶ 문장삽입
  명시적 형태로 드러나 있지는 않지만 주어진 문장과 바로 앞 문장의 내용은 일종의 'not A but B'의 상관적 구조를 지니고 있다. 즉, 루이 플렉스너의 연구 결과는 "장기기억이 단기기억보다 더 강하다는 단순한 의미가 아니라 오히려 두 기억이 전혀 다른 생물학적 원리에 입각해 있다."는 것을 보여주었다는 게 되는 것이다. 따라서 주어진 문장이 Ⓐ에 들어가면 '서로 다른 생물학적 과정'이라는 것이 새로운 단백질 합성 과정인 것으로 뒤이어 설명된다.

2 ④   ▶ 내용추론
  경험의 반복은 기억에 관여하는 뇌의 생화학적 변화와 해부학적 변화를 수반하여 장기기억의 생성을 촉진한다고 하였으므로 ④는 타당한 진술이다.

06 2018 숭실대

우리가 빨간 코 순록 루돌프(루돌프 사슴코)가 특별하다는 것을 이미 알고 있지 않았다면, 루돌프의 밝게 빛나는 코는 홍해에서 발견되는 화려한 색채를 가진 산호의 유전 물질이 매우 우연히 전달되어 생긴 것일 수도 있다. 아마도 그 유전 물질은 루돌프의 어머니가 루돌프를 임신한 동안 바다에 불시착한 사고로 산호에 긁혔을 때 어머니의 혈류로 들어갔으며, 그런 다음 그 DNA가 태내의 새끼에게로 전달되었을 것이다. 어쨌거나, 그것은 존스홉킨스대학의 한 영리한 과학자가 추측했던 내용으로, 이것이 그 유명한 안개 자욱한 크리스마스이브에 산타와 그의 썰매를 안내해줬던 루돌프의 코를 설명해줄지도 모른다. "이동성 유전인자는 바이러스에서 유래한 것으로, 상당히 많은 양의 DNA를 잘라서 숙주의 게놈에 삽입할 수 있는 놀라운 능력을 갖추고 있습니다."라고 존스홉킨스대학의 생물학 교수인 스티브 파버(Steve Farber)는 말했다.
대부분의 아이들과 아마도 많은 부모들은 크리스마스의 그 사랑스런 동물을 그 모습 그대로 받아들일지도 모르지만, 과학자들은 우리가 우리 주변 세계를, 비록 소중히 여겨온 크리스마스 동화책에 나오는 세계일지라도, 이해하길 원한다. 의혹을 미루기보다, 과학자들은 곧잘 우선 먼저 동료들이 검토한 연구를 살펴보고 그들이 목격한 것에 대한 어떤 확실한 설명이 있는지 알아보거나, 아니면 그들 스스로 직접 실험을 한다고 파버는 말했다. 루돌프 문제는 산호 DNA를 확인하기 위한 유전자 검사를 해보는 것 정도로 쉬울 수도 있다. 그리고 루돌프의 자손 또한 산호 DNA를 포함하고 있는 동일한 유전자 재배열을 지니고 있을 것이다.
"당신이 현재 체계에서 일어날 것 같지 않은 것들은 기꺼이 무시한다면, 저는 이런 일이 일어날 수

reindeer n. 순록(馴鹿)
result from ~이 원인이다, 생기다
one-in-a-million a. 백만에 하나 있을까 말까 한, 아주 진기한, 특별한
transfer n. (유전자의) 전달
genetic material 유전 형질(形質)
coral n. 산호
bloodstream n. 혈류, 혈류량
scrape v. 긁다, 찰과상을 내다
calf n. (사슴·코끼리·고래 따위의) 새끼
sleigh n. 썰매
cherished a. 소중하게 간직한
suspend v. 중지하다
witness v. 목격하다; 입증하다
craft v. 정교하게 만들다

있는 여러 가지 방법을 제안한 것입니다. 저는 그냥 재미로 하고 있을 뿐입니다."라고 연구원인 바(Bah)는 덧붙였다.

rearrangement n. 재정리, 재배열
forgo v. 삼가다, 그만두다

1 ③ ▶ 빈칸완성
루돌프의 코가 빛나는 이유가 산호 DNA에 의한 것일 수도 있다고 스티브 파버는 추측했는데, 산호 DNA가 있는지 확인하기 위해서는 유전자 검사를 해야 할 것이므로 빈칸에는 ③ genetic이 적절하다. ① 실험의 ② 종합적인 ④ 환경의

2 ① ▶ 글의 제목
"루돌프를 임신한 어머니가 산호에 긁혀서, 산호 DNA가 혈류로 들어가 태내의 루돌프에게 전달되어 루돌프가 밝게 빛나는 코를 가지게 되었다."고 가정하고 있으므로, 이 글은 '루돌프의 코가 밝게 빛나는 이유'에 대한 설명이라고 볼 수 있다. 따라서 ①이 글의 제목으로 적절하다.

3 ④ ▶ 내용파악
루돌프의 밝은 색 코는 화려한 색채를 가진 산호의 유전 물질이 전달되어 생긴 것이라고 가정하고 있으므로, 루돌프는 발광 유전자를 가지고 있다고 볼 수 있다. 따라서 ④가 정답이다.

07 2013 중앙대

인간의 유전자 풀을 개선하겠다는 제안은, 그 근대적 형태로서 우생학(eugenics)이라는 이름을 갖게 되었는데, 이는 프랜시스 골턴(Francis Galton)이 1883년 '좋은'이라는 의미의 그리스어 *eu*와 '출생'이라는 의미의 *gen*을 합성하여 만든 신조어였다. 다윈(Darwin)의 저술들을 탐독한 뒤, 골턴은 계량적인 특성들의 유전, 특히 지능의 유전에 관심을 갖게 되었다. 1865년 이후로 계속해서, 그는 자연선택에 의한 인간특성의 진화를 선택적 번식에 의한 진화로 대체할 수 있다는 사상을 주창하였다. 자기 자신이 화려한 가문 출신이었던 골턴은 가문들 속에 지적이고 성격적인 특성들이 흐르는 방식에 깊은 인상을 받았다. 그런 특성들은 유전된다고 확신하고서, 동물 교배에 대한 자신의 지식을 이용하여 그는 '여러 세대에 걸친 현명한 결혼'은 '매우 재능이 뛰어난 인종들을 출현시킬' 수 있고 그리하여 우수하지 않은 자들의 과도한 교배로 인해 초래되는 것으로, 사회 전체를 위협하고 있다고 그가 믿고 있던 '평범함으로 회귀'를 차단할 수 있다고 결론지었다.
골턴의 사상은 많은 저명한 사상가들에 의해 받아들여지고 발전되었다. <연구 결과 사회경제적 조건이 발달함에 따라 개인 간의 유전적 차이가 상존함에도 불구하고 평균적인 지능 점수 역시 향상된다는 점이 밝혀졌다.> 그러나 사회진화론자들과 마찬가지로, 초기 우생학자들은 그들이 바람직하지 못하다고 여기는 특성들에 대해 자신들의 개인적이고 문화적인 편견들을 반영하였고, 그리하여 처음부터 상당히 인종 차별주의적이고 계급에 기초한 편견들이 한 역할을 하였다. 20세기 초 우생학 운동의 영향력 있는 주도자였던 데번포트(Davenport)는 뉴잉글랜드 주민들을 기준으로 삼아 미국의 모든 사회집단에 대해 그 출신 국가와 상관없이 비교를 행함으로써 이러한 인종 차별주의적인 접근의 전형을 보였다. 데번포트와 그가 설립한 우생학 기록 사무소(1910년부터 1944년 사이에 미국의 가문들에 관한 방대한 정보 데이터베이스를 수집했음)의 다른 사람들에 따르면 특정한 집단들은 인식 가능한 유전적 요소를 지닌 사회적 특성들로 구별할 수 있다고 한다. 이를테면 이탈리아계의 폭력성, 유대계의 상인정신, 아일랜드계의 극빈 상태 등은 전형적이라는 것이다.

suggestion n. 제안, 제의, 의견
eugenics n. 우생학
breeding n. (번식을 위한 동물) 사육, 육종, 품종개량; 번식; 가정교육
draw on ~에 의지하다, ~을 이용하다
judicious a. 현명한, 신중한; 명민한
thwart v. 방해하다, 좌절시키다
reversion n. 복귀, 역전, 되돌아가기; 격세[복귀] 유전
mediocrity n. 보통, 평범함
prominent a. 저명한; 현저한, 두드러진
exemplify v. 전형적인 예가 되다, 예증[예시]하다
irrespective of ~와 상관없이
influential a. 영향력 있는, 영향을 미치는
identifiable a. 인식 가능한, 알아볼 수 있는
mercantilism n. 상업주의
pauperism n. (구호가 필요한) 빈곤 상태

1 ③ ▶ 글의 흐름상 어울리지 않는 문장 고르기
ⓒ의 내용은 사회경제적 조건의 개선에 의해 지능 점수가 사회 전반적으로 향상될 수 있음을 기술한 문장으로 우생학의 기본 가정과 상충된다.

2 ④ ▶ 내용일치
이 글에 따르면 인종차별적 편견은 우생학의 시작부터 자리 잡고 있었다.

08 2021 한국외대

오늘날 과학자들은 실제로 도덕이 인류의 출현보다 수백만 년 앞선 먼 진화적 기원을 갖고 있다고 지적한다. 늑대, 돌고래, 원숭이 같은 모든 사회적 포유류들은 진화에 의해 집단협력을 증진하는 데 적합하게 된 윤리규범을 갖고 있다. 예를 들어, 늑대 새끼들이 서로 놀 때는 '공정한 게임'의 규칙이 있다. 새끼 한 마리가 등을 대고 굴러서 항복한 상대를 너무 세게 물거나 계속 물면, 다른 새끼들은 그와 놀지 않을 것이다. 침팬지 집단의 경우, 우세한 침팬지들은 약한 침팬지들의 재산권을 존중해 줄 것으로 기대된다. 만약 어린 암컷 침팬지가 바나나를 발견하면, 심지어 우두머리 수컷조차도 대개 자기가 먹고자 바나나를 훔치려 하지는 않는다. 만약 이런 규칙을 어기면, 그는 지위를 잃을 가능성이 있다. 유인원은 무리 안의 약한 유인원을 이용해먹지 않을뿐더러 때때로 그들을 적극적으로 돕는다. 밀워키 카운티 동물원에 살던 키도고(Kidogo)라는 수컷 피그미침팬지는 심각한 심장 질환을 앓고 있었고, 이 때문에 몸도 약하고 정신도 혼미했다. 키도고가 처음 이 동물원으로 이송되었을 때, 그는 방향감각이 없었고(자꾸 엉뚱한 쪽으로 걸어갔고) 인간 관리사들의 지시도 이해하지 못했다. 다른 침팬지들이 키도고의 어려움을 이해하자 개입했다. 그들은 종종 키도고의 손을 잡고 어디든지 그가 가야할 곳으로 그를 이끌었다. 만약 길을 잃으면 키도고는 큰 소리로 조난신호를 보냈고 그러면 어떤 유인원이 도와주기 위해 달려왔다.

1 ③ ▶ 글의 제목
이 글에서는 "인간만이 윤리규범을 갖춘 것이 아니라 동물에게도 윤리규범이 있고, 이것을 통해 상호협력을 증진해서 생존적응을 높여가고 있다."고 설명하고 있다. 따라서 ③이 이 글의 제목으로 적절하다.

2 ② ▶ 빈칸완성
앞 문장에서 키도고가 똑바로 걷지 못하고 관리사의 지시를 이해하지 못한다고 했는데, 이것은 키도고가 처한 '신체적·정신적 어려움(predicament)'을 의미하므로 ②가 빈칸 Ⓐ에 가장 적절하다. ① 특권 ③ 인격 ④ 선호

3 ① ▶ 내용일치
이 글에서는 동물에게도 윤리규범이 있어서 집단협력을 가능하게 한다고 설명하고 있는 것이지 윤리규범과 집단협력을 비교하고 있는 것이 아니므로 ①이 본문의 내용과 일치하지 않는다.

pre-dating a. 연대가 앞선
adapt v. 맞추다, 적응하다
dominant a. 우세한, 지배적인
alpha male 우두머리 수컷
for oneself 자기를 위하여
confused a. 혼란스러운, 분명치 않은, 당혹스러운
orient v. 일정한 방향으로 향하게 하다; (새로운 상황에) 적응시키다
orient oneself 자기 위치를 똑바로 알다
intervene v. 개입하다, 가로막다
predicament n. 곤경, 궁지
distress signal 조난신호
primate n. 영장류
similarity n. 유사성
prerogative n. 특권, 특혜

09 2017 홍익대

불과 10년 전에는, 생물학적 인종 개념이 마침내 최후를 맞이한 것처럼 보였다. 인간의 전체 유전자 코드를 지도로 만들어낸 인간 게놈 프로젝트가 우리의 유전자로 인종이 식별될 수 없다는 것을 증명했던 것이다. 게놈 서열 초안을 발표했던 2000년 6월 26일, 빌 클린턴(Bill Clinton) 대통령은 "인간은 인종과 관계없이 99.9% 똑같습니다."라는 유명한 선언을 했다. 널리 오해하고 있는 바와는 달리, 우리는 유전적으로 식별할 수 있는 인종집단으로 자연스럽게 구분되지 않는다. 생물학적으로는, 하나의 인류만이 존재할 뿐이다. 인간에게 적용되는 인종은 정치적인 구분이다. 인종은 만들어낸 생물학적인 구분에 근거해 사람들을 사회적 위계질서로 분류하는 하나의 통치 방식이다.
그러나 생물학적인 범주로서의 인종이 사라졌다는 보고서들은 시기상조였다. 인간 게놈 서열 분석으로 등장한 과학(유전체 과학)은 시대에 뒤떨어진 방식(인종)의 관에 마지막 못을 박는 대신, 인종에 근거한 유전적 변이에 대한 관심을 되살리는 것으로 구체화되었다. 일부 과학자들은 새로운 게놈 이론들과 컴퓨터 기술들을 통해 발견된 유전학적 유사점들이 낡아빠진 인종 분류와 일치해서, 인간의 인종별 차이점들은 실재하며 의미심장하다는 것을 증명한다고 주장하고 있다. 또 다른 과학자들은 약물반응에 있어서의 차이들뿐 아니라 건강과 질병에 있어서의 엄청난 차이들도 설명해줄 수 있는 인종 간의 유전학적 차이들을 찾고 있다. 그에 따라 지금까지 인종에 근거한 생명공학기술들이 폭발적으로 많이 생겨났다. 2005년, 미국 식품의약국(FDA)은 흑인 환자들의 심부전을 치료하는 BiDil이라는 최초의 특정 인종을 위한 약품을 승인했다.

meet one's end 최후를 맞이하다, 숨을 거두다
genome n. 게놈(세포나 생명체의 유전자 총체)
map v. ~의 배치를 찾아내다
identify v. (본인·동일물임을) 확인하다; 식별하다
unveil v. 밝히다, 공개하다, 발표하다
draft a. 초안의
sequence n. 서열 v. ~을 일정한 순서로 배열하다
misconception n. 오해
hierarchy n. 위계질서
demarcation n. 구분
demise n. 사망; 소멸
premature a. 너무 이른, 시기상조의
coffin n. 관, 널
obsolete a. 쓸모없어진, 시대에 뒤진, 구식의
resurgence n. 재기, 부활

1 ③	▶ 글의 주제
	이 글은 인종을 유전학적으로 구분하여 범주화할 수 있느냐에 대한 상반된 주장을 소개하고 있으므로, 글의 주제로는 ③의 '인종의 유전학적 범주화를 둘러싼 논쟁'이 적절하다.

2 ③	▶ 내용추론
	첫 단락에서 '인종은 유전학적 근거가 없는 것으로서 국가 권력이 국민을 통치하는 조작된 방식'이라고 언급한 후에, 이어진 둘째 단락에서 '그런데 그 유전학적 근거가 재조명되고 있다'고 말했을 뿐이다. 따라서 ③의 "국가 권력이 국민을 인종으로 분류하는 그 조작된 방식에 더 이상 의존하지 않았다."는 추론은 할 수 없다.

3 ①	▶ 빈칸완성
	빈칸 앞에서 '최초의 특정 인종을 위한 약품'이라고 했으므로, 빈칸에는 '특정 인종'인 '흑인'과 '약품'과 관련 있는 '치료'를 언급하고 있는 ①이 적절하다.

genetic variation 유전적 변이
novel a. 새로운
correspond to ~에 일치하다
antiquated a. 한물 간, 구식의
staggering a. 깜짝 놀라게 하는, 엄청난
inequality n. 불평등, 불균형, 불균등
common struggle 단결 투쟁
state power 공권력
resuscitate v. 소생시키다, 부활시키다
criminal suspect 피의자

10 2018 성균관대

연구에 따르면, 최근 수십 년간 야생동물의 '생물학적 소멸'은 지구 역사에서 6차 대량 멸종이 진행 중이며 앞서 걱정했던 것보다 더 심각하다는 것을 의미한다. 과학자들이 일반 종과 희귀 종 모두를 분석한 결과, 수십 억 개의 지역 또는 지방 개체군들이 사라졌다는 사실이 확인되었다. 과학자들은 인구 과잉과 과소비를 그 위기의 원인으로 보며, 대처할 수 있는 기회의 시간이 얼마 남지 않은 가운데 그 위기가 인간 문명의 생존을 위협한다고 경고한다.

예전의 연구는 종들이 수백만 년 전보다 훨씬 더 빠른 속도로 멸종하고 있지만 그래도 멸종의 예는 상대적으로 드물다는 것을 보여주어서, 생물의 다양성이 점진적으로 감소한다는 인상을 주었다. 그 대신, 새로운 연구는 더 넓은 견해를 취하여, 서식범위가 줄어들면서 전 세계적으로 개체 수가 감소하고 있지만 다른 어딘가에 존재하는 그런 많은 일반 종들을 평가한다.

1 ②	▶ 부분이해
	6차 대량 멸종이 현재 진행 중에 있으며 걱정했던 것보다 심각하다고 했고, 예전의 연구에서는 종들이 수백만 년 전보다 훨씬 더 빠른 속도로 멸종하고 있다는 것을 보여주었다고 했으므로, 6차 대량 멸종의 속도가 느려지고 있다고 한 ②가 옳지 않은 진술이다.

2 ①	▶ 빈칸완성
	종이 빠른 속도로 멸종하고 있다고 한 다음, 역접의 접속사 but이 나오면서 멸종되는 종은 상대적으로 드물다고 했으므로, 그것이 주는 인상은 '종이 서서히 감소한다'는 인상일 것이다. 따라서 빈칸에는 ①이 적절하다.

biological a. 생물학의, 생물학적인
annihilation n. 전멸, 절멸, 소멸
wildlife n. 야생동물, 야생생물
mass extinction 대멸종(大滅種)
under way 이미 시작된[진행 중인]
severe a. 극심한, 심각한; 엄격한
threaten v. 협박하다, 위협하다
survival n. 살아남음, 생존, 잔존, 존속
window n. (잠깐 동안의) 기회, (기회의) 창
extinct a. 멸종한, 사멸한; 폐지된
take a broad view 거시적으로 보다
assess v. 평가하다, 사정하다
shrink v. (규모·양이) 줄어들다
gradual a. 점진적인, 서서히 일어나는
biodiversity n. 생물의 다양성
disappearance n. 사라짐, 소실, 소멸; 실종
partial a. 부분적인, 일부분의, 국부적인; 편파적인
enduring a. 지속하는, 영속적인; 내구성이 있는
continuity n. 연속, 연속성, 연속 상태, 계속

11 2015 고려대

우리들 중 많은 사람들이 에너지는 흩어지려고 하는 확고한 성향이 있고 그렇게 함으로써 높은 질의 형태에서 낮은 질의 형태로 이행하는 성향이 있다고 하는 열역학 제2법칙을 어느 정도 잘 알고 있다. 생명, 즉 생물권도 이와 다르지 않다는 증거가 점점 늘어나고 있다. 생명의 복잡성은 열역학 제2법칙을 반박하는 것이어서, 개인의 심리적 경향에 따라 어떤 신적 존재나 미지의 자연적 과정이 작용한다는 것을 시사한다는 말이 종종 있었다. 그러나 생명의 진화와 생태계의 역학은 주로 에너지를 흩어버리는 쪽으로 작용하면서 열역학 제2법칙의 명령을 따르고 있다. 그들은 밝게 타오르고 나서 사라져버리는 식으로 열역학 제2법칙을 따르는 것이 아니라, 화학에너지를 저장하고 지속적

thermodynamics n. 열역학
unwavering a. 변함없는, 확고한
propensity n. 경향, 성향
disperse v. 흩어지다, 해산하다
transition n. 변천, 이행
biosphere n. 생물권
contravene v. ~와 모순되다; 부정하다, 반박하다

448 김영편입 영어 독해 기출 2단계

으로 태양의 변화도를 감소시키는 안정적인 신진대사의 순환을 통해 그렇게 한다. 광합성을 하는 식물, 박테리아, 조류들은 태양으로부터 에너지를 얻어 모든 먹이 그물에서 핵심을 형성한다. 다른 종류의 생물들은 이들 '생산자'를 소비하여, 이용 가능한 에너지를 최대한 활용한다. 그렇다면, 인간을 포함한 사실상의 모든 생물들은 변형된 태양광선이고, 에너지 흐름 속의 일시적인 경유지인 셈이다. 열역학적 관점에서 보자면, 생태적 천이(遷移), 즉 오랜 시간에 걸쳐 어떤 생태 공동체의 종(種)의 구조가 변화하는 현상은 에너지 획득과 분해를 극대화하려는 하나의 과정인 셈이다. 마찬가지로, 생물량과 생물의 다양성이 증가하는 것뿐 아니라, ― 해부학적 형태와 신진대사 경로와 영양적 상호작용이 점점 더 복잡해지는 것에서도 보여주고 있듯이 ― 생명체가 지난 35억 년에 걸쳐 더 복잡해져 온 경향 또한 단지 대부분의 진화론자들이 여전히 주장하고 있는 자연선택 때문인 것만은 아니고 좀 더 많이 태양의 흐름을 붙들어놓으려는 자연의 노력 때문이기도 한 것이다. 생명체의 특징인 이러한 느린 연소 덕분에 생태계는 외부적, 내부적 교란에 반응하여 변화하면서 오랜 시간에 걸쳐 지속될 수 있는 것이다.

deity n. 신(神), 신령
dynamics n. 역학; 동역학; 역학 관계
mandate n. 권한; 지시, 명령, 지령
dissipate v. 흩뜨리다, 흩어버리다; 소멸되다
metabolic a. 신진대사의
gradient n. 경사도; (증감률 등의) 변화도
solar gradient 태양의 변화도(지구로 들어오는 태양 방사선에 의한 지구의 온도·습도 등의 변화도)
photosynthetic a. 광합성의
algae n. 조류(藻類: 물속에 사는 하등 식물의 한 무리)
core n. 핵심; 정수; 중심
transmogrify v. 변신시키다, 탈바꿈시키다
ecological succession 생태적 천이(군집 구조가 시간이 지남에 따라 점진적으로 안정된 구조를 향해 변천해 나가는 과정, 시간의 흐름에 따라 군집의 조성이 변화하는 과정)
degradation n. 비하, 수모; 하락, 강등; 분해
anatomical a. 해부학상의
trophic a. 영양(營養)의
biomass n. (특정 지역 내의) 생물량
grab v. 붙잡다, 움켜잡다
persist v. 고집하다; 지속하다, 존속하다
perturbation n. 동요; 교란, 혼란

1 ③ ▶ 동의어
contravene은 '부정하다, 반박하다'라는 뜻이므로, disprove(반증하다, 논박하다)가 가장 의미가 가까운 단어다. ① 분명[명확]하게 하다 ② 확증하다 ④ 단언하다

2 ② ▶ 내용추론
"생명의 진화와 생태계의 역학은 주로 에너지를 흩어버리는 쪽으로 작용하여 열역학 제2법칙의 명령을 따른다", "화학에너지를 저장하고", "태양으로부터 에너지를 획득하고", "생명체가 지난 35억 년에 걸쳐 더 복잡해져 온 경향은 좀 더 많이 태양의 흐름을 붙들어 놓으려는 자연의 노력 때문이다" 등의 진술을 종합하면, 거의 모든 생물들이 에너지의 흐름 속에서 에너지를 획득하고, 저장하고, 흩어버리면서 열역학 제2법칙을 따른다고 볼 수 있다. 따라서 ②가 정답이다.

3 ③ ▶ 빈칸완성
'모든 먹이 그물의 핵심'이라는 말은 그것을 통해 모든 생명체들의 먹이 순환이 시작된다는 것을 의미한다. 모든 생물들이 태양 에너지를 광합성하는 생물들이 핵심이 되는 먹이 그물에 의존하고 있다는 것이므로, 모든 생물들은 에너지 흐름 속에서 '변형된 태양광선' 다시 말해 '태양광선이 변형된 형태로 일시적으로 경유하는 장소'라고 말할 수 있을 것이다. waypoint는 '어떤 과정이나 여정 중간에 머무는 지점'을 의미한다. ① 영원한 소우주 ② 고립된 누에고치(보호막) ④ 영원한 저장고

4 ④ ▶ 글의 목적
이 글은 생명의 복잡성이 열역학 제2법칙과 모순되는 것이 아니라 오히려 거기에 부합하는 측면으로 볼 수 있음을 설명하는 글이다.

---

12   2022 중앙대

외부에서 보면 인간은 기분 좋게 대칭을 이루고 있다. 팔, 다리와 눈의 오른쪽과 왼쪽이 균형이 맞는다는 뜻이다. 그러나 몸 내부로 들어가면 이야기가 달라진다. 심장은 왼쪽에, 간은 오른쪽에 있다. 폐와 신장 역시 비대칭이다. 이제 연구자들은 발달 중인 장기들이 제자리를 찾는 것을 돕는 유전자를 분명하게 규명해냈다.

과학자들은 발달 중인 둥근 배아의 초창기 대칭을 깨뜨려 장기들이 어느 한쪽을 택하도록 돕는 다른 유전자들을 밝혀냈다. 그러나 연구자들이 이 유전자를 추적한 방식은 독특했다는 것이 발달생물학자 대니얼 그라임스(Daniel Grimes)의 말이다. 그의 말에 따르면 연구는 장기 형성이 왜 일부 사람들에게서 엉뚱한 방향으로 가는지를 더 잘 이해할 수 있게 해줄 수 있다.

발달생물학자들은 심장과 또 다른 장기들이 중심을 벗어난 곳에 자리를 잡게 되는 현상이 초창기 배아에 일시적으로 형성되는 좌우형성체(left-right organizer)라는 일군의 세포 때문이라는 것을 오랫동안 알고 있었다. 1998년, 생쥐 연구를 기반으로 일본의 연구자들은 형성체 세포의 하위 집단 위에 위치한 털 같은 부속기관인 회전 섬모(twirling cilia)가 배아 체액을 오른쪽이 아니라 왼쪽으로 보냄으로써 장기들이 제자리에 형성되도록 돕는다는 가설을 제시했다. 이 배아 체액은 그 왼

pin down 분명히 정의하다
pleasingly ad. 기분 좋게
asymmetric a. 비대칭의
embryo n. 배아
track v. 추적하다
unique a. 독특한, 고유한
go awry 실패하다, 예측에서 벗어나다
off-center a. 중심에서 벗어난
organizer n. 형성체
twirl v. 회전하다
cilia n. 섬모

쪽에서 특정 유전자를 활성화시켜, 그 다음 성장하는 것들을 바꾸어 놓는 것이라고 일본 학자들과 또 다른 학자들이 추정한 것이다. 훗날 연구자들은 어류와 개구리에게서도 똑같은 현상이 발생한다는 것을 발견했다.

그러나 놀랍게도, 발달 중인 병아리와 돼지 속에는 회전 섬모가 달린 이런 세포가 전혀 없다. 그런데도 이들의 심장은 여전히 한쪽에서만 형성된다. "문헌에 혼동을 주는 결과들이 많아 이 결과들을 조화시키기가 어렵습니다."라고 그라임스가 말한다. 그와 다른 학자들은 이 소위 운동 섬모(motile cilia)가 동물의 진화 초기에 진화를 거쳤지만 동물 가계도의 가지에서 손실되어 조류와 "짝수 발굽을 가진" 돼지 같은 포유류에게서는 없어졌지만 인간에게서는 남아 있는 것이라고 생각한다.

발달생물학자인 브루노 리버세이드(Bruno Reversade)와 크리스토퍼 고든(Christopher Gordon)은 이 불일치가 몸의 대칭을 깨는 원인이 되는 새 유전자를 추적하는 방법에 힌트를 줄 수 있지 않을까 궁금히 여겼다. 이들과 동료들은 발달 중인 생쥐와 어류와 개구리 속에서 활동하지만, 더 이상 배아 체액이 없어 그런 유전자가 필요하지 않은 돼지와 조류의 발달 단계에서는 활동하지 않는 유전자들을 찾아보았다.

연구자들은 이런 유전자 다섯 개를 찾아냈다고 이번 달 『네이처 유전학(Nature Genetics)』지에 발표한다. 리버세이드는 이 유전자들 중 셋은 체액이 유도하는 대칭의 소실에서 중요한 역할을 한다는 사실이 이미 알려져 있었기 때문에 자기 팀의 연구 방향이 올바른 쪽으로 가고 있다는 것을 알고 있었다.

appendage n. 부속물
speculate v. 추정하다
reconcile v. 조화를 이루다, 화해시키다
even-toed a. 발굽 개수가 짝수인
hint at ~을 암시하다
induce v. 유도하다, 유발하다

1 ① ▶ 글의 제목
글이 둘째, 셋째 문장을 보면 몸 장기의 비대칭이 언급되고 있고 그다음 문장에서 "이제 연구자들은 발달 중인 장기들이 제자리를 찾는 것을 돕는 유전자를 분명하게 규명해냈다."라고 한 다음 이와 관련된 실험 결과가 과정과 결과까지 나오고 있으므로 제목은 '몸의 대칭을 깨는 유전자 탐색'이라는 ①이 적절하다.

2 ② ▶ 내용추론
좌우형성체는 배아 단계에 일시적으로 형성된다고 했으므로 ①은 틀린 추론이고, 발굽이 짝수인 포유류의 경우 회전 섬모가 진화 과정에서 소실되었다고 했으므로 ③도 틀린 추론이며, 리버세이드와 고든이 몸의 대칭을 만드는 유전자를 다섯 개 규명했다고 했으므로 ④도 틀린 추론이다. 셋째 단락에서 "생쥐 연구를 기반으로 일본의 연구자들은 회전 섬모(twirling cilia)가 장기들이 제자리에 형성되도록 돕는다는 가설을 제시했다."고 했으므로 ②가 맞는 추론이다.

13 2019 아주대

Ⓐ 최초의 뇌는 약 5억 년 전에 지구에 출현했으며, 4억 3천만 년 동안 서서히 초기 영장류의 뇌로 진화했고, 그로부터 7천만 년을 더 진화하여 최초의 원인(原人)의 뇌가 되었다. 그 후, 어떤 일이 일어났고, 곧 인류의 뇌가 될 원인의 뇌는 200만년이 조금 넘는 시간 동안 전례 없는 급격한 성장을 겪으면서 부피가 두 배 이상 늘어났다. 그리하여 1.25파운드였던 호모 하빌리스의 뇌에서 거의 3파운드인 호모 사피엔스의 뇌로 변했다.

Ⓑ 만약 핫퍼지(초콜릿 아이스크림)를 주로 먹으면서 매우 짧은 시간 안에 몸의 부피를 두 배 늘린다고 하더라도, 다양한 신체 기관의 부피가 똑같이 늘어나지는 않을 것이다. <새로 생긴 군살은 아마도 배와 엉덩이에 주로 몰릴 것인 반면, 혀와 발가락은 상대적으로 호리호리한 상태 그대로 있을 것이다.> 마찬가지로, 인간의 뇌의 크기가 급격하게 커졌다고 해서 현대인들의 새로운 뇌가 구조적으로는 이전의 뇌와 완전히 같고 크기만 커지도록 모든 부분의 부피가 공평하게 두 배로 늘어난 것은 아니었다. 오히려 전두엽으로 알려져 있는 뇌의 특정 부분이 비대하게 커졌다.

Ⓒ 과학자들은 전두엽이 손상된 환자들이 종종 표준 지능 검사에서는 좋은 결과를 보이지만 계획을 세우는 것과 관련된 검사에서는 심각한 장애를 보여준다는 사실을 알게 되었다. 과학자들은 심지어 그 환자들이 그날 오후 늦게 무엇을 할지를 말하는 것도 사실상 불가능하다는 것도 알게 되었다. 이러한 발견으로 인해 우리는 전두엽을 우리들 각자가 현재로부터 떠나 미래를 미리 경험할 수 있게 해주는 타임머신으로 여긴다. 인간과 꽤 비슷한 전두엽을 갖고 있는 다른 동물은 없으며, 인간이 미래를 생각하는 유일한 동물인 것도 이 때문이다. 전두엽에 관한 이야기는 우리에게 사람들이 상상

leisurely a. 한가한, 느긋한, 여유 있는
evolve v. 서서히 발전하다, 진화하다
primate n. 영장류의 동물
protohuman n. 원인(原人)
unprecedented a. 전례 없는, 미증유의; 새로운
spurt n. 분출, 뿜어 나옴; 급등
mass n. 부피; 크기; 질량
transform v. 변형시키다; (성질·기능 등을) 바꾸다
various a. 가지가지의, 여러 가지의
structurally ad. 구조상, 구조적으로
identical a. 아주 동일한; 같은, 일치하는
disproportionate a. 불균형의
frontal lobe (대뇌의) 전두엽(前頭葉)
notice v. 알아채다, 인지하다
impairment n. 장애
involve v. 수반하다, 포함하다; 연루시키다

속의 내일을 어떻게 떠올리는지를 말해주지만, 그 이유는 말해주지 않는다.

1 ④ ▶ **글의 제목**
인간이 다른 동물과 다르게 미래에 대한 계획을 세우고 미래를 마음속으로 그려볼 수 있는 것은 전두엽이 발달된 덕분임을 이야기하고 있는 내용이므로, ④가 정답으로 적절하다.

2 ④ ▶ **내용추론**
전두엽이 손상된 사람들은 '미래를 계획하고 상상하는 능력을 잃게 된다'고 했다. 이것은 '시간이 흘러가는 것을 이해하지 못하는 것'과는 다른 개념이므로, ④가 추론할 수 없는 진술이다.

3 ② ▶ **문장삽입**
주어진 문장은 "새로 생긴 군살은 아마도 배와 엉덩이에 주로 몰릴 것인 반면, 혀와 발가락은 상대적으로 호리호리한 상태 그대로 있을 것이다."라는 의미이므로, "부피가 늘어나더라도 신체기관의 부피가 똑같이 늘어나지는 않는다." 내용에 대한 부연설명으로 볼 수 있다. 그러므로 주어진 문장은 ❷에 들어가야 한다.

4 ⑤ ▶ **뒷내용 추론**
글의 마지막이 "전두엽에 관한 이야기는 우리에게 사람들이 상상 속의 내일을 어떻게 떠올리는지를 말해주지만, 그 이유는 말해주지 않는다."로 끝나고 있으므로, 본문 뒤에는 사람들이 미래를 미리 생각하는 이유인 ⑤에 대한 내용이 이어질 것이다.

assume v. 추정하다, 추측하다, 가정하다
vacate v. 비우다, 퇴거하다, 떠나가다
conjure v. (마음에) 그려내다, 생각해 내다

---

14 2015 홍익대

다윈(Darwin)과 그의 뒤를 이은 여러 세대의 생물학자들에게 진화는 '변이를 수반하는 계통'으로 생각되었다. 먼저 '계통'이라는 말을 생각해보자. 진화에 대한 이러한 개념에 따르면, 진화는 계통적으로 연결돼 있는 유기체의 개체군인 혈통 안에서만 발생한다. 생물학적인 의미에서, 개체군은 번식의 측면에서 상호작용하는 유기체 집단이다. 개체군 속의 유기체들은 번식을 통해 새로운 세대를 만들어내는데, 마찬가지로 그 새로운 세대도 번식이라는 상호작용을 통해 또 다른 세대를 생겨나게 하며, 그 또 다른 세대 또한 번식이라는 상호작용을 계속해서 하게 된다. 이러한 과정은 시간적으로 확장된 개체군을 잇달아 만들어내는데, 나중에 생겨난 개체군은 먼저 생겨난 개체군으로부터 번식이라는 과정을 통해 계통을 잇게 되며, 그렇게 개체군이 시간적으로 연결돼 있는 것이 바로 혈통이다. 혈통 내에서, 후손은 부모로부터 특질을 물려받는 경향이 있으며, 그 결과 후손은 혈통 내에서 친족이 아닌 유기체들에 비해 부모를 더 많이 닮는다. 그렇다면, '계통'이란 부모와 후손 사이의 유전적 유사성을 특징으로 하는 유기체의 혈통을 가리킨다고 할 수 있다.

'변이'는 혈통 안에서 특질 혹은 형질이 확산되는 데 있어서 일어나는 여러 세대에 걸친 변화를 일컫는다. 기관이나 일부 형태에서부터 행동 유형에 이르기까지, 유기체가 가진 눈에 띄는 특성은 모두 형질이 될 수 있다. 개체군에 속해 있는 유기체들이 번식 과정을 거쳐 새로운 세대를 만들어냄에 따라, 한 세대에서 다음 세대로 전해지는 형질의 빈도에는 변화가 있을 수도 있고 없을 수도 있다. 가령, 어느 인간 개체군의 한 세대에서 갈색 눈이 65%, 녹색 눈이 25%, 파란 눈이 10%인데, 이러한 눈 색깔의 비율이 다음 세대에서 달라졌다면, 그 혈통에는 '변이'가 있었던 게 된다. 따라서 다윈과 그의 뒤를 이은 여러 세대의 생물학자들에게, 진화는 혈통 내에서 여러 세대에 걸쳐 전해지는 유전적 특질의 빈도 변화를 의미했다. 이러한 정의에 따르면, 개개의 유기체가 일생동안 겪는 변화는 진화와 관련이 없다는 사실에 주목하는 것이 중요하다. 오히려, 진화는 유기체가 가진 특질의 빈도 면에서의 혈통 내의 여러 세대에 걸친 변화에만 있는 것이다.

1 ① ▶ **내용파악**
첫 번째 문단의 네 번째 문장에서, "생물학적인 의미에서, 개체군은 번식의 측면에서 상호작용하는 유기체 집단이다."라고 되어 있다. 이것과 가장 의미가 비슷한 내용을 만드는 ①이 빈칸에 적절하다.

evolution n. 전개, 발전; 진화
descent n. 가계, 혈통, 출신
modification n. 수정, 변경, 변화
lineage n. 혈통, 계통; 계보
reproduce v. 생식하다, 번식하다
interact v. 상호작용하다, 서로 영향을 주다
spawn v. (물고기·개구리 따위가) 알을 낳다, 산란(産卵)하다; 생산하다
temporal a. 시간의
offspring n. 자식; 자손; (동물의) 새끼
inherit v. (재산 따위를) 상속하다; (체격·성질 따위를) 물려받다, 유전하다
characteristic n. 특질, 특색, 특성
hereditary a. 유전에 의한, 유전의
distribution n. 분배, 배분; 살포; 분포
trait n. 특색, 특성
observable a. 관찰할 수 있는, 눈에 띄는
property n. 재산, 자산; 성질, 특성
morphology n. 형태학
frequency n. 횟수, 도수, 빈도
definition n. 한정; 정의(定義); 설명

2 ① ▶ 빈칸완성
빈칸 앞에서는 '개개의 유기체가 일생동안 겪는 변화는 진화와 관련이 없음'을 언급하고 있고, 빈칸 뒤에서는 '유기체가 가진 특질의 빈도 면에서, 여러 세대에 걸친 변화에 대해서만 진화가 있음'을 언급하고 있다. 그러므로 '오히려'의 의미를 가지면서, 앞서 언급한 내용과 다르거나 반대되는 내용을 도입할 때 쓰는 Rather가 빈칸에 들어가야 한다. ② 그런데 ③ 그럼에도 불구하고 ④ 그러나

3 ③ ▶ 내용추론
변이가 유기체들이 항상 환경 적응에 도움이 되는 쪽으로만 일어나는지는 본문의 내용을 통해 알 수 없다.

4 ② ▶ 뒷내용 추론
본문에서는 다윈과 그의 추종자들이 생각하는 진화에 대한 개념을 설명하고 있다. 본문에 언급하고 있는 진화의 개념이 모두 다윈과 그의 추종자들의 주장 혹은 이론임을 감안하면, 이어지는 글에서는 진화의 개념과 관련된 다른 이들의 이론이나 주장, 혹은 다윈이 생각한 진화의 개념에 대한 오류나 문제점에 대해 다룰 가능성이 높다고 볼 수 있다.

15 2020 아주대

Ⓐ 많은 설명자들은 개가 되기를 원하는 늑대가 인간이 제공하는 쓰레기 더미에서 열량의 노다지를 처음으로 활용했다는 것이 가장 가능성 있는 시나리오라고 주장한다. 기회주의적인 행동을 통해, 그 신생 견종들은 접근 허용 거리가 좁혀지고 민첩하게 도주해야 할 일이 줄어들고, 종간 사회화를 위해 강아지의 발육 시기가 더 오래 연장되고, 위험한 인간들도 또한 점유하는 지역을 그들과 나란히 더 자신 있게 점유하여 살아가는 그런 환경에 행동적으로, 그리고 마침내는 유전적으로 적응되고자 했다.

Ⓑ 차별적 순화(길들이기)를 위해 여러 세대에 걸쳐 선택된 러시아 모피 여우에 대한 연구는 가축화와 관련된 많은 형태학적, 행동적 특성들을 보여준다. 이 여우들은 일종의 원시 "마을 개" 출현의 모형이 될지도 모르는 것으로, 유전적으로는 늑대에 가깝지만 행동적으로는 늑대와 아주 다르며 가축화 과정을 촉진하려는 인간의 시도에 대해 더 수용적이다. 개들의 번식을 계획적으로 통제함으로써, 그리고 의도하지는 않았지만 강력한 결과들을 얻음으로써, 인간은 (공진화) 이야기의 초기에 등장하는 다양한 종류의 개들을 만들어내는 데 공헌할 수 있었을 것이다. 인간의 생활방식이 개들과 연관되어 현저히 변했다. 유연성과 기회주의는 인간과 개, 두 종 모두에게 중요한 것이고, 두 종은 여전히 진행 중인 공진화 역사 내내 서로를 형성해간다.

Ⓒ 학자들은 기술 문화에 관한 좀 더 생성적인 담론을 형성하기 위해 여러 버전의 이런 이야기를 이용하여 자연과 문화의 명확한 구분에 의문을 제기한다. 다시 모레이(Darcy Morey)는 그 이야기가 처음부터 끝까지 차별적인 번식에 관한 이야기이므로, 인위적 선택과 자연적 선택 사이의 구별은 무의미하다고 믿는다. 환경 역사학자 에드 러셀(Ed Russell)은 개 품종의 진화는 생명공학기술 역사의 한 장을 차지한다고 주장한다. 그는 인간 작인(作因)(작인으로서의 인간)을 강조하며, 유기체를 조작된 기술로 간주하지만, 개의 적극적인 역할을 인정하는 방식으로, 그리고 인간 문화와 개의 계속되는 공진화를 전면에 내세우는 방식으로 그렇게 한다.

Ⓓ 공진화는 생물학자들이 습관적으로 하는 것보다 좀 더 광범위하게 정의되어야 한다. 분명히, 꽃의 생식 구조와 꽃을 수분하는 곤충의 기관과 같은 가시적인 형태들의 상호 적응은 공진화이다. 그러나 개의 신체와 마음의 변화를 생물학적인 것으로 보고, 인간의 신체와 생활의 변화를 문화적으로 보고, 그래서 공진화에 관한 것이 아니라고 보는 것은 잘못이다. 적어도, 나는 인간의 게놈에는 개를 포함한 인간의 반려 종들의 병원균들에 관한 상당한 양의 분자 기록들이 포함되어 있다는 생각이 든다. 면역 체계는 자연 문화의 작은 부분이 아니다. 면역 체계는 인간을 포함한 유기체들이 어디에서 살 수 있고 누구와 함께 살 수 있는지를 결정한다. 독감의 역사는 인간과 돼지와 가금류와 바이러스의 공진화 개념을 빼놓고는 상상조차 할 수 없다.

1 ③ ▶ 글의 제목
이 글은 '개가 가축화된 이래로 인간과 개 모두가 공진화적 변화를 겪고 있다'는 예를 들

interpreter n. 설명자
bonanza n. 노다지
opportunistic a. 기회주의적인
emergent a. 신생의
hair-trigger a. 예민한, 민첩한
flight n. 탈출, 도피
window n. 관찰할 기회
parallel a. 평행한
tameness n. 길들이기
morphological a. 형태학적인
domestication n. 가축화
further v. 촉진하다
receptive a. 수용적인
the name of the game 중요한[불가결한] 것, 주목적, 본질
generative a. 생성적인
foreground v. 특히 중시하다, 최전면에 내세우다
pollinate v. 가루받이[수분]하다
alteration n. 변화, 변경
molecular a. 분자의
pathogen n. 병원균
fowl n. 가금

면서, '자연적(유전적, 생물학적) 요소와 인간의 문화가 상호작용해 공진화를 이끌어 낸다'는 요지를 전개하고 있다.

2 ② ▶ **문법적으로 옳지 않은 표현 고르기**
ⓑ의 and 앞은 behaviorally quite different from wolves에서 but 앞에 나온 명사인 wolves를 생략한 것인데 명사만을 생략할 수는 없고 '전치사+명사'구인 from wolves를 생략하거나 from을 쓰면 them으로 하여 from them으로 나타내야 한다. 즉 앞에 나온 명사를 뒤에서 그 명사만 생략할 수 없다는 것이다. 다만 앞에서 명사를 먼저 생략하고 뒤에 명사를 나타낼 수는 있다. 그러면 genetically close to but behaviorally quite different from wolves로 된다. 따라서 ⓑ의 and 앞을 behaviorally quite different나 behaviorally quite different from them으로 고쳐야 한다.

3 ⑤ ▶ **내용일치**
B 단락에서 '러시아 모피 여우들은 유전적으로는 늑대와 가깝다'고 하였을 뿐 개가 유전적으로 늑대에 가깝기보다 러시아 모피 여우에 더 가까운지는 알 수 없고 이에 대한 논란이 있는지도 알 수 없으므로 ⑤는 잘못된 진술이다. 한편, A 단락에서 '그 신생 견종들은 종간 사회화를 위해 강아지의 발육 시기가 더 오래 연장되고'라고 했는데 이는 원래의 늑대는 새끼로서의 발육 시기 즉, 젖 떼는 이유기가 더 짧았다는 말이므로 ②는 올바른 진술이다.

4 ⑤ ▶ **부분이해**
문맥상 '늑대 중의 일부가 개가 되는 가축화 과정을 설명하는 가장 그럴듯한 가설(시나리오)'이라고 볼 수 있다.

13 동물·식물

01 2019 중앙대

슬로베니아의 연안에 서식하는 일반적인 큰돌고래의 몇몇 비정상적인 행동이 9년간의 연구를 통해 밝혀졌다. 이들 종의 한 개체군 내에서, 큰돌고래들은 두 개의 집단으로 나뉘어졌고, 두 집단은 하루 중 서로 다른 시간대에 사냥을 함으로써 서로 접촉을 피했는데, 이는 해양 포유동물들 안에서는 알려져 있지 않은 사회적 전략이었다. 연구원들은 돌고래의 등지느러미 사진을 이용해서 돌고래를 개별적으로 식별했다. 그들은 38마리의 돌고래를 여러 번 관찰했으며, 각각의 돌고래가 목격된 시간, 날짜, 장소를 꼼꼼히 기록했다. 그 해양 포유동물들은 각각 19마리와 13마리로 구성된 두 개의 주요 집단으로 나뉘었고, 6마리는 느슨하게 제3의 집단을 이루었다. 좀 더 큰 집단의 19마리는 이탈리아 '반도'의 동북부 최상단에 위치한 트리에스테 만(灣)에 저인망 어선을 따라가면서 몸을 물 밖으로 내미는 경향이 있었는데, 이는 사냥을 하는 것 같았다. 두 번째 집단의 13마리는 트리에스테 만에 있을 때 어선과는 전혀 무관하게 있었다. 그 돌고래들은 같은 지역에서 사냥을 했음에도 불구하고, 서로 마주치는 경우가 거의 없었음을 연구원들은 발견했는데, 이는 좀 더 큰 집단은 현지 시간으로 오전 7시에서 오후 1시에 그 지역에 있었던 반면, 좀 더 작은 집단은 오후 6시에서 오후 9시 사이에 모습을 드러냈기 때문이었다. 사냥하는 바나를 나눠 갖는 돌고래 집단에 대해 기록한 다른 연구들도 있었지만, 이 바다 포유류들이 바다를 시간별로 공유한다는 것을 보여준 것은 이번이 처음이다. 비록 연구원들은 돌고래들이 왜 또는 어떻게 이런 시간 일정들을 잡는지는 모르지만, 동물들이 같은 장소에 있지 않다는 사실은 비우호적인 접촉을 줄어들게 할 것이고 먹이에 대한 직접적인 경쟁을 감소시킬 것이다.

uncover v. 폭로하다, 공개하다
bottlenose dolphin 큰돌고래
dorsal a. 등(쪽)의
fin n. 지느러미
sighting n. 목격
hang out 어울리다, 사귀다; 몸을 밖으로 내밀다; 자주 출입하다
trawler n. 저인망 어선, 트롤선
cadre n. 핵심 그룹의 일원
timeshare v. 시분할(時分割)하다
diminish v. (수량·크기·정도 등을) 줄이다
unfriendly a. 비우호적인, 불친절한
encounter n. 만남, 조우

1 ②   ▶ 글의 제목
이 글은 슬로베니아의 연안에 서식하는 큰돌고래의 몇몇 비정상적인 행동에 대한 내용, 즉 "같은 개체군에 있는 돌고래들이 무리를 지어 생활을 하지만, 한 집단에 속한 돌고래들이 다른 집단에 속한 돌고래들과 서로 다른 시간에 바다를 사용함으로써 두 집단의 돌고래들이 서로 접촉을 피한다."는 내용을 소개하고 있다. 이로 인해 각 집단의 비우호적인 접촉이 줄어들며 먹이에 대한 직접적인 경쟁을 감소시킬 수 있다고 했으므로, 글의 제목으로 가장 적합한 것은 ② '바다를 시간별로 동료들과 공유하는 돌고래'이다.

2 ③   ▶ 내용추론
연구원들은 돌고래의 등지느러미 사진을 이용해서 각각의 돌고래를 확인할 수 있었다고 했으므로 ③이 정답이다.

02 2021 경기대

호주에는 독을 쏘는 나무가 7종이 있는데, 그 가운데 가장 심한 통증을 일으키는 것은 아마도 "Dendrocnide moroides"일 것이다. 이 작은 관목은 빛이 가득 들어오는 열대우림의 개간지에서 자라며, 잎의 너비는 최대 50cm이다. 이 잎들은 가는 털로 덮여 있어서 촉감이 부드러워 보인다. 하지만 피부에 닿게 되면 그 잎들은 통증을 유발하는 독소를 주입한다. 이 독소는 즉시 효과를 발생시켜 30분 안에 최대 강도에 도달하며, 수일 혹은 수주에 걸쳐 지속된다. 털이 피부에 박히는 경향이 있기 때문에, 환부를 문지르거나 씻는 것은 얼얼한 통증을 완화시키는 데 거의 도움이 되지 않는다. 이 식물들의 근처에 있는 것만으로도 위험한데, 왜냐하면 이들은 심각한 호흡기 손상을 일으킬 수 있는 입자로 근처의 공기를 가득 채우기 때문이다. 독소가 매우 강함에도 불구하고, 이 식물은 몇몇 곤충 종(種)과 붉은 다리 왈라비라 불리는 유대류(有袋類) 동물의 먹이가 되고 있다.

species n. 종(種), 종류
stinging a. 찌르는, 쏘는
shrub n. 키 작은 나무, 관목(灌木)
clearing n. (산림을 벌채해 만든) 개간지
rainforest n. 다우림(多雨林), 열대 다우림
fine a. 가는, 미세한
come into contact with ~와 접촉하다
inject v. 주사하다, 주입하다
toxin n. 독소(毒素)
take effect 주효하다, 효험이 있다

1 ③   ▶ 빈칸완성
'심각한 호흡기 손상을 일으킬 수 있는 입자로 근처의 공기를 가득 채운다'고 했으므로,

이 식물의 부근에 있는 것은 위험할 수 있을 것이다. 그러므로 nearby와 같은 의미를 만드는 ③이 정답으로 적절하다. in the vicinity of는 '~의 부근에'라는 의미이다. ① 존재 ② 유사성 ④ 출현

2 ①　▶ 내용파악

"이 독소는 즉시 효과를 발생시켜 30분 안에 최대 강도에 도달하며, 수일 혹은 수주에 걸쳐 지속된다."라고 했으므로, ①이 정답으로 적절하다.

3 ③　▶ 내용파악

"털이 피부에 박히는 경향이 있기 때문에, 환부를 문지르거나 씻는 것은 일월한 통증을 완화시키는 데 거의 도움이 되지 않는다."라고 했으므로, 남아있는 그 식물의 털을 제거하도록 해야 할 것이다.

---

intensity n. 강렬함, 강함, 격렬함; 강도, 세기
persist v. 고집하다; 지속하다, 존속하다
rub v. 문지르다, 비비다
affected a. 영향을 받은; (병 따위에) 걸린, 침범된
relieve v. (고통·부담 따위를) 경감하다, 덜다
lodge v. (탄알 등을) 쏘아 박다; (화살 등을) 꽂다
hazardous a. 위험한
nearby a. 근처의 ad. 근처에, 바로 옆에
particle n. (아주 작은) 입자[조각]
respiratory a. 호흡의, 호흡을 위한
potency n. 힘, 세력; 능력; (약 따위의) 효능, 효력
consume v. 소모하다; 먹다, 마시다
marsupial a. <동물> 유대류(有袋類)의
pademelon n. <동물> 왈라비

03　2017 한국외대

콘스탄틴 슬로보드치코프(Constantine Slobodchikoff) 교수와 그의 동료 교수들은 그 영리함에 대해 알려져 있지 않은 설치류인 프레리도그의 의사소통 체계를 해독해 왔다. 그러나 슬로보드치코프 교수팀은 프레리도그에게도 복잡한 언어가 있다는 증거를 갖고 있으며, 그들은 이 언어를 파악하는 일에 착수했다. 프레리도그가 어떤 포식동물을 볼 때에는 고음의 찍찍 소리로 서로에게 경고한다. 훈련이 돼 있지 않은 사람들의 귀에는 이런 프레리도그 소리가 전부 같은 소리처럼 들릴 수도 있지만, 동일한 소리는 아니다. 슬로보드치코프는 이런 경고음은 프레리도그 언어를 해독하는 데 있어 '로제타스톤(Rosetta Stone)'과 같은 것이라고 말하는데, 이런 경고음이 사람들이 이해할 수 있는 상황 속에서 발생하여, 그 의미를 해석할 수가 있기 때문이다. 그의 연구에서, 슬로보드치코프는 경고음과 포식동물의 접근에 따라 프레리도그들이 이로 인해 도망치는 행동을 기록했다. 그리고는 근접한 포식동물이 없을 때에, 녹음한 그 경고음을 재생시켜서, 프레리도그들이 도망치는 반응을 영상으로 촬영했다. 녹음한 경고음 소리에 따라 도망치는 반응이 포식동물이 있을 때의 반응과 일치한다면, 이것은 의미 있는 정보가 경고음 안에 암호화되어 있다는 것을 의미한다. 그리고 실제로 의미 있는 정보가 내재되어 있는 것으로 보인다. 슬로보드치코프는 경고음 안에 포식동물들마다 관련된 서로 다른 (독특한) 경고가 있다는 것을 밝혀냈다. 이런 경고음은 심지어 포식동물의 색깔, 크기와 모양까지도 구체적으로 명시해준다.

1 ①　▶ 글의 주제

프레리도그가 다양한 경고음을 통해 서로 의사소통한다는 것을 전제로 프레리도그의 언어라고 할 수 있는 의사소통 시스템을 연구했다고 했다. 따라서 주제로 적절한 것은 ①이다. 한편, 포식동물에 대한 경고음에 대해서만 다루었고 다양한 감정에 대한 언급은 없으므로, ④는 주제로서 부적절하다.

2 ①　▶ 부분이해

로제타스톤에 있는 비문(碑文)은 고대 이집트 상형문자를 해석하게 만든 유일한 단서였다. 프레리도그의 의사소통 체계를 해독할 수 있는 실마리는 포식동물에 대한 프레리도그의 경고음뿐이다. 이런 경고음을 로제타스톤과 비교한 것은 이것만이 프레리도그의 의사소통 체계를 해석할 수 있는 유일한 단서이기 때문이다.

3 ③　▶ 빈칸완성

녹음한 경고음 소리에 따라 도망치는 반응이 포식동물이 있을 때의 반응과 일치한다면, 이는 경고음 안에 의미가 내재되어 있다는 것을 뜻하는 것이다. 따라서 ③ "의미 있는 정보가 경고음 안에 암호화되어 있다."가 빈칸에 적절하다.

---

colleague n. 동료
decode v. (암호를) 해독하다, 번역하다
prairie dog 프레리도그, 개쥐
rodent n. 설치류 동물
smarts n. 지능, 지성, 명민함
predator n. 포식자, 포식 동물
high-pitched a. 고음의
chirp n. (새·벌레의) 찍찍 소리
alarm call 경고음, 비상 신호
subsequent a. 뒤의, 차후의; 다음의
response n. 응답, 반응
comparable a. 유사한
reflex n. 반사행동
encode v. 암호화[기호화] 하다
distinct a. 별개의; 명료한, 뚜렷한
specify v. 일일이 열거하다, 명확히[구체적으로] 말하다, 명시하다

04　2022 단국대

인간에게 위험한 것으로 간주되는 상어는 식인 상어로 알려져 있는 것과 식인 상어로 일컬어지는 것의 두 부류로 분류되어야 한다. 식인 상어로 알려져 있는 종(種)은 극소수다. 이 중에서 백상아리는 가장 사납고 위험한 것으로 인간에게 알려져 있다. 호주 사람들이 종종 화이트 포인터(the white pointer)라고 부르는 이 상어는 세계의 나머지 지역에서는 다양한 이름으로 알려져 있는데, 그 이름들에는 화이트 데스(the white death), 그레이트 화이트 샤크(the great white shark), 그레이 샤크(the grey shark), 그레이 데스(the grey death), 그레이 포인터(the grey pointer) 등이 포함된다. 의심할 여지없이 이 상어는 근래에 바다가 낳은 것 중에 가장 끔찍한 괴물이다. 그것은 길이가 거의 40피트인 것으로 기록돼 왔는데, 1930년대 후반에 하와이 제도 연안에서 39피트짜리가 포획된 예가 있고, 빅토리아의 포트 페어리(Port Fairy)에서 포획된 또 다른 것은 길이가 36피트로 추정되었다. 이런 동물은 틀림없이 무게가 몇 톤 이상 나갔을 것이다. 백상아리는 세계의 모든 바다에서 발견된다. 백상아리는 열대 및 아열대 지역에서 여전히 흔하고 또 자주 마주치지만, 보다 차가운 물에서 가장 많이 번식하고 있다.

사람들이 처음으로 배를 타고 바다로 나간 이래로 사람들은 백상아리를 알고 있었고 또 두려워했던 까닭에, 가장 억센 선원들에게조차 공포심을 심어주었다. 아마도 이 거대한 상어의 "유령 같은" 하얀 모습으로 인해 이 상어가 나쁜 평판을 얻게 됐을 것인데, 왜냐하면 이 거대한 동물에게는 뭔가 비현실적이고 불길한 점이 있기 때문이다. 백상아리는 며칠, 심지어 몇 주 동안이나 항해하는 배들을 따라다니는 것으로 알려져 왔는데, 용골(龍骨) 부근이나 선미 가까이에서 조용히 떠다니면서 지켜보고 또 기다린다는 것이다. 사람들이 돛단배를 타고 다니던 옛 시절에 그 굶주린 괴물이 바다 밖으로 몸을 내밀어, 힘없이 있는 선원을 바람이 잦아들어 멈춘 배의 옆으로부터 낚아챘다는 기록이 남아 있다.

1 ④ ▶ 내용일치
"백상아리는 보다 차가운 물에서 가장 많이 번식한다."고 했으므로, 상대적으로 기온이 더 낮은 지역에서 더 흔히 발견할 수 있을 것이다. 따라서 ④가 정답으로 적절하다.

2 ④ ▶ 빈칸완성
백상아리가 두려움의 대상이었음을 부연해야 하므로, "강건하고 억센 선원들에게조차 공포심을 심어주었다."라는 흐름이 되는 것이 가장 자연스럽다. 최상급이 아니라 원급 표현이라면 억세고 강인한 선원보다 우둔하고 바보 같은 선원에게 공포심이 더 잘 심어지겠지만, 최상급 표현일 때는 우둔하고 바보 같은 선원은 말할 것도 없고 가장 억센 선원에게조차 공포심을 심어주었다는 의미로 해야 적절해진다. ① 가장 우둔한 ② 가장 키가 큰 ③ 가장 따뜻한

reputed a. 유명한, ~라 일컬어지는
ferocious a. 사나운, 잔인한
specimen n. 견본; (동식물의) 표본; 예(例), 실례
estimate v. 어림잡다, 견적하다
prolific a. 다산(多産)의; 풍부한
encounter v. 우연히 만나다, 조우하다
tropical a. 열대지방의
semitropical a. 아열대의
instill v. (사상 따위를) 스며들게 하다, 주입시키다
sinister a. 불길한; 사악한
vessel n. 그릇; 배; 항공기
keel n. (배나 비행선의) 용골(龍骨)
stern n. 고물, 선미(船尾)
snatch v. 잡아채다, 낚아채다
helpless a. 스스로 어떻게도 할 수 없는, 무력한
becalm v. 바람이 자서 (범선을) 멈추게 하다

05　2018 한국외대

식물들은 빛이 나뭇잎을 지나면서 걸러질 때 발생하는 빛의 양의 감소나 적색광 대 원적색광(R:FR) 비율의 감소와 같은 다양한 단서를 통해서 경쟁 식물들을 감지할 수 있다. 그러한 경쟁 단서들은 세 가지 유형의 회피반응, 즉, 주변 식물보다 더 크게 자라 주변 식물에 그늘이 지게 하려는 것이나, 그늘에 잘 견디게 되어 빛이 제한된 상황에서 생명작용을 더 잘 하게 적응하는 것이나, 주변 식물을 피해 옆으로 자라는 것 등을 유발한다. 그러나 식물들은 이 회피반응들 중에 선택하여 경쟁 식물들의 상대적인 크기와 밀도에 맞게 반응할 수 있는가? 이 질문에 답하기 위해, 연구자들은 서로 다른 여러 빛-경쟁 환경을 본뜬(모방한) 실험 장치를 사용했다. 그들은 세로 줄무늬의 투명한 녹색 필터들을 사용했는데, 이 필터들은 빛의 양과 R:FR 모두를 감소시킨다는 점에서 경쟁 식물들을 모방한 것이다. 이 모방한 식물(녹색 필터)의 높이와 밀도 모두에 변화를 줌으로써 연구자들은 있을 수 있는 다양한 빛-경쟁 상황을 식물들에게 제공할 수 있었다. 그 결과는 식물들이 실제로 최적의 방법으로 경쟁에 대응할 수 있다는 것을 보여주었다. 모방한 경쟁 식물들(녹색 필터)이 키가 작고 빽빽이 모여 있다면, 식물들은 수직으로 가장 높이 자라는 것을 보여주었다. 그러나 키가 크고, 넓은 간격을 두고 있는 이웃 식물들 아래서는 식물들이 옆으로 가장 멀리까지 자랐다. 마지막으로 모방한 이웃 식물들이 키가 크고 빽빽하게 모여 있는 상황에서는 수직으로도 측면으로도 그 모방한 식

detect v. 발견하다, 알아내다, 감지하다
cue n. 신호, 단서
reduction n. 축소, 감소
ratio n. 비, 비율
wavelength n. 파장
filter v. 여과하다, 거르다
induce v. 유발하다, 초래하다
avoidance response 회피반응(예기되는 자극을 피하려고 하는 반사행동)
outgrow v. ~보다 더 커지다[많아지다]
shade v. 그늘지게 하다, (빛이 바로 닿지 않도록) 가리다
shade-tolerant a. 응달에서 자라는, 내음성의

물들보다 더 많이 자랄 수 없다보니, 식물들은 가장 높은 내음성(그늘에서 가장 잘 견디는) 행동을 보여주었다. 이 연구의 결과는 식물들이 이웃 식물들의 밀도와 경쟁 능력을 평가해서, 그에 맞추어 반응할 수 있다는 것을 보여준다.

1 ③ ▶ 내용일치
연구자들은 세로 줄무늬의 투명한 녹색 필터를 사용했는데, 이 필터들은 빛의 양과 R:FR 모두를 감소시킨다는 점에서 경쟁 식물들을 모방한 것이라고 했으므로, ③이 정답이다.
① 내음성은 '음지에서 견디는 힘'으로 주변 식물들이 키가 크고 밀도가 높아지면 식물이 내음성을 키운다고 했다. 경쟁 식물을 피해 옆으로 자라는 것은 주변 식물들이 키가 크고, 넓은 간격을 두고 자라는 경우이다.

2 ① ▶ 내용파악
경쟁 식물의 키가 크고 밀도가 높은 경우에는 식물들은 그늘에서 견디는(내음성을 향상시키는) 선택을 한다고 했다. 따라서 이런 상황에서 더 높이 자란다고 한 ①은 식물의 회피반응의 예로 적절하지 않다.

3 ③ ▶ 부분이해
"식물들이 이웃 식물들의 밀도와 경쟁 능력을 평가해서, 그에 맞추어 반응할 수 있다."라고 했는데, 이는 식물들이 다양한 크기, 밀도를 가진 주변 식물들과 살아가야 하기 때문에 상황을 분석해서 자신들에게 유리한 방침을 선택할 수 있다는 것을 의미하므로 ③이 정답이다.

---

adapt to ~에 적응하다
sideways ad. 옆으로; 옆에서
density n. 밀도(빽빽한 정도)
competitor n. 경쟁자, 경쟁상대
experimental a. 실험의; 실험[시험]적인; 경험적인
setup n. (실험 등의) 장치, 설비
simulate v. ~을 가장하다, ~인 체하다; 흉내 내다; 모의 실험하다
vertical a. 수직의, 세로의
transparent a. 투명한; 속이 뻔히 들여다보이는, 명백한; 솔직한
mimic v. 흉내 내다, 모방하다
vegetation n. 식물, 초목
optimal a. 최선의, 최상의, 최적의
laterally ad. 측면으로, 좌우로; 비스듬히
shade tolerance 내음성(耐陰性: 식물이 약광 조건에서 생존하고 생장하는 능력)
evaluate v. 평가하다, 측정하다
tailor v. (목적·기호 등에) 적응시키다, 맞추다
accordingly ad. (상황에) 부응해서, 그에 맞추어

---

06 2020 서울여대

갈등은 사회적으로 살아가는 모든 동물들에게 볼 수 있으며, 음식, 공간 또는 짝짓기 상대와 같은 부족한 자원을 두고 발생한다. 그러나 20세기 후반에, 동물의 갈등에 대한 우리의 견해가 바뀌었다. 오래된 견해에 따르면, 위협과 또 다른 공격적인 과시는 개체들이 일정한 거리를 두도록 하고 안정적인 위계질서 속에 개체들을 배열함으로써 실제 폭력을 줄이는 것으로 여겨졌고, 현장 연구는 이러한 견해를 뒷받침하는 것처럼 보였다. (인간의 경우) 무기가 우리의 희생자들을 우리로부터 멀어지게 하여, 복종하는 표현과 그 외 다른 폭력에 대한 자연적인 제한행위를 효과가 없게 만들기 때문에 인간만이 동족을 죽인다고 말해졌다.

우리는 현재 이 견해가 틀린 것임을 알고 있다. 이 견해가 지속된 부분적인 이유는 동물이 죽이는 것을 목격할 기회가 부족했기 때문이었다. 개코원숭이 무리가 인간과 같은 폭력 사망률을 가지고 있다 하더라도, 단 한 건의 살해를 관찰하는 데도 수 세기가 걸릴 수 있다. 그러나 현장 관찰이 축적되면서 살해에 이르는 폭력이 많은 종(種)들에서 목격되었다.

한 예는 경쟁적인 유아 살해인데, 하누만 긴꼬리원숭이에게서 처음 연구되었다. 긴꼬리원숭이 무리의 핵심에는 친족 관계인 암컷들과 새끼들이 있다. 수컷들은 일 년 혹은 그 이상 머무르지만 결국 떠난다. 어느 틈엔가 새로운 수컷이 등장해서, 이전의 수컷들을 몰아내고, 이전의 수컷의 자리를 차지한다. 그들은 곧 생후 6개월 미만의 모든 새끼 원숭이를 죽인다. 암컷은 한 동안 저항하지만, 성공하지 못하며, 곧 다시 가임기가 되고, 새로운 수컷과 짝짓기를 하게 된다. 경쟁적인 유아 살해의 다양한 형태는 침팬지, 사자, 들개, 그리고 다른 많은 종에서 설명된다.

1 ③ ▶ 글의 주제
첫 번째 문장에서 갈등은 사회적으로 살아가는 모든 동물들에게서 볼 수 있다고 한 다음, 이전에는 인간만이 같은 종족을 죽인다고 했는데, 동물들도 동족을 살해한다고 하면서 긴꼬리원숭이의 예를 들고 있다. 새로운 집단에 들어간 수컷 원숭이들은 이전의 수컷이 낳은 새끼 원숭이들을 죽인다고 한 다음 다른 동물들에서도 이와 같은 것이 설명된다고 했으므로, 이 글에서 주로 다루고 있는 것은 ③ '동물의 폭력성'이다.

---

scarce a. 부족한, 적은, 결핍한
mate n. 친구; 짝
aggressive a. 침략적인, 공격적인
space v. (사물들 사이에 일정한) 간격을 두다
arrange v. 정리하다, 배열하다; 조정하다
submissive a. 복종하는, 순종하는
restraint n. 제지, 금지, 억제
persist v. 고집하다, 주장하다
competitive a. 경쟁의
infanticide n. 유아살해
transient a. 일시 머무르는
drive off ~을 쫓아버리다
fertile a. 생식력 있는

2 ④ ▶ 내용파악
20세기 후반에 "갈등으로 인해 동족을 죽이는 것은 인간뿐이다."는 견해가 잘못된 것으로 드러났는데, 이는 동물들도 갈등으로 인해 동족을 죽이는 일이 발생한다는 것이다. 따라서 ④가 정답이다.

3 ② ▶ 내용일치
마지막 문장에서 "경쟁적인 유아 살해의 다양한 형태는 침팬지, 사자, 들개, 그리고 다른 많은 종에서 설명된다."고 했으므로 침팬지도 긴꼬리원숭이처럼 유아살해를 하는 것이 목격되었다고 할 수 있다. 따라서 ②가 정답이다.

07 2015 경기대

병에 걸린 나무가 조난 신호를 보내는 소리를 여러분들은 아마도 결코 듣지 못할 것이다. 그러나 한 무리의 과학자들은 그 외치는 소리를 들었으며, 그들은 일부 곤충들도 나무가 내는 소리를 들으며, 마치 죽어가고 있는 동물에 이끌리는 독수리처럼 그 곤충들도 소리를 내는 나무에 이끌리는 것으로 생각하고 있다. 연구원들은 미국 산림청과 함께 바싹 마른 나무의 껍질에 센서를 붙인 후에 구조를 요청하는 신호를 분명하게 들었다. 참여했던 한 과학자에 따르면, 가뭄에 시달리고 있는 나무들 대부분은 그들이 겪고 있는 고통을 50~500 킬로헤르츠 대역의 소리로 전한다. 기계의 도움을 받지 않은 인간의 귀가 감지할 수 있는 대역은 20 킬로헤르츠까지에 불과하다. 붉은 떡갈나무, 단풍나무, 스트로부스 소나무, 그리고 자작나무는 모두 나무 표면에서 발생하는 진동의 형태로 각각 조금 다른 소리를 만들어낸다.

그러한 진동은 나무에 세로로 나 있는 관다발 속의 물관이 그 속에 너무 적은 양의 물이 흘러서 깨지는 경우에 발생한다고 과학자들은 생각한다. 이렇게 금이 생긴 물관들은 독특한 진동 패턴을 밖으로 내보낸다. 일부 곤충들은 초음파 주파수 대역에서 서로 의사소통하기 때문에, 그 나무들의 진동을 감지하고서 약해진 나무들을 공격하기도 한다. 현재 연구원들은 그 소리가 곤충들을 끌어들이는 것인지를 알아보는 실험을 물이 고갈된 화분에 심은 나무를 가지고 하고 있다. "물이 부족한 나무들은 또한 그렇지 않은 나무들과는 다른 냄새를 풍기며, 온도의 변화를 겪습니다. 그래서 곤충들은 소리가 아닌 다른 무언가에 반응하고 있는 것일 수도 있습니다."라고 한 과학자는 말했다.

sicken v. 구역질나게 하다; 병나게 하다
distress n. 고민, 걱정; 고통
vulture n. 독수리
fasten v. 묶다, 붙들어 매다; 고정하다
drought-stricken a. 가뭄으로 고통을 받는
torment n. 고통, 고뇌; 고문
detect v. 발견하다, 간파하다; 탐지하다
pine n. 소나무
birch n. 자작나무
vibration n. 진동; 동요; 전율
column n. 기둥
length n. 길이; 세로
fracture v. 부수다; 금가게 하다
ultrasonic frequency 초음파 주파수
potted a. 화분에 심은, 단지에 넣은
thermal a. 열의, 온도의
respond v. 응답하다, 대답하다

1 ③ ▶ 내용파악
"가뭄에 시달리고 있는 나무들 대부분은 그들이 겪고 있는 고통을 50~500 킬로헤르츠 대역의 소리로 전한다."라는 내용이 있으므로, 나무는 물이 부족할 때 조난 신호를 보낸다고 할 수 있다.

2 ② ▶ 내용추론
첫 번째 문단 후반부에 "가뭄에 시달리고 있는 나무들 대부분은 50~500 킬로헤르츠 대역으로 소리를 내지만, 인간의 귀가 감지할 수 있는 대역은 20 킬로헤르츠까지에 불과하다."는 내용이 있으므로, 인간은 기계를 사용하지 않고서는 나무에서 나는 소리를 들을 수 없다고 추론할 수 있다.

3 ① ▶ 동의어
torment가 '고통', '고뇌'라는 뜻으로 쓰였으므로, '고민', '고통', '(육체적인) 아픔'이란 의미의 agony가 동의어에 해당한다. ② 환경 ③ 필요조건 ④ (손짓·몸짓으로 하는) 신호

4 ② ▶ 내용파악
첫 번째 문단에서 "일부 곤충들은 나무가 내는 소리를 듣는다."라고 했고, 두 번째 문단에서는 "물이 부족한 나무들은 그렇지 않은 나무들과는 다른 냄새를 풍기며, 온도의 변화를 겪는다. 그래서 곤충들은 소리가 아닌 다른 무언가에 반응하고 있는 것일 수도 있다."고 했다. 하지만 '색의 변화'에 대해서는 본문에서 언급하지 않았다.

08　2011 고려대

코스모스는 열대 식물의 하나로 대략 20여 종에 이른다. 코스모스는 키가 크고, 우아하고, 늦게 꽃이 피며, 다양하고 깃털모양의 잎을 갖고 있는 일년생 혹은 다년생의 식물이다. '코스모스(cosmos)'라는 말은 그리스 용어 *kosmos*라는 말에서 비롯된 것으로, '장식 혹은 아름다운 것'을 의미한다. 그리고 만발한 그 사랑스럽고 우아한 코스모스를 보고 나면, 이 꽃이 정말로 이름이 잘 지어졌다고 생각할 것이다. 코스모스는 열대와 아열대 지역 아메리카가 원산지이다. 코스모스의 아메리카 원종(原種)은 더 따뜻한 고지대인 멕시코에서 온 것으로 알려져 있다. 미국에서 자란 초기의 종들은 추위에 견딜 수 없었다. 왜냐하면 코스모스는 햇빛을 좋아하기 때문이다. 코스모스가 씨앗이 여물기도 전에 서리를 맞아 죽는 일이 종종 있었다. 그러나 새로운 종의 코스모스가 개발되어 이제는 여름철 꽃뿐만 아니라 가을철 꽃도 되었다.

코스모스가 늦게, 다른 많은 식물들이 제 할 일을 다 했을 때 꽃이 핀다는 사실은 정원사와 꽃 애호가들에게 코스모스를 더 가치 있게 만든다. 왜냐하면 코스모스는 첫 서리가 내릴 때 참으로 진가를 발휘하기(만개하기) 때문이다. 잎이 얇은 이 늦게 피는 별모양의 꽃은 화단이나 담장에 아주 매력적일 뿐만 아니라 꺾은 꽃은 실내 장식을 위해 아름다운 꽃다발이 된다.

미국에서 가장 일반적으로 재배되는 종은 7내지 10피트의 높이로 자라지만, 일부 종은 그렇게 키가 크지 않다. 코스모스는 부드러운 줄기를 갖고 있으며, 밝게 빛나는 화려한 꽃들은 노란색 화반(花盤)을 갖고 있다. 방사형으로 갈라진 꽃잎들에는 흰색, 연분홍색, 빨간색, 자주색, 조개껍질 색, 노란색, 오렌지색을 포함한 다양한 색이 있다. 사실상 청색을 제외한 거의 모든 색이다. 초기의 원시 종들은 직경이 대략 1인치인 꽃들을 갖고 있었다. 그러나 다양한 육종업자들은 이 매력적인 식물을 연구해서 일부 경우에는 줄기를 짧게 하고, 꽃의 크기를 증가시켰으며, 일부 꽃은 하나씩, 다른 꽃들은 다발로 자란다.

1 ③　▶ 부분이해
"첫 서리가 내릴 때 진가를 발휘한다."라는 말은 "첫 서리가 왔을 때 코스모스는 만발한다."라는 의미이므로 ③이 정답이다.

2 ①　▶ 내용추론
②는 '다년생(perennial)'이라는 말에서, ③은 "만발한 그 사랑스럽고 우아한 코스모스를 보고 나면, 이 꽃이 정말로 이름이 잘 지어졌다고 생각할 것이다."라는 말에서, ④는 "코스모스의 아메리카 원종(原種)은 더 따뜻한 고지대인 멕시코에서 온 것으로 알려져 있다."라는 말에서 각각 추론할 수 있다.

3 ④　▶ 내용파악
두 번째 단락의 마지막 문장에서 "잎이 얇은 이 늦게 피는 별모양의 꽃은 화단이나 담장에 아주 매력적일 뿐만 아니라 꺾은 꽃은 실내 장식을 위해 아름다운 꽃다발이 된다."라고 했으므로 ④가 정답이다. ② 코스모스는 열대와 아열대 지역 아메리카가 원산지라고 했다.

4 ③　▶ 내용파악
세 번째 단락의 첫 번째 문장에서 "일반적으로 재배되는 종은 7내지 10피트의 높이로 자라지만, 일부 종은 그렇게 키가 크지 않다."라고 했으므로 ③은 본문의 내용과 맞지 않다. ① 일부 꽃은 하나씩, 다른 꽃들은 다발로 자란다고 했다. ② 방사형으로 갈라진 꽃잎들에는 흰색, 연분홍색, 빨간색, 자주색, 조개껍질 색, 노란색, 오렌지색을 포함한 다양한 색이 있지만 청색은 제외된다고 했다. ④ 코스모스는 부드러운 줄기를 갖고 있으며, 밝게 빛나는 화려한 꽃들은 노란색 화반(花盤)을 갖고 있다고 했다.

---

genus n. 종류, 부류, 속
tropical a. 열대의, 열대 지방의
herb n. 풀, 초본
annual a. 일년의; 해마다의; 일년생의 n. 일년생 식물
perennial a. 지속하는; 다년생의 n. 다년생 식물
feathery a. 깃털 같은, 깃털 모양의; 가벼운
foliage n. 잎; 무성한 잎
ornament n. 장식
in bloom 만발한
native a. 태어난 곳의; 토착의; 원산의; 타고난
semitropical a. 아열대의
upland n. 고지
glory v. 의기양양하다, 자랑으로 여기다
frost n. 서리
ripen v. 익다; 무르익다
come into one's own 진가를 발휘하다, 정당한 명성[지위]을 얻다
blossom n. (특히 과수의) 꽃; 개화, 만발
filmy a. 매우 얇은, 박막성의
decoration n. 장식
primitive a. 원시의; 원시적인
cluster n. 송이, 다발

09 2016 서울여대

코모도왕도마뱀은 수천 년 동안 인도네시아의 일부 섬에 서식해왔다. 한 이야기에 따르면, 어떤 비행기가 불시착으로 코모도 섬 근해에 착륙했던 제1차 세계대전 기간에 코모도왕도마뱀이 처음 발견되었다고 한다. 그 이야기는 어떻게 조종사가 헤엄쳐서 코모도 섬까지 가서 무서운 거대한 도마뱀들에 둘러싸였는지를 말해준다. 이 이야기는 실제로 액션영화에 나오는 이야기 같은 느낌이 든다. 그러나 이 이야기는 실제로 지어낸 이야기다. 우리는 코모도왕도마뱀이 언제 처음 발견되었는지 정확히 알지 못하지만, 코모도왕도마뱀의 존재는 1926년에 처음 확인되었다. 이때는 탐험가 더글러스 버든(Douglas Burden)이 탐험대를 이끌고 코모도 섬에 갔었던 해이다. 더글러스 버든은 미국 자연사박물관에 재직하고 있었다. 그는 탐험에서 돌아오는 길에 죽은 코모도왕도마뱀 견본 12마리와 살아있는 코모도왕도마뱀 두 마리를 가지고 왔다.

코모도왕도마뱀은 세상에서 가장 큰 살아있는 도마뱀이다. 일부 코모도왕도마뱀은 길이가 3m이며, 무게가 130kg 이상 나갈 수 있다. 이것은 코모도왕도마뱀이 지구상에서 가장 무거운 도마뱀이라는 것을 의미한다. 코모도왕도마뱀은 머리가 길고, 주둥이는 짧으며, 피부는 비늘로 덮여있고, 다리는 짧으며, 꼬리는 크면서 힘이 강력하다. 현재까지 발견된 가장 큰 코모도왕도마뱀은 길이가 3.13m이고, 무게가 무려 166kg이었다! 코모도왕도마뱀은 그들이 서식하는 코모도 섬에서 최상위 포식자다. 코모도왕도마뱀은 짐승의 썩은 고기, 보다 크기가 작은 도마뱀, 야생말과 돼지, 몸집이 큰 물소, 그리고 때때로 운이 나쁘면 인간에 이르기까지 거의 모든 것을 먹어치운다! 코모도왕도마뱀은 일시적으로 시속 20km로 달릴 수 있긴 하지만, 이 파충류들은 대개 인내심을 발휘하며 위장을 한 채 먹잇감을 사냥한다. 코모도왕도마뱀은 한 곳에서 몇 시간이고 머무르면서 먹잇감이 나타나기를 기다릴 수도 있다. 운이 없는 그들의 희생양이 지나갈 때, 코모도왕도마뱀은 그 희생양을 공격한 다음 조각조각 찢어버린다. 코모도왕도마뱀의 침에는 50가지 이상의 박테리아 종(種)들이 들어있다. 만일 먹잇감인 동물이 코모도왕도마뱀에 물렸는데도 도망칠 경우, 보통 상당히 빠른 시간 안에 패혈증으로 죽게 된다. 만일 이렇게 먹잇감이 패혈증으로 죽게 될 경우, 코모도왕도마뱀은 우수한 후각을 이용해 죽었거나 죽어가는 동물을 추적해서 위치를 알아낸다. 호랑이와 같은 많은 맹수들은 먹잇감의 25~30%는 먹지 않는다. 이들 육식동물들은 위(胃), 가죽, 뼈, 발은 남긴다. 그러나 코모도왕도마뱀은 낭비가 적어서, 먹잇감의 약 12%만을 남길 뿐이다. 코모도왕도마뱀은 뼈, 발, 털, 그리고 살가죽을 먹으며, 심지어 위도 먹는다! 코모도왕도마뱀은 자기 체중의 80%를 먹어치울 수 있다. 그러나 코모도왕도마뱀이 겁을 먹거나 불안을 느낄 경우, 그들의 위 속에 있는 내용물을 토할 수 있다. 이것은 코모도왕도마뱀들의 몸을 가볍게 만들어줘서, 보다 쉽게 도망칠 수 있게 해준다.

1 ② ▶ 내용파악
어떤 비행기가 불시착으로 코모도 섬 근해에 착륙했던 제1차 세계대전 기간에 코모도왕도마뱀이 처음 발견되었다는 이야기는 지어낸 이야기라고 했다. 반면 "코모도왕도마뱀의 존재는 1926년에 처음 확인되었다. 이때는 탐험가 더글러스 버든이 탐험대를 이끌고 코모도 섬에 갔었던 해이다. 더글러스 버든은 미국 자연사박물관에 재직하고 있었다."라고 본문에 언급되어 있으므로, ②의 '미국 자연사박물관에 재직했던 탐험대의 대장'이 정답이다.

2 ③ ▶ 내용파악
"코모도왕도마뱀은 겁을 먹거나 불안을 느낄 경우, 위 속에 있는 내용물을 토할 수 있다."라고 했으므로 ③이 정답이다.

3 ② ▶ 내용파악
"만일 먹잇감인 동물이 코모도왕도마뱀에 물렸는데도 도망칠 경우, 보통 상당히 빠른 시간에 패혈증으로 죽게 된다. 만일 이렇게 먹잇감이 패혈증으로 죽게 될 경우, 코모도왕도마뱀은 우수한 후각을 이용해 죽었거나 죽어가는 동물을 추적해서 위치를 알아낸다."라고 했으므로 ②가 정답이다.

Komodo dragon 코모도왕도마뱀
crash n. (비행기의) 추락, 불시착
lizard n. 도마뱀
myth n. 신화; 지어낸 이야기
existence n. 존재, 실재, 현존
expedition n. 탐험대
specimen n. 견본; (동식물의) 표본
snout n. 코, 주둥이
scaly a. 비늘이 덮인; 비늘 모양의
predator n. 포식자
carrion n. 짐승의 썩은 고기; 부패
water buffalo 물소
reptile n. 파충류
camouflage n. 위장
patience n. 인내(력), 참을성
prey n. 먹이, 사냥감
rip v. 콱 잡아 찢다
saliva n. 침
blood poisoning 패혈증
carnivore n. 육식동물
hide n. 가죽
wasteful a. 낭비하는; 사치스런
scared a. 무서워하는, 겁먹은
nervous a. 불안해[초조해] 하는; 신경이 과민한
throw up 토하다, 게우다
content n. 내용물
vomit v. 토하다
trace v. 추적하다

10 2021 아주대

A 붉은 다람쥐는 혼자 있기 좋아하고 텃세가 강한 종(種)이지만 유콘(Yukon)에 서식하는 이들 다람쥐에 대한 22년간의 연구에 따르면, 해마다 같은 종의 다른 다람쥐와 이웃하여 살아갈 때 생존 가능성이 더 높고 자손의 수도 더 증가한다고 한다. <놀랍게도, 이 발견은 그 다람쥐와 이웃들이 친척 관계인지 여부는 중요하지 않았고 그 대신, 이러한 건강상의 이점이 친숙함, 즉 같은 다람쥐와 얼마나 오랫동안 이웃하며 살았는지 그 시간에 달려있음을 보여준다.> 데이터에 따르면 이러한 이점들은 나이가 많은 다람쥐에서 더욱 뚜렷했으며, 해가 바뀌어 다음 해까지 자신의 모든 이웃들을 유지할 때 노화의 영향을 급격히 상쇄할 수 있었다.

B "붉은 다람쥐는 각자의 영토에 살면서 서로 신체적 접촉을 거의 하지 않지만, 친숙한 이웃의 가치를 고려할 때 우리의 연구는 그들이 경쟁자들과 협력할 수도 있다는 정말 흥미로운 가능성을 시사합니다."라고 엑서터 대학의 박사 후 연구원이자 제1저자인 에린 시라쿠사(Erin Siracusa)는 말한다. "이러한 협력의 양상이 식량 자원을 공유하는 것인지, 포식자를 이웃에게 경고하기 위해 적극적으로 경보를 울리는 것인지, 혹은 약탈자로부터 주변 영토를 방어하기 위해 심지어 잠재적으로 연합까지 형성하는 것인지, 우리는 알지 못합니다. 그러나 나는 우리의 연구 결과를 바탕으로 독자 생활을 선호하는 그들의 특성에도 불구하고 붉은 다람쥐들이 사회적 상호작용에 참여하며, 중요한 사회적 관계를 가질 수 있다고 주장합니다."

C 무리를 이루어 사는 동물들에게 사회적 관계가 중요한 역할을 한다는 것은 알려져 있지만, 시라쿠사는 같은 종의 개체들과 물리적으로 거의 상호작용하지 않고 홀로 영역을 지키며 살아가는 종에게 사회적 관계가 어떤 영향을 미치는지 알아내는 데 관심이 있었다.

D 시라쿠사는 이보다 앞서 다람쥐들이 자신의 정체를 밝히기 위해 내는 "딸랑이"라고 알려진 방어적 소리를 통해 부분적으로 확립되는 안정적 사회적 관계를 맺은 붉은 다람쥐일수록 서로의 영토를 침해하거나 서로가 숨겨둔 먹이를 몰래 훔칠 가능성이 적다는 사실을 관찰하였다. "이들 영토의 경계에 동의할 만큼 오랫동안 서로 옆집에 살게 되면 '좋아, 우리는 이 영토의 경계를 설정했어. 우리는 서로가 어디 사는지 알고 있어. 우리는 더 이상 이런 경계를 두고 싸우면서 시간과 에너지를 낭비하지는 않을 거야.'"라고 말하는 일종의 신사협정을 맺게 된다고 그녀는 말한다. 친숙한 이웃들 간에 공격성이 감소하는 이 현상은 "친애하는 적"이라고도 알려져 있는데, 이전에 다른 많은 종들에서 확인되었지만 연구자들은 이 현상을 건강상의 이점과 쉽게 연관시키지는 못했다.

1 ⑤ ▶ 내용파악
연구의 핵심 내용은 붉은 다람쥐들이 동종의 이웃과 인접하여 오래 지낼수록, 공격성은 감소하고 아울러 수명과 번식으로 대표되는 건강상의 이점까지 누린다는 것이다.

2 ③ ▶ 내용파악
B 단락에서 언급되고 있는 '영토 방어를 위한 연합 구성'의 상대는 '친숙한(familiar)' 이웃 다람쥐이지 낯선 신입 다람쥐는 아니다.

3 ① ▶ 문장삽입
해당 문장에서 언급된 지시내용 'these fitness benefits'가 포함된 부분을 찾아야 한다. 문맥상 이는 ❶ 바로 앞에서 언급된 '해마다 같은 종의 다른 다람쥐와 이웃하여 살아갈 때 생존 가능성이 더 높고 자손의 수도 더 증가하는 것'을 가리키고 있음을 알 수 있다. 또한, 다음에 잇따라 이어지는 '이러한 이점들은 나이가 많은 다람쥐에서 더욱 뚜렷하고, 해가 바뀌어 다음 해까지 자신의 모든 이웃들을 유지할 때 노화의 영향을 급격히 상쇄할 수 있다'는 문장은 주어진 내용을 상술하는 일종의 '뒷받침하는 세부사항(supporting details)'이라고 볼 수 있으므로 ❶이 주어진 문장이 들어가기에 가장 적절하다.

4 ④ ▶ 문법적으로 옳지 않은 표현 고르기
waste가 타동사로 사용되어 '낭비하다'는 의미일 때 waste something on something 또는 waste something (in) doing something의 문형으로 나타난다. 그러므로 ⓓ는 fighting over these boundaries로 고쳐야 문법적으로 적절하다.

---

solitary a. 혼자 있기를 좋아하는, 혼자서 잘 지내는
territorial a. 텃세[세력권]를 주장하는
pronounced a. 확연한, 명백한
offset v. 상쇄하다
predator n. 포식자
potentially ad. 잠재적으로
coalition n. 연합
usurper n. (권력·지위 등의) 강탈자, 횡령자
defensive a. 방어적인
rattle n. 달그락거리는 소리
identify v. 알아보게 하다
intrude v. 침입하다; 방해하다
pilfer v. 좀도둑질하다
cache n. 은닉처
aggression n. 공격; 공격성
fitness n. 건강

MEMO

MEMO

MEMO